Heroes of
Unwritten Story

Heroes of Unwritten Story
The UAW, 1934–39

Henry Kraus

Foreword by
Nelson Lichtenstein

University of Illinois Press
Urbana and Chicago

This book is printed on acid-free paper.

Library of Congress Cataloging-in-Publication Data

Kraus, Henry, 1905-
    Heroes of unwritten story : the UAW, 1934-39 / Henry Kraus.
        p.   cm.
    ISBN 0-252-02035-9 (cloth)
    1. International Union, United Automobile Workers of America (A.F.
of L.)—History—20th century. 2. Trade-unions—Automobile industry
workers—United States—Case studies. 3. Strikes and lockouts—
Automobile industry—United States—Case studies. I. title.
HD6515.A82I575   1993
331'.04292'0973—dc20   93-6938
                                                                CIP

The title of this book, like that of my first book about the UAW, *The Many and the Few,* is drawn from two companion verses of *The Mask of Anarchy* by Percy Bysshe Shelley. The long poem was written in fiery protest over the massacre of workers at Peterloo, Manchester, England, on August 16, 1819.

xxxvii
Men of England, heirs of Glory,
Heroes of unwritten story,
Nurslings of one mighty Mother,
Hopes of her, and one another:

xxxviii
Rise like Lions after slumber
In unvanquishable number,
Shake your chains to earth like dew
Which in sleep have fallen on you—
Ye are many—they are few.

Contents

Part Three. The UAW Defeats Factionalism and Starts Anew

Illustrations follow page 310.

Foreword

Nelson Lichtenstein

As this century nears its close, trade unionism in the United States holds little fascination for the vast majority of Americans who exchange their time and labor for a paycheck. It is not simply that less than one in six are members of a union or that the labor movement has little power and less prestige. No, the disinterest, if not the outright hostility, held by so many Americans arises out of a far more profound difficulty: the incapacity of the labor movement—and of American society in general—to project a transformative vision capable of mobilizing and motivating the thousands of women and men whose hopeful expectations are the real building blocks of a powerful union movement.

It was not always so. In *Heroes of Unwritten Story* Henry Kraus returns us to the formative years of the United Automobile Workers, a union that more than any other embodied the promise and the politics of the labor movement at flood tide. Kraus was a dedicated union activist during the 1930s, a founder of the UAW and the foremost labor journalist of the autoworkers' early struggles. He therefore had his note pad out, but not just as a reporter or a publicist. Even before the dramatic sitdown strikes of 1936 and 1937, Henry Kraus knew that his comrades and he were making history on the grand scale. Thus the detail and texture that make this volume so rewarding after sixty years are a product both of his hopeful expectations in the 1930s and of a more traditional sort of research Kraus completed during the last decade.

Henry Kraus had the time and money to complete this book because in 1984 the MacArthur Foundation awarded him one of its very handsome, five-year fellowships. He was then seventy-nine, a resident of Paris, and the author, often with his wife, Dorothy, of several remarkable books on medieval art and architecture written during more than twenty years of independent research on the Continent. The anonymous scholars who recommended Kraus to the foundation may well be surprised to note the subject of this volume. But if they open its pages they will find that the life work of Dorothy and Henry Kraus—as scholars, as writers, and as socialists—embodies an organic vision that links the aspirations and life experience of those who carved the stonework on the Gothic cathedrals of France with the twentieth-century production workers who cut sheet steel in the Fisher Body plants of Cleveland and Flint.

Henry Kraus was born on November 13, 1905, in Knoxville, Tennessee, but grew up in Cleveland. His father, Adolph, was an 1889 immigrant from Austria; his mother, Liza Moste, left Rumania a year later. Of Jewish origin, both were socialists, partisans of Eugene V. Debs, and active trade unionists in an era when the Cleveland Federation of Labor stood well to the left of other big city labor bodies. Kraus's father was a barber and recording secretary of his well-organized local for more than twenty years.

At the University of Chicago and then Western Reserve University, from which he graduated with a master's degree in 1928, Kraus majored in mathematics and science. He taught high school mathematics, but his interests flowed more toward literature, music, and art. After his marriage to Dorothy Rogin in 1928, the couple spent almost two years in Europe. Upon their return they found the country in depression, and the working class of northeast Ohio beginning to stir. Henry Kraus joined neither the Socialist nor the Communist parties, but he was clearly a man of the left and for more than thirty years counted as a friend and sometime mentor that remarkable organizer Wyndham Mortimer, whom Kraus rescues from obscurity in *Heroes of Unwritten Story*.[1]

During the last two decades, historians of American labor have devoted much talent and energy toward an understanding of working-class life and politics in the Great Depression. No union has enjoyed greater scrutiny than that of the United Automobile Workers, whose dramatic history and excellent archive at Wayne State University have generated numerous books and essays. Historians have probed the shopfloor dynamics of the struggle between shop stewards and foremen, the racial and ethnic conflicts that have both energized and divided the union, the impact of mass culture, the function of the new labor law, and the role of ideological radicals and conservative managers in shaping the structure and politics of the industrial relations system that emerged at the end of the 1930s.[2]

Kraus is familiar with much of this literature, but his work rests solidly within the great tradition of the historical narrative; indeed, he sometimes uses the word *chronicle*, with all its medieval allusions, to describe his kind of writing. His subjects are those union pioneers—men like George Addes, Robert Travis, Ed Hall, Walter, Roy and Victor Reuther, Richard Frankensteen, and the steadfast Mortimer—who sought to enlarge and channel the aspirations of working-class Americans in order to build a trade union movement that might confront and defeat the nation's most powerful corporations.

Their story is told in a perceptive, highly textured, almost novelistic fashion, with much attention offered to their personal virtues, individual foibles, and the play of happenstance. The cadre that built the United Automobile Workers was naturally divided by politics, circumstance, and ego, and Kraus offers a striking portrait of the men and women in conversation, debate, and battle. Although his work is not a memoir, his part in this history is hardly absent, for Kraus makes clear, in his understated way, how central he was to the success of the union-building project itself. *Heroes of Unwritten Story* ends in 1939 with Henry Kraus on his way to the Michigan northwoods to begin writing what would eventually become his first book, the classic history of the Flint sitdown strike, *The Many and the Few: A Chronicle of the Dynamic Auto Workers.*

But Dorothy and Henry Kraus were not quite finished with the UAW. The union had sent Wyndham Mortimer to Southern California, and in 1940 he coaxed the Krauses there to help him organize the wave of young workers flooding into the booming aircraft industry. Their efforts reached a tragic climax in June 1941 during a strike at the giant North American Aviation plant in Inglewood, where more than a quarter of all fighter aircraft were built. California aircraft organizers saw this spirited workstoppage as but another in the great cycle of working-class mobilizations that had begun early in the depression, but the confrontation at North American Aviation came when the approach of war had turned the political tide against labor militancy. In Washington, high officials in the military and the new mobilization agencies denounced the strike as a communist-inspired sabotage of defense production. Buckling under this pressure, UAW officials in Detroit declared the strike a wildcat, and then President Roosevelt sent in the army to break up the picket lines and arrest scores of unionists.[3]

Kraus soon took a job in a San Pedro shipyard and in his spare time wrote articles on the importance of engaging workers' creative participation in war production. He finally published *The Many and the Few* in 1947, at a time when the UAW's bitter factional fight had been resumed, culminating in the ouster of the left and Walter Reuther's consolidation of power in the union. Kraus observed Reuther's rise with great concern. He rejected the new UAW president's anticommunism, and he thought his leadership far too accommodative toward the big automakers. Though *The Many and the Few* hardly strays from the dramatic events of 1936 and 1937, the book's celebration of rank-and-file militancy served as a weapon in the arsenal of Reuther's factional opponents. Indeed, the two most important, Vice-President R. J. Thomas and Secretary-Treasurer George Addes, wrote an introduction lauding the book "as a herald of the future, when the common people shall fully possess their heritage."[4]

In 1951 Kraus published another piece of contemporary social history,

In the City Was a Garden. This second chronicle recalled the community spirit and everyday struggles of the men and women who lived in the San Pedro housing project where the Krauses had helped build a militant and creative residents' council during the war. Neither of these postwar books found a publisher, so the Krauses published and distributed both themselves. Meanwhile, Henry Kraus scrambled for work both in Los Angeles and New York. His career as a labor journalist had been largely foreclosed by his identification with the left, so in 1955 he took a job as a medical news reporter. The couple soon moved to Paris, where for seven years Henry Kraus wrote articles and features for World Wide Medical News Service. They kept their American citizenship but closely followed the fortunes of the left in France. When the trade unions joined the student revolutionaries in the great factory and university occupations of May–June 1968, Dorothy and Henry Kraus hurried to the big Renault plant in Billancourt to share their own experience with this new generation of sitdowners.[5]

Returning to his youthful enthusiasm, Henry Kraus found the medieval churches of France utterly fascinating; soon he devoted almost every free moment to a firsthand study of the monuments. As a laborite radical and a self-taught historian, he began to see these medieval structures in a fresh light, which highlighted the social context and documentary character of twelfth- and thirteenth-century art and architecture. He discovered that many early artisans were independent personalities whose distinctive impress upon the carvings and paintings of the Middle Ages could be noted through careful observation and study. Thus, in their unique exploration of the misericords—those carvings beneath the purposefully uncomfortable wooden seats found in the stalls of cathedral choirs—Dorothy and Henry Kraus found an entire secular world of people at work and at play, of domestic cats, carnival freaks and randy priests, of sailors and moneylenders, cobblers and teachers, of pipers piping and young women dressing. He proved a prolific author, publishing *The Living Theatre of Medieval Art* in 1967, *Gold Was the Mortar: The Economics of Cathedral-Building* in 1979, and, with Dorothy, *The Hidden World of Misericords* in 1975 and *The Gothic Choirstalls of Spain* in 1985.

These books made Henry Kraus world famous, which attracted the attention of the MacArthur Foundation, which in turn gave him the opportunity to return to Michigan and to the rediscovery of the men and women whose lives are now retold in *Heroes of Unwritten Story.*

Notes

1. Biographical information taken from Henry Kraus to Nelson Lichtenstein, May 29 and June 13, 1993.

2. Sidney Fine, *The General Motors Strike of 1936–1937* (Ann Arbor: University of Michigan Press, 1970); Peter Friedlander, *The Emergence of a UAW Local, 1936–1939: A Study in Class and Culture* (Pittsburgh: University of Pittsburgh Press, 1975); Steve Jefferys, *Management and Managed: Fifty Years of Crisis at Chrysler* (Cambridge: Cambridge University Press, 1986); August Meier and Elliott Rudwick, *Black Detroit and the Rise of the UAW* (New York: Oxford University Press, 1979); Roger Keeran, *The Communist Party and the Auto Workers Unions* (Bloomington: Indiana University Press, 1980); John Barnard, *Walter Reuther and the Rise of the Auto Workers* (Boston: Little Brown, 1983); Ronald Edsforth, *Class Conflict and Cultural Consensus: The Making of a Mass Consumer Society in Flint, Michigan* (New Brunswick: Rutgers University Press, 1987); Christopher Johnson, *Maurice Sugar: Law, Labor and the Left in Detroit, 1912–1950* (Detroit: Wayne State University Press, 1988); Nelson Lichtenstein and Stephen Meyer, *On the Line: Essays in the History of Auto Work* (Urbana: University of Illinois Press, 1989); Steve Babson, *Building the Union: Skilled Workers and Anglo-Gaelic Immigrants in the Rise of the UAW* (New Brunswick: Rutgers University Press, 1991); and Stephen Meyer, *"Stalin over Wisconsin": The Making and Unmaking of Militant Unionism, 1900–1950* (New Brunswick: Rutgers University Fress, 1992). The memoir literature includes Wyndham Mortimer, *Organize!: My Life as a Union Man* (Boston: Beacon Press, 1992); Frank Marquart, *An Auto Worker's Journal: The UAW from Crusade to One-Party Union* (University Park: Pennsylvania State University Press, 1975); Victor Reuther, *The Brothers Reuther and the Story of the UAW* (Boston: Houghton Mifflin, 1976); and Margaret Collingwood Nowak, *Two Who Were There: A Biography of Stanley Nowak* (Detroit: Wayne State University Press: 1989).

3. James R. Prickett, "Communist Conspiracy or Wage Dispute?: The 1941 Strike at North American Aviation," *Pacific Historical Review* 50 (1981): 215–33; Nelson Lichtenstein, *Labor's War at Home: The CIO in World War II* (New York: Cambridge University Press, 1983), 56–64; Mortimer, *Organize!* 166–193; and UAW, Proceedings of the 1941 Convention, Buffalo, August 4–16, 243–68, 400–449.

4. Henry Kraus, *The Many and the Few: A Chronicle of the Dynamic Auto Workers,* 2d ed. (Urbana: University of Illinois Press, 1985), xxv. In his own 1947 Preface, Kraus also noted the book's "vital contemporary context." The most thorough account of the postwar faction fight is found in Martin Halpern, *UAW Politics in the Cold War Era* (Albany: State University of New York Press, 1988). In later years Kraus's viewpoint became more nuanced toward Reuther and his brand of trade unionism. In 1993 his judgment was that "while the UAW's rank and file activity had fallen far off, the union had won a number of improvements, particularly in such things as health care, pensions, etc., which I largely credited to Walter's leadership and ideas." Kraus to Lichtenstein, June 15, 1993.

5. Henry Kraus, *In the City Was a Garden: A Housing Project Chronicle* (Los Angeles: Renaissance Press, 1951); Kraus to Lichtenstein, May 29, 1993.

Introduction

I entered the auto union by its back door. In fact, when I first sought it out early in 1934, it was not as a union primarily but as an aggregate of workers whom I wanted to get to know for other reasons. I was a would-be writer who was very conscious of his shortcomings. I had worked on a novel for more than a year and appraised it negatively because of its subjectivism, its self-indulgence. I despised the breed I had written about, to which I belonged, to be sure, and decided that I must shift my sights to a different group, the working class, what I called the "real people."

After marrying, Dorothy and I had gone to Europe, where, after several months of desultory seeking, we discovered art. Whatever else the two years spent in the museums and churches of France, Germany, and Italy did for me, they were time lost for my career. It was certain that I did not want to write about art! We came back home to Cleveland in July 1930 in the depth of the depression. But we both got part-time jobs, Dorothy as a coach of working women at a branch of the YWCA, I as a translator of medical articles for research staff members of the Crile Clinic. Our earnings permitted us to rig out a little garret with a few pieces of Salvation Army furniture and I began to write my novel.

After reaching my adverse judgment about it, I set out walking all over the city in search of those "real people" whom I had decided I must get to know. I associated them with the depression victims, going down into the "Gulley" of the Cuyahoga River, where a number of Hoovervilles had sprouted. These hovels that men lived in were jerry-built from a great assortment of castoff debris and topped by corrugated metal roofing; meals came from gleanings out of garbage cans and from backdoor begging expeditions. I was moved although disturbed by this communal life that thrived under such miserable conditions.

But along my route I met other victims of the bad times who were unwilling to accept so degrading a solution to the problem of living. They were organized into what were called Unemployed Councils, which used aggressive methods to force the local authorities to add to people's borderline existence. I ran into a demonstration of such a group one day outside a welfare office that occupied an old two-story house in a rundown section of Cleveland. There were several dozen people gathered at the foot of the stairs, listening to a speaker. He was telling them that the office personnel had refused to meet with their committee because Fridays were set off for such hearings and this was only Wednesday.

"We can't tell that to our empty bellies!" the little fellow in shirtsleeves jibed caustically, standing defiantly on the stairs just beneath a policeman who held his club firmly in his hand as though ready for use. I was not aware that the office had called the neighborhood police station, but soon after I arrived a patrol wagon appeared. The protesters were well trained and just stood quietly by as a couple of officers ran up the stairs and, grabbing the unresisting orator under each arm, dragged him down and threw him into the rear of the truck. Then they followed up with a random selection of half a dozen of his comrades and drove off swiftly.

The rest of the crowd stood around for a while before dispersing. I had retreated to the other side of the street at the appearance of the paddy wagon. My urge, no doubt, was to separate myself from the group of protesters. I was not proud of myself for doing this though it was true that I was not a part of what was going on. What stuck in my mind afterward at any event was the amazing self-discipline that the group, especially the diminutive speaker, had shown throughout the incident. Putting up a resistance would have only brought on a more violent response.

My meanderings left me sufficient time to become acquainted with the new crop of writers who had appeared during our two-year absence. Most were of left-wing persuasion, products of the depression—John Dos Passos, Erskine Caldwell, James Farrell. Soon after, I joined the John Reed Club at the invitation of a friend, an alumnus like myself of Western Reserve University. I had read John Reed's *Ten Days That Shook the World* and my appreciation of it was heightened by the film I saw a bit later that Serge Eisenstein had drawn from the book and retitled *October* in more direct reference to the Russian Revolution of 1917. A small movie house had recently opened in Cleveland that featured the remarkable Soviet films of that early period, films directed by Eisenstein, Pudovkin, Trauberg, and others.

When the club heard of our having been to Europe and studied Gothic art there, I was asked if I would give a talk on the subject at one of the monthly meetings. I agreed to do so, although reluctantly. There was, I observed, a spiritual depth in Gothic art, surpassing almost all other styles, which was magnificently reflected in such artists as Giotto, Duccio, and Cimabue. Modern Christian art, however, had lost that inspiration, and I referred to the great hall of nineteenth-century paintings at the Vatican Museum, which I described as a "chamber of horrors." Modern artists, I explained, clearly needed a new faith, like communism perhaps, to inspire their work.

The members listened politely, except for one person by the name of David Martin, who tended to assume a didactic posture in the club. He accused me of advocating a reactionary, anti-Marxist concept. Communism, he declared, was based on dialectical materialism and not on spiritual belief. My ideas would lead the workers down a blind alley. Hadn't I heard that Marx called religion the opium of the people? Actually, I had and I resented being reminded of it although I could not claim to be acquainted with Marx's writings. I was not talking about belief in God, I insisted, because I was an atheist. Nevertheless, if you wanted to grasp the inspiration of the early painters, you had to accept them as they were, whereas modern faith would indubitably have to be built on different ground.

The discussion ended amicably and Dorothy and I assimilated into the club for a time. In the main, members were people with merely cultural interests who only rarely possessed professional-grade talents. There were two graphic artists whose work was good but blatantly propagandistic. The prize of the group was a married couple named Auville who composed Appalachian folk songs which, accompanied by a banjo, they sang before unemployed groups all over town. I can still remember some of the words to "The Miner's Son," whose father gives him some sharp advice:

> The Son:
> Just a boy without work, I decided,
> Along with some friends of mine,
> To answer the call of my country
> And with the Home Guards to sign. . . .
>
> The Father:
> The miners will strike from starvation,
> They'll march on that old picket line.
> The Home Guards will be called out to break them,
> If you're with them, you're no son of mine!

The one group I missed in the club were professional writers, though almost everybody admitted with a bit of coaxing that they "wanted to write." Talking about it with them merely brought back to me my own unhappy experience. However, I said nothing to them of my quest for "real people" since they might consider it belittling. During the summer of 1933, something occurred that helped me solve this dilemma. The Unemployed Council announced a statewide "Hunger March" to Columbus. I decided to join the march and proposed it to the John Reed Club as a worthwhile activity that would link us with the working class. It aroused very little enthusiasm. There was one exception, a young chap by the name of Dave Hilberman, a talented cartoonist who was later picked up by Walt Disney and who became one of Disney's most imaginative artists. It was very lucky for me that he agreed to go along because I never could have had the rewarding experience that I enjoyed on the week-long march were it not for him. Every evening after the hundred or so marchers had had their frugal meal (unless the food was supplied by some county official more conscientious or maybe more intimidated than the others in whose fairgrounds we stopped over for a night), a program was presented that Dave and I had worked up with a group of young people.

It consisted chiefly of a playlet that I would scribble down at supper time of the events of the day. At times they were not lacking in drama, drawn from the tiffs we had had with the state police, the sheriffs, or other authorities. Our footlights were made up of the crossing beams of our two rattletrap supply trucks. Dave would start off with a program of what he called "Chalk Talks," consisting always of a "boss" who by a few dexterous strokes was transformed into a bank robber, his fat belly into a bag of loot. Meanwhile I gave our young actors a run-through of our playlet. These became a roaring success once we had discovered a big, fat fellow whose nickname was, appropriately, "Skinny" and who agreed after much arm-twisting to assume the permanent role of the sheriff.

Skinny was a natural addition to my gallery of "real people." He was quite willing to talk about himself, and I jotted down everything that he told me in my pocket notebook, which thereafter became the indispensable instrument of my trade. He told me, for instance, how he had lost his hair (although he was only twenty-six) due to drinking. But he was cured, he assured me, after he joined the Unemployed Council, which appeared to fill his whole life thereafter.

Quite a bit different, yet of particularly nostalgic interest for me, was a small clan of Italian friends who formed a little community of their own due to the fact that they spoke hardly a word of English. Nevertheless, they were always in high spirits and were overjoyed when I began practicing my elementary Italian on them. I often walked along with them, and they taught me their revolutionary songs, which made up for our faltering conversation:

> Avanti popolo a la riscossa,
> Bandiera rossa, bandiera rossa!
> Avanti popolo a la riscossa,
> Bandiera rossa vogliamo far!
>
> Bandiera rossa la trionfera,
> Bandiera rossa la trionfera,
> Bandiera rossa la trionfera,
> E viv' il comunismo e la libertà!

[Forward, people, to the Revolution,
The Red Flag! The Red Flag!
Forward, people, to the Revolution,
The Red Flag will make us free!

The Red Flag will our banner be,
The Red Flag will our banner be,
The Red Flag will our banner be,
Long live communism and liberty!]

My interest in Joe Dallet bore upon my present plans because he was a steel worker from Youngstown, the first contact I was to make with anyone from the mass production industries. He would cut me short whenever I made advances to him, however, which I attributed to the fact that I was an "intellectual," which he as a member of the Young Communist League did not distinguish from "the bourgeoisie." Years later I read that Joe Dallet had joined the Abraham Lincoln Brigade to fight in the Spanish Civil War, where he was, I believe, one of the first American volunteers to be killed in action.

I never did go back to the John Reed Club after the march. Things had happened in the meantime in the big world that were really going to change my life. Roosevelt had introduced the National Recovery Act (NRA), and workers in the heavy industries began their march toward unionism. Soon after, I found my way through the back door into the White Motor local of the auto union, and my search for the "real people" had come to a happy end, or I should say a happy beginning.

A Note on Sources

Major sources used in this book have come largely from my own documents and personal papers. I had not seen the part of them that the Wayne State University Archives acquired in 1965 for twenty years until I spent several months each summer from 1986 through 1989 renewing my acquaintance with them. I also consulted other collections and oral histories at the time, which enabled me to add vital details to various subjects or to check the veracity of my recall. Particularly helpful were contemporary UAW journals, especially those I had edited: the Cleveland *United Auto Worker,* the *United Automobile Worker,* and the *Flint Auto Worker.* Together they covered the period from 1935 to 1937.

In general, however, it has been informal sources that have been the most meaningful. I acquired very early the habit of keeping notes about my experiences in the UAW. Whether or not I had an immediate use for them, I saved these jottings, which eventually were transcribed onto six-hundred single-spaced typed pages that I called Annotations. They have been the prime source of the present work. Correspondence with friends who were, like myself, participants in the UAW were carefully preserved and have proved an important adjunct. Letters exchanged with my wife during short periods of separation were especially helpful. Both of us were deeply involved in the UAW and what we considered important to write about then has often remained so forty or more years later. Dorothy's notes and papers concerning women's activities have been a precious source to me for that phase of the work.

Early on, in a kind of literary urge, I began to gather personal interviews, starting with the first auto workers I got to know at White Motors in Cleveland. Later my recordings evolved into a type that was little different from the formal oral histories. From 1934 to 1938, I conducted several dozen interviews of both kinds. Most were of people with whom I worked closely in the union and learned about in the process. I conducted extensive interviews with only a few of them, including Walter Reuther, Dick Frankensteen, Ed Hall, Bud Simons, Kenneth Malone, and several others. All of the interviews came early in my career, except for that with Kenny Malone, whom Neil Leighton and I queried in 1986, when I had the opportunity to check certain details regarding the Chevy 4 sitdown.

Personal Interviews

A partial list of persons whom I interviewed, and the years in which the interviews occurred, includes:

1934: Wyndham Mortimer, Ed Stubbe, and Richard Reisinger, all from White Motors.

1935: James Roland and Robert Travis, Toledo Chevrolet; Louis Spisak and Robert Bates, Cleveland Fisher; Elmer Bernhardt, Ashtabula Bow-Socket.

1936: Lloyd Jones, Murray Body; Russell Merrill and Forrest Woods, Studebaker; Bud Simons, Walter Moore, and Joe Devitt, all of Fisher One, Flint; George Lehman, White Motors.

1937: Walter Reuther; Ralph Dale and Bill Cody, Seaman Body; Jerome Strauss, Cleveland Fisher; Charles Killinger, Flint Buick; Karl Prussian, De Soto; Joseph Shears, Flint city commissioner.

1938: Richard Frankensteen; George Addes; Paul Miley; Ed Hall; Victor and Sophie Reuther; Stanley Nowak; George Edwards; Nicholas (Mike) Dragon, Dodge; Steve Jensco, Cleveland Fisher; Maurice Sugar, UAW attorney.

1986: Kenneth Malone, Chevrolet 4.

Acknowledgments

First, I wish to express my gratitude to those UAW friends who cooperated unstintingly during our often-lengthy interviews. My deep regret is that now, when my book is finally appearing, so many of them are no longer here to learn how very helpful they were in its preparation.

My sincerest thanks go likewise to the Wayne State University Archives, which has been a singularly important source. Access to it has been facilitated in every possible way by Director Philip P. Mason, Assistant Director Warner W. Pflug, and their remarkable staff, including Margery S. Long, Kathleen Schmeling, Thomas Featherstone, and others.

I am also grateful to my friend Neil O. Leighton of the University of Michigan at Flint, who, along with much other invaluable assistance, helped make available readable transcriptions of difficult voice recordings of important oral histories of co-participants in this story.

My work in the Detroit and Flint archives, which lasted many months, was made possible by a special financial aid of the MacArthur Foundation, of which I am a Fellow and to which I convey my lasting appreciation.

And last but never out of mind, I wish to acknowledge the unique role played by my wife and dearest friend, Dorothy Kraus, who participated with me in many of the reported events and then stood by, patiently, encouragingly, during the tough task of their being put on paper.

Part One

The UAW Fights the AFL for Self-Rule

Looking for a Strike: I Discover a Union

1

It was not until I got to the White Motor plant on St. Clair Avenue near 79th Street in Cleveland that morning in early March 1934 that I asked myself what I actually intended doing there. My misgivings arose as soon as I got off the streetcar and looked around, wondering which part of the massive structure to head for. Suddenly my inner conviction failed me, and a mental snag seemed to call my entire project into question.

I might have turned right around that moment and fled had I not noticed some way down the street a wide open gate into which a driveway ran. Without any other choice, I headed that way, turned in, and walked up the paved road along a five-story red brick building. A hundred yards ahead, a broad transverse structure riveted my attention. The factory! I hurried toward it.

Whether or not this was where I was supposed to go, the steel sliding doors were invitingly open. No one was there to challenge me as I entered into a large vestibule; off a little way to the left stood an elderly man in drab work clothes, probably the watchman. He turned a perfunctory look at me and, without stopping, I went toward him, wanting to get close enough to make myself heard in the steady heavy rumble that filled the area.

"No strike yet?" I asked without thinking that it was the one question that might have roused his suspicions. But he looked at me without guile as he shook his head. "The committee's in with the management," he replied in a loud whisper that sounded like a long-practiced adaptation to the noise. "They've been in for a couple of hours already."

It was nothing, but it was a revelation and an opening to learn more. Almost any question might do. "What's the problem?" I asked. "The papers haven't been very clear about it."

He smiled, almost conspiratorially, I felt. "Money," he said, his lips warping. "Company still claims it's broke."

"Don't they always?" I observed, throwing in my full lot with a matching sneer.

"Yes, but they can't get away with that any more the way they used to, stalling for months and months. You see that piece in the paper recently where the big shots' bonuses were posted?"

"No, I didn't notice that one," I admitted self-reproachingly.

"Well, it was on an inside page," he excused me, "like as if the paper had to print it but didn't want to make too much of it. But somebody or other noticed it and the news went through the plant like a dry-meadow fire. Mister Bean got one-hundred-and-thirteen thousand dollars. *One-hundred-thirteen-thousand dollars,*" he repeated, his strongly English-tinted voice taking on an almost joyous ring. "Boy, the guys were mad. You could have closed the whole works down that day in ten minutes," he commented triumphantly. "It minded me of the good old days back home."

A sudden commotion coming from the passageway linking the factory and the office building interrupted his nostalgia. Two men emerged and paused by the door. One, about forty, black-haired, and mustached, was visibly very angry. The other, ten years older, who wore glasses, listened to his sputtering words without comment.

"That's Wyndham Mortimer," my friend whispered close to my ear, denoting the older man. "He's chairman of the grievance committee. His folks were English-born," he slipped in adroitly with a lift of the eyebrows. "The other one's Dick Reisinger. He's vice president of the local."

Reisinger broke away from his partner suddenly and without taking the slightest notice of us shot past as though he was starting a marathon, kicking the floor as he went and cursing in unrestrained rage: "Son-of-a-bitch! *Son*-of-a-*bitch!*"

Mortimer stood looking after him with what struck me as a worried smile. I had the sense that he might be embarrassed because of my presence, and I felt at a loss myself. It was like finding oneself in the middle of a family quarrel and not knowing the first thing of what it was all about.

Reisinger stopped abruptly on his return prance and pierced Mortimer with glaring eyes. He wore a tiny Charlie Chaplin–type mustache that was hardly noticeable above his blood-red lips. "Don't worry, I'm going to fix his clock for him!"

The older man took hold of his arm. "No, Dick, it'll do more harm that good. It's too bad it happened that way but arguing among ourselves won't help it any now. We've got to stress the positive side of what we've gained."

Reisinger was plainly unconvinced and darted off, disappearing into another passage. It seemed hardly the time to plead my own minor cause even though I felt rather encouraged by the elderly man's reasonable manner.

Reaching a quick decision, I approached him. "Mr. Mortimer," I began swiftly, "I'd like to explain to you that I came here expecting that there'd be a strike and I wanted to offer the union my help putting out leaflets or something. I realize that there won't be a strike after all, but I still could help. I don't want a job," I added hastily, veering nervously into my prepared speech. "As a matter of fact, I might learn something myself that way. I have a strong feeling that these big factory unions are going to become important in this country."

I had to keep my eyes from his face and was unaware how he might be taking my words as they gushed out. Maybe I had already said too much though I had wanted him to understand that I had really done quite a lot of reading and thinking about unions in recent months. But it all sounded very stiff and artificial coming out that way, even infantile.

What I did not realize at the time, however, was that much of the experience of these new unionists was equally strange and baffling to them, and that they might even consider my offer as something altogether natural. In the case of Wyndham Mortimer, there was much more besides that fitted my curious ploy into a pattern of fool's luck, for he was exactly the kind of man, as I would soon enough learn, who could comprehend the kind of overture that I was making. Suddenly I noticed in amazement that he was nodding. "I think it's a fine idea, Mister. . . ."

"Kraus," I exclaimed. "Henry Kraus."

"I'll introduce you to our local president, Mister Kraus. He'll be down any minute."

But when George Lehman appeared, he had other things on his mind. He was a bright-eyed, breezy man of about forty-five but clearly under strain at the moment.

"Where's Dick?" he asked, his eyes darting about. "Gone upstairs, I suppose. He was sure mad." He shook his head, smiling nervously. "Heck, Mort, you realize we had to make a quick settlement there."

"That's not the point, George, but I don't think we ought to discuss it here."

"The stewards were tickled to death," Lehman reassured himself. "It didn't take them more than five minutes to make up their minds. Then did you see the way they piled out of the cloakroom and rushed off to pass the word throughout the shop?"

Mortimer's face was noncommittal and he turned to me to cut the conversation short. "George, this young man, name is Kraus, came here to offer us his services. Wants to get some experience in a union, he says, doing publicity. I thought maybe you'd want to talk to him."

Lehman approached me with a quick smile and open palm, eager to make an ingratiating gesture. "Sounds like a great idea, Mr. Kraus. Why don't you come around to our next meeting?"

"That's what I was hoping to do."

"We meet twice a month on alternate Fridays, at the Metal Trades Council. You know where that is, at the old Moose Hall on Walnut Avenue. I'll tell the sergeant-at-arms at the door about you." He turned to Mortimer. "Say, Mort, maybe we ought to have him come down to the beer bust we're planning. We could introduce him to all the boys. What do you think?"

Mortimer brightened slightly, on my account, I felt. "Yeah, that might be a good idea."

It was almost too good. Agitated, I shook hands and hastened off, wanting to think it all over and take the measure of my success. I seemed delivered into a new community, a new life, and was frankly intimidated about being able to match up to its swelling, unforeseeable demands.

• • •

It was the "beer bust" that was most instructive to me, even if Wyndham Mortimer, who had proposed the idea as a get-together with the officers of the other auto locals, had much to complain about the way it was arranged. George Lehman had turned the job of preparing the invitations over to AFL representative George McKinnon, who simply neglected to contact any of the other auto locals. It was a basic policy of the Federation, I would soon enough learn, to keep such groups apart.

Mortimer frankly admitted his outrage at the neat way he had been outdone and promised himself that it would not happen again. "All we had were carpenters and plumbers, pipefitters and blacksmiths," he said. "They ate our food and drank our beer. It cost us about a hundred bucks and we didn't even meet one solitary auto worker."

His displeasure was probably accentuated by the fact that he was a confirmed teetotaler, and although President Roosevelt's 3.2 beverage could hardly be taken seriously, consumed in quantity it eventually produced a noisy, convivial crowd. It also loosened tongues and before the evening was over I heard all about what had happened at the meeting between the company and the union committee that caused the rift whose backwash marked my introduction to the union.

Dick Reisinger, who had apparently made things up with Lehman, was my chief informant nevertheless. He was a sharp-witted, educated man from a middle-class background who had been declassed by the depression, as were a number of other workers I was to meet. His experience had definitely slanted his thinking to the left, which as yet found its major outlet as a suspicion of the AFL's intentions toward the auto workers and a more recent alertness to George Lehman's close alliance with its officials.

As the English watchman had informed me, the union's demands for wage adjustments had lain in abeyance for a number of months while the union continued to honor the company's "proofs" of astronomical losses that only union cooperation and the winning of government contracts could set back on a positive course. When the huge managerial bonuses were announced, probably no one on the workers' side tried to figure out how much their aggregate would divide off among two or three thousand men. In fact, that information was not pertinent because the argument of "equality of sacrifice" was at play at the time.

The union's demand put forward the previous November for the restoration of the 1929 wage scale had been yanked out of limbo, along with a series of additional adjustments on piece work for those who earned more than 50 cents an hour. The minimum wage of 56 cents that was asked for was no less than 13 cents above the base specified in the Auto Code of Roosevelt's National Recovery Act (NRA). The forthright union team, piloted by Mortimer and Reisinger, their logic braced by resentment, argued that the code *minimum* did not mean "maximum" and had taken steps to strengthen the union's position on this critical occasion.

This consisted of two measures. One was to set a deadline for the company's answer for 10 A.M. on March 1, above which it was understood that the threat of strike hovered. The other step was much more unusual and contrary to AFL practice. The committee stripped itself of the right to call off the ultimatum in case the company made a substitute offer that the union negotiators themselves might find acceptable. That right was placed in the power of the seventy-five union stewards, who, accordingly, at 9:30, wiped their hands on their grease cloths and from their various stations throughout the plant began trooping down to the locker room, the previously agreed-upon rendezvous.

It was at this point that George Lehman made his unexpected gesture. Reaching into his coat pocket he brought out a sheet of paper containing a brace of figures and some writing that he himself apparently had prepared. He handed the page to George Smith, the plant manager.

While the company official was swiftly absorbing Lehman's memo, Lehman attempted to explain its contents to his teammates, but his face was drained of color. The company had already more or less accepted a 51 cent minimum, so he stressed other features. But the men sat in stunned silence. Only Ed Stubbe lost control, his heavy jowls flushing angrily. "You know you got no right to do that!" he assailed Lehman and meant to go on but Mortimer, sitting next to him, yanked sharply at his sleeve and he caught himself up.

Smith quickly indicated a tentative agreement, eager himself to forestall an argument within the committee that might invalidate what to him was a satisfactory new offer. Mortimer as chair of the committee was the only other union man to comment, speaking as much to the attention of his own president as to the company official: "But it still has to be approved by the stewards." And with that the committee rose abruptly and left the room.

There was much in Reisinger's narrative that left me in the dark and his replies to my eager questions revealed the sharp-edged subtlety of his thinking. For one thing, I would have expected the stewards to show more spunk. Weren't there any angry voices among them calling for a rejection? I asked him. "No! Because the rest of us shut up. We didn't exchange a word between us but we all knew that's what we had to do. What else could we do, get into a fight with George in front of them and split the union to hell? What a way to start a strike, huh, the first strike maybe that most of them had ever been in!" And he pushed the blood blister on his lower lip forward in a belligerent gesture that was habitual to him. "Besides," he toned his anger down and smiled shrewdly, "the guys weren't really as disappointed as all that. They thought, an 8 cent raise meant $6.40 extra in every two-week check. Boy, that ain't hay." Then his anger flared again. "The only son-of-a-bitchin' thing about it was the way George pulled it off, kicking us all in the teeth, acting like a goddam AFL stooge." And he shoved his blood-red underlip forward yet again.

• • •

Dick Reisinger and others in the local leadership took it for granted that the pressure on Lehman came from the Metal Trades Council (MTC), in particular from George McKinnon, who was President Bill Green's personal representative in charge of Cleveland's auto locals. But they were not quite willing to accept the idea that the man who had worked with them for years (Reisinger especially considered him a close friend) had become so submissive to AFL influence as to be willing to surrender the local's own independent judgment and right of decision.

In the following two years I came to know George Lehman quite well and considered him an intelligent and decent man. He later agreed to do an interview ("have a talk") when I told him of my plan to write a history of the Cleveland locals, a project that would change and greatly expand in the succeeding years. I interviewed several other men at White's and at other plants but never came upon anyone who struck me as a more trustworthy witness. Of course, he did have a definite ideological viewpoint that colored his narrative, but knowing what it was meant that I could take it into account.

At the time I got to know him, George Lehman was beginning to think that Wyndham Mortimer's impact was basically bad for the union. This troubled him all the more because he had been as responsible as anyone in getting Mortimer, about six months earlier, to bring his competitive group to join the AFL local. This group was affiliated with the communist-controlled Trade Union Unity League (TUUL).[1]

Several of the most important leaders of the AFL local were of German-American extraction, an ethnic group that was strongly represented in Cleveland. There was, however, little that seemed to link George Lehman or Dick Reisinger or Ed Stubbe with that background until they reminisced about their early years with their families. Stubbe did not speak English until he went to school, but this would not account for his linguistic shortcomings, which were those of any sparsely educated American boy. More surprising and most gratifying to me was the fact that he (as well as Lehman) had come from a pro-union and even socialistic background: indeed, both still spoke warmly of Eugene V. Debs. In Stubbe's case, the radical attachment had ceased when the socialists opposed World War I.

During his early years at White's, George Lehman had engaged in swift ladder-climbing. Smart and ingratiating, he became a straw boss while still in his early twenties and five years later was set up as a foreman on the night shift. When the crisis came, this shift was eliminated, and he was sent back on the line. After work started up in 1932, he and his wife lived in the expectation that he would get his foreman's post back, but that never happened. Then the company changed owners and Lehman grew bitter. Making the logical leap in thought, he concluded: "It was nobody but White Motors itself that organized the union!"

It might be correct to say that Lehman's political inheritance came to the fore when the National Recovery Act brought its exciting message to the White Motor workers. That was the way he described it when telling me about the first meeting he attended at the MTC on July 14, 1933. Harry McLaughlin was the leading speaker and Lehman was much taken with his platform performance. He told me how McLaughlin's slogan "Join the union of your craft" had appealed to him. Strangely, Lehman made no reference even then to the actual significance of the slogan and was probably only thinking of the pleasant sound of the words and not of the message of craft-unionism that it carried, of splitting factory workers into a dozen disparate groups. But somehow I could not help thinking that Lehman's obliviousness concealed his identification with the idea, an assertion of social separation from the vulgarity often associated with manual labor. His close co-workers were, like himself, skilled men, machinists and inspectors. Although he did not deny a place in the union for unskilled hands, he saw in unskilled workers a kind of class difference, a lack of some quality required in those that one chose as friends.

Lehman, Reisinger, and Stubbe were early recruits to the AFL local, with George Lehman taking the lead by choice of the Federation's organizers. A first open meeting, held on July 28, 1933, and reported by the *Cleveland Plain Dealer,* was attended by four hundred men, half of whom had signed application cards. The men cheered Roosevelt, and an auto worker by the name of John McCarthy sang a song "of me own makin'" dedicated to the

President: "Onward we will go—with Franklin Delano!" At a second meeting a week later, it was announced that the local had reached six hundred members (certainly an exaggeration) and that the national office of the AFL had been asked for a charter.

All these were signs of spectacular success in terms of union organization. The White Motor local must have been considered adequately established when officers were elected and it began holding business meetings on August 11. Termed "temporary" because the charter had not yet arrived, the officers were not essentially changed when that event took place. Lehman, predictably, was designated president; Dick Reisinger, vice president; Charley Walsh, Lehman's closest friend, treasurer; and Ed Stubbe, chair of the trustees. Extremely popular, Stubbe was nominated for every post but declined them one after the other. Finally, in accepting that of head trustee, he explained for the benefit of his "gang": "I want to have my eye on the money. This is one union that's gonna be run straight!"

Soon enough he gave proof of his vigilance, although some thought the act was uncalled for, when the secretary, Anthony L. Rohman, put in a bill of $66 for preparing all the local's books. Stubbe arbitrarily cut it down to half that sum, explaining that all the officers gave a lot of their time for free. Rohman summarily quit his post, which was fortunately taken over eventually by Reisinger.[2]

The Federation's organizers were particularly proud of the White Motor local, boasting that it was already the biggest unit in the MTC. But their nurture of it was vigilant, for as craft unionists they could not quite trust this great amorphous animal, even when it had only a couple hundred members. George McKinnon attended every meeting, sitting at the platform table to the right of and slightly behind George Lehman and in reach of his ear. Indeed, Lehman was glad to have him. The job of union president was intimidating to him despite his long membership in the Masons, where he had seen innumerable meetings conducted. He purchased a copy of *Roberts' Rules of Order,* which he studied diligently on weekends, but it took months before he commanded the "Order of the Day" and could run through it in proper sequence without constant ocular control guided by his index finger.

After the early flush of success, Lehman began to worry about the local's lack of progress. The time arrived, soon enough, that new members stopped coming in, or at least ceased paying their entry (initiation) fee. The high point of the local's membership is impossible to ascertain. Financial statements do not appear in the minutes (which begin on August 25, 1933) until October 6, when events altered the local's status.

George Lehman suspected the reason for the slackening of the union tide; it was that other organization in the field. However, it was not a come-lately outfit that played a dog-in-the-manger role in cutting into the AFL unit's numbers. The fact was that Wyndham Mortimer's TUUL local had started organizing at about the same time as Lehman's. Both had been growing simultaneously though their major concentrations were in different departments, and membership for both began falling off at about the same time. The fault was the split, which discouraged the workers.

• • •

The TUUL union was probably bigger than the AFL local, as Mortimer seems to have thought, for he had not waited for governmental sanction to get it started. As a matter of fact, he had been talking union to all who would listen for many years. The son of a coal miner who was a staunch union man, he began his working life as a miner when he was twelve. He considered it contradictory that a law must enunciate the "right" for workers to organize a union. He ironically minimized the significance of the NRA in talking with his fellow workers, a mistake that I also made. Many of these men firmly believed that "Section 7-A" had given them something that they had not had before. When I met him, Mortimer no longer tended to argue on this issue, recognizing no doubt the subjective gains of NRA, which had instilled in workers the courage to organize and a belief that many of them had never had before in the importance of unions.

In 1920, during the post–World War I flurry of organizational fervor, Mortimer and a sizable group of his fellow workers at White's had gone down to AFL headquarters to ask for help in getting their plant unionized. An organizer went the rounds, ticketing the men as "belonging to" six different internationals.[3] When Mortimer, citing his experience as a coal miner, argued that industrial workers must function as a unit, the AFL man said: "Well, you could have a shop council." Mortimer replied that it was not the same thing at all, that it would be like "organizing for permanent disorganization."

In 1932, a year before the NRA, when White Motors had been taken over by the Morgan interests and was streamlined with piecework and its inevitable speedup, Mortimer led another group down to the AFL. But Harry McLaughlin, secretary of the Central Labor Council, was downright offensive, qualifying mass production workers as ignorant "hunkies" who could not appreciate the blessings of American unionism. Mortimer and his friends recalled this insult a year later when the NRA excitement coursed through the plant. Fortunately, they felt, there might be an alternative to the AFL, when earlier in 1933 they had read in the papers about the big strikes that were conducted in Detroit at Briggs Body, Hayes Body, and other factories. Mortimer and Bill Dieter, his shop companion since 1919, one day set out to contact the equivalent of this Detroit auto union in Cleveland.

Its headquarters were downtown, on the second floor of a dingy old flatiron building. In the hall above the stairs were painted huge figures of a black worker and a white worker clasping hands, the whole executed in the style of proletarian gigantism that left-wing artists affected at that time. On the outer door upstairs was painted "Joint Council of Industrial Unions," while on one of the inner doors were letters illustrating the Communist party's dual outlook on trade union work: "AFL Rank and File Opposition Center."

Joseph Zack, the TUUL secretary, greeted the two men effusively. So the auto workers were in motion at last! Oh, he had waited a long time for this day. He rubbed his pudgy hands and giggled, as if to show his splendid teeth. Naturally, they wouldn't have anything to do with the AFL fakers, he went on, supplying their thoughts for them. They can't fool even the American workers all the time. Yet he had no application cards for Mortimer and Dieter to distribute in the plant when they asked for them. "What do you want application cards for?" he queried, shrugging. "Call your workers to a meeting. Talk over your grievances. Get them into motion. That's the only thing to do."

It was arranged that they would have a meeting in the TUUL hall that coming Friday. Mimeographed slips that Mortimer's teen-aged daughter made to announce the meeting were passed out in the shop. But when he came down early on Friday to see that all was in order, he was dismayed to find the hall already occupied by a meeting of the Unemployed Council.

"So what!" Zack exclaimed enthusiastically. "So you'll meet together with the Unemployed Council. Do you think the problems of the employed and unemployed workers can't be discussed together?"

Mortimer had already begun to realize that it did not pay to argue with Zack. In a sweat, he dashed about the neighboring area until he found a vacant hall in the Painters Union headquarters. The janitor insisted on getting the $6 rent in advance but Mortimer did not have it. After a long discussion he convinced the man that the money would be collected at the meeting. When he got back to TUUL headquarters on Payne Avenue, a big crowd was gathered outside. Some had gone home but most had remained and hopped into their cars or walked up to Euclid. When the meeting started at 8:30, nearly two hundred workers filled the small hall.

Mortimer took the chair because no one else would and started by raising the primary question of affiliation. He felt, he began, that the men had to decide two questions: Did they want a union and should they join the AFL? Most of those present had been influenced by Mortimer's ideas. One old German, Paul Novak, explained what seemed the prevailing sentiment by shouting, "I don't give a damn vot kind of union it is so long it isn't dot goddam AFL!" The decision was unanimous but for one hand against the Federation. Mortimer gave a pep talk about the Auto Workers Union

(TUUL) and the victories it had won in Detroit the previous February. A collection of $6.20 was gathered for the hall rent, and another meeting was scheduled for the following week.

The drive was on. As soon as application cards were available, the men began spreading them around in the factory. Truckers or others who had the run of the plant were the best for this job. Within two weeks, five hundred men had signed up but only a fraction had paid their initiation fee or dues, which many doled out a dime at a time. All of this called for a lot of book-keeping and Mortimer found that most of the detail fell on his shoulders. Certainly TUUL headquarters were little help. When dues stamps ran out, Zack saw no reason why they could not use initiation stamps instead until a supply of the others arrived from Detroit. When Mortimer told him that the fellows were asking about a charter, Zack extended his short arms in a disgusted gesture. "My God," he demanded, "what do they think a union is, a Masonic lodge?"

In the end, Mortimer lost patience with Zack's slipshod methods. "You don't think workers are going to pay money out without getting something to show for it," he told him testily. "Most of them aren't sure where their family's next week's food budget is coming from. It's a sacrifice for them even to pay a quarter for their dues."

Zack's carelessness was probably more than a personal deficiency, it was as much a reflection of his exuberance about the tremendous organizational impulse that the country was experiencing. He was aflame with the vision of "a period of great struggles." In fact, he could not see any organization in a plant of the size of White Motors as at all possible unless it was achieved through a "battle." "Haven't you elected a committee yet?" he asked the men at one of the meetings. "What are you waiting for? Do you want the company to invite you?" He was sure that the workers relished this sort of coarse humor.

"What good is it," one man replied truculently, "if the company turns the committee down? What if they all get fired?"

"What do you mean 'fired'?" Zack demanded with contained wrath. Then, suddenly, he was galvanized with fury, puffing his cheeks and pounding a balled fist on the table. "Fire the committee?" he repeated. *"Over . . . our . . . dead . . . body!"* The men looked thrilled and one or two cheered. But a few remained dubious, Ed Stubbe among them.

Stubbe had come to this meeting by mistake. He had been given a couple of announcements at the plant, one of them by Dick Reisinger, an inspector on the line like himself. He shoved both of them into his pants pockets and when he took one of them out after work, all he noticed was the address. "That guy must be nuts!" Stubbe said out loud and raced for the door. Bill Dieter, Mortimer's friend and someone Ed Stubbe knew from the plant, was at the meeting and extended a card, which Stubbe shoved brusquely aside as he left the hall.

Downstairs, he ran smack into Charley Walsh, whom he knew very well and whose presence there confused Stubbe. Suddenly, he felt that he had to explain to him why he was at the meeting. "Dick Reisinger asked me to come down tonight but I ain't seen *him* around."

"You came to the wrong meeting," Walsh confided to Stubbe, bending over his ear in a manner that he had. "The AFL local is up on 62nd Street, at Dunlevy Hall. This is the communist outfit here. I'm keeping tabs on them." He fingered his jacket pocket open to reveal a small notebook. Charley Walsh was mysterious. I was later told that he had been a kind of private cop, working for department stores sniping shoplifters. Those who told me about him did not consider this kind of work as a mark against the man, just as most workers, I was horrified to learn, thought of Pinkertons as admirable, sort of G-men who tracked down big crooks and kidnappers.

Most of the AFL group began to take on George Lehman's worries about "that other gang." Walsh tried to laugh them off, insisting that their membership was declining. "I've been getting the communist bug into the ears of some of their best guys," he said.

Chris Schaum, a trustee, agreed: "Most of their fellows don't even know it's a communist union. All we gotta do is *tell* them."

Lehman thought they were whistling in the dark. "There's no use kidding ourselves," he said. "This man Mortimer has got a real drag in the shop. I've talked to a lot of guys about him. They don't any more believe he's a communist than you or I are. I think I'm going to talk to the man." Lehman took the bull by the horns soon after and stopped Mortimer in the plant's downstairs vestibule at lunch hour to tell him that his group would like to talk things over with Mortimer's some time.

"Sure, any time you say," Mortimer told him. Lehman suggested that they go down to the Metal Trades some evening and meet Harvey Brown, the Machinists' vice president, who was a kind of godfather of the AFL local at White's. "After all, you've had so much more experience with unions than we have," Lehman observed shrewdly. "It wouldn't be a fair match with only us against you."

"I don't mind meeting Harvey Brown again," Mortimer said. "We had a long talk once years ago," he added, squinting his eyes in humor. In truth, Mortimer had been growing concerned about the progress of his own group. The "red scare" was having a demoralizing effect on his members and he found himself spending most of his time counteracting its influence. The AFL attack had become virulent. Leaflets distributed outside the plant called on the workers to "Choose between Franklin Delano Roosevelt [who, it was falsely claimed, had "endorsed" the AFL] and Joe Stalin."[4]

Even before Lehman had spoken to him, Mortimer was halfway inclined to favor a merger if satisfactory guarantees could be had from AFL officials regarding raids on the local's members. When the day arrived for the meeting with Harvey Brown, he felt that his group must take the offensive on the jurisdictional question because it was the only way to establish a fellow feeling with the AFL men. Hence his first question to Brown concerned what assurances he would give that, once the merger took place, the craft unions wouldn't start splitting the White local into a dozen parts. In an amazingly tactless response, Brown threw himself into a lengthy defense of craft unionism, ending by quoting passages marked with place slips in some books stacked on his desk.

The meeting broke up without issue. But it did have the effect of starting a hot discussion among the AFL men about their "federal charter," which had been promised them some time ago. Why was it being held up? Some of the things Brown had said made men like Dick Reisinger and Ed Stubbe skeptical. Even Lehman was disturbed. They asked for a showdown.

A couple of nights later, local officers were again called down to the Metal Trades, where they were met by Jim McWeeney and other organizers. They were very polite, too polite, and the White men learned from them that their federal charter was actually in doubt. The AFL leaders had been playing this charter up to the point that the auto unionists regarded it as an impregnable, factorywide industrial union setup. This it was never meant to be; it was only a kind of bait that would attract factory workers during the big organizational surge, who would be distributed among the craft internationals as soon as possible.

McWeeney explained these facts about the AFL's plans very explicitly to the White Motor men. All nonproductive workers, such as maintenance men, truckers, and sweepers, would be put into a local of their own; all machine hands would pass into the Machinists Union; and so on and so on. The White local delegation, who had expected other tidings, were shocked, infuriated, and spoke their minds out freely. It was all a goddam racket, they shouted, and Reisinger, Stubbe, and several others bolted from the office.

McWeeney ran after them and brought them back after much coaxing. "For God's sake, don't do anything rash," he pleaded. "I'm willing to take the responsibility and let youse boys keep your present setup. What's more, I'm going to get youse your federal charter even if I bust trying."

Reisinger thought that McWeeney was putting on an act but the federal charter did arrive shortly afterward and the merger of the two groups followed. Even before that event, the sense of security that the federal charter had brought the White Motors local was shaken by a letter. Dated October 2, 1933, four days before the scheduled amalgamation, it contained a message from AFL Secretary Frank Morrison, who sternly ordered Local 18463 to transfer its tool-and-die workers to the Machinists Union. And a number of skilled workers started receiving claiming letters from various other craft unions. "They'll have to come in and get them!" Reisinger hissed, protruding his blood-red lip.

• • •

Wyndham Mortimer had waited for the grant of the federal charter to the AFL local before taking up the merger with his TUUL group. When he did, it was not easy to put the idea across and required hours of debate, as he has freely admitted.[5] Joseph Zack considered Mortimer's decision an act of betrayal. After a long argument, when he realized that he could not change his mind, Zack veered to an amazing new tack. "All right," he told Mortimer, "go into the AFL, but only to smash it!" "I couldn't do that," Mortimer replied. It was not the last piece of advice that he was to receive from Zack, who tried to keep epistolary contact with him. However, as far as I know, he never saw him again.

The local's minutes record three things that took place on October 6, 1933, all landmarks in its history. One was the merger; another was the election of a financial secretary, memorable not because Mortimer was a candidate but because he was an also-ran, the only time that I know of when he was defeated for office in the local. The third and most significant event was the union's decision to set up a grievance committee instructed to open negotiations "immediately" with the company. Mortimer was appointed one of its five members by President Lehman, who whispered to Dick Reisinger, "I want you to meet with the committee after adjournment and get it started, but especially I want you to see to it that Mortimer is made the chairman."

It is doubtful that Lehman's reason for this surprising move was to show appreciation to the new group for having come into the local. Honors for that step had already been bestowed when the TUUL members were invited to go up front en masse to take the obligation. The entire assembly rose while the applicants stood, their right hands over their hearts, and responded "I do" to the pledge. The audience intoned, "I bear witness." Then Lehman gave the new members the password of the year—"Five days a week"—and instructed them about the required manner of saluting the guard at the door, palm up or palm down according to whether they were entering or leaving. Lehman then shook hands symbolically with Mortimer and hundreds of pairs of hardened palms applauded enthusiastically.

Financial reports in the minutes provide a lucid picture of the vivifying effect that the merger and the decision to start negotiations had on the local's bank balance, which rose from $540 to more than $3,000 in the three months following.

The company officials were no doubt informed about the union's still modest numbers but did not take aggressive advantage of the fact when soon after the merger the negotiating committee came to meet with them. George Smith, the plant manager and company spokesman, who turned out to be a rather decent opponent, assumed a customary manner of approach, linking the company's fortunes with those of its workers. White's had lost $8 million during the depression and was still operating in the red, he said. There was a limit as to how long that could go on. Ashton Bean, the company's president, he added, and "the rest of us" were doing everything under the sun to get more orders, particularly to get started on "the new model" that would have to compete with the lower-priced trucks that were in the market. "But we can't do that unless you help us," Smith emphasized. "It isn't fair for a national organization like the AFL to make demands on a small company while sparing its powerful competitors like General Motors, Ford, and International Harvester. As it is, we're complying with all the requirements of the code."

The union negotiators were silenced by the seeming strength of these arguments. Lehman smiled nervously and glanced at Mortimer's imperturbable face as though hoping that he would pick up the challenge and take the burden from him. Some of Mortimer's friends had said that Lehman's purpose in putting Mortimer at the head of the committee had been to put him on the spot, to get him to "stick his neck out." From having talked to George Lehman later, I am certain that this was not the case. He regarded Mortimer highly, he asserted, and in those early days was delighted to have him "in my corner."

Mortimer cleared his throat, and the whole group switched their eyes toward him. What could he say? There was no gainsaying Smith's reasoning. "We're well aware of the company's problems, Mr. Smith," he began, "and we thank you for being so frank with us. We're glad to return the favor. You see, Mr. Smith, you're implying that a man's suffering is the same as a company's. It isn't. The only way you can compare yourselves with us is that we all need food and clothes and shelter. A couple years ago, the house on which my wife and I had been paying for fifteen years was threatened with foreclosure. Well, we saved it with the help of a couple hundred of our neighbors—but that's another story."

He opened a slip of paper that he had been clutching. "This sheet," he resumed, "tells how much I earned at White's in one year, from June 1932 to June 1933. It was one hundred and thirty-six dollars." He looked straight into the company official's eyes. "That's enough money to starve on, Mr. Smith, but it's not enough to do piecework on a machine. As for the code, it's not the minimum hourly wage, but the annual earnings that count in a family's budget."

There was a pause which Smith broke by changing the subject to the union's request for recognition. "We're always glad to meet with representatives of our workers, gentlemen, and to take up any matters that you wish to bring to us. I'm willing to put the time aside once a week on the same day and hour, if that's all right with you."

The only thing that Mortimer's humanistic plea accomplished was that Smith did not raise the question of shared sacrifices again until the first "crisis" rose between the company and the union and then he quoted the same figures to the press. However, the union men felt that they had learned something about negotiating at that first session. Thereafter, they came to each meeting primed with several concrete problems, leaving no openings for tendentious discussions.

The company settled all grievances out of hand that did not cost anything or cost much, for example, changing the starting hour in the morning from 7:00 to 8:00 or paying workers who had to prepare their own jobs, which the "set-up men" were supposed to do and for which they got paid. It was only fair that the pay go to the production men.

Some grievances were about patently unfair practices yet it was difficult to get management to admit this. One common practice in those early days concerned piecework earnings, which were ostensibly guaranteed by a minimum hourly wage (base rate). The company had a trick of juggling the figures from day to day, drawing off the "excess" of the piecework earnings on one day and adding it to another day that had fallen below the minimum. The result was, as Mortimer pointed out, that the "guaranteed minimum [43 cents] actually became the maximum."

Workers knew that money was being taken out of their pockets by such "petty larceny" practices, as they called them. But it was impossible to stop such practices until a union was established that was "willing to go to bat for them." One would think that a self-respecting company would have corrected this "small" vice of its auditing department without having to be prompted by the union. The fact was that many thousands of dollars were often involved in such seemingly negligible cases when the multiplying factor of 2,500 workers entered into the calculation.

To cure this vice the union committee asked that piecework earnings be posted day by day, then, at the end of the two-week pay period, workers could figure out for themselves exactly how much was coming to them. One day, Smith announced to the grievance committee, as recorded in the local's October 31 minutes, that a solution had been found. He introduced a "Mr. O'Donnell," who explained that in the future "they were going to give the men small stubs of the piecework tickets so that they could figure out what they earned."

There occurs among the grievances cited in the local's minutes of this period one case that foreshadowed what was to become a spectacular subject of controversy. It was natural that the first negotiations were almost exclusively concerned with money because of the near-starvation level to which earnings had fallen during the depression. But an item that takes an entirely different tack appears in the minutes of October 31, 1933: "Report was made to him [George Smith] of two men in [Department] 1A2K who were told that they were going to be replaced by new men, and that as far as we knew, it was not justified."

Concealed in these few obscure words was a reference to the large number of skilled workers in their fifties and even older who had worked many years at White's. We can judge by this notice that they were beginning to be discharged and young men put in their places. Others in their forties and fifties were not even called back to work because the Auto Code's provisions on "seniority" gave them no protection, having been devised by the manufacturers and signed by AFL President Bill Green.

An additional issue of plantwide importance was the question of money. According to the local's minutes, on November 17, 1933, after a thorough discussion, the local adopted a motion that the company be asked to restore the wage scale of 1929. A reply was called for in four days though the word *strike* was not mentioned. The major thrust of the union's demands was the Auto Code's 43 cent minimum, which was to be raised to 56 cents. In addition, the rates of skilled workers were to be increased from the existing 70 cent ceiling to a dollar an hour. Ten days later, on November 26, when there still was no reply from the company, the local decided to put pressure on it by making the strike threat overt. The "test strike vote" that was taken at two separate meetings covering both shifts gave overwhelming assent to the strike, 1,087 to 78, and the company was once more given four days to reply.

But there was no strike, although neither the 1929 wage scale nor any across-the-board raise was granted. Certain wage adjustments were made "on classified jobs . . . where inequalities may exist," and the company promised to pay the minimum rate on all work, even if piecework earnings fell below it. It will be recalled that George Smith had already consented to do this. But the significant difference was that his verbal accord now appeared in a signed letter dated December 11, which carried the crucial words "the White Motor Company *agrees*" [emphasis added]. It was tantamount to "recognition" in the union's view, even though that recognition was limited to "members of Federal Local Union No. 18463." But it was the only union named, and it was indeed the only one that functioned in the plant.

A telling revelation of what members thought about the settlement is given by a simple little sentence in the local's minutes of December 15: "Committee given a rising vote of thanks." Other factors should not be ignored in the search for a total picture of the event, however. Most impressive no doubt was the wire that President William Green had sent in reply to the local's strike vote of November 26, a vote that George McKinnon had announced to Green. With great solemnity, the AFL representative read the telegram to the crowded local meeting: *"Under no circumstances permit a strike until public officials have opportunity to adjust controversy"* [emphasis added].

Lehman followed Green's behest by reading pertinent sections on strikes from the Federation's manual, to which McKinnon added his own personal observations, outlining the dire consequences of disobedience of Green's counsel: "If you ask other unions for help, their doors will be closed to you. How long do you think your local treasury will last without such help? How long could any of you keep food on your table from the money you've got in the bank or that you could borrow from your families or friends?"

Wyndham Mortimer did not call for defiance of Green's order. With the unification of the local hardly a month old, he was well aware that it was too fragile to go into a protracted strike in the face of AFL opposition. What he could have thought of Green's intrusion was another matter, depriving the local as it did of the strength the huge positive strike vote could have furnished in its negotiations with the company. Reisinger and Stubbe told me later that they had considered Green's action a "sellout." Their shift to Mortimer's general trade union outlook probably dated from this event.

Despite the accommodation reached at White Motors, several issues remained in suspense, leaving a brooding discontent that would break loose again on March 1, 1934. In Smith's letter, which George Lehman read slowly and meticulously to the December 15 membership meeting, there was one wording that the men would continue to think about and discuss. Smith promised that wage increases would be granted *"when and as* the company is no longer compelled to endure the tremendous losses sustained during the last three years" [emphasis added].

The membership listened in respectful silence to Smith's listing of those losses until suddenly they broke into a lusty round of boos when he declared: "In spite of this, the Company recognizing that your wages have been greatly decreased, especially because of the spreading of employment, gave an increase of somewhat better than 10 percent last August." The White Motor workers were sick and tired of hearing this 10 percent raise being vaunted; they well knew it had been preceded by a bevy of cuts, as high as 30 percent, in piece rates. The false boast, repeated once again in Smith's letter, left a bitter taste with them, and cast doubt on both the company's arithmetic and its promises.[6]

The Growth of
the White Motor Local

2

It took fewer than three months for the White Motor local to lose its faith in the company's promises. The reason for this cannot be ascribed to the malice or insurgency of any group among its members. On the contrary, the company itself was to blame, its official family in any case.

What was granted to the White Motor men on March 1, 1934, was not considered ample, especially when they learned through the grapevine that it had probably been reduced by a half by their president's illicit action of offering a "compromise" to the company—an offer to which the rest of the committee had not consented. We can be almost certain that the inspiration for this act came from the AFL organizers, who took such arbitrary decisions of union officers for granted.

As it happened, only a few days later President William Green would become involved in a strike-breaking act on a massive scale during an experience that came to be known as the "March events of 1934," which engaged automobile manufacturers, the national AFL, NRA officials, and President Franklin D. Roosevelt. Company union spokesmen should also be mentioned, although they could hardly be considered as acting independently. A number of them were transported and housed in Washington in company-paid Pullmans. In the end, Green and his lieutenants from Detroit, Flint, Pontiac, and Lansing surrendered all the demands of the auto workers one after the other and diverted the threatened strike into a vertiginous rout.

It is no exaggeration to say—and the AFL has often said so itself—that the auto locals of Michigan, particularly those of General Motors, which had burgeoned to a hundred thousand members within weeks, went to pieces faster than they had assembled. AFL auto unionism would no doubt have totally disappeared at that time were it not for the resistance of a few plants in outlying centers at Toledo, Milwaukee, South Bend, and Cleveland, which by aggressive action against their employers and disobedience of the tactics that their AFL leaders proposed were able to survive.

Although the White Motor local had no part in the March disaster, the union was constantly confronted by constraining rules and decisions stemming from this unhappy event, against which it fought with courage and persistence, eventually erecting an opposing defense that was superior to that gained by most other auto locals. The White Motor local's readiness to struggle could already be sensed during the period between the December 11, 1933, agreement and the March 1, 1934, near-strike crisis.[1] The local's minutes for the intervening months reveal a steady concern with working out and putting before the company more equitable conditions in the categories of hours, overtime pay, piece and day rates and especially seniority.

On April 27, 1934, two months after the "settlement" with which this book began, the local's grievance committee presented to the company a more detailed group of demands, including a set of rules covering seniority, which the union proposed as a substitute for the utterly unsatisfactory provisions of the Auto Code. Everybody was surprised when George Lehman added a man who worked in the office, Frank Klavon, to the bargaining group for this important encounter. Dick Reisinger soon after told me the reason. It was stunning news. Lehman had decided not to run for reelection in August (the AFL had other things in view for him), and Klavon was to be Lehman's successor. Lehman and the Metal Trades leaders had it figured out that Wyndham Mortimer would be the most likely opponent for their candidate.

Since my arrival on the scene, I had been trying to serve the union, with little success, as voluntary publicity agent, which gave me the cover for my deepening interest in its various manifestations. The choice of Klavon was hard for me to fathom because he had attracted very little attention until recently, as far as I could see. He was bright enough and pleasant to look at, not yet forty and glib of tongue. Another thing about him, however, would never have occurred to me had Reisinger not mentioned it. Klavon had been for years a fellow Mason of Lehman's and rather high in the organization for so young a man. I myself, to be sure, had already set my sights on Mortimer and was suddenly seized by anxiety. "Do you think Klavon has a chance to win?" I asked Reisinger offhandedly, without designating the opponent I was thinking of. Reisinger considered seriously for some moments. "It's hard to say. He might make a strong run. His experience in the Masons wouldn't hurt him in the least. He'd know how to handle the chair and that's important to the guys."

What the grievance committee prepared was still far from a full-blown contract. The White Motor leaders were too sensible to tackle so vast a task so early and decided to concentrate instead on the selection of a few of the important problems that were most pressing. There were only a half-dozen of these, which can be paraphrased as follows:

1. Wages of workers on an hourly basis were to be computed daily instead of semimonthly.
2. Pieceworkers were to earn at least 20 percent above the hourly rate.
3. Overtime work should be paid for at the rate of time-and-one-half.
4. Seniority should be calculated from the original time of hiring; lay-offs and rehirings would be made on that basis, the man with the longest work record being laid off last and rehired first.
5. Salaried foremen were not to do the work of men who were on an hourly basis.
6. Members of the union would refuse to work with any worker who did not join the union within thirty days (equivalent to the closed shop).

The local's discussion of two or three of these points was particularly lively. Reisinger seemed to anticipate this by reading them slowly and emphatically. When, for instance, he rendered the wording on rehiring, he stressed with a sort of pride the provision that the committee had come up with to forestall a familiar abuse, to the effect that an employee should go *"back on the same work from which said employee was laid off"* [emphasis added].

This brought a spontaneous cheer from the members. Active, pro-union men were not the only ones who tended to be victimized by transfers. Non-complaining "weak sisters" were just as apt to be gulled, and older workers especially were picked on with the aim of getting them to quit their jobs voluntarily so the company would be relieved of charges of discrimination. There was no discussion on several demands that everybody favored though they would be hard to get, for example, the bonus for overtime that eventually would become one of the important accomplishments of the new union movement. The prohibition of salaried men doing work belonging to hourly workers was directed at the company's practice of calling foremen in on weekends to do "rush jobs," when many veteran White men had not yet been rehired.

I was pleasantly surprised when several members discussed piecework in an anomalous way. Rather than ask for a bonus of 20 percent for it, they called for the elimination of piecework altogether. The reaction was enthusiastic and I recalled having been told that White Motors had introduced the piecework system only after the depression. Apparently, a lot of the old-timers looked back nostalgically to the time when White's had acquired a reputation for being an "Old Men's Home." Such a reversion was unrealistic, to be sure, but the passion of the speakers did not seem to take that into account. Lehman warned them that the local had to "go slow" on this issue because the entire industry was involved. "We've got tough competitors," he asserted, "and truck-buyers don't give a damn about good workmanship any more or the fact that White's can bring up an old truck from some purchaser in Africa that's done a million miles and is still running."

Lehman likewise cautioned on the question of the closed shop (point 6 on the list of problems to be addressed), warning against "flash strikes" that could close the whole plant. "Why should 2,000 men suffer when one man is stubborn?" he asked. But such common-sense arguments failed to impress a number of the men, including pugnacious leaders like Ed Stubbe. Feisty unionists heatedly took after the "hitchhikers" (men getting all the benefits of the union without paying dues), describing the tactics they used to make life miserable for anti-union cranks. For example, one morning in the strongly organized engine shop, the men notified their foreman that they were going to walk out at noon unless a certain belligerent character was transferred out of the department. They went through all the acts of getting ready but plant manager George Smith cut the thing short by removing the stubborn holdout.

George Lehman argued that the closed shop was illegal according to the Auto Code. "It protects the free decision of the workers to join any union of their choice or no union at all," he said. "That's not the way I see it, George," Dick Reisinger replied. "Section 7-A of NRA was meant to protect workers from being forced into the damn company unions, not to protect pro-company stooges!" And Ed Stubbe had a less intellectual but even more effective comeback. Red-gilled and puffing, he shouted at Lehman: "You say the company can't agree to force workers to join the union. Maybe *they* can't, *but we can!*" A clap of thunder greeted his fiery words.

The fourth point on the list—seniority—did not arouse any discussion, because the committee's carefully prepared wording had already been read to the members and approved by them. Moreover, the subject had been endlessly discussed in the press, and auto workers were aware of the nullifying factors of "dependents" and "merit" (skill, efficiency), which had been rammed into the Auto Code by the manufacturers, with the passive blessing of Roosevelt. No one expected that the local could put across its foolproof quantitative plan without a battle, but neither was anyone aware of how soon such a struggle would threaten to break out.

On the morning of April 27, 1934, when the committee entered George Smith's office to present their demands, the company had contrived to take a jump on the union by posting the announcement of a 5 percent raise on all piece and day rates. This was a good deal less than the company expected the union to ask for but the idea no doubt was to weaken its request under the principle that "5 percent in the hand is worth 20 percent in demand." Smith then proceeded to take up the whole list, point by point: "This one we can do" (point number 1); "this one's okay" (point number 2). He continued to sift through the pages without committing himself further, however, until he came to point number 6 (closed shop).

"On this point," he said firmly, his lips tight, "all I can say is that you're sure to come to blows with the company on it . . . and that you're bound to lose." He went on to explain that it was illegal under the Auto Code and gave much the same argument that George Lehman had presented to the local. Dick Reisinger took wry pleasure in pointing this out to me in private after the negotiations. "I'm telling you this off the record, Henry, because if it comes out it could only have come from me. I slammed back at Smith exactly the way I had done at George at the meeting. George was nervous too because he realized that he had given the very same arguments." And he looked at me finely to see if I had caught his point.

The newspapers' handling of these negotiations provided me with a first-hand lesson about what a union's publicity agent could expect from the "capitalist press" in any situation of relative importance. I was waiting for the committee when they came out of the company office into the ground-floor vestibule. I explained that I felt it was advisable to try and get some publicity on the union's demands before the company could contact the papers.

Reisinger turned over to me a typed copy of the six demands, and Mortimer and he stayed with me for ten minutes before going back to work, giving me some words about the discussion that had taken place. They seemed pleased with its results. They also told me about the raise that the company had posted just before they entered Smith's office.

I went off to the main library downtown, where I read the demands over several times before writing my copy.[2] It was by far the most important assignment I had undertaken since "joining" the union two months previously. As it happens, I kept a scribbled original of my release, which I copied twice more legibly (I could not type yet), one copy going to the *Cleveland Plain Dealer,* the other to the *Press.*

In listing the six demands, I took advantage of the need to shorten them by eliminating entirely the introductory clause to the one asking for the 20 percent piecework "prime" because I found its wording objectionable: "In order to create an incentive for pieceworkers to give their best to your company, piecework prices shall be computed so that pieceworkers shall make not less than 20 percent over and above the hourly rate per day."

I felt no compunction in making the cut since the wording contained no essential factual material and was nothing but a plea by the union that was close to begging. I could not think that Reisinger could have been responsible for such weasel words. More likely, it was Joseph Summerell, the recording secretary and a strong Lehman man, who deserved that honor.

Of much greater importance, I felt, was the lead that I was to give the article. Without too much time to think about it, I decided to make it the demand for the closed shop. I did this mainly because of the animated debate it had produced at the local meeting and because it seemed to reflect the members' genuine, militant spirit. Thus I was able also to bring into my story the threat of the engine plant to strike that afternoon if the single anti-union holdout did not join. It was a piece of red-hot news in the making.

But neither newspaper used this feature of my story; more amazing still, they did not even mention the local's demand for the closed shop. The desk man at the *Plain Dealer* seemed distraught when he read the piece and he called the labor editor over, a man by the name of Lavelle, who skimmed rapidly over the six demands. "I agree," he said, "we'd better not say anything about number 6, forcing men to join the union after thirty days. That's illegal."

"I don't understand," I replied, nettled by his repetition of the same argument that everybody was using. "All I'm saying is what the men are asking for."

"Yes, but it's certain that the courts will find it illegal, so I advise you to leave it out."

"How can I do that if they voted for it? That makes it news, doesn't it?"

"Maybe so," he conceded, "but you still don't want to turn public opinion against you. Just think what people will say about the union trying to dictate that to the company."

I realized that simple logic would not move him and after leaving tried to figure out why he was so set on the matter. Was it because of the strike that was going on at the Fisher Body Plant? Judging from the newspapers, the whole city was greatly agitated by the strike and all the union was asking for was recognition. But the management would not so much as meet with it and threatened the union with an injunction unless the strike was called off. Printing a story that featured a demand for a closed shop at White Motors, I told myself, would be like throwing raw meat to the Fisher Body strikers.

I went next to the *Cleveland Press* and in a somewhat subdued mood handed my article to a young man. "Who wrote this?" he asked.

"I did."

"It's darn good." He went to confer with an older man, who looked toward me several times as they spoke. Then the young man came back. "It'll go in just the way it's written."

But it did not. As though they had conferred with each other, both papers avoided any mention of the closed shop demand or of the debate I had inserted into the story between George Smith and the union representatives over its legality. But neither paper forgot to include the company's "voluntary" raise of 5 percent.

The White Motor Company's reply of May 12 arrived within a week of the negotiations and was presented to the local at a special meeting held on May 18. By prearrangement among the grievance committee members, acceptance of the company's grants was recommended even though half of the union's demands were turned down. What was gained however (and without a strike), including the company's 5 percent raise that no one credited as "voluntary," was considered important enough to defer the rest for the future.

The company's letter met with success when read to the meeting. This impression was strengthened by the verbal reports of the committee members, who explained the importance of what was being gained and stressed the wisdom of the local's "strategy" in not going after everything all at one time. In illustrating the point, Frank Klavon's description of Smith's first reaction to the union's demands made an especially big hit with the members. On Lehman's advice, Klavon had prepared his account with care, telling how, when the committee handed Smith its memorandum, he snapped the pages up and ran his eyes swiftly down one sheet after the other, gobbling up the words. When he finished reading, he slammed the papers on the desk and exclaimed, his voice a mixture of displeasure and concealed surprise, "There's no demand for a wage increase!"

There was a smile of controlled mirth on Klavon's lips as he looked around at the men, whose questioning eyes were set on his. Then he gave a big vaudevillian wink. "We all know that the company has its stooges in the union so that they can get firsthand reports about our plans. But those guys slip up sometimes, and they must've told the company that we were putting in for a big raise. Well, I guess there'll be an increase in the ranks of unemployed stool pigeons after this!" This observation brought a burst of gleeful laughter, which I must confess I did not share with a full heart. The company's offer was accepted unanimously.

• • •

It was hardly two months later that this seeming peace was broken by a series of provocative acts on the part of the company. The acts centered around the question of seniority, an issue upon which White Motors had refused to make any concession in the recent negotiations.

On July 6, Wyndham Mortimer reported a large series of layoffs among older workers who had a minimum of eighteen years of service in what was called the parts department, a kind of supply store that furnished replacement parts to owners of old White truck models. These men were too old to work on the line but were highly competent to handle this task. They had "grown up at White's" and knew all the models from the company's beginning by heart. Thus they could suggest substitutes for parts that customers ordered that were similar to current catalog numbers but not found in the stacks, parts about which younger workers would be totally ignorant.

There were thirty older men involved who were summarily discharged. Because hundreds of others in their late forties or fifties still worked at White's, the layoffs set off a wave of fear in the plant. President Lehman announced that if the company turned down the grievance committee's proposals in behalf of the discharged parts employees, a meeting of the executive board would be called to decide on a strike-vote meeting of the local. A member of the grievance committee named Furman added a suggestion that hours in the department be shortened before any other layoffs took place, a stopgap, share-the-work measure.

Although the entire local was united around a defense of the thirty laid-off parts plant workers, the union itself was no longer as unified as this affair might indicate. A split that started with the March 1 near-strike had now reached the point where a polarization had set in between the Lehman-Walsh-Klavon and Mortimer-Reisinger-Stubbe groups. This brooding factional spirit broke out sharply on June 15, over the question of designating delegates to a Detroit conference at which a National Council of all federal auto locals in the country would be chosen, a group slated to play a historic part in the union.

Although limited to an "advisory" role to a national director whom William Green would appoint, the council was offered as an answer to the increasing clamor among the auto locals for an international union. It was hoped, too, that it might reverse the continued decline of the auto union, particularly in the Michigan area, that had set in following the AFL's disastrous retreat during the March events. An outbreak of strikes in April, concentrated mainly at Fisher Body plants, had gone for naught, again due to poor Federation leadership. This resulted in a series of secession movements among auto locals in Kansas City, St. Louis, and, most dangerous of all, in several centers of Michigan.

The last development was led by Arthur Greer, president of the Hudson local of Detroit, reportedly the biggest auto union in the country. Greer had become closely associated with Richard Byrd, the labor representative on the Auto Labor Board (ALB) set up by the March settlement, who aided him in gathering recruits for his breakaway movement. Among those that became entangled in its web was the Fisher Body local of Cleveland, after its short strike of April 1934 was ended by empty promises and intimidation on the part of Federation officials.

It was a major assignment of the AFL organizers of Cleveland to help the Federation prevail at the June conference. To George McKinnon and James

McWeeney of the Metal Trades Council, this meant primarily to see to it that loyal delegates were sent to the Detroit session in order to assure the election of George Lehman as one of the eleven members of the National Council. They feared Wyndham Mortimer as a competitor for this post and were not certain either what part he might play in the disruptive plans of Arthur Greer. Mortimer's early role in the TUUL local at White's marked him in their eyes as a likely convert to any "dual union" movement, whatever its program or ideology.

Their decision was, with George Lehman's certain collaboration, to keep Mortimer out of the Detroit conference altogether. This had to be done at the local's June 15 meeting since the conference was scheduled for June 23. The letter asking the local to send delegates was no sooner read when Ed Gockel, a familiar of Lehman's who usually carried out such chores for him, popped up and moved "that President Lehman appoint three delegates to the Detroit Convention [*sic*]." However this motion is surprisingly recorded in Joseph Summerell's sparse minutes as being withdrawn. The reason is not given but my memory fills the gap because it has stored up loud complaints about the procedure indicated, describing it as "undemocratic," and even hinting that the president was beginning to take too much power upon himself.

So a new proposal was made by Ed Gockel, "that the president be sent to Detroit accompanied by a committee of his choosing on approval of the local." But at this point, a well-remembered and astonishing outburst by George Lehman himself occurred, and the motion was forgotten, as well it might be for there was plenty of turmoil raised for the next half-hour or so.

The dramatic incident might seem to deserve fuller treatment but is confined in the minutes to merely four trenchant words: "President Lehman resigned verbally." But I clearly remember the exciting action that followed, about which the minutes are totally silent. Pointing his gavel toward Vice President Dick Reisinger, who was standing by the door at the rear of the hall, Lehman called out in a clear voice that sounded like the peal of doom: "Brother Reisinger, will you please come forward and take the chair!"

When Reisinger had done this and Lehman had deliberately lifted his jacket from the back of his seat and put it on, he called out, his head turned to the assembly, "Brother Chairman, I want to announce that I am resigning as president of this local." He then raised his straw hat from the table and, holding it in his hand, walked toward the stairs at the far right of the platform, rapidly descended them, and then continued up the outer aisle to the rear of the hall.

There was a great commotion, out of which only a few details emerge for me. Some members were standing and shouting, offering motions or other observations to the new chairman, though I cannot recall what they might have been. I do remember my state of perturbation and of seeking out the figure of Wyndham Mortimer, who was at his usual place in the fifth or sixth row and looking extraordinarily composed. I was also aware of elongated Ed Gockel, flapping his thin arm at Reisinger and shouting at him. Reisinger pounded his gavel repeatedly, then astonished me by pointing it at Gockel. "Brother Chairman," the latter finally made himself heard, "I move that President Lehman's resignation should be rejected." The motion was seconded and declared adopted without discussion, but Lehman, hat in hand, stood at the door, shaking his head.

"I will not withdraw my resignation," he repeated several times, emphasizing a different word each time, I noted curiously, as though it were a role he was rehearsing. I became aware of several of his friends calling out to him, a couple of them approaching him at the door. Finally, he made up his mind and began walking slowly down the center aisle and remounted the platform. He carefully placed his straw hat on the table and, taking the offered gavel from Reisinger, he declared, putting great reluctance and hurt into his words: "I agree to take back my resignation."

Only then did it occur to me that the entire scene was a prepared performance. Without further explanation, he proceeded to carry out the previous motion, which almost everybody else had probably forgotten: "I want to announce my appointment as the delegates to accompany me to the conference, Brothers Reisinger, Stubbe, and Walsh, with Brothers Mortimer and Schaum as alternates."

The motion to approve was instantly made by Ed Gockel and seconded. And the little plot was at the point of success when a shout coming from a heavyset man of forty standing in the aisle suspended final action. "How about discussion, Brother Chairman?" And without waiting for Lehman's answer, the man, whom I knew as a great admirer of Mortimer's by the name of Whitcomb, went on to make his point. "I imagine that as an alternate, Brother Mortimer won't be going to the conference," he said, his voice heavy with sarcasm. "That means that you will be depriving this local at this important gathering of the one person who knows more about unionism than any other man at White's. Does that make sense to you, Brother Chairman?"

George Lehman looked at him for some long moments, balancing the gavel in his hand. One wondered as one looked at the crowd whether the earlier pandemonium would resume. But the crowd remained absolutely silent, and then an amazing thing happened that I have never been able to explain and I doubt that anybody else has either. The minutes recount the decision of George Lehman's closest friend in a few naked words: "Brother Walsh begged to be excused, and Brother Mortimer was approved to take his place. Motion made that this Committee be accepted. Carried."

Thus, contrary to the McKinnon-McWeeney plot, Wyndham Mortimer was able to go to the June 23 conference after all. The idea of the plot is not based on fantasy, but can be seen in an unsigned report prepared at the Detroit AFL office several months later by some unknown functionary.[3] The report appraises the qualities of the National Council members and observes that George Lehman "was elected largely by efforts of McWeeney who wanted to be sure [that] left-winger [would] not secure post."

It was all a matter of controlling Cleveland's votes at the conference. McWeeney and McKinnon were aware that the key lay with the two big locals, White Motors and Fisher Body. But the snag was that the latter was in revolt against the AFL after the fiasco of its recent strike, which had been broken with the aid of these two men, McWeeney and McKinnon. What could prevent Mortimer from joining with the Fisher representatives at Detroit and wrecking their plans for Lehman? It was safer to keep Mortimer out of Detroit altogether. Lehman's selection of Reisinger and Stubbe as delegates was clearly meant to split the opposition. With Mortimer absent, the AFL group doubtlessly felt that they could handle his friends.

• • •

The 156 delegates from seventy-seven auto locals attending the two-day session at Fort Wayne Hotel found its bonds tautly drawn before ever they arrived. Although one-third of the resolutions that had been offered by various locals called for the creation of an international union, these were totally disregarded in favor of the AFL's plan for the National Council, which was without acknowledged power of any kind, not even so much as to decide the dates of its meetings. The plan for the council was docilely presented to the delegates by Clyde Cooke of Lansing, appointive chair of the resolutions committee. Cook's clandestine activity as a Pinkerton spy would not be exposed for a couple of years, but he did this stint dutifully by polemicizing that the time for the International was not yet ripe because auto workers did not earn enough to pay higher dues.

The arguments that William Green offered against the International were hardly more sincere. He did not oppose it on principle, but for various reasons of expediency. Auto workers needed more time, he declared with avuncular concern, to gather experience and finances, to develop trained leaders. If an international were set up now, it would rip the locals apart in a fight for office instead of permitting them to concentrate on economic problems. I have notes gathered from several of those attending the conference, according to one of which the delegates were "impressed" by Green's polemic. Nevertheless, the National Council merely skimmed through with a narrow majority.

Locals or delegates who favored other plans were not allowed to offer arguments in their behalf. No motion or even amendment could be made from the floor. Only prefabricated proposals on this and other subjects enjoyed that privilege. A few vain attempts were made to elude this strict prescription. Russell Merrill, president of the strong Studebaker local of South Bend, whose resolution for an international union was shunted aside, made a spectacle of himself in flaunting an open copy of *Roberts' Rules of Order* toward Chairman Bill Collins and was ordered to resume his seat.

Wyndham Mortimer had a bit more success with his two sallies. One, which offered a substitute for the National Council, was ruled out of order but not before he had a chance to characterize the council as "a form without substance, nothing but a rubber stamp." The description stuck with it thereafter. Then, once the National Council was declared adopted, Mortimer was on his feet with a second motion: that the council's first order of business be to make plans to create an "international industrial union" no later than November 1934. Collins sneeringly identified this motion with the leaflet that had been passed out at the hotel entrance "by the Communist Party." Actually, the leaflet was signed "Auto Workers Union" but thereafter the delegates would know that the term *industrial union* was linked with Moscow. Nevertheless, a number of them sought out Mortimer afterward and exchanged addresses with him.

The most exciting event of the conference was the grandstand play of Arthur Greer, president of the big Hudson Motors local, in launching his secession movement. He had established caucus headquarters at the nearby Tuller Hotel and sent letters to other locals, inviting them to attend sessions there two days before the conference opened. As many as a hundred delegates accepted the invitation. It remained merely for Greer to pick the proper moment or excuse to stage his departure from the conference. It was easy enough to decide on since Hudson's resolution calling for an autonomous international was among those brushed aside. When finally Greer rose to leave, fifty delegates (one-third of the total) went with him, representing plants in Detroit, Flint, Pontiac, and Lansing, a basic segment of the industry in Michigan.

Bill Collins's farewell to them sounded hollow: "No secession or radical movement is going to change the principles and the policies of the American Federation of Labor." A virtuoso speaker whom Collins presented to the delegates made a far more effective plea on the dangers of insurgency. He was Homer Martin, a former Baptist preacher turned labor leader from Kansas City and unknown to the audience. Tall and pleasing of feature, it was his picturesque, parabolic language that was most attractive. He told how his local had disregarded the advice of Federation officials and even quit the AFL before going on strike. Inevitably, it was lost. "For months," he perorated, with tears visible in his eyes, "we have had hundreds of our workers walking the streets of Kansas City while their families were starving." His meteoric appearance at the conference would not be forgotten.

Arthur Greer's caucus chamber at the Tuller was impressive, not only because of its size and furnishings—Mortimer described its central table as "the longest damn table I ever saw in my life"—but also because the caucus's receiving hosts included all three members of the Automobile Labor Board (ALB), which President Roosevelt had established in the March settlement with the aim of controlling the ebullient auto workers. Mortimer "looked into" the caucus by arrangement with the rest of the White Motor delegation and had a sizzling exchange of thoughts with Leo Wolman, the ALB's "impartial chairman," until by his own account he was submerged by Wolman's "Mississippi River of words."

George Lehman was elected National Council member from Cleveland over Wyndham Mortimer. Bill Collins's open red-baiting and the whispering campaign that was freely developed by the Federation's organizers had evidently done the trick. Nothing that Mortimer told me about the conference suggested that he was disappointed or indeed that he had ever thought that he had a chance to be elected. On the other hand, he expressed great pleasure to have found so large a sentiment for an international union.

· · ·

But no pressure for it would come from George Lehman. While realizing the debt he owed to McWeeney and McKinnon, he was deeply impressed by the personalities of President Green and Bill Collins and was completely won over to their view regarding the need for delay in granting the International Union to the auto workers. His attitude toward Wyndham Mortimer had become one of convinced antagonism. He agreed with McKinnon and McWeeney that Mortimer's standing in the local must be combated and he set himself the task of fostering more actively the election of Klavon to the local presidency in September.

Meanwhile, the situation of the older workers in the parts department continued to deteriorate. The company refused to compromise on the issue of the layoffs and turned over the negotiations to its president, a man by the name of Dahl who was notorious for his tough, sarcastic style. I recall an incident about him that was told to me by one of the union's negotiators. The local had added an office worker who could take shorthand to the grievance committee, and at the following meeting Dahl was handed a typed verbatim copy of the previous session. He hit the ceiling. "Jesus Christ!" he growled. "I couldn't play football with you guys. You'd kick me in the balls every time!" Thereafter, the company had its own stenographer at the meetings, a spiteful hint that it did not trust the union's recordings.

Dahl's outbursts did not intimidate the grievance committee. It does not require long years of negotiating experience for workers' representatives provided with guts to learn how to handle a contention with their company. Fact is fact. Truth is truth. Occasionally it did help, however, for one of them to explode in anger as a show of force reflecting the power behind them.

Ed Stubbe fitted well into this role, which came naturally to him, a man with a nasty temper that thrived on practice. In spite of the limitations of his vocabulary, he was at times absolutely inspired in his sharp retorts. A typical case was that of an elderly worker who had been fired. At Stubbe's request the department superintendent was brought in. He argued that the man was "dumb," just couldn't learn to do his work properly. "How long would you say he's worked for you?" Stubbe asked innocently, tilting his heavy jaw.

"Oh I don't know exactly, fifteen-sixteen years."

"Huh!" Stubbe erupted. "Worked for you sixteen years and you're just finding out he's dumb? I don't know who's dumb, him or you!"

There was the other style of negotiation, too, Mortimer's style that quietly emphasized the facts. During his many years at White's, by his open efforts to organize a union and even joining the company union during the twenties to challenge the sincerity of its claims, he had acquired a reputation as an intellect, and company representatives were reluctant to tangle with him. Curiously, they avoided red-baiting him lest he involve them in a discussion of "Marxism," although they were not above making little jabs at his previous attachment to the communist-led Auto Workers Union. Thus George Smith, when discussing the closed shop, cast a quick look at Mortimer and said, "We can't tell a worker what union he should join. Maybe he wants to belong to the IWW . . . or the TUUL!"

After a number of sessions, the union committee realized that the company meant what it said and had no intention of retreating from its rigid position. The laid-off parts department men were still out and there was no telling when new victims would be tagged. According to the local's decision of June 15, a "special meeting" was scheduled at which a warning strike vote would be taken.

Ed Stubbe had postcards multigraphed to announce the meeting, which took place on the torrid evening of July 12. George Lehman was away in Detroit attending the first session of the National Council and Dick Reisinger was in the chair. Wyndham Mortimer made the report for his committee, after which there came a spate of rather desultory discussion that consisted of a few questions and answers. There was no excitement among the workers, either because of the heat or the fact that such votes had become familiar.

A motion to end discussion and take the strike vote was adopted and Ed

Stubbe mounted the steps to the platform, the ballot box under one arm and a briefcase with ballots in his hand. He was beginning to pile the latter on the table for distribution when the front door burst open and huge George McKinnon barged into the hall and came rumbling down the center aisle. "Just a second up there!" he shouted. "You can't take a strike vote. You didn't follow the proper procedure."

Breathing heavily, he stomped noisily up the stairs, taking a stance on the edge of the platform before the table. Wheezing from emphysema, he explained to the huge gathering that a sealed letter should have been sent to the members, according to AFL rules. "You'd be liable to a suit by the company if you tried to pull a strike on the strength of this ridiculous postcard," he threatened.

Then he turned around and shoved the postcard into Stubbe's face. "And what kind of a signature is this?" he demanded. "S. L. U. 18463. That stands for Socialist Labor Union!" he yelled, switching around to the audience again, who were beginning to react angrily to these accusations. A couple of husky young fellows, including Harry Frowen, a Mortimer enthusiast, headed for the platform and ran up the stairs.

Stubbe, blazing red with fury, was trying to explain how the mistake was made. He had telephoned the printer and dictated the letters to him. "I gave him 'F. L. U. 18463,' the way it should of been."

"What difference does it make?" McKinnon shouted. "I think you fit the bill anyhow. The way you been acting, you could be a communist!"

"And you're a bastard!" Stubbe yelled.

McKinnon hauled off as though to hit Stubbe when Harry Frowen whacked him on the ear, drawing blood. The huge man howled, swerved around in quest of his aggressor, and saw him racing down the stairs. He tore off after him. Stubbe grabbed up the ballot box and his other things and followed, forgetting to take the local's charter propped up below the table. His job as head trustee was to bring the charter up from the office and return it there after a meeting, where it was locked in a case.

The crowd had already begun to filter from the hall. Dick Reisinger followed them with questioning eyes while holding the gavel suspended. Then he rapped a few times with it on the table. "The meeting is adjourned," he announced, but no one paid the slightest attention to him.

I had hardly kept up with all these happenings. I sat in my seat, frozen with dismay. Someone near me said in a clear voice, "Well, another good union shot to hell!" and the words described my deepest fears. That evening I telephoned Mortimer and asked if I could see him at the plant at lunch time. When I met him in the vestibule I was stunned by his relaxed appearance.

"How did the men take it?" I asked.

"They were disgusted."

"That's all?"

"What else did you expect?" he asked, raising his brows slightly.

"Don't they realize what they're up to? They're out to smash the union or at least to expel you and some of the others."

He looked at me and shrugged. He thought I was exaggerating, I realized. "Well, what do you think we should do?"

"I don't know, put out a leaflet maybe explaining the whole thing. The local can't just stand by and let them get away with tactics like that. It's an invitation for more. They've wrecked two of the federal locals already, as you know."

"Yes, but the White Motor local is different," he said, squinting in firm defiance. "I suggest that we just wait awhile. Things are bound to quiet down."

Mortimer was right but it was not because George Lehman willed it so. When he got back from Detroit, the first thing he did was announce the temporary suspension of the grievance committee and then he went in and had a session with George Smith by himself. At the July 20 meeting he was in the chair, in a cool but somehow foreboding mood. Without introduction or explanation he announced, "I'll let the grievance committee's standing rest with the rank and file." The statement brought a momentary silence. What did he mean? Not everybody in the hall (it was a much smaller meeting than the previous one, which confirmed my fears) knew what he was referring to, or even that he had suspended the committee.

Slowly, an angry murmur began to spread among the men. Reisinger was first to take the floor. "You know very well, George, that we were just carrying out the plan that was agreed to on June 15 when you were in the chair. So what's all this about suspending the grievance committee when it was George McKinnon who barged in like a bull and broke the meeting up!"

Then Whitcomb spoke in his sardonic way. "It strikes me like a big conspiracy to get rid of our committee just when we need them most. Rather than lay them off we should be giving them all a medal of appreciation. I move that we give them a vote of confidence and tell them to go in there and battle with the company till we win!"

There was a roar of approval, and my chill of apprehension dissipated. "That's okay by me," Lehman said coldly. "I was just asking the local for its decision since there was some criticism of the committee's action at the last meeting." There was a grumble of disagreement and return of anger. Lehman cut the matter short by saying that he would attend all grievance committee meetings thereafter and had asked McKinnon to do the same.

The AFL organizer did not appear until the local's following meeting and then he seemed almost contrite. He was very sorry, he said, about the little tiff with Brother Stubbe or that he had called him an insulting name. Actually, Stubbe had demanded this public apology "so as to straighten things out with my gang" or he would never talk to McKinnon again.

The augmented grievance committee went back into negotiations the following week. But the company's attitude remained negative and on August 20 a new strike ballot was approved, this time strictly "according to Hoyle" (or according to George McKinnon, who was present at the meeting). The vote for the strike was 1,879 to 139, and the company was given until the following Monday morning to make up its mind. The men would work for an hour and, if there was no agreement, they would pull the switches, pack their tools, and walk out.

But once again there was no need for these final acts. What the minutes call "a tentative agreement" was approved by the local on August 22 and began to be carried out immediately. The laid-off men were all to have individual hearings in the presence of their foremen and the union's full grievance committee. In the first four cases, two men were rehired outright and two others were turned over to Leo Wolman, chair of the Auto Labor Board as arbiter. Mortimer was opposed to this move because he was dubious about the ALB's record on discrimination cases and mistrustful of Wolman, especially after meeting him during the June 23 conference. He was overruled, however, by Lehman, who considered the case of Fred Heistler, one of the two men being heard by Wolman, as invincible.

The verbatim account of Heistler's earlier appearance before the management, which I read, is, at any event, extraordinarily impressive. He described case after case where younger salesmen could not fill an order in the parts "store," which he was able to do by suggesting some astute substitution. All right, the company representative, a Mr. Metheis, admitted, Heistler's "order interpretation" was okay, but he lacked "sales ability," which Metheis defined as "something inherited." When Heistler disproved this claim also, Metheis shifted his shortcoming to something more abstruse, "good personality." This, too, went by the boards before Heistler's unanswerable proofs.

Finally, Heistler lost patience, pointing to the hypocrisy of the company's recorded excuse for his layoff after twenty years' service as "inefficiency." "This is a very false reason they put on my layoff card," he asserted bitterly. "I think it should be stricken out from the records as it might be detrimental to my seeking employment in the future."

When Fred Heistler's case (and that of another layoff, Parker Kelly) was turned over to Leo Wolman for arbitration, George Lehman chose Frank Klavon to present the arguments in another move to give him airing before the local elections, which were only two weeks away. The two men had decided to charge "anti-union discrimination" in the two cases, which Mortimer argued was a mistake because the whole series of layoffs followed the pattern of the company's fixed policy of replacing older men regardless of their efficiency, personality, or even union membership. Mortimer revealed this basic policy in a sharp exchange with Art Reitz, the company's personnel director, in the course of the Heistler hearing:

> Mortimer: Is it not a part of the company's policy to replace a certain number of old men each year with younger men?
> Reitz: No, that can be proved by the people we hired in the last nine months.
> Mortimer: Do you recall a short time ago your making a remark to me about the company's having a very difficult problem on their hands and that unless they got some new blood in the organization, it was liable to die of dry rot?

Reitz insisted that "experienced old men" were still being hired, but he did not explain why so many others were being fired.

The appeal to Leo Wolman gave him a chance to vaunt White Motor's liberal attitude toward the union (which was true enough compared to the general run of automobile manufacturers), and hence to decide that the two discharges were "not improper," which did not necessarily follow. The decision was read to the November 2 local meeting, where members castigated it as "biased and unfair." Dick Reisinger, then the recording secretary, asked for the privilege of penning a reply to Leo Wolman, the opening sentence of which might be considered a final judgment of the auto workers on the Auto Labor Board: "In a moment of weakness we were prevailed upon to submit these cases to you and may God forbid that this union ever have any more such moments of weakness!"[4]

• • •

Given my affinity for the White Motor local, which after only five months seemed to me as having lasted for years, it was hard for me to understand how an active union man could consider any other attachment (sport, church, fraternal order) more important. George Lehman's retirement from the local's presidency remained a mystery to me until I began to hear that his wife was making trouble for him for becoming more and more withdrawn from family life. "It's either me or the union," Reisinger quoted her as saying to Lehman. However, I later also heard rumors that something else might have been involved, her fear that George was "running around with other women," which was reportedly fed by gossip coming from Charley Walsh's wife and to her from Walsh himself. I was getting to know what seemed to be a new kind of free-wheeling world which, though I could regard it as preparatory to my writing career, was hard to accept in reference to people I knew, even if I differed with them in trade union outlook.

It was a shock of a different kind for me to learn that Frank Klavon had hesitated to accept Lehman's suggestion that he run for president and especially his reason. Klavon was moving up fast in the Masonic order and feared that his becoming so prominent in the union might hurt his standing there. But apparently this concern was taken up in higher circles and it was made clear to him that just the contrary might be true, that the organization would be proud to have a member as the head of so important a union.

Lehman had taken Klavon down to the Metal Trades Council and the organizers there were delighted with him. This, too, had its elusive side for me since I had assumed that Catholics and Masons were sworn enemies. Was the explanation of this seeming contradiction that they both hated "communists" even more? Some idea like that must have bolstered Lehman's belief that Klavon would beat Mortimer though there were surely more Catholics than Protestants among White workers. In any case, Lehman, the shrewd politician, began systematically to throw things Klavon's way that could attract favorable attention to him.

On the night of the election itself he asked Klavon to read the letter that Leo Wolman had written to him to acknowledge the receipt of Klavon's request that the chairman of the Auto Labor Board take up the Heistler-Kelly cases. It was nothing, and nobody applauded—but it was publicity. By an inverse shrewdness, Lehman had whispered to Dick Reisinger that he was going to ask him to deliver the report for the grievance committee that evening, the point being to keep Mortimer out of the limelight, as I understood it.

I was surprised when Lehman asked me to act as one of the tellers. He had been unfailingly friendly with me and I gave him no reason to be anything else. But paranoid as I was, I suspected at times that he had read my thoughts and wondered if there wasn't something else involved that evening. I took my place on the platform while the curtailed meeting proceeded, seated at a small table by Ed Stubbe's side.

"You gonna be a teller?" Ed asked me.

"Yes."

"Good!"

"I think we ought to rule off some pages to help record the votes," I told him. Stubbe had no ruler and just a couple of sheets but George McKinnon came up to us just then and I asked him if we could get some more paper down in the office. "Sure!" he said and with embarrassing eagerness hustled across to the stairs.

Two other tellers were added and a lot of people milled about on the platform as the ballots were tallied by our two groups. Very soon, Mortimer began pulling far ahead. My mathematical sense of probability told me that his election was foregone and I could pay attention to some of the other elections. Dick Reisinger, for reasons of his own, had allowed his nominations for both vice president and recording secretary to stand. Some of his followers had been confused and it was apparent to me that he would not win a majority in either case. There would have to be a runoff, but I knew he would beat Joseph Summerell for recording secretary.

Bill Dieter, a working companion of Mortimer's for fifteen years, was being badly beaten for sergeant-at-arms. He was a sweet and intelligent man but timid and I felt sorry for him though I had not really expected him to win. Ed Stubbe was not a candidate because his post of head trustee was for a three-year term. He would now have as fellow trustee George Lehman, who had cannily decided to maintain his presence on the executive board that way and was winning overwhelmingly. The few runoffs went as expected, with Reisinger beating the incumbent Summerell handily and Paul Jahn, a fervid unionist who suffered from an inferiority complex but was very popular, replacing Reisinger as vice president.

The most important post, the presidency, needed no runoff because Mortimer beat Klavon two to one. The crowd that had waited to hear Stubbe's announcement of this result cheered and whistled. A representative of Bill Green's office, Thomas N. Taylor, affectionately dubbed "T. N. T.," swore in Mortimer while whispering to him, "You sure have a strong pull in that shop, Mort." Then he gave him the gavel, and Mortimer turned around toward Lehman and passed the gavel over to him, asking that he "keep it as a memento of the members' gratitude for your faithful service in the first year of the union's existence."

Somewhat later, Lehman had a chance to reply to Mortimer's gracious words by congratulating him personally for his victory. "Mort," he said, sincerely, "I don't know where you get your drag!" But then, to hide his chagrin at Klavon's defeat, he danced a little jig. "Me, I'm free! Whoopee!"

But the rest of his group looked sadly desolate. Klavon was vague-eyed and all the others avoided looking at him. Ed Gockel, an extraordinarily devoted unionist (as well as Mason), who attended all meetings of the Cleveland Federation of Labor and the Metal Trades Council as a White delegate, never failing to bring back lengthy reports to local meetings of "do not patronize" lists, strike reports, or candidates endorsed, was beside himself with hurt and anger for being defeated for a minor office and broke out in a startling and untypical burst of obscenity: "They can fuck themselves before I'll do anything more for this goddamn union!" But Mortimer reappointed him to his former charges and Gockel continued to bring in his excellent reports.

George McKinnon was stunned by the defeat and whispered confidentially to me, "This isn't a fair election. Only 250 voting out of 2,200 members." Others of the Lehman crowd began making similar observations. The election should be declared illegal, it was argued, because it was held on the

erection floor did not wait for the union committee's consent to take action. They felt that they had been given a run-around for more than a month and decided on their own to call it quits. On October 9, at 8:10 A.M., before even starting work, section 411P pulled off what was later called a sitdown strike.

The erection-floor grievance stemmed back to September 13 at least, when the committee had transmitted to the company the request of these workers for a raise in the hourly rate to a minimum of 70 cents. The work was rugged and the men felt that a pay adjustment was called for. The company promised to get active on it but did nothing despite repeated reminders by the committee.

Mortimer and Reisinger were immediately notified of the strike in section 411P and contacted George Smith in the presence of a representative of the erection-floor men. The plant manager told them that he would not discuss the matter with them until the strikers had gone back to their jobs but changed his mind when the unionists informed him that they were prepared to extend the action. Smith then asked for a delay of twenty-four hours to gather the data necessary for a settlement. Meanwhile, workers in section 413P had joined the sitdown.

That afternoon, management assured the committee that steps had been taken to improve the piecework rates on the erection floor and that the men there would be able to make their 70 cents an hour "in the future." When this report was presented the following morning, the workers found it unsatisfactory and said they would continue their strike until given "something concrete and not just promises." Mortimer suggested, however, that to make the strike fully effective they must enlist the support of all workers in the plant because eventually everyone would become involved by the stoppage. Arrangements must therefore be made to take an overall strike vote.

The strikers were asked to return to work until the evening of October 15, when the union's executive board would schedule a special membership meeting to take the strike vote. The men offered some resistance to these suggestions but in the end were convinced and went back to work. The executive board set the wheels running for the strike ballot. To lend authority to the threatened action, the Metal Trades Council was contacted and George McKinnon and Thomas N. Taylor, the representative of President William Green's office, were invited to accompany the grievance committee in its next meeting with the company.

The company may have been aware of these preparations but what must have impressed them even more was the tenacious spirit of the erection-floor workers, which might easily have caught on with the men in other sections of the factory. When the enlarged grievance committee went into the company office on October 11, at 3:30 P.M., they were highly pleased to see the evidence supplied by the cost department that the erection-floor rates had been duly raised. They were informed furthermore that workers would "receive" their earnings every day (that is, would be shown how much they had earned). These arrangements, the committee was assured, would be permanent, and further improvements would be made.

A meeting of the grievance committee with several representatives from the erection floor was held that evening at the Metal Trades Council. When the company's actions were reported to them, these spirited workers were still a little dubious but accepted the offer and themselves proposed that the local's special (strike-vote) meeting should be cancelled. They were perfectly willing, they said, to wait for the local's regular meeting on October 20 to take "further action" if this was thought necessary. Meanwhile, the added delay, they declared ironically, "would give the board and the men a better chance to see if these earnings would continue or if it was only a two-day flash."

• • •

An encouraging feature of the erection-floor action was that both groups in the union were united in carrying it out. This, unfortunately, was not the case in other important incidents that occurred in the period following the elections. In fact, a difference of interpretation happened as frequently as did agreement and almost anything seemed capable of widening the rift. The worst occurrence of this nature took place in the parts department and what was most unusual about it was that it involved the discharge of George Furman, a member of the grievance committee, who, although aligned with the Lehman group, was not supported by them in his trouble.

Furman was a militant unionist and his misstep consisted of trying to help older workers by encouraging them not to overextend themselves in order to prove that they could still "cut the mustard." This he did among his own group of order-fillers. From 1931 to early 1933, the company contended, these men had averaged 480 orders filled each eight-hour day. Starting in October 1933, this average dropped to around 430 orders and the company accused Furman of having deliberately instigated the slowdown. They put a secret check on him on August 2, 1934, and found that he had filled 303 orders in the morning and only 133 in the afternoon. He was fired soon after, and a company representative testified that within weeks the order-filling was brought back to the daily level of 480.

In this case, it was a lack of militancy that strengthened the company's hand. This was not true of Ed Stubbe, who was all for calling a strike on the issue. However, Frank Klavon termed Furman's conduct "sabotage" and George Lehman declared righteously at a local meeting, "We're not going to support somebody who plays dirt on the company and then comes running to us to fight for him!" His words got big applause and the motion to reopen the case was voted down. Even though Mortimer never left any doubt about being willing to take firm steps to get Furman reinstated, he admitted to me that Furman had done "something dishonest."

This made me think that something was involved in the incident that I did not understand but that might be clear to any worker. Still, the lack of solidarity cut me to pieces. No one asked who had set the pace in the first place. Was the level of 480 filled orders a law of nature? What if it had been established by speedup methods in 1931 and 1932 before the union existed and when widespread unemployment made workers willing to do anything to hold onto their jobs? Furman had merely wanted to reduce the speed to a more decent pace, a rate that unions in the future would insist on having a share in determining.

One would have thought that the Lehman-Klavon group had the wind in its poop. This was not exactly true if memory serves me. It was just that the group had become a conscious opposition, ready to question anything that the new leadership proposed if they could make a point against them. For example, when a letter was read inviting the local to send a delegate to a conference in Washington supporting unemployment insurance, Lehman amended the motion to comply by asking that "the local find out who is at the head and who is backing this conference" (minutes, October 19).

Secretary Reisinger made an "investigation" and gave a favorable report on December 7. A motion followed that the president and the secretary be sent as delegates but Lehman challenged the motion, saying that he, too, had looked into the matter with the help of the Metal Trades Council and discovered that communists were behind the conference. Otherwise, why would they be calling for support of the Lundeen Bill, which everybody knew the communists were backing?

Mortimer turned his gavel over to Vice-President Paul Jahn. It was amazing, he said, how the AFL persisted in opposing this essential measure without offering any suitable solution of its own. A great number of AFL unions had nonetheless endorsed the Lundeen Bill but it had no chance of being adopted by Congress unless a big campaign was put on to support it. Were the communists in favor of it? Maybe so, but did that mean the local must automatically be opposed to it? "I imagine that a lot of communists like ice cream, or hot dogs," he said, "but some people are so prejudiced that if they were drowning in mid-ocean and a Russian ship offered to pick them up, they'd refuse to be saved." The quip brought laughter, but there was only a small crowd present and the "opposition" had mobilized for the occasion. The motion was defeated, 52 to 44. Ed Gockel rose in his seat and gave out a whoop of joy.

I would eventually learn to differentiate between those matters about which the White Motor unionists would be apt to draw "correct" conclusions and those about which they might fail to do so. Whereas the workers' reactions to certain social or political subjects were likely to cause disappointment to a person like myself, they would, on the other hand, almost unfailingly be right on basic union questions. Another occasion illustrated this dichotomy quite remarkably. It was during a local meeting under "Good and Welfare," when someone suggested that a letter be sent to the Cleveland Chamber of Commerce protesting its support for William Frew Long. Long was a notorious supplier of labor spies to employers and had put together a union-busting group called the Secret Seven, which had been gaining a lot of publicity of late. Dick Reisinger said that nothing would give him greater pleasure than to write that letter, and he ended with a hot, sputtering attack on Long, whom he called "Labor's Enemy No. 1."

A ruddy man with an Irish brogue and a ward-heeler's stance, whom I had never seen at a meeting, asked for the privilege of carrying a copy of the letter in person to William Frew Long, who lived in Macedonia, Ohio, close to where he himself lived. That way the union would save the price of the stamp, he explained sarcastically. This brought laughter, on the waves of which the man went on talking after readjusting his features suddenly to a mask of solemnity. "You've just passed a motion," he said, "to send a letter to the biggest enemy that labor's got. Now I'm going to ask you to send a letter to labor's greatest friend. I mean Father Charles E. Coughlin!" This brought a burst of applause, and the man went on. "I listen to Father Coughlin every Sunday and I want to say that at times he carries me close to tears when I realize how he exhausts himself in the cause of labor." His voice turned mawkish, and its pitch rose as he concluded, "He is the greatest man since Jesus Christ!"

There were some titters but they halted when someone made a motion, to which there were a dozen seconds, to send $50 to Coughlin's radio fund. Then someone else said, "We ought to make it a hundred," but no one took him up on it, and at that point I noticed Mortimer handing the gavel to Paul Jahn. I thought, "Oh, no! You'll just be throwing yourself to the wolves!" But Mortimer did not heed my silent plea. "I'm against sending any money to Charles Coughlin," he started bluntly. "Let's spend it instead on organizing our own unorganized plants and we'll be getting something for our money."

The audience seemed to be stunned by Mortimer's stern words. They were accustomed to him as a mild-spoken man who never used emotion as an aid to getting his ideas across. I noticed a few friendly faces that seemed to be questioning him doubtfully. What did he mean? Why was he attacking Father Coughlin that way? "I'm opposed to sending money to Charles Coughlin," Mortimer went on, "because he has never done anything for the working man; he's never done anything for you and me."

A few objections were raised and a cry of "That's not so!" "Tell me one thing then," Mortimer replied quickly. "Has he ever supported a strike? Why doesn't he speak out for unemployment insurance?" There was a pause of momentary quiet, followed by a clear, loud call: "How about the World Court?"

This brought a murmur of approval that Mortimer disregarded. "How about it? It wasn't Charles Coughlin who defeated the World Court in any case," he asserted.

The objections now came loud, near to boos, and it was clear that Mortimer had lost his audience, indeed, he himself seemed ready to call it quits. "Oh I'll admit that Charles Coughlin is an effective speaker," he said, "but it's *what* he says that counts. They say that Adolf Hitler is an effective speaker, too!" And then the boos broke loose and he had to wait for them to subside before putting in his last word. "I don't mind your booing. All I'm asking is that you try to remember what I'm saying here tonight. If there's no further discussion, I'll call for the question."

As the aye vote seemed to benefit from an angry roar, Mortimer asked for a rising tally. Ed Stubbe announced the count as 158 to 116 in favor of sending the money. I was amazed to see Lehman and his friends all standing up against the motion. Lehman sought out my eyes and seemed to be asking for my approval, but I realized that all it meant with him was that a Mason was voting against a Catholic priest and nothing more. His true political views had been revealed by the vote on the Lundeen Bill.

What I learned from such experiences was how much patience was required for anyone who had set out to "educate the workers." Yet Mortimer had a lot of patience. He had been talking to his fellow workers all his life and I could see the results in some of the men at White's. Even a man as strong-minded as Dick Reisinger seemed to take Mortimer's ideas on faith and their close association only went back little more than a year or so.

As for myself, I had a long way to go in the matter of patience. I might be riding the waves for a while, then something would happen and I would be in the mopes again. For example, the night of the Joe Louis–Max Schmeling fight coincided with a local meeting and the officers decided to adjourn after an hour so that the men could go down to the beer hall and listen to the fight over the radio. I was not much of a boxing fan but Joe Louis had brought me as close to becoming one as would ever happen. The beer hall was already jammed when we got there; no seats were left and most of us had to stand to drink our beers.

The fight started and the crowd was soon so highly charged that it was hard to hear the voice of the announcer.[1] The men had to be shouted down time and again until the third round, when the tenseness of the fighting momentarily froze the listeners into silence. When Louis was knocked down the first time, a tumultuous roar broke out and did not let up. Everyone crushed around the radio stand and Louis quickly went down again. When he was counted out the men completely lost control, hollering, pounding each other on the arms and back and laughing until the tears came.

I could hardly believe my senses. It was the Nazi Schmeling, Hitler's friend, whom they were cheering. Suddenly I felt sick in the heat of the place and needed to vomit but the toilet was occupied so I hurried outside and over to the curb. I walked all the way home, wanting to weep more than anything. Arriving at our studio I was glad to find Dorothy had not yet come in. I went right to bed, determined not to tell her what had happened when she did arrive.

• • •

The White Motor local conducted no educational program. Yet some of the new officers were aware of the need to explain important elements of the union's program, at least to key members like departmental committeemen (stewards). I was surprised (and secretly flattered) when George Lehman asked me if I would prepare a memorandum on the "merit clause." The National Council had asked him to do this in connection with suggested changes in the Auto Code, which was coming up for renewal.

More to the point, Dick Reisinger busied himself with a group of committeemen preparing a new set of seniority provisions, a subject of perennial interest at White Motors, with its large body of older workers. The minutes record, for example, that when Reisinger's group had completed a tentative version of the new wording, copies went to all committeemen, who were asked to hold meetings in their departments and bring suggestions to a general session on November 19. The group was responsible for one original idea—a "permanent disability clause"—that was considered important enough to be presented to the company.

Similarly, after work on December 7, Mortimer conducted a seminar with the committeemen, which I was allowed to attend, on the international union. Although one would imagine that the workers were tired after putting in their eight hours, they were full of life, and the attendance was amazing. Mortimer stuck to essentials, describing the two basic forms of already existing internationals—the one functioning among widely scattered workers in a particular craft, the other among workers who had various types and skills and were employed in a single factory. Thus, he clarified graphically how the latter form was preferable for auto workers on a practical basis despite what AFL leaders said about its being a "communistic" idea.

Actually, within the controlling body of the AFL, its Executive Council, the subject of the international had begun to be a matter of sharp discussion. It was a legacy of the great organizational wave resulting from the NRA that had brought hundreds of thousands of new workers into AFL ranks. Not all of these had been lost by neglect or mishandling. The desires of these workers, it was true, received minor consideration from the leaders of the craft unions. Of much greater importance to these leaders was the fear that the new organizations could challenge their hegemony over the Federation.

Several strong AFL internationals that were themselves organized along industrial lines took a leading role in encouraging that system among the newly recruited workers. John L. Lewis's United Mine Workers was its chief exponent at the AFL's San Francisco Convention in October 1934, where the question was debated heatedly. His strategy was to increase the Executive Council from eight to twenty-eight members, his idea being that this would bring several industrial unions into the council and thus weaken the stranglehold that the crafts had on it. Lewis realized that it was necessary to make important concessions to gain this end, one of which was to accept damaging qualifications in the international charters that were to be offered to the auto workers and the other groups in the basic industries.

It is pertinent to explain that in October 1934, auto workers did not regard Lewis with the reverence they accorded him during the great sitdown strikes of 1937. For one thing, his reputation among many auto workers who were former coal miners was that of a labor leader who conducted his own union with an iron hand. Reports that came out of the San Francisco Convention did not improve their opinion; it was said that he had supported without reservation the Executive Council's self-defeating international charters that were proposed for mass production workers. According to the October 12 *Cleveland Plain Dealer,* "Lewis was on the floor answering every question raised against the proposal," insistently assuring the leaders of the craft internationals that the resolution "by no means . . . intended to disrupt, reorganize or impair the efficiency of the established unions in the skilled trades." It all impressed us as pure demagogy since the Executive Council's announced plan not only would split great segments of workers away from the auto international (which it had already done to several of our federal auto labor unions) but would also place it under rigid tutelage for an unspecified period.

The White Motor local almost missed sending a delegate to San Francisco since the officers had felt that little good could come of it. Jim McWeeney offered to carry its proxy to the convention, asking Mortimer, "Why waste your money sending your own delegate?" Mortimer felt like replying, "Giving you our proxy would be worse than losing our money," but he did not want to hurt the feelings of the foolish little man. It took a leader of another federal local, Coleman Taylor, who worked at National Carbon, a supply plant, to remind Mortimer of the importance of the auto locals sending delegates. He told Mortimer that he himself was going and would even be paying his own way with the help of a collection from fellows in his shop since the local could not afford it. Taylor said that they all felt that the industrial union group ought to have as loud a voice as possible at San Francisco.

Mortimer felt a prick of conscience about his remissness. Unfortunately, it was too late to bring the matter up before a regular meeting but he suggested instead to Dick Reisinger, Ted Reiff, and several other officers that it ought to be taken up at a special session of the executive board, subject to final approval by the members. Meanwhile, the delegate's name could be inscribed on the call and sent to San Francisco. Charley Walsh, acting on an impulse that took everybody by surprise, nominated Ed Stubbe as the delegate, giving the other officers no time to consider whether he was the proper candidate for this responsibility. The nomination was unanimously approved.

The choice of Stubbe was not the best though no one whom I talked to thought that but I. Mortimer evidently sensed Stubbe's inadequacy, because he prepared a resolution on the International that the executive board could approve and that Stubbe could present in the local's name. It included provisions for full industrial jurisdiction of the International in automobile manufacturing and parts plants as well as democratic control of its affairs. This was the banner under which our campaign was to march thereafter.

I never had the gumption to apologize for having insulted Ed Stubbe in judging him unsuited for the job. I was not thinking of Mortimer as the person who should have been sent since he had told me that he was not the proper one to go. Mortimer would have been the last one to red-bait himself out of assuming some important duty but he felt he was too well known to AFL officials since the June 23 conference and to appear at San Francisco would give Bill Green the opportunity to squelch him properly and thus harm the fight for the International.

In San Francisco, Ed Stubbe sat in the rear of the big auditorium with a group of federal union delegates (including three or four from auto locals) all week long, not actually listening to the endless speeches, for they induced a kind of waking somnolence in him.[2] On the last day of the sessions he told the fellows that he was leaving them. "I'm gonna get the floor today," he said. "I'm gonna speak from the platform." He picked up his briefcase and went up front, right beneath the podium, where he had identified a group of seats, some of which were always vacant, among the crafts. At a chosen point during a pause in the proceedings, Stubbe rose abruptly and shouted in his booming voice, "Point of information, Brother Chairman!"

President Green looked down at him, standing there among his craft-union friends, and smiled. "What is your point, Brother?"

Stubbe mumbled something that he meant to be unintelligible.

"I can't hear you, Brother," President Green said.

Stubbe did not reply this time, just made a dash for the platform, up the stairs and straight over to the center. "What is it you want?" a man sitting at a table asked him as he passed. Stubbe knew the man to be Matt Woll (an AFL officer), for Stubbe had done nothing all week long but case the whole setup. He was almost tongue-tied but managed to mention the number of the White Motor resolution. What he wanted to know, he muttered, was whether the convention was going to take it up. Woll looked around in some confusion and Stubbe seized the occasion to slip over to the microphone. He gawked at it for a few tense moments and suddenly heard his own voice speaking back at him: "Back in Cleveland we auto workers want some real democracy. We want the craft unions to leave us alone so we can run our own business."[3]

Then he stopped and he could hear his friends in the back, clapping. This encouraged him to speak some more, remarks that he repeated glibly to me afterward, although I wondered if he had really said them or if he had let his fantasy accommodate his memory. He recalled how he had invited the AFL to call a convention "as soon as possible and not later than December 1"; to establish an International Union of all automobile and parts workers; and more that was taken directly from Mortimer's resolution, which Stubbe had evidently memorized and could actually have repeated. Then, he recalled, an old man from the Seamen's Union—"I think his name was Ollander"—stood on the floor below him and told the AFL bigshots: "We'd better start listening to these fellows. Remember there are hundreds of thousands of them."

Ed Stubbe reported back to the local on two successive occasions since he felt that he had to give the members the fullness of his impressions. But the crux of it was summed up in a few despairing words: "I wish ten thousand auto workers could have been there with me just to see how little chance we got under that setup!"

It was, nevertheless, "under that setup" that the Cleveland federal auto locals had already begun during the previous August to take steps to foster an international union that they meant to be very different from the one that the San Francisco Convention was to lay out for them in October. The initiative came from the Fisher Body local, largely through the energetic drive of a member, Peter Specht, who had been a delegate to the UAW's June 23 conference at Detroit.

Angered by the AFL's failure to establish an international union at the San Francisco Convention, as were many other delegates, Peter Specht got his local to call a regional conference in Cleveland on August 18 to take the initiative out of the Federation's hands. All nine Cleveland locals responded, including White Motors. George Lehman, still president at that time, decided to send two trusted accomplices—Edwin Gockel and Leslie Bailey—to the conference to do a little handy spying.

They did more than that. They engaged in the discussion and their names are attached to the call that the twenty-three delegates present issued to a national conference in Cleveland on September 16. Here would be elected, the call declared, "a temporary International Board . . . which shall call a National Constitutional Convention as early as possible [and which] shall be the highest authority for administering the national affairs of the union until the time of the convention."

It was regrettable that Lehman kept secret from his local the Fisher Body local's call to the regional conference. Had Wyndham Mortimer or Dick Reisinger known about it and been able to attend the meeting, the call to the September 16 conference would never have assumed the fantastic form and wording that it did, with references to "constitutional convention," "international board," and other terms that were naive and inappropriate. It was never their intention to promote the International except by authorized procedure. Any other course would have courted violent AFL reaction and been self-defeating.

• • •

September 16, 1934, was a bright Sunday and an auspicious day for me to be finding myself at the broadest gathering of auto locals that I had yet attended. The small ground-floor conference hall was early filled with "delegates," most of them from the Cleveland area, but quite a few from Detroit, Flint, and even Milwaukee had driven in the previous evening and lodged with friends. There were a number of the Cleveland group that I met for the first time, some of whom I would get to know very well in the coming months. One surprise visitor needed no introduction; George Lehman took a place at the rear of the hall and sat there, alone in silent dignity.

The most important groups from out of town were the delegation of five from the Flint Buick local, led by Charles Killinger, and another of two from Seaman Body–Nash of Milwaukee, one of whom was its newly elected president, Anthony Weileder. My own notes are of little help in identifying any of the other non-Cleveland men, but Bud Simons of Fisher Body One who was at the conference much later supplied the names of several others who had attended from Flint.[4] These included his friend Joe Devitt from Fisher One, and Louis Leader, Walter Reed, and a man from Chevrolet named Griffith, whose trip was paid for by the Socialist party, as was Walter Reed's, according to Simons.

The conference was just getting started when a huge bus appeared outside the windows, parked, and began letting its passengers off. There were about two dozen of them, who somehow looked like soldiers under discipline as they lined up silently in double file alongside the big vehicle. The word went swiftly through the hall: It was Arthur Greer and his group, Arthur Greer, the president of the great Hudson local of Detroit, whom nobody had been expecting. Some men in the hall saw the arrival as a happy harvest, but most must have known better.

Mortimer certainly did, and, moreover, he definitely appeared to know what had to be done about this apparition. Abruptly leaving the chair, he hurried to the door, whispered a few words to one of the Fisher Body guards, and went outside, where he engaged in a lengthy conversation with Greer. We would learn shortly that Mortimer told Greer that the gathering was a conference of auto locals of the American Federation of Labor and that no arrangements had been made for visitors. Greer then showed Mortimer a copy of the printed "Official Credential," which bore Greer's signature and those of several other men who had been "duly elected to represent" their locals at the conference.

"Yes," Mortimer told Greer, "but the heading here says 'American Federation of Labor.' Are all of you here affiliated with that organization?" He knew the answer to that question of course because it was notorious in auto union circles that, shortly after Greer made his dramatic exit from the June 23 conference in Detroit, he and his associates had taken steps to formalize their action. His own Hudson local, together with Oldsmobile of Lansing and Yellow Truck of Pontiac, had on August 15 established the Associated Automotive Workers of America, while a number of other units were on the verge of joining. By September 9, Greer had assembled a group of twelve locals that elected temporary officers and an executive board and set a constituent convention for September 22, when the longed-for international union could be brought to life. These were the men who now appeared in Cleveland to offer their big red apple to our conference.

"I'm not going to make the decision in this situation by myself," Mortimer told Greer. "I will suggest to the delegates inside that we set up a committee before which you and your group can appear. The committee will make its recommendation to the body whether you should be seated and it will be up to them to reach the final decision."

Greer nodded unctuously and Mortimer came back into the hall. The committee was quickly designated: William Kics of Bender Body; Ralph Rocco of Fisher Body; Coleman Taylor of National Carbon; Elmer Bernhardt of Bow-Socket at Ashtabula; and Mortimer himself. They withdrew, and the meeting was turned over to John Soltis of the Hupp Motors local, a middle-aged former coal miner and a devoted trade unionist. A delegate from Detroit suggested that, while waiting for the committee to report, individuals who had some firsthand knowledge of Arthur Greer should be called upon to inform the conference about him.

All agreed that it was a good idea and some interesting information was immediately forthcoming. Greer, it was reported, had been a foreman at Hudson for many years and was more recently active in forming a company union there, which he served as president. When the AFL began having some success at the plant, Greer decided to go into it and was soon president of that local. It was said that he continued under the new set-up to have very friendly relations with management, had the run of the plant, and had easy access to the company office. Many unsophisticated members considered these things important in a union leader, as much as were the half-dozen barrels of beer that he supplied for the members' pleasure after every meeting.

Meanwhile, at the hearing, which took place in a small anteroom adjoining the hall, Arthur Greer's urbanity would have seemed to contradict these dubious reports. He pictured the appearance of his group at the conference as being dictated solely by a sincere desire to rid the auto workers of the AFL's dictatorial control and to establish a great and independent international union. "If we have made a breach of conduct in coming here, we beg this committee and the delegates to excuse us," he declared earnestly. "We have scheduled a conference of our own for next Sunday in Detroit and we would be very pleased if you and other members of your locals would come there. They will all be greeted with open arms and no questions asked." Mortimer disregarded this invitation in his reply, which bristled with indignation:

> Mr. Greer, you talk about this question as though it is just a friendly difference of opinion. Your decision to walk out of the Detroit conference had all the earmarks of being carefully thought out. Since then you've carried your plan to its logical conclusion by seceding from the AFL and forming an international of your own. And now you've come here today with only one possible objective: to get us to join your big gamble. But a labor organization is nothing to gamble with, Mr. Greer. It involves the lives and welfare of thousands of people. To seat you at our conference would be a dangerous step and you surely realize that. Well, you've made your own choice, Mr. Greer. Now you will allow us to make ours. That will be *my* recommendation to the delegates in the other room.

Greer and his two companions left the room, and the other members of the committee decided that the question required no further discussion, voting unanimously to turn down the request of the Greer delegation, even for visiting privileges.

"The committee," Mortimer reported upon its return to the hall, "is unanimous in its decision, which is the following. Since Arthur Greer and his delegation are not members of the American Federation of Labor, it is our opinion that they have no legitimate place at this conference. We move that this recommendation should be adopted by the body."

John Soltis asked for the second and discussion (of which there was none) and then for the vote by a count of hands. I was startled to find that about ten delegates raised their hands in opposition to the committee's recommendation. But my eyes were drawn especially to George Lehman, who seemed amazed at the entire procedure. The realization that he should be witnessing this remarkable scene gave me great pleasure. For the rest, events happened too fast for me to catch more than two or three of those who voted for the Greer group.

The would-be delegates were invited into the hall to hear the verdict, which they had already guessed, no doubt. They took it quietly, but as they filed out, one man stopped near the door. "I just wanted to leave you with one thought," he declared in a sing-song voice. "Seek the truth and the truth will find you out."

• • •

There was a sense of accomplishment after that unpleasant episode was over. Yet the response was less than enthusiastic when Mortimer proposed that the conference adopt an "economic program" that he had been working on that would give depth and wider appeal to the International that it was promoting. I too felt personally rebuffed by this opposition since I was partly responsible for the idea, having told Mortimer about the new Auto Code on which the National Council was working and for which George Lehman had asked me to prepare a memo on the merit clause. There was an introductory sentence in Mortimer's proposal explaining that the conference "went on record not only for an International Union but for one with an aggressive organizational and economic program that would guarantee a decent living to the men working in the industry." Then came several points: strict rank-and-file control of the International; a thirty-hour week; a dollar minimum for production workers; progressive scales for skilled workers; reinstatement of discharged unionists; full seniority rights; unemployment insurance (Lundeen Bill); and no discrimination against women, blacks, and youth.

When this program was opened for discussion, its hottest opposition came from Tony Weileder of the Seaman Body local, the mystery man of the conference who carried great prestige for having recently been elected president of his big local against virulent opposition from the AFL. The word had gone around that Weileder was a "progressive," which would have implied that he would react favorably to the economic program. Instead, he brought up the most superficial arguments against it, such as the notion that it would distract attention from the fight for the International Union or turn some against it who would otherwise favor it.

Those supporting the economic program, particularly Mortimer, made the point that the contrary was true, insisting that it would strengthen that fight by giving it a more serious purpose and answering the charge that the International Union was nothing but a job-seeking venture. As Mortimer spoke, I was amazed to see a sarcastic smirk on Tony Weileder's face. Impetuously, I got up and took a seat next to the big fellow and began whispering to him. "You seem to have something against Mortimer," I said. "He's a real progressive guy and he's been fighting for a union for fifteen years at White Motors." But the sneer broadened on Weileder's unfriendly face and he snapped back at me, much too loudly for comfort: "What the hell is he, a member of the S.L.P.?"[5] "What's that?" I asked, looking around nervously. Noticing that several delegates nearby had turned toward us, I left him.

There was no more discussion and the economic program was voted down. The afternoon session was well along the way and in dismay I knew that only a vote for reconsideration would save the important statement. I moved around, distraught, trying to light on someone who might know Weileder and get him to change his mind. Unfortunately, Mortimer had come to the conference without any other White Motor men. Dick Reisinger would have been a life-saver. Finally I struck on Coleman Taylor, whom I did not know too well and who had shown antagonism to me, I felt, due to my not being a worker. He was standing by a window, and I went over to him and explained the matter to him, asking him if he could talk to Weileder.

"That crazy bastard!" he commented. I returned to my seat but watched him tensely for some time as the session seemed to be coming to an end. Suddenly he left his post and walked quickly over to where Weileder was sitting and bent over and said something to him. Surprisingly, Weileder rose, and they went out of the hall together. I took a deep breath. Indeed, they soon came back, and Weileder was smiling.

Taylor made the motion for reconsideration and Weileder spoke in favor, "explaining," incredibly, that he had misunderstood the economic program when it was first presented. There was no other discussion and within five minutes the program was adopted unanimously.

As George Lehman probably reported it to them, the Cleveland conference must have created a great blur in the minds of the AFL leaders. He had left our meeting right after the Greer group had been turned away, looking as though this decision simply overwhelmed his thinking. Did he understand that Mortimer had acted on principle in the matter, I wondered, or was he trying to figure out some twist of self-interest in it? It would be beyond him to think that Mortimer had acted as a loyal friend of the AFL.

• • •

The second rank-and-file conference took place, as prearranged, in Flint on November 10. It was attended by forty-three delegates from eighteen locals, eleven of which were officially represented. There was one discouraging feature about this conference: Not one of the Flint locals had taken formal action to attend it, the most disturbing absence being that of the Buick local. Charles Killinger, who led the five-man Buick delegation to Cleveland, had been one of the most enthusiastic boosters of the movement. After getting back to Flint, however, he fell under the heel of the AFL organizers there and was eventually expelled from the union.

It may never be known why Mortimer himself was not ridden out of the AFL during this period. Bill Green was inclined to take this step on several occasions and yet never carried it out.[6] The Federation's leaders probably apprehended what Mortimer might do if he were totally free of their control. They had unsuccessfully sought an understanding about him with the White Motor management, although it was likely, they felt, that he would carry most of the plant with him if he were expelled from the union. The AFL's position in the auto industry was too weak to take such a risk, particularly after Mortimer's strong position among the city's other auto locals had become evident through the rank-and-file conferences and in the Cleveland Auto Council, which was founded soon after.

Another factor that no doubt protected Mortimer was the threat of the Greer movement, which for some time worried the AFL as much as did the insurgents in its own ranks. When the Cleveland conference under Mortimer's leadership refused to tie up with Greer and sent him packing, AFL leaders may have felt relieved and possibly even grateful to him for his unexpected and eloquently expressed loyalty for the Federation though they were not certain that they could depend on it.

Meanwhile, many tasks were left for us to carry out, each of which might loom up as a critical hurdle on our path to the essential goal, the International Union. Next on the list was the third rank-and-file conference, which was scheduled for Detroit on January 26, 1935. It was the first one to which the Mortimer-Reisinger-Stubbe group decided to send an official delegation and it was during the struggle that developed on this issue that their full leadership of the local was established. The clash opened unobtrusively enough at the local's meeting of December 21, 1934, where the call to the Detroit session was read. It was signed by eighteen officers from six Cleveland locals, including five presidents.

The White local's endorsement was given without apparent objection, as attested by the minutes: "A motion was made that this local participate in all conferences of the committee for the formation of an industrial union in the auto and parts industry in the AFL; unanimously adopted." And Chairman Mortimer then appointed five delegates to the Detroit conference, with the local's approval, likewise unanimously given. But this unanimity was only possible, it turned out, because of George Lehman's absence from the meeting.[7] On January 4, 1935, however, he was very much present and the situation was changed. He had arranged to bolster that meeting by sending postcards to the entire membership, inviting them each personally, a very unusual procedure that implied some extraordinary motivation. It was not until under "Good and Welfare" that he revealed what it was, when he moved to reconsider the decision of the previous meeting to send delegates to the Detroit conference.

Lehman's arguments were cut-and-dried. In eighteen months he had absorbed a good deal of Federation jargon, which he could deliver with a tone of unanswerable authority, calling our rank-and-file movement a "dual organization" and maintaining that it was "opposed to the principles and policies of the American Federation of Labor."

"We must be reasonable," he asserted. "We can't get everything in one day. Look at the Fisher Body local, they're the noisiest supporters of this movement. Why don't they spend their time and energy organizing their shop and winning conditions for their workers? I'm asking you to rescind the action of the previous meeting." There was very little applause despite Ed Gockel's effort to raise a claque. Another Lehman supporter whom I did not know asked the chair a naive question for which he had probably been coached, Did the Detroit conference have the approval of the AFL?

"If you mean the Executive Council or President Green, the answer is 'No,'" Mortimer replied. But the point of the question became clear when AFL representative Thomas N. ("T. N. T") Taylor, who was sitting in the front row, heavy-browed and livid, rose and started moving slowly toward the stairs. "I didn't intend talking to you about this," he began, disregarding the incongruity of his words, for why else would he be there and why had George Lehman sent out the postcards? "However, now that it's been brought up, I want to say that not only does this movement *not* have the approval of the American Federation, it has its utter condemnation."

Then Taylor attacked what he called "the ideas behind this movement" and assailed its leaders, calling them "upstarts and know-nothings." The AFL had been going on for a long time, he said, and would continue to exist with them or without them. I was astonished by the feebleness of his contribution, yet he had an effective way of speaking, breaking his words up into syllables and emphasizing selected ones. Applause was weak, however, as he descended the stairs and resumed his seat.

Mortimer then took over, arranging some papers on his desk to show that he had anticipated this attack and meant to answer it in full. He knew that though he had the support of his people on this question, it was important that they should know in detail the essentials of what was involved. He started by reading the San Francisco resolution on the promised international charters to show how the AFL expected to run these organizations, appointing all officers, determining policies, and taking charge of funds. "This should not surprise us," he commented, "when we consider who it is that makes up the Executive Council who are fostering these internationals. Many of them are the very same craft unionists who claim jurisdiction over us. Let me read to you a few words from the November issue of the *Machinists Monthly:* 'Self-preservation is the first law of nature and the I.A. of M., which is thoroughly competent to protect the interests of those over whom it claims jurisdiction will not stand idly by and, without protest, permit the *Federation or any other organization, to trespass upon its jurisdiction* except in a most *limited* way'" [emphasis Mortimer's].

"With this viewpoint dominating the Executive Council," Mortimer continued, "what are the prospects of success in our efforts to establish an international that will give us that unity in the auto industry that Brother Lehman spoke of?"

He paused for a few moments and studied his audience, which had been listening intently. "Brother Lehman," he resumed, "called our movement promoting an International Union within the AFL a 'dual organization.' Now Brother Lehman was a visitor to our first conference here in Cleveland on September 16 and he witnessed how we turned down the request to attend the conference of twenty-five delegates from Michigan led by Arthur Greer, president of the Hudson local, for the very reason *that they had seceded from the AFL and were therefore not eligible to sit in on any conference of ours.* . . . Who's talking about disunity? Isn't it the AFL's crazy system of organization that is disuniting us? Why didn't they give us an industrial union in the first place instead of the federal locals? Because they intended to split us up. We know and they know that that's the truth, the pure and simple truth. And that's the reason for these conferences, to make sure that the International Union that we get is the one we need and want."

When Mortimer stopped, there was loud and prolonged applause and no need for further talk, but he called on others by name, apparently to show that his thoughts were shared widely. "Brother Spalt," a politically minded man, compared the AFL's attempt to dominate the International with fascism, which he defined as "rule from the top." Dick Reisinger continued this idea by referring to the American system of democracy, which allowed Congress to overrule the president. Ed Stubbe came back once again to the San Francisco Convention, where all those craft leaders were dead against giving an industrial union to the auto workers, he said. Ed Gockel, the only Lehman man to speak, said that all members were obligated to follow Federation policy by having taken the pledge when they joined the AFL.

John Soltis, vice president of the Hupmobile local and a frequent visitor at White Motor meetings, took the floor to give a token of the view of Cleveland's other auto locals. He was an old-style rabble-rouser, with pointed finger and kindling eyes: "The only way to revive faith in the AFL is for them to give us an International Union," he shouted. "I've been in the AFL thirty-one years and I'm heart and soul for it. By the eternal God, we want the AFL but we want it to be ruled by the rank and file!"

Before calling for the vote, Mortimer explained the procedure carefully twice because it was a negative motion: "If you vote 'yes' on the motion to reconsider, it means 'no' on sending delegates. And if you vote 'no' on the motion, it means 'yes,' we'll send delegates to Detroit." He called for a rising vote, and no more than fifteen or twenty men in a small rectangle around Lehman stood up on the "yes" count. The whole mass of several hundred rose noisily for the "no" vote, applauding while still on their feet.

They had no sooner sat down when T. N. Taylor got up: "I want to notify this local that I will write a letter tonight memorializing President Green of your action taken after the AFL's position was clearly explained to you."

A quiet settled on the big crowd as Taylor left the hall. George McKinnon added to the sense of menace that had been left in everybody's mind by warning Mortimer after the meeting that "they'll take your charter away." But this threat had been sounded before and did not seem to frighten anyone. Rather, what stuck in the thoughts of all was the thrill of victory. The men in the shop could not stop talking about it. This enthusiasm was to give the Detroit conference a special atmosphere that glowed with confidence and maturity.

• • •

I made every effort to assure my own attendance at the third conference. I had missed Flint due to lack of funds but was determined not to miss Detroit. Dick Reisinger suggested to Mortimer that the five White Motor delegates should all chip in a few dollars to pay my expenses but I would not hear of it. I was working on a WPA job that paid $15 for a twenty-hour week;[8] my wife Dorothy earned an equivalent amount as a coach of working women at a branch of the YWCA. It was just enough for us to get by on; most White Motor men were not earning more. The White delegates went to Detroit by train and put up at a medium-priced hotel that Lehman used when he attended National Council meetings but the local could afford it. Ed Stubbe's bill to San Francisco had been $500 and, though it brought whistling from some of the opposition, he could account for every cent he spent.

The other locals all drove to Detroit and stayed at very modest hotels. Fortunately, there was room for an extra passenger in one of the Fisher Body cars and the space was offered to me. There was no other group that I would be happier to be with despite the standoffish attitude of some of its officers since I felt that concessions must be made to bring this local closer to the other groups. Their plant was one of GM's crucial bodymaking units and might have an important future role to play. I noticed that the Fisher men were younger than the White Motor leaders, at least ten years on the average, and different from the rather staid White men. I told myself that the difference lay in the much tougher work they did, which was probably true.

I was delighted at the beginning of our journey by the talk in the car, which became animated after I told the story of the big Taylor versus Mortimer debate. My companions had read about it in the papers, especially about McKinnon's threat of the local's expulsion. "That fat tub-of-lard," Scotty Campbell sneered, "he's always expelling locals every other day!" I asked how Fisher Body got along with the AFL leaders. "Louis Spisak [the local president] likes them fine," Jack Barskites said, sliding a meaningful sidewise look at me from the wheel. "Taylor especially; he thinks he's a brain."

These men seemed apt at that kind of gossip or in revealing internal rivalries. But before long I realized that I could not get them to discuss serious things for any length of time, the way one could with the White Motor crowd. I could see that they wanted to relax. It was the end of a week of grind and they were on vacation. I wondered when they would bring the liquor out. It was as we were leaving Rocky River that a change came over them and their talk became obscene. It was as though morality was only something attached to a particular place. One clicked his tongue and said: "It'd be nice to get a strange piece of tail in Detroit!" and the others laughed. As it turned out, a porter in the hotel found the means of satisfying their yen, shocking me to the point that I accepted the offer of a Detroit delegate to set me up the next night in his apartment. I was punished for my prudery by the discomfort of my cot, which was without linens and had a blanket of coarse wool that left the allergic skin of my throat and chin aflame.

The changed spirit that prevailed at the Detroit conference was reflected in its major resolutions. It was almost as though we had had a hint from somewhere within the Federation's structure that we could expect an altered attitude toward our program. Though the conference discussion was still bitter in its criticism of the AFL leadership—their "no-strike" policy and their dependence on the "strike-breaking arbitration boards"—the final resolutions dropped most of that contentious line. Emphasis was now on our positive program and the means by which it must be brought about. Most remarkable of all was the leading role that we assigned to the National Council in all of this.

Our demands remained pretty much the same: the International, the convention that would establish it, and the economic program, which had now evolved into a full-fledged Auto Code that I had a hand in fashioning. We could hardly expect the AFL to be enthusiastic about one significant addition, a complete outline of a plan for preparing for and conducting a general strike. But in the very first "Resolved," the initiating role was put into the hands of the National Council, which was to "convene a national auto workers conference" to put the vast action on wheels. And the National Council was likewise called upon to play a key part in convoking the "constitutional convention which can establish the new international."

But attendance at the Detroit Conference was not in keeping with this fervent plan. About twenty locals were registered there, and the majority were represented by a single delegate or even only one "visitor." A considerable number of other auto unionists, however, from Detroit and elsewhere in Michigan appeared at the Danish Brotherhood Temple, seemingly eager to meet the "Cleveland group" about which they had been hearing. We were just as eager to see them and find out why they had not been joining our movement.

We came away from these contacts, however, thinking that the AFL auto unionists of Detroit were "scared of their own shadows," as Reisinger put it. Another inescapable impression was the weakness of the unions there. Eighteen months of impotent, uninspired leadership had left its toll. The Greer secession had taken part of the Michigan auto workers in tow. The independent Mechanics Educational Society of America (MESA), a vital union, had absorbed a considerable number of the tool-and-die workers. The massive Chrysler plants seemed under the clutch of a well-organized system of company unions and the Ford workers were enclosed in the company's vast and heavily guarded feudal fortress.

It would seem that only a miracle could restore vitality to the AFL auto union in Michigan. It would be several weeks before we would know of President Green's grandiose plan for a spectacular late February tour of the major automobile centers to help propagandize a general strike vote that could be put into his hands for action. The tour was already a preciously guarded secret of the National Council members, whom UAW Director Francis Dillon had put on notice to prepare themselves to come to Detroit for an indefinite period and be in permanent session, awaiting the call for a "titanic action."

George Lehman hinted at these great things to come shortly after our return to Cleveland from the Detroit conference. He appeared at a meeting of the White Motor local, a man utterly changed from the one we had seen on the occasion of the debate between T. N. Taylor and Mortimer. It was as though Lehman were trying deliberately to erase its contentious impressions. The atmosphere of the meeting itself was remarkable, too, as I wrote on a page that I have saved:

Tremendous crowd. Took up our three resolutions; they passed overwhelmingly. First resolution, for conference to plan convention, passed with a roar. Then the resolution for the strike. Someone said: "You vote for a strike but you don't say what you're striking for." A burst of laughter. Another young chap said: "I'm for striking everybody, the railroads too." Big applause. . . . There was an immense emotional force present, great tension. It's the high pitch of production and all the resentment for past grievances seems ready to explode. I've never seen anything like it, such unison, a really transcendent force, something unexpected and grand.

Then I described the singular change in George Lehman: "Lehman tries to recuperate lost popularity. Someone asks Mortimer what the National Council's opinion of the resolutions was. Mort replies curtly that Lehman is opposed to our movement for the International. Lehman gets up: 'I was opposed to your *methods* but now you're going about it through the right channels. I can tell you that I'm prepared to take this resolution [on the strike] to Detroit next week and do my best to put it through.'" The broad hint almost bowled me over. Perhaps others shared my thought that it really was not the wording of our resolutions that had made the difference, as Lehman implied. At any event, his startling acquiescence made us feel that maybe we were getting somewhere after all.

Even more striking was Lehman's change of attitude in reacting to a fourth resolution that had not originated at the Detroit conference. It concerned only the Cleveland unions, which had decided to form an Auto Council. Lehman had erroneously reported the establishment of such a body to his National Council back in August 1934. The latter had attacked the Auto Council as being "unauthorized" and "communistic" and ordered participating locals to abandon it.

How would Lehman react to the subject now? When the motion was made in favor of the resolution, he said not a word about his previous error, nor did he try to oppose its adoption. Considering the explosive mood of the big meeting it would have done him little good. A humorous incident reflecting this mood occurred when the section was read asking that each local pay a cent per capita to the council, the total collected going to help organize the Fisher Body union. As a member protested, "We are the strongest union. Why should we go and make somebody bigger?" a tremendous "Boo!" drowned out his denial of solidarity.

The AFL's Bogus Plan for a National Auto Strike 4

The resolution that the White Motor local adopted on February 15, 1935, for the Auto Council was actually a one-page constitution that had several peculiarities. Those who prepared it were clearly in a rush to get it out, so bare are its seven sections. One could, on a fast reading, think of a dozen other things that should have been included in such a document, and the first section seems curiously out of place: "Section 1. That the delegates of Greater Cleveland and District, and those that shall affiliate with same, shall set up a Council *in sympathy with the movement now in progress for the formation of an International Union* on the basis of Industrial Unionism" [emphasis added].[1]

Understanding old documents is sometimes impossible without knowledge of their background, which in this case was bizarre. The Auto Council, when Mortimer proposed it to the other Cleveland locals, met with little enthusiasm and even some resistance. The argument was that the council would weaken the fight for the International by taking minds off this basic goal. Mortimer pointed out that, on the contrary, the council would strengthen this drive by welding locals into a firmer unit. "Talking in the name of an Auto Council will give us a lot more prestige than being only some loose committee," Dick Reisinger added.

This contention took place at one of the frequent informal sessions that officers of the Cleveland locals active in the movement for the International held between our rank-and-file conferences. Fortunately, the rather detailed minutes of one of these meetings, that of February 12, 1935, have survived as written by George Booth of the Hupmobile local, the acting secretary.

That it was not the only gathering of its kind is attested by my own memory and by various notes, as well as an early sentence in George Booth's three-page report: "Minutes of previous meeting read and accepted with two corrections." Whatever they were, they indicated that the Auto Council was finally approved. Indeed, one recorded motion makes an oblique reference to the polemic on the question in offering a compromise solution that was evidently satisfactory to the two contesting viewpoints: "Brother Krause [*sic*] makes motion that this District Council and [the] International Committee be combined into one organization and carry on the work as outlined by both bodies."[2]

This motion was passed unanimously by the six locals represented at the meeting and another session was scheduled for a few days later, on February 16, when officers would be elected. The content of my motion was, to be sure, the same as section 1 of the Auto Council resolution proposed to the White Motor local meeting of February 15. Copies of this resolution were sent to all the other locals, which in short order voted their approval.

My role in this affair may seem strange and should be explained. Not only did I attend these meetings but I also spoke at them and even offered motions to be acted upon (the one listed earlier was not the only one I made at that same meeting). I had never done this at White Motors though I gave regular "publicity reports" at its meetings after George Lehman surprised me by calling on me to do this soon after I was introduced into the union. It was not until much later, on February 7, 1936, that in recognition of my "good services" I was made an "Honorary Member of the Local . . . *without voice or vote*" [emphasis added]. I never received such an acknowledgment from the Auto Council despite the far more active role that I played in it or, more correctly perhaps, because of that role.

It was natural for an auto local to be stricter about such matters because the problems it handled were often of primary economic importance. The Auto Council was a loosely assembled body without official standing. Nevertheless, it soon assumed several pivotal functions and sought out individuals willing to take them on. I was a natural choice because I could never avoid a searching eye. From the start, I was considered an accredited member of the White Motor delegation. The minutes show me as often engaging in discussions, being put on various committees, and making reports. It all strikes me as very strange today.

Soon, however, a post fell to my lot that made me an essential functionary of the Auto Council. The idea was mine, in fact, and it turned out to be one of the council's most important offices. The notion was already in the making at the February 12 meeting, which was so rich in organizational ideas. Once more it appears in the form of a motion by Mortimer: "That this Council goes on record in favor of supporting a newspaper to cover the organized automobile and parts workers of Cleveland." A delegate by the name of Kozak from the Willard Storage Battery local immediately offered a supplementary motion: "That each local-affiliate be asked to back this newspaper and that each local shall elect a committee of three to work upon and for this paper."

The idea for the paper was mine but it was not unique because several other groups around this time started putting out intermittent local sheets, usually mimeographed, on the initiative of some energetic member. UAW Director Francis Dillon himself spoke about launching a newspaper in a letter he wrote to the National Council, assuming that its members would dutifully accept the obstacles that would first have to be overcome before this project could be realized. The auto union's membership was frail, and consequently funds were insufficient. Mortimer had not found a solution to the financial problem but I suggested a plan to him how this might be accomplished on a modest scale and he had agreed that the council should try it out.

The idea for a paper had occurred to me while I was helping Louis Spisak, president of the Fisher Body local, put out a special issue of the *Labor Digest,* a small-sized tabloid that had been started in June 1934 under Paul Miley, the leader of the hapless strike that the AFL had broken. The result was a surge of the company union, which had every aid of the management, including the exclusive use of the plant's bulletin board. *Labor Digest* was the local's answer to this monopoly; the tabloid continued to appear for some months until a big drop in members left no funds for such extravagances. The sudden decision by the Auto Labor Board (ALB) in February 1935 to hold representational elections in the plant gave Spisak an excellent excuse for reviving the little tabloid during the campaign. He announced his plan to the February 12 meeting of the Auto Council and I offered him my services, which he accepted.

One of the last numbers of the earlier series, that of September 6, reported Spisak's accession to the presidency on Paul Miley's despondent retirement. Spisak's inaugural message must have cheered the company. "Of this union the management should have no fear," and he expatiated on what its major purposes would be: to improve the moral, intellectual, social, and (happily, not forgotten) economic conditions of the workers.

I wondered how anyone could expect workers to support so spineless a program. I decided that perhaps the program made such dull reading that it could not hurt too much to print it. The problem was how to alter this sheepish approach in the one issue I would be helping to get out before the elections. It would not be an easy task, I realized, because the AFL was calling on workers to boycott the voting, an act that would require greater courage on their part than merely posting a void ballot.

With a display of confidence that I did not feel, I suggested to Spisak that we ought to tell the workers that the Auto Labor Board vote was not the key issue. We should remind them, I said, that the union just a week earlier had sent the company a series of important demands, a fact that the ALB ballot was merely obscuring. What the union wanted to know, and what the workers ought to know, was what the company had to say about the 20 cent raise, the reduction of hours, and the other things that had been asked for.

Spisak nodded eagerly and said that he had planned to write exactly that kind of article. That worried me because I had wanted to do it myself and could just imagine how he would garble it. But he came back the next morning with an excellent piece, concentrating on the raise and giving it a clever title: "Unto Caesar." I could hardly believe my eyes as I read it.

It is imperative that we receive substantial increases in wages at once. . . . We are willing that the owners make a fair profit on their investment. We are compelled to sell our bodies but to continue working for the present wages we must also sell our souls. This we refuse to do.

Raise the wages! We care little whether the raise is announced through the labor union, the company union, or the Union for Social Justice [the Coughlin organization]. We care not whether it is first printed in the *Labor Digest,* the seemingly well-financed *Searchlight* [the company union paper], or the humble but aggressive *Spark Plug* [the communist shop paper]. The wages must go up. They must go up substantially. . . . Unless wages are increased we give a solemn warning to the Caesars of the Automobile Empire. Beware of the Ides of March.

As I read, I could already see where the article should go: into the inside fold at the left and on the full page facing, the "Proposed Agreement" would be presented point by point in bold-face type: the six-hour day, thirty-hour week, a minimum weekly wage of $30 for the unskilled and $35 for the skilled, and seniority based on service.

Encouraged, I took over the rest of the makeup of the little tabloid, thinking of the readers at whom it was aimed, workers not given to careful reading habits. Bigger headings, more prominent type, and balanced distribution were necessary, and I put a boxed reprint of the union's election slogan on page one, center:

DO NOT VOTE FRIDAY, FEBRUARY 22. . . . .
WE PROTEST THE METHOD OF THIS ELECTION
6-HOUR DAY, 8-HOUR PAY: KEEP DEPRESSION AWAY!

I suggested to Spisak that twenty thousand copies of this message be printed on small cards for distribution at the shop gates and to be put into the hands of workers in the factory. This might bring a howl from the foremen, but, considering what they permitted company union stooges to get away with, they had their answer.

The fact was that the company intruded openly and unabashedly all through the day of the balloting. Foremen campaigned for company union candidates and distributed printed lists of their names (the ALB ballots were not permitted to identify affiliations). They concentrated especially on people who did not vote, threatening those who abstained with losing their jobs, circulating continuously in their departments, and growling reminders to vote.

Still, the response threatened to be so poor at one point that the management decided to halt work for eighteen minutes to encourage the poll because many men were putting on a great show of work-eagerness during the voting period, heads and torsos bowed over the moving assembly lines, plainly too preoccupied to leave. Toward the end of the balloting, a loudspeaker let loose, manned by members of the regional labor board, to give an official sanction to the voting: "This election was called by the Automobile Labor Board under direct orders of President Roosevelt" and, cloaking the foremen's aid to the company union, "You are free to vote for anyone you choose."

The excited union men who came to local headquarters after the day shift brought word that the boycott had worked like magic. This seemed particularly true in the strong pro-union departments. One fellow told us, "The way things were in the press room, it was more dangerous to vote than not to vote!" This was Paul Miley's department, where, despite his loss of heart after the 1934 strike, he had kept the union spirit alive among his men. Another man from the press room said that in his section only four voters were counted out of four hundred workers: "And what I mean, we really kept our eyes peeled!" Everybody at headquarters was jubilant. Spisak predicted an 80 percent boycott. "Even the Commies are plugging for us!" Ralph Rocco commented, displaying the recent issue of *Spark Plug*.

Counting the ballots would take place at the Amsterdam Hotel downtown. The day shift's votes would be counted first and then the night shift's ballots would be brought down. It was expected that the tally would go on until the early hours, and I had offered to be there throughout, serving as an official witness for the union. It was a hard vote to record because none of the candidates was identified as belonging to any group and a worker could vote for someone without stating his "labor group preference." One suspected that this was done to give company union men a mask.

After the counting was over, I went home and spent the rest of the night analyzing the vote. As a basis of comparison, I used the cumulative figures that newspapers had been publishing since ALB elections began in Detroit on January 26. Overall, the Detroit boycott total was 12 percent and that at Cleveland Fisher more than two and a half times as much, 32 percent. The company union candidates whose lists had been widely distributed by the supervision totalled only 6.4 percent of the vote.

The Cleveland results were among the best in the country. Three other

General Motors groups, including Toledo Chevrolet (chapter 6), disregarded the AFL ban and ran candidates, all of whom received significant votes.[3] Sidney Fine concludes that the boycott was an error. This was my own viewpoint after my experience at Cleveland Fisher and, far more so, two years later, when Dick Frankensteen told me about the brilliant manner in which the Chrysler workers of Detroit exploited these ALB elections to build their unions (chapter 10) and gave me materials to document this. The Chrysler unions were independent until 1936, when through Frankensteen's urging they affiliated with the UAW, in which he long played an outstanding role.

One might wonder at the decision of Federation leaders to conduct this boycott. The ALB's announcement of the elections early in December 1934 seems to have taken them by surprise, and they reacted more from fear and anger than from wisdom. Coming only a month after Roosevelt extended the Auto Code without heeding the AFL's often-repeated request to be allowed to propose changes in it, the sudden call for the ALB ballot must have struck William Green and Dillon as a sheer provocation. Green's grand tour of the auto centers, which was decided upon in mid-December, may well have been in response to the ALB's decision. When the first elections were held on January 26, it was probably no accident that they were begun in Detroit, where the auto union's weakness was notorious. The very next day the AFL "withdrew" from the Auto Labor Board.

This could not, however, prevent the elections from taking place; the problem was how to make the results appear the least catastrophic. Bill Green had in an off-guard moment revealed that the federal auto locals had only twenty thousand dues-paying members (twenty thousand more being "delinquent"). Hence the national strike vote that was to be taken during his tour was in danger of being refuted by a poor AFL showing in the ALB balloting. The result would be to negate the effectiveness of the Federation's plan to gain a powerful support for Green's bargaining position with the auto manufacturers without actually having to call a strike to back it up, which Green certainly did not intend to do.

The result of the Fisher Body ballot would give a big push to the Green tour, which started off auspiciously at Cleveland with an enthusiastic meeting of three thousand auto workers. Louis Spisak was overjoyed by this concordance in which his local had so propitious a place. It seemed to be in recognition of this that President Green granted a lengthy interview to a group of Fisher officers on that same day. I saw Spisak soon after and he was still glowing from his successes. He told me of his plan to put the *Labor Digest* out every two weeks thereafter and invited me to his home for dinner. I accepted though I had no intention of agreeing to the proposal that I sensed he would make to me on that occasion.

This decision was strengthened by my visit to his house, particularly by the collection of Coughliniana that I saw displayed there: a pile of the radio priest's pamphlets and a book of his Sunday talks. Self-consciously, Spisak sought to mitigate this attachment by showing me a copy of *Partners in Plunder,* which panned the AFL "terribly," he said, and Lincoln Steffens's autobiography, which he called a "swell book." Then, without realizing it, he ruined the good impression he might have made on one by praising T. N. Taylor, who he thought was "wonderful," a real "square shooter." I was aware of the play this man and other AFL leaders were making for the Fisher Body group in trying to build a base among the Cleveland locals to counteract the White Motor influence. Spisak had even arranged for a personal desk for Taylor at the Fisher local headquarters.

After dinner, which was served by his intellectual wife, a school teacher, Spisak continued to unbend, to the point of telling me of his ambition to run for the city council.

"That's a fine idea," I said, "on a Labor party ticket."

"No," he countered, "as an independent."

For some reason or other I took a little dig at him: "Okay, run as an independent, so long as you don't run as a Coughlin party candidate. That would antagonize the Protestants," I added with a meaningful smile.

Louis Spisak had taken it for granted that I would stay with him and the *Labor Digest* and felt put down when I told him that it was our plan to put out a paper for the Auto Council that would be independent of any individual local.

He thought for a little while, then asked, "Well, why don't you put out the *Labor Digest* for the Auto Council in that case?"

"Do you think George Reichow [a Fisher Body member I had met] would agree to act as business manager?" I said, an idea I had already thought about.

"I don't know, I'll ask him."

We put out a couple of issues that way, still in the small *Labor Digest* format, but Spisak seemed to lose interest in the paper once it was out of his hands. He was very much relieved when I suggested a way out for him, arguing that so important a local as Fisher Body ought to have a paper of its own while I would try to put out a separate one for the Auto Council. Spisak did not feel close to the council and probably never would, but I was surprised when George Reichow said that he would like to work with me.

• • •

My plan was already prepared and I presented it to the next meeting of the Auto Council. We would double the size of the *Labor Digest,* I said, and could put out a four-page issue of twenty thousand copies for $60. This could be paid for by our local committees gathering sixty one-inch ads at

$1 each. Advertising should not be hard to get if committees canvassed their plant neighborhoods and solicited beer halls, restaurants, groceries, drug stores, and other places they patronized.

"There will be no other expense," I added. "The tough job will be getting those ads but we can't afford to pay the go-getters a percentage since that would mean we'd have to get more ads and that would eat up our space. As for articles, I suggest that each local appoint a shop editor who will be in charge of turning in reports of meetings, negotiations, or any other interesting stuff. These articles should be signed, to give them authenticity. That's about it, the rest we'll learn by experience. Oh yes, one more thing. Fisher Body will probably continue to publish *Labor Digest* as a local paper. I suggest that we change the name of the Auto Council's paper to the *United Auto Worker.*"

I was startled and truly moved when the last remark brought a spontaneous burst of applause. What was even more gratifying was that it was followed up immediately by concrete offers of help. As usual, Ed Stubbe took the lead: "Don't worry about ads, Hank," he cried, giving me the nickname that stuck thereafter. "I'll guarantee you ten bucks a month myself." It was a promise he kept, though at times he used rather rough tactics to do so. He had bottomless contempt for merchants who took the auto workers' money in trade but then refused to spend a dollar for an advertisement in the *United Auto Worker.* Once at a meeting of the local Stubbe gave an enthusiastic pep talk to demand that members stop patronizing Sam's Cigar Store on the corner of St. Clair Avenue and 79th "due to their unfavorable attitude toward our paper." The threat must have worked since a couple meetings later Stubbe announced pompously that Sam's Cigar Store had been taken off the unfair list.

There were other aces at the game of ad-gathering; one of them, Robert Fulgham, of the Murray Ohio local, was so good that our editorial board soon decided to ask him to deduct $10 or $15 a month for his expenses. It was permissible to go back on one's good intentions, I told myself after discovering that volunteer efforts were not always dependable, leaving us short once or twice on our printer's bill. With a brashness I never could have mustered for a personal need, I even mentioned the fact to an Auto Council meeting. "I'll take care of the printer," an officer from Bender Body declared, almost angrily. Then he explained, "I'm in a couple of fraternal organizations that get their printing done there." When I next went to the print shop, the owner treated me deferentially. But I paid him the money we owed him anyway with the White Motor $20 per capita check to the Auto Council that Mortimer had signed over to him as a "loan" to the newspaper.

Another reason why we fell short on the printer's bill now and then was because of an extravagance on my part. We had been publishing for three or four months when we began getting requests from locals in various centers, one of them in Oakland, California, for some copies. I, the proud editor, would ship as many as several hundred papers and was too sensitive to mention money. Soon, however, the requests became too frequent and too big, and I had to set a price with the printer: $2.50 for a thousand copies, railroad shipping cost included. Surely, I thought, they could afford to pay that. But I was amazed to learn that some of them could not. "Any date will be all right," they would say, meaning leftover copies, as though a newspaper published for and by auto workers would have to be interesting however outmoded the content.

One request really surprised me. It was from Elizabeth Birds, the secretary of the Detroit Ternstedt local, who asked for a little delay in paying for the thousand copies that she ordered. She also suggested shyly that we send leftover copies from previous issues, which the local would pay for eventually. It was only later, when I got to know this remarkable young woman, that I learned that her local had fewer than a hundred members for the eight thousand workers, the majority female, in that General Motors plant. It delighted me beyond reason when she told me that they used our paper, carefully doled out, as an organizational tool.

Somewhat later Sister Birds wrote me a letter that I put into the paper because it was so instructive about the sacrifices an outsider was prepared to make to circulate it:

Dear Brother Kraus: The *United Auto Worker* certainly got a hot reception at Ternstedt when another union member and myself distributed it two weeks ago. The company apparently got a jolt at seeing such a paper in front of their plant, so they had the police pick us up. The police promised that we would never be able to get a job at Ternstedt again. I didn't expect to get back after not allowing my local to be broken up, so I don't lose any sleep worrying over it.—Well it will be a tough job organizing Detroit, but it will have to be done.

Elizabeth Birds continued, nevertheless, to be active in the union and before the South Bend Convention in April 1936 she took a step that has been recorded in UAW history. She quietly surrendered her choice as delegate for the Ternstedt local to Walter Reuther, who thus became eligible for election to the International's executive board during the following critically important year.

• • •

In the Auto Council elections that took place on February 16, 1935, the White Motor group, especially myself, was surprised to learn that Mortimer would have opposition for the presidency: John Soltis. It was hardly a question of favoritism on our part. Mortimer was the natural candidate. He was president of the biggest local in Cleveland, which also was one of the three or four outstanding auto unions in the country and one of a small minority that had won a signed agreement, including recognition, full bargaining rights, and a number of other important improvements. In addition, the White Motor local, Mortimer specifically, had given courageous leadership to the movement for the International Union.

We felt that Soltis was not a serious candidate for the post as long as a man like Mortimer was available. But *was* he available? Whatever Reisinger, Stubbe, and the rest of us thought, Mortimer was reluctant. I, more than the others perhaps, tended to forget that he was fifty and had to work eight hours a day at a compelling, exhausting job. The presidency of a big local was exigent enough as an after-work avocation. Mortimer averaged at least two nights a week on union work, he told me and as I knew, and every weekend some local (and not only auto workers) asked his help in working up a contract or in some other task. When he went to an evening meeting, he did not spare himself the double drive home, for he was a devoted family man and would not miss eating supper with his wife and daughter. Each trip from and to Euclid Village was thirty miles. Mortimer told me that he needed seven hours of rest a night but often had to make do with a good deal less.

I have often wondered in later years what gave me the presumption to decide this question for Mortimer, for it was I who conducted his "campaign." A complicating factor was that every local had five votes and a single delegate could cast them all. Hence, a small local that had as few as two or three hundred members (about the average) had the same vote as the mighty White Motor local, which had more than two thousand. Only Fisher Body had as many as five hundred members during this period when almost eight thousand workers were in the plant.

In the contest for the presidency, Mortimer's supporters were sure that he would win hands down, but I was far from being that confident. I was sure of only four of the nine groups: White Motors, Bender Body, Willard Storage Battery, and National Carbon. The last group was represented by Coleman Taylor, whom Mortimer knew from his Auto Workers Union (TUUL) period. There were other locals that had a TUUL background, like Bender Body and Murray Ohio. But these early groups were destroyed at the beginning of the NRA period by newspaper red-baiting and police violence that usually operated in cahoots with the AFL. The present leader of the Bender local, William Kics, was a bright, progressive-minded man of Hungarian extraction, the national background of a large part of its membership. Mortimer had been helpful to Kics in bargaining with his management or in giving him advice over the telephone.

Ed Simpson, the leader of the Willard local, was an active member of the

Socialist party and likewise had great admiration for Mortimer, particularly for his intellectual quality and self-acquired learning. I recall how Simpson fascinated the Auto Council by his account of Mortimer's debate with Jim McWeeney at his local. Mortimer had helped the executive board draw up its demands, which were presented to the company. The company proved adamant, however, and the local called a meeting to take a strike vote. In his speech at that meeting, McWeeney simply advised delay. Mortimer was called upon next. "'A strike vote is a warning,'" Ed Simpson quoted him, "'that you the workers will remove your labor power unless the company is reasonable. It is meant to give support to your demands through the only weapon that you possess. What in heaven's name is the point of giving a warning to the company *by delay?*'" The Auto Council delegates chuckled delightedly. "McWeeney and some of the guys were standing around after the meeting," Simpson commented. "You, Mort, had left so you didn't hear what he said. You know the funny way he has of expressing himself. He said: 'First I talked, then Mortimer talked, and after he finished, you'd think the ceiling was gonna fall down on our heads!'"

A fifth group with some likely Mortimer supporters was Fisher Body. Louis Spisak seemed to like Mortimer but was concerned about his left-wing reputation and aware that AFL representatives like T. N. Taylor feared and even hated him. But Spisak was eager to keep in Mortimer's good graces and had invited him to speak at one of the Fisher meetings. Mortimer offered to return the courtesy by inviting Spisak to speak at White's, but for some reason or other Spisak sent Jack Barskites, the local's financial secretary, in his place. I was not sure of Bob Bates's vote, either. He was slow-talking, feet-dragging, and tall, a devotee of the International Union but little else as far as I could make out. I was quite sure, on the other hand, of the support of Sam Griff, a graduate lawyer who was forced to postpone his career because of the depression. I was suspicious of Griff at first when he told me that he had invited Arthur Greer to our Cleveland conference the previous September. But Griff did seem to have a sincere regard for Mortimer after seeing him in action there, so he said.

It was harder for me to act as precinct captain in countering John Soltis's support. I knew that he was popular with several of the local leaders and for good reason, always responding to any request for help. Because Hupmobile, his plant, had been closed for a number of months, he had a lot of time on his hands. The status of his local was ambiguous. Eventually, Hupp would go out of business but in the meanwhile Soltis had convinced the local to stay alive by paying a minimum per capita tax so that it would be in a position supposedly to get going again "when the factory reopened." Soltis was not troubled with finances because of the layoff since, as he explained, he received compensation for an injury he had received in the coal mines.

As for the other locals, I knew that the Baker-Raulang parts plant was definitely in Soltis's corner because he was much involved with its long quest for a federal local charter. I could make no conclusions about either Murray Ohio or Ashtabula's Bow-Socket though I figured that even if both these locals gave their five votes to Soltis, he would still not have enough to win. The voting followed almost exactly the pattern I had laid down, except for one surprising and ridiculous circumstance. Coleman Taylor of National Carbon (five "sure votes" for Mortimer) did not show up for the meeting that Sunday morning at 10 and he had sent no one to take his place.

Without the slightest twinge of conscience, I decided to try to stall the voting as long as possible. Inadvertently Elmer Bernhardt of the Bow-Socket local fell into my plot by raising a question that precipitated a discussion lasting a quarter of an hour. I followed through by asking for a clarification on how the ballots would be counted in case there was a split among a local's delegates, suggesting that their votes be tallied individually. This killed another fifteen minutes and Coleman Taylor finally appeared. The elections took place immediately and Mortimer defeated John Soltis by only three votes, 24 to 21. Mortimer's sole comment was, "Well, I'm in the chair already so I guess we'll just keep going on to the other officers."

Soltis, who was designated vice president by unanimous ballot, seemed to be very pleased by that choice. Apparently, he had not expected to be elected president and, not realizing how close he would come to it, was satisfied to have done so well against an important candidate like Mortimer. By some kind of mutual understanding, Bob Bates of Fisher Body got the post of secretary, a concession to the thin-skinned sensibilities of that local, which had never established congenial relations with the other unions. It was a kind of snobbishness and although no one could deny that this plant was far and away the most important one in the area, the local's strength was utterly out of keeping with that fact. Bates, who I discovered later was an outcast in his own local, proved to be the right person to break down its isolation.

• • •

Whatever the private qualms I may have had in the process, the establishment of the Cleveland Auto Council was of immense significance for the events that followed soon after. President Green was scheduled to inaugurate his grand tour in Cleveland on the day after Mortimer's election, and Mortimer had already been designated for a special role on that occasion at the Auto Council's prescient February 12 session.

In anticipation of Green's visit, the Auto Council had voted on February 12 to address a "letter or telegram" to "His Honor," with back-up messages to Francis Dillon and George McKinnon, asking for (1) a meeting between

Green "and a committee representing ten locals of auto and parts workers";
(2) that Brother Mortimer represent these locals "on the speaker's stand";
and (3) that Brother Mortimer be the "representative speaker for Cleveland's auto and parts workers at the mass meeting."

In the letter that George Booth, acting secretary of the Auto Council, sent
the following day, February 13, he curiously left out any reference to the
second and third requests. This may have been due to carelessness but since
Booth had written the original motions in his own hand into the council's
minutes of February 12, that explanation is not very likely. The typed letter
is headed "14005 Coit Rd.," which was the Fisher Body local's headquarters. An apter explanation, therefore, is that Booth allowed one of the officers there, or even more likely T. N. Taylor, the AFL representative who had
a desk at the headquarters, to edit the wording, thus cutting down Mortimer's suggested role.

These omissions did not speak well for the reception of our committee
on that important day. The only request granted to it actually was the meeting with Green but even this occurred almost by accident. The elected committee (comprised of Mortimer, Soltis, Kics, Coleman Taylor, Jack Barskites, Merle Moccabbee of Murray Ohio, and Kozak of Willard), together
with a number of other auto union activists including myself, went to the
Gillsy Hotel, where the pre-meeting luncheon was to take place. We arrived
a good half-hour ahead of time to make sure that Green would find an occasion to meet with us.

We stood around outside in the automobile entrance court waiting for
him and after some minutes Francis Dillon appeared in a big, chauffeur-
driven limousine that halted by the door. Dillon was sitting in the back and
made no move to get out. The committee hurried up to the car and Mortimer tried to get Dillon's attention through the partly rolled-down window.
"What the hell do *you* want?" he demanded after a while, glaring out at
Mortimer. Mortimer kept his temper and bent closer to the window to say
something to him but before he had finished the car suddenly drove off.

A number of AFL officials had witnessed the ungracious scene. A business agent of the Machinists who seemed to know some of the auto workers approached us and said to Mortimer, "For Christ's sake, what goes on
here?" When Mortimer told him, he looked around incredulously. "Don't
worry," he said. "I'll get you a meeting with President Green." The grudge
against Dillon seemed to be general.

All the auto union men (there must have been twenty of us by then) strag-
gled on into the hotel. We assembled outside the door to the banquet hall in
order not to miss Green in case Dillon tried to slip him in by some side entrance. Somehow we were not surprised to see George Lehman and Charley Walsh wearing white aprons and acting as bartenders at a big table in-

side the hall. They seemed too embarrassed to take notice of us. Both were rather glare-eyed and Lehman had a bouncy step for keeping his balance as he moved about.

It was not until a quarter of an hour or so before the luncheon began that we got notice that Green would see the committee. We rushed down a corridor twenty-strong, finally running into Dillon, who was standing outside the door of a cubbyhole-sized room inside which Green was visible. "This is too big a mob!" Dillon shouted. "He can't see any more than six of you."

In the commotion that followed, the committee as such was almost lost sight of as six men were separated out. We were all afraid that the time would be up before Mortimer could have a chance to talk to Green. I stayed back at the door, but Bill Kics grabbed hold of me: "Here, you've got to be in on this!" I tried to resist but he pulled me in with him.

Mortimer was standing close to Green, and they already seemed engaged in a sharp exchange. I heard little of it, merely noticed a peculiar feature of Green's face, as one is apt to do when one sees a celebrated person up close. It was his nose, rather round-tipped and boyish, and I curiously associated it with Huckleberry Finn's nose, which I must have seen in a sketch in some juvenile edition of that story. Green's nose was pink and sprinkled with tiny globules of perspiration, and it seemed to be throbbing with held-back wrath. "Once you get your International," he was saying to Mortimer, "you'll be sorry you ever asked for it and you'll be running back to us for help."

I stared at Green incredulously, feeling ashamed for him and thinking, "What a childish thing to say!" Mortimer tried to say something but Green broke in again. "What you want to think about is your workers' economic conditions. They're far more important than the International, which is occupying all your time."

Mortimer managed to get a few words in at this insulting provocation. "We've been doing exactly that, Brother Green, but our managements all tell us that they can't do anything more for us until the rest of the industry is organized." But Green wasn't listening. He was saying something else, which I did not hear, while poking a finger at Mortimer's solar plexus. Then he moved his head back as though to study the effect of his words on Mortimer while fixing him with a cold look of hatred that stunned me.

The monologue was swiftly ended. Green was spirited away and the next thing I knew we were all at a couple of big tables in the banquet hall, far away from where the important people sat. One might easily forget what the whole thing was about, that the minds of the half-million auto workers were at stake and that they still had to be reached and won.

At the mass meeting itself we were all stunned by Bill Green's performance. The *Plain Dealer* in its evening edition said that three thousand auto workers were in the audience. It was the first time I had heard him speak, and nothing had prepared me for the broad-shouldered belligerence of his style. I was impressed particularly by the frontal manner of his attack and his expanded chest and big, balled fists, reminders that he, too, had been a miner. "The automobile workers of this country have an opportunity to join with us in this great historic struggle," Green cried, then pausing for a moment and raising his fist, he shouted the thrilling words that I heard for the first time: *"We have just begun to fight!"*

Even more amazing was Dillon's speech, which he delivered with melodramatic effect. He glared ferociously, set his jaw, gathered his eyebrows, and prepared to tear the unseen enemy limb from limb. He called forth a whole range of acts and decisions from his auditors. He called on all those who condemned the Auto Labor Board for its many iniquities to rise, and everybody did so. Then Dillon called for a standing vote in favor of a general strike ballot to be taken in the automobile industry and for President Green to be the auto workers' representative in the negotiations that would follow. The audience cheered as they clattered to their feet while cards were being passed around for all to sign.

It was the strike call that they were acclaiming and I was thrilled. But at that very moment I quickly thought about the shrewd manner of its presentation. The call was meant to tie the hands of the insurgent auto workers in case any group of them should think of jumping the gun. Even if, as a result of the AFL's incitement, a strike did come, Bill Green would be there, on the ground floor, in a position to accept any "reasonable offer" so as to drive the strikers back to work.

• • •

A succession of happenings in the next days and weeks kept the momentum rolling. Though probably not appreciated by the AFL leadership, the White Motor local adopted a resolution on February 20, three days after the mass meeting, calling for a general strike in the auto industry, which was meant to put some extra pressure on the issue. On February 23, Mortimer and a delegation from five locals of the Auto Council appeared at Detroit headquarters and asked for a hearing with Director Dillon, which was surprisingly granted without ado.

Mortimer told Dillon that the Cleveland locals were still very much concerned about the International Union because their interview with President Green had been unavailing on the subject. The locals would like to know the latest word about the International because all kinds of rumors were circulating. Dillon was unbelievably gracious, perhaps still under the glow of the splendid Cleveland meeting. He assured the delegation that an announcement of the International would soon be issued. However, he added, they would all agree that it was advisable that the date and other details should be left in abeyance while the strike vote and President Green's big tour were proceeding.

On March 16, Francis Dillon wrote a letter to the Cleveland Auto Council (although he addressed it to "President Mortimer of the White Motor local"), corroborating what he had told them tentatively on February 23. "President William Green," he stated, "has assured the National Council that he has been authorized by the Executive Council of the American Federation of Labor to issue a Charter to the United Automobile Workers as an International Union. However, in view of the tense situation prevailing in the automobile industry, the National Council requested and the Executive Council agreed, that . . . the issuance of the Charter will be held in abeyance until the present crisis is past."

There was an additional cause for satisfaction in the letter: the "recognition" of our Auto Council. Although wrapped in limitations ("such Councils . . . are purely voluntary in character, are not chartered and have no authority to collect dues or levy assessments"), we greeted it as a welcome go-ahead signal for all the work we had undertaken as interlopers, which we could now do without fear of sanctions.

The National Council was in session when the Cleveland delegation arrived in Detroit, involved in what would be the most exciting experience that this pathetic body would ever have. The mutual correspondence during this period reveals states of mind that veered from ecstatic excitement to despondency and back again.[4]

Ed Hall of Wisconsin asked that the National Council be called into "constant session." To lend support to his own synthetically contrived crisis, Francis Dillon gave partial consent to this suggestion by arranging a full outline of discussions. First came the overall strike plan that he had devised. It would start with the strike vote of all the AFL's 176 federal auto locals but the walkout itself would concentrate on General Motors plants. Cleveland would take the lead, followed by Toledo, Kansas City, St. Louis, Janesville, Wisconsin, and Norwood, Ohio, by which time Flint would be ready to go.

The strike vote started ten days later, on March 4, with eight hundred members at Cleveland Fisher endorsing the strike overwhelmingly. The White Motor local voted in similar fashion the following day. National Council members had all gone home and Dillon's hyped-up tension was past. He was back to his soothing utterances to the effect that this ballot by no means meant that a strike was actually contemplated. The automobile manufacturers must have taken him at his word since they haughtily turned down the AFL's request for a pre-strike conference.

Cleveland's Unions Take the AFL at Its Word

5

Long before things had reached this sad state, the Cleveland group had given up on the national AFL and all its vaporous plans. More than ever, we realized that any accomplishment would depend upon us. Even the granting of the International Union was not for this season. Only on the economic front could something still be saved, possibly. March had not yet ended, and production was going at a good clip. There was still time enough for the rank-and-file unions to pick up the baton that William Green had let fall from his trembling hands. This had been attempted by a few unions in 1933 and 1934; maybe 1935 would be a more propitious year.

For one thing, the agitation that Green and UAW Director Francis Dillon had stirred up in Cleveland could be used to good purpose. The auto companies had been given a real scare, our people reported from the plants. We had to take advantage of this, and the Auto Council and our paper could help. Both had been launched at an appropriate moment coinciding with an extraordinarily active period among our affiliated locals. The first issues of the *United Auto Worker* reflected this animation. An unwary historian might attribute the ebullience to President Green's grand tour and the national strike vote. Unfortunately, that conclusion would be wrong. It was from their own propulsion that Cleveland locals were prepared to move and everything that happened thereafter served their momentum.

When he announced the projected strike vote to the Cleveland groups, UAW Director Francis Dillon had bade them to prepare for it by presenting lists of demands to their companies, the idea being to win a head start in the wake of Green's passage. Our locals needed no such prompting since steps of this nature had already been undertaken with the help of the senior leaders of the Auto Council. Some of these locals had gotten off to bad starts during the early period, often due to the poor advice of AFL organizers, and consequently were in a relatively weak position.

I was able to gather some notes about experiences of this kind at the Auto Council. Merle Moccabbee, president of the Murray Ohio local, told me of an incident involving George McKinnon that was hard to believe. The latter was sitting in on an early negotiation with their management when the company surprised the union by bringing in a counterproposal. The men had hardly had the time to read the paper, to say nothing of studying it properly, when McKinnon declared enthusiastically: "Well, boys, I just know you're going to accept this agreement. I'm sure it's the best that the company can offer."

The time for such incidents was past, however, as was the time when the federal locals looked up to the Federation's representatives as oracles. It was not only that they realized that the AFL men lacked experience in the mass production industries; by March 1935, there had also been a significant qualitative change in local leaders themselves. They had set their wits against their employers and become seasoned by their failures and occasional successes. Moreover, these leaders had benefited from the aid of more seasoned men in other locals. Wyndham Mortimer was an outstanding example. At negotiations in particular, he brought them a sense of confidence due to his great experience, which enabled him to provide new answers to nubby problems.

Two years later, when I interviewed George Lehman, I asked him frankly what he thought of Mortimer. Lehman had by this time retired from union activity and gone into church work with his wife. He replied that he had always had the highest regard for Mortimer, who by then had been the International's vice president for a year. "However," he added, "I didn't like it when he began building his caucus with Reisinger and Stubbe and Ted Reiff and Dieter. I thought he was planning to take the local back out of the AFL and into that dual union of his. I realize now that that was foolish but it's what I feared. But as a union thinker Mort was tops. The idea he thought up which we were able to put across in 1934 of plantwide seniority was the most important thing that we ever accomplished."

The fact that I did not fully appreciate at the time this important quality in Mortimer was due to my lack of understanding of technical problems in the shop. I could have learned more about them from him and the others had I been motivated sufficiently. But I was more interested in something else, local politics, which Lehman criticized—but which he had always played adeptly himself. The economic aspect of trade unionism, however, was its most important function, as any worker could have told me.

That the auto unions were so politically oriented in the early days was a consequence of their insecure situation brought on by their constant struggle for self-rule against the continuing challenges of the AFL leaders. For example, the problem of the union at Cleveland's Baker-Raulang was that it had no charter. This medium-sized parts plant was first organized in 1933 by the communist-led TUUL, which had the audacity to call a strike against a rigidly stubborn company. The strike was crushed by police in collusion with AFL officials, who then took the group over with the frank intention of parcelling its workers out to a baker's dozen of craft unions, as had been done at several other plants. This did not turn out to be as easy at Baker-Raulang as was expected, however, due mainly to the aggressive leadership of a tough young man, Elmer Davis, who boasted of his bootlegger's background, when he had helped run liquor across Lake Erie from Canada.

Jim McWeeney tried to offer the Baker-Raulang group a charter from the Auto Rebuilders Union. But Elmer Davis all but spat on it and was no more gentle with the documents tendered by the Machinists, the Painters, and several others. His stubbornness seemed to have paid off when McWeeney finally told him that the group would get a federal charter. "That's more like it!" Davis shouted, clapping the diminutive labor leader on the back with his huge palm. McWeeney took advantage of his enthusiasm to slip in a word of caution. "I don't want you to get impatient on me again since it may take some time. Meanwhile you'll turn your funds over to the Metal Trades Council for safe-keeping till you can elect officers who can be bonded."

Elmer Davis nodded, while telling himself he'd be a goddam fool to give up such a good bargaining foil. "Bring me that federal charter first," he told McWeeney silently and set himself to outwait the little organizer's patience. It was around this time that Davis made contact with the Auto Council, which happened at his first meeting to be preoccupied with the problems of getting the *United Auto Worker* started. Suddenly Davis erupted: "I sit here and it gets me sick to listen to you guys arguing like a bunch of schoolboys. Jesus Christ, don't you have anything more important to do?"

Everybody looked at Davis in amazement, which he thought was admiration of his toughness. I snapped at him angrily, "Maybe some day, Brother, you'll be glad to have a newspaper where you can print your side of the story!" He apologized afterward and we soon became friends. He reported his charter troubles to the Auto Council and said that he had decided to go to Detroit and seek out Director Dillon in his own lair. He almost got into fisticuffs with the burly auto union chief, who to get rid of Davis promised prompt service on the charter. "Don't worry, I'll get it for you within three days," Dillon vowed.

But the elusive federal charter was once again not forthcoming, not in three days and not in three months. The Baker-Raulang local nonetheless put in its demands to the company, as did all our other locals during that period. To get a toehold advantage during negotiations, the company made a fake sticking point of the charter. "How can we sign a contract with you when you don't even have a charter? You're not even a union!"

So the not-even-a-union went on strike for three-and-a-half days. Then the company signed the agreement after all, probably satisfied to have a local without status to deal with since it could always take advantage of that shortcoming.

• • •

For about six weeks, virtually all of the Cleveland auto locals went through strikes. One after the other they came, with at times two or even three running simultaneously. The locals had all gone through the same procedure: preparation of demands, a letter to the company, negotiations refused or stalled, a five-day ultimatum, and, finally, the strike. For the entire period I was constantly on the go, from picket line to picket line, so that I had to take several "sick leaves" from my WPA job.

I took my responsibility as editor with an urgent conscientiousness. Locking step with the pickets, I interviewed them one after the other, scribbling their remarks in my hardback notebook as we made the round together. I was not the only picket-line devotee. Solidarity was already a deeply shared entity and since a number of plants were relatively close to each other, any one that was struck could depend on visitors from others that were working, especially before and after shift, bringing cigarettes, tobacco, and money, coins gathered in tin cans the day before in their departments. The rich White Motor local paid its unemployed members a dollar a day plus carfare to picket voluntarily at these strikes.

Since the *United Auto Worker* came out only once a month, it could hardly be a dispenser of "hot news," though a couple of times at longer-lasting strikes a previously written story *in their own paper* would bring cheers from the pickets. I brought written reports from our struck locals to the daily press in downtown Cleveland whenever I had a chance, talked to the men at the news desks, and actually got reporters out to a strike now and then. The headlines in the *Plain Dealer* and the *Cleveland Press* for the period read like a John Dos Passos novel:

May 1:   Bender Body strikes.
May 2:   Murray Ohio strikes.
May 3:   Willard Battery strike averted when company agrees to negotiate on contract.
May 5:   Murray Ohio strike settled; terms.
May 7:   Ashtabula Bow-Socket strikes.
May 9:   Willard negotiations fail; 3–400 vote strike.
May 18: Willard negotiations at impasse.
May 19: Willard strike ends as company agrees to arbitrate wage increase.

May 20: White Motor negotiations at impasse.
May 21: Bender Body settles; terms.
May 21: White Motor strikes.
May 24: National Carbon strikes; Coleman Taylor warns on Berg-
hoff strikebreakers.
May 25: White Motor negotiations progress.
May 27: White Motor strike praised for good order.

There are few things more exciting to union members than a first strike and most of our strikes were that kind. Even though the Bender Body local had Mortimer's help in working up its demands, it was putting them out on the platter that brought the thrills—and the chills. The Bender list was more "original" than others; an innovation at Bender called for wage minimums at three levels—50, 55, and 66 cents—with skilled rate raises to match of 5 to 14 cents an hour. Foremen were specifically barred from cutting these rates on any account, as they arbitrarily had done in the past. The work week was fixed at forty hours but had to be cut to twenty-four before layoffs could take place. Nothing else was forgotten: seniority, recognition, or a signed contract.

The strike apparatus was meticulously laid out beforehand by Bill Kics (Kish) and his committee. Twelve picket captains were designated, and there were four men to a squad. Squads were changed every three hours and every member was required to picket every day. There was no violence in the strike but this was because strikers were so well prepared. Yet violence seemed bound to come on one occasion when the company asked that seven great gasoline tanks be completed for delivery. When the union refused, the company hired a strike-breaking group to move the tanks. Word of this came to the local hall, where a meeting was taking place, and two hundred men "flew" (Bill Kics's word) to the plant. The company changed its mind.

Violence was the hardest aspect of a strike for me to accept. I wondered how I would act when faced with it and tried to work myself up mentally so as to conduct myself properly when it came. You never knew when or where violence would present itself. The White Motor strike was declared a model of peace and gentlemanly conduct, but White was a large plant with more than two thousand workers. Size alone was no protection, however, because size might call forth a great show of belligerence. I did not witness the most turbulent of our strikes, the one at Bow-Socket, because the small plant was in another city. But Elmer Bernhardt gave me a remarkable account of events. He himself did not appear to be a violent man; he was about forty, spare and lanky with loose-hanging arms, wan features, and gray eyes. He made me think of Abe Lincoln. The strike had been going on for fourteen days, and the union men were picketing peacefully.

Then the company sends up to Cleveland and asks McGrath [a strike-breaking outfit] to get some "guards" down. They called in the union committee and told us: "You fellows go right on picketing, only you got to do it across the street." I said: "We're staying right where we are." Then McGrath stopped by the union tent and said: "We're bringing some Cleveland men in tomorrow. We don't want any trouble with you boys. But we'll be ready if it comes." I said: "So will we." So next day when the busses come we were out there full force, with clubs and sticks and bricks, and boy we had a battle royal. We had the ambulances going for half an hour. The sheriff he got hurt too. So they let us stay on picket.

• • •

The Fisher Body shutdown was hardly a strike. It was a halfhearted attempt to take advantage of the Toledo Chevrolet walkout of April 23 that forced General Motors to close a number of other plants. But the timid Cleveland leadership took too long in making up its mind. When finally the executive board decided in "secret session" on April 29 to strike the following day, the company was promptly informed about it and jumped the gun, locking the gates on the workers who arrived that morning.

Lincoln Scafe, the plant manager, promised Louis Spisak, the local's president, not to try to run scabs in but militant members demanded action. They raised the famous slogan "Turn the lockout into a strike!" and the executive board had no choice but to comply, declaring the strike on May 1 (an unintentional coincidence) and ordering pickets to be set out on the following day. Bob Bates, the head of the strike committee, drove around all night trying to recruit men. About fifty responded the following morning and he placed two or three to a post all around the vast factory grounds.

When I arrived at local headquarters around 10 o'clock, Bates was high with excitement, his eyes bloodshot from lack of sleep. His shag of unkempt black curly hair stood erect. He greeted me with effusive pleasure and immediately put me in charge of assigning picket reliefs, a meaningless task since there were no pickets to send. There were some men hanging around at headquarters, however, keeping warm because it was cold outside and raining. Besides, almost everybody felt that picketing was useless since the company had shut the plant (this was the AFL "line"). The men thought they were doing their duty in just waiting for something to happen. I told myself I'd have to write a piece in the next issue of the paper on the importance of picketing a locked-out plant. The men were holding a big gab-fest on the question.

"Are we on strike or not?"

"It's a lockout, it ain't no strike."

"Whadya mean lockout, didn't the executive board call it a strike?"

"Well, if it's a strike, where's all the pickets?"

"We're beginning to put pickets out."

"Where are they? You can't even see them for the rain!"

"We're just kidding ourselves, there ain't no strike."

"Yeah, the company got the jump on us."

"That's right, we're one day behind."

"Okay, then," a young fellow shouted angrily, "if the company called you back, would you go?"

"Hell, no!" the answer came, swift and unanimous and spirits perked up for a while.

Bob Bates asked me to make the rounds with him. Despite the rain, the pickets at the first post seemed in a good mood. They were clustered under a big umbrella latched to a lamp-post. What looked like a coke bonfire was burning in a covered iron barrel. When we parked, the conversation, which was in a Slavish tongue, halted, and the men smiled shyly at us.

"Everybody okay?" Bates asked breezily.

"Ya! Ya!" one replied.

"That's great. If you need anything, let us know."

"Those guys are all communists," Bates said as we drove away, giving me a look between a leer and a smile.

"How do you know?"

"We've had our eye on them. They make it easy for us because they always stick together. You know this guy, Mike Evko, he's on our strike committee. He's one of them too. Smart guy. One time he was talking at a meeting and he says, 'Like Comrade Campbell said,' and he covers up as fast as you could blink. 'I mean Brother Campbell,' he says, 'I always say "Comrade" because that's what we called each other in the American Legion, where I belonged after the war.'"

Bates chuckled as we went on to the next post. "Well, we put a couple of guys on Mike's tail, and one by one we picked them off. We got a marker on about thirty of them. It's okay as long as they behave themselves. But the first wrong thing they do, we'll lower the boom on them."

The Fisher Body local benefited extraordinarily from the Toledo Chevrolet strike, which gave a new zest to the union spirit in the plant. Many members, who had fallen away after AFL officials had broken the strike of the year before, returned to the fold, and for several days workers jammed local headquarters to sign up. Ralph Rocco said that he got a cramp in his hand from inscribing the new members in the ledger. Steve Jensco, in an oral history that I did with him three years later, estimated that membership in the local surpassed the two thousand mark at the time. Both Rocco and Jensco were members of the local's executive board.

One morning when the lockout strike was in its last days, Bates asked to talk to me in private. We went to a nearby restaurant to get away from the hullabaloo and had no sooner sat down when he started off in his slow delivery. "I like that idea of yours of the flying squadrons."

"It's not my idea, it's Mortimer's," I corrected him. "He mentioned it at that time when he spoke here at your local meeting."

"No matter but I think it's a great way to organize. I know a dozen fellows up Detroit way who could organize all of Michigan with me in three months' time using that method."

"Are they auto workers?" I asked, feeling a strangeness coming over me because of the way he kept studying my face.

"Not all of them. They helped me organize the Ku Klux Klan some years ago up that way."

I caught my breath and tried to keep the blood from flushing my face. "I thought they were anti-labor," I said, innocently.

"Aw, don't believe everything you hear! They got the anti-immigration law adopted, didn't they? That saved us from having millions more of unemployed."

I decided not to let the thing rest there regardless of how he took it. "I still think it's bad for the union to bring subjects up that cause religious antagonism."

"It's not us that brings them up!" Bates countered heatedly. "Fellow I work with started raving about Father Coughlin. I talked against him and he got hot. 'Now wait a minute!' I says. 'I got nothing against the Catholic religion or the Catholic people but it's the Catholic *Church* that's dangerous because it wants to take over our government.' That's why the Protestants have got to get organized," he commented. "They've got the Catholics outnumbered four to one but they're weak because they're all split up." And the KKK will bring them all happily together, I told myself, trying to calm my emotion with irony.

"I told Spisak that," Bates said. "He's Catholic, you know. I noticed that he and some of the other officers didn't trust me. But after I talked frankly to them, I think they changed their minds." And he gave me his open face of sincere conviction.

"But they're no longer around now, are they, I mean the Ku Klux Klan?" I asked, somehow hoping for a confirmation.

Bates smiled. "They're just like the Masons. They've grown up."

I was in internal commotion after our talk and wondered whom I could turn to for reassurance. I thought of Elmer Bernhardt, for whom I had had a high regard until recently, when I felt that he was indulging in some lefthanded red-baiting in asking if I knew Andy Onda, head of the communist-led Unemployed Councils. I said that I had heard about him but went no further. Bernhardt said that Onda had spoken at the May Day meeting in Ashtabula and had made a great speech but let the matter drop when I failed to react. I reproached myself afterward for being so suspicious. Bernhardt was an honest man, I felt, and completely loyal to the working class.

The next time I met him, soon after I had my shocking conversation with Bates, Bernhardt started talking about stool pigeons! He was delighted with having just uprooted one because of the fat black pen the man used. Bernhardt took it out of his jacket pocket to show me.

"They use these," he explained, "to get a guy's finger prints by making him sign his name or something. When he flashed this one on me, I said to him, 'Lend me your pen, will you?' and I took it away from him and wouldn't give it back. He realized the game was up and slobbered all over me about his wife and two kids. So I told him I wouldn't squeal on him if he'd tell me things. There are other guys in this local I've been watching that I want to find out about."

"Anybody I know?" I asked, my heart pounding.

"Well, I'm suspicious of Barskites and Grossman," he said. "I noticed that this stoolie, I'll just call him 'F,' had a grudge against Grossman. So I decided that he was probably playing for another team, maybe the 'Pinks,' and that 'F' was jealous of him because he was earning more money."

"How about Bob Bates?" I asked very quietly.

"Yeah, Bob Bates, too," Bernhardt replied without even having to think.

So I decided to shoot the works. "What do you know abut the KKK, Elmer?"

His face brightened all at once and he arched his shoulders. "I'm a past King Kleagle myself!"

When I left him, my head was ready to burst. We seemed to be building a united front of stool pigeons, KKKers, and communists!

• • •

I stayed away from Fisher Body for several days, spending time at the other plants that were on strike. One afternoon I was out at Willard Battery when Bob Bates drove up, stopping his car some twenty yards up the street from where I was walking the small oval picket with Joe O'Neill, a young officer of the local. I noticed several other men in Bob's car, but I only recognized Bethel Judd. Bates came out alone and headed toward us, and I started to walk in his direction.

"Haven't seen you around for some time," he said as we shook hands. "What you been up to?"

"Gathering stuff for the next issue."

"What's it going to be about?"

"Strikes." I smiled. "Say, that gives me an idea. How about an article from you about Fisher Body? You're head of the strike committee, after all."

"That might be an idea," he said, without conviction.

Something was up and I waited for him to tell me. Then I noticed that Bates had a card palmed in his big hand.

"You seen this?" he asked, looking sharply at me.

I took the card from him and ran my eyes quickly over the few mimeographed words. It was an invitation to a meeting at 7 that evening at the Ukrainian Hall. It was signed in caps, EDUCATIONAL COMMITTEE.

"What's it all about?" I asked.

"You sure you ain't seen it?" he repeated, taking the card back from me.

I looked him in the eye. "No, I haven't. Who put it out?"

"Scotty Campbell was handing them out secretly after the meeting this afternoon."

"Oh," I said, getting the wind of it all at last. "Is Scotty the head of the local's educational committee?"

"We don't have an educational committee."

"So Scotty is trying to set up one of his own, is that it? What a damn fool thing to do!"

Bates seemed convinced about me and even relieved, I thought. "Here we've had this big success," he said, "and the local is really going to town. We've signed up four to five hundred men in the last week alone. We're not going to let them start their monkey business!"

"It's really too bad," I said, feeling immediately that my condemnation was inadequate. "What do you count on doing?"

His mistrust was roused again. "We know what we're going to do," he said sinisterly.

My eyes flickered toward the parked car, then I took a flyer. "You going down to that meeting tonight?"

He did not answer, but I assumed he had. "I'll go with you," I said. "What time will you be leaving?"

I was not sure that Bates liked the idea of me inviting myself but I did not leave him a choice. We arranged that I would meet them outside union headquarters at six-thirty, which gave me time to call Dorothy and also to get a bite to eat.

While in the restaurant I tried to figure out what I must do. I was surprised that I was not frightened. It seemed to me that I had already won a point by getting Bates to let me go with his group. Actually, I felt almost as disturbed about the conduct of Scotty Campbell and his friends as I did about Bob Bates's reaction. I realized that the communists at Fisher Body might be more backward than I had supposed when I found their shop paper, the *Spark Plug,* calling on the workers "to back the AFL officers in the union" while congratulating those officers for "demanding that Dillon set a date for a general strike in auto." Now, all of a sudden, judging from Scotty Campbell's stupid leaflet, they seemed to be resuming their traditional role of an "opposition group."

To me, such a shift in their line did not make sense under the existing circumstances. The communists in the Fisher Body local participated freely in all of the local's activities and several held posts on committees. This was a radical alteration of the situation that had prevailed the previous year during the strike of April 1934, when Dick Reisinger and I had witnessed suspected communists forced to leave the picket line and told to "make yourself scarce." Soon after, a young woman "comrade" who was selling *Daily Workers* had her papers roughly seized and burned in the street. In sharp contrast, I had recently overheard one of the kibbitzers at the Fisher local headquarters suggesting that they call on the Unemployed Council for help as a solution of the picket problem. "Hell," he said, "they come out on their own last year and offered to supply as high as five hundred pickets any time they were needed."

When Bob Bates's car drove up a few minutes early, it struck me as a good sign that only three men were in it, Bates, Bethel Judd, and another fellow who was not familiar to me. My sense of relief vanished, however, when I opened the rear door and noticed a couple of baseball bats on the floor.

Bob was at the wheel, and the other man was up front with him. Judd, whom I knew slightly and who had always struck me as a decent chap was in the back with me. All three men sat glum and silent as though full of nasty thoughts. What could I say to them to make them snap out of it?

"The Willard negotiations are still going on and the arbitration on wages should start up any time," I offered, just to fill the void. But no one showed the least interest. "That's a nasty company," I went on nevertheless. "It was company guards that sideswiped Charley Cook's car and went right to work on him."

"All companies are the same," Bethel Judd suddenly commented, to my delight.

"You said it, Brother," I observed eagerly. "Maybe White Motors is different, but we'll have to wait till the strike starts to know for certain."

"They going on strike too?" he asked, turning his head toward me as though surprised.

"Oh yes, I'm sure. They asked for a delay because this new president had just come in. The local gave him a week. Even if he got a month he wouldn't know any more than he'll know at the end of the week, it seems to me." Judd chuckled and I was pleased, not having realized that what I said might be considered humorous. Judd was a sharp one all right, I told myself happily, feeling all at once more assured about the prospects of our trip.

When we arrived at the hall, however, things again became tense. Bates parked on the other side of Superior but made no move to leave the car. The men didn't say a final word to each other and this, too, seemed a good sign, though perhaps they had decided on a course of action earlier. I kept sitting, too, as though to give them priority but actually because I felt that remaining with the bats might discourage the men from picking them up. I had decided to try to argue them out of doing so.

Without a word, Bates opened his door and we all piled out of his big, secondhand Oakland together. I stood close to him as we examined the dilapidated building. Then, Bates leading, we started to cross the street in a close group. The bats had been left in the car.

The hall was broader than it was deep. There was no platform, only a table in the front at which Scotty Campbell stood, gavel in hand. The twenty or so men present occupied seats in the first three or four rows. They all turned toward us as we entered noisily and several showed their pleasure at seeing us. Mike Evko particularly smiled broadly, as though he might have been expecting us.

I recognized a few others but knew only Joe Chaka by name. He was a personable young chap built like a boxer. I had once overheard him giving Louis Spisak a hard time for defending Bill Green. "I don't care how brilliant you think he is," Chaka told Spisak. "I just don't trust any so-called labor leader who is paid $20,000 a year!"

Bob Bates chose the last row in the hall and let the rest of us pass in front of him to our seats. I made sure to occupy a place next to him. No sooner had I sat down than he bent his lips to my ear and whispered, "I know every last one of them!"

Scotty Campbell, who looked pleased with himself, rapped his gavel on the table. "We might as well begin," he said.

I stood up and raised my hand. "Brother Chairman," I said, "could I have the floor?"

Scotty stared at me without answering and I smiled back at him. I could almost feel the tense silence of Bob Bates and the other fellows in our group, which may have given us all an appearance of complicity. It was Mike Evko who broke the silence with his heavy accent. "Brother Chairman," he called out very loud, "Brother Kraus is asking for the floor."

In an automatic gesture, Scotty Campbell pointed the gavel at me. "Brother Chairman and Brothers," I began, talking deliberately,

I'd like to make a motion, but before doing so I want to say a few words. I just saw one of your cards a couple of hours ago, and I decid-

ed to come down here to give you my opinion. To set up an educational committee of Fisher Body local members is a commendable thing.
But don't you think that that should be done by the local union itself?
I've been watching this local for some time, and I believe it is one of
the most democratic and well-conducted locals in the Auto Council.
It deserves your full cooperation, as it does that of every other union
member. Therefore, I want to move, Brother Chairman, that your educational committee should be dissolved and that you should adjourn
this meeting immediately.

"I second the motion, Brother Chairman," Mike Evko called out even before I had finished. And I was surprised when someone else shouted "I call
for the question!" Scotty Campbell stood as though transfixed.

"The question has been called for, Brother Chairman," still another voice
cried out, with the relish that the new unionists always extended to these
punctilios of parliamentary procedure.

Perfunctorily, Scotty took the vote and my motion was adopted without
opposition. As though this was all they had come for, the small audience
rose, smiling good-naturedly, and headed for the door, not even looking at
us as they passed.

Bob Bates and his friends made no attempt to talk to me as we went down
the high stairs. Apparently, he and his companions had not yet made up their
minds about the meaning of my gesture. Would they realize that it was the
proper thing to do, as I was prepared to argue? The important point was to
stop Scotty Campbell's nonsense cold "without doing damage to the union,"
I would tell them. I realized, however, that they might end up being angry
with me for having done it all on my own. At that moment I did not much
care what they thought. I felt as though a load had been lifted from my chest.

I said goodbye to Bates and his men at the car and said I would take the
streetcar home. I walked straight toward the car stop to discourage any of
the others who were hovering around on the sidewalk nearby from coming
up and trying to open a discussion. Let them mull it over by themselves, I
told myself, and recognize their own foolishness.

• • •

When White Motors workers were getting ready to strike for the first
time in the company's thirty-four years, Francis Dillon, the AFL's plenipo-
tentiary for the automobile industry, happened to be in town as the featured
speaker at a meeting of the Fisher Body workers. Hearing about the projected action of the White local, he got into a car and drove out to the plant with
George McKinnon. We were told that Dillon had announced that he would
settle the "trouble" without any difficulty, disregarding the drawn-out nego-

tiations that had already taken place, compounded by three weeks of further delay that the company requested to give its new president, Robert F. Black, time to become acquainted with the situation.[1]

The negotiating committee was in the president's office when the AFL officials arrived and noticed them through a window as they drove up. "Go on down there and see what the hell they want," Mortimer whispered to Dick Reisinger. "Head them off before they come up here and make a mess of things."

There was little danger of that, however, because the committee itself had asked for the local to tie its hands in case the company did not come across with a settlement by the deadline, 10 A.M. on May 21. This was sanctioned in the pro-strike vote of 1,300 to 67. Thus, they meant to avoid the sort of thing that George Lehman had pulled at the last minute when, a year earlier, he put across a one-man settlement (chapter 1). Still, at the meeting the previous night Lehman had the brass to propose a motion to empower the committee to call off the strike if the company made a satisfactory new offer. His motion was "angrily rejected" by the local, the minutes record.

Dick Reisinger caught the burly AFL men as they came up the walk toward the administration building. "I hear you've got a situation here," Dillon said sententiously.

"That's right," Reisinger bristled.

"Well, let's go on up, we can settle this thing."

Reisinger, a medium-sized man, stood athwart the path of the corpulent officials. "Nobody's settling anything except our membership!"

Dillon eyed him for a good long time. "Okay, if that's the way you feel about it," he said pityingly, "but don't expect any help from us in that case." He turned abruptly and strode back down the walk.

Reisinger in his feeling of triumph could not resist a parting shot. "Don't worry," he shouted, "we'd much rather do without!" He was thinking of adding some nasty crack about the "help" the Toledo Chevrolet strikers had recently received from Dillon, he told me, but decided it was better to restrain himself.

When I got to the factory on May 21, it was still a half hour or so before the deadline. It was past certain that the strike would occur; if it did not, I certainly would have felt cheated. At the moment, however, I was thinking of the violence that had marked a number of the city's strikes in the past weeks and I was apprehensive.

But the reality proved to be the antithesis of these paranoid thoughts. I was right at the gate when the men marched out. "Marched" is the proper word. There was something almost martial about their bearing. It was the first strike for them all and they were silent and conscious of the gravity of their action. Yet they were also proud, as though saying by their manner, "This is how a great union conducts itself!"

Inside the plant, there had not been the slightest disturbance, not even among the "half of one percent of company stooges." When, at the deadline, no word of a settlement was forthcoming from the office, the men shut off the power on the various lines, put their tools away, wiped their hands, pulled off their overalls, and paraded toward the doors. Few had bothered to bring their lunches, so certain were they that the strike would come. Some had worn their street clothes all morning.

The way the strike began was the way it continued. It was so extraordinarily peaceful that newspapers began to make a model of it. Because strikes were apparently inevitable, why not alter the habitual approach of vilifying them all by differentiating between the decent ones and the rowdy kind? The company itself took the lead, with full-page advertisements praising the conduct of its workers: "There could be no stronger proof of the morale of White workers and their kindly feeling for the company than the peaceful way in which they laid down their tools and walked in orderly fashion from the factory."

Of course, the management insisted, the union was wrong in its demands.[2] But they would not attempt any coercion on that account. The factory would remain closed. This was in sharp distinction to one of our other shops, National Carbon, where the company had promptly run to the courts to ask for a restrictive injunction and had begun to hire strikebreakers. The White management, by contrast, bought bats, balls, and gloves for the workers, who laid out a diamond on the parking lot. They, in turn, asked for brooms and shovels and rubbish carts so they could keep the streets around the factory tidy. Police were noticeable by their absence, no doubt at company request. Formal picket lines were impossible to maintain despite the complete corps of squads and captains that the committee had established. The atmosphere was one of relaxation, almost festivity.

It occurred to me that it must have pained AFL officials that a strike led by Wyndham Mortimer should be so exemplary. But the strike also tended to clash with some of my own preconceptions. I had long been troubled by the pro-company orientation of many of the older White workers. How would they ever learn the true meaning of the class struggle if not now, during a strike? Much as I feared it, I almost hoped for violence, just a little of it, enough to prove the hollowness of the company's mawkish pronouncements. Failing this, the union ought to say something to expose their hypocrisy. I was disgusted with the negotiating committee when they turned down my proposal to write a proper answer to the company's unrelenting propaganda.[3]

I undoubtedly regarded my class-struggle ideas as revolutionary and was more than a little surprised to learn that the Communist party did not quite agree with them. I felt rather flattered one morning when John Williamson, the CP state secretary, telephoned to ask if he could see me. He had obtained the number of our Fine Arts Building telephone from the John Reed Club, he explained. When he arrived at our studio half an hour later, he was accompanied by another individual, whose name I did not catch but whom I got to know later in Detroit as "Bill" (B. K.) Gebert.

I was pleased to learn that Williamson wanted to discuss the strike with me, but realized after he had gone that he had probably hoped to get some thoughts across to the strike committee through me. He was concerned, he said, about reports in the press that the committee had accepted the company's offer to inspect its books in order to prove the company's claimed inability to pay wage increases that the union demanded. "Of course, you couldn't merely turn down such an offer," Williamson observed. "But the workers ought to be told that the company has ways of doctoring its books. Besides, why should the men suffer for the company's bad years? Before the depression, when they made their tremendous profits, did they offer to share them with the workers?"

There was no disagreement between us on that score but what he said made me feel the worse for not being allowed to put out a strike bulletin, especially when he seemed to hint that the *United Auto Worker* might be the proper medium for such a message. "By the way," he said, "talking about papers, I want to compliment you on the one you're putting out."

I was ashamed to tell him about the local's ban on my news-dispensing during the strike, so I abruptly shifted the subject by describing how George McKinnon had been ousted from company-union negotiations. He had been designated as President Bill Green's personal representative but the company had countered by bringing in William Frew Long, head of the Associated Industries, the local strike-breaking outfit. The union men threatened to abandon the talks but the hassle was settled by leaving both men out.

"Dick Reisinger told me he could hardly keep from bursting out laughing when McKinnon said he'd be glad to leave if his presence stood in the way of negotiations," I chuckled. But Williamson surprised me by his reaction. "It's not right. It sets a bad precedent. Maybe some day you'll want to get an honest representative of the union in."

Gebert had remained silent, smoking one cigarette after another, which he carefully inserted into a long holder after rooting out the stub. But at times he would shrug his broad shoulders or shake his head in undisguised displeasure. "Such a strike I've never seen," he finally observed, puckering his eyes. "The pickets clean the streets. The company gives them bats and balls. I'm surprised they don't send the foremen on the picket line!"

His condescending tone suddenly infuriated me. "So what if the company tries to pull the wool over the men's eyes by tactics like that? It won't help them in the least."

"Still I'm suspicious about a strike which the capitalist press praises so much."

"That's because of the local situation," Williamson interposed. "The papers want to stir up sentiment against the workers in the Industrial Rayon strike and other struggles where there has been violence, as though they were to blame for it."

The publicity surrounding the settlement of the White Motor strike was even more offensive to me in its class-collaborationist emphasis. I should have been pleased by the spotlight of publicity given to Mortimer by the *Cleveland News* account were it not for its objectionable setting.[4] Six-inch pictures of Mortimer and Robert F. Black were mounted tandem-fashion on the front page accompanying a feature article headlined "Cleveland's White Motor Plan for Settling Labor Wars Gaining National Attention." Then, after the vicious anti-union paper had released its venom on the horrors of strikes, it made a beatific exception of this one, "settled on a basis of human understanding. While the pickets were sweeping off the sidewalks in front of the plant, executives and union leaders conferred quietly in downtown anterooms. They didn't glare across tables at each other. There was logic, reason and courtesy in those little speeches. Men were being men."

The dictated inspiration for this vision was the full-page advertisement that the company ran in the *News* and the city's other daily papers: "MEN in a Common Cause Settle their Differences like MEN." "There are no wounds to heal," it elated. "No unpleasantness to be forgotten. White and its workers have simply been through a period of mutual striving toward a common goal."[5] And, because so much virtue deserved its reward, the company's statement ended by announcing that, despite the strike, it had "booked the largest single week's business on new trucks and busses since 1929."

As for the agreement, aside from its undeniable gains, one thing stuck in my craw: the demand for the general wage increase was denied. Actually, it was dropped by the committee after the union's auditors examined the company's books. But full and unequivocal seniority rights were granted despite the company's initial toughness on the issue, as was recognition of the union, time and a half over eight hours, the promised elimination of Saturday work, piece rates guaranteed at 20 percent above the hourly wages, and other concessions. All of this was embodied in a straightforward written contract, which must have satisfied the workers because two thousand of them voted almost unanimously to accept it. Despite Francis Dillon's rebuffed services, the national UAW office vaunted the contract as one of the finest yet gained by auto workers.

The Toledo Chevrolet Strike:
Preview of the Flint Sitdown

The Toledo Chevrolet strike was about a week old when I got the chance to see it close up. We had all been inspired by this great event even though its importance was not fully grasped at the time. Moreover, we had our own strikes in Cleveland, all of very minor weight compared to Toledo's but in the disjointed condition of the union we had given them disproportionate attention.

Elmer Davis asked me if I would care to drive to Toledo with him, and I leaped at the chance. John Soltis, his mentor, was with us, as well as two others whose identity I have forgotten. We were fortunate to arrive in time for a meeting of strike leaders and picket captains, about 150 in all. George Addes, the financial secretary of the big amalgamated local to which the Chevrolet unit belonged, was up front answering questions. The strikers were tough, seemingly mistrustful and I wondered what it was all about.

Addes, a dark, handsome man who seemed much too well dressed, looked embarrassed, even apologetic. It would have been impossible to foresee the stellar role he would play in the greater UAW though he was already quite important in Toledo, judging from the papers. One fellow asked Addes bluntly, "When are we going to have another issue of *Strike Truth?*" The query brought a hand. The reply was lame. "You've got to trust your local executive committee, fellows," Addes said. "You gave us the power to put it out at our discretion."

The reply was booed but Addes was saved by the announcement of our arrival, which was cheered. We were beckoned to the front and Soltis was called on to speak. He was peculiarly unsure of himself. I realized that he had suddenly become aware of the fact that he could not tell these tough men about the blessings of unionism, the usual patter he gave his listeners. He searched the ceiling with his eyes but found no inspiration there. Elmer Davis was no better though the strikers displayed exaggerated appreciation for both.

I was shocked when they called on me next and I tried to get out of it but was pushed to the front. I pulled off my cap, which I had worn so as to look like a worker, balling it in my hand against my nervousness. "I'm no speaker," I excused myself. "I'm just a reporter."

"Go on and speak!" someone yelled and I realized that I had no choice.

"The president of my local, the White Motor local, asked me to tell you that we're sending you a check for fifty dollars," I began uncertainly. But the news was better than any rhetoric and it brought a cheer. Encouraged, I decided to hold onto that topic, recalling an article in the *Cleveland Press* that vaunted the vote of the Chevrolet company union to go back to work. "The original idea," I resumed, "was to send you two hundred bucks but then the newspapers said that you were going back to work, so we cut it down."

There were fierce yells: "That's a lie!" "It ain't true!"

"We knew the pressure you men have been under to force you to end the strike and we were afraid that you had given in. But since coming here, we know better. So I guess we'll have to send you the rest of those two hundred bucks to help you keep fighting for a real settlement."

After the meeting, the men gathered around us, and I took notes. George Addes was brought over to me and I asked him a couple of questions to get some direct quotes. He was forthcoming until I asked: "And will all decisions be brought back to the rank and file?" Then he grew cool and distracted and left soon after. Later I learned that my question was hardly applicable to this democratic union.

But the strikers were exuberant, several of them taking hold of me and telling me what to say in my paper. They gave me a copy of *Strike Truth* and a lot of clippings.[1] Then they took us around to give us a view of their set-up. The strike was remarkably well organized. Picket posts were supplied with tents and stoves, indicating that defense operated through the twenty-four hours. And more than that, they had learned from the fiercely violent Auto-Lite strike of the previous year that anything might happen in Toledo and were apparently showing that they were ready when and if it came.

All the entrances to the plant, including the doors to the shipping areas, were bolted and heavily chained from the outside. This was for protection against the steps taken by the company to send blueprints and equipment to other plants that could undertake production of the halted Chevrolet transmissions. It was Sunday and there were many visitors whom the strikers were intent on informing about their struggle. A number of bulletin boards filled with reading matter and photographs were attached to street posts. One great poster that attracted much attention contained a gallery of cutouts of heads of five of the "most despised" foremen attached to the huge bodies of rats.

Elmer Davis was eager to get away and avoid the late Sunday afternoon traffic back to Cleveland. But when he got into the car, a number of strikers kept tagging along with us, slowing us down. One asked me, "Don't you think it's good parliamentary procedure to put out another issue of *Strike Truth?*" I did not know exactly what he meant but I said, "Of course it is, it's a great idea!" He was delighted. On the way back, I tried to puzzle out his peculiar use of words and concluded that one of the strikers might have made a motion at a meeting that another issue of the paper should be gotten out and the officer in the chair perhaps had said, "Brother, your motion is out of order, it's contrary to parliamentary procedure."

The Toledo Chevrolet strike of May 1935 has never received the attention it merits. Perhaps it came too soon before the stupendous Flint sitdown of 1937 and was thus obliterated by it. The enormous influence it had on the Flint strike, in which several of its leaders and many members became active, is generally ignored.

The Toledo Chevrolet strike was led by an extraordinary group of radicals, who were in revolt throughout its duration against the ultra-conservative AFL officials, particularly Francis Dillon. Its three outstanding leaders were James Roland, Robert C. Travis, and Joseph Ditzel. Roland was unquestionably a disciple of A. J. Muste, co-founder of the American Workers party, who was in Toledo through that entire period. Ditzel was an active Socialist party member, whereas Travis was unaffiliated despite later attempts to link him at the time to the Communist party by what one might call "association by anticipation."[2] I met Travis during the Chevy strike (as I did Roland, Ditzel, Kenny Cole, and other Chevrolet leaders) and saw him two or three times, once in my home, in the period directly following it. He never gave the slightest intimation that he was a communist nor that he was a Musteite, either, however highly he praised Roland for his trade union know-how and guts.

Organization efforts at Chevy had heated up when Roland was fired for union activities. The union was not strong enough to reply, so his case was put in the hands of the Auto Labor Board. But Roland got tired of its stalling and decided to take direct action on his own by establishing a one-man picket line. He painted a big sign and nailed it to a two-by-four, mimeographed a batch of leaflets, and began walking before the main gate one bright morning. The incoming men who knew him greeted him enthusiastically and soon there was a crowd and he began delivering a pep talk to them. He planned to return at the noon hour but after arriving home received a wire from the ALB setting the date for a hearing. He was ordered rehired almost immediately.

The Chevy unit did a land-office business after Jim Roland's scoop. There were several hundred members in the union when the ALB set up representational elections for April 9, 1935. Fred Schwake, secretary of the amalgamated local to which Chevy belonged, told the men about the AFL's idea of boycotting the ballot but they replied that they thought it was bunk. "It doesn't make sense to tell workers to do *nothing,*" Bob Travis said, "you have to tell them to do *something,* whatever it is." Someone proposed the idea of running the same candidate in every district, an idea that was accepted enthusiastically. Schwake agreed to be that candidate; he got the top vote in every one of the eight districts, an overall total of 62 percent.

The ALB runoffs were set for two weeks later, April 24, but Roland and his friends decided not to wait for them, their idea being always to keep one step ahead of the company. They set up a contract committee of no fewer than forty members representing every section of the factory. These men hammered out a full body of demands, five of which were considered major: recognition, a signed contract, full seniority purged of nullifying provisions like the merit clause, a 10 percent wage increase and 70 cent minimum, and the thirty-six-hour week.

By April 16, the contract was sent to the management, who, despite the AFL union's splendid showing in the ALB election, disregarded its request for an early meeting. The shop committee realized that the company needed some persuasion and asked the men in the shop to grant them the power to call a strike if the committee felt negotiations were not progressing. On April 22, the company brought out a counterproposal that made a slight impression on the union bargaining committee. Offered were merely a 5 percent raise and a few other concessions on minor points. All five of the union's key demands were disregarded.

The committee asked for a few hours to consider the counterproposal though actually their minds were already made up about it. Negotiations were supposed to be resumed the following day, but the committee, meeting late that night, decided to take the company by surprise. Because they had the power to do so, they voted unanimously to strike the plant in the morning. Those attending the meeting took a pledge of secrecy, yet the nine-man committee was stunned to learn on coming to work that morning that the company must have been informed about their decision and had prepared an answer to it in the form of a counterproposal which was distributed to incoming workers.[3]

The committee was deeply disturbed by the revelation that one of their members was a company spy. All through the strike this troubled them and Bob Travis had not forgotten about it almost two years later when, with a small, selected group, he planned the famous seizure of the Chevrolet 4 plant at Flint. The presence of spies among the stewards was taken for granted and even entered into the final strategy.

• • •

Nevertheless, the strike started at the designated time, and a majority of the men vacated the plant voluntarily. The company sent those who remained home soon after since it could not operate with the split force. It also canceled the second shift, declaring that it would keep the factory closed for the duration.

The peaceful nature of the strike was the result primarily of the strength and discipline of its organization, which was immediately evident to visitors. The discipline was established on the first day, being based on the strict principle of universal participation. Everybody was expected to picket (all strikers being registered on six-hour tricks) and to engage in every struggle.

The day that the strike began, the committee was tipped off that the company had loaded several freight cars with completed transmissions, for which the Toledo plant was the sole supplier for Chevrolet and Pontiac assemblies.[4] Several thousand of these units were needed every day and, lacking them, assembly plants would begin to close all over the country within a week. The strikers halted that first shipment as a token of their control. The railroad men put up the "blue flag" and Chevrolet pickets played horseshoes between the tracks for the duration.

But that was only half the strikers' problem since General Motors promptly began to shift transmission production to other plants. To prevent this, at least in part, it was necessary to avoid the transferring of pertinent equipment, as well as blueprints and specifications, from Toledo. The strikers established a narrow watch on exits and chained and bolted doors. When the band of company-loyal men who had remained in the plant were allowed to leave a few days later, it was almost as prisoners, hands over heads and clothes closely ferreted.

Nevertheless, General Motors was soon able to start transmission production at two places: at the Buick transmission department in Flint, where minor changes in the pattern permitted the prompt manufacture of Pontiac units; and at Muncie, Indiana, where an abandoned factory that had been closed for three years was rapidly refurbished at the cost of $800,000, according to the company, and put to work on May 7 with four hundred employees turning out Chevrolet transmissions. By May 12, reported the *Detroit News,* this production allowed the reopening of the St. Louis assembly plant.

In both cases, a sharp conflict about how this strike-breaking work should be handled developed quickly between Francis Dillon and the Toledo strikers, and, one might add, with almost everybody else in the AFL. Dillon even disagreed with the mild-mannered T. N. Taylor, who had gone to Muncie to "investigate the situation" and who declared in the *Cleveland Plain Dealer* on May 6 that if General Motors produced transmissions at Muncie, "we will try to close down the plants (wherever they are used)."

The Toledo strikers, according to the *Union Leader* on May 3, suggested the more direct action of hitting at the source by sending masses of pickets to Muncie. But Dillon quickly put a clamp on such a notion, reported the *Detroit News* of May 9.

To help quicken the pace of support of other GM locals, the Toledo men undertook a number of visits to other automobile centers. In the earliest of these, on April 26, just a few days after their own walkout began, twenty-five strikers went up to Detroit to picket the big Chevrolet plant on Holbrook Avenue. But the demonstration was smothered by the seasoned Detroit police, who seized their banners and leaflets and escorted them to the city limits. The trip to Norwood, Ohio, was, on the contrary, a huge success. Jim Roland swung the strike vote there with his speech, bringing the big crowd to their feet with his cry, "One settlement for all!"

The Toledo strikers sent missions to other centers but their chief point of concentration was the Buick plant, which not only had the magic appeal of being in the heart of the General Motors empire in Flint but which also constituted the greatest danger to their own strike. Jim Roland decided to take a big delegation to help stir things up there.

He delivered a spirited appeal to a meeting of three hundred Buick workers to join the Toledo strike. These activities were to become one of the major objectives of the Chevy local's strategy and were meant to force General Motors, which continued to refuse to negotiate with the strikers until they went back to work, to come to the conference table. It was a method that the Flint sitdown, through Bob Travis's impulsion, would use to telling effect.

When Dillon heard that things were getting hot at Buick and that the strike there might prove impossible to avoid, he came rushing up to Flint and, with the aid of the completely controlled executive board, was able to get the agitated local membership to continue delaying their strike pending the outcome of the Toledo negotiations. He pledged solemnly that if the Toledo conferences resulted in a breakdown, he would hasten back and himself assemble a strike meeting. It was hardly a serious promise because he knew in his own heart that he was prepared to accept and force the Toledo strikers to endorse almost any concessions that General Motors demanded.

• • •

For eighteen days, GM President William Knudsen kept stalling the opening of negotiations with the Chevrolet strikers while the corporation was getting its anti-strike movement underway. At the core of General Motors' plan was an expedient that was to be widely used during the 1937 sitdown at Flint, Anderson, and elsewhere. It was the notorious Flint Alliance ploy in embryo, its purpose being to contest the Toledo strikers' claim of speaking for a majority of Chevrolet workers, especially to contradict the representativity of their negative vote in turning down the General Motors counterproposal.

The back-to-work movement was started on April 29 by ten Chevrolet employees who dubbed their organization the "Independent Workers Association" and began distributing petitions approving the company's terms. Apparently, the response was not encouraging because the petitioners began taking signatures from members of the supervision and a couple of them even got the idea of invading the rich pastures of the Chevrolet picketers. They were surprised (and newspapers were indignant) when they were chased and given some rough handling.

With great fanfare the IWA group called a mass meeting of their own on May 4. A standing vote of the claimed 1,600 people present at the meeting was taken, and 1,400 were declared to have endorsed the back-to-work proposal. Thus General Motors had in hand its own offensive weapon. The "majority" of Chevrolet workers had spoken. The strikers represented but a tiny minority. William Knudsen, who had heretofore refused to meet with the strike committee until the men had gone back to work, now demanded that they must also agree to a plantwide vote on the company's counterproposal.

The strike committee was sharply opposed to the ballot even though they were confident that they could win it if they consented to participate in it. There were, however, one or two members of the committee inclined to vacillate. Hence, to keep their ranks solid the committee consented to the vote. The poll was held on May 8 and was limited to production workers. The result was an overwhelming victory for the union: 1,251 to 605, with 369 abstentions.

Negotiations began on May 11 at 9 A.M. and lasted eighteen hours until 3 the following morning. It was time enough to attain a more satisfactory consensus than the one that was reached. The basic weakness in the union team (comprised of eleven members) lay in Dillon's eagerness to compromise, to surrender demands that the committee considered fundamental. All he was interested in, they felt, was to get a settlement, whatever its content, that he could rationalize later. Repeatedly, he took debatable positions without consulting them. On one occasion Jim Roland called for a recess and the matter was fought out bitterly until Dillon consented to allow the rank and file to have the final decision on any agreement that would be reached.

The committee fully expected the strikers to turn down and send back to the negotiating table the final terms that Dillon found acceptable, some of which they considered beneath contempt. The terms contained only one additional concession of any consequence to the original GM offer: the pay raise was upped from 5 to 8 percent and the minimum wage from 50 to 54 cents. The company would also allow the committee to discuss the speed of any job the workers considered excessive but without granting the union any sanction in adjusting such grievances. The rest was a balance sheet of negatives. All the major demands of the union were rejected.

The strikers' meeting was scheduled for the evening of May 13, and on the day before Dillon issued two separate statements to the press. One expressed his "unqualified acceptance" of the agreement; the other was a virulent attack on the leaders of the strike, whom, according to the *Detroit News,* he qualified as "those who presume . . . to speak in the interest of the workers the language of a Soviet dictatorship."[5]

The enraged strike committee thereupon considered themselves free of any obligation toward Dillon and spread the word among the strikers to vote the "agreement" down. Jim Roland chaired the meeting that evening and representatives of the locals from Norwood, Flint, and Cleveland (Louis Spisak) were seated on the platform.

When Dillon appeared, a resounding roar of boos greeted him as he walked deliberately to the stage and assumed his place there. He rose soon after and began to read the agreement. When he had finished, Roland, probably by previous agreement, recognized a striker who offered a motion that the document be reread and discussed section by section and that only strikers should be allowed to speak. Dillon took the floor again, nevertheless, declaring that the agreement had to be voted on as a whole, either accepted or rejected. The thunderous outcry in answer continued without let-up. It was apparent that the strikers were determined not to let him speak. After ten minutes, he picked up his coat and stalked out of the hall, shouting, "You're out! You're out!"

The meeting continued as best it could in the throb of excitement that possessed all those present. The strike committee led off in the discussion of the "contract," all members calling for its rejection except for Ben Bonner, who was generally considered the one conservative on the team. While this was going on, leaders of the big Toledo local, alarmed by Dillon's threat of lifting their charter, were making hectic efforts to get him back to the hall.

In the end, Roland and the rest of the committee let themselves be convinced about calling Dillon back. What was the difference, they told each other, they'd let him speak and then they'd vote him down. George Addes rushed to Dillon's hotel, where the irate official had gone. He needed very little coaxing because he realized immediately that he had won the match, and smiling triumphantly he posed with Addes for the newspaper photographers.

When Dillon reentered the hall he was loudly booed again but this time he was allowed to speak and, despite many interruptions, never lost his temper, assuming the attitude of a wise parent toward disorderly youngsters.

This at least was the way he presented himself in the eight-page report he prepared a few days later for distribution to all federal auto locals in the country.[6]

"What about wages?" someone was quoted as asking.

"I am not discussing wages . . . this must be adjudicated and arrived at through joint conference."

Voice from the audience: "What about a signature?"

"A signature, Brother, is a different matter. The company agrees to deal with a committee of your union as the representatives of your union." Boos from audience. "Just a moment, please. It isn't my fault that all your shop don't belong to your union. That's your job. My advice is to accept this and go back into the shop."

Audience: "No."

"Has it come to the point that when a man who has the responsibility of interpreting things that have to do . . . with the welfare of women, with the welfare of kiddies. . . ."

Audience: "You are holding a club over our head."

". . . because they won't sign it, they will never sign it. . . . You can hiss all you please, General Motors will not sign your contract."

And Dillon terminated with words that suddenly transformed the earnest, reasoning tenor of his plea to a cold and naked threat: "If you refuse to accept this offer within forty-eight hours you will regret it and I mean that and I am prepared to prove it." And he left the hall, this time for good.

As the ballots were being distributed and all through the voting, several officers of the parent local kept addressing the strikers, urging them to vote yes on the agreement. Even Louis Spisak, though only a visitor, took the floor to call for acceptance, probably at the instance of his friend T. N. Taylor. The most damaging influence on the result, as everyone later agreed, was that of Fred Schwake, whom the Chevrolet workers had chosen eight times to be their spokesman. Schwake kept reminding them of the loyal support they had received from the amalgamated local. Now, if it lost its charter, its ten thousand members would suffer the consequences though they were not involved in the strike.

Schwake probably caused many of the strikers to abstain from voting, as the low total of ballots cast, 1,107, indicates, whereas newspapers reported that 1,500 strikers were present. The hundreds of non-voters were apparently too disturbed by the broadside of these other appeals to vote for the continuance of the strike yet could not in conscience approve of General Motors' terms. The vote was 732 to 385 for acceptance, with probably four hundred abstainers.

Jim Roland and the other strike leaders were shocked beyond belief. "Are you yellow mice or are you men?" he yelled, glaring at those who in their shame were hurrying to leave the hall. He completely lost his self-control and walked around thereafter as though in a daze.[7] Several hundred dead-enders remained for hours, standing around looking at each other, cursing, some weeping. All agreed that they would reestablish the picket line the following morning and prevent anybody from going back to work. But Travis, Ditzel, and the others, even Roland, changed their minds during the night, agreeing to go back into the plant with the rest and continue the fight from there.

Francis Dillon made the most extravagant claims for the accomplishments of the Toledo strike, basing them mainly on the magic of his relationship with the General Motors top brass. He boasted about it to Bill Green, stating that he had "never . . . before been treated with greater courtesy nor observed a more favorable reaction . . . than I have observed upon the high executives of this great corporation." And he ended by pronouncing a fantastic prediction: "I am confident," he exulted, "that the United Automobile Workers are upon the way to the achievement of great things."[8] Closer to home, the *Union Leader,* the Toledo Federation's newspaper, printed a bitterly contradictory view of Dillon in its May 12 post-strike banner issue; the lead editorial was headed "Mussolini-Hitler-Dillon."

In a news item in the July 1935 issue of our *United Auto Worker* Jim Roland summarized the strike at my request. He ended philosophically: "If we would have had an International at the time of the recent Chevrolet strike in Toledo, we would have secured a signed agreement covering all the General Motors plants, that is of course if we had democracy in our International."

The AFL Imposes an Unacceptable International on the UAW

7

Jim Roland's allusion to the International Union in the *United Auto Worker* was not fortuitous. The subject had been broached recently by the AFL leadership itself in the form of a referendum addressed to the auto locals. We were taken by surprise and inclined to think that the survey would be used to elude the granting of the International by some ruse or other.

The early news we received about the canvass was discouraging. One of the biggest locals in the country, the great amalgamated Toledo unit, had voted it down, according to Thomas J. Ramsey, Toledo's National Council member, who circulated the bad news to the entire organization, giving his own interpretation for the negative vote. I printed Ramsey's letter and a seething reply by Dick Reisinger side by side in the July 1935 *United Auto Worker.*

But the inner-page debate was rendered passé by the last-minute "News Flash" that I ran on page 1 of the same issue: "By an overwhelming vote the Toledo Federal Auto Local, representing 12,000 men, rescinded its former action and voted for the International. Welcome to our ranks, Brothers of Toledo!"

These ranks had been rapidly swelling in recent days because the same issue listed among the positive "voices that we have not heard before" those of Norwood, St. Louis, Pontiac, South Bend, Flint, and Detroit. In the end, the vote was overwhelming, and the convention was set for August 26, 1935, in Detroit. The Cleveland group remained wary nevertheless, remembering that several key questions had to be settled. I summed them up in one sentence of the lead editorial in the July 1935 *United Auto Worker:* "We know what kind of an International we will fight for: one absolutely controlled by the rank and file, with all officers elected on the convention floor and all policies democratically determined."

An accompanying article in the same paper presented a more immediate reason for our wariness. It told of the Detroit UAW office's expulsion of George Darner and Joseph Woods (as well as the entire St. Louis local) for the critical remarks they had passed on Director Francis Dillon's conduct of the Toledo strike. The subhead read: "Progressive Local Known as Leader of Fight for the International," a warning that the same peril might be looming for other militant groups and leaders.

And there were further indications that Dillon was preparing for the Detroit Convention by making a frontal attack on various individuals and groups that would be expected to give him trouble at its sessions. Several of the Cleveland locals were likely targets: White Motors, Fisher Body, and Bender Body. During the Toledo Chevrolet strike, Dillon had come to Cleveland and threatened the Fisher local with loss of its charter if it did not make some of its allegedly anti-AFL officers behave.

Dillon felt good about his accomplishments on that occasion and wrote a self-congratulatory report about them to William Green. Green had earlier enjoined Dillon to talk "direct and plain" to the recalcitrant unions of Cleveland and singled out Wyndham Mortimer for special attention. Mortimer, said Green, should be booted out of office if it could be shown that he was a communist. Dillon evidently felt that there would be no difficulty on that score and told Green that he intended returning soon to Cleveland to carry out the tough counsel.[1]

The disciplining of Mortimer did not take place, however, and as we look back on the circumstances we can see the probable reasons for this. Soon after, the White Motor strike, one of the most successful strikes in the automobile industry of the period, occurred. The Cleveland papers, it will be recalled, put it up as a model of labor-company relations, devoting commendatory editorials to it and running streamer headlines on their front pages. This created altogether too brilliant a setting for Dillon, with his profound deference for employers, to blemish.

If Mortimer was shielded, other militants were not as fortunate. The suspension of Charles Killinger from the Flint Buick local was almost exactly like the ouster of Darner and Woods. The action took place after the forced settlement of the Toledo strike on June 19, when the Norwood (Cincinnati) local invited Killinger to speak on "Industrial versus Craft Unionism," a topic that he, a former miner, relished. But he was very careful to keep clear of personal references, he later told me, because word had been going around about Dillon's campaign against progressives. The big audience (about 750, Killinger said) enjoyed his talk immensely. Many asked questions at the end during the discussion period. Inevitably, the question of the Detroit Convention came up and Killinger was asked what he thought about Dillon's chances of getting elected. He was on the spot and tried to turn the question around by asking: "Would you support Dillon for president?" There was a roar for an answer: "No!" That was all that he ever said about

Dillon, Killinger insisted, but when he got home, there was a letter from Dillon to the Buick local, accusing Killinger of having made slanderous attacks on him, Green, and the AFL.

After much bickering by the Buick executive board, a trial committee set a date for a hearing on the matter, asking Dillon to be there. He did not appear, however, and the board decided that there was no case. Dillon, nonetheless, ordered that Killinger was not to be admitted to local meetings, which rendered him ineligible for election as a delegate to the convention.[2]

The expulsion of Anthony Weileder and Stephen Breidick, president and secretary of the important Seaman Body local of Milwaukee, was the most significant pre-convention coup for the Dillon forces. Not only did it carry the local with it but it also produced the individual who became Dillon's most puissant supporter in Detroit. Ed Hall had not attracted too much attention before that time. Like the rest of the National Council members, he had been kept in check by Dillon's fear of the rise of a challenger from their ranks. But the preparations for the convention allowed Hall to develop the kind of talents that Dillon sorely needed in the outlying regions.

Hall ran up and down Wisconsin, attending all local meetings and spreading wild tales about the "reds" of Toledo and Cleveland and the danger of their taking over the new International Union. He scared the locals into isolating their own "communists," thus succeeding in bringing a herd of thoroughly cowed delegates to Detroit, among whom the few independent spirits were tied in a knot by an incredible "rule" that Ed Hall contrived, requiring a statewide unit vote on all issues.

Solid hold on the Wisconsin majority was made possible by the Weileder-Breidick expulsion, which Ed Hall's machine (Seaman Body was his own local) engineered by what the American Civil Liberties Union characterized as gangland terror.[3] The authenticity of this description was verified by Hall himself, who later narrated the details to me, as did two other local officers, Bill Cody and Ralph Dale, with whom I became friendly during the Flint sitdown in 1937. Cody's role in carrying out the plot against twenty-two leading members of the local is worthy of note since it consisted of his reading a letter from President William Green to the meeting which sanctioned the Weileder-Breidick expulsion in advance by reminding the members that all communists were agents of the Third International. Also foredooming the decision was a gag rule that was adopted "unanimously" and provided that any member who defended the accused men would be expelled automatically.

• • •

That AFL officials were able to add Jim Roland to the list of outlaws to the convention required the collaboration of the executive committee of the big Toledo local, which essentially ran the organization. The controlling majority of the committee had their own factional reasons for wanting to get rid of Roland and simply arrogated the power to do so. They announced simultaneously their right to choose the local's delegates to the convention, from which Roland was thus likewise banned.

These authoritarian acts almost had a fatal effect on the development of friendly relations between the Toledo local and ourselves. By siding with Roland in his differences with his local, we lost sight of the fact that the main fight was against Dillon and failed to realize that George Addes, Ellsworth Kramer, and other Toledo officers, whatever their attitude toward Jim Roland, could be as inimical to Dillon's policies as we were ourselves.

Our solidarity with Roland was buttressed by the fourth rank-and-file conference, which we held at Toledo a day before the convention opened. It was more a pre-convention caucus than a continuation of the meetings that had been started in Cleveland the previous September. Because the purpose of these meetings was to promote the International Union, there might have seemed little point to this one, now that the convention was just around the corner. But everybody was agreed that it was important to get together and discuss the strategy that progressives should follow at the sessions.[4] In fact, we in Cleveland had printed a four-page pamphlet for distribution among the delegates.

The Toledo conference proved to be a heartening encounter, not the least reason being the two new and important unions, Toledo Chevrolet and Norwood, that had joined our group. A number of delegates from other locals were also present, notably a man named Tom Johnson from the Ford River Rouge plant. Hal Richards of Cleveland, who represented an Auto Rebuilders local, was also much appreciated, having just written a stunning article for the July issue of *United Auto Worker* about the first automobile international, with which he had been personally associated. Organized in the pre–World War I period, it was subsequently crushed by greedy AFL craft groups.

Of the eighteen locals represented at our conference, the stars of the show were undoubtedly the Toledo delegation, which in addition to Jim Roland included Bob Travis, Joe Ditzel, and several others. By unanimous vote Roland was chosen chair. The gesture was meant not only to honor the host group but also to render homage to its brilliant accomplishment in the recent strike. Roland was flushed with surprise and pleasure as he took the gavel to loud applause.

The better I got to know the young Chevrolet leaders, the more I admired their high quality. I had not seen such fresh talent in any other group and attributed it to the remarkable struggle they had conducted against General Motors—and Francis Dillon. The "sellout" had not spoiled that alertness and the men went back into the shop more militant than ever. The management had collapsed like a stuck balloon, granting most of their demands. Some of the men, Bob Travis, for example, received wage hikes as high as 50 percent. It was a pleasure now to work in the shop, Kenny Cole said.

Mortimer opened the Toledo conference with a roundup of the issues and read extracts from our printed pamphlet. Some of its material was way out of line from what the majority of the convention would be thinking but it is worthwhile to note that a good part of the program would become the active blueprint of the International after it won autonomy the following year. The union must prepare "for strike action if necessary next season," the brochure said, which would be capped by a "national agreement with the automobile employers." It warned about the AFL charter that was being granted, which limited the union's right to take in only production workers. It likewise demanded the election of all officers and board members from the convention floor, adding that those chosen must be ratified by a referendum of the entire membership of the union, a rule that the UAW never adopted.

There was a lively discussion on these and other subjects. I have found mention in my notes of one motion that now sounds curious since it castigated the recently adopted Wagner Labor Act. In taking this stand our conference must have disregarded the protective features of the law and reacted solely to the two years of bitter disappointments that had given auto workers a deep mistrust of all substitutes for the settlement of labor disputes in lieu of the workers' own militant action.

The Toledo conference turned out to be the most lively one that we had yet held. This was due no doubt to a considerable degree to some of the new representatives present, especially Tom Johnson, the delegate from Ford. He was obviously an experienced unionist though he tended to speak of himself with humorous abnegation, causing mirth when he explained that he had recently "cancelled [his] connection with Ford at Harry Bennett's invitation."

Before the conference broke up, Roland raised the issue of his differences with the Toledo local. The Chevrolet unit, he explained, was putting in a protest with the credentials committee on the way the Toledo delegates had been chosen. They were not elected by the membership, as was laid down in the convention call, but by the local's executive committee. "I don't know if I'll even be able to get in as a visitor," he declared ironically.

This announcement brought a sharp outburst from the gathering. Everyone agreed that the Toledo executive committee's action should be challenged when the report of the credentials committee was read to the convention. The question was, Who could best do this? Someone—I believe it was Mortimer or Reisinger—suggested that the challenge ought to come from the Norwood local, which was not yet identified with our movement and therefore could not be accused of having an axe to grind. Tom Hoskins, a bright and outspoken member of that group, volunteered immediately for the job and the conference adjourned with its first direct intervention on the convention floor all lined up.

• • •

The intervention was never carried out, however. I did not learn the circumstances of how that happened but I believe that Tom Hoskins's generous offer was later vetoed by the other Norwood delegates who were reluctant to put themselves on the spot by antagonizing the powerful Toledo local. We ourselves were to have second thoughts about what our relationship to its leaders should be as the convention's fast-moving events forced us to reexamine more carefully Jim Roland's description of the Toledo leaders as "a bunch of reactionaries."[5]

From Roland's account of how the Toledo delegates were chosen, I had concluded that the Chevrolet unit was not assigned a single place among them. I was surprised, therefore, to find Bob Travis and Ben Bonner sitting in the midst of the big Toledo delegation at the convention. A number of other shocks were reserved for us on this same account. One stemmed from the AFL setup itself, as Mortimer revealed when he told me that he had been designated a member of the resolutions committee. As a matter of fact, several other men in our caucus were named to other committees. All of which might have given us a feeling of really belonging, although it would have been naive to think that the convention was not under strict control. A solid majority of all committees, to be sure, was in the hands of Dillonites.

I caught another proof of this domination as I sat watching attentively on the first day of the convention, my box seat at the right side of the hall giving me a clear view of both the platform and the delegates' tables. One individual sitting off by himself at an end of the podium struck me as a person of importance. He did not talk to anyone but merely looked about, his eyes roving deliberately from person to person. He made no attempt to mask his curiosity. He was solely interested in the delegates and it was plain that he knew those who were important or at least worth knowing more about. I could share his interest regarding Russell Merrill of the Studebaker local, for example, or Carl Shipley of Bendix. But the man's eyes returned over and over to one man in particular and read his face with great intensity. It somehow scared me to watch him for it was none other than Wyndham Mortimer whom he studied. Soon after, I learned that the man on the podium was Meyer Lewis, a close advisor of William Green.

The platform was suddenly invaded by a cluster of people arriving in Dillon's wake. Soon after William Green arrived, amid applause. Without delay, Green presented Dillon with two gavels (why two?) and then tendered him the International Union's "charter," an act that I took to mean that the whole thing was already settled. Auto workers would have to accept anything that went along with this precious parchment. And that was exactly what President Green said in the first ten minutes of his interminable speech, which dragged on after that for at least an hour. It was as though, out of kindness, he wished to spare auto workers the strain of uncertainty by coming quickly to the nub of the morning's business:[6]

1. *Jurisdiction:* Eligible for membership in the auto union were merely those "directly engaged in the manufacture of parts (not including tools, dies, and machinery) and assembling of those parts into completed automobiles." Excluded were "any other employees engaged in such production plants" (which, I told myself, meant maintenance men, inspectors, electricians, painters, laborers, etc.) or employees in "job or contract shops" (which could cover parts plants of any kind).

2. *Election of Officers:* "That for a temporary period determined by the Executive Council, the officers to function under the charter thus issued [will] be designated by the President of the American Federation of Labor."

All the rest of Green's speech was devoted to pleas for the delegates' acceptance of the rugged jurisdictional restraints, which he, no doubt, considered the most controversial part of the grant. Because he could not accord them a compromise substitute and because he could not boast of any organizational gains (with only twenty-five thousand dues-payers and eighteen contracts, twelve of them in Ohio and not a single one in Michigan),[7] Green vaunted the more esoteric prizes that the AFL had brought them, legislative ones particularly. He dwelled at length on the Wagner Labor Act, which our progressive conference in Toledo had so flippantly rejected.

In fact, I felt that he might be referring to our defiant action when he described in detail his appearance before the Senate committee that conducted hearings on the bill. He ended with an angry, impassioned pitch, telling how he had to combat spokesmen for the Manufacturers Association and the Communist party, who, he rhetorically implied, were working hand-in-glove. "I ask you, my fellow workers, as a trade unionist who has gone through this movement for over thirty years . . . I ask you to listen to me, speaking out of the accumulated experience of years, to have nothing to do with them. . . . When they talk to you ask them why they came to Washington and stood up with the Manufacturers Association opposing the Wagner Disputes Bill. . . . Ask them why they did that and if they cannot give you an answer—and they *can't*—tell them: 'Out the door, we want nothing to do with you!'"[8]

It was an effective performance, I felt. Self-consciously, I gazed around the hall, scrutinizing the features of a number of the delegates whose opinions would carry weight in this body. Somehow—and it was an immense relief—I did not find them to be very much roused by President Green's emotion, not enough, apparently, to make them forget the unwelcome package he had just laid into their laps: the jurisdictional mess and the rejection of the free election of officers. To the second, he did not devote a single word of comment.

Why not? I asked myself in surprise. Did the AFL strategists consider this matter already in the bag? We had no idea of how strong the response had been in the big locals to the National Council's pre-convention resolution asking that Green appoint Dillon to the presidency. All we knew was that council member George Lehman had presented the resolution to the White Motor local, where it had been defeated. But that was no criterion. The Dillon office might have other proof of wide support for the measure. There was Ed Hall with his solid block of Wisconsin votes, and, as far as we knew, Dillon could have picked up many others in South Bend, Toledo, and other places.

The convention adjourned immediately after Green's speech to let delegates cogitate on all the "inspiring and instructive" thoughts that he had left them, as Dillon put it. The hall was vacated in a few minutes. I sat in my box seat, feeling at odds with myself. Suddenly, I noticed George Addes all alone in the Toledo section, just sitting and staring at the table. Then, abruptly, he did a curious thing. He threw his pencil in an angry gesture at his convention folio.

Addes had tended to snub me since I had asked him a foolish question during the Chevrolet strike, an action I often regretted thereafter. There was something I liked about him. He seemed always preoccupied with his thoughts. It was about time I tried to make it up with him, I told myself, in some way encouraged by his gesture. I entered the aisle and walked up to him. "What's the matter, Brother Addes," I asked, "do you feel as disgusted as I do?" For an answer he picked up his pencil and threw it down again: "Son-of-a-pup!"

There was that expression again, that disguised obscenity that religiously trained workers, mainly Catholics, used. Intuiting what was ailing him, I took the bull by the horns. "You're concerned about Bill Green's taking the election of Dillon for granted, aren't you?" I asked.

Addes looked up at me at last, surprised by my perspicacity, perhaps. "Don't worry," I said firmly. "This convention will *never* elect Dillon president." A slight smile dawned on his dark and handsome face as, without replying, he gathered his things and headed for the exit.

• • •

I told our group about my encounter with George Addes. Maybe we ought to be careful about writing the Toledo delegation off, I suggested.

Dick Reisinger, who had a way of getting around and talking to people, said that something seemed to be cooking between Studebaker and Toledo, a deal about sharing candidates.

A minor incident that occurred at the next morning's session was picked up by the papers and blown into a big event, which it was to us in any case because it proved that there was an antagonism between the Toledo delegation and Dillon. It came up when the convention committee's report on rules was read and an amendment was offered to add the "question of privilege" to the rules, which was promptly done. As though it was a signal to him, Fred Mayberry, a young delegate from the Toledo local, was instantly on his feet and on a point of "privilege" moved "that all general organizers who are paid by the American Federation of Labor be instructed and compelled to remain away from the hotel and the convention."[9] There was a splash of applause, and Dillon angrily ruled the motion out of order. But Mayberry's point had already been made as far as many delegates were concerned. They wanted to run their own convention and, by extension, their own International as well.

It was not the most auspicious moment to begin what turned out to be the crucial debate of the convention.[10] Nevertheless, nothing could have assured Dillon of a more favorable setting and the gears were already grinding. The resolutions committee had the floor, and its chair, Forrest Woods of the Studebaker local, was reading the proposal calling on the AFL to "appoint" Dillon to serve the "first term" as president of the UAW.

It was the very same resolution that the National Council had prepared and sent out to all locals some weeks before but the delegates listened to it excitedly as though it came as a surprise. They did not have long to think about it, however, because the moment that Woods's reading had ended, Carl Shipley, president of the big Bendix local, was on his feet with a typed sheet in his hand. Once more on the claim of "privilege," he offered a substitute motion that "a special order of business be declared for the purpose of nominating and electing officers of this International Union from the floor of the convention and that said nominees . . . [must] be members of the Automobile Workers Union."

When Shipley finished reading his short text, the tension in the hall suddenly broke out in a gust of sound compounded of excited words and expressions of pleasure, while all eyes sought out Dillon, who kept tapping his gavel lightly on the table. It was plain that he was overwhelmed with surprise, not only by the motion but also by the person who had presented it. I realized this later when reading in the newspapers that he had threatened to strike Shipley in the hotel lobby, calling him "a skunk and a quitter." It was apparent at the present moment that Dillon was at his wits' end, and, probably by prearrangement, he called on Green to be "gracious enough" to take the chair, alleging that he could not make rulings in the coming debate because he himself was "involved as an individual."

Green took over but seemed incapable of making the forthright ruling that Shipley's substitute was out of order, which it probably was and which Green did anyway after a protracted discussion, most of which was taken up by his own verbose and repetitive arguments. He made beneficent pleas to "my dear boys," urging them not to be "young men in a hurry" and kept dangling the financial help that the AFL was prepared to give, which, it turned out, was merely Dillon's salary and office expenses—the price of this unwelcome gift! Green pledged that they would not have to bear overlong with Dillon. "He will serve only temporarily, perhaps not longer than one year." And they would be allowed to elect all their other officers and their executive board, who would be "clothed with full power to direct and administer the affairs of your International Union."

A dozen delegates discussed the section of the AFL resolution on the election of officers after Shipley's substitute was ruled out of order, and when Ellsworth Kramer, president of the Toledo local, and Russell Merrill, head of the Studebaker unit, joined Mortimer in opposing it, the incredible probability suddenly struck me that the resolution might be defeated. I could not make my thoughts go any further than that. The idea was too fantastic. The AFL would never let it happen.

I had prepared my notebook for recording the roll call.[11] Delegates voted one by one, a process that dragged the count out interminably. Few seemed aware of any tendency that was showing up in the ballot. Excitement came only when the spokesman of one of the larger delegations, which usually voted in a bloc, cast his group's tally in loud, accented words that seemed to imitate the manner of big political conventions. Sometimes these announcements brought outbursts of pleasure or surprise or even unleashed conflicts in a delegation. This happened in the White Motor group when George Lehman cast his vote for Dillon despite the local's firm instructions for a bloc vote against his candidacy. Dick Reisinger reacted immediately, bending over to Lehman and saying something to him out of his twisted mouth, to which Lehman did not reply.

The biggest stir occurred when the Kenosha Nash local of Wisconsin cast its solid twenty-two votes against the resolution. This brought a display of ferocious anger from Ed Hall that he made no attempt to disguise. The convention was my first view of the man whose arrogance was so excessive that I felt he was putting on an act, despite the fact that it merely confirmed accounts that we had received of his virulent assaults on Tony Weileder and other progressives in the Seaman Body local.

The Kenosha vote was particularly gratifying to Mortimer and me because we had been in contact with this group for several months. I had received a letter from Paul Porter, the editor of *Kenosha Labor,* a recently launched and excellent newspaper, asking me to put him on the mailing list of the *United Auto Worker.* This I did immediately and Porter returned the favor. When the UAW convention was announced, he wrote to ask Mortimer to prepare an article for *Kenosha Labor* on the key issues that would be coming up. The paper was privately published, we later learned, but it was supported by the progressive Central Labor Council, which included a group of left-wing socialists who favored a united front of the left.

At Detroit, we made contact with several members of the Kenosha delegation and were delighted to learn that practically the entire group was in agreement with us on major issues. They were, however, under terrific pressure from Ed Hall and had to keep an eye on several of their "weak sisters," whom Hall was trying to buy or scare off. The vote on the resolution endorsing Green's appointment of Dillon as UAW president showed us that he had thus far failed. As the vote count neared its end, the word spread outside the hall, bringing a rush of delegates back to their seats. My own tally was by no means perfect, but the majority was so strong that I knew that any errors I had made could not overturn it. I conveyed the fact with careful signals to our group.

A heavy silence fell on the assembly as John Nafe, secretary of the credentials committee, stood on the platform, looking at the sheet in his hands. "The vote on the resolution," he announced in a trembling voice, "was 112.8 votes for and 164.2 votes against." A shout of triumph rang out from many throats and a number of the opposition delegates rose, cheering and clapping.

President Green's voice could hardly be heard as he translated Nafe's announcement into an official decision: "The report [resolution] has been defeated." The convention was adjourned until the afternoon but that session never took place. Dillon later admitted that he had been overwhelmed by the result. At any event, the AFL leadership would have needed more time to decide on their next step.

• • •

The pro-Dillon delegates were sent out to missionize among the opposition, supplied with a bag of lies and libels with which to ply fallible contacts. If they spent money for drinks, they'd be remunerated, Ed Hall told them. The AFL strategists had studied the roll-call tally and drew conclusions about the major points at which they had to hit. The vote of 164.2 to 112.8 sounded overwhelming but actually was not, they told themselves. The key was Kenosha, which had broken the Wisconsin unit rule, the only local out of ten to do so. If its twenty-two votes were brought back into the

Dillon column, the count would show marked improvement: only 142.2 to 134.8. A mere shift of five other votes would bring a victory, so the heat was poured on Kenosha.

But the Dillon command had other stratagems. Even I became one of their designated targets. Actually, I had caught the signal while I was sitting in my box on the third morning, a wary eye fixed on Meyer Lewis, who had gone into a paroxysm of calculated activity. Suddenly, I noticed that Lewis flashed a look and slightly twisted his head toward a delegate from Flint named Arthur Dubuc, a dumpy little man puffed up with his own importance. Plainly, I had been discussed and Dubuc nodded acknowledgment. But, curiously, it was another man, an AFL menial, who soon after entered my box and told me that I had to leave. He took away my badge and conveyed me to the door.

Ed Simpson and Bill Kics were just entering at that moment and howled when I told them what had happened. Mortimer and Ed Stubbe soon followed and before long eight or ten people were involved in my cause célèbre. But the session started, and I was outside the hall, eating my heart because I had counted on observing Dillon's attitude after the defeat and maybe reading in it a hint of Green's next move.

When Arthur Dubuc came up to me soon after, he gestured mysteriously to indicate that we were being watched. Finally, he found a quiet corner down a side passage where there were a couple of vacant chairs. "I like to be private," he whispered, cupping his hands behind his ears to designate snoopers. "You put out a good paper," he said. "I like it very much."

"Thank you," I replied to the transparent falsehood. It was certain that Meyer Lewis's interest in me was of a different order.

"I read what this Brother Mortimer write in it, it is very good," the little man continued, ostensibly in the same vein but the name of Mortimer put me on the track.

"You know," he resumed with dramatic emphasis, "some people said nasty things to me about him—and I believed them." Then he added with excessive anger, "but it's all lies! I know that since I serve on the resolutions committee with him. He is very fine man, very intelligent, very very intelligent."

I nodded seriously. "We in Cleveland all feel the same way."

Dubuc bent closer to me. "That's why I'm talking to you now. I been speaking to a lot of people. They think Mortimer is the best of all of them. Why don't he run for office? He'd make a fine president."

I laughed, modest in Mortimer's behalf.

"I mean it," he insisted emotionally. "I swear to God I'm sincere."

"I realize that but Mortimer is not ambitious."

"That don't make any difference. You gotta talk to him. You gotta tell his friends to talk to him. It be a shame if we let somebody else like this Homer Martin get elected. I know him for years. He don't know nothing."

I was getting bored and made an awkward attempt to change the subject. "You've got a peculiar accent," I said with an apologetic smile. "Are you French?"

Dubuc opened his eyes wide with unaffected pleasure. "You recognize that from my accent? I'm Canadian French, what you call Canuck."

"Moi, je parle français un peu," I said deprecatingly.

"Tu parle français? Tu l'as étudié à l'école?"

"Oui, mais ma femme et moi nous avons vécu en France pendant plus d'une année."

Dubuc was overjoyed. "You're the first American I met who can talk French." He rose, seized my hand, and shook it fervently. He must have considered that his task was done.

"Don't forget what I told you," he said, preparing to leave. "You talk to Brother Mortimer about that. You tell me later what he says."

Before the afternoon session began, I was told to appear before the credentials committee; a whole crowd from the Cleveland delegation was there, too. When my case came up, the chairman cut it short by explaining that my expulsion was an error. They had mistaken me for the publisher of a communist paper, who had tried to sneak into the convention. "Brother Dillon himself intervened in your behalf," the chairman explained, handing back my badge.

Actually, my eviction must have been on the AFL's ledger, but, when carried out, the action was already inopportune because the Dillon strategy had changed. The campaign for officers was underway, and trying to get Mortimer to run for president was a play to split the opposition vote. He was not the only candidate, however. The big Studebaker local was backing another, truly serious prospect, Homer Martin.

Homer Martin was a mystery. His trade union record was almost purely negative. A Kansas City preacher turned auto worker for obscure reasons, he had been fired from his job after a few weeks for talking union. Thereafter, he made all the mistakes possible: dragging his union into a secession movement; instigating an ill-timed strike that ended in a mass of discharges; and, finally, finagling a deal with the AFL to bring his broken union back into the fold, for which he was rewarded with an organizer's job. But Martin had one thing that made his supporters forget about his shortcomings: glamour.

At Detroit, Martin looked the part of a president. In those days, auto workers did not earn the kind of money they did later and even when they wore "Sunday clothes" they didn't look well dressed. Besides, it was very hot in the hall and the men went around in their short-sleeve shirts. Martin, however, was always fully garbed in a glowing white summer suit and never without a tie. It was part of the picture the fellows bought: the preacher who had embraced the cause of the workers but who remained a man of God.

In the lobby there was always a gathering about Martin, as though he were a visiting celebrity or even a Hollywood star. I noticed, however, that he never talked very much although he always showed his perfect teeth. No one seemed to ask him searching questions, as would have been natural to do with the man who was probably going to be their president. But delegates seemed content just to hear his voice, as though that could reveal something about his reputedly brilliant speaking ability. Not once during the sessions did he take the floor.

Ed Simpson and I were in the lobby once when Martin entered. Ed told me that he had heard that Martin was a socialist, which was his way of attaching the quality he esteemed most highly onto this attractive personality. "Let's go up and talk to him," Ed suggested. After shaking his hand, he impulsively broached the question of Martin's candidacy but Martin parried the thrust. "I'm not a candidate for anything, not even dog-catcher," he said, showing his brilliant teeth that almost looked "store-bought" up close.

"But a lot of people think you're going to run against Dillon," Simpson insisted.

Martin shook his head. "Oh no, I wouldn't be so presumptuous. I consider Brother Dillon a tremendously experienced union leader. I couldn't possibly compete with him."

"But somebody's got to do it," Simpson persisted. "Dillon may be experienced but his heart and mind aren't with us. He's been a disaster for the auto workers!"

"Well, you've got to consider the circumstances that he's had to face. I think he tried his best and angels couldn't do more than that."

It was plain that the conversation was getting nowhere and when Martin's eyes started darting around, Simpson decided to let him off the hook. "Well, Brother Martin," he said, putting out his hand, "it was nice talking to you."

Martin was hardly out of earshot when Simpson vented his disgust: "What a slimy character. Who ever got the notion that he was a socialist!"

• • •

The idea began to grow on the Cleveland group that the choice of candidates for the International's officers was taking place without our having any part in it. Whether we liked it or not, this dubious man was apparently slated to become our president. We had been so involved with policy and program that this essential feature of the union that we thought we were creating had simply evaded us. Now, suddenly, we asked ourselves whether it was worthwhile keeping Dillon out of office if what we got in his place was Homer Martin.

It was less disturbing to learn that the leading contestant for the other important post, that of the secretary treasurer, was George Addes. Bob Travis told us that the Toledo local was backing him and a number of its delegates were quietly politicking for him. Indeed, the local was not making a secret of it, having rented a big room on the sixteenth floor of the Fort Shelby Hotel, where free drinks were served to delegates, especially to wavering Dillonites. With Addes's candidacy boosted by his local's thirty-eight votes, the next step was obvious.

It was necessary for the Toledo delegates to talk to the Studebaker group about matching up candidates. With the backing of the two strongest locals in the union, a total of eighty-eight votes would be corralled. As a matter of fact, the Studebaker politicos had had the same idea, so the matter was handily arranged. After that, it was necessary only to keep the snowball rolling. The other big bundles of votes were considered first and thus, for the first time, the basically conservative Toledo men made an approach to the Cleveland group. Ellsworth Kramer sought out Dick Reisinger and proposed backing Mortimer for the executive board in return for our support for the two officers. "We have to fill the places of the two National Council members from Ohio," Kramer explained. "You'll probably want to put Mortimer in that ass-licker Lehman's place and we'll turn over Tom Ramsey's post to Norwood and consider it a bargain!" And so it was arranged.

The deal added approximately fifty votes, including a number of small progressive locals, to the officers' aggregate, which thus attained almost half the convention total. Building up a reserve came next. Unfortunately, the big Kenosha local with its solid twenty-two votes could not be offered the executive board post from Wisconsin because the truculent Ed Hall had that state tied up. However, it seemed likely that Kenosha would go along with the anti-Dillon slate anyway. Other possible arrangements were more aleatory, such as what would happen to Indiana's National Council member. Though Forrest Woods was a popular figure, Studebaker realized that they would have to sacrifice the post to win support for a voteless candidate like Homer Martin. They could never get Russell Merrill to swallow Carl Shipley of Bendix for the executive board.[12]

The AFL's only direct intervention in the contest was to hit at Homer Martin. It was a chore that Ed Hall assumed with relish. Several confrontations in Green's presence were arranged. Martin's role was to play innocent, telling how the Studebaker men had approached him on their own a long time back. "I made a solemn promise to them," he declared, giving his words a pious sanction.

Hall decided that it was time to rip into Martin's hypocritical mask since Green was hardly in a position to do so. "Listen, you dumb son-of-a-bitch, quit playing around with us. You're the only one who can decide if you run or don't run. If they want to nominate you, let them. All you have to do is decline the nomination." Martin looked helplessly at Green, his eyes filling with tears.

This was, of course, Ed Hall's version, which I heard from him a good deal later when I was well aware of his flair for exaggeration. But such an account sounded entirely credible because the tone Hall used with Martin, even after Martin was the International president, frequently fringed the offensive.

It was during the debate on the jurisdiction issue that the delegates first demonstrated their basic unity. Not a single speaker whom I could remember (the *Proceedings* merely list their names) of the thirty or more who took the floor was in favor of the Executive Council's offer.[13] It was no surprise to hear Mortimer repeat his already famous observation about the AFL's craft-studded jurisdiction plan fitting into the auto industry "like a square peg in a round hole," or that Carl Shipley provided a brilliant topical argument that outflanked one of the AFL's proudest boasts. "Regardless of the laws of the AFL, we now have the Wagner Act which says that organizations having a majority shall be the sole bargaining agencies in their factories," as he is quoted in the *Detroit News* of August 29.

But what utterly amazed me was to find even Ed Hall taking a defiant stand on the issue: "I don't care what policy is laid down by the AFL Executive Council. *Our* members are going to remain in *our* local!" The statement brought cheers from the assembled delegates and I noticed a number of the opposition applauding lustily. While accepting the AFL's jurisdictional limitations, escorted by protests to President Green and to the fifty-fifth AFL convention, and instructing the UAW officers to "take [further] action as may seem advisable," the delegates lofted a red flag of defiance over the issue by unanimously adopting a motion inviting John L. Lewis to come and address their convention.[14]

• • •

As the convention continued, it became encouragingly evident that the progressive group was breaking out of its ghetto. The change of attitude toward Tom Johnson, whom Dillon had been able to isolate at first by circulating the slanderous rumor that he was a Ford serviceman sent in to disrupt the convention, was especially evident. The lie faded by its own improbability as well as because of Johnson's attractive personality, his straightforward manner, and the resolute way he faced down Dillon's insinuations.

Dillon simply refused to recognize Johnson. Even when there were no other claimants to the floor, he would run his eyes all over the hall while letting Johnson stand. Johnson would patiently hold his ground, periodically calling out, "Brother Chairman!" in a calm sing-song until Dillon gave way. Then he would growl: "What do *you* want?" and Johnson would raise his point of information or other business.

Our progressive caucus had established the practice of holding a short meeting every day at the end of the afternoon session. We discussed the highlights of the day and what was likely to follow on the next. Tom Johnson played an important role at these meetings because he was very well posted about the substance of the convention, having read all the resolutions and constitutional proposals. He had more time to do this than the others because he did not seem interested in the politicking that was going on.

It was at the afternoon session following the debate on jurisdiction that he raised a question that was like a splash of cold water on our self-congratulatory mood. "We've still got the biggest battle to fight," Johnson reminded us, "the election of officers." The convention was past the halfway mark, he said, and it was probable that Bill Green would bring in his answer the next day.

"What's he going to say to the delegates after stalling two whole days? Is he going to say, 'Well, boys, you voted down the National Council's resolution which the AFL endorsed, so I guess we have no other choice than to allow you to go ahead and elect your officers'?" Johnson paused as a heavy silence took over, a worried thoughtfulness that knitted brows.

"No," Johnson answered his own question, "we all know that Bill Green is not going to say that. Is he going to go back to the original resolution that we voted down and appoint Dillon and let us vote for all the others? I may surprise you but I don't see him doing that either and for the very reason that we've shown ourselves to be so strong. It's more likely that he'll say that in voting down the AFL's generous offer we've proven our lack of maturity and that the Executive Council has no other recourse than to retain the status quo for another year or so."

There was a general outburst of anger and disbelief. "He wouldn't dare do that!" Ed Simpson declared with conviction. "We'd just tell Green to go peddle his papers somewheres else!" Elmer Davis shouted.

"You mean you'd just walk out? Pull another Art Greer fiasco?" Johnson asked. "I don't think the UAW could outlive another split like that. Look at what's happening here in Detroit with this new Coughlin union. But that's aside the point. Just consider the facts. We've won a tremendous victory here. We've established a unity in our ranks that we didn't think was possible. It would be tragic to throw it all away now by acting like a bunch of kids."

But the men were not in the mood for reasonable arguments, except for Mortimer, who, nevertheless, expressed only a tentative agreement with Tom Johnson's disheartening prediction. "I'm not sure that things are going to turn out the way Tom says," he declared. "But after my years of experience with the AFL, I wouldn't be too surprised. It would just mean that Bill Green had decided that if he can't subjugate the auto workers he'd prefer to destroy the union. And I agree that we mustn't allow him to do that if we can help it."

Tom Johnson picked this wisp of encouragement up eagerly. "Listen, Brother Mortimer, you men on the resolutions committee were faced by the same alternatives on another issue: Do we get full industrial jurisdiction now or do we quit? What did you decide? You decided that we should accept the charter, even with those lousy provisions, *under protest,* and to carry that protest to the highest court of the AFL. Well, I think that we must do the very same thing on the question of officers."

The two questions were not "the very same," of course, but nobody had anything else to offer, so the men were in a glum mood when the meeting broke up. Johnson was slow in getting started, as he gathered his things. His face looked gray and drawn and I decided to stay with him, feeling that he might appreciate having company just then.

As we walked down the hall to the elevators, he suddenly said, "Jesus Christ, what I need is a double shot of liquor and I need it bad!" Then I remembered what Mortimer had told me about Johnson's background of alcoholism. He seemed to guess my thought. "You don't drink, do you? Well, I've been a regular booze hound in the past. But I haven't touched the stuff for six months and this isn't exactly the time for me to break that record." And he gave me a spurious smile.

• • •

From President Green's first words the following afternoon, it was apparent that Tom Johnson had guessed right about his decision. Somberly predicting that the UAW was in danger of being torn to pieces if abandoned to itself, he told of having consulted a number of the locals' representatives "for whose judgment I have profound respect" and concluded that if elections were allowed, it would be "sure and certain that you would go out from here divided, divided in your allegiance, divided in your opinions, divided in policies. So, my friends," he concluded, "in order to avoid [these dangers] I have decided to follow literally the instructions of the Executive Council, that for a temporary period . . . the officers . . . shall be designated by the President of the American Federation of Labor." And he began reading their names. "I announce first the name of Brother Francis J. Dillon as your temporary president." A deep groan issued from the assembly as Green hurried on: "I announce the name of Brother Homer Martin, Kansas City, as his assistant and vice-president. I announce the name of Brother Ed Hall of Milwaukee, Wisconsin, as secretary-treasurer."[15]

A pensive silence took hold of the delegates as they heard these other names, and, no doubt, there was bated curiosity about who Green would come up with for the executive board. But indignation fairly exploded when the delegates realized that Green had chosen to retain all the old National Council members, people who had distinguished themselves by servile obedience to Dillon and who deserved no more consideration than did Dillon himself.

Green had hardly finished when Ellsworth Kramer was on his feet. "I move that this convention rescind the action that we took on Monday in accepting the charter offered to us by President Green and ask him to take it back again," he declared in tense defiance.[16] There was a cheer that drowned out Bob Travis's prearranged second. "The motion is out of order," Dillon shouted. Kramer did not sit down, however. Holding his ground while looking Dillon straight in the eyes and spreading his arms wide, he spoke words that struck me as beautifully appropriate: "I appeal to the rank and file."

Dillon needed many more words to say the little that he had to say, which was that the matter was not debatable. "The charter has been granted [and] is binding upon the convention," he concluded. A number of delegates began shifting in their seats and some rose out of the Toledo delegation at first and then others followed. This was the moment that our progressive group had feared. My eyes darted about the hall and I noticed that several men from the Cleveland tables were on their feet.

Then Dillon spoke again: "As the president of your union, clothed with the authority to speak, I must now say that if there be those here who cannot conform to the terms and provisions of this document, then they must leave." It was insane. It was sheer provocation. Fortunately, no one took him at his word immediately. Delegates began shouting to each other. I could see Mortimer, Reisinger, John Soltis, Bill Kics, and others engaged in heated arguments with men near them. It seemed touch and go whether the assembly would break up and start for the door.

Then, suddenly, I noticed Tom Johnson on his feet, a sheet of paper shaking in his hands as he yelled for the floor. Dillon glared at him, swinging his gavel as though prepared to pound him out of order at his first syllable. But Johnson disregarded him and began reading, loudly and with strongly accented words: "Brother Chairman, I move that this first constitutional convention of the United Automobile Workers of America vigorously protest the action of the Executive Council of the American Federation of Labor and President Green in appointing not only our international president and secretary-treasurer but our executive council as well and we instruct our officials to appeal its decision to the Fifty-fifth convention of the American Federation of Labor."[17] It was none other than Fred Mayberry of Toledo, the first delegate at the convention to revolt against Dillon's authority, who rose to second Johnson's motion.

The delegates grew suddenly still as though waiting to see what Dillon would do with this new motion. The stout man set his jaws grimly but the expression in his eyes showed that he was taken aback and he held his gavel aloft indecisively. Green literally had to push him aside to take over the authority of the podium. "The motion just offered by Delegate Johnson is clearly in order," he declared. "You have a right to appeal and I think if your motion would be framed so as to appeal first to the Executive Council and then if necessary to the convention of the American Federation of Labor, you would be clearly within parliamentary procedure."

Tom Johnson nodded his head vigorously to indicate that he would rewrite his motion to include Green's suggestion and sat down at his place to do so. He wrote at a rapid-fire clip but after several minutes it appeared to me that it was getting overlong and I realized that he was adding something. I looked at Green to see if he was aware of that but Green, the man of many words, was in no hurry. Rather, he seemed pleased to be able to elucidate Johnson's protest and the way it would be processed.

He interrupted it only when Tom Johnson rose again, prepared to read his rephrased motion, the original one having been withdrawn with the consent of its seconder, Fred Mayberry.[18] As Johnson read, I realized that he had not only rounded out his text but had also taken advantage of the break to add an entirely new section. What would it be, and what would be Green's reaction? I wondered apprehensively.

After repeating with deliberation his original statement with the addition only of several sharp adjectives, Tom Johnson glanced swiftly at Green's face and then quickly read these significant words: *"We hereby elect in this convention a committee of seven from the floor which will be entrusted with the responsibility of appealing his decision* [emphasis added] to the Executive Council and to the Fifty-fifth Convention of the American Federation of Labor."

Fred Mayberry seconded the new motion and Carl Shipley quickly added an amendment that the expenses of the committee be paid by the International. It all happened so fast that President Green seemed to have no time to find fault with Tom Johnson's altered text. He merely suggested that Johnson include the amendment in his motion, which was done with a nod and which, in effect, gave the seven-man committee Green's sanction. A number of other delegates, most of them top officers of leading locals, took the floor to associate themselves with Johnson's idea, showing that they had caught onto the crucial significance of his committee. It shattered Green's ban on their conducting free elections, which they were going to be able to hold after all. The motion as amended was adopted.

• • •

The voting for the committee was set as the first order of business on the following day, the rest of the present afternoon having been put aside for acceptance speeches by Green's appointees. This gave the delegates the chance at last to hear the famed forensic talents of Homer Martin. I described his speech in my notes as "fulsome" and "sentimental" but also recorded that "it got tremendous applause." Its vacuousness can be judged from the *Proceedings,* although the delegates never noticed that, not even reacting to Martin's long panegyric on Dillon, which contained such mawkish pearls as "I don't believe that a man ever lived who bore a greater burden."[19] It was his revivalist, preacher's style, familiar to many, that enraptured them. He struck a histrionic pose, standing tall and handsome, fists balled, chin set forward, eyes glaring, his strong voice aimed at all the ambient though unidentified enemies. As one delegate that I overheard commented when Martin finished: "Boy, can that baby speak!"

It was not until Saturday morning, on the last day of the convention, that the Committee of Seven was elected,[20] the scheduled voting on Friday having had to be put off due to an "error" in the printed ballots containing the names of nominees. Tom Johnson's name had been left out, and another man with the same surname and a different initial—F. Johnson, a delegate from the Flint Buick local—had been substituted. My ebullient friend Arthur ("Frenchy") Dubuc, one of Dillon's appointed tellers, insisted aggressively that the other name was correct because he had recorded it when the nomination was made. But the storm of protest compelled Dillon to order the first ballots destroyed and new ones printed.

The long delay accomplished one thing, however, it permitted the leading anti-Dillon locals (Studebaker, Bendix, Toledo, Norwood, and White Motors) to agree on a slate. John Milkent, the candidate of the Kenosha group, was left off the slate for some reason, probably to make places for two men from Michigan. One, Tom Johnson of Detroit, was an obvious choice;the other, John North of Grand Rapids, belonged to our caucus.

The seven-man slate (which also included L. R. Richardson of Studebaker, Shipley, Addes, Hoskins, and Mortimer) gathered no less than 72 percent of the total vote cast (1,300 of 1,805); 78 percent if Milkent's vote was included (1,409 of 1,805). The pro-Dillon group did not run a slate of their own because they were reluctant to show their weakness, but neither did they boycott the vote, casting their ballots for two added nominees—Walter Wells and Jack Kennedy—as well as three delegates from the anti-Dillon group: Merrill, Kramer, and Milkent. The aim of this diversion was obviously to split our votes and, if possible, to get such marked left-wingers as Mortimer and Johnson defeated. It was a vain attempt because the lowest vote on the anti-Dillon slate (North with 154) was almost fifty votes higher than the highest tally of the also-rans (Milkent with 109).

The results were no sooner announced when peppery Ellsworth Kramer offered a motion that "the seven elected men be the official delegates of the UAW" at the AFL convention. A number of speakers eagerly took up this proposal but Dillon had had the time to quiet his agitation and find the argument to squelch Kramer's mischievous suggestion, explaining that "the seven elected members were elected for a special purpose and not as delegates to the convention."

However, the discussion showed that the delegates had already assigned a far greater importance to the "seven," as indeed they themselves would quickly apprehend. As the sole democratically elected body to come out of the UAW convention, they realized their authority as the indisputable spokesmen of the auto workers. This role would be fully established at the AFL's Atlantic City Convention in October, where their right to speak freely was won by the direct personal and physical intervention of the formidable John L. Lewis.

The seven men met before the convention adjourned and elected Mortimer chair and Johnson secretary of the committee. They exchanged addresses and promised to keep in touch until they met again in Miami for their rendezvous with the AFL Executive Council.

Mortimer and I had driven to Detroit in his old car to save me the expense of the railroad fare (the four progressive White Motors delegates, Mortimer, Reisinger, Ed Stubbe, and Ted Reiff, had also shared my hotel bill) and we decided to stay over in Detroit a few extra hours to attend the meeting of the "Coughlin Union" on Belle Isle. We had no intention of lingering still another day to take in the AFL Labor Day picnic at the same place. Dillon was billed as the featured speaker and the prospect of listening to the gush of praise that he would be getting was a contrary incentive.

According to the newspapers, no more than a few thousand attended the Belle Isle picnic, whereas the Coughlin Union's meeting, which we attended the day before, drew a mass of twenty thousand. Mortimer and I were hardly pleased to see such a vast number of Detroit auto workers, presumably responsive to union organization but actually drawn by the treacherous oratory of the radio priest. While we were waiting for Coughlin to arrive, application cards were distributed and we saw, not without pain, great numbers of them signed and gathered up in baskets. It was all too much to bear finally and though we were curious to see Coughlin, we decided that the rousing reception he would undoubtedly receive would be too high a price to pay. After half an hour, or less, we decided to leave and drive directly back to Cleveland. "We'll avoid the heavy late afternoon traffic that way," Mortimer said in an absolving explanation that fooled neither one of us.

Most of the way back to Cleveland, I mentally composed the leading editorial that I decided to run in the upcoming convention issue of the *United Auto Worker*. I had even chosen the editorial's title: "Father Coughlin's Union Will Split Auto Workers."[21]

Part Two

The UAW Wins Its Greatest Victories

The Industrial Unions
Support the UAW's Protest 8

For the following four or five months, Cleveland impressed us as being the center of the world—*our* world. It was a purely subjective feeling, yet there was a certain truth in it. This microcosm, however circumscribed, was, during that period, invaded by numerous prominent people who brought with them the sense of an extraordinary accretion of importance.

The first thing that took place after our return to Cleveland was the election of officers at the White Motor local, which in a symbolic way confirmed the "victory" we had won at the Detroit Convention. The pro-Dillon group sustained a crushing defeat and the event marked a coup de grâce to George Lehman's career. Everyone had assumed that his "retirement" from the local's presidency the previous year was to be permanent. That he decided to be a candidate in the local's September elections was no doubt due to a change of plans about him by the AFL leadership, which may have sought a bigger career for Lehman originally but now found that he had to reestablish his base at White Motors and regain control of that important local.

The White Motor elections turned out to be a plebiscite that raised their significance to a national level. On August 13, before the convention, Lehman had presented the local with the National Council's resolution calling for endorsement of Dillon's appointment as president. It was turned down resoundingly after a number of indignant members swamped Lehman's pro-Dillon arguments. "If we can elect the President of our country, we should be able to elect the president of our International," one speaker argued. The wording of the resolution was enough to defeat it; its praise of Dillon for "his ability to handle our problems in a very capable manner" brought guffaws.

The members did not want to take the chance that their elected delegates would fail to carry out their wishes on this fundamental question, so they accompanied their veto of it with instructions that the delegates must also vote down the preposterous suggestion at the convention. Lehman had chosen to disregard this bidding, as we know, seeming to think that he could do this with impunity, or at least that he could ride the waves against the storm of criticism that his defiance would probably bring. But it was amazing that he decided to run for the local's top office only a week after breaking his word to the local.

News had got around in the plant about Lehman's broken pledge but Wyndham Mortimer and the other officers had agreed to hold the elections at the beginning of the meeting so that any personal attacks on Lehman might not affect the result. Mortimer beat him two to one (414 to 212), and Lehman carried all his friends along with him to defeat. Dick Reisinger won over C. Griffith for secretary (431 to 173); Paul Jahn whipped the popular Chris Schaum for vice president (279 to 224); and the vociferous Ed Gockel, one of Lehman's fellow Masons, was bested for a one-year trustee by Bill Dieter, Mortimer's closest friend in the plant.

The biggest shock was the defeat of Charley Walsh, the Lehman family's friend, whose curious antics had at times acutely irritated Lehman. Walsh had held the important post of treasurer since the formation of the local but he was beaten by Ted Reiff, a strong supporter of Mortimer, by a close score of 318 to 286. Walsh's upset would certainly have been more emphatic had he not broken from Lehman in the Dillon vote at Detroit, an act the members no doubt marked down in his favor.

• • •

The sweeping victory in the White Motor elections heightened the positive mood that we had brought home from Detroit. My leading front-page editorial in the September issue of the *United Auto Worker* stressed this feeling, summing it up in the one word—unity: "No more are we scattered like the autumn leaves. We are knitted together in one solid organization, 35,000 strong. And we pledge our last ounce of strength in support of any and all progressive efforts on the part of our International officers to build our organization into an effective power."

We truly felt that it was the "great tact" that the delegates had shown in the face of calculated provocation that had saved the union from a disastrous split. Our forbearance, the editorial continued, had already inspired Akron's rubber workers in facing down President William Green's analogous attempt to impose an unwanted president upon them. "The rubber workers may thank the stiff fight that our auto worker delegates put up for obtaining their own more satisfactory terms," I wrote.

This event in Akron occurred only a few weeks before the UAW's Committee of Seven was to meet with the AFL Executive Council, which put the committee in what they felt was a very strong position to protest the auto workers not having been allowed to elect their own officers. The council was in session at Atlantic City, making preparations for the convention that would open a few days later. The UAW committee assumed that they had an appointment with the council but when they arrived at the specified time they found that it had not yet assembled.

Actually, the Committee of Seven never received a real hearing in Atlantic City. After Green arrived and the session opened, "Big Bill" Hutcheson, president of the Carpenters International, who, Mortimer has reported, "gave every impression of speaking for the Council," asked the purpose of the committee's visit. When Mortimer told him in a few carefully chosen words, Hutcheson observed sarcastically: "Maybe what we should do is recall [your] charter and when you have organized the industry we can then discuss the question of a charter."[1]

Mortimer refused to get trapped by this attempt to shift the subject. "We are not here to discuss a charter," he said. "The charter has been issued. We are here to demand our democratic right to elect our own officers. That is the only question at issue." This was, of course, the fact since that was the convention's mandate to the Committee of Seven.

It was in no way helpful when President David Dubinsky of the International Ladies Garment Workers Union (ILGWU) chose that moment to ask Mortimer how many members of the committee were communists. Mortimer refused to answer the offensive question, declaring sharply that "it was out of order." The hearing ended right there and Green told the committee that their protest would be considered and the council's decision would be passed on in due time.

John L. Lewis's absence from this meeting dismayed the UAW delegation, who felt that he would have intervened in their behalf. It is my feeling, however, that his absence may have been voluntary since Lewis would not have wanted to get embroiled with the other members of the council on this subject just a few days before the opening of the AFL convention. He and the other Mine Workers officers were preparing a spectacular maneuver which they must have wanted to come as a complete surprise to the craft leaders.

This coup would go far beyond the auto workers' contestation with the AFL leadership and it was up to them to shift emphasis and fit into the new situation. It is significant, however, that Mortimer, in an article he wrote for the September issue of our paper, had concentrated on the question of industrial versus craft unionism, almost as if he anticipated the subject of the great debate at the AFL's convention. He even drew the same implicit conclusion to this basic issue that Lewis would make: "The immediate and burning problem is one of organizing all the unorganized workers in the auto and parts plants."

At the time, we were not aware of previous occasions when the Executive Council had discussed the auto workers' problems in Lewis's presence, nor of his support in those discussions. One such incident, as early as February 1935, is partly reported in the Executive Council's minutes and reveals Lewis's support for key measures of our progressive program. The minutes describe the appearance before the council of a delegation comprised of Francis Dillon and three members of the UAW's National Council. Their ostensible purpose was to ask the AFL to charter an international union but in discussing their proposal they themselves furnished self-defeating arguments against it.

Forrest G. Woods of Studebaker, whom we were to meet six months later at the Detroit Convention, argued that it would be five years before auto workers would have the kind of leaders who could handle the International Union's affairs. The same line was taken up by Michael J. Manning of Detroit and by Dillon himself. Why, then, did the UAW ask for an international? Dillon explained that there was constant agitation for it from the communists and from "rump organizations," which, he hoped, the council would help him squelch.

Lewis was infuriated by such shilly-shallying, as Manning told me in an interview two years later. However, Lewis's contempt for the UAW delegation did not keep him from preparing a plan for the auto workers and from presenting the plan to the Executive Council for adoption after Dillon's delegation had left Washington. Lewis urged that an international charter be issued immediately to the auto workers and that Green would appoint temporary officers. These officers, however, would be supplanted by permanent ones who would be elected at a convention to be held within three to six months. Meanwhile, at the peak of production in March, the UAW would initiate a great organizational campaign, which the AFL must help with money and men. Lewis offered, in the name of the United Mine Workers, to start the kitty going with $5,000. The motion caused a great commotion among the craft unionists on the council, to whom Lewis ironically referred in a remark that would become famous: "Contention over the fruits of victory [should] be deferred until we have some of the fruits in our possession."

George Harrison of the Railway Clerks offered an amendment to Lewis's motion establishing the jurisdictional limitations that President Green would force on the UAW convention in August in Detroit. The amendment was adopted, eleven to three, and the motion as amended by a vote of twelve to two. Thus Lewis (joined by Dubinsky) had voted against his own motion, or, as he called it, his "emasculated resolution." And the craftsmen had encased the UAW International in a carapace that would, they felt, protect them from the wild demands of an irresponsible mass of unskilled workers.

• • •

When the AFL convention opened on October 10, 1935, in Atlantic City, the UAW's Committee of Seven could hardly foresee the broad proportions that their protest would assume or the powerful champions it would win. The members of the committee were also completely ignorant of the intricacies of the inner-AFL relationships and of the rules by which its conventions were run. Except for a couple of former miners or sons of miners, they knew practically nothing about John L. Lewis aside from the fact that he was attached to industrial unionism, which they took for granted. Mortimer told them about the "captive mines" that steelmakers often possessed as part of their vast enterprises, mines that were unorganized and hence constituted a great threat to the UMW.

For a number of days, nothing seemed to happen at the convention. John L. Lewis did not appear at the miners' table until the beginning of the second week. As far as the committee knew, this was the convention's habitual rhythm and they tried their best to make the idle days count. As a kind of introduction, they had prepared a letter, which they deposited at each delegate's place, containing an account of their controversy with the AFL. Though it was four pages and 1,600 words long, the committee innocently described the letter as "a brief review of the facts."[2]

Reading the letter today, one wonders how the committee might have thought that the delegates, with many serious problems before them, could have been tempted to read so much as a paragraph of this bloated text. "We are chiefly concerned with the selection of capable national officers," it declared earnestly, "officers with the courage, the patience and the ability to organize the industry" (meaning Homer Martin, no doubt). The statement ended with a call for a special convention to be held no later than March 1, 1936, where these paragons could supposedly be elected.

Fortunately, a more adequate report of the auto workers' dilemma was distributed two days later in the September issue of the *United Auto Worker*, which may have been more helpful. Devoted almost entirely to the Detroit Convention, the issue contained three articles and two editorials covering various aspects of the sessions. I had sent Mortimer a bundle of a thousand copies, which Elmer Davis (a delegate representing his own local) distributed with dramatic aplomb, telling each delegate to "Read this paper if you want to know the truth about the auto workers!"

The edition seemed made to order for the occasion. Though I had not thought of the AFL convention in preparing it, the contents give the impression of being a special appeal to that audience, judging by two headings: "President Green Ignores Majority Vote: Appoints Dillon First President" and "Committee of Seven Elected: Will Carry Protest to AFL Convention in October."

Mortimer's article on page 2—"Craft Jurisdiction: A Serious Problem"—would also be eye-catching to the delegates, the more so perhaps because of the moderate tone of the title. Readers' curiosity would be rewarded by the conversation that Mortimer reported between President Green and himself at Detroit:

> Mortimer: In our union at White Motors we have, for instance, a blacksmith shop. Under our new charter, will the Blacksmiths claim jurisdiction over these members?
> Green: Yes, they may.
> Mortimer: Then as president of this local union, must I consider it my duty to force these blacksmiths out of the United Auto Workers, where likely as not they will join the M.E.S.A. or remain unorganized?[3]
> Green: Do not force anyone out of your local union. . . . The Blacksmiths have jurisdiction, it is true. But this is a matter we can safely leave to the future.

We never thought that this exchange would furnish a preview of the leading subject of debate at Atlantic City. Nonetheless, many delegates who read it surely would have been surprised by Green's liberal attitude. Some, on the other hand, might have been comforted to note the attachment that the new unionists displayed for the AFL. The editorial on the same page was headed "Father Coughlin's Union Will Split Auto Workers" and contained this declaration of loyalty: "There is no question, the true home of organized labor in this country is the American Federation of Labor. All friends of labor must know this."

• • •

It has been said that industrial unionism carries within it a great progressive potential. Yet the UMW had not distinguished itself in this sense from the generality of the AFL crafts. The new movement to which the UMW gave leadership would indeed assume an extraordinarily fresh outlook: dynamic, courageous, enlightened. But these features were offshoots of such recent social and political impacts as the Great Depression and the rise of fascism. That the new industrial-union movement would develop these tendencies so positively was largely the result of the grim struggles it was to conduct against powerful industrialists, whose basic responsibility for many of the country's retrogressive impulses became apparent in the process.

Whatever the case, John L. Lewis would demonstrate a sophisticated progressivism at Atlantic City.[4] I was not aware that he had any background for this kind of outlook. Men like Sidney Hillman and David Dubinsky were far more reputed in this respect and both would rouse feelings of affinity among auto workers with left-wing tendencies. It may have been that Lewis's manifestations of this type attracted more attention because they were unexpected. And yet his deft manner of linking union issues with liberal concepts revealed an undeniable familiarity with such subjects.

This was especially noticeable in Lewis's speech in the famous debate of industrial versus craft unionism, which he had prepared with conspicuous care. "There is a great reservoir of workers here numbering millions and millions of men and women," he urged, "and back of them great numbers of millions of dependents, who want the AFL to adopt a policy that will be sufficiently flexible and sufficiently modern that it will permit them to join with us in this great fight for the maintenance of the rights of workers and for the upholding of the standards of modern democracy." Then, suddenly, his deep voice seemed to ring out in a homiletic throb: "Now prepare yourselves by making a contribution to your less fortunate brethren. Heed this cry from Macedonia that comes from the hearts of men. Organize the unorganized and in so doing make the American Federation of Labor the greatest instrumentality that has ever been forged in the history of modern civilization to befriend the cause of humanity and champion human rights."[5]

I was not there and so did not hear the speech but those who did glowed when they described it. What most stirred them, I felt, was that the Miners' leader was talking about them. From his very first words they felt it, when Lewis described the San Francisco Convention, where the Executive Council had presented its deceptive plan to establish international unions. The auto delegates who were there were shocked when Lewis supported this plan, and their fears were justified when it reappeared at the Detroit Convention in the form of the crippling jurisdictional grant imposed upon them.

Now, Lewis would tell them why he had taken that contradictory position on their charter, which he called a "breach of faith and a travesty of good conscience."[6] "At San Francisco," he frankly admitted, "I was seduced by fair words. Now, having learned that I was seduced, I am enraged, and I am ready to rend my seducers limb from limb." Nevertheless, he made a last appeal to these "seducers" on behalf of the mass production workers. "If these men are going to fight voluntarily for their rights . . . and are willing to assimilate the punishment that may be inflicted upon them, why not let the rest of us, who will not shed any blood personally, let them make their rules, so that they may have a chance to win?"

Yet far from indulging in such permissiveness, "Big Bill" Hutcheson of the Carpenters would not even let these workers speak. W. W. Thompson, an officer of the Rubber Workers, was on the floor, trying to tell about the hardships that the Executive Council's restrictive charter had inflicted on his organization when Hutcheson demanded that Thompson be called out of order because the question of industrial unionism had already been settled. When President Green docilely complied, Charles P. Howard of the Typographical Union (soon after to become a cofounder of the CIO), followed by Lewis, defended Thompson's right to tell his story.

"This organization introduced a resolution," Lewis explained, "calling the attention of this convention to [their] specific problems in the hope that it might influence the minds of the Executive Council. It does not deal entirely with the question of industrial unionism as decided by this convention. It deals with a problem in Akron, Ohio, and elsewhere, and certainly in my judgment . . . these delegates . . . have a right to tell the convention their own particular problems in relation to it. This thing of raising points of order all the time in minor delegates is rather small potatoes."[7]

Whereupon Hutcheson, who weighed at least two hundred fifty pounds, took up the gauntlet. "Mr. Chairman," he said, "I was raised on small potatoes. That is why I am so small." After the laughter, he resumed contemptuously: "Had the delegate who has just spoken about raising points of order given more consideration to the questions before this convention and not attempting, in a dramatic way, to impress the delegates with his sincerity, we would not have had to raise the point of order at this late date." Hutcheson rounded out his taunt in a private growl at Lewis as Lewis passed his seat on the way back to the Miners' table. What the newspapers called "an obscenity," Mortimer, who was seated close by, identified as "You dirty bastard!"

Lewis struck Hutcheson a single blow on the chin that sent him sprawling between the tables. For a few minutes it looked as though there would be a general brawl as numerous delegates leaped to their feet, overturning chairs to confront adversaries. The Miners were outnumbered, and a group of new unionists by an automatic impulse rushed to their table to defend Lewis and the other leaders. Mortimer reports that during the fray Ed Wharton of the Machinists dashed by him, swinging his folding chair and yelling "Kill the son-of-a-bitch!" Mortimer grabbed him, and they milled about for a while. Later, Wharton apologized for "having lost his head."[8]

• • •

When peace was restored, the chairman took a vote on the appeal by W. W. Thompson to his decision, declaring Thompson out of order. Green's dignity narrowly escaped by a vote of 108 to 104, in a show of hands. But the face-saver was meaningless because the auto workers soon after began to discuss their own jurisdictional protest, which they did without restraint and in an atmosphere of peace and dignity. Lewis chuckled over Mortimer's shoulder: "You notice how quiet they are now? You don't see them trying to stop you fellows from speaking any more!"

The UAW speakers were from most of the big locals—Studebaker, Bendix, Toledo, and White Motors—those that had been strong enough or shrewd enough to resist company unions and spies, to fight off police violence and injunctions, and, not the least, the spurious claims and meddling of their "brothers" from the crafts. Many others had succumbed, as Thomas Killeen reported:

> In 1933, we organized Federal Labor Union 18763, comprising employees of the Budd Manufacturing Company. . . . A strike was called . . . of the men in the automobile plant. . . . There was a pattern-makers' department 100 percent organized. [But] they had a company union in that plant [and] the shop delegate from the patternmakers' local was and is a member of that company union. His name is George Zimmerman. I asked Mr. Leach [Lynch], who I think is the president of the Pattern Makers, in Philadelphia, why the patternmakers did not come out and support us. He said he thought they could do more for us on the inside. . . . [Our] local disintegrated and at the present time there is no Local No. 18763.[9]

George Addes told of a similar situation at his Willys-Overland plant in Toledo: "When we first organized our local we got into a dispute with the Machinists. We worked together for a while until they wanted to take everybody over and leave us the sweepers in the plant. When we turned men over to the Machinists Union, what happened? There isn't [one] member that is in good standing with [their] local union. We are carrying these men in our contracts in each and every plant in Toledo. In the Willys-Overland plant we have drop-forge men and they are under contract although they are not paying any money into our organization."[10]

Wyndham Mortimer, speaking with the conscious support of a solidly unionized plant, with full recognition and a signed contract, could give his words a ring of authority: "We believe we are the only ones who can do the job [of organizing the industry] and do it . . . within the American Federation of Labor. . . . [But] we are determined upon one thing, whether you like it or not—we don't intend to give our members up without a battle."[11]

The pedagogical Carl Shipley, on the other hand, decided to give the tool-minded delegates a graphic lesson in the reasons why craft segregation of auto workers was impossible on an assembly line: "You have a line of production that starts up at that door with a piece part. When it finishes down here it is completed. . . . They might have a punch press, a washer, a welder, then somebody is rubbing off the high spots, the metal finish, and down here somebody else is painting. . . . If anybody in this house can segregate the trades in the plant he is a Moses—it is impossible. For that reason we ask complete jurisdiction over every worker in the industry."[12]

It was during this lengthy debate that the industrial unions, which were soon to set up the CIO, took their stand with the mass production workers represented at the convention. One of the first to pronounce in their favor was an officer of the Typographical Union. The man, whose name was Simons, described himself as formerly "a firm believer" in craft unionism, yet during the last two years he had come to appreciate that the problems of the labor movement were changing fundamentally: "Today I realize what these young members have to contend with. . . . The strictly craft organizations, I feel, have been forced upon them to such an extent that it is weakening their organization and discouraging their membership. The American Federation of Labor should help them and if necessary we should change this hard and fast policy of craft unionism."[13]

Sidney Hillman of the important Amalgamated Clothing Workers (ACW),[14] which would also become a cofounder of the CIO, suggested that craft unions, which could not themselves organize the auto industry, should agree to a three-year "moratorium" on their jurisdictional claims in order to allow auto workers to do the job. He made an impassioned plea on the political importance of unionizing the mass industries, which were controlled by a "reckless combination of capital will" that would "bring in fascism" when capital thought doing so would serve its purpose.

The greatest excitement, I was told, was produced when the powerful Van Bittner, one of Lewis's impressive group of associates, took the floor and in a strong, deliberate voice said, "I rise at this time to support the Automobile Workers."[15] Something about that simple statement and the way it was delivered gave the UAW men a sense of total commitment. Several of our delegates repeated it to me with slow emphasis as though reciting the words of a poem learned in school, or words from some historic speech such as "Four score and seven years ago."

Reading Van Bittner's statements in the *Proceedings* provides something of the earnestness and sincerity that had impressed the men. Bittner had a way of reducing abstractions to concrete terms that made them instantly convincing. For example, he disposed of the question of jurisdiction, which was full of arbitrary complexities, with one sharp blow:

> What jurisdiction does the American Federation of Labor have over men that are not members of any union? So the quibbling has been about nothing. It seems to me that the . . . automobile workers have their hands full in fighting General Motors, Chrysler, Ford and the automobile barons . . . instead of having to come to this convention . . . and beg and plead, if you please, for the right to organize the au-

tomobile workers of this country. . . . Instead of . . . turning down [their] plea . . . we should be thinking of getting up a war chest here so that we can organize these industries and bring them within the American Federation of Labor.

These words set things into proper perspective for the auto delegates. Their overriding thought was that of the powerful friends they had won. The big resolution on industrial unions had been crushed by a roll-call count of 18,024 to 10,993. But the auto delegates thought only of the second tally that spoke for great masses of supporters, more than a million workers, whereas the crafts' total dwindled to insignificance, being made up of a dispersed multitude of small groups that the Hutchesons and Whartons carried in their hip pockets.

• • •

Our auto delegates were, in a different way, as enthusiastic about the rank-and-filers whom they had met from other mass industries as they were about meeting the famous leaders of the older unions. About fifty delegates, most of them young men, quickly formed a compact group that boosted their power despite their insignificant voting strength.

Through the initiative of the radio and allied delegates, a caucus of the new unionists was called at the beginning of the Atlantic City Convention, on October 8. It was attended by delegates from the radio, electrical, metal-mining, cement, chemical, auto, rubber, and other mass industry groups, most of which were allowed a single vote at the convention but would eventually constitute important units of the CIO. The group discussed organizational problems and took stands on burning issues of social and political moment, for which many of them had presented resolutions to the convention. The group's decision to vote against the anticommunist amendment to the AFL consistation, which the Executive Council had called for in its annual report, revealed the progressive viewpoint that prevailed among them.

One of their most efficacious activities was to establish themselves as missionaries. They made the rounds of the hotel lobbies during pauses in the convention sessions and, evidently with the approval of UMW leaders, buttonholed all those wearing badges, trying to win votes for industrial unionism by recounting their own problems and experiences. They asked for help and, above all, for understanding. In this manner they succeeded in forging personal bonds that would soon be expressed in dozens of localities, especially in the Central Labor Councils, where local union delegates were often beyond the dictates of their hidebound international officials.

Political leftists found the fifty-fifth convention more congenial for proposing progressive measures than had been the case in years. The support for a labor party was particularly heartening and would make its mark in the UAW's special convention six months later. The Textile Workers conducted an energetic campaign on its behalf. The meeting this union organized in one of the convention halls was addressed by officers of the ILGWU and ACW, as well as other representatives, including Wyndham Mortimer. Six internationals had endorsed the Textile Workers' resolution for a labor party, and the resolution won a respectable vote from the convention delegates.

It was disappointing to the progressives when the UMW did not join the list of endorsers though Thomas Kennedy, a UMW officer, felt called on to explain the reason: the danger of dividing supporters for the reelection of Roosevelt the following November. This type of opportunistic rationalization carried little weight with progressives, who knew that something would always stand in the way of breaking with the two-party system. They had the chance of testing the commitment of other pro-industrial union associates when the decision was made to run Emil Costello, a leader of the Kenosha-Nash local, against Matthew Woll for the Federation's third vice presidency, which Woll had held unchallenged for twenty-five years. But the vote for Costello was very small; some members of the auto group even put in a blank ballot and Carl Shipley actually cast his for the arch-reactionary.

Yet it was not on such issues that the Atlantic City Convention must be judged, as even the most politically advanced of the UAW men admitted. Just observing the pathetic isolation of Francis Dillon told them how far they had come in a few weeks. The UAW president could not even get Green to "introduce" him to the assembly, despite Russell Merrill's intercession on his behalf. The latter, out of pity, let Dillon sit beside him though the other auto delegates strenuously objected to giving him that kind of recognition.

One sad note was brought home to me from Atlantic City that gave me many sleepless hours. It was about Tom Johnson's "disappearance" early in the convention. Members of the Committee of Seven began passing the word around that AFL goons had drowned Johnson to keep him from making trouble at the convention. Mortimer told me the true circumstances of Johnson's disappearance. One day, the landlady in Mortimer's rooming house told him that a man had been asking for him during convention hours. By her description, Mortimer knew it was Johnson. "All I want you to tell Mr. Mortimer is that nothing happened to me and that I'm all right," he told her.

Reading the *Proceedings* of the convention reveals Johnson's active participation, if not actual presence, at the sessions. Both of the personal resolutions he entered had been adopted. One was on the preparation of an organizational drive in the auto industry (page 675); the other was an exposure of Father Coughlin's role in fostering a dual auto union (page 793). Thus, even when absent, Tom Johnson continued working for the auto workers.

The issue of autonomy, the Committee of Seven's formal reason for being at the convention, was never settled there, not even behind the scenes. Their resolution was referred to the Executive Council at the end of the convention on a motion of the resolutions committee along with all other undecided measures and the council voted that no further action on the particular case was necessary.

President Green had kept promising the UAW committee that he would have an answer on autonomy for them before the convention adjourned. Yet he still had nothing definite when they went to him on the convention's last day. He pledged, however, that if they would trust him he would get the Executive Council to grant him the power to terminate the probationary period at his discretion. He said he would make it a matter of record by slipping in a mention somewhere. This he did, stating that the auto workers' appeal would be taken up at the Executive Council's first session the day after adjournment.

"We don't want to continue that probationary period any longer than seems necessary," Green told the committee, "and if we can have discretion to deal with the matter we will deal with it effectively." But the men did not know whether to trust him or to insist on forcing the matter to the floor because they didn't want to make fools of themselves in trying to explain things to their rank and file in case there was a slip-up. Lewis advised them against taking the latter course, however. "If Bill Green promised that he'll do it," he told Mortimer, "you can depend on his word."

As it happened, however, Green delayed two months before informing the committee of the Executive Council's positive decision though it added a stipulation "that the matter shall not be consummated until [its] January meeting . . . when further consideration" would be given it. There was nothing to do but accept this further delay, during which UAW activists concentrated on getting locals to repeat their demands for the new convention to be held "not later than March 1st" lest another high production period should pass without taking the necessary "militant action" that only a new rank-and-file leadership could be trusted to carry through.

Lewis Chooses Cleveland to Launch the CIO

9

The events of the Atlantic City Convention profoundly stirred Cleveland's UAW activists, giving them the certainty of early success. An eagerness for action took hold of our group, which is reflected in the October 1935 issue of the *United Auto Worker,* which I pieced together from the excited outpourings of returning delegates. The extravagant headline, "Industrial Unions Make Great Gains at AFL Convention," is accompanied by a defiant bottom-page streamer: "Let the Crafts Keep Their Jurisdiction—We'll Keep the MEN!"

Such self-assurance appears presumptuous today, considering that almost two-thirds of the Atlantic City votes had gone against the industrial-union bloc. But no one could have argued us out of our belief in the superior strength of our side. This confidence was consecrated when the Committee for Industrial Organization was announced a month later. Wyndham Mortimer had been invited to informal meetings of industrial union leaders at Atlantic City, where tentative plans had been aired. These hard-headed realists had no illusions that their spirited fight would have jarred the Executive Council loose from its prejudices. "A record of twenty-five years of constant, unbroken failure," as John L. Lewis put it, had made backwardness a habit.

In Cleveland we took up the challenge of the situation without hesitation. For us, an organization drive meant essentially unionizing the Fisher Body plant. The problem, however, was still the local's leadership. With Bob Bates, now the president, lackadasically controlling the situation, we were forced to contrive a setup that would take matters out of his hands. This was accomplished through a citywide organization committee of the Auto Council, made up of two members from each of the nine locals and the Fisher Body's entire executive board. Bates was cozened into permitting the committee's chairmanship to be handed over to the energetic Elmer Davis, who announced that his local had donated $100 to the drive and reported self-importantly that he had already spoken to John L. Lewis at Atlantic City about coming to Cleveland to speak at a great mass meeting.

The inference was that Lewis had accepted, which did not happen to be true. More recently, Mortimer had written to him in the name of the Auto Council and Lewis had replied with his "regrets." Mortimer then suggested to the council that the United Mine Workers head might change his mind if a delegation were sent to Washington to speak to him in person. Davis immediately proposed himself for the committee and vouched for his local's willingness to pay his expenses. No other local besides White Motors could afford to do as much, so the delegation was limited to Mortimer and Davis.[1] At the last minute, Homer Martin, the UAW's new vice president, who had recently come to Cleveland and seemed to have no other responsibilities, asked if he could go along, and Mortimer readily assented.

Lewis was still hard to convince despite the fervor of Elmer Davis. The UMW leader argued his "great press of business," as the *United Auto Worker* reported in its December 1935 issue. But "after an hour-and-a-half's discussion," he finally changed his mind. It seems apparent that Lewis's initial reluctance was because of his uncertainty that Cleveland's auto workers, however sincere, were sufficiently experienced to make a success of his first public appearance as spokesman of the new movement. But the idea nevertheless attracted him, and it was probably Mortimer's suggestion that Lewis could also speak in Akron on the afternoon of the same day that finally convinced him. Moreover, he decided to keep his eye on the project by sending Adolph Germer, the CIO's first organizer, to Cleveland to supervise our preparations.

• • •

The news set us going. Several committees got to work. Dick Reisinger headed publicity and I helped him put out a whole assortment of handbills, placards, and letters to a list of AFL locals that Trent Longo, a progressive leader of the Painters Union, made up for us. We prepared releases for the English and the foreign press; Hungarian and Slovenian translations were arranged by Bill Kics of Bender Body and Mike Evko of Fisher Body. A corps of young unionists from White's and Willard's were enlisted to talk to meetings of important craft locals and sometimes got themselves in vitriolic debates with contemptuous business agents. Joe O'Neill, the personable young vice president of Ed Simpson's local, made a big hit by starting off his talks with an old Irish air sung in his pleasant, high-pitched, nasal voice. My wife, Dorothy, also got involved through a recently formed group of actors that put on a playlet called *Union Label* at AFL meetings.

As expected, the AFL officialdom proved tougher to convince. Mortimer wrung a reluctant endorsement of the meeting itself from the Cleveland Federation of Labor (CFL) but his invitation to them to share the platform with the Mine Workers' leader was gingerly declined by Secretary Lenehan, who argued that he had to remain neutral in the jurisdictional quarrel. When John P. Frey, the craft-union spokesman, arrived in Cleveland a few days before the Lewis meeting, however, Lenehan and his friends forgot their "impartiality." But the attendance at the Frey gathering was pathetic despite the fact that ten thousand handbills had been distributed at a CFL meeting to announce it. An audience of only three hundred gathered to hear Frey list the "inconsistencies" in Lewis's program. Would Lewis relinquish jurisdiction over miners working in the captive mines? Frey demanded. Would he surrender the miners who worked for Henry Ford to the UAW? I was there and silently replied to all Frey's quips.

During the week before the Lewis meeting, Reisinger's publicity campaign shifted into high gear. He staged auto parades to start at all the plants, especially at Fisher Body, at quitting time. A couple of loud-speaker trucks wound their ways through the city's working-class areas on the weekend of January 16. A big pre-meeting rally was scheduled for the previous Sunday afternoon and featured several important CIO speakers from out of town, the principal luminary being Julius Hochman, second in command to David Dubinsky of the International Ladies Garment Workers Union (ILGWU).

I was especially interested by the arrival of the ILGWU leaders because Mortimer had given me the impression that Dubinsky was not overly enthusiastic about the CIO and I wanted to know why. Aside from Hochman, I met Charles ("Sasha") Zimmerman and Rose Pesotta, a sparkling personality who would be with us for many weeks during the Flint sitdown of 1937. All of these people were left-wingers and their conversation was marked by political sagacity. I was surprised to learn, however, that they were critical of John L. Lewis, a view that reflected, I felt, Dubinsky's attitude.

The ILGWU leaders felt, for example, that Lewis had made a grave mistake in resigning from the AFL Executive Council, an act that we in Cleveland had regarded as unavoidable once the Committee for Industrial Organization had begun to throw its weight around. The ILGWU visitors maintained that Lewis should have stayed in to fight, the implication being that he had left poor Dubinsky all alone, like another Daniel facing the lions' rage.[2] Similarly, Lewis's offer to Green "to return to your father's house" and head the CIO movement was regarded as flippant and to have belittled the whole program, arousing reservations about what Lewis really intended doing with the organization after it was built up.

My chief assignment in preparation for the Lewis meeting was to put out two issues of our paper, which would be used as the primary publicity appeal to the city's auto workers. Elmer Davis had been after me for a classy announcement of the meeting but I felt that this could be better accomplished by a special issue of the paper in December 1935 to explain what the meeting was all about. In other words, it would give readers some basic facts about the great new movement. In this respect I was eager to develop an idea I had been working on that gave what I considered a unique interpretation to the big debate that had taken place at Atlantic City.

The idea had occurred to me while I was studying the convention's *Proceedings,* in particular the distribution of the votes on the industrial-union question.[3] Newspapers had announced that the "minority" resolution proposed by John L. Lewis and Charles P. Howard was defeated two to one and had drawn the conclusion that the AFL membership was opposed to industrial unionism by that lopsided margin. But I realized from my analysis that this was utterly wrong and was amazed that no one had caught the obvious evidence to the contrary.

The misinterpretation stemmed from two totally neglected groups in the AFL voting system. The first consisted of the seventy-one federal labor unions at the convention, the great majority of which were organized in the basic industries. All were chartered as junior dependents of President Green's while awaiting their eventual disposition, supposedly as international unions. At the convention, these locals were assigned a token ballot of one vote each. In reality, they spoke for uncounted tens of thousands of members and had voted overwhelmingly for the minority resolution.

The second group was of a different kind. Its delegates, somewhat smaller in number than the first group, occupied an ex officio position in the AFL structure and likewise only carried a single vote each. Yet their enormous importance could not be measured quantitatively, but, as leading officials of the state and city federations, their votes on any critical subject would, undoubtedly, constitute an invaluable basis for an opinion survey of the groups they represented.

What had called my attention to this group were the interventions of two of its leading representatives that could be read in the Atlantic City Convention's *Proceedings* during the debate on industrial unionism. One representative was of particular importance to auto workers since he was Frank X. Martel, head of the Detroit Federation of Labor, which represented many times more union members than the UAW could yet boast of in that hub of the automobile industry.[4] Yet Martel had taken up the cudgels for the auto workers' resolution on jurisdiction.

The second individual who caught my notice in the *Proceedings* represented an important state federation, Ohio's, and was designated as "Delegate Donnelly." He had taken the floor not long after the Hutcheson-Lewis battle, which was touched off by Lewis's support of United Rubber Workers' delegate W. W. Thompson's right to speak. Donnelly had somehow been lost sight of in the great hurly-burly, and when peace had been restored, President Green had simply gone on to other business. Donnelly rose to a point of order that seemed to have an admonishing ring: "The floor belongs to Delegate Thompson!"[5]

The positive votes of these two men on the industrial-union question gave me the idea of counting the "yes" and "no" totals of all the city and state federations. It was a surprise to find that a majority in each case had voted in favor of the industrial-union motion: 14 to 9 and 22 to 18, respectively, for an overall total of 36 to 27. On the strength of this finding I prepared an article for page 1 of the December *United Auto Worker* headed "Majority of AFL Membership Favors Industrial Unions for Mass Production Workers."

I realized that a thorough explanation was necessary of what might be considered a brazen claim. The official vote, I explained, was faulty because the officers of the big internationals who had cast it for their hundreds of thousands of members did not truly represent the opinions of those members on this question. "What means besides a direct referendum do we have of demonstrating this?" I asked.

We had the ballots of the representatives from the state and city federations, I replied. "These delegates are supposed to represent not the particular internationals of which they may happen to be members—but the *entire AFL membership* of the city or state by which they are sent." Then I quoted the actual votes of these units and drew the inescapable conclusion: *"In other words, a distinct majority in each case voted for industrial unions for the mass production workers."*

• • •

There was not much fallout after my article appeared, I noted with a twinge of hurt pride and decided that I must avoid such esoteric discussions in the future. But I did not pine long because there was so much to do. We all worked as though success or failure of the Lewis meeting depended on each of us. When the day finally arrived, there still seemed that much was left undone and I am sure that others were as pleased as I was that the Akron meeting came first so we in Cleveland had time to catch up on any essentials that had been overlooked.

Arrangements had been made for a motorcade of the Cleveland auto locals to Akron. There were about twenty cars in the parade that followed the front car containing Lewis, Germer, and Mortimer. All of the cars were plastered with our posters and banners, and drivers tooted their horns emphatically at the outskirts of Akron as though to announce the great new message we were bringing to working-class America.

The meeting was vivifying. The great hall was packed, electric with excitement. Akron was a one-industry town, which made a difference in such a gathering. It was as though all the workers had piled out of their plants at Goodyear, Firestone, and Goodrich and come straight to the meeting. They responded to Lewis's words in unison. Again and again they burst into cheers of resounding approval when he castigated the craft leaders for being "incredibly selfish," for being "extraordinarily short-sighted from the point of view of their own organizations." His strong features relaxed momentarily in an ironic smile of shared understanding.

Then, suddenly, my heart began pounding as I realized that he was talking directly to me, quoting almost word for word from my article: "The majority vote of representatives of state and city federations in favor of the industrial union issue at the Atlantic City Convention of the Federation of Labor clearly demonstrates that could a vote be taken of the individual members of the Federation, it would be overwhelmingly in favor of industrial unionism for the basic industries."

The mood on the return from Akron was carefree and congratulatory but the sudden coming of darkness reminded us of our own big meeting and our worries resumed. It had been scheduled for 8 P.M., too late for a Sunday, in order to accommodate the Akron gathering. Workers would be thinking of having to get to work early the next morning. A blizzard was already heading off Lake Erie as the crowd started to arrive. Fortunately, the Music Hall was almost full, but the meeting was not half over when people began leaving. Mortimer, who was chairman, could not bring himself to insist that the preliminary speakers, who included Mayor Harold Burton and several important local union leaders, should cut their talks short.

In addition to these perturbations, I was especially worried about the play that was to be given just before Lewis's speech since I was the one responsible for scheduling it. My wife's People's Theatre had, on my suggestion, written to the program committee and offered to do a new one-act piece called *Private Hicks,* which Albert Maltz had based on the Toledo Auto-Lite strike of 1934. I considered it appropriate, as did the rest of the committee except for Adolph Germer, who gave no reason for opposing it. But his veto was summarily overridden at my instigation.

However, as the meeting dragged on I regretted my initiative more and more. I had a wild urge to ask Mortimer to shift the play to the end of the meeting but was afraid that the suggestion would cause too much commotion and so did nothing. The play got underway. Howard da Silva, a well-known Broadway actor who was out of work and visiting his family in Cleveland, had agreed to direct it and take the leading role. Several days earlier I had asked him to keep the performance down to twenty minutes and had received the impression that he would do so. But after awhile, I began to realize that the text had been kept intact, complete with every word, pause, and gesture.

I kept looking around toward John L. Lewis, who was sitting in the second row next to Adolph Germer. Lewis's powerful body was rigid, and his eyes were glued on the actors. It was plain that he was not enjoying the piece and was probably wondering why it had been scheduled. Had Germer told him about the circumstances? I heard the loud sound of expelled breath from their direction and was certain that it came from Lewis, showing his impatience or worse. Picking myself up, I desperately headed for the exit at the right side of the stage and ran up the inner stairs. I stood in the wing, waving my arms frantically to attract the actors' attention. But no one responded and the play crawled on to the bitter end.

After Lewis was introduced and began speaking, I resumed my seat, close to collapse. I heard little of the speech, being aware only of his sweeping page after page aside that he decided to skip. It seemed to me that the audience, especially those in the balcony, were leaving in droves, making a horrible din with their clacking seats. At the end of his speech, Lewis got a standing ovation nevertheless, which somewhat restored my sense of balance.

People gathered around up front after the meeting, auto workers and friends, all in a delighted mood. No one seemed to have noticed anything untoward about the last stages of the meeting. Lewis remained on the platform, surrounded by an eager crowd. He was talking to a couple of reporters who had folded copies of his speech in their hands. I was surprised to find not the slightest sign of displeasure in the UMW leader and decided that he was confident that he would have a good press anyway, which proved to be the case both locally and nationally.

Among those waiting to talk to Lewis, I noticed a number of UAW members whom we had invited from other cities. The *Cleveland Press* would report that fifty men from out-of-town locals were at the meeting. Many came up to me to shake my hand, men from St. Louis, Kenosha, Norwood, Toledo, Detroit, and other places. Ed Simpson introduced Allan Strachan, the newly elected president of the Detroit Auto Council and a socialist, as Ed whispered proudly. Strachan had brought four other council delegates with him.

It struck me all at once that this concourse of UAW representatives was one of the most significant features of the meeting. Only then did I recall the cheer that had gone up when Lewis had suddenly paused, then declared in a ringing voice that if, some day in the future, the AFL dared to expel the UAW for infringing on the claimed jurisdiction of other unions, "You can rest assured that the United Mine Workers will walk out with you!"

As I read the speech later, I found a strong note of defiance in it. It struck me as being a message addressed to the Executive Council in reply to their recent arrogant demand that the CIO should immediately dissolve—"should cease to function." But it was much more than that. The factional references were only a minor element as far as I was concerned, meant to flavor a serious and even scholarly address. Lewis had declared that

> Industrial unionism contemplates the elimination of industrial and financial autocracy, excessive profits to a few, and a redistribution of industrial output which will assure steady employment and adequate compensation to all classes of industrial workers. . . . Political action by organized labor will also be increasingly necessary . . . to safeguard the fundamental . . . rights of industrial democracy and . . . in order to secure legislative and perhaps constitutional sanctions for its economic program. Success in the organization of our basic industries will bring with it the political power which the labor movement has hitherto lacked for the attainment of these objectives.

As one reads these words today, one is struck not only by their aptness for the great organizational task at hand but also by Lewis's prescience regarding the course that the movement would take in the years to come. As for my previous misgivings, they were all forgotten, especially in light of Lewis's gracious manner toward our group which took him to his train. He was beyond doubt very pleased with the day and parted from us with the warm exhortation "to keep up the good fight."

Lewis was especially cordial with Mortimer, smiling and covering their handclasp with his other hand. I remembered that smile when reading his speech the next day and noted its reference to the former miners in the ranks of the auto workers. "As a result of their previous training and experience, I hope that they may be of service to you," he had said, and I could not avoid thinking that he had Mortimer in mind when making that remark.

● ● ●

The announcement of the UAW's South Bend Convention came right after the Lewis meeting, hence most of us linked the two events, attributing the Executive Council's long-delayed acquiescence to their fear of the growing activities of the CIO among mass production workers.

Some UAW activists took the Executive Council announcement as a signal to start the scramble for International posts. Homer Martin, who should have felt assured of his choice as president, was one of the most animated of the politickers. In fact, we heard that there had been a get-together of out-of-towners at Martin's hotel during the afternoon of Lewis's visit when the entire Cleveland group was in Akron.

We were perturbed when we heard of this meeting, which Martin had arranged under our very noses. He had come to Cleveland several weeks before, on the invitation of the White Motors local, which had asked the Detroit office if he could officiate at the presentation of their new International charter. Martin had to be reached in Kansas City because Francis Dillon had not permitted him to establish his office in Detroit, we would learn later.

We were surprised when Martin remained in Cleveland after the presentation. It was clear that he had no other assignment but we were content to have him and did whatever we could to make him feel at home. We all realized that we would have to live with the man eventually and considered it a good occasion to get to know him better. I saw quite a lot of Martin during those weeks, accompanying him in his car during his visits to the various locals when he spoke at their Friday night meetings.

Martin kept showing us his brightest side. One evening, after he, Dorothy, and I had dinner at the Mortimers, he sat at the wheel of his car for some time before switching on the motor. "You know," he said finally, "I just love that man!" Not long after that, he confided to me his determination to support Mortimer for the vice-presidency. "If I'm elected president," he said hesitantly as though the eventuality still seemed unrealistic to him, "I've got to have Mort with me. I just couldn't do without him."

Something soon happened, however, that made Martin change his mind. Ed Hall, his fellow officer, had a big row with Dillon. At first it was hard for us to believe that it was a real brawl since the two men had been linked so intimately at the Detroit Convention but soon enough we realized that the dispute was serious.

I did not get the full explanation of what had taken place until much later. When, several weeks after the convention, Hall asked Dillon to set the date that he could come to Detroit and get to work, Dillon told him to remain in Wisconsin; he was sure that Hall would be happier there. How could the secretary-treasurer of the UAW function away from Detroit? Hall asked. "Oh, don't worry about that," Dillon replied, "I can handle both jobs myself."

Dillon told Homer Martin pretty much the same thing, as I had learned from Martin himself, who had accepted the news without complaint apparently. He seemed to have nothing else to do but wait for his checks to arrive in Kansas City. "They were always weeks late," he assured me, "till my family was in need and my coat was so torn," he added in his imaginative way, "it was half falling off my back."

But that was not Ed Hall's way of solving the imposed dilemma. After taking a couple of pleasant weeks to arrange his affairs, he came to Detroit without saying a word to anyone, found an apartment, then telephoned his wife and told her to hire a moving van to pack and truck their things. It was only when they were installed that he appeared at the International office and announced himself to Dillon, who told him to turn right around and go home. "Listen, Brother," Hall replied, "I'm here because the UAW constitution says that's where I'm supposed to be and I'm not taking any contrary orders from you or anybody else. I want to remind you that you and me both were appointed to office by President Green and I intend to act accordingly."

The office relationship, thus inauspiciously begun, never prospered. Hall literally had to fight for every square foot of space, every piece of furniture or equipment, every chore that was properly the secretary-treasurer's. By good fortune, Dillon's office manager, Mrs. Collyer, was tired of his abusive ways and cooperated quietly with Hall.

The blow-up came over a strike at the Walker-Ajax Company, located in Racine in Hall's own state of Wisconsin. He was fully informed about the strike, which had been going on since September. Dillon had authorized it while Hall was still there, but soon after Hall came to Detroit, Dillon decided without consultation that the strike had to be called off. The decision came just as the company had begun to show signs of weakness, Hall said, even making plans to move out of town. But the mayor of Racine assured the union that he would give them police protection if they tried to prevent this. The state administration, too, had been fully cooperative and supplied strikers with relief from the outset of the strike.

Not long after establishing himself in Detroit, Hall learned from Mrs. Collyer that Dillon was going to Racine. Hall telephoned union headquarters there and told the men to sit tight until he himself arrived. When he blew in on Dillon at his hotel room the following day, it took the burly man some time to recover his self-composure and to announce that the strike was over.

"I've settled it," he said.

"What did you get?" Hall asked innocently.

"The company agreed to take all strikers back without discrimination."

The strike had been precipitated over four company-minded men who refused to join the union but the local had added some other demands, none of which were mentioned in the settlement, Dillon admitted.

"The thing is, we want the strike settled," he said. "You've got to go in there tomorrow and tell the men to go back to work."

"If that's all the company is offering, I'll be damned if I do!" Hall replied.

"Then you'll be fired!"

Hall let out a horselaugh.

Amazingly, when Dillon came out of his conference with Walker, the company's head, the following day, he had a completely new agreement containing most of the other points that the union had demanded. Dillon was puffed up with pride and invited Walker to attend the local meeting with him.

The crowd was noisy and insulting, shouting wisecracks that they directed equally between Dillon and Walker. The settlement itself was deemed satisfactory but when Dillon asked for the vote, the strikers demanded that Ed Hall be allowed to speak first. Dillon had to agree to this in the end.

Hall started by explaining that he was not opposed to the settlement but wanted to tell a few facts about how it was obtained. And he laid it all out for them. The crowd bellowed and stomped in fury. Dillon was lucky to get out of town with a whole skin, Hall said.

• • •

The two officers' relationship with the UAW president grew steadily worse. Ed Hall convinced Martin that they ought to go down to Miami and put the facts of their conflict with Dillon before the Executive Council. They could make a strong argument for the council to hasten its decision to terminate the "probationary period" and give Dillon the boot. "The Council had better come across," Hall blustered, "or goddam it, we'll just call a convention of our own. We've got every important local in the country with us, so how can we lose?"

It was a lot of bravado, they both knew, as they thought of facing some of the redoubtable characters on the Executive Council. Then, suddenly, it occurred to Hall and Martin to invite Mortimer to go to Miami with them. He could speak on behalf of the Committee of Seven.

There had been rumors about trouble in the Detroit office but Mortimer had no idea of how bad things really were until he heard the facts from Hall and Martin. The idea of going to Miami to put a fire under the Executive Council sounded reasonable. In fact, the suggestion that Mortimer should make the trip had already been made at the Auto Council. His consent to accompany the officers would now make it unanimous in favor of the new convention. However, the three men were not vouchsafed a meeting with the council though they were able to talk to President Green. He told them that he had been given the power to call the convention "not later than April 30."

Hall and Martin were out of control after that. They both felt that they had to make a big splash to draw attention to themselves. Hall in particular knew that he had to remake his reputation after being involved in saving Dillon's skin at the Detroit Convention. A golden opportunity presented itself at that very moment, that of intervening in a blusterous squabble that Dillon had started with the big Toledo local.

The contention concerned the local's charter.[6] Some weeks earlier, the Detroit office had begun sending out new International charters to all units. Toledo received nothing but a letter bearing a special notice to the effect that it would henceforth be "the adopted policy of the International" to issue charters only to single plants. Toledo's amalgamated local had no fewer than thirteen factories under its aegis, eleven of which held individual contracts with their managements. The local felt strongly attached to this form of organization, attributing much of its remarkable success to the cohesion it had attained through it. Hence, it refused point-blank to be divided. When Dillon issued a time-setting ultimatum, the local voted to withhold its per-capita tax.

Dillon then agreed to grant the local a single charter for sixty days to give the various units time to set up their separate organizations. The local insisted on a full charter without any strings. Several of the companies began taking advantage of the union quarrel, alleging legal obstacles to the renewal of their contracts and even using the dispute as an excuse for refusing to conduct collective bargaining. At this stage a serious situation involving the Chevrolet unit occurred that further weakened the local's position.

The Chevy group had wanted to sever its link with the big local for a long time but its leaders were reluctant to do so just when the local was in trouble. But a new situation arose at the change of models in November that made matters urgent. The unhappy truth was that the militant Chevrolet men had allowed themselves to fall into a company trap. Their relations with the management after their strike had been impeccable for six months, so when Alfred Gulliver, the plant manager, told them before the autumn layoff that the new model would require some "readjustments" in the equipment, the union leaders took him at his word. "The company will hire as many men as before," he assured them.

The old machines were moved out and new ones brought in. No one paid any attention to them until the factory reopened and it was discovered that the new machines were mainly repairing facilities. When work started up again, hardly one-third of the original 2,361 workers were rehired. When he was reminded of his promise, Gulliver responded gleefully: "Yes, but I didn't tell you *where* they would be hired!" The men were to be rehired at Muncie and Saginaw, where the Toledo machinery had been shifted. These were non-union plants, where rates were as low as half of those prevailing at Toledo.

It was a cruel, hard winter that the Chevy workers lived through that year.[7] This was the case for workers who had been kept on as well as those who had been discharged since these loyal union men decided to share the work "in order to keep the union intact." Their slogan was "Everybody works or nobody works!" Without complaint, my Chevy friends told me all about the hardships that this remarkable group voluntarily assumed in carrying out their pledge. But the union was preserved and served as one of the big drive's most dynamic forces, making its greatest contribution to the Flint sitdown of January 1937.

Francis Dillon made a virtue of the Chevrolet group's necessitous circumstances by granting it a separate charter, as Local 14. Having set this precedent, he refused to make further concessions to the big Toledo local. Ed Hall eagerly stepped into the situation. "The UAW constitution gives the secretary-treasurer the power to issue charters," he told William E. Siefke, the secretary of that local. "I'm preparing yours and you can come in and get it when it's ready."

But Dillon got word about the arrangement and broke into Hall's office at night and stole the charter. Whereupon Hall ordered Mrs. Collyer to prepare another. Dillon fired her for insubordination and Hall rehired her immediately. When the new charter was ready, Hall turned it over to Homer Martin and informed the Toledo local that he would bring it to them in person and would take care of the presentation ceremonies as well. Martin made a rip-roaring speech from all reports but he also said some imprudent things. "Auto workers throughout the country have repudiated Dillon," he declared. "We have taken over control of the International office."

The two officers' reckless words and actions, brought to our attention from several sources, seriously troubled us. Although the *United Auto Worker* firmly defended the right of the Toledo local to have its charter, we felt that Hall and Martin were taking unnecessary risks that involved the whole union at a time when discretion would be in order. What would prevent President Green, if he was looking for an excuse, from suspending the two officers for irresponsibility and even putting off the convention? There was probably only one circumstance that was working for us, the incredible ineptitude of Green's top appointee, Francis Dillon.

Green called the three men to Washington, where a truce was compacted with all belligerents in effect holding one hand concealed behind their backs. "I'll agree to go back and tend to my business," Hall blustered, "but only with one understanding. The first time Dillon sticks his head in my door, I'll blow his goddam brains out!" Hall recounted his own story some time later, so linguistic embellishment was to be expected. I knew, however, that when I worked for the International he did keep a gun in his desk; so did Homer Martin, for that matter. A permanent padlock was put on the communicating door between the two offices after the men returned from Washington and things continued in that manner until the South Bend Convention.

• • •

The election campaign had begun heating up for that long-awaited event. Mortimer lead the race for vice president. Toledo Chevrolet had even expressed its preference for him as president. In fact, Adolph Germer, who had acquired considerable prestige in the UAW by this time, also inclined toward Mortimer for the post, perhaps reflecting John L. Lewis's viewpoint. But few insiders felt that Mortimer could swing any of the big conservative locals like Toledo, Studebaker, Bendix, Seaman Body, or even Norwood, where we had recently discovered a group of pro-company elements among our former friends.[8]

Several weeks before the convention, a caucus was held in South Bend to address some of these issues. It was called by the Committee of Seven and was attended by a mass of representatives from as many as a hundred locals. It could have passed for the convention itself. Something approximating a platform was adopted at the caucus, as presented by Mortimer in the name of the Committee of Seven. Some of the planks had already been popularized over the past two years by the Cleveland-based rank-and-file movement and the *United Auto Worker.*

1. A great organizational drive centered on Michigan and concentrated in General Motors.
2. An International based on industrial unionism, continuing the fight for an unrestricted charter while functioning as though we had one.
3. Trade union democracy, to be established through constitutional changes and expressed in the phrase "Take power from the president and give it to the executive board."
4. Unity with the independents, for one all-inclusive union in the auto industry.
5. A labor party, or "independent political action," as some preferred to call it.

There was a strong sense of purpose at the caucus. Still, there was also a good deal of politicking going on, which was to be expected. The caucus found a sensible consensus in the contest for the vice-presidency by endorsing the proposal for three vice presidents without getting embroiled in designating specific candidates. But this did not prevent some pernicious rumor-mongering, of which, as it happened, Mortimer was the chief butt. It was no surprise that red-baiting was its medium and no doubt that Homer Martin, operating through several of his supporters, was the secret fomenter of this nastiness, the prime agitator being Elmer Davis. Why this devious person should have thought it necessary to slander Mortimer in order to foster Martin's candidacy was something that neither Mortimer nor I could comprehend at the time.

Homer Martin's overt attitude toward me, or, more precisely, toward the *United Auto Worker,* left nothing to be desired in the period before the South Bend Convention. He got the Kansas City and St. Louis locals from his district to order bundles and to send in reports (on my request) of their activities, which I published. He even cited the paper in his vice-presidential report to the convention. But these gestures were likewise imbued with hypocrisy; I learned later that he was simultaneously dickering with other people about taking over the editorship of an International organ, as well as with printers in several cities to assume its publication.[9]

One or another of these plans would probably have succeeded were it not for one simple fact about which I myself was not fully aware: the great popularity that the *United Auto Worker* had acquired which peaked during the last months before South Bend. The list of locals that sponsored the paper that was printed at the top of page 1 gives a certain evidence of this. The number rose issue by issue, from nine, to thirteen, to eighteen, to twenty-four, and finally to twenty-eight for the pre-convention issue, as high as 90 percent of the union's membership. The circulation rose to thirty thousand for that edition.

Somehow, I took Ed Hall's praise of the paper more seriously than I did Homer Martin's, no doubt because I felt more assured of Hall's sincerity. In a speech he made at a Cleveland rally just before South Bend, he caught me by surprise by complimenting our "little paper for establishing some semblance of contact among the locals." He told of a contrary case of a small union twenty-five miles from Milwaukee that had been wiped out by a strike without anyone in the UAW ever hearing about it because of the lack of a "little paper" like ours.

Dillon himself showed how much the existence of our "little paper" galled him in a letter of March 11, 1936, addressed to members of the lame-duck International executive board.[10] It is pertinent to quote the letter because it anticipated an important incident of the South Bend Convention:

> I enclose herewith a copy of a publication entitled "United Auto Worker" which has just this day come into my possession.[11] It is my desire that you read the articles contained therein in their entirety, giving special attention to the one titled "Toledo Union Granted Charter."
>
> This paper, in my judgment, gives expression to a philosophy and ideas which render difficult if not impossible the proper operation and development of our Union. Everything is criticism, ridicule and the cultivation of suspicion and distrust of one another. There is nothing constructive and no expressed disposition to cooperate and assist in the development and maintenance of our general organization.

Nonetheless, Dillon must have felt insecure in the Toledo charter affair since he admitted in his letter that he was preparing "a detailed and complete report" on the subject for submission to the convention. Alas, it would come too late to do Dillon any good.

The South Bend Convention: The UAW Takes Full Control 10

Everyone was taken by surprise, including Francis Dillon, I was convinced, when, on the first day of the convention, President William Green announced the termination of the probationary period of the International Union and suggested that the election of officers take place immediately.[1] The "anti's" had expected to have to fight on this issue because they had no intention of abiding Dillon as chair of the assembly for any length of time if they could help it. Too many important things had to be disposed of and they wanted to be free of his disruptive tactics. Or, more frankly, they simply did not want him around.

Yet the burly man seemed to take his effacement with resignation. He sang a swan song of untypical good humor: "This morning I am placed in a rather unique position for I am a citizen of the great state of Indiana and on my way through the city from Detroit to my home, I knew that you would all be happy to have me stop here and say a few words of welcome to you also." Laughter turned into loud hand-clapping as he added: "I think I should not say in your presence that under no circumstances would I consent to be a candidate for any office within the gift of the United Automobile Workers of America."[2]

But that was as far as it went on either side. One had but to glance at Dillon's fifty-page *Report* to be reminded of the profound chasm between us that only a moment of impressionability had bridged. He actually thought that this stored wisdom would influence the delegates' thinking and even offered them extra copies of the report to take home. But that was not all Dillon left behind. While remaining in South Bend for several more days, ensconced in his hotel room, he sought to influence the course of the convention through a handful of his supporters, men so thoroughly repudiated for the most part that any position that they took on a subject acted as a negative barometer to the majority.

Their inept efforts caused irritation or anger and also mirth. The delegates roared when huge Roderick MacDonald, trying to present a credible image of his "hard-working" chief, said, "Here is a man I know, Francis J. Dillon, that lived like a goldfish in a goldfish bowl."[3] Final judgment on the man came when the committee on officers' reports recommended that his magnum opus be "filed." Al Cook, one of his stalwarts in Flint, begged for a touch of consideration.

> Delegate Cook: If there is no objection on the part of the committee, Mr. President, I wish to add . . . that it was *"accepted"* and filed.
> President Martin: Does that meet with the approval of the committee?
> Committee Chairman Richardson: No.
> The report of the committee was unanimously adopted.[4]

There were, however, two or three more reputable men who were adherents of the retiring official. One of them, Russell Merrill, I found difficult to fathom. The recent junction of his company, Studebaker, with White Motors had given Dick Reisinger the idea of inviting Merrill to speak at a local meeting. His speech was excellent; Merrill surprised us with a detailed report of his local's aggressive policies, especially with its support for a Farmer-Labor party. Reisinger's purpose was to talk convention politics with him, particularly to woo Merrill's support for the proposal of three vice presidents in the International, as well as to accept being on a slate with Mortimer. But Merrill had replied to all of this with a frozen smile.

His loyalty to Dillon was possibly bolstered by a tragic personal event. Shortly after Merrill's visit to White Motors, his family was in a terrible automobile accident in which his wife was killed. He came to the convention from his hospital bed, on crutches, his arm in a plaster cast, and accompanied by a solicitous retinue of followers.

His opposition to the three vice presidents, we finally realized, had no other objective than to retain the AFL's hold on the UAW. His plan for accomplishing this appears in the resolution the Studebaker local had submitted, outlining the manner in which the convention should proceed.[5] It was a strange subject for a resolution. In it, the local "respectfully requested" that Green allow the first day to be given over to speeches, that on the second day, as soon as the assembly convened, he was to terminate the probationary period and "immediately following," a "special order of business" was to be declared for the nomination, election, and installation of officers.

Evidently, some snag forced a change in this neat plan. At any event, our side would have been too alert to fall into this trap. We were, of course, glad that the union should be freed so expeditiously of Dillon's heavy hand. But we very well knew that that was only the beginning. After Homer Martin was unanimously chosen chairman of the convention, delegates settled down to business, which meant taking care of a few highly essential details preparatory to the election of officers.[6]

First came the report of the credentials committee. Everyone knew about one hot issue it would present, that involving the seating and voting strength of the big Toledo union, Local 12. Like all the convention committees, the credentials committee had been designated by Dillon and followed his line on this prickly issue, as he had explained it in twenty pages of his report.[7] The committee proposed that the local's voting strength be based on per-capita tax payments of the past six months, as was the case of all other locals. But Toledo had refused to pay its per capita for half of that time after learning of Dillon's attempt to split it into ten locals for the obvious purpose of undermining its strength.[8] The missed per-capita payments would average the vote down to only half the local's actual importance.

Progressives and other anti-Dillonites had decided to disregard the technicalities of the case and give Toledo its full vote without delay. This action would be taken on the minority report of Bob Travis, a member of the credentials committee, whom Dillon had put there in the expectation that he could count on the hostility of the Chevrolet unit (that Travis headed) to the big Toledo local, to which it had formerly belonged. He was mistaken. After several attempts to skewer Travis's report had failed, it was adopted.[9] A spontaneous demonstration broke out as the full Toledo 12 delegation took their seats and progressives saw the victory as a promising harbinger of the course that the rest of the convention would take.

It was hardly matter-of-course, however. The vote on the three vice presidents, which came up soon after, saw a number of shifts in the lineup of forces. The issue had been much discussed before the convention, but no particular argument had proved completely convincing. The most persuasive one urged was that of giving representation to the most prominent groups in the organization, which would lend it cohesion and balance.

It had been hoped that a slate could be arranged that would win universal support. Together with Homer Martin and George Addes, who had been linked since the Detroit Convention, three other outstanding men with the most important followings—Wyndham Mortimer, Ed Hall, and Russell Merrill—seemed to round out the group that was needed for a satisfactory joint leadership. But Merrill's refusal to go along wrecked this accommodation. The reason for his obstinacy was only a short-lived mystery, however, which subsequent events dispelled.

It was the AFL's viewpoint that swayed Merrill's thinking, its basic motive being to keep Mortimer out of office. If that could not be accomplished by defeating the proposal for the three vice presidents, then it would be done by running their strongest man—Merrill—against him. Thus the two goals were interchangeable, and both were directed against the same person, whom the Federation felt it must at all odds keep out of the top UAW leadership.

What surprised me most about this whole strategy was Merrill's docile role in it. I had come to think of him as very intelligent though, admittedly, I had little to go by in support of this opinion. My disillusionment in him for involving himself in this imbroglio was no doubt due to the poor view I had of the AFL crowd with whom he was voluntarily associated though I should have realized that Merrill could hardly be blamed for all their imbecilities. One of their stupidest brainstorms was a letter purportedly written by communists that was mailed to all delegates and had been put into their hotel boxes.[10] The names of the delegates, it was clearly evident, could only have been supplied from the AFL office before the convention's daily *Proceedings* had published them.

The arguments of the letter were revelatory of the Federation's thinking at its most simplistic level. In it, the communists allegedly hailed the "radical change" in the organization that could be expected in the way strikes would be increasingly conducted by certain candidates for International office:

> These strikes are not to be fooled with. They must be called often and handled with enough courage to let the bosses know we mean business. The man we have in mind to handle such situations is Bro. Homer Martin. . . . He is our choice for our International president. . . . Bro. Wyndham Mortimer of Cleveland is our choice for vice president. He has been active in our movement for many years and has our utmost confidence. . . . With those two men there can be but one thing happen, that is, a close knit organization that will enforce the demands of the workers thru the only medium the bosses know—STRIKE!"

Homer Martin handled the matter adeptly: "I recall an old scriptural saying that reads: 'They fear the light because their deeds are evil.'" Then he told of the wire that he had received from Earl Browder, national secretary of the Communist party, who identified the letter as an obvious forgery as it bore no return address, signature, or name of a responsible committee. The wire made a categorical denial: "OUR PARTY HAS TAKEN NO STAND ON QUESTION OFFICERS YOUR UNION."

• • •

We were by no means certain about how the vote would go on the question of the three vice presidents. Only Ohio (Toledo and Cleveland) gave it their solid support, while South Bend seemed just as strongly against it. Ed Hall's Wisconsin group was split on the issue, with Racine and even Kenosha (now controlled by a Dillonite), except for three delegates, voting in the opposition camp.[11] Kenosha was a painful surprise to us because it had been solidly anti-Dillon during the Detroit Convention.

Forrest G. Woods of Studebaker was the most impressive speaker on the "anti" side. "My contention is," he began in his legalistic manner, "that [considering] the financial state of our union . . . we cannot stand the drain." Then he added, more effectively, that he was opposed to the attempt "to place favorite sons in salary-paying positions." Russell Merrill found a more graphic way of saying the same thing—"Do we have to give a piece of cake to [every] section of the country so that [we] might have harmony?"—and replied with biting sarcasm, confirming the split between his erstwhile protégé Homer Martin and himself: "Our industry has not been organized in the last six months as it should have been organized. Whose fault is it? Is it because we didn't have five officers? If three officers can tear down an organization as they've done since the Detroit Convention, put five in there and you won't have any organization left next year!"[12]

The big guns of our own side were silent until Ed Hall took over, Mortimer evidently feeling too sensitive to speak where self-interest was involved. He got the floor just to pass the ball over to Dick Reisinger, who invoked the harmony that the spread of leadership would bring as well as the prestige that the title of vice president would give to a man in dealing with management.[13]

It was during this discussion that Walter Reuther spoke for the first time at a UAW assembly. His name had already become known to the delegates because his right to represent the Ternstedt local had been challenged before the credentials committee: "Never employed in the Ternstedt plant since this [International] was established." However, the decision was favorable: "Your committee has conducted a hearing and determined from Brother Reuther's testimony, corroborated by that of Sister Tombor . . . that he had worked in the Ternstedt plant under an assumed name during. . . . December 1935 and January 1936 and that he is therefore eligible in our International [convention]."[14]

Shortly after ridding himself of this snag, Reuther spoke on the five-officers issue. "Brother Woods," he said, "has talked about economy. It seems his big mistake was that he tried to judge the future by the past. What we have to do is to try to judge the future by the *possibilities!* [the emphasis is in my memory]. If you vote for five officers you vote for the thing that will make it possible to weld us into a powerful militant International Union."

Mortimer in the *United Auto Worker* and in *Kenosha Labor* had taken up the officers' issue as a budgetary matter. The union would not lose by adding two officers, he pointed out, because the progressives were proposing that all officers' salaries should be cut to $3,000, for a total of $15,000.

Under the AFL-Dillon arrangement, the three men had been paid $15,500. Ed Hall used these statistics to make an impassioned workingman's speech that brought continued bursts of approval. "I am an auto worker," he said in his gravelly voice, "and I was making 85 cents an hour when President Green took me out of my job and gave me eighty-six dollars and fifty cents a week. Who am I that I should receive eighty-six dollars and fifty cents a week?" he demanded angrily. "It's ridiculous! I've told every man I've talked to that I would gladly split my salary to put another man on the job who could help organize the auto workers."[15]

It seemed to me that the "pro" speakers had made a much better impression than the anti's but it was impossible to figure out the vote from that circumstance alone. Locals did not vote as individuals on such matters, but there were many imponderables nevertheless that resulted in split delegations that one could not know about. Even if the resolution passed by a safe majority, the hurdle of the elections still had to be achieved. To us, this was a matter of utmost importance because the progressives' influence on the future course of the union was at stake. It was true that at Detroit we would have been delighted with far less but things had evolved enormously since the Detroit Convention.

Before the balloting began, a last-ditch attempt by the anti's to amend the motion for the three vice presidents was defeated by a much bigger margin than any of us expected, 143.54 to 89.18.[16] Yet the resulting tonic feeling was fragile. Homer Martin was elected president without opposition and the nominations that followed immediately for first vice president brought me new perturbations.

Mortimer, Merrill, and Carl Shipley of the Bendix local were named in quick succession and though the third nomination was a surprise, I found nothing in it to worry about. Such was not the case with another nomination, however, that of Ed Hall, who was proposed by a Cleveland man, Frank Scheepers of Elmer Davis's local. We were well aware by this time of Davis's duplicity, but the move struck me nonetheless as sinister. My eyes went swiftly to Hall and I literally held my breath as he calmly rose— and declined the nomination.

In itself, this gave no absolute assurance about how Hall's Seaman Body delegation would vote but it did to me. All of a sudden everything shifted back to normal and the roll-call ballot turned out better than we could have hoped.[17] Mortimer took 60 percent of the vote, winning not only the entire Seaman Body delegation but also several others of which we had not been sure. A number of additional locals unexpectedly supported him, including several from Detroit and even the treacherous Elmer Davis himself.[18] Closer analysis would verify the fact that most of his surprise supporters were brought into Mortimer's column by Hall. Our people did very well by him too for the second vice presidency. But it struck me as more meritorious for Hall to win over the hard-heads of the Seaman local or conservatives like Jack Kennedy of the Detroit Chrysler unit than for us to hold progressives in line once they were convinced.

Significantly, all three races for the vice-presidencies were personal defeats for Merrill. He not only lost his own contest but his candidate against Hall, John Milkent of Kenosha, was also overwhelmed by a three-to-one vote (179.7 to 59.48), while Alton Green, a Studebaker man, lost 134.4 to 95.7 to Walter N. Wells, president of a small Detroit local, Detroit Gear. Wells had been put on our anti-Dillon slate as a substitute for the defaulting Russell Merrill. He actually was a more representative candidate than Merrill would have been despite the much bigger formal vote that the latter carried, for Wells's election gave Michigan a place among the five top offices of the International.

• • •

If one were limited to the *Proceedings,* one might be apt to miss the true ebullience of the South Bend Convention. Enlightened measures were often little more than listed after having been adopted without discussion because everyone took them for granted. This was the case with the resolution for the Farmer-Labor party, for example. In the contrary sense, important decisions were sometimes masked as negative triumphs, whereas they were defeats of retrogressive measures that might have hampered the free development of the union. The most dangerous of these was a resolution "that the International Union notify all its affiliate locals to immediately expel from its membership all known communists."[19]

This rabid proposal was a particularly bitter pill for most delegates of the Cleveland group to swallow. It was presented by one of our locals, Baker Raulang, a further proof of the reactionary trend of my former friend Elmer Davis. Yet it enlisted several important supporters, who considered it advisable, however, to soften the brutality of its provisions. Russell Merrill, for example, offered a substitute that became the subject of debate: "that no known communist be permitted to hold office in the International Union or in any local union nor be a delegate to any convention."

What was amazing about the supportive discussion was its almost juvenile character. Even so important a person as F. J. Michel of Racine had nothing better to offer than an ancient AFL bromide: "I have always known since the start of our organization that communism was here to wreck the labor movement."[20] And the scholarly Forrest G. Woods followed with "documentary" proof of this claim, citing a recent congress held "in Russia" of the "Third Internationale" [sic], which "formulated policies to be followed out by communists throughout the world."[21]

In a typical intimidating gesture, Woods asked for a roll-call vote on the resolution. But the "red" issue had become so timeworn in the auto union that the average progressive no longer felt apologetic on the subject, which a year earlier would have been thought to be dictated by self-defense.[22] Ben Bonner of Toledo-Chevrolet promptly asked the speaker through the chair "if he has any real authoritative information on that or if he is quoting [William Randolph] Hearst or somebody like that." Woods replied sternly that he was quoting from the *Daily Worker,* "though I do not have the paper here."[23] This ended the polemic in favor of the resolution and opened the field to the large number of those who spoke against it, most of whom identified themselves as noncommunists or even anticommunists. One of the first was Eldon Matthews of the South Bend Bantam local, who had supported Merrill for vice president.

> We had a little squabble out here at Bendix and our honorable mayor said: "Throw out the communists and we will deal with you." We had one man who was a communist but there never was a labor man who was more conscientious. We did not throw him out. On his own initiative . . . he resigned. The same honorable mayor . . . what did he do? . . . He had the police force lead in the strikebreakers. [Suddenly he choked up and could not go on for a while.] I can not express in words what I want to say because it burns me up so darn bad to hear this [talk]. . . . I have lost two or three jobs through being branded as a communist. I am not a communist but about one more job and I'll be damn good communist.[24]

This was a common experience, as Jack Thompson of the big Toledo local remembered when telling of the famous Auto-Lite strike of 1934. "We had a bunch of workers who came down here and helped us out in our strike and the first thing they had in the papers was: 'There are communists in town.'. . . I am a good American citizen. I answered the call of my country and I will again if necessary and if you want to call those men communists then you can title me a communist as well."[25]

Bob Travis reported a surprising position that the UMW had taken on a similar resolution at its recent convention. "You all know how violently opposed John L. Lewis is to communism. However he advocated nonconcurrence . . . due to the fact that it would place in the hands . . . of the coal operator another weapon to be used against labor."[26]

A number of speakers warned against a witch hunt if the resolution were adopted. Ed Simpson said: "If we . . . go around to find known communists, we might just as well forget about a campaign to organize the unorganized."[27] Henry Mack told of resigning the chairmanship of his local's educational committee "when reactionaries . . . went around spreading the word that [he] was teaching communism" while leading a discussion class that was based on an International pamphlet on shop stewards.[28] That was the way it went, on and on. I had not been aware of how current this topic was or how enlightened so many auto workers were about it though it is possible that their tongues were loosened by the freeness of the discussion.

Members of the Merrill-Michel group seemed to weaken in their resolve to brand and weed out communists as a result of the debate.[29] Delegate Ralston of Studebaker wanted to blot all mention of it from the record and the defeated candidate John Milkent called for the reduction of the whole thing to one simple "resolved" in the original resolution: "That the United Automobile Workers of America go on record against communism."[30] That meant that anyone could read any meaning into the resolution that he or she wished. Finally, Forrest Woods proposed a way out that was accepted since, as he explained, you had to say *something* to keep Hearst from yapping since the subject of communism had been raised: "That this International Union . . . hereby express our unalterable opposition to Fascism, Nazism and Communism and all other movements intended to distract the attention of the labor movement from the primary objectives of unionism."[31] The statement was adopted without expressed opposition.

• • •

The convention sessions were to take on a more positive character thereafter, which was the way the delegates were to remember the gathering. For two days visiting speakers from allied organizations opened delegates' eyes to the broad new movement they were entering. Most important were the representatives from several of the powerful CIO unions that had pledged help with the great organizational tasks. These speakers were nothing like the burly old AFL piecards whom they had often come to know in their own localities. Two representatives, Rose Pesotta and Powers Hapgood, were already engaged in organizational work for the CIO, both having participated in the recent Goodyear strike at Akron.

Although she had been active in the International Ladies Garment Workers Union (ILGWU) for two decades and was one of its vice presidents, Pesotta looked very young. She surprised us all by referring back to the discussion on communism, giving it an unexpected turn in warning the delegates not to ignore a much more serious "ism"—fascism—that had infected a great local of her organization in which many Italians were members.[32]

There were a number of other representatives from the industrial unions at the convention who seemed to give it a definite CIO character. Some of the more conservative delegates grew concerned about this and the CIO leaders themselves cautioned the more effusive individuals among our people against assuming an antagonistic stance toward the AFL. Even the Executive Council's restrictive jurisdictional rule was allowed to stand, with the tacit understanding that each local would work "between the limitations" while the International's officers continued efforts to change them.[33]

A dramatic demonstration of the desire for a harmonious relationship with the Federation came in the form of an outraged reaction to a banner headline in the Hearst-owned *Chicago Herald-Examiner* on Tuesday, April 28: "Forty Thousand Auto Workers Quit Labor Federation—Green Appointee Out as President." Walter Reuther seized on the occasion to make a big play at the convention in a well worked-out gesture that was a howling success. He picked a moment of pause in activity to go running down the middle aisle, holding the paper high above his head. Homer Martin adeptly stepped away from the microphone and Reuther gave a scorching talk, ending in a motion that all delegates put across a boycott of the Hearst papers published in their own areas.

There were shouts of angry approval and Forrest Woods offered an amendment that the Hearst reporter be "debarred from the convention hall," which raised the agitation a couple of notches. But the newspaperman could not be found, which gave Reuther a chance to counsel a wiser course of action. "I don't think this body should go on record opposing the reporter: he has to work for a living. The story in the paper is okay. The headline was prepared by the editorial bigshots in Chicago. There is one thing that we can do here however, we should work on this reporter to get him to join the Newspaper Guild."[34]

Although he was new to the union, Walter Reuther was to become one of the best-known delegates at the convention. He often took the floor on key issues, showing a surprising grasp of things for a novice. His personal initiative, together with the backing of progressives in the Michigan delegation, resulted in his election as one of the four executive board members from that state. But Reuther continued to be harassed throughout the convention by Dillonites and other reactionaries. A motion, made after his election, that he be investigated was defeated.[35] And President Martin told the convention near adjournment time that he himself had made "a very careful investigation of the facts" and had concluded that Reuther "stands clear in his records as an automobile worker, as a delegate and as a qualified officer of the International."[36] Yet that was not the end of the matter.

• • •

Second in interest only to the presence of the CIO representatives at the convention was that of the fraternal delegates from the three independent auto unions (AIWA, MESA, and AAWA).[37] Dick Frankensteen represented the AIWA and Art Greer represented the AAWA. But since Matt Smith, its general secretary, had refused to appear for the MESA, its Detroit district

committee sent John Anderson to take his place. For us, Anderson represented the most important segment of that body's membership, the tool-and-die
workers. Smith had demanded jurisdictional assurances from the UAW before opening discussions with it, which he must have known the UAW could
not grant.

John Anderson gave a lively account of the MESA in his talk.[38] Early in
1935, he said, the MESA had two thousand tool-and-die workers at Ford
who tried to negotiate with the company. But Ford had put them all into one
building and simply locked them out. "We were not strong enough to fight
that battle alone," he concluded, ending in a surge of conviction that carried
his audience with him: "If I was a guy that talked about God a great deal, I
would say: 'I hope to God when I come back next year, it is not as an independent trade unionist but as a delegate from the American Federation of
Labor in the auto industry with better than 100,000 membership.'"

Art Greer's attachment of his AAWA to the UAW had no obstacles to
overcome from his docile members, who were mainly concentrated in the
Hudson plant.[39] Nevertheless, in his speech I was struck by a certain discomfort in the man as well as by the fatuity of his words. He sounded like a
collegian (he must have been in his fifties) talking at a national gathering of
his fraternity: "I don't know how to express myself but I really am just bub-
bling over. . . . I can go back [to my people] and tell them that the spirit of
fraternity and democracy just fairly oozed from this convention." I could
understand the man's uneasiness several months later when he was exposed
as a Pinkerton agent. His new role must have created demands that were
hard for the elderly spy to fill.

The most important of the three independents was undoubtedly the
AIWA, which was concentrated in the Chrysler plants of Detroit, where the
UAW had practically no membership. A serious handicap, however, was
Father Coughlin's association with the group, which Frankensteen tried to
play down because he was aware of the antagonism that both the AFL and
CIO had expressed toward the radio priest. But he was pleased to discover
that Homer Martin felt differently about Coughlin, eagerly accepting Fran-
kensteen's suggestion that he be invited to speak at the convention.[40]

Coughlin, supposedly, was in South Bend "by coincidence" and Frankensteen arranged a "secret" meeting between the priest, himself, and Homer Martin, probably at Coughlin's hotel.[41] Shortly thereafter, Martin told
Mortimer that he was thinking of inviting the priest to speak at the convention. Mortimer protested vigorously and I believe he also got Ed Hall and
several of the CIO representatives to add their vetoes. So Coughlin had to
content himself with appearing at the smoker that the South Bend program
committee had organized for male delegates.

I was among those who boycotted the party but news reports quoted quite a bit of Coughlin's speech, indicating that Frankensteen had also arranged for reporters to be admitted to the smoker. Coughlin had evidently been asked to bear heavily on the amalgamation question, for he is quoted as saying "Away with the independent unions!" and the like. Having no doubt read in the papers about the debate over communism at the sessions, he observed that it was the fault of "lousy capitalism" that communism existed at all in this country, adding a slick wisecrack that brought laughter and applause: "Still I would rather be a lamp-post in South Bend than a commissar in Moscow!"

Although I had reservations about Frankensteen, like everyone else at the convention I fell under the charm of his geniality. He was tall and heavyset though more muscular than stout, a vestige of the athletic career that a decade earlier had made him one of Detroit's most famous scholastic heroes. The depression, fighting the speedup at the Dodge plant, an early marriage, and the rapid expansion of his family had ended the promise of that bright background but not his irresistible vitality or combativeness, traits that enabled him to create the AIWA in the teeth of a company-sponsored works council.

Aware of the bad name this works council background had given his union, which AFL leaders like Francis Dillon and Frank X. Martel had maliciously propagated, Frankensteen threw a defiant challenge back at them: "Never was there an overt act to try to win us into the Federation. No one came out and said, 'Fellows, we feel we have something that is just what you are fighting for.' All we received was slams." A company union? he demanded and in eloquent detail replied by describing the courageous and truly brilliant manner in which the plant-based works council had been transmuted into an independent "outside" union. "We got these men and women workers together; we met and decided on the things we wanted to fight for . . . the hours, the wages and the various conditions that trade unions [struggle] for." After a battle, the top management representatives agreed to meet with the union's executive committee. "They met with us and bargained with us. They were afraid of our strength," Frankensteen asserted with pride. "We made gains. We had 12,000 raises put through, five to twelve cents an hour, in the Dodge plant."

Never losing the rapt attention of his audience, Frankensteen continued. Then, all at once, he stopped and directed a mischievous smile at them. "I have told you this not because I wanted to brag about our organization . . . but because I wanted you to know something about the people it is going to be my effort to bring into the labor movement of the Federation." This totally unexpected, simple remark brought the convention to its feet, cheering. "I want to go a little further," Frankensteen resumed after the hall had grown quiet again. "I can only speak for myself [but] I say that it shall be my recommendation that this body has an autonomy that is equal to ours, that you have democratic proceedings and . . . I cannot see any difference between you people and the people I represent: We are all workers. . . . And I will recommend to my body that our place is in this movement."[42]

It was the pinnacle of the convention, which seemed to have found its meaning in this wholehearted expression of unity. Ed Hall, who possessed a sharp sense of the right thing to do at the proper time, asked for the privilege of offering a resolution from the convention floor "that an additional seat be added to the general executive board, to be filled by a representative of the independent groups, if and when these independent organizations affiliate with this International."[43] The resolution was adopted with a cheer. Hall had cautiously refrained from mentioning the eventual recipient's name but everyone assumed that it would be Dick Frankensteen.

• • •

Despite this salute to unity, there still remained controversial issues to be settled, or, more properly, issues that were not decided without controversy. The contention that produced the most heat, curiously, was the minor question of the next convention city. The rejection of Milwaukee at Detroit had been a chastisement of the Wisconsin delegation, particularly of Ed Hall, for their role in the imposition of Dillon as head of the UAW. At South Bend, many of the same delegates who had voted against Milwaukee wanted to make amends for this factional act out of consideration for Hall's remarkable conversion and the positive part he had played throughout the present assembly.

I believe that Mortimer himself was swayed by such thoughts. In any case, he found real pleasure in learning that Hall was a fair-minded and intelligent colleague with whom he could work harmoniously. Moreover, Mortimer did not think the chief argument in support of Flint as the convention city—that it would help organize its plants—could be taken seriously. "The fight will take place, I believe, long before this convention is held."[44] Hall echoed this thought in even stronger terms: "I cannot conceive a convention organizing General Motors. . . . I think that before the next convention takes place that General Motors will know damn well that we are not running away from them."[45] This was no empty bluster because both men at their own request would, soon after the convention, initiate the drive against General Motors, Mortimer in Flint and Hall in Anderson, Indiana.

• • •

In the important election of international executive board members, partisan spirit was even more rampant though the antagonism of the two groups was limited by the fact that the choice of representatives was made by districts. This meant that the designation of more than half of the members was virtually uncontested. It was true of progressive-led Ohio, where John Soltis of Cleveland and Willis Marrer of Norwood were readily picked, and of three other districts where erstwhile supporters of Dillon were chosen: Michel of Wisconsin; Merrill of Indiana, who swamped a challenger from his own local, the bright young John Bartee; and the indestructible Fred Pieper of Atlanta, who represented the South. In addition, Delmond Garst of St. Louis, a zealous supporter of Homer Martin, was of unknown but predictable viewpoint.

I happened to have a decisive influence in the choice of one of the five remaining places, the representative for the East. It was a case of meddling for which I would never forgive myself. About a month earlier, I had received a letter from a man named Frank Tucci of the Tarrytown General Motors local, asking me to send him a bundle of the *United Auto Worker*.[46] It was his second letter in which he also announced that his local had endorsed the paper and elected him as delegate to the convention. I was delighted to hear this because it evidently meant the passing of Otto Kleinert, an appointee of President Green's to the board and long a staunch supporter of Francis Dillon's.

When we met at South Bend, I found Tucci very friendly but incredibly innocent, and I considered it my duty to find a few minutes now and then to explain to him the major issues before the convention. There were only two delegates from the eastern district, each of whom had but a single vote, thus representing a hundred or fewer members.[47] When the board elections came up, I spoke to Tucci and, seemingly against his desire, convinced him to run.

But the other man also decided to be a candidate. Accordingly, it was a dead-heat race even before it began, with the spectacular count of one to one. Someone suggested that the two candidates should flip a coin, but I advised Tucci indignantly to veto the idea and proposed a more serious solution: to check the per-capita payments of the two locals during the preceding six months. We consulted Ed Hall's records, and luck was on our side. Tarrytown averaged some twenty-odd dues-payers per month while his opponent's local averaged only eighteen. My naive new friend thus became a member of the eleven-man controlling body of the International.

This incident of impromptu comic opera was matched only by Fred Pieper's election without opposition. Nevertheless, delegates, especially the progressives, took the elections of board members very seriously. Part of our program had been to increase their powers and limit the International's president's, an office that Dillon had loaded to serve his designs. These measures would have fateful repercussions in the future.

In the choice of Michigan's four board members, this awareness was of overriding consequence and resulted in a furious debate on the convention floor. In the end, the issue reduced itself to the technical question of whether board members should be chosen by the state as a whole or by what were called geographical regions, each grouped around an important automobile center: Flint, Detroit, Pontiac, and Lansing. It would seem that the individual regions should be allowed to make their own choice, which in later years became the practice.

Yet the majority of Michigan's delegates at South Bend felt they could not ignore other considerations. Chief of these was the fact that if the handful of Flint's delegates were allowed to elect their own board member, the office would inevitably fall to one of the pro-Dillon leftovers, several of whom were suspected of being spies or company agents and would, in fact, be revealed as such a few months later by the La Follette Committee's investigators.[48] The majority group at the Michigan caucus therefore decided to elect their board members by a statewide vote.[49] The meeting was held under the "impartial chairmanship" of Second Vice President Ed Hall, who arranged for detailed minutes to be kept by Helen Tombor, also a delegate. The minutes eventually were entered in the convention's *Proceedings*.

Thirty-odd Michigan delegates were present at the caucus, as well as five absentees, who would be allowed to hand in their ballots later. Each delegate was "required" to vote for four candidates. Delmar Minzey and Herbert Richardson, both from Flint, refused to vote and announced their intention of protesting the election before the convention. The vote was tabulated and the following results announced: Walter Reuther, thirty votes; Lester Washburn, thirty votes; Lloyd Jones, twenty-nine; J. J. Kennedy, twenty-eight; Ed Ayres, five; and Gerald W. Corkum, two. Ed Hall declared the top four candidates elected, pointing out that "even if the five absent delegates, as well as the two who refused to vote, would vote they could not change the final outcome."

Several things are evident from these results. First, the almost equal tallies of the winners indicate that there had been an agreement on their selection. Second, three of the four winners were from Detroit and only one, Lester Washburn, from another region, Lansing. Nominees from Flint and Pontiac did not even figure in the contest. The candidacy of Walter Reuther surprised many progressives, who had been given to understand that Allan Strachan would be Detroit's third candidate in addition to Jack Kennedy and Lloyd Jones. How this change came about I never knew though I imagined it must have been a Socialist party decision because both Strachan and Reuther were said to be members of that party.

• • •

Because of the great amount of time consumed in remaking the constitution, time greatly prolonged, moreover, by Martin's eagerness to impress the delegates with his fairness and patience, a mass of important resolutions had to be rushed through in the last two days. One concerned the decision on the International's publication, a decision in which I was very interested.

I knew that different locals, mainly those from Cleveland, had offered several resolutions that named the *United Auto Worker* specifically. In fact, the Cleveland Auto Council had adopted one such resolution and then encouraged the locals to follow suit, presenting the UAW with a neat package of paper and editor. I must take some of the blame for this blundering approach because I had early started the practice that encouraged it though the practice was intended for a different reason. Whenever out-of-town locals ordered bundles of the paper I would write to them and ask that they endorse it. If they did so, I would add the locals' names to the list on the masthead. My obvious purpose was to give the paper prestige and effectively counter any antagonistic measures that Dillon might take against the *United Auto Worker*.

I was pleased when my friend Joe Ditzel asked for my suggestions in wording the resolution that the publication committee, of which he was chair, had to prepare. I had already discussed the matter with the Cleveland delegates whose locals had submitted resolutions on the subject and we agreed to put the *United Auto Worker* into the background, especially to leave my name out lest it appear that the committee was trying to anticipate the choice of the editor, a prerogative of the officers and the executive board.

Accordingly, the committee's resolution mentioned the Cleveland paper directly only in the final resolved: "that this convention go on record in appreciation for the pioneering work done by the Cleveland paper of the above name and respectfully requests that the Cleveland Auto Council relinquish the name of its paper to the International publication."[50] The request was granted immediately by Mortimer as chair of the council and the resolution as a whole was open for discussion.

Curiously, it was only the name that occasioned any disagreement, a change to the *United Automobile Worker* being supported by several delegates.[51] The reason offered by Roy Speth of the Seaman Body local—that the title should conform to the name of the International—was legitimate. My only objection was that the proposed title was ungainly. The committee felt the same way; one member from the Kenosha local by the name of Stander evoked the titles of other CIO journals such as the *United Mine Worker* and the *United Rubber Worker* in support of his preference.

Joe Ditzel agreed and added another motivation for his attachment to our name. It was, as he said, in recognition "of the wonderful work done by the paper," which he as a dedicated progressive and officer of the Toledo Chevrolet local naturally espoused. But this desire to reward a paper by preserving its name was a subtlety that few delegates would share. With most of them it was probably a question merely of not wanting a name for their paper that somebody else had used.

The considerable list of enlightened resolutions endorsed by the convention reflected a level of political and economic sophistication of which I had been unaware.[52] The resolution on the Farmer-Labor party was adopted by unanimous vote after a minimum of discussion. Yet it lacked nothing in clarity and class-consciousness, as I would have expected from a resolutions committee chaired by Dick Reisinger. The resolution assailed both major parties as "parties of big business [which] equally break strikes and otherwise continually encroach upon the rights of labor."[53] And it urged all subordinate bodies of the UAW to give "the strongest and widest support to the setting up of national, state and local Farmer-Labor parties."

A resolution in broad defense of civil rights was endorsed[54] and repressive measures condemned (such as the anti-freedom of speech gag bills, the Tydings-McCormick disaffection bill, the Dies anti-alien bill, and the Kramer sedition bill), whereas the investigation of labor spies by the Senate's La Follette Committee was warmly endorsed. President Franklin D. Roosevelt was asked to express "our contempt for the tyrannical regime of the Hitler government" by declaring a boycott on the Olympic Games in Berlin. Freedom for the Scottsboro Boys was demanded. And the continued imprisonment of Tom Mooney and Warren Billings was "denounced with wrathful indignation." The National Youth Administration was also supported.[55]

A number of changes were approved in the UAW constitution to eliminate retrograde provisions inherited from Dillon, including membership requirements of U.S. citizenship and "moral character." A deeply different "philosophy," as Dillon would call it, was manifested on the question of the membership of foremen in the UAW.[56] As proposed in the White Motor local's resolution, foremen were banned categorically from membership, a decision previously left to the discretion of the local. In his report to the convention, the former president had urged companies to hire "trained and experienced labor men who are fully qualified in every respect to serve faithfully and efficiently as Directors of Personnel."

The great organizational drive that would be launched after the convention, and was in the minds of all delegates, aroused their thinking on questions of wage rates, working conditions, negotiations, and other such matters. Widespread opposition to piecework, for example, was translated into a resolution of uncompromising firmness: "That the delegates assembled in convention go on record as being opposed to all piecework, premium or bonus systems and favor the straight day work rates for all workers."[57] The resolution was adopted unanimously. As for the organizational campaign itself, the resolution the White Motor local offered was inspired by John L. Lewis's heralded program and proposed the raising of a great war chest of $250,000, $75,000 of which was to come from the UAW locals themselves.[58]

Bob Travis had set aside his idea of a national council of General Motors locals, which he had proposed in the convention edition of the *United Auto Worker* since he had come to realize that the locals' overriding priority was to complete the organization of their own plants. The UAW was abysmally weak in General Motors. Ed Hall's records of dues-payers for the previous six months listed only four GM locals with as many as a hundred members: Norwood (700); Janesville (450); Toledo (400); and Kansas City (150).[59] The five great factories of Flint, with their forty-five thousand workers, totaled fewer than two hundred members and the fourteen other GM units in the country counted four hundred.[60] Travis's council could thus speak for only 2,500 of General Motors' 250,000 workers, and he must have realized that it would be premature to try to set the council up at the convention. Yet the idea was not forgotten and the union adopted it the following year. It eventually became an important element of the UAW's administrative structure and its relations with the corporation.

• • •

The final transaction of the convention occasioned an unusual incident that left many delegates with troubled thoughts. I no longer remember why the endorsement of Roosevelt for a second term should have been put off to the very end of the sessions. The resolutions committee in the person of Dick Reisinger had just been dismissed with thanks by President Martin, who then added, "Now we are ready to discuss the matter Brother Shipley has in mind."

What Carl Shipley had in mind was that his local's Resolution Number 147, calling for FDR's endorsement, should be considered by the delegates.[61] His motion that this order of business should be adopted was seconded and carried and he then read the resolution. The question rises why the resolutions committee itself had not been allowed to handle the matter. Was it an afterthought? Had the committee found it impossible to conciliate various divergent thoughts about it? Curiously, I never seemed to find out the reason then or later. The reasons given in the resolution are no help:

> WHEREAS: Since President Roosevelt has, since becoming President of these United States, consistently favored legislation favorable to the majority of our people, and
> WHEREAS: It is our belief that such humanitarian action should be taken into serious consideration in the selection of the next President.

The discussion was sparse for so weighty a proposal, giving the impression that the delegates wanted to get discussion over with and go home.[62] The arguments against were more numerous than those in favor. A few were firmly for or against but most were indecisive.

It was not until John Bartee of the Studebaker local spoke that one could understand the reasons for the vacillating offerings of the previous speakers. "I can hardly see," he said, "how this convention . . . can go on record as supporting President Roosevelt after some of the things that have happened to the automobile workers in the last two years."[63] Then, opening a sheet of paper, he explained that it was a copy of a letter that Arthur Young, a steel mogul, had written to his lobbyist in Washington when Section 7-A of the Auto Code had come before Congress. Bartee read: "'My personal opinion is that it isn't going to bother us very much. If . . . the National Labor Relations Board try to horn in on us in any situation, I think we have our fences pretty securely set up.' In other words," Bartee explained, "Mr. Arthur Young . . . knew that Section 7-A was not going to be enforceable when it was passed. And what did General [Hugh] Johnson do [about it]? He went to Detroit—and he was an appointee of President Roosevelt—and he gave away all the rights we had under Section 7-A in the merit clause."

The delegates listened with profound attention as these words from the past tolled heavily. Bartee went on: "Then we will consider Clay Williams. Who was he? He was the man sent to Washington." But Delegate Byrd broke in: "Point of order—let him stay on the resolution." Bartee was a congenial person. He paused as though wondering whether he should reply to this challenge and evidently decided against it. "Well," he concluded, "I just feel that we haven't got everything that is coming to us as working people and I believe if the President had been someone like [California] Governor [Culbert] Olson or Norman Thomas, people who have labor at heart, and if he had had the courage to fight he could have done us a lot more good. It is certain that we don't have a person of that type to vote for in 1936, so I think that this question ought to be voted down."

There was no other speaker who asked to follow this pertinent and impassioned plea. I looked around in surprise. Did it mean that the delegates had been convinced? It did not seem possible but when the vote was taken, the vocal "no's!" drowned out the echo of the previous "aye's!" Carl Shipley asked for a division of the house and the result was even more conclusive. The standing delegates looked at each other, hardly crediting the truth of what had happened.

I became aware soon after of a buzz of activity taking place on the platform, especially in the right wing, where Adolph Germer had established himself and was talking to several people. A couple of them sidled over to the podium to talk to Martin. Powers Hapgood of the United Mine Workers was speaking at the time, telling the delegates how the UMW had built up its power by defying the craft unions. "The reason we got [our] jurisdiction," he cried out in his curiously high-pitched voice, "is because in those twelve years we had *taken* jurisdiction and taken all the men in the coal mining industry into our ranks."[64]

There were cheers and stamping at these defiant words. Leo Krzycki, who was the next speaker, had a more topical story to tell, about the recent formation of the Farmer-Labor-Progressive Federation in Wisconsin, the first of its kind in the United States.[65] While he was speaking I noticed Martin slipping away from the chair and joining Germer in the wings. An animated dialog between them followed though Germer did most of the talking. I could almost tell what he was saying from his gestures. His head was bowed toward Martin's, his cheeks puffed in anger, his cowlick falling over one eye. Martin listened uneasily. When he came back to the chair his face was pale, his manner distraught. "I have just been speaking to Brother Germer about a very important matter, the matter of the resolution that was passed [voted?] on this afternoon and rejected by a small majority. Many of those that are close to affairs realize that in the President of the United States, labor had at least been given a chance and a helping hand never before afforded it. By permission of this body, because of the effect that it may have on the future of our organization, I have considered the request of several delegates that the matter be reconsidered."[66]

As the rereading of the resolution and the other details of the motion were taking place, I looked around at some of those who had opposed it and realized that none would say a word against it, even though I could see in several an incensed reaction to Germer's loaded threat. It was not the substance of Martin's appeal but its pathetic nature that had swerved them, I felt. He was asking desperately for help in a tough quandary, and it was a point of loyalty to give it to him.

When the motion to adopt the resolution was passed without discussion, Walter Wells, the third vice president, quickly moved that the previous action be wiped from the records. He soon after explained to me his true feeling about the incident: "Now I was in favor of the resolution in the first place but what happened shows how those strong organizations are going to try to control us!"

After the vote, Germer left his alcove, looking grim but self-satisfied. I scrutinized him with displeasure, consoling myself with the thought that the reality of the event was the opposite to what he thought or how he would tell it. The auto workers had actually taken a clear-cut and courageous position. They had voted down Roosevelt for all the sins he had committed against them during two long years. Germer and I would have some sharp set-tos on this score during the months to come.

• • •

The South Bend Convention ended soon after, and it was time to draw up its balance sheet. There was so much good to record, it was hardly credible. Above all, we had an International Union that was sturdy and forward-looking beyond our most visionary dreams. That it should have come so quickly in the end was due largely to the emergence of the CIO. That was the key to remember, I told myself, that and not the few mishaps we might have met along the route.

The Organization Drive
Gets Underway

When the newly elected officers arrived in Detroit after the convention, they were suddenly faced by the enormity of their task. After all the talking and planning, the propositions and resolutions, they were overwhelmed with the job of putting them into motion. Where to begin, what to do first? After being fiercely critical of the AFL for having delayed the convention until it was too late to "do anything," the officers were, if they asked themselves, delighted to have those few inactive months before the new season began. The time permitted them and the union to get ready for their responsibilities.

One available record illustrates this tentativeness: the International's journal, which I was asked to edit, at least for the first numbers. True, it is my own version of the situation that is reflected in it but I believe that it gives a fairly objective picture of the prevailing sentiment. The organizational drive was the paramount task, as I and the paper saw it and my problem was to reach the workers with something to which they could relate. After their disastrous experiences with the AFL, the desire for the union had to be reimplanted in them.

A serious personal problem was the insecurity of my status. After the late May edition, which was occupied entirely with an account of the convention, I had to return to Cleveland because Homer Martin could not bring himself to give me his confirmation.[1] I did not get back to Detroit until June 21 and he still was undecided, asking me if the newly appointed educational director, Merlin Bishop, could not assume the post of editor as well if I came in from Cleveland for a week every month to do the "technical job" of putting the paper together. I looked at him and shook my head.

Thus the July issue had to depend mainly on inner-union developments and other things I could pick up from the officers' mail baskets. What perturbed me most was that I had no time to get anything from inside the plants.

I realized, of course, that in July and August work was at a low ebb. Yet even after August when lines were already throbbing, the paper still shows little that reflects that activity, for the union was simply not there.

I tried to make up for the lack of content with boastful headings—"Organization Drive Gains in Detroit District," "Progress Made among Foreign-Born in Flint," "Parts Plant Has New 100% Local"—but these were innocent compared to the double banner I gave Ed Hall's report from Anderson, based on the alleged recruitment of a hundred metal polishers in the Guide Lamp plant: "AUTO UNION SMASHES GM STRONGHOLD." This bombast was in keeping with the general idea of treating the paper as a propaganda medium. In order to impress the workers, we felt that we had to convince them of brilliant successes. Exaggeration was an unavoidable temptation. The International's press releases made extravagant claims of accomplishments despite the efforts of Frank Winn, our publicity man, who had had excellent journalistic training in Texas, to tone them down.[2]

The paper remained unrestrained until the facts began to catch up with the style. Long before that happened, however, a front page almost got me into real trouble. It was at the time when the AFL suspended the CIO unions and I put out a defiant August issue that I hoped would commit Homer Martin, whose attachment to the CIO tended to waver. The headline shouted "'CIO GOES ON!'—LEWIS." The article reminded readers that the UAW's executive board had unanimously endorsed Martin's action in aligning the union with the CIO, a step "in keeping with a convention decision as well as with the overwhelming sentiment of the International's membership."

The matter was still unsettled a month later when I prepared the September issue before going to Mackinac Island for a week with Dorothy, who was afflicted with hay fever. I used a heavy black heading that kept the pot boiling on the suspension: "PROTESTS SWEEPING AFL!"[3]

When I got back to Detroit, I learned that I had almost lost my job. Ed Hall was the cause of the trouble. He had come to Detroit and, in typical fashion, brought all the Anderson bundles, 2,500 copies, back with him. "What the fuck can I do with a heading like that!" he growled. Wyndham Mortimer calmed him down and got me off the hook by reminding Martin that I had shown the final page proofs to both of them. Nonetheless, my position remained tenuous for quite some time and I was put under the tutelage of Adolph Germer.

As far as the paper itself was concerned, the incident was therapeutic. I acknowledged to myself that Ed Hall was right. We were no longer fighting the AFL. We were trying to reach workers who did not know the first thing of what the ruckus was all about. My years of involvement in the fight for the International had left me with an abstract heritage that was light-years away from the needs and thoughts of the rank and file.

• • •

Though dormant in the plants, the union was by no means inactive during this period. Among the vital administrative tasks that were undertaken were the absorption of the independent unions and the setting up of the organizational staff. The first group of Detroit organizers was named and placed under the directorship of Dick Frankensteen, who had helped to expedite the merger of his Automotive Industrial Workers of America (AIWA) into the UAW. What was considered the union's outstanding task—organizing General Motors—was also launched, with Mortimer volunteering to tackle the major target, Flint, and Ed Hall picking the important GM center at Anderson, Indiana. Organizers were also established at the General Motors plants in Atlanta, St. Louis, and Cleveland, where executive board members were put in charge.[4]

Bob Travis's idea of setting up a council of GM locals, a notion he had quietly spread among the delegates at South Bend, was approved by the executive board early in August, when representatives from seventeen locals met briefly and decided to call a broader meeting within a month. This was held on September 12, and a "permanent" GM Council was constituted and a standing committee comprised of Travis, Delmond Garst, and Bill Munger, our new research director, was instructed to prepare a national program of demands. Homer Martin announced to the press, prematurely, many felt, that the UAW would seek negotiations with General Motors through this council.

Other organizational undertakings were initiated in Detroit. One was devoted to the numerous Polish workers of the city and was headed by Stanley Nowak, a scholarly young man who had started at an early age working in the automobile industry. Another was launched among the city's tool-and-die workers under the guidance of John Anderson, whose post was part of the merger agreement offered by the UAW to the Mechanics Educational Society of America (MESA). A third effort, which attracted little attention at the time, was begun almost on a personal basis by Walter Reuther on Detroit's vast West Side, totally barren of organization though possessed of such important plants as Ternstedt, Cadillac, Fleetwood, Kelsey-Hayes, and Ford. Reuther, though a board member, was "forgotten" when Martin named the organizers.

Despite the favorable early circumstances, the merger of the three independent unions within the UAW did not come off without some tangles. This was especially true of the MESA, where Matt Smith, its general secretary, remained obdurate to the end. Shortly after South Bend, the UAW's officers invited leaders of the three groups and their wives to a "banquet" at the Verdi Cafe in downtown Detroit. Smith boycotted the affair, but leaders of the MESA district council came and invited the UAW to send a delegation to its next meeting.

Matt Smith was there, to be sure, and as the UAW group led by Mortimer sat in the lobby of the MESA office, waiting to be called in, they could hear him loudly declaiming about the UAW's officers. Martin, Smith said, was an ardent supporter of Dillon until the rank and file turned against that "pot-bellied strike-breaker."[5] Hall was a "scab-herder," Smith added; every time he spoke his name he had to rinse his mouth with disinfectant. Dick Frankensteen he called a "bond salesman posing as a labor organizer." John Anderson, the Communist party's former candidate for governor, he declared, had tried for three years to wreck the MESA and succeeded only in wrecking himself. Smith's only decent word was for Mortimer: "a good man keeping bad company." He summed up, "These are the self-styled messiahs who are going to lead the Detroit workers into the promised land." These last words were left hanging, and the group outside could hear loud noises of shifting furniture, then some shouted words, and what sounded like a whack on someone's physiognomy. It was Anderson, who had plastered Matt Smith across the mouth with the "back of his open hand." It was a light blow, Anderson insisted, for he was concerned with his bad temper and the fact that Smith was a small man. Smith quickly retreated behind the front desk and a motion was made and adopted to admit the UAW delegation.

Without prelude, Mortimer presented the UAW's offer: a separate charter for each MESA local with full autonomy assured; a paid-up membership book in the UAW for a paid-up book of the MESA; and the right of the tool-and-die workers to choose their own UAW organizer. The council delegates approved the terms without discussion. They represented four locals in Detroit with approximately a thousand members. Three of the groups, including Anderson's key local of seven hundred members, rapidly voted to amalgamate. Smith had to cheer himself with retaining one small unit and the national headquarters.[6]

Amalgamation of Arthur Greer's Associated Automobile Workers of America (AAWA) was cut and dried. The group was comprised of the Hudson local and a few contacts in other factories, all that was left of the once vaunted "international" that Greer and Richard Byrd had projected at the time of Greer's dramatic secession from the AFL at the June conference in 1934. Only a couple of hundred dues-payers were actually turned over to the UAW though Greer never ceased to claim that the AAWA had several thousand members. He was put on the UAW's payroll anyway, evidently by previous agreement, but no one knew what his assignment was as he moved about International headquarters on padded feet, unless it was to search out those evanescent masses.

The procedure of merging Frankensteen's AIWA into the UAW was more formal than that of the other groups. Its locals were loosely linked, and the AIWA general council insisted on setting up a committee of fourteen representatives from the various units to supervise the procedure. Each local would vote individually on the merger at a membership meeting, it was decided. Frankensteen was afraid of losing several of them and was reduced to asking help from Charles Coughlin to swing the decision though in private he would insist that the radio priest no longer had any hold on his members. Coughlin agreed to send Frankensteen a personal wire to read at the meetings, which he did with dramatic emphasis: "There can be but one union for success. I urge you to amalgamate."

Coughlin had his own reasons for wanting to placate the AIWA leaders, who had angered him when they refused to allow their organization to join the National Union for Social Justice (NUSJ). This had almost resulted in a break. Now he had a new—and, to him, highly important—reason to win back the union's loyalty: to gain its support for the presidential candidacy of William Lemke.

I was present at what was probably the key meeting on the merger of the AIWA, that of the Chrysler-Kercheval local, where the situation was complicated by the friction that had developed because of a competitive UAW local led by board member John Kennedy. The AIWA unit was headed by Roland J. Thomas, who presided at the meeting and made a good impression on me with his gruff, working-class manner. "You've all read in the capitalist papers," he declared, "how Chrysler doubled his fortune last year. Has anybody in this audience doubled *his* fortune? I know you started with zero last year and two times zero is still zero!"

Dick Frankensteen read Coughlin's wire and then reported on Coughlin's visit to South Bend. "In the past," he said, "I've been as prejudiced against the AFL as anybody. But after being at the UAW convention, I decided that it is wrong for us to stay apart. Your own plant is the best example of this. Two groups, all workers, but disunited. I say to you, we have no right to a separate existence. It won't be until we get all the workers together that we will be able to control the wage rates of the automobile industry."

The final speaker, Martin, added little of moment to the question, his best words being, "We stayed on the inside and kicked. You kicked from the outside. Together we got rid of those whose policies stood in the way of organization. And they're out to stay!" Nevertheless, the audience asked a number of questions that reflected mistrust of the AFL and, by extension, the UAW.

"Can the AFL tell you to go out on strike?"

"In case of a strike, will negotiations be conducted by one man?"

"Why does the AFL charge such high dues?

Frankensteen had prepared Martin on the dues question, which seemed like the major stumbling block to leaders of the AIWA, whose members paid only 50 cents a month against the UAW's dollar. They were afraid that they might lose as many as half of their members on this issue alone. Martin did not take an apologetic stance on the question, however, but told about the large number of organizers being put on the payroll at the same wage the average auto worker earned, $40. "We've just got to organize the auto industry," he declared, setting his jaw grimly. "Everything depends on it. As for the question that that brother over there asked. When you go out on strike, nobody has the power to conduct negotiations except your own committee. And the committee must submit the company's offer to you the members for your approval. That's written into our constitution."

By May 25, Dick Frankensteen was able to announce to the press that eight of AIWA's twenty-six locals had voted to affiliate with the UAW. This included two important Chrysler units at Kercheval and Highland Park and six of the eleven divisions of the great Dodge factory.[7]

• • •

After the merger was completed, I began to spend a lot of time with Frankensteen because he made good copy for the paper. He was also an effective street-corner speaker and carried a sturdy box around in his car. He would stand on the box when he spoke at plant gates during the change of shifts. Evening meetings in parks were even better because the summer of 1936 was very hot and the days were long. The only problem was, How to draw a crowd? Frankensteen had a bright idea.

The election campaign was on and Frank Murphy, the former mayor of Detroit, was running for governor on the Democratic ticket. Frankensteen told me that he had met Murphy several times and felt that he had made a good impression on him. "What if I ask him to speak at our next meeting at Chandler Park?" he asked. To my amazement, Murphy accepted the invitation enthusiastically, evidently convinced that the UAW had a much bigger following than actually was the case. Fortunately, I have saved a couple of pages of scribbled notes from this meeting, containing a few of the future governor's remarks. One of those which I noted down brought cheers from his largely working-class audience: "My friends, I believe in organized labor."

The UAW put on an appropriate show for the occasion, with Homer Martin, Adolph Germer, and John Kennedy as the other listed speakers. Dick Frankensteen chaired the meeting and it was here that he surprisingly announced his candidacy for the Michigan House of Representatives, telling his listeners what he would do for the auto workers if elected. He stressed the occupational ailments and the blatant lack of state injury and occupational compensation legislation.

When introducing Murphy, Martin predicted, "A time will come when we will hang our banner in the city hall, in the state capitol, in the White House at Washington, reading: 'Human Rights Above Property Rights!'" Murphy responded by recalling an incident from his career as mayor of Detroit: "I told those gentlemen of the automobile companies that I would not use the welfare question to break their strikes." He ended with a compendious remark that amounted to an all-inclusive populist platform: "I believe in progressive legislation that will bring security to all the unemployed, to all the wretched and the unfortunate."

A side comment in my notes reminds me of an unpleasant experience I had of being taken for a spy at the Chandler Park meeting, an experience that reveals the workers' morbid preoccupation with this subject at the time. At the beginning of the meeting when union application cards were being handed around, Frankensteen explained that they would not be gathered up at the meeting because stool pigeons were present. "Just fill it out at home and put it in an envelope and mail it to the Hofmann Building," he advised.

I was sitting on a bench, pad and pencil in hand and flanked by two other men, when suddenly I became aware that a number of others nearby were glaring at me and seemed to be edging closer. I stopped writing and was relieved when Mike Dragon, Frankensteen's friend from the Dodge trim department, came over, slapped me on the back, and smiled. "Hi, Hank!" he said. I realized that he wanted to show the others that I was okay and smiled back at him before resuming my note-taking. My bench companions left in a hurry.

Frankensteen paired the park meetings with a weekly radio talk over WMBC every Friday night at 10:15. He asked me to help him prepare his speeches but he needed no such assistance. His histrionic talent served him even when invisible. Yet he enjoyed practicing his talks before me and gobbled up my compliments, which were sincere enough.

During the great heat wave of July, Frankensteen was able to find for the first time in the campaign an agitational subject from "inside" the plants. He picked up his facts from former comrades at Dodge as well as from the newspapers, which were full of gruesome details. For a week straight, the thermometer soared above 100 degrees, and, as the auto plants continued to operate even though with a reduced staff, workers fell at their stations like flies. According to the papers, more than three hundred died in Detroit during the three- or four-day heatwave, and five hundred deaths were reported in the state of Michigan.

Spontaneous movements for slowing down the lines or closing the plants sprang up everywhere and the sparse union members were hard put to take advantage of their opportunities. At Murray Body, a committee in one of the departments, including a single covert union man, contacted the superintendent and demanded that work be halted early. The official replied that no exceptions could be made: "We have to get the work out!" Thereupon, the workers shut the line themselves and went home. Consternation seized the management when several other departments followed them out. Much the same thing occurred at other plants, including Dodge.

Frankensteen devoted his weekly talk to this subject. "Today in one plant," he began, "hundreds of men and women were carried out of their factories on stretchers. Ambulances could not give sufficient service to take care of those human beings who were falling like June bugs to the floor. . . . Mr. Management—and I know that you are listening—and you do know whom I mean—this coming Monday, if conditions are as they were today, *that killing speedup will stop!* And you won't be talking to one department at a time either but to the whole plant. We refuse to see our people killed off for your blood dollars."

Frankensteen adopted the practice of singling out one company during each broadcast, sending a wire to the object of his remarks an hour or two beforehand. The following week he made a bitter attack on the violently anti-union owner of the Fruehauf Trailer Company, who had recently won a court ruling that overturned a decision of the National Labor Relations Board (NLRB) condemning the union-wrecking activities of a company operative.[8] Fruehauf commented appreciatively that his company would now be freed from the interference of "outside influences" and that it was "loyalty between employers and employees and not agitation" that kept the factories going.

"Was your spy Martin an *inside* influence?" Frankensteen demanded with grinding irony. "Was his spying on his fellows the way you consider being loyal to your workers? Mr. Fruehauf, how can you have stooped to the practice of listening at the key-hole and then speaking of loyalty? There is no law on earth that can free your conscience for the nine men that you discharged for taking advantage of their God-given right to join a union. . . . Mr. Fruehauf, may God have mercy on your soul!"

Before long, the fiery monologues began to generate feedback. The people at WMBC said that they would have to check Frankensteen's talks before his broadcast because of protests that the station had received about them. It was a primary union policy to resist censoring resolutely and Frankensteen had already had experience with this sort of thing. He finally agreed to let the WMBC staff have a copy of his talk half an hour before he read it. They had first asked for it a day in advance, then two hours ahead of time, but Frankensteen stuck to his guns, demanding point-blank whether they wanted him to send the copy to the company he targeted each week and save WMBC the stamp. I argued that he would be tying his hands that way, but Frankensteen reassured me. "Don't worry, I can always slip something in that isn't in the script. Then too," he added with a conniving smile, "I'm an actor, you know, and a lot can be added to the text by the way you read it."

Participating in these talks, and in anything that Dick Frankensteen did, was great fun. I actually spent too much time with him even though I was not needed. Moreover, my own work was becoming more and more demanding, so in a way it was a relief when WMBC decided to cut off the talks. Frankensteen protested blusteringly but was actually pleased. "That proves that I was getting to them," he gloated. I replied dourly, "But they stopped you anyway!" Yet I told him of what Mortimer reported about the Flint radio station, which simply refused to sell him time, if only to advertise a meeting. In fact, everything connected with the UAW was banned in Flint. There was also an ordinance there that prohibited leaflet distribution, so that flyers became illegal and had to be smuggled into the workers' hands by other means. Curiously, authorities let themselves be tied up by their own regulations in permitting the union to get around the ban by increasing the size of the leaflet and printing a newspaper instead. As for the radio bar, it, too, was evaded eventually by a brand-new medium—the sound car—which was to prove the union's most redoubtable weapon.

• • •

The Polish division of the Detroit organizational staff continued to use the radio without interference. No doubt the fact that Stanley Nowak's broadcasts were delivered in Polish made instant control difficult if not impossible. The weekly talks were very popular and received wide notice. I went to Hamtramck a couple of times during their delivery over station WEXL and was delighted to find that the stores all along Chene had loudspeakers barking the union's message out on the street while workers stood about listening intently.

Nowak was a triple-threat man; in addition to his broadcasts, he gave lectures to all kinds of groups and edited a language weekly, *Glos Ludowy.* When the drive began to take shape, he also had to find time to take over the organization of a couple of plants. Together with Leo Krzycki, who was on permanent loan to the UAW from the Amalgamated Clothing Workers, he organized a citywide Polish committee of fraternal, professional, and small business representatives who helped the union to reach out to the enormous Polish communities of Detroit and Hamtramck.

It was no exaggeration for Nowak to maintain, as he did in the *United Automobile Worker* in September 1936, that "it is practically impossible to organize the auto industry without organizing the Polish workers." He backed his statement with statistics showing that tens of thousands of Polish men and women were employed in the auto plants, their proportion running as high as 40 percent in a single factory. These workers became the nucleus of the plant organizing committees that Nowak set up.

As the retooling season started, John Anderson, now also on the International's payroll, launched a drive in the job shops. In important ways, the problems of the tool-and-die makers were little different from those of production workers, among whom what was euphemistically called "technological improvement" was making its relentless way. There seemed to be no limit to the voracity of the machine. Special skills were only a relative shield in its wake. In 1935, as the union pointed out from figures of the Michigan State Welfare Commission, only 3.4 percent of the tool-and-die men were more than fifty-five years of age, while the three thousand of these workers on the welfare rolls revealed the ominous end of the road for ever-increasing numbers of those still working, unless they organized aggressively to combat their dismissals.

By autumn, the International had put nine full-time and as many part-time (read "half-pay") organizers on the payroll, distributing them parsimoniously among the selected concentration points.[9] Although this number was several times more than Dillon had ever employed, it hardly met the demands of the UAW's ambitious program. The CIO was asked to help but pleaded other responsibilities. The UAW's own fund-raising drive—its goal was $75,000—had attained little more than a fifth of that target by the end of the year.[10] The UAW was paying for its zooming organizational requirements largely from the increasing dues received from new and "renewed" members.

But the bustle at the International's headquarters gave the impression that things were really getting underway. Detroit's locals, however skeletal, did not need hired help to instruct them about how to organize. Many were guided by political left-wingers who helped set up committees of volunteer organizers who quietly began operations inside the plants. I got to know many of the organizers when they came to headquarters for supplies of brochures or for the International's journal to distribute inside the plants or at workers' homes. Now and then, I would help them to prepare a special leaflet that they could not afford to print themselves.

I got to know Bill McKie, an acknowledged communist, that way. I had met him at the Detroit and South Bend conventions but we had only exchanged a few words. He was a retiring, elderly man whose heart and mind seemed keyed on one single objective: organizing the Ford workers. He had been fired from the plant long ago and was, no doubt, on welfare when the International decided to pay him $10 a week. This gave him a sense of heightened responsibility, if that was possible. One day, after I had arranged to put out a leaflet that McKie had prepared, he told me that he was working on a big article on Ford based on personal experience, which he updated by talking to his dozens of contacts inside the plant. The article featured the devastating Ford speedup and was studded with specific examples of how output had been increased in the past two years while pay rates had been lowered. I published the account in the August issue, devoting the whole upper half of a page to it.

Lloyd Jones, one of the four board members from Detroit, was another contributor with whom I developed a personal relationship. When the blow-up about the notorious Black Legion came at the end of May, he told me that he had some experience with that organization during the Motor Products strike. I got him to talk about it and the result was a quite remarkable article. Jones had the gift of gab, I told him admiringly. He giggled youthfully and said that his parents had discovered that when he was just a child. He had become a preacher at the age of nine. Then, it turned out, he could cure people by the laying on of hands.

"My God," I exclaimed, just managing to keep my incredulousness under control, "why did you give it up?"

"Because it began to fail me."

"How come?" I asked.

"I lost my faith," Jones replied with a simplicity that shamed me.

I felt embarrassed about querying him further but he himself explained his religious life to me. He had begun to rebel against the implied discrimination contained in the Scriptures, which denied people of today the privileged experiences that those of biblical times had enjoyed. There were no answers to the terrible modern debacles that could come like a blast of thunder from heaven. There were no miracles to soothe pain and end misery. Self-proclaimed prophets like Coughlin and Huey Long were nothing but fascists who exploited people. This was the explanation of Lloyd Jones's conversion to unionism.

Another of my editorial contacts was hardly as gratifying as knowing McKie or Jones though he was certainly interesting, if difficult to get along with. Fred Pieper, the board member from Atlanta, earned only $25 as an International organizer but seemed to have no problem in coming to Detroit often and for relatively prolonged visits, buzzing around headquarters, holding closed-door conferences with Martin, and preparing memoranda for submission to the executive board.

Pieper had always avoided me and I thought I knew why: an allergy to my leftist outlook. I could understand this when I thought about his own record as an unfailing advocate of Dillon's line and of the most reactionary measures that had come up at the Detroit and South Bend conventions. Also revealing was the letter that a delegate named Henry Mack had turned over to Mortimer at the pre–South Bend caucus in March. The letter was addressed to Pieper from the red-baiters of the Norwood local who were in league with him, Elmer Davis, and others to get Mortimer defeated for the vice-presidency.[11]

I was surprised one day to find Pieper approaching me at my desk in the cubbyhole I shared with Frank Winn. Pieper was all smiles as he offered me some multigraphed sheets that he identified as copies of the "little newspaper" he was putting out for the Atlanta local. He was that local's financial secretary. "I thought maybe you could find something in it that you could use in the *United Automobile Worker*," he suggested.

It required no effort on my part to show him that I was pleased by his friendly approach. I had decided that the huge task of organizing the auto workers required the united efforts of all UAW activists regardless of their ideological outlook—all except stool pigeons, of course.

I read the issues of Pieper's *Bulletin* and was amazed at their ingenuousness. If he had made some of the same observations to me in personal conversation I would have concluded that he was stringing me along. In particular, I had to read his second *Bulletin,* dated July 1936, several times before concluding that it was serious: "Recently there was a 'strike' of some 15 or 20 minutes duration over on the metal finishing line at Fisher. Approximately 20 metal finishers, non-union, quit their work about one o'clock on 'days' because Mr. Schwarzwalder 'done 'em wrong' by cutting off a man in the department, thereby requiring more work to be done by each remaining worker. We are confident that, had the metal finish line been composed of union men, such a distressful situation to the management would not have occurred. *The white principled way is the only way*" [emphasis added]. Nevertheless, I praised the *Bulletin* and asked Pieper what he would suggest that I should use.

"I'd like to write an article about what I regard as the most important task that we've got—to educate the workers," he replied. I did not consider that idea exactly a burning issue but encouraged Pieper to go ahead. A couple of days later he brought the article in and I published it as it was written but for one deletion that he himself made after I offered a negative remark about it. I read the sentence to him: "'When workers first join unions in the South we really must class them as a liability until they can be educated because too often they drop out and become highly critical of the union.'"

"Even if that's true," I commented, "would you really want to print it?"

He jerked his head as though he had been slapped, then, grabbing the page from my hand, he scratched out the condemned words.

I could hardly believe that it was workers' education that Pieper would be discussing with Martin during their lengthy huddles. Soon enough though, we began to realize what this devious character was up to and that Martin was in league with him: Pieper wanted to get into Flint! All the suspicious elements up there were in on the plot, besides. Yet Pieper never surfaced when the matter came to a head and a big Flint delegation came down secretly to Detroit to meet with the officers—all except Mortimer since he was the one they wanted to get rid of.

I have described this incident in *The Many and the Few;* its upshot was that Mortimer decided to leave Flint, despite the fact that he had been making considerable progress there, in order "to keep peace in the family."[12] Martin made the mistake, however, of letting Mortimer choose his successor, which he did with the help of George Addes, who suggested Bob Travis. Martin was taken aback but he was too eager to get Mortimer out of Flint to raise any objection. But Pieper was frantic and started immediately working on Travis to get him to ask for him as his assistant in Flint. Travis warded him off with innocent excuses.[13]

But Pieper stayed on in Detroit, occupying himself with other ideas that fed Martin's paranoia while lining up board members to resist the growing strength of the "left." He singled out Walter Reuther as its most dangerous member and managed to reopen the question of his legitimacy as a board member. In this he was helped by another pro-Dillon man who, as a member of the credentials committee at the convention, had already opposed Reuther.

Dewey Smith had "connections" at the Ternstedt plant and was able to report to a meeting of the executive board that the management there was unable to find the assumed name that Reuther had given at South Bend as having used at Ternstedt. Reuther replied that of course he had given a false name because he knew that Smith would get in touch with the company and he wanted to confuse them all. The majority of the board sided with Reuther out of solidarity and voted that the affair should be dropped permanently. Pieper had no choice but to accept their decision.

However, soon after that, he shifted his attention to the AFL-CIO controversy. Pieper was too cagey to oppose the UAW's affiliation with the CIO that summer but when this decision soon after engaged the auto union together with the other CIO affiliates in the AFL Executive Council's suspension, he began to make dark observations about all the trouble the CIO was getting them into. Other members of the board treated the matter lightly. Dick Frankensteen made everybody laugh when he said, "It took me only a month after joining the UAW to get you kicked out of the AFL!"

Martin himself seemed hardly more concerned, as Frank Winn and I learned when we tried to get him to issue a statement on the suspension. I wanted to use it in the current issue of the paper, and Winn, who had Archie Robinson of the *Detroit News* waiting for something hot to put into the evening edition, lost his pains as well as his patience. The board was in session and in the end it voted unanimously to remain "loyal" to the CIO, while Martin, in a statement that was too late for the evening edition, asserted inanely that "no action of the union was in conflict with the purposes or ideals of the AFL."

Martin's loyalty to the CIO had lasted about two months before he began to connive with Fred Pieper to get the UAW, by action of the executive board, to "secede" from the CIO. It was hard to understand his motive for getting involved in this little conspiracy though, on afterthought, it was strangely like his conduct two years later, when he came close to destroying the UAW. It is certain, however, that Pieper could not have succeeded in working up this plot along with the other board members in his clique had he not had the go-ahead from Martin.[14]

• • •

As the organizing momentum began to quicken, several events occurred almost simultaneously that proved to be of immense importance to its success.[15] These were the exposure of the Black Legion, the beginning of the La Follette Committee's investigation of spies in the auto plants, and the "discovery" of the sitdown strike. The fortuitous arrest, in Detroit, on May 12, 1936, of a man named Dayton Dean as a suspect in the murder of an equally obscure individual, Charles A. Poole, started unreeling the gruesome story of the Black Legion, a story that continued all through that scorching summer of 1936.

Once broken down by the police, Dean was eager to talk. What he had to say sounded utterly maniacal until it was corroborated by fellow members of his sanguinary group. Two of them had reported that Poole beat his wife, which was considered worthy of retribution by the Legion, sworn to defend "white womanhood" and other canons of "100% Americanism."[16] Dayton Dean was the trigger man and he calmly narrated the gory details of Poole's assassination to the police. In the days that followed he confessed other atrocities of his group, including the slaying of Silas Coleman, a black worker, an act that was decided upon at a drinking party in which Legion wives participated. The purpose, as one of the men expressed it, was to learn "what it feels like to shoot a nigger."[17]

However shocking these early revelations were, it was only for a short time that they could be considered the wild barbarities of a demented, self-intoxicated little group since other disclosures soon linked them to a widespread conspiracy of fascistic character totaling tens of thousands of members in numerous communities of southern Michigan and northwestern Ohio. Membership in the Black Legion was concentrated among civil servants, including some high officials in the crime detection and prosecution departments. Implicated, for example, was Duncan C. McCrea, Wayne County prosecuting attorney, who shrugged off the accusation by admitting having signed a Legion card unknowingly during the 1934 election campaign.

McCrea, who was probably very eager to rehabilitate his tainted reputation, sent an official request to Ohio Governor Martin L. Davey for the extradition of the Black Legion "commander," Virgil Effinger, from Lima. Davey replied that he needed time to consider such an action. McCrea waited for awhile, then sent a squad of police officers to Lima, armed with a fugitive warrant and under orders to pick up the wanted man. They were not successful because Effinger managed to "disappear," aided by Lima's police force.

This interstate imbroglio had a repercussion in our own International office when a few weeks later Adolph Germer presented me with a wad of materials that the Norwood UAW local had sent him in support of Governor Davey's reelection. Germer asked me to feature the material on the front page of the UAW paper, along with a large photograph that had also been sent. The major point I was to make, he told me, was to tout Davey as having consistently refused to call out the National Guard during strikes. I replied that I could not take responsibility for giving a candidate such acclaim in the official journal unless the International's officers had endorsed him. Germer reminded me that an important UAW local had done so, and that I could write the article that way. I said that I personally would never write it under any circumstances and asked him if he had forgotten the role Davey had played in the Effinger case. Germer became so furious that I thought he would have me fired outright. A compromise was somehow reached between us and he agreed to do the story himself in the form of an interview by an unnamed questioner. I cut it down to a moderate size and stuck it at the bottom of page 3, giving it an ironic head that I thought would rile Germer: "Finds Gov. Davey's Strike Record Good."[18]

Although nominally a socialist, Germer had strong leanings toward the Democratic party and his support for Roosevelt was unquestioning. I felt, on the contrary, that it would be wrong to give FDR a blank check after the near defeat of his endorsement at the South Bend Convention. The paper must, on the other hand, avoid anything that might help Alf Landon win the election. In the end, I confined my comments to a monthly column that focussed ironical attention on the Republican candidate's policies. I called the column "G.O.P. Jitters" and, because the forty-nine-year-old Landon's youth was constantly vaunted over the aging president, I introduced the series by approving a reporter's suggestion that the Republican cognomen should be changed from the Grand Old Party (GOP) to the Grand Young Party (GYP).

In my second column, I dealt with Landon's nomination acceptance speech, pointing to the devastating slip of the pen made by his "Wall Street ghost writers," who had assured industrialists that under Landon's administration their employees would be "free from interference from any source."

Such assurances had brought howls of protest from union leaders and "G.O.P. Jitters" listed a number of items from the press proving "the anti-labor and pro-capitalist bias" of Landon and his supporters.

Adolph Germer was apparently taken with my column and offered to do the next one on John D. Hamilton, the national director of Landon's campaign. It was a strong piece of writing that delighted me, especially because I would not have dared to pen such an article myself. Hamilton had roused Germer's wrath by demanding that David Dubinsky, who had been named a Democratic presidential elector for the state of New York, should be removed on the grounds that his union, the ILGWU, had given $5,000 to "communistic Spain." I gave the piece a full page and titled it "Landon's Stooge Brands Self Fascist," which was an accurate description of Germer's tirade:

> If Hamilton and Landon and Knox [the vice-presidential candidate] are against helping the victims of fascism in Europe they must be against the Spanish republican form of government, recognized by the United States and other countries and they must be in sympathy with the rebel forces who are trying to destroy that government by force and violence. It is a reasonable assumption that should such a disaster as the election of Landon and Knox befall the United States, we may look for the rise of a fascist movement and fascist dictatorship in our country. In that event the fate of the labor movement in the United States will be the same as the fate of the labor movement in Europe—total destruction.

The anti-union activities of the Black Legion were directed by an amazing character who seemed to have been drawn from fiction. His name was Isaac White, but he was better known as "Peg Leg" because of his wooden stump. He was identified by this prop, during the big exposure of the Black Legion, as having participated in the murder three years before of George Marchuk, the secretary of the communist-led Auto Workers Union (TUUL) at Hudson. Peg Leg's major activity, however, was to conduct a broad system of espionage on behalf of the automobile companies, which he called an "Intelligence Department." He explained that the service was a "courtesy proposition," offered to all managements menaced by strikes, which by Legion definition were "anti-American."

In March 1934, when the AFL was supposedly contemplating a national strike in the auto industry, Peg Leg admitted having paid a visit to the Hudson Motors Personnel Department. There he presented a typed list of the most dangerous strike fomenters in the plant, five of whom he identified as communists. One of the people on the list was John Bielak, leader of the metal finishers. A day or two later, this claim was ostensibly corroborated when Bielak led a short stoppage that won a raise in his department. The company had tried to fire him, but workers threatened to shut the plant down if it did. The following evening, Bielak's foreman, Bill Moore, invited him to a rendezvous, about which he told his wife. Late that night, his body was found lying in a ditch on a dark road. A union application card had been stuck beneath Bielak's head.

Alerted by Bielak's wife at the time, the police questioned the foreman but readily accepted his gratuitous explanation that the shooting was an inner-communist affair, a punishment of Bielak for having quit the party. Two years later, in 1936, the case was reopened, but Police Inspector John Navarre repeated the original motivation, which he insisted had been proved by an investigation. This whitewash was sharply contradicted by William Weinstone, head of Michigan's Communist party, who denied that Bielak had ever been a member.

More recent examples of union involvement with the Black Legion were reported in several UAW locals but the International never investigated them. The pity of it was that significant leads were not followed through in such an important center as Flint.[19] The fault, to a considerable extent, lay in the factional maneuvers of Homer Martin against his first vice president.

Not long after Mortimer got to Flint, he began to hear talk that some UAW leaders were members of the Black Legion. He did not take these rumors seriously until these men began to obstruct his organizational efforts though, as he told himself, he did not see much difference between their doings and the skulduggery of ordinary stool pigeons.

The disrupters were sent into temporary retreat when Harold Hubbard, a former officer of Fisher Body No. 1, publicly confessed his Black Legion membership and identified other UAW leaders at that plant as co-members.[20] Hubbard's disclosures corroborated Mortimer's accusations against the Legion, which he made in a memorandum addressed to the International officers.[21] Of the twelve members on the Flint local's executive board, Mortimer was able to identify four as suspected (later confirmed) Black Legionnaires or spies.

Mortimer's subsequent difficulties with Homer Martin and his forced retirement from Flint put an end to his discoveries about the Black Legion in the union there. This was particularly unfortunate because Mortimer's continued investigations could have brought light to a phase of this virulent group that has remained largely uninvestigated: the relationship of General Motors with the fascistic Black Klan. The La Follette Committee published a letter written by a GM official to a colleague who was organizing an anti-CIO front among the nation's big industrialists. "Maybe you could use a little Black Legion in your country," the official suggested. "It might help."[22] The link between the Fisher One supervision and the Legion was accidentally discovered on a quiet Saturday afternoon by Marie Schlacter, a future UAW leader at the plant, who saw a forelady (Nellie Compton) and some foremen sewing and fitting out some black hoods and cloaks.[23]

At Pontiac, the proof of a close link between the Black Legion and some leaders of the auto union was deliberately suppressed by Homer Martin under circumstances that were highly disturbing if not suspicious. Revelations of a far-reaching involvement with the Legion in Pontiac were made by another one-man grand jury who identified dozens of high-placed individuals in the community and in government. Tice Woody, head of the GM Truck local at Pontiac and formerly national president of the AAWA, made a sensational confession of his own previous membership in the Legion while implicating other officers of the independent union, including Arthur Greer and Richard Byrd, labor's repudiated representative on the Auto Labor Board.[24]

Around this same time, Homer Martin, a featured speaker at a great civil rights rally at Cass Technical High School in Detroit, thrilled his three thousand listeners by pledging that "There are no limits to which we will go to expose and stamp out this menace!"[25] Yet when faced by the other officers with evidence on Art Greer, Martin refused to take action against him, declaring: "I will not stand for red-baiting but I won't tolerate black-baiting either."

I myself had told Martin about the Black Legion's role in the Motor Products strike, which I learned about while helping Lloyd Jones prepare his article for the *United Automobile Worker.*[26] Jones revealed that the group was called the "Invisible Eye of Labor" and that its organizer was a striker named Esquire Lerne Cessnor. Almost all strikers joined the Invisible Eye in the hope that doing so would strengthen the strike. Even Catholics were allowed to join, Jones said, who mentioned such important future UAW leaders as Jack Kennedy and Loren Houser as having been members; they met three times in Kennedy's basement.

Cessnor gave each man who joined the Invisible Eye of Labor a small paper bullet the size of a 410 shotgun shell and would tell them: "We now hand this shell to you as a brother. Beware that the next time it won't be as your worst enemy." Then the initiate would swear an oath that Jones recognized at the time of the exposures as the same that was printed in the newspapers: "In the name of God and the Devil, one to reward and the other to punish . . . I pledge and consecrate my heart, my brain, my body and my limbs . . . to the obedience of my superiors, and that no danger or peril shall deter me from executing their orders; that I will exert every possible means in my power for the extermination of the anarchist, the communist, the Roman hierarchy and their abettors."

The automobile manufacturers did not make wide use of the anti-union services of the Black Legion in their plants.[27] There was one promising arrangement initiated by Alvan Macauley of Packard Motors that several other companies adopted but they were all evidently scared off by the exposure of the Legion. Packard's leading operative in this activity was a Black Legion member named Frank Rice, who used Peg Leg's "Intelligence Department" to help coordinate his work. His method was to con the names of applicants for employment and weed out those identified as undesirables. He joined the MESA, AAWA, Communist party, Socialist party, and other organizations from which he made up extensive lists of members. Other Legionnaires involved in this stool-pigeon work met regularly at Rice's home to compare notes. A number of them were given jobs in the plants from which they reported.

This method was not essentially different from the one used by the established spy agencies except that it did things in reverse order. It had a great advantage over the latter which depended on the slow and perilous process of "hooking" its operatives. The Black Legionnaires not only volunteered their services but also usually believed in what they were doing. They considered it a patriotic duty to help foil the subversive activities of the "communistic" unions. Fortunately, such anti-union efforts were never fully developed or the UAW's organization drive might have had a redoubtable obstacle in the way of its success.

Despite the sensational disclosures of the summer of 1936, no concrete legal measures were undertaken against the Black Legion organization as such. Scapegoats were made of a handful of subalterns: several dozen police officers, firemen, and sheriff's deputies were discharged while the higher-ups who were named got off with lame excuses or hypocritical mea culpas. Nevertheless, the great commotion did have an important salutary effect through the great public horror and anger it aroused. The dangerous incipient fascistic movement was catapulted into retreat, its remaining adherents in disarray.

• • •

Routing stool pigeons out of auto plants was not the specified task of the Subcommittee of the Committee on Education and Labor of the U.S Senate, popularly called the La Follette Committee after the name of its chair, Robert M. La Follette (D.-Wis.). Such a project had never been undertaken by an agency of the federal government and the committee's official task was expressed in more general terms in Senate Resolution 266 of the 74th Congress: "A resolution to investigate violations of the right of free speech and assembly and interference with the right of labor to organize and bargain collectively." But the committee's anti-spy purpose was undoubtedly in the minds of the person who proposed S.R. 266 and of the small group of determined men who carried out its work.

In the Michigan auto unions, several La Follette investigators became well known. This was particularly true in Flint, where the brilliant efforts of Charles Kramer and Benjamin Allen must be credited with having played a significant part in preparing for the great sitdown victory. There was nothing cut-and-dried about this work. The investigators learned as they went along. Stalled by some legalistic obstruction, they found an extralegal evasion. Some obstacles, however, could not be bypassed.[28]

One thing that investigators could not achieve was to oblige General Motors or other corporations to admit collusion with the spy-herding agencies. But there was plenty of secondary evidence of the truth of this conclusion. Investigators were more successful in extracting information from the spy-herders themselves though experienced groups such as Pinkerton often side-stepped their efforts. This happened to Harold Cranefield, who sought to subpoena the reports of Pinkerton's operatives but failed until he got the idea of subpoenaing the janitor of the Pinkerton Detroit office building. The subpoena demanded the company's waste paper and Cranefield thus obtained heaps of revealing materials, often torn into tiny bits, which he pieced together in hours of assiduous labor.

The greatest success of the LaFollette men was in digging out the spies since it was in this work that union leaders could help them.[29] Bob Travis worked closely with the investigators during the period before the Flint strike, designating suspects at particular plants and furnishing other aid that facilitated their task. When alerted by Harold Cranefield's attempts to get their spies' reports, the agencies began to require the spies to deliver information by long-distance telephone. Charles Kramer, however, thwarted this evasion by subpoenaing spies' telephone bills, which itemized out-of-town numbers. He was able to identify in that way two Corporations Auxiliary spies, John Stott and Richard Adlen, out of the four suspected men whose names Travis had provided.

Ben Allen's correspondence shows that he was aware of the anti-union activities of the Black Legion. In one letter of December 16, 1936, he asks for subpoenas for five Detroit men who were "presumably" Legion members: Ted Henderson, Paxton Simmons, John Carlson, Tex Stanley, and the person whom Lloyd Jones identified as the head of the Invisible Eye at Motor Products: Squire Larue [sic] Cessnor. Allen also wrote about another auto worker, Troy Segar, on December 5: "This gentleman works at the Chevrolet plant in Toledo and was, if he is not still, a colonel of the Black Legion in that city and was active for the Black Legion in trying to break the strike in 1935. I understand his name was listed in the Toledo papers in this connection and he is getting rather nervous and is inclined to fly. Please send me this subpoena before he disappears."

It strikes me as important to mention though it is difficult to convey, the sense of security that it gave us to know that the La Follette Committee was always there to call on whenever the union's legitimate rights were obstructed.

• • •

Progressives, especially left-wingers, did not expect to get much help from leaders of the Democratic party during the UAW's organizational drive. At most, they asked for assurances from assertedly friendly candidates to vote against the many repressive bills in the hoppers of state legislatures and Congress. From men running for executive posts, progressives sought pledges especially that troops or the police would not be used against strikers. This was the whole content of the letter that Dick Frankensteen received from Rudolph G. Tenerowicz during Tenerowicz's campaign for mayor of Hamtramck, a letter Frankensteen read to all his meetings and asked me to publish in the paper.

The eyes of the UAW's progressives were focussed hopefully on the future, as was exemplified by a few burgeoning Farmer-Labor parties. These groups, and especially the auto worker candidates they backed, received a lot of attention in the *United Automobile Worker.* At least half a dozen such parties were in the field during the 1936 elections. It was my pride to think that they were inspired by the resolution adopted at the South Bend Convention, where one "resolved" urged UAW members to help develop these parties. It was remarkable that so many members had taken this urging to heart.

The most promising farmer-labor movements in which UAW people were involved were at South Bend and Detroit. South Bend succeeded in establishing a permanent party on a broad united front basis, holding a two-day convention, working out an excellent platform, and fielding a full roster of state and county candidates. The participation of members of the Studebaker and Bendix locals had a good deal to do with this success, the efforts of John Bartee being particularly noteworthy. He was nominated to run for U.S. congressman, and L. R. Richardson, Forrest G. Woods, and Harry Marlett (of Bendix) also ran for state and county offices.

Michigan's Farmer-Labor party had a promising start. At first based in Detroit and Wayne County around the broad community movement that was built up during two brilliant campaigns conducted in 1934 and 1935 by the labor lawyer Maurice Sugar and recently joined by a number of progressive-led UAW locals, the party's claim to its dual title was validated when the strongly organized upstate Farmers Union joined it before the state convention that was held at Owosso on September 12, 1936.[30] The gratification caused by this prestigious addition was cut short, however, when it became known that the big farmers' delegation was chiefly concerned about putting the name of William Lemke on the party's vignette.

Charles Coughlin's directing hand was, of course, behind this maneuver because his Union party had failed to qualify in time to get Lemke's name on the state ballot. Several days before the convention, accordingly, Coughlin's National Union for Social Justice (NUSJ) applied to affiliate its claimed fifty-seven thousand members into the Farmer-Labor party. This was refused and the NUSJ's check was returned, together with a stiff statement that pulled no punches. An all-night session of the party committee before the opening of the convention failed to placate the pro-Lemke delegates, however, and the sessions opened on Sunday morning in an atmosphere of impending storm that even a newcomer like myself could sense.

After a volcanic debate accompanied by a bedlam of catcalls and yelling from the balcony, where the Coughlinites had installed themselves, the delegates, by a vote of about two to one, turned down the motion to seat the Coughlin people. Then, the seven hundred representatives of the Farmers Union withdrew and set up a rump convention in the high school auditorium next door. Surprisingly, the Coughlinites who followed them out did not join their assembly but gathered once more in the balcony, where they conducted a convention of their own.

This was in keeping with the intention of Charles Coughlin to maintain his Union party independent of any other associations, his sole interest being to get Lemke's name on the Michigan ballot. If this meant destroying the Farmer-Labor party, so much the better. The rump group, which had cherished hopes of uniting with the powerful NUSJ, was stunned. Nevertheless, they proceeded to "nominate" William Lemke and his running-mate. The gathering in the balcony did the same, taking advantage of the offer of the so-called Third party that had been organized by a small group of extreme right-wingers. Thus the name of William Lemke would be available to Michigan's voters even if the Farmers Union's attempt to take over the Farmer-Labor party was successfully challenged in the courts.

The Farmer-Labor party did not, in any event, break up—not then anyway. They put a full slate of candidates on the ballot, including twenty-one members of UAW and AFL locals. Maurice Sugar was the candidate for Congress in one Detroit district, Fred Van De Putte of tool-and-die Local 155 in another, and Bill McKie in a third. LeBron Simmons, a black lawyer, ran for the state senate, and my friend Lloyd Jones for sheriff.

Maurice Sugar's biographer Christopher Johnson, in commenting on his campaign, says that Sugar's supporters worked "less ardently" than they did for Roosevelt and that his attempts to win labor support "failed rather dismally."[31] Sugar's attitude toward Roosevelt may have been at fault since he made a sharp sectarian attack on the president in a preelection radio talk and finished third in the race for Congress, which would seem to indicate that only forthright support for FDR could have been politically rewarding at the time.

Witnessing the Owosso fiasco opened my own eyes to some of the sharp realities of the day. The dangers of the Lemke candidacy, reflected in the personalities of some of his rabid, flag-waving, red-baiting supporters, scared and disillusioned me about my own negative, recondite approach to the election and forced me to reexamine my attitude toward Roosevelt. This process, which came too late to do any good, reached its acme during the president's tour of the Midwest in October. He concentrated on visits to the industrial centers and arranged to slow his passage at great factories, where workers would shut down their lines and crowd to the windows to cheer him.

Roosevelt's trip through Michigan was one continuous triumph. In the auto centers, where we were trying so hard to reanimate the workers, those same workers put on spontaneous demonstrations of overwhelming enthusiasm. In Lansing, thirty-five thousand came out to hear FDR speak from the rear platform of his train. Flint, with its pathetic UAW membership of 136, put more than a hundred thousand people along his path. In Pontiac, where we had no members at all, there was a "tremendous gathering," according to the *Detroit News* of October 15, 1936. It described the cheering crowds in the hub city as rivaling the Armistice Day throngs, those at Lindbergh's visit after his transatlantic flight, or the World Series jamboree of 1935. The *News* estimated the number of people lining the streets from Hamtramck to Detroit at five hundred thousand. Frank Winn and I, who followed the president's motorcade in the press section, doubled that figure.

There were 250,000 gathered in City Hall Square to hear Roosevelt's speech, to hear him lashing the auto manufacturers for thinking only of their own profits while ignoring the dire problems of their workers. They roared their approval but they also listened intently, as I did, for I could not fault a single word of what Roosevelt said. I had never before had so convincing a political experience. Roosevelt's victory was assured, I told myself. But beyond that certitude was my realization that the UAW's fate was linked with FDR's victory, my conviction that success was within our grasp.

The First Victories:
Preparing for the Titans   12

When the great sitdown strikes came to the automobile industry in the autumn of 1936, the UAW leaders did their best to prove that they were not "revolutionary." Strikers were instructed to deny any such inference, inviting reporters, community personalities, and political officials to visit the occupied plants to see for themselves how solicitous the sitdowners were about the property over which they had temporary custody.

Nevertheless, the sitdowns were unquestionably radical in background though few American workers who participated in them were aware of that fact. Sitdowns stemmed from the harrowing rise of fascism in Germany and Austria during 1933 and 1934, which found its first revolutionary response in the October 1934 revolt of the Asturian miners in Spain, where factories and mines were seized and held for several weeks by armed workers until they were driven out by sanguinary assault.

Less turbulent and longer lasting was the reaction in France, which in May 1936 elected a united front left-wing government under a socialist prime minister, Léon Blum. As this Front Populaire group was preparing to take office, the workers who supported it burst spontaneously into an unprecedented wave of sitdown strikes that spread swiftly throughout the country.[1] The majority of participants did not belong to any union. From June to September, membership in the Confédération Générale du Travail (CGT), the nation's leading labor organization, climbed dazzlingly from sixty thousand to 4,400,000. We in the UAW could not possibly have been insensitive to this sensational event.

Walk-out strikes had been common enough in the United States since 1933, but they were often accompanied by violence. Not so the sitdowns of France, which were as peaceful as a picnic. Pictures showed the strikers eating and sleeping in their factories, playing cards and reading, making music and dancing. Incredibly, we read, they held out at the Renault automobile plant for several weeks, their demands sounding very much like our own, including the forty-hour week with adjusted wages and "the right to go to the lavatory without losing our job."[2]

Though this distant happening made a deep impression on us, we were in no way prepared to follow its example at the time. But we did absorb the lessons of the sitdown as a technique, especially its advantages in such employer-ridden centers as Flint, Pontiac, and Detroit. We stored the idea of the sitdown away for the proper moment. What was our surprise, when, as the new production season was getting underway among the feeder plants of Detroit, we heard of dozens of spontaneous strikes sputtering—-and most of them were sitdowns!

It was a hectic time for our organizers as they chased after these wild-cats, seeking to make contact with the strikers. Most often the stoppages would be over before they could reach them. If a single union member, or even a sympathizer, was in the group and could get to a telephone, the union's sound car would be outside the plant within an hour or less—if the stoppage lasted that long—to cheer strikers inside with an unexpected, friendly message.

In an article I prepared for the October 1936 issue of the *United Automobile Worker,* I described this wave of strikes, linking them with the sitdown, which I also referred to as a "Chinese strike." I wrote: "Several successful sitdowns which have occurred in the past few weeks in Detroit, in each case in an unorganized plant, attest to the fact that the non-union workers in this hub of the industry are more than ripe for a real militant organization."

I then described in some detail a sitdown at the Jacobs Manufacturing Company, which had occurred on September 11 to protest against incredibly low earnings of 20 cents an hour. "This is for piecework," I explained, "paying at the rate of 3 cents a hundred," whereas other companies doing the same work paid 9 or 12 cents a hundred. The management promised an increase within two weeks and the men went back to work. But when September 25 came, the company refused to keep its word, threatening to close the plant if the workers persisted in their demands. One of the Jacobs workers contacted UAW headquarters and we prepared a handbill that was printed that evening and passed out the following morning. Its message read: "Your sitdown strike won you a promise. Only organization can enforce that promise!" The leaflet called for a meeting in two days and my article summarized the result: "Now an organization in this parts plant which hires five hundred men is underway."

That was the way things were during those early autumn days of 1936. Everything was still very tentative at Peninsular Moulding, at Allen Industries, and at how many other plants that we never heard about? One thing we could be sure of, however, the companies were worried, even frightened, and did not know what to do about this agitation. Some made small concessions to forestall further trouble. A few made their grants contingent on the promise that "the workers would have nothing to do with the union." We were highly pleased by this "requirement" because it did no good and also, as I wrote, it "shows . . . the great fear that the bosses have for the auto union."

• • •

The first major event of that eventful autumn occurred at the Dodge plant. In August during the layoffs, the management had notified several thousand workers that due to "technological improvements" their services would not be required when the new season opened. The premature announcement with its unpleasant euphemism was meant presumably to give laid-off employees a chance to seek new jobs elsewhere.

The cause of the labor displacement was a major change in body form that had been partially introduced the previous season and was now being universally applied. This was the all-steel "turret-top" that was pressed out in a minimum of sections, thus eliminating a number of operations and the workers that went with them. The full effect of the change was not to be felt that year because increased production would take up much of the slack. But it would be encountered later when production dropped off again.

The union was in no position as yet to go to bat on such an issue, which required firm solidarity between those victimized and those fortunate enough to escape. But when it became apparent that the Dodge management intended using the huge displacement as a cover for discrimination, the situation changed swiftly. The company had assumed that workers' personal fears for their jobs would play havoc with collective loyalties. The UAW determined to prove that the company was wrong.

When large numbers of workers brought their layoff letters to the Dodge union headquarters on Jos. Campau, it was soon discovered that the major target was the older workers though they were not the only ones involved. Highly paid displaced men were refused transfers to other jobs unless they accepted beginners' pay. Still others reported that the discharges were being used to mask a generalized speedup of 10 to 15 percent. It was evident that management counted on the willingness of the more energetic younger workers to put up with the required extra effort since doing so meant that they could keep their jobs.

Most insidious was the way the deliberate breakdown in seniority was merged in a welter of favoritism toward pro-company employees. In departments unaffected by the displacement, loyal union members were called in last and were subjected to harassment by their foremen. Three leading rank-and-file unionists were singled out and fired under provocative circumstances. One of them was Mike Dragon, Dick Frankensteen's friend, who, on the day he returned to work, was approached in the locker room by a man who engaged Dragon in an argument. "I suppose you're going to tell us that the union was responsible for getting the bonus?" he sneered. His reference was to a 10 cent raise that the union had requested for months and that the company had finally granted disguised as a "bonus" at the very end of the previous production season.

"Of course it was responsible for getting the bonus," Dragon snapped back. "You know damn well it was." That was all he said because he considered the other man a stooge who was trying to bait him. Shortly after work began, however, Dragon was called off the job by a plant policeman, conducted to the office, and told that he was discharged "for agitation." The two other men were fired under similar circumstances and the three cases thus became linked with the union's general response to the management's provocative program of layoffs.

With the first batch of almost a hundred seniority violations in their hands, the union committee headed by Dick Frankensteen asked the company to open negotiations with it. The request was granted but discussions proved fruitless, even though the union limited its grievances to violations in seniority incurred during the layoffs. The company agreed to only a handful of adjustments and the union's request that hours of work be reduced until all laid-off workers were returned was also turned down.

Negotiations went on for meeting after meeting. It was clear that the management considered itself in an impregnable position. Finally, after one session that seemed no different from any of the others, a union spokesman announced to the press: "We are prepared to strike. We do not want to strike but if it becomes necessary we shall do so." Preparations were already underway. A banner committee and a food committee were set up, and it was announced that a flock of kitchens were being rented, evidently to take care of feeding the twenty-three thousand anticipated strikers.[3]

On October 15, the union-company conference was announced as the "final" one by the union's side, which brought Allan Haywood, a top official of the CIO, to the session. The union negotiators offered to drop all other demands in return for the company's agreement to arbitrate the cases of claimed discrimination. But the company remained obdurate, and after several hours of barren discussion the union conferees rose and, in a dramatic gesture, issued a twenty-four-hour strike ultimatum.

It was the day of Roosevelt's visit to Detroit and the UAW car returning to headquarters became engulfed in immense traffic in the wake of the motorcade carrying the President to the city center from Hamtramck, from whose obscure little railroad station he had chosen to enter Detroit. The union delegation had the sense of being embraced by the tumultuous throng of workers and their families that lined the streets and the earlier, gloomy thoughts of the union men dissolved in a feeling of hopeful strength.

It became part of the union's legend that it was this enormous demonstration that decided the stubborn Chrysler Corporation to change its mind. At any event, the following morning its vice president, Herman Weckler, telephoned Dick Frankensteen to announce Chrysler's acceptance of the union's proposal. The Dodge management then called the factory's works council, a majority of which belonged to the union (Frankensteen was its chair), to an afternoon meeting where, in an act of sham dualism, the same announcement was made.

The works council had been established in early 1935 in an election conducted by the now-defunct Auto Labor Board. The AFL, it will be recalled, had boycotted these elections but the unorganized Dodge workers had decided to participate in them through the medium of a grass-roots movement led by Frankensteen and several other sharp-witted and courageous workers who thought they could make the council function. They were quickly disillusioned and established an outside organization with which, through a series of shrewd tactical maneuvers, they eventually supplanted the company union.

It was a great personal satisfaction to me when Mike Dragon and the other men who had been fired were made part of the settlement and put back on their jobs. I wanted to give a high account of this achievement in the Dodge security special edition of the *United Automobile Worker* that I put out a few days after the strike threat ended. I asked the three men if they minded the publicity and, though aware of the risk, they heartily consented. I featured them together, arms about shoulders, in a three-column photo, beneath which I put a photostat blowup of an affidavit asking *"Who Won the Chrysler Raise?"*

The affidavit was sworn by Frankensteen and two other union negotiators and cited five company men who were present at a conference when F. J. Lamborn, the directing head of the Dodge Company, admitted "that the only reason that these . . . men were discharged was because they had said that the union was responsible for getting their raise."[4] The fact that the union insisted on the rehiring of the men at the threat of strike was proof of the significant heightening of the Dodge workers' union consciousness and loyalty. It was, likewise, a demonstration of courage that would hearten other workers, we felt, and serve as an inspiriting example during the coming season.

● ● ●

It had not occurred to the CIO leaders that the UAW would or even could take the initiative in the organizational drive away from the steel workers.

No one in the auto union thought in terms of priority; we were solely concerned with the problems facing us and they were more than a handful. At any event, we were gratified when, shortly after Allan Haywood's visit, Philip Murray and John Brophy arrived for a two-day conference. All UAW organizers and board members were called to Detroit for the get-together, and citywide stewards' meetings were assembled to hear addresses by the CIO chiefs.

During their visit, the UAW leaders put pressure on the CIO men for financial help or at least to pay the salaries of additional organizers. Our own fund drive was lagging and George Addes was worried about the International's dwindling bank balance. I thought of talking to Phil Murray but nothing could have made me mention money. I wanted to tell him about something else that I considered of great importance but I did not think that my position in the union gave me sufficient prestige to approach Murray. I had thought repeatedly of just going up to him and starting right off, "Brother Murray, I would like to talk to you about something that should interest you." But the idea remained a daydream. The moment I saw Murray in person, smiling his gracious, icy smile, I froze. Then Dick Frankensteen furnished me with what seemed to be an opportunity. He had arranged to have Murray speak to the Dodge workers at the main gate at lunch hour and asked me to go along. The drive out to the plant did not prove conducive to my getting Murray's ear, however, because he sat up front with Dick while Frank Winn and I were in back. Besides, he appeared much too preoccupied for me to venture an approach.

In the *United Automobile Worker* of November 1936, a photo, clipped to mask the sparseness of the crowd, reminds me of the incongruity of the situation at that meeting. Murray stood on the back bumper of Frankensteen's car while Frank Winn and I held up a sign: "Dodge Workers Welcome Philip Murray." Those "Dodge Workers" consisted of exactly two dozen (counted) people, including a young newsboy and a hotdog vendor. The meeting almost ended before it began when a policeman grabbed Murray and started to pull him off his perch. Frankensteen rushed over and broke the officer's grip. "Do you know who this man is?" he shouted. "He's Philip Murray!" The crowd surged closer, out of curiosity, I am sure, rather than protective anger. But the officer quickly backed away, muttering something about "blocking the sidewalk" and "a permit."

Somehow, Murray was feeling good on the trip back and I found an opening by making the others in the car laugh at my description of the policeman's "terror" in learning of Murray's identity. I then launched immediately into my prepared talk about the turbulence that was coursing through the auto plants. The auto workers were *hot,* I explained. There had been nothing like it seen in years. They were no longer afraid to assert themselves. They talked back to their bosses and stopped working if they didn't get satisfaction. "I think we're going to see some real action in the auto industry," I asserted and stopped short to give Murray a chance to ask a question. But his features retained their normal composure. "Very interesting," he observed blandly.

I felt deeply disappointed with myself for some time after, realizing that I had not reached the man. Nevertheless, I remained convinced of the truth of what I had tried to tell him. There was no doubt that a profound change had occurred among the auto workers that autumn. The union's situation inside the plants was completely altered as well. Most of the many stoppages were led by members and the union nuclei were lodging themselves in the most hostile soil.

Even so notorious a union-busting outfit as Briggs Body had been drawn into the surge despite the worst efforts of a spy system that was second to none outside of the Ford Service Department. Daily stoppages were reported at Briggs; one had started with two or three small pockets of welders and swelled like a great wave until 1,500 men were involved. No company, "good" or "bad," was immune to the agitation: Packard, Hudson, Chrysler. The entire drop-forge division of Chevrolet Gear and Axle, 137 men, joined the union in a body after cracking the speedup in a spontaneous action. Hudson workers invented a new version of the sitdown, dubbing it the "skippy." When management increased hood production from 140 to 160, the men simply let every seventh hood pass by untouched.[5]

Although union men in particular plants seemed to be in control of things, the situation as a whole was chaotic. Everyone was waiting for something to happen. Where would it be? People at headquarters knew as little about that as anyone else. Detroit was still outside the pale for most, whether officers or staff. Our thoughts were centered on General Motors and General Motors did not mean Detroit. One day Homer Martin thrilled me with the announcement that the executive board had asked that a special GM edition of the paper be put out. I sat right down to prepare a letter to those locals, listing the kind of information that we would need.[6]

• • •

A few days later, my cup was overflowing when Bob Travis came down from Flint, bringing me a batch of pages covered with handwriting. "We've decided to put out a special Fisher One paper," he said with quiet assurance. I ran my eyes over the material. "This looks fine," I told him, "but there isn't nearly enough for a paper." I thought for a moment. "Are you going back up today?" I asked. "Okay, I'll go with you and stay the weekend. Meanwhile, do you think you could phone up there and arrange for me to meet a few of the guys tonight? Any time at all; just tell them to bring stuff from the plant, as long as it's *facts*."

This first issue of the *Flint Auto Worker* was easier to put out than I had anticipated because I was able to fit most of the material into a single slot.[7] Everything the men brought, everything they talked about, resonated with the speedup. I had heard a lot about the speedup in Detroit but it somehow did not have the same intensity, was not impregnated with the deep emotion that I found at Fisher One.

I had brought a batch of subject fill-ins with me and got much more from Bob Travis. "Tell them about the union," he hammered away as he was driving. "Tell them how democratic it is. Tell them about the officers and board members all being auto workers right out of the plants. Tell them about the CIO."

The Fisher One issue came out as scheduled on Monday morning (though I was already back in Detroit) and it was distributed immediately, Travis wrote. The following weekend we put out a Chevrolet-Flint tabloid in the same way and the week after that, one for the local as a whole. Meanwhile, material for the "General Motors Special" had been pouring in so copiously that we had to expand the issue three times, ending with sixteen pages. There were success stories out of Anderson, Cleveland, St. Louis, Atlanta, and Detroit. Just before the paper was to go to the press, I had to redo the lead article on page one and all of page three to describe the exciting "dress rehearsal sitdown" at Fisher One, a situation that forced the reinstatement of three welders: the Perkins brothers and Joey Urban. The incident started the Flint organization on its historic course.[8]

Of course, this was not the big strike for which we had all waited. That was still a good six weeks off. It was not even a full-fledged strike, only an incident. The first real sitdown in the auto industry occurred in the Bendix plant at South Bend. It was a surprisingly limited affair to have taken on such importance.[9] Its motivation was anachronistic: the favoritism shown by the management for a company union. The UAW local demanded a representative election, by the National Labor Relations Board, to settle the issue, but the company obtained a restraining order and held up the voting for month after month.

On November 17, after Roosevelt's great election victory, a spontaneous stoppage broke out in several departments at Bendix with the express purpose of forcing the company's hand and spread swiftly throughout the plant. The management responded by ordering workers to turn in their tools (an unusual request) and go home. Taken aback, the workers obeyed. More than half of the crew were on the way out of the plant when several union leaders woke up to what was happening and began dashing madly through the factory, yelling "Don't give up the plant! Everybody stay in and protect your job!" About a thousand did, including a majority of the factory's three hundred women workers.

There was bedlam in the plant on that first night. Nothing to eat, nowhere to sleep and it was cold. On the second day Bendix added to the discomfort by turning off the heat, a tactic most other companies adopted in succeeding sitdowns. The strikers' families replied by bringing blankets, woolen underwear, and sweaters. They prepared mounds of sandwiches and pails of hot coffee. On the third day, there was cooked fruit for breakfast and roast beef and mashed potatoes with gravy for lunch, the *United Automobile Worker* reported from a sitdowner's diary.[10] The strike took on a number of the pleasant social characteristics that typified this picturesque technique everywhere.

Negotiations began but got nowhere until the union agreed to evacuate the plant after six days of occupation. Vincent Bendix entered the talks at that point, and, after an all-night session, a tentative agreement was reached.[11] The strike ended two days later, with the company union emasculated by a clause giving the UAW local the final word on any issue in dispute. Little seemed to have been gained and it was hard to make it look important. Frank Winn in his press release could only vaunt the wide national publicity received by the "unique combination of sitdown and lockout."[12]

But the real significance of the sitdown lay in the production problems it caused for a large number of manufacturers, whose supplies of indispensable Bendix parts were cut, reported the *Detroit News* on Novenber 24: Buick, Chevrolet, Olds, Nash, Studebaker, Packard, Hudson, Essex, and— Ford. Bendix was the sole supplier of Ford's brakeshoes and we later learned about the punitive action that Henry Ford took against Bendix because of the snarl the strike caused in his production. John Gillespie, an agent of Ford's in charge of outside parts suppliers, told Dick Frankensteen that representatives of the company came to South Bend during the stoppage to reclaim Ford's brakeshoe dies. "We cannot take any more chances with you," they allegedly told Vincent Bendix, "since it's plain that you don't know how to control your labor force." They then turned the dies over to Kelsey-Hayes Wheel in Detroit, which had not had a serious labor disturbance in many years. But late 1936 was a poor time for self-willed employers to try to outthink their employees.

Ford's action at Bendix had the unwonted effect of lifting a secondary strike into a position of high consequence that it shared with two other strikes of that crucial period, all of them linked with Ford.

• • •

Responsible leaders of the UAW agreed that the General Motors locals, despite signs of growing tension in several of them, were far from ready for a general strike in that corporation.[13] This was not the opinion of Fred Pieper, however, and as early as October 30 he precipitated a sitdown at the Atlanta Fisher Body plant. On October 27, the management there had posted the piecework rates for the 1937 model, an act that provoked a storm of protest when it was found that the rates averaged cuts of 20 to 25 percent. The union committee immediately asked for a meeting with the management, which was refused. A sitdown erupted but was called off when the company changed its mind and after a short session promised to adjust the rates within a week.

When this period had almost run out, Pieper sent a frantic letter on November 7 to all General Motors locals to ask for assurances of support in the event that a strike was called in Atlanta.[14] "We are fully aware," he wrote, "that to close this plant without being in a position to close all other plants would spell defeat." He asked that the locals advise him by wire or airmail letter about their decision as well as "the exact condition of your respective organizations." A request to be told the number of members in each local must have struck most of them as dubious. I do not know of a single local that gave Pieper that information though several did promise supportive action. And Kansas City actually struck, albeit under peculiar circumstances of its own.[15]

This response was far from Pieper's expectations. The deadline given the Atlanta management had passed when he decided that his local would go into action on its own and face the other units with the fact. He devised a dramatic gesture to spark it off. As two officers of the local, C. H. Gillman and a man named Smith, later reported it to me, Pieper alone went in to see the plant manager and told him that all members would put on their union buttons a couple days later. If the supervision made any trouble, there would be a strike. He then called a meeting of the union, which greeted his announcement with cheers, especially when he reported that workers at Flint, Detroit, Norwood, and other centers were "raring to go": "If every General Motors plant in the country isn't struck within a week and twenty-four hours, you can take me out and horsewhip me!"[16]

But Pieper had forgotten to notify George Addes to send a thousand buttons to Atlanta to be distributed among newly recruited members and which would be used in the anticipated challenge. Its fixed date could not be changed and the wire Pieper sent to Detroit could not get the buttons down in time for the demonstration. This meant that only a fraction of the union's strength was exhibited and the great display turned out to be a show of weakness rather than strength. Emboldened by this failure, the management fired several button-wearers in the trim department. It was probably very much surprised when workers not wearing the button struck, followed by workers in other sections. When the sitdowners voluntarily left the plant two days later, they proudly exhibited their buttons, which had by then arrived.

Despite the encouragement of Homer Martin, who, without the approval of the other officers, wired all GM locals "to stand by for action," the help that Pieper had promised his people never came. He went into hiding when he began to hear of threats that some hotheads intended to carry out the punishment that Pieper had asked for. Several days later he showed up under the protection of one of the other officers, Smith, who let it be known that he was carrying a .38, which bulged noticeably in his jacket pocket.

Pieper made peace with the union pickets at the plant by explaining in his glib, excited manner that the reason the Flint workers were holding their strike off was because they were waiting until Michigan's newly elected, pro-labor governor Frank Murphy had taken office, adding, with a mythomaniacal fantasy that brought cheers, that all other General Motors locals in the country had agreed to contribute two hours' pay a week for the Atlanta strikers while waiting to join their ranks.

He was probably counting on getting those locals out on strike before his wild promise would fall due and he almost succeeded, with the zealous collaboration of Homer Martin. At the board meeting where this took place, Pieper chose his time carefully to propose a motion for an immediate national strike in General Motors, just when Dick Frankensteen, who he knew would oppose it, was in negotiations at Midland Steel.

Pieper's motion took the progressives on the board by surprise since the lineup of the board due to Frankensteen's absence was six to five in favor of the strike. The general officers, who were opposed, had no vote on the board during this period. The progressives stalled by calling for a half-hour recess, meanwhile rushing Adolph Germer out to Midland Steel to bring Frankensteen back to the meeting. They figured that if he would tie the count, Homer Martin, the only general officer with a vote on the board, would be too craven to cast the deciding ballot for a national strike because doing so would give him the direct responsibility for any adverse consequences that might arise from it.

The correctness of this reckoning seemed to be verified when, early in the half-hour pause, Martin stepped out "for a few minutes" and did not return. Ed Hall, the second vice president, took the chair since Wyndham Mortimer was also away at the Midland negotiations. As soon as Frankensteen appeared, Hall called the board back into session. He had Pieper's motion re-read and took the tally. It was six to six, and he, as acting chair, cast the deciding vote against the strike.[17]

• • •

The Midland Steel sitdown, the first use of this novel tactic in Michigan and the first victorious major strike of any kind in Detroit, came as a huge surprise to UAW leaders, who had paid little attention to this plant, no doubt because John Anderson, an acknowledged communist, was in charge of it. The Midland local had been inherited from the MESA but was in bad condition when turned over to the UAW due to the factionalism that had been whipped up by supporters of Matt Smith. Favored by the combative mood of the workers that season, Anderson had succeeded in reorganizing the plant. A series of demands were presented to the company on November 14, and, after a week of unsatisfactory negotiations, the union set a strike deadline for 11 A.M. on November 24.

Dick Frankensteen and I accompanied Anderson and the large committee into the conference that morning, when E. J. Kulas, the company's president, made a last-minute counteroffer that was an obvious stall. The committee promptly turned it down. Kulas then asked for additional time but Anderson replied that the committee's hands were tied because the workers had voted to shut the power off at the deadline if there was no agreement. At this point Frankensteen intervened for the first time, urging that the company officials' request be granted. Anderson glared at him but decided not to contradict him in the committee's presence. The delay was accepted and the men ran back into the plant to spread the word.

On the drive back to headquarters Anderson ripped into Frankensteen in cold fury. "You've got a lot of guts breaking in that way. For all we know you may have wrecked the strike. What's to keep Kulas from declaring a lockout tomorrow morning the way Bendix tried to do?" Frankensteen was contrite. "All I could think of was the Motor Products strike that nearly wrecked the AIWA," he explained. "I've been terrified of strikes ever since."

Anderson smiled somewhat ironically, evidently realizing that he had gone too far in chastising Frankensteen. "Well, you'd better get over that," he observed, "because we're going to have to call a lot of them before we organize this industry. . . . I'll tell you what, Dick," he added placatingly. "I mentioned a lockout because that's what I would do if I was Mr. Kulas. But there's one thing you can usually depend on and that's that the boss will be a little dumber than you are."

As it turned out, the delay proved a stroke of luck. When we arrived at headquarters, we found George Addes leafing through the latest page proofs of the La Follette Committee's exhibits. "Check it for Midland Steel," Anderson suggested. "Kulas swears that they don't have any spies in the shop and says if we find one there that he personally will kick him out of the plant," he added disgustedly.

Nevertheless, we hunched over Addes's shoulder as he searched out the pages for Midland Steel. The La Follette Committee had written, he said, that Midland had a contract with one of the spy groups that maintained an office in Detroit. Addes stopped at an early exhibit, No. 1835, which contained a roll of "Undercover operatives employed inside plants by National Corporation Service."[18] He slowly ran his fingertip down the list of names printed in small type, none of which Anderson recognized. Addes was ready to flip the proof page when Anderson let out a sudden whoop. "Wait a minute!" he said and pointed to a tiny footnote referring to a group of identification numerals without names. He read out in a triumphant voice: *"James Howe is one of these!"* None of us knew the name but Anderson quickly enlightened us. "He's the sleazy bastard who won the membership recruiting drive we just held. Signed up forty-four members, three times as many as anybody else! Would you believe it?"[19]

We looked at each other in stunned silence, our minds a rout of clashing thoughts. Mainly we were relieved that the strike had not gone through that morning as originally intended since the union clearly had to do something about this discovery first. Jim Howe was undoubtedly the most popular man in the union, Anderson explained. He was in charge of the tool crib and everybody knew him. Fortunately, he was not on the committee, having always refused such responsibilities. He did his dirty work in other ways.

"Listen," Anderson continued, "that bastard has given us more headaches than anybody. I just thought he was a dumb cluck but I had to go easy with him because of his drag in the shop." Howe had fought against letting blacks into the union, Anderson said, because he didn't want to have to sit next to a "stinking nigger" at the meetings. Just a few weeks earlier he actually offered a motion barring blacks from membership. Anderson had pointed out that such a motion was in opposition to the UAW's constitution. Besides, he added, with 250 blacks in the plant, it would be suicidal to keep them out just as the union was preparing to strike. "In fact," Anderson said, "when we've brought some of them in and I want all of you to help, I'm going to propose that we put one of them on the negotiating committee," which was done.

Jim Howe docilely accepted the voice of authority with a bogus smile. He then turned his disruptive tactics to the three hundred women workers at Midland. He had a couple of obscene cracks about them that the men enjoyed: "Women are good only for two things, frying fish and fucking." Anderson did not have enough time to countervail this pernicious propaganda and when the strike came, no women were in the union. This did not seem such a calamity to the committee. It had been decided to keep women out of the sitdown because of the trouble that had been stirred up over the question in the Bendix strike.

Before we left George Addes's office the decision of what to do about Jim Howe had been reached. You could not just announce his treachery to the whole crowd. That could rip the union apart. The thing to do, Anderson said, was to face him personally with the evidence and scare the life out of him. Then three or four of the most solid union men would be told so they could keep their eye on him. It was also agreed that the strike would start the following morning without giving the company any previous warning. The committee had the power to decide when the strike began. They would announce it to the workers just before reopening negotiations with Kulas, who would be given the same eleven o'clock deadline to make up his mind.

Howe's partial unmasking was to take place that evening at a big pre-strike meeting for stewards. I brought a photographer along, ostensibly to get a picture of the whole group for the paper. Then I asked for a close-up shot of a few leaders. Jim Howe remained modestly in the background.

"Come on, Jim, you've got to be in on this!" Anderson prodded jovially.

"Sure, Jim, what you so bashful for?" somebody else urged and there were cheers when the sheepish man assumed the place of honor between Anderson and Frank Carr, the plant chair, as the bulb flashed several times.

While the stewards met, we pulled a few of the leading men into a side room and told them about Jim Howe. They were shocked at first, then looked mistrustfully at Anderson; one or two began to argue. But when they were shown the printed evidence, the fact began to sink in. One elderly fellow, a foreigner, began to cry. "My best friend," he moaned.

When we thought all were convinced we brought Jim Howe out and Anderson put the screws to him in the others' presence. You could tell that they saw him with new eyes and were quickly persuaded. Howe was cagey but not clever enough to hide his shock. Anderson gave him a choice. He would either confess or be exposed to the stewards then and there. Finally, Howe broke down though he insisted vehemently that he had not done one single thing against the union. "I swear to Holy Christ I haven't!" he said, raising his right hand. He was a Catholic and the head of the spy agency, Carl Myers, had enlisted him by telling him that all they wanted was his help in ferreting out communists. Jim Howe hated communists and considered it a windfall to be offered $50 a month to help expose them. He had eleven children, the eldest still in his teens, and the money would be a godsend. After working twelve years at Midland, life was still a hand-to-mouth affair for Jim Howe and his enormous brood.

• • •

The sitdown at Midland Steel started on the Friday morning after Thanksgiving, at eleven o'clock on the dot. The committee was in the office and you could feel the heavy vibration die away as the big machines went down. The discussions continued for several hours as the company offered a few more minor wage concessions that got nowhere. I had taken a sandwich and an orange with me from home and told Dorothy that I probably would not be back until late. She asked me where Midland Steel was located and I told her frankly that I didn't know because I'd always been driven there. "It's somewhere on the east side," I said.

The talks broke up toward the end of the shift and the committee members went back into the plant to join the sitdowners. A number were crowded at the windows, yelling down gaily to the second-shift workers gathered on the sidewalk. "Go on home!" someone yelled from above. "Don't you know the plant's on strike?"

A rope with a basket attached came dangling down over a windowsill, with money in it for cigarettes.

"Send us up your lunch buckets while you're at it!" one of the strikers called.

"You may need them!" someone below bantered.

"Sure, we're going to stay here till Christmas!"

When I left the building, a lot of women were coming out at the same time. Anderson was standing on the steps, trying to make himself heard by the second-shift people assembled in the court. He announced a meeting at Slovak Hall nearby, which would be strike headquarters for the duration. "The meeting will start at four o'clock," he said. "We'll tell you how the company has been stalling. Let's get over to the hall as soon as possible. It's on Strong and Frontenac."

The crowd broke up promptly and began moving. When the large court around the entrance stairway had partly cleared away I suddenly noticed my wife in the midst of a group of women. I walked over toward her but she gave me a quick warning look and turned her back on me. So I just joined the crowd on the sidewalk and went to the hall.

Dorothy told me later that even before I left that morning she had decided to go out to the plant to get a look at the sitdown. I had told her that first-shift women would be asked to leave but we did not discuss the matter. As she stood alone in the court, the women began coming out, she said. Most went home, but about a dozen remained, forming a compact group and talking among themselves. Dorothy quietly joined them and no one said a word to her, assuming that she, too, was a worker. They appeared to be contemptuous of the strike though it was plain that they were eaten with curiosity about it. It began to drizzle and it looked as if the group was going to break up and go home. "Why don't we go to the union meeting?" Dorothy quickly seized the initiative. "This strike might last several days so we ought to find out what it's all about at least."

"Do you think they'd let us in?" one of the women asked. "We're not even members."

"What difference does that make?" Dorothy replied angrily. "You work in the plant, don't you?"

Curiosity won out, and the cluster of women started walking the short distance to the hall. Quite a crowd was already inside and they took seats at the rear of the auditorium to attract as little notice as possible. But John

Anderson, who was up front waiting to open the meeting, called attention to them. "I'm very pleased to notice that some of the girls have come along to the meeting and I want to welcome them." Dorothy's companions were flustered but visibly pleased by the outburst of applause his announcement produced. They listened raptly as Anderson made a short report of the failed negotiations and then shifted to an explanation of what the second-shift group could do. "You're going to have it easy compared to the guys that are sitting in, who voted unanimously that no one will leave the plant as long as the strike lasts except for illness of themselves or their families. But I'm sure that you too will want to make your contribution to winning this strike and there's plenty of ways that you can help."

He began listing them. "We've got to organize a picket line to protect those body frames that are stacked up in the yard. The company might even try to move them and we've got to let them know that we're not going to allow that to happen." He moved his eyes over the stern faces of his auditors. "Then, too, we've got to get everybody to join the union. All of you have got some friends who aren't members. Talk to them and make them join up. They're going to share the benefits of this strike, so it's the least they can do."

Dorothy meanwhile was talking to the women. What did they think about offering to make sandwiches for the sitdowners? she asked. "Sure," one of the bolder ones replied, "it's going to be a long night in that plant tonight." With a little coaxing the young woman made the announcement to the meeting though she was too timid to stand up. When the women all rose together to get started, there were cheers.

There was a kitchen attached to the hall but no supplies were on hand, nor any dishes. The women chipped in the money they had, but it was hardly enough to pay for bologna and bread to make a thousand sandwiches, plus coffee, cream, sugar, and paper cups. Yet they found storekeepers more than willing to give them credit when they heard what the groceries were for. One woman reported that a baker offered to furnish the strikers a dozen loaves a day for free.

"How did you accomplish that?" Dorothy asked.

"I just chiseled it out of him," she replied, making with her eyes.

This was the origin of the name for the most contributive group of the strike, the chiseling committee. It was so successful that, even when hot meals began to be served, at least half of the cost of supplies was covered by the committee's efforts. The rest came from small-change gifts, a large part of it garnered on Saturdays and Sundays when the chiselers (men and women) made the rounds of beer joints. Detroit's first sitdown proved so popular that it did not cost the International a cent, and when it ended, the local was able to donate the committee's $200 "profit" to the UAW's strike fund.

• • •

Feeding seven hundred men three hot meals a day was no job for amateurs, however fervent. Dick Frankensteen and Dorothy went the following morning to see Frank Martel, leader of the Detroit Federation, who put them in touch with the Cook's Union. There, by lucky chance, they met Max Gazan, who was to become the cook for a number of the UAW's sitdowns, including Flint's. He had been chef at a leading businessmen's club, which was hardly the proper background for the task that faced him. But another member who offered to join Gazan was experienced in feeding big groups because he had cooked for the army. Neither man would hear of being paid until the union insisted on it after the strike began to drag out.

The second-shift strikers who were involved in helping in the kitchen, delivering the food, and in the chiseling made up but a small part of the twelve hundred or so workers on the outside.[20] Many stayed at home but a surprisingly large number came to Slovak Hall every day and sat around all afternoon, no doubt expecting the union to keep them posted about the strike. Actually, negotiations had not started up again but it seemed to me that it was the union's responsibility to do something about these men. I spoke to John Anderson about the matter and he said he had asked Nat Ganley, an officer of Local No. 155, the mother local of Midland, to prepare a strike bulletin. "Maybe you can help along with that," he suggested.

"I'm not looking for something to keep *myself* occupied," I replied, nettled. "I was thinking about the guys who sit around here all day long. I thought that there ought to be a meeting for them or something."

"Je-sus, no meetings for me!" he vociferated. "Once negotiations start, I'll have my hands full."

So, much as I disliked appearing before a crowd, I decided to take the responsibility upon myself until I could turn it over to someone else. I gathered all the newspapers, marked them, added some galleys from the coming issue of the *United Automobile Worker,* and, after lunch, when the men began streaming into the auditorium, I went up front and stood smiling at my unsuspecting auditors. "Brothers," I called out, "I've got some things here that you might like to know about."

No one was as surprised as I was when the effort turned out a success. It was favored by the popularity of the strike, the remarkable press it had. Strikers were overjoyed to learn that people as far away as Chicago or even New York were talking about the Midland sitdown. I read interesting extracts, peppering them when appropriate with sarcastic comments that delighted my captive audience. I tried to get them to talk themselves but few volunteered. We began to have many visitors, however, and if I knew them I would call them up front and put them through the paces. Among the most interesting was George Edwards, Frank Winn's friend and recently the president of the National Students Union. He was gratifyingly responsive and came right up front to talk on "What's wrong with the American schools?" This was undoubtedly his first strike and he loved feeling part of it. He came back again and again and soon enough Dorothy found work for him to do.

The biggest crowds, of course, came to the plant itself to get a view of the sixth wonder of the world. The gabbiest of the sitdowners put on performances from the windows, reciting some original doggerel or playing a harmonica, then they would run down a basket to pick up the gifts, mostly cigarettes or change. Some wives used the basket for hot, cooked meals that they continued to bring from home, never believing that anybody else could feed their men properly. But most of the strikers claimed that they were gaining weight from Max Gazan's meals. One black called down to hefty Dick Frankensteen as he arrived one morning with the union negotiators: "Now don't you settle this here strike! I never ate so good in all my life and I gained ten pounds already."

It was after work that the biggest crowds came from the many plants in the area. Traffic grew dense as visitors drove slowly past the jammed windows, honking their horns. The biggest demonstration was put on by a couple of departments from Dodge that Mike Dragon organized. The newspapers said that three hundred autos were in the caravan that tied up traffic on Mt. Elliott Avenue for fifteen minutes.

These exchanges of solidarity had importance in addition to publicity value because a number of workers in other plants were being laid off who might be inclined to hold a grudge against the union. Chrysler Corporation units were particularly affected: Plymouth, De Soto, Chrysler-Kercheval, and Dodge, a total of fifty-three thousand workers, it was reported. The supervisors began to make anti-sitdown propaganda because of these layoffs and the union at Dodge retaliated by serving notice that they would refuse to assemble frames produced by any other than Midland Steel workers.

Ford typically chose to use direct action (as it had done at Bendix) to pick up its Lincoln-Zephyr frames stacked in the Midland yard by sending down several trucks filled with Harry Bennett's goons. But the union sentries were on the job, armed with iron bars and prepared for a battle that promised to be bloody.[21] Negotiations were going on at the time and U.S. conciliator James Dewey threatened Ford with federal sanctions for interfering with them. The trucks were withdrawn.

No more successful was the patently company-inspired red-baiting swipe at the UAW representatives that was issued by a mythical "Committee of Midland Steel Strikers Who Are Opposing Communism within Our Ranks." The unsigned leaflet asked, "Why not elect your own men from the shop to represent you?" But everyone, especially the management, knew that the negotiating committee was made up of fourteen stewards, one from each department, elected by the rank and file.

The throwaways were distributed by a group of youngsters who even got to pass them out at Slovak Hall, apparently under police protection. It was the oddest feature of the incident. The boys remained in hiding until the officers appeared, then quickly got rid of their leaflets and ran out of the building. The police left right after. As soon as I realized what had happened, I dashed outside and caught their car as they were preparing to drive away. When I asked pointblank who had requested that the police furnish protection for the distributors of the anti-union leaflet, the police seemed sincerely nonplussed and showed me their docket: "Fight at Slovak Hall— 3 o'clock."

"Did you see any sign of a fight?" I asked.

"No."

They asked me for a copy of the leaflet and read it without making much sense out of it, as far as I could see.

Later, one of the union men known as "Frenchy" furnished me with the license numbers of the three cars that had brought the distributors and then carried them off. One was an Ohio license—U976Q—that the LaFollette investigators identified as belonging to the Essex coupe of Carl J. Myers, head of the Detroit office of the National Corporation Service, Jim Howe's "hooker," whose name was also listed on the La Follette Exhibit No. 1835. A sympathetic pharmacist nearby told Glen Snyder—a member of an astonishing union family in which the father, daughter, and two sons were all stewards—that the driver of one of the cars had used the store's telephone several times to call a man named Higgins, who was the law counselor on the company's group of negotiators. This evidence seemed to prove conclusively that the management was directly involved in this unsavory affair.

Negotiations finally got started on November 30, three days after the sit-down began. The company put up stiff resistance, making concessions slowly. Wages were chiefly at issue, Midland's offers being anywhere from 2.5 to 14 cents short of the union's demands. The company was toughest with the machinists, a key, militant group asking for 80 cents an hour. A blanket raise in the base rates of 10 cents was eventually granted (except for welders, who got only a nickel), whereas a minimum of 66 cents an hour for men and 58.5 cents for women was guaranteed. The company also agreed to pay time and one-half over eight hours a day and forty-five hours a week (the five hours being worked on Saturday), and conceded straight seniority as well as recognition of the union.

Talks were stalled on the union's demand for the elimination of piece-work, the company maintaining that it could not shift to straight day work until the following season. Then it consented to do this "as soon as possible." It was not until the very end that it pledged to start making the change "immediately" while raising all piecework rates 10 percent in the interim.

All through these negotiations a small group of determined stewards hung tough. The International's representatives, especially Anderson and Mortimer, were reluctant to contradict them though they did point out to them that the terms were in general better than those existing in other local plants. The union leaders discussed among themselves some pertinent lateral issues. How long could the men be expected to be away from their families and live under such uncomfortable conditions? A week? Ten days? Meanwhile, the circumstances at home would be deteriorating. Bills would be falling due, and the union was in no position to furnish financial help. Winter was approaching.[22]

Aware of the union's monetary pressures, Dorothy and the other women decided to hold a fund-raising dance. The problem was where to get a band. Frank Martel suggested that they call on the Musicians Union and told them when their board met. Without previous notice, Dorothy and three of her prettiest chiselers broke in on the meeting at the union's ornately furnished office, where half a dozen well-dressed Italians greeted them in great surprise.

Dorothy explained the situation and the pecuniary reasons for the dance. "But we don't want a scab orchestra," she said, "and we can't afford a union one." The chairman replied that the union had a strict rule against giving free performances; otherwise they would be swamped by requests. But this was no ordinary request, Dorothy said, it was for a strike for a living wage. Many of the men earned less than 50 cents an hour, the women as little as 35 cents.

"That's very, very little," another man admitted. There was an exchange of whispers and the chairman asked the women to please wait outside. In a few minutes he joined them, and, smiling happily, he reported that their request had been granted.

The strike ended before the fund-raising dance was held, so it was turned into a victory ball. The five-piece orchestra was excellent and the musicians seemed to be enjoying themselves as much as anybody. They broke into medleys of operatic tunes now and then, with one humming a lyrical bel canto accompaniment. Dorothy and I were delighted that a group of blacks had come though they did not mix with the whites and just stood along the wall near the entrance. She was surprised, however, when one of the group asked her for a dance and noticed the others watching her as he approached. She quickly accepted.

They had danced no more than a minute or two when Dorothy became aware that several white men drawing their partners had begun to close in and bump into them without even trying to make it look accidental. She looked up angrily when one man bent down to her ear and hissed "Nigger lover!" Other couples began to notice that something was up and, expecting trouble, started to move away from the center of the floor. Dorothy noticed that other blacks were heading for the door and asked her partner if they might sit down for awhile. But the whites blocked them off. Just then John Anderson, who had probably been warned of trouble, arrived and Dorothy quickly whispered a few words to him. He nodded and called out gaily: "All right, let's keep the floor clear for the dancers. Come on now, everybody dance! Everybody dance!"

I was not aware of the incident until it was over since I was downstairs taking care of the bar. But Dorothy's troubled account struck me with dismay. Once more I was reminded that union success was no assurance of social enlightenment. It was bitter to remember that in my glowing round-up of the strike published just the day before in the December 10 *United Automobile Worker,* I had hailed the "strong unity shown between the white and colored Midland workers." This was all the more remarkable, I said, because just a few weeks before the strike "there had been much opposition to taking the Negroes into the union." And I ended boastfully: "Nothing now can disturb the complete solidarity of the Midland men and women!"

My reference, of course, was to Jim Howe's opposition to blacks and it suddenly occurred to me that he had been successful after all. He had fully earned his Judas shekels! I was disgusted with myself for having thought that his regeneration was sincere when he would greet me now and then with his eager "How'm I doing?" Poor moron, I would tell myself, it isn't his fault that he's so dumb!

John Anderson had no such illusions and prepared carefully for Jim Howe's expulsion in order to avoid any surprises. I missed the event and had to learn of it second-hand because I was in Flint putting out an issue of the *Flint Auto Worker.* Anderson asked Bill Munger, the UAW research director, to read the La Follette evidence of Jim Howe's guilt at the meeting. Howe brazened it out by insisting that he was always trying to help union members by settling their grievances with their foremen. He must have noticed some assenting looks and sought to clinch the matter by using the sympathy plea about his eleven children. But Anderson cut him short. "How about the hundreds of kids of the rest of the Midland Steel workers?" he demanded. "Did you think about *them* when you were helping the company rob their dads of their rightful earnings?"

Jim Howe never came back to the plant after his expulsion and a few days later it was learned that he had skipped town, eleven youngsters and all. The big story I wrote about him featured a four-by-six-inch blowup of the picture that had been taken at the stewards' meeting before the strike, to serve as a warning to other unions to be on the lookout for him.

• • •

If the Midland Steel strike was chiefly a Chrysler headache insofar as its ultimate effects were concerned, the sitdown at Kelsey-Hayes Wheel was primarily a Ford affliction. Underlying it was a memorable throat-slashing contest between the River Rouge curmudgeon and his ancient enemy, the Michigan Employers Association.

The Kelsey-Hayes sitdown was not nearly as sturdy as the Midland strike, with its seven hundred immovable squatters and the strong supporting force outside. The Kelsey strike was precipitated before the union was able to establish itself fully and the plucky little group of 250 sitdowners, including fifty women, had to keep themselves continuously mobilized against the threat of being driven out of the plant.

The Kelsey-Hayes union was a unit of the West Side Local that Walter Reuther and a few others had initiated in the summer of 1936. Its theoretical jurisdiction covered the entire union wasteland of Detroit's West Side, including the gigantic River Rouge plant, Cadillac, Fleetwood, Ternstedt, Kelsey-Hayes, Universal Cooler, and dozens of small parts shops. All union members from these plants were pooled into a local of seventy-eight dues-payers. A store on Michigan Avenue was rented as a headquarters with a $300 loan from the International and the slow, drop-by-drop process of organization was begun.

Kelsey-Hayes was chosen as the local's "concentration point"—"because we had our 'mass base' there, thirty-five members," Reuther would comment ironically.[23] They found some ancient sound equipment that they mounted on the top of a car and every day at the noon hour and at the change of shifts Kelsey workers were harangued with the union's message. Finally, it was thought that sufficient groundwork had been laid and Reuther decided to hold an open meeting for each shift. A leaflet was meticulously drawn up and distributed at the gate. Three workers came to one meeting and five to the other. Reuther got the message; open meetings were abandoned and the sound car began pounding away again.

The Kelsey union strategists decided that some other approach must be used. Why not a "quickie" stoppage? It did not require much cogitation to choose the brake department (No. 49) for the trial because the union was strongest there, with eight members on the first shift and three on the second. The plan for a ten-minute stoppage was laid out. Someone suggested that it should start with the sham fainting "from exhaustion" of one of the women, who had had a real blackout a few months earlier.[24]

The stunt was to occur just before the change of shifts so the union could have the benefit of all its eleven members in the department.[25] Every step of this famous action was mapped out to the last detail, even to the words that would be used in answering the foreman. "Call Walter Reuther in here," the union members would say and then refuse to discuss the matter any further. It is amazing how closely the events followed this blueprint.

At the appointed hour Reuther was sitting in the local's office, nervously waiting for the telephone call and telling himself that the fate of the union could depend on the success of the little stratagem. The time that it should have taken place had passed, something must have gone wrong. Reuther was beginning to wonder how he could find out what had happened when the telephone rang. His caller announced himself as Paul Danzik of the Kelsey-Hayes personnel department.[26] "What's happening in the McGraw plant?" he demanded sharply.

"How should I know?" Reuther replied.

"They've stopped work over there. They told me to call you up."

"What can I do?"

"Go talk to them!"

"Well, you'll have to come down and pick me up. I don't have my car here today." Reuther felt fully in command already and succeeded in sounding unconcerned.

Danzik came right after him and they drove to the plant. The second-shift workers were milling about outside because management had grown panicky and locked the gates. The entire first shift had gone down when word of the stoppage spread and many of the workers streamed into the brake department. Hundreds of them had gathered there when Reuther and Danzik arrived. The scene that followed has been told countless times. Danzik pointed to a heavy crate that was extended lengthwise on the ground. "Okay, get up there and talk to them," he said.

Reuther began to talk fast because he knew that Danzik would not like what he would say. Why had Department 49 stopped work? he asked. Because of the terrible killing speedup. Because of the low wages. Because of the unhealthy working conditions. He detailed all the grievances he could think of and could hear Danzik sputtering angrily down below and tugging at his trousers. "Hey, you're supposed to get them back to work!" he growled.

"Sure, but I've got to organize them first," Reuther replied. Meanwhile, union members were busy passing out application blanks as Reuther went on talking, boasting about the fact that the company had to call on the union to get the work started up again. "Just think of what it'll mean to all of you when we get the whole plant organized!" he declared proudly. And all the while the personnel man kept pulling at his pants.

Finally Reuther came to the point. The strikers would agree to evacuate the plant but the management must promise to negotiate with the committee the following morning, Friday, December 12, at nine. Paul Danzik was ready to agree to anything to get the strikers out of the factory. As they were leaving, the union leaders passed the word around that there would be a meeting that night to elect an expanded negotiating committee and decide on a program of demands.

It was the first real meeting of the Kelsey unit and everyone felt good after the "big" victory. The committee was chosen and demands reviewed, calling for a 5 cent blanket raise, larger increases for low-paid workers, reduction of the speedup, and improved working conditions.

When the committee appeared at the president's office the next morning, they found Chester Culver of the Employers' Association with him and in evident control. George Kennedy paid little attention as the union group outlined its demands and, after a long and aimless discussion, the committee left the conference to report back to the workers gathered in the brake department about the company's negative attitude. This started the sitdown going again, which was once more terminated by the management's agreement to resume negotiations the following Monday morning, December 14.

The company, however, had other plans worked out for that weekend and Chester Culver had undoubtedly had a hand in their preparation. The fact was that Detroit's manufacturers were deeply worried about the ebullient spirit of their workers, which had peaked after the Midland Steel strike. They felt that firm action was called for, especially to put a stop to the seizure of plants. The events of the following weeks would show that their fears were well-grounded, however inadequate their countermeasures were. Kelsey-Hayes, Alcoa, and National Automotive Fibres all struck at about the same time and other factories were getting ready to erupt.

Part of Kennedy's reply, announced next day, was spectacular, taking the form of a 75 cent wage minimum for all employees, men and women. Simultaneously, the "Employees Association," using company facilities, sent wires to all Kelsey workers, calling a meeting at 2 P.M. on Sunday, the obvious purpose being to associate the virtually defunct company union with the big raise. It also explained George Kennedy's flippant treatment of the union committee, whose position, he presumably assumed, would now be totally undermined.

This did not take place, however, because the alert union leaders did not let it happen. They countered with a call for a union meeting, also on Sunday morning but three hours earlier than the company union gathering. Here the company's 75 cent offer was boldly declared to be the result of the union's growing power, which, of course, was true. But that was only the beginning. What about the hundreds of workers in the higher wage brackets? What about the speedup? What about time and a half for overtime? What about recognition?

At one o'clock, just before the union meeting adjourned, Walter Reuther announced that all members would form a line outside four abreast for a march in unison to Dom Polski Hall. The company union's meeting, he explained, had been called under false pretenses because all Kelsey workers had been sent wires. "I hope you've brought those entrance tickets," he said. "In any case, we're all going in together."

The suggestion was approved with cheers and laughter as telegrams were raised in a number of hands. Led by Reuther and Frankensteen, the big union crowd was among the first to arrive at the hall, which filled rapidly after that. The UAW leaders sat and stood quietly as John H. Cowgill, president of the company union, and five other officers mounted the platform. Cowgill had no sooner opened the meeting when Chet ("Moon") Mullins, a union stalwart, shot to his feet and shouted, "We demand the democratic election of the chairman!"

Cowgill disregarded him but others took up the call while Reuther and Frankensteen, accompanied by a squad of husky Kelsey strikers, ran forward and leapt onto the platform. There was a short scuffle but the organized union group prevailed. The handful of company union men ran off, leaving the overflow meeting under UAW control with an even bigger crowd outside that Vic Reuther, Walter Reuther's brother, held together with his sound apparatus, reporting decisions made inside.

Unanimous votes were taken to dissolve the company union, support the UAW's program of demands, to ask full pay in addition for time lost in the two stoppages, and to turn the lockout into a strike should the company shut the gates the following morning contrary to its pledge and refuse to negotiate with the union committee, as the *Detroit News* of December 14 reported.

This last vote may have forestalled the action that it anticipated. Nevertheless, on Monday, when the committee found the company resuming its dilatory tactics, the strike began in earnest. Most workers left the two plants either immediately or shortly thereafter and the union wound up with a force of scarcely three hundred sitdowners (although claiming more) to conduct the siege. The leaders felt that it would be easier to control the sitdown with this smaller number since the plan was to occupy only one of the two buildings. They issued a bulletin in line with this idea, asking the two other shifts to remain outside and help the sitdowners from there.

The union also asked the fifty or so first-shift women to leave and was surprised when they flatly rejected this discriminatory suggestion.[27] They had helped to start the strike, they declared, and intended to see it through. A separate billeting section was set off for them and a company matron was asked to stay on as a chaperon. Curfew was set at 10:30 P.M. and guards were posted at the door leading to the women's sleeping quarters. But in every other respect the women engaged fully in the sitdown.

Outside, too, women played their part. Aside from the usual activities on the commissary side, they kept the auxiliary picket line alive, particularly during the first two or three days. One dismal early winter day, the line almost disappeared and Sophie Guzik and a few of her friends came to the meeting at Falcon Hall, the strike headquarters, wet through from the rain and feeling disheartened.[28] Sophie Guzik was a blond, strongly built Polish woman of twenty-one or twenty-two. She grew steadily angrier as she stood in the rear watching the "damn-fool" men sitting around, smoking and talking and not even listening to the speakers. She asked for the floor. "We girls just come from the picket line," she said. "There was less than twenty of us there. I don't see what all you men are doing sitting around here. What if Henry Ford's thugs come and break into the plant? Then where will we be?" She had to stop when tears filled her throat.

The men listened in silence to Sophie's tense sincerity, then the chairman asked her to come forward and repeat her talk in Polish. She had regained her composure and spoke passionately, without sparing the language. The audience hung their heads and fumbled with their hats but broke into riotous applause when she ended. And early the next morning the line was bolstered by sixty new male picketers.

There was a delay in getting hot meals to the Kelsey sitdowners because strikes in Detroit had come so fast that it was hard for the UAW's kitchen to keep up with them. The Alcoa sitdown started several days ahead of Kelsey's and the Midland Steel kitchen equipment and staff were adapted to feed the 660 occupants there. It was different when Kelsey struck soon after since extra cooking was required and food had to be transported several miles from where Max Gazan and his assistants prepared it.

Dorothy had proposed to Dick Frankensteen the idea of establishing a central commissary around Woodward Avenue to take care of all the strikes. He agreed but the suggestion was vetoed by George Addes for the usual reason, lack of funds. Frankensteen offered to put Dorothy on the payroll instead, which she turned down indignantly. "That's not why I made my suggestion, Dick," she told him.[29]

Instead she shifted her activity immediately to Kelsey-Hayes, which somehow impressed us all as being more important than the other striking plants. I cannot say why exactly this was so but our friendship with Reuther and the progressive role he played in the union certainly had something to do with it. During the first two days, the Kelsey sitdowners had been fed only sandwiches and coffee and a lot of complaints were coming in, Reuther told Dorothy. He showed her a letter he had just received at the union office. It was tense and peremptory: "Do not make any more delay if you have to go buy enough to feed the 200 in here."

One wondered why it had been sent to the office rather than being turned over to the sitdown committee or its message given directly to Reuther. And why was it unsigned? Reuther was disturbed nonetheless and criticized Dorothy as though she was responsible for the delay. But she controlled herself, realizing that he was under pressure. She kept the letter, suspecting that it had been sent by a company union stooge or a spy.[30]

Using the Midland group as a model, Dorothy encouraged the Kelsey outsiders to form a chiseling committee that could gather supplementary supplies for the occasions when prepared meals were late in coming. This Kelsey-Hayes group left an excellent and informative record of its work, with more than a hundred reported donors. Included also are the names of thirty members, women and men, listed as teams of two or three: John and Clara; Jackie—Peter—Anthony; Clint—Louise—Gilbert. "Brosko" was credited with bringing in sixty sandwiches on his own. The kind of supplies collected (money being a minor item) indicates the partial function they were meant to serve: wieners, blood sausages, hamburger meat, mountains of bread, and gallons of milk. One housewife donated six gallons of home-made jam. The Warsaw Music Store gave a record.

• • •

The union seemed to have done everything necessary to organize the strike, but one thing was lacking: no collective bargaining was going on. When the sitdown began on December 14, negotiations were broken off abruptly and not resumed.[31] The company gave its reason to the press, de-claring that it would not negotiate so long as its plants were occupied. On December 17, this assertion was repeated, and on December 21, when the strike was a week old, Walter Reuther and Dick Frankensteen sent George Kennedy a wire charging the company with being solely responsible for making thousands of workers idle through its recalcitrant conduct.

The sitdown was developing into a contest of endurance. How long could the strikers hold out? How long could the company? Kelsey-Hayes pro-duced wheels, rims, hubs, brakes, and other parts for a number of auto man-ufacturers, including Ford, Chevrolet, Studebaker, and Pierce-Arrow. They all put the screws on the company as their supplies began to fail. Henry Ford's clamor was the most menacing of all. Despite his denials, his assem-bly plants throughout the country began to close down and even the Rouge giant was sustaining perturbations.

Ford's hatchet man Harry Bennett had the entire Detroit officialdom hop-ping because of Ford's dilemma. He got Mayor Frank Couzens to agree to go to the Kelsey plant with George Kennedy to try and talk the sitdowners into reason. But the UAW leaders would have none of this high-toned, class-collaboration. Labor-hating police commissioner Heinrich Pickert declared that he was willing to undertake a forceful eviction but that his hands were tied by county prosecutor Duncan McCrea, who was riding high after the Democratic party's sensational victory in the recent elections. "There is no statute covering such a strike," McCrea told Pickert, according to the *Detroit News* on December 20, "so we have to go back to the common law. Under the common law, so long as a strike is peaceful, the police have no authority to interfere. The employees are in the plant by invitation, so there can be no trespass."

To Ford, this was an invitation to manufacture violence, which would give the police the excuse to intervene. Meanwhile, he announced that he would seek a writ in the circuit court to permit sheriff's deputies to reclaim his brake dies for him. Whatever method would be used, the sitdowners prepared to resist it by erecting a barricade three feet high against the main gate with dollies, into each of which they loaded two tons of hub castings.[32] A long human conveyor passed the materials hand to hand from inside the plant to the gate.

While this was going on, a police scout car was parked across the street, its radio playing "Silent Night, Holy Night." At the same time the women pickets seemed to be adding to the hallowed note by decorating a Christmas tree that had been set up near the gate. They stood around it as its candles were being lighted, singing carols. The menus for the Christmas dinner that Max Gazan intended cooking were distributed among the sitdowners. Dorothy had them professionally mimeographed on maroon cardboard, showing St. Nicholas wearing a cook's hat, and ordered three hundred pounds of holiday fowl for the *plat de résistance,* "stuffed roast Vermont turkey."[33]

The sitdowners were not disarmed by the police display of holiday spirit. A couple of days before they had experienced a trial run of violence when the company brought a dozen strikebreakers into the plant under police protection. The strikers entrenched themselves behind the single communicating door running from the employment office and the first aid station (where the thugs were assembled) into the factory proper.[34] The outside picket captain meanwhile sent SOS calls to several big locals that were meeting that night. There was a humorous story about the Hudson local, which was in session when the call came and the man answering the telephone said, "Okay, we'll put it on the agenda." "Agenda, hell!" the irate striker yelled into the mouthpiece. "We need help now!"[35]

As car after car came tearing down the street and screeched to a stop, the plug-uglies lost their nerve. So did the police, apparently, when the pickets yelled to them that at the first blow they would climb over the fence and do battle inside the plant. The armed sitdowners were on the other side of the corridor, and Merlin Bishop, the UAW's educational director, barked at the cops insultingly, then, remembering the course in "workers' education" he was giving during the sitdown, he turned to the strikers near him and cried:

"Look at those policemen! They're supposed to preserve the peace. But are they? No! They're inciting the hoodlums to violence. Strikers, this is *real* workers' education!"

The big crowd outside grew more and more agitated, demanding that the thugs be removed or they would go in and get them. The police surprisingly agreed but insisted that the pickets open a path for them. After this was done and the strikebreakers were escorted away in patrol wagons, the sitdowners came out and fraternized with the great crowd of cheering visitors through the wire netting. All were confident that the victory had been assured by this night's splendid solidarity.

In fact, things began to change soon after. The following morning Dick Frankensteen had a surprise telephone call at the local's office, where he and Reuther had been sleeping on folding chairs for several nights. The call was from Frank Martel, who asked the strike leaders to come right away to the Federation, where John Gillespie was waiting to speak to them. Franken-steen had already met Gillespie during the Midland strike and knew him as a sharp, unscrupulous person whose sole purpose was to keep Ford supplied with parts. He didn't much care what it took to do so and the feeder compa-nies all feared and hated him.

Gillespie went right to the point, asking the UAW men to give him their lowest terms. They told him that the two chief things were wages and the speedup. They also wanted a written assurance that the 75 cent minimum was not a fraud, insisting besides on corresponding adjustments for the higher brackets. Gillespie said that he did not see why those terms could not be met. Henry Ford believed in paying decent wages, as everybody knew, he reminded them haughtily. "Of course I can't contact George Kennedy myself," he laughed. "He and I aren't exactly on the best of terms. But there is somebody else who will talk to him." By his look the union men realized that he meant Harry Bennett and were pleased by this evidence that Ford was ready for a peaceful settlement.

These were the circumstances under which the union's negotiations with the Kelsey-Hayes management were finally resumed.[36] Both Reuther and Frankensteen described the proceedings, which at times took on the char-acter of social drama. Chester Culver of the Employers Association was present in person, while Harry Bennett used the telephone. The union men would put forward a demand, and, after some discussion, Kennedy would seem ready to agree to it. Then Culver would call him out of the room and Kennedy would return with his backbone stiffened.

Then the union leaders would go out, call Gillespie, and complain that Kennedy was stalling. A minute after they returned to the conference room the company president would be wanted on the telephone. It was Bennett, evidently, and the hapless Kennedy would come back looking like a whipped cur. He began to soften again to the union's demands but Culver would stop him, call him out, and the farce would start all over again. When Frankensteen and Reuther described the negotiations they would always refer to the vacant chair in the conference room. It was where Henry Ford's ghost had sat.

The final draft of the compromise settlement was drawn up in Harry Bennett's office at Rouge. Gillespie brought it down to the union leaders, who then went about the complicated business of getting it approved by the strikers. Several hours were consumed in satisfying the fifty members of the outside strike committee, their main complaint being that Kelsey-Hayes had not made a statement specifically mentioning recognition. What would prevent the company from disregarding the terms as soon as the strikers went back? As Sophie Guzik expressed it, "I say if they sign with the union, okay. If not, we stick!"

The UAW leaders explained that the company's failure to put the word *recognition* into the statement was due to a personal idiosyncrasy of Henry Ford's. But the company agreed to meet regularly with the union representatives for collective bargaining, they pointed out, and cited the other important concrete terms of the memorandum, which repeated the 75 cent minimum grant, thus tying it up definitely with the strike. The company also conceded two more of the union's chief demands in the short phrase: "The matter of overtime pay and of wage increases for all men over 75 cents per hour will be adjusted." And it agreed to take all strikers back without discrimination.

This was not a whole lot, Walter Reuther conceded, but it was a good beginning. Beyond that, the most important thing to come out of the strike was the union itself, strong and united. That meant much more than a few words on a piece of paper. A majority of the committee finally gave the settlement their approval.

But the sitdowners proved far more difficult to convince. After the routing out of the strikebreakers they were inclined to be overweening, as though forgetful of the tremendous support they had received from the other unions on that occasion. With fewer than three hundred inside defenders, they were in a weak position to resist a new attack, which would surely come from Harry Bennett's redoubtable servicemen, mobilized to reclaim Ford's brake-shoe dies and probably backed by an army of sheriff's deputies and police.[37] The UAW's strategy, moreover, ruled out prolonged sieges of secondary plants where the hazards of defeat exceeded the potential gains of a more complete victory. A General Motors strike at Flint was looming more imminently every day, demanding the careful husbanding of the union's strength.

The inside leader hardest to win over was George Edwards, who was convinced that the sitdowners could hold out for higher terms. Walter Reuther and I stood at the plant gate arguing with him for an hour or more on that bleak late afternoon. I felt bitter that one so new in the union should hold so stubbornly to his untenable position, willing to risk the union's broader options, so carefully prepared, in a subordinate contest that might easily end in a shattering defeat.

"What if the company refused to adjust the higher wage brackets after we go back to work?" he demanded. "How do you expect a skilled man to continue working for 82 or 84 cents an hour when sweepers and truckers will be getting 75?"

"That's just the point!" I cried. "How *can* you expect them to? Do you think the management does?"[38]

Reuther finally wrung a reluctant acquiescence from Edwards, who insisted that he come over the fence and help sell the deal to the sitdowners since his own heart was not in it. This was done and the strikers packed their things disconsolately. One heard the word *sell-out* uttered here and there.[39] Others were thinking of the cackling company stooges and foremen they would have to face down and the hard time they would have convincing the "weak sisters" in the union that they had won a victory.

These dismal thoughts must have vanished from their minds as they heard the dim roar of the approaching though still unseen procession of second- and third-shift men and women coming from the meeting at Immanuel Aid Hall, where they had approved the settlement with a minimum of opposition. They were headed by Vic Reuther's sound car and accompanied by a large mass of visitors from other UAW locals who had been invited to come and witness the celebration.

The sitdowners came out of the plant and stood waiting behind the gate. It was midnight when the marchers began arriving, some carrying red torches in token of the holiday season as well as the victory. Each successive contingent let out a roar of greeting to the front-line fighters. There had been no need for subtle dialectics to convince the marchers that a trail-blazing victory had been won, and, as the courageous sitdowners, women and men, came through the gate to receive their acclaim, they could hardly have withstood the force of this conviction.

The UAW was modest in its claims about the Kelsey-Hayes settlement when the strike was ended. Walter Reuther termed it an "armed truce" in order to keep the pressure on for the important issues that still remained to be negotiated, as was specified in the agreement. Soon, however, the positive accomplishments, in particular the 75 cent minimum, took precedence over all else and gave its full sense to the significant victory that the Kelsey sitdowners had won.

The Great
General Motors Sitdown

13

When Wyndham Mortimer went to Flint in early June 1936, his most redoubtable impediment was the spies.[1] Those who followed him around the
city, whether he was afoot or driving his old Dodge, amused him more than
they troubled him. Those in the union were the real problem, as they
promptly set themselves athwart his huge task of organizing workers at
Flint's five great General Motors plants.

There were more than forty thousand men and women in these factories
and few more than a hundred were union members. Moreover, according to
the data later released by the La Follette Committee, a considerable number
of these workers were paid spies.[2] Mortimer soon enough became aware of
their existence. When, for example, he asked for volunteers to arrange for
the distribution of the International's journal, the two individuals who immediately responded were Arthur ("Frenchy") Dubuc, eventually identified
as a Pinkerton agent, and Dick Adlen, a Corporations Auxiliary spy. The
result was that Mortimer was soon hearing that the workers were not receiving the papers, most of which were thrown down an abandoned elevator
shaft in the union headquarters building, the remainder sold for scrap.

Mortimer realized that if he were to have any success in his work he
would have to set up an independent union apparatus. He took personal
charge of all membership records, had the combination of the safe changed,
opened a private banking account, and discharged the office secretary.
Those he recruited were told to stay away from the Pengelly Building, the
union headquarters.

He conducted his campaign almost entirely door to door. He also sent a
weekly letter to several thousand former members who had dropped out in
March 1934 when the AFL had collaborated with the Roosevelt administration in scotching the movement for a general strike in the automobile
industry.[3] The torrid heat wave in July, when assembly lines kept pounding

away, causing a great number of deaths according to the newspapers, resulted in many spontaneous work stoppages and stirred up an incipient pro-
union sentiment.

The local officers, outraged by their exclusion from Mortimer's activities, dropped even the sham of cooperation. They demanded that he turn
over to them the names of all new members and to permit them to examine
his secret bank account. Mortimer lent a deaf ear to these importunities and
continued imperturbably with his program when his enemies received help
from a totally unexpected source, Homer Martin.

The UAW president had been more than pleased when Mortimer had
proposed to him that he go to Flint, believing that he was undertaking an
impossible, heartbreaking task. Martin had second thoughts about this,
however, when Mortimer's efforts began to meet with some success and
gave a sympathetic hearing to the Flint local's disruptive elements who
complained to him that Mortimer was building a "red empire" while shun-
ning the cooperation of all "honest union members."

Martin invited a delegation of these people to Detroit to present their
charges before a secret session of the general officers. He conveniently "forgot" to notify Mortimer of the meeting, which turned into a kind of trial of
him in absentia. Ed Hall and George Addes promptly realized what was taking place.

"How many members did *you* bring in last week?" Hall grilled each of
the Flint men in turn. The entire group could not account for a single recruit.
Whereupon Hall let out a stream of characteristic invective and Addes delivered his most scabrous oath: "Son-of-a-pup!"

Notified by the other officers, Mortimer came to Detroit soon after, but
he surprised them by announcing that he had decided to leave Flint, "to keep
peace in the family." "I can't fight General Motors and the president of the
UAW as well," he told them. "All I ask is that we send a good, dependable
man up to take my place."[4]

"How about Bob Travis?" George Addes proposed. Mortimer agreed.
Travis was the man he himself had wanted to recommend. Martin had had
other plans but was so delighted to get Mortimer out of Flint that he fell in
eagerly with the suggestion. Thus the first serious rift in the UAW leadership, forerunner of the virulent factional conflict that later plagued the
union, was patched up for the time being.

• • •

The Flint disrupters were given a rude awakening when, on Travis's arrival, he let it be known immediately that Mortimer's entire organization
plan, including its methods of secrecy, would be retained. It was, in fact, one
of his undercover groups—at Fisher One—that soon after began setting the

pace in the union's drive. This would have been next to impossible had Mortimer confided in the old union clique at the plant. One of them, Harold Hubbard, had confessed membership in the infamous Black Legion that summer, implicating several other former officers, Plez Carpenter, Bert Harris, and Jerry Aldred.

The secret union's nucleus was of an entirely different stamp. At the center of the group were three friends—Bud Simons, Walter Moore, and Joe Devitt—political left-wingers who had greeted the opening of the union drive with fervor.[5] Working cautiously, they laid its foundations in their own department—the "body-in-white"—while others got underway elsewhere, reported the *Flint Auto Worker* in November 1936. There were seven short spontaneous stoppages at Fisher One during one week. Some were caused by the company's wage "adjustments," more of them by the speedup. Everywhere the crews had been reduced while the speed of the line was maintained. In some cases, group and piece rates were cut as much as 40 percent.

I happened to be in Flint for the first time, getting out the initial issue of the *Flint Auto Worker*.[6] Travis and I visited Bud Simons at his home at 2 in the morning following his shift. Simons was almost weeping with eagerness to get going. "Honest to God, Bob," he said, "you've got to let me pull a strike before one pops somewhere that we won't be able to control!" While driving back to the hotel, Travis picked a worker up who was waiting for a bus near the Fisher plant. He was a young chap but looked all done in.

"Working overtime?" Travis asked him.

"Yup."

"How is it?"

"Terrible."

"Speedup, huh?"

"That's it."

"I never worked in a plant," I said, "what's it like?"

"I don't know," the young fellow searched for words. "You just get to feeling so poohed out you don't know if you're sick or exhausted or just plain disgusted."

The little encounter gave me my lead: the speedup. Everyone I spoke to in Flint had the same story to tell. You did not hear nearly as many complaints about wages.[7] It was always the speedup, the horrible speedup. Flint workers had a peculiar grey, jaundiced look that long rest after the exhausting week's work did not efface. The speedup was the one element that found a common ground of resentment. It was the speedup that organized Flint.

• • •

Travis realized that Simons was right, the time was getting ripe. The moment was approaching when the spark would have to be put to the tinder.

He laid the groundwork for action by setting up a system of key men in each department where the union had members—about forty in all. He gave each a "volunteer organizer" card with the International's seal on it. "Boys," he said solemnly at a meeting in someone's basement, "the whole future of the Flint workers depends on you. I know you're not going to let them down. Whatever happens, stick together. And remember—*nobody gets fired!*"

The first union-led sitdown in Flint took place three days later after the supervision eliminated one worker from a group of "bowmen."[8] Two were brothers, typical farm boys from midstate, named Perkins. Another was a scrappy little Italian-American, Joe Urban. None of them were in the union, but they had been reading in the UAW paper about the recent Bendix sitdown in South Bend and just stopped working. A foreman and a superintendent came hurrying over to start them up again but the fellows asked that something be done about the speedup. The talk went on until there was a gap of twenty jobs. It made them nervous to be responsible for such disorder in the line, so they finally agreed to continue for that night. But tomorrow afternoon, they told each other, they'd talk to the day shift fellows about it.

When the Perkins brothers came to work the following evening, they found their cards missing from the rack. In their places were tell-tale notices: "Report to the employment office." They went, and, sure enough, their money was waiting for them. But the union committee had anticipated this contingency, having talked it over with Travis after the previous night's shift. It was decided that this might be the right moment to come out into the open. If anyone was victimized over the little stoppage, the entire "body-in-white" department must be closed down.[9]

After the two brothers showed the committee members their red cards, the latter ran up to the department and spread the word: "The Perkins boys were fired. Nobody starts working!" The whistle blew. Every man stood at his station, tense and unmoving. The foreman pushed the button, and the skeleton bodies, already partly assembled when they got to this point, began to rumble forward. But no one lifted a hand. All eyes were riveted on Bud Simons, who stood out in the aisle by himself. The bosses ran around like mad. "Whatsamatter? Whatsamatter? Get to work!" they shouted.

The superintendent stopped by the bowmen. "You're to blame for this!" he snarled.

"So what if we are?" Joe Urban cried. "You ain't running your line, are you?"

The superintendent grabbed Urban and started for the office with him. They went down almost the entire line while the men stood rigid, watching them. Simons, a torch-solderer, was near the end and they were just passing by him when he called out, "Hey, Teefee, where you going?"

The superintendent, taken aback by the impertinent question, replied: "I'm taking him to the office to have a little talk with him." Then suddenly he got mad. "Say, I think I'll take you along too!"

"No you won't!" Simons said calmly.

"Oh yes I will!" and he grabbed hold of Simons's shirt.

Simons yanked himself loose. Then, all at once, by this simple act of insurgence, Teefee became aware of the long line of silent, inimical men. Seizing Joe Urban, he hastened off with him. Simons yelled, "Come on, fellows, don't let them fire little Joe!"

About a dozen men shot out of the line and started after Teefee, who dropped Urban like a hot poker. The men returned to their places and all stood waiting. When Teefee returned, he was accompanied by Bill Lynch, the assistant plant manager, who went straight up to Simons. "I hear we've got a little trouble here," he said in a chatty way. "What are we going to do about it?"

"I think we'll get a committee together and go in and see Parker," Simons replied. Lynch agreed and Simons began to select the committee, choosing no fewer than eighteen men, including Walter Moore but leaving Joe Devitt behind to see that the bosses would try no monkey business.

Evan Parker, known for his tough, army sergeant's style, was smooth as silk when he greeted the committee. "You can smoke if you want to, men," he said. "Well, what seems to be the trouble?"

Simons took the lead. "Mr. Parker, it's the speedup that the boys are complaining about. It's absolutely beyond human endurance. And now we've organized ourselves into a union. It's the union you're talking to right now, Mr. Parker."

"Why that's perfectly all right," Parker said affably. "Whatever a man does outside the plant is his own business."

The men were almost bowled over by the great man's amiable manner but when he turned to other members of the committee for their opinions, seeking to break them up into so many individuals, Simons saw that he had to put an end to it. "We might as well come to the point, Mr. Parker," he broke in. "The Perkins boys have got to get back to work and that's all there is to it!"

"That's what you say," Parker snapped.

"No, that's what the men say. You can go out and see for yourself. Nobody is going to work until that happens."

Parker knew that was true. Joe Devitt was seeing to it. He finally agreed that the Perkins brothers could return on Monday. This was Friday night and they had already gone home. There was no sense holding up thousands of workers until they were brought back in. It sounded very reasonable and

Simons saw the danger. Who knew what might happen until Monday? "They go back tonight," he insisted.

Parker was fit to be tied. "Those boys have left!" he shouted. "It might take hours to get them back. Are you going to keep the lines tied up all that time?"

"We'll see what the men say," Simons replied, realizing that some backing from the rank and file would be helpful at this juncture. The committee scooted out of the office and back to the shop, where Simons jumped onto a bench as the men crowded around him. He told them in detail of the discussion that had taken place with the plant manager. Pride and courage mounted into their faces as they listened.

"What are we going to do, fellows," Simons ended, "take the company's word and go back to work or wait till the Perkins boys are right here at their jobs?"

"Bring them back first!" Walt Moore and Joe Devitt began yelling, and the whole crowd took up the cry.

Simons seized the favorable moment to make it official. "As many's in favor of bringing the Perkins boys back before we go to work say aye!" There was a roar in answer. "Opposed, nay!" Only a few voices sounded, the company-minded men and the foremen, who had been circulating among the workers trying to influence their vote. Simons turned to them. "There you are," he said.

Parker got the news and decided to terminate the matter without further delay. He contacted the police and asked them to bring the Perkins brothers in. One was at home, but the other had gone out with his girl. The police short-waved his license number to all patrol cars. The local radio station cut into its program several times to announce that the brothers were wanted back at the plant. Such fame would never again come to these humble workers.

By chance, the second brother caught the announcement over the radio in his car and, bewildered, came to the plant. When told what had happened, the unappreciative chap refused to go to work until he had driven his girl home and changed his clothes. A thousand men waited another half-hour while the meticulous fellow was getting out of his Sunday best. When the two brothers came back into the shop at last, accompanied by the committee, the workers let out a deafening cheer. Simons called the Perkins boys up on an impromptu platform. They were too shy to even stammer their thanks.

"You glad to get back?" Simons coached them.

"You bet!"

"Who did it for you?" Simons hoped that they would say the union.

"You boys did."

Simons then gave a short talk though also refraining from mentioning the union. "Fellows, you see what you can get by sticking together. All I want you to do is remember that. Now let's get to work."

The men got the double meaning of his last words and from that moment the barriers were down at Fisher One. Organization shot out from body-in-white into paint, trim, assembly, and press-and-metal. Even the women in cut-and-sew began heeding the call. The management itself seemed ready to admit that the union had come to Fisher One, reported the *Flint Auto Worker* in its December issue. It began to bargain regularly with the committee; numerous grievances were corrected, wage raises and speed reductions won. Meanwhile, the stewards system was being perfected and union buttons began sprouting like dandelions everywhere.

• • •

Strategically, it was not improper for the Fisher One plant to take the lead in the union drive. The body plants were especially vulnerable to organizational efforts because the size and cumbersomeness of car bodies made it impossible to store them in anticipation of strikes. What was extraordinarily favorable at the time was the fact that the union was in a position to set into the balance the two most important body plants in the General Motors complex, Fisher One and Cleveland Fisher.

Both were "mother plants," according to GM terminology, being responsible for the fabrication of the greater portion of Chevrolet and other body parts, which were then shipped in knock-down form to assembly plants throughout the country. In particular, the great dies and enormous presses used to stamp out the mammoth simplified units of the new turret top bodies were concentrated at the Cleveland and Flint factories.

Cleveland Fisher had experienced two unsuccessful strikes, in 1934 and 1935, and the workers had suffered heavy reprisals. Two thousand were laid off, victims of the corporation's policy of decentralizing away from union hot spots. It was felt, consequently, that this plant would be in no position to take the lead in the projected contest. There was a serious question, in fact, about whether, when Fisher One led off, Cleveland Fisher could be depended upon to follow through.

These workers took strategy into their own hands, however, on December 28, when a surprise sitdown in one department spread swiftly through the entire factory. The local's officers were overwhelmed and decided immediately to get in touch with Mortimer. As it happened, he was in Flint when Louis Spisak, the president, finally reached him. He and I were with Bob Travis in his hotel room when the call came in. Mortimer put his hand over the receiver; his smile was as wide as his face. "Cleveland Fisher is on strike," he said. "They're sitting in."

Travis and I began to dance around in the small room. Then we got anxious and hung over the telephone. "Tell him not to settle till you get there! Tell him to sit tight and agree to nothing!"

Mortimer nodded. "Okay, Louie, I'll come right down. Don't worry, everything will be all right. You'll get all the support you need. If they try to put the heat on you, tell them you have no authority to act, tell them the situation has been taken over by the national office. You can tell them I'm coming down to take charge."

Mortimer heaved a big sigh after hanging up. "Boy, there's a weak sister! It looks like the mayor and all the city fathers are after him to settle the strike. The company knows what the score is, all right."

We packed Mortimer into his car. "Don't forget, Mort," we repeated urgently. "No settlement without a national agreement!" And thus was born the strike's first slogan.

• • •

The new season had opened in Cleveland as everywhere else in General Motors with widespread wage-slashing coming in the form of piecework "adjustments." These grievances broke out into a number of short stoppages during December. Finally, after much delay, a conference between the management and the union committee was scheduled for the morning of December 28. But at the last moment the company postponed the meeting until that afternoon. So slight a thing, a matter of a few hours. But to the workers, who carried the memory of years of accumulated grievances, it had the effect of a last straw. A complaint of the strongly organized quarter-panel department was to have come up for discussion. When these men heard of the postponement, they said, "To hell with this stalling!" and yanked the power off. The steel stock, metal assembly, and trim departments followed in rapid succession and in a few minutes the great factory was dead.

The strike started at 1 P.M. and in less than two hours Mayor Harold Burton had arranged a conference between the management and Louis Spisak at the city hall. Spisak quickly agreed to the mayor's plan calling for evacuation of the plant by the sitdowners, resumption of work, and immediate opening of negotiations. However, when he conveyed the proposal to Paul Miley, steward of the quarter-panel department and now the sitdown's leader, Miley turned it down.

When Mortimer arrived on the "Mercury" from Detroit, reporters were waiting for him at the station. They told him of Mayor Burton's plan and asked him for comment. "That's out!" he replied adamantly, giving the papers their headline. "The union will demand that the Cleveland dispute be settled on a national basis."

Lincoln Scafe, the plant manager, complained pathetically that the union committee had "run out" on him. Mayor Burton said that he was "still willing to meet" the union representatives whenever they desired to do so. But federal mediator James Dewey, who had been hastily called to Cleveland, left soon after, describing the situation as hopelessly deadlocked.

• • •

It was now up to Fisher One to follow through and a further lucky break, coming this time, too, on a silver platter from the company, facilitated the confirmation of the second major feature of the strike plan. Early on the evening of December 30, Bob Travis received a telephone call from James ("Chink") Ananich, a Fisher One worker, who had slipped out of the plant to make the call. This time also I happened to be present.

"They're moving dies out, Bob," he said excitedly.[10]

"You sure?"

"Yeah! The boys in the press room working near the doors by the railroad dock say they got crank press dies on some trucks and they're loading a flock of freight cars."[11]

Travis made up his mind instantaneously. "Okay, they're asking for it. Tell the boys there'll be a stewards' meeting at lunch time. Bring everybody down."

There is hardly anything about which a unionist is more sensitive than a runaway shop. In Travis's own experience the memory was fresh of how General Motors had slipped two-thirds of the jobs right from under the workers at Toledo Chevrolet in reprisal for its defeat in the strike of May 1935. Present always in his mind were the suffering and despair that this act had caused. The role that Travis and many volunteers from his local would play in the Flint strike was directly traceable to this tragic experience.

After Ananich hung up Travis called the Fisher One union office. "Put the flicker on," he told the secretary, referring to the big, red, two-hundred-watt bulb over the window. When it was on, the men in the plant across the street knew that something was up and there would be a meeting.

At 8 P.M., the workers streamed out of the plant for lunch hour (actually, thirty minutes). In four minutes the union hall was filled with an expectant crowd. The report of the moving of the dies had evidently spread around by this time. Travis got right down to brass tacks. "Boys, I'll make this snappy," he said. "I understand there's something happening over there on the press room dock."

"That's right," one of the men called out, "they're taking dies out of the press room. They got four or five cars lined up there." The men from the die room corroborated this.

"Well, what are we going to do about it?" Travis asked, looking slowly about the room.

There was a sort of cold pause. A chap raised his hand. "Well, them's our jobs," he said quietly. "We want them left right here in Flint."

"That's right!" several others exclaimed.

"Boys," Travis said, still holding himself back, "I'm not going to tell you what I think you ought to do. In my plant in Toledo, General Motors walked off with fifteen hundred jobs a year ago and in Cleveland the Fisher Body boys struck just Monday to save theirs. What do you want to do?"

"Shut her down! Shut the goddam plant!"

The cry was taken up by the whole room until it was nothing but one big shout.

"Okay, fellows, that's what I wanted to hear you say. Now the important thing to remember from here on out is—discipline. Roy [Reuther] and I will come in after you've got the plant down to help you get everything organized.[12] Bud Simons and the rest of the committee will be in charge but you'll have to enlarge the committee so as to get representation from all departments. Remember, absolutely no liquor. And tell the girls in cut-and-sew to go home and come around to Pengelly headquarters tomorrow morning. We'll have plenty of work for them to do. Okay, good luck!"

"Everybody stays in till the warning whistle!" I yelled from the closed door.

"That's right," Travis said. "We don't want any stooges tipping the company off ahead of time."

The men stood still facing the door. It was like trying to chain a natural force. They began crowding forward and finally broke past me and through the door. They made a race for the plant gates, running in several directions toward the quarter-mile building that bordered the main highway from Detroit.

Travis and I waited outside watching the windows, stamping anxiously on the cold pavement. The starting whistle blew. We listened intently. There was no responsive throb. Was it right? we asked each other with our eyes. Had they pulled it off?

"Here's where the fighting begins," Travis said between tight lips. But we could notice nothing of the sort going on inside the plant. Several minutes passed. Then, suddenly, a third-floor window was flung open and there was Ananich waving his arms. "Hooray, Bob! She's ours!" Then other windows went up and smiling workers pushed their heads through.

"Was there any trouble?" we shouted.

"Naw!"

A little later, the women came out wearing overalls and working caps. And there was a straggling male here and there. But the great majority of the three thousand men remained voluntarily inside the plant that first night.

• • •

After leaving the union hall, one group of men had rushed back to the railroad dock to stop the movement of the dies. A locomotive was just backing up to the platform to hook on to the flatcars. "There's a strike on!" the men yelled to the engineer.

"Okay!" he replied and waved to the brakeman to never mind and the locomotive chugged off again.

The job of organizing the strike was enormous and the situation inside the plant was tumultuous during the first days as a result. One of the first steps was to confine the sitdown to one building, the north unit, and to merely subject the south unit and the press shop to a constant patrol. At first, the foremen were not excluded from the plant until it was found that they abused this privilege, urging workers to leave or eavesdropping on the strike meetings. They were told to go.

The strike committee of seventeen and other leaders toiled ceaselessly during the first days, as secretary Harry Van Nocker's strike journal amply testifies.[13] The problems that rose were a gauge of the complexity of the life and functions of the sitdown. All the sitdowners had to work, putting in six hours' strike duty a day, three hours on and nine off, fitting in as near as possible to their regular shifts.

The strikers insisted meticulously on the observance of all plant rules concerning maintenance and safety. Their strict care of the company property under their temporary wardship was meant to emphasize, perhaps unconsciously, the legality of their strike in rebuttal to the revolutionary motives with which inspired propaganda sought to cloak it. One day the strikers were shocked to find several of the finished bodies marked by deep file scratches. The comment of Bud Simons at a strike meeting was significant: "That was done by a stool pigeon because who else would do such a disgusting thing?"

Food was a fundamental feature of the sitdowners' life, as the International had learned in its earlier experiences with this strike medium. The Flint strikers were served three warm meals a day, prepared across the road in the restaurant of a sympathizer, Ray Cook, that was turned over gratis to the union for the duration. In charge of the kitchen was Max Gazan, the former chef of the swank Detroit Athletic Club, who had worked with my wife Dorothy at the sitdown kitchens of Midland Steel and other Detroit plants.[14] Preparation and distribution of food was only one of the strike's phases that the outsiders handled; others were publicity, welfare and relief, pickets, and defense, all directed from the Pengelly Building headquarters.

For the men in the plants, the long days and nights of the six-week vigil grew very heavy at times, making pastime a major function of the strike. The basement was the center of social life. Here three ping-pong tables were going all the time. Cards and checkers were played everywhere in the plant and the strikers boxed, wrestled, and kicked a football around outside. Throughout the strike, Merlin Bishop and Eugene Faye of the UAW's education department taught classes in the history of the labor movement and parliamentary procedure, but only a small number of men attended the sessions.

The hour before strike meeting every evening was devoted to entertainment. The union-conscious Contemporary Theater of Detroit put on a group of labor plays for the men and got a big hand. But best of all they liked their own hill-billy orchestra that early began to broadcast its nightly programs over the loudspeaker for the benefit of the many outsiders who gathered to listen. The hopeful spirit of the strike was expressed by the group's sprightly theme song, which had been adapted to the tune of the well-known song "The Martins and the Coys."

> Gather round me and I'll tell you all a story,
> Of the Fisher Body Factory Number One:
> When the dies they started moving,
> The union men they had a meeting,
> To decide right then and there what must be done.
>
> CHORUS
> These four-thousand union boys,
> Oh they sure made lots of noise,
> They decided then and there to shut down tight.
> In the office they got snooty,
> So we started picket duty,
> Now the Fisher Body shop is on a strike.

· · ·

With the strike taking strong root in Flint and Cleveland, its national momentum picked up with spectacular speed. Atlanta and Kansas City, which had struck several weeks earlier, were still out, and on December 31 a sitdown started at the important Guide Lamp plant in Anderson, Indiana. On the same day the union struck at Norwood in Cincinnati, the men walking out of the plant.

But the corporation's counterattack was not long in getting underway. The Fisher One strike, which was matched on the same day by a sitdown at Fisher Two, was no more than three days old when General Motors lawyers entered the circuit court of Genesee County and in drumhead justice style, without a show cause hearing or other previous notification to the union, secured an injunction.[15] The writ not only ordered the strikers to leave the Fisher One and Two plants, but also forbade them from picketing them after they had left.

The union simply disregarded the injunction and made a farce of Sheriff Tom Wolcott's effort to read it to the strikers. Larry Davidow, a Detroit attorney hired by Martin, was sent to Flint to confer with the union leaders about it. His views were very disquieting to us. The next step, he explained, would be for the judge to issue a bench warrant against the strikers and their leaders, charging them with contempt for disregarding the writ.

"What do we do then?" Travis asked suspiciously.

"There's nothing you can do. You'll have to obey the order. Otherwise the sheriff can deputize an army of a thousand men if necessary to take the plants over."

"You mean just walk out of the plants and hand the strike over to General Motors on a silver platter!" the strike leader demanded incredulously. "I'll be damned if I'll do that!"

But Davidow's advice was not final on the matter. Lee Pressman, the CIO's chief counsel, and Maurice Sugar, the well-known Detroit labor lawyer, set themselves to explore other possibilities out of the dilemma. Was there, Pressman asked, a state law in Michigan governing the eligibility of judges to try cases in which they were personally interested? Yes, Sugar replied, there was such a provision. He got an assistant to check the statute books for its exact wording. It was contained in section 13888 of the code: "No judge in any court shall sit as such in any case or proceeding in which he is a party or in which he is interested."

Well, Pressman said, maybe it was far-fetched, but what if the old geezer who had issued that ex parte injunction was a General Motors stockholder?[16] A telephone call to an associate in New York sent him hastening to the General Motors Building with a request for the corporation's list of stockholders, A to D. The result was far more exciting than the attorneys could have hoped. Not only was Judge Edward D. Black of Genesee County a General Motors stockholder, but he actually owned 3,365 shares of the stock, which according to the current market quotation were worth $219,900. The union blasted this damaging discovery before the public eye. The injunction, it argued citing precedents, was without legal force and would be disregarded.

The rejected injunction was by no means the sole item in GM's antiunion arsenal, however. During the first days of the strike, City Manager Jim Barringer assembled a top-secret meeting of all General Motors' moribund works council (company union) representatives whom the plant managers regarded as "safe" and outlined a plan to them for a back-to-work movement. The plan was duly approved and soon after launched amid a fanfare of publicity under the title of the "Flint Alliance for the Security of our Jobs, our Homes and our Community."

The task of organizing the Alliance was turned over to a friend of Barringer's, George Boysen, a former mayor of the city and for many years the paymaster at the Buick Motor Company. Headquarters were opened in the heart of the city and within hours the organization claimed thousands of members. Membership was not confined to workers. Businessmen, store-keepers, housewives, and even school children were signed up to swell the lists.

The organizers of the back-to-work movement disclaimed any violent intentions. "We merely wish an enrollment for its moral effect toward smothering the strike movement," the head of the Flint Alliance announced, and to "restore peace in Flint and men and women to their jobs." Yet secondary signs were soon abounding that the strike-quelling organization had a relentless impulsion toward forceful action.

The leaders of the company side needed violence, moreover, that would destroy the eminently peaceful impression of the sitdown. An attack on Fisher One with its hundreds of defenders was out of the question. But in the city's other sitdown plant, Fisher Two, a Pinkerton spy who was among the original strikers had come out to report to the company that no more than a hundred men were in occupation. This plant would be an easy objective.[17]

Fisher Two was not a key plant, nothing like Fisher One, certainly.[18] There were a dozen other units like it working on Chevrolet bodies in scattered centers. Hence, to recapture this plant would mean little to the corporation in a strategic sense. It would mean a great deal psychologically, however. Even if the attempt were unsuccessful, the resulting violence would serve as motivation for calling in the National Guard.

That this was the primary purpose of the plan was later admitted by several local officials. City Commissioner Joseph Shears, for example, in an interview with me, quoted Captain Caesar Scavarda, who was in charge of the state police in Flint, to that effect. The idea was to force Governor Frank Murphy's hand by creating a situation that was ostensibly beyond the city's control. The governor would then have to declare martial law and suspend all union meetings and other activities. The strikers would thus be starved out and the plants repossessed at point of gun. The back-to-work movement would take care of the rest.

The plan, as worked out with precision by City Manager Barringer, was put on the rails in the early evening of January 11. First, the union transporters carrying "dinner" to the Fisher Two men were stopped at the gate by the plant guards. Unlike the Fisher One sitdowners, the occupants of the smaller plant had allowed the company guards to remain in possession of not only the main entrance but also of the entire ground floor. The strikers occupied only the second floor, which meant that food and other supplies had thus far been delivered to them at the pleasure of the company. By shutting the gate, the company notified the sitdowners that it had changed its mind and was virtually saying, "Get out or starve!"

This the strikers had no intention of doing. By arrangement with the outside pickets, a twenty-four-foot ladder was brought to the factory, and food was run up to the second floor that way. It was only a momentary solution, however, because the guards formed a flying wedge, overcame the small group defending the ladder, and confiscated it. Then other things began to happen. All traffic approaches to the factory were blocked off by the police while owners of parked cars within the immediate area were told to remove them. Thoroughly aroused by these moves, the union hastened all available pickets to the plant as well as the sound car that a Chevrolet worker guided over a small unpaved road and past the police cordon.

It was clear that the sitdowners must immediately gain possession of the gate. If the police could get inside the plant during an attack, their advantage would be enormous.[19] Strike director Bob Travis hastened out to Fisher Two to take charge of this task. Over the sound car's loudspeaker he encouraged the insiders to get going. They selected twenty of their biggest men, all armed with plant-made billies, to do the job. The burly squad descended the stairs while the rest of the men clustered around the stairhead, listening. The exchange of words below was brief. "I want the key to the gate," the squad captain snapped.

"My orders are not to give it to anybody," the chief of the guard replied.

"Well, we want that door opened," one of the men said. "We've got to get food in here."

This was the signal. The men took a firmer hold of their clubs and moved toward the doors. "Get the hell out of there!" they warned, and the guards sidled away with alacrity. They disappeared before anyone could notice where they went. Actually, they hurried to the women's restroom on the ground floor and locked themselves in while their captain got to a telephone and called police headquarters to report that they had been "captured" and were being held prisoner by the strikers.

Meanwhile the sitdowners' special squad had gone up to the locked doors, put their shoulders to them, and pressed. There was a sound of ripping wood and the doors flew open. The men ran out and a great cheer went up from the pickets. Many others came down from upstairs and the sitdowners and pickets mingled joyously, shaking hands and pounding each other on the back. But the self-congratulatory mood was short-lived as one of the pickets suddenly cried out: "Here comes the police!"

Several squad cars, sirens shrilling, headed from north and south and screeched to stops in front of the plant. A dozen heavily caparisoned men, who looked like some sort of prehistoric beetles, piled out and ran toward the main gate, pulling their gas helmets over their faces as they ran.[20] Several gas grenades exploded, forcing the pickets to break and dash for safety while the insiders scrambled back into the plant, slammed the doors shut, and barred them. The police were there that moment. One smashed a pane, inserted his gas gun, and shot a shell inside.

Curiously, the attackers had not approached the sound car during this action and Vic Reuther started shouting over the microphone: "Pickets, back to your posts! Men in the plant, get your fire hose going!"

The pickets did not need the summons. They had been only temporarily discomfited and had gone but a short distance. Inside, the sitdowners had unwound a fire hose and dragged it to the door. It was a little short but they let fly anyway, blowing the cops back with the force of the stream. The men upstairs poked another hose through a window and played it on the police in the street while two-pound car-door hinges began raining down on them. The officers, several of them drenched through and through, retreated unceremoniously toward the Flint River bridge, out of range of the water and the hinges.

The sitdowners and pickets yelled in wild triumph. The men on the ground floor hauled out cases of empty milk and pop bottles for the pickets to use in case of another attack and those upstairs dumped quantities of hinges onto the sidewalk for them. Thus the second wave of police found the plant's defenders completely prepared and very quickly took to their heels, this time with the pickets close behind them. Several hard-pressed officers drew their pistols as they ran and discharged them indiscriminately into the ranks of their pursuers. Some began to fall. Those near them stopped to carry them back, but the others kept on, swept forward by the emotion of the battle.

• • •

The police did not attack again, contenting themselves with firing gas shells from the bridge down into the pickets' ranks or at the sound car. Several ambulances had arrived and the wounded men were carried off. Fourteen had bullet wounds; one had been critically hit by a pistol shot in the abdomen. He was Earl De Long, one of the city's striking bus drivers who had joined the auto workers' struggle to their own.

Large crowds of onlookers witnessed the entire battle, standing at both ends of the street. They were unquestionably sympathetic with the unionists and as those in the sound car directed a steady call to them to join the pickets some began coming over. Vic Reuther's voice rang out with particular appeal, alternately rising above the turmoil of the exploding guns and sounding like the very soul of courage:

All during these days the Fisher Body workers have been sitting down peacefully protecting their jobs; yes, and religiously guarding the machines at which they earn their livelihood. Not a scratch has marred a single object inside the plant until tonight when the police shot their gas and bullets into it in a cowardly attack upon these unarmed and peaceful men. . . . You police, you weren't hired by the citizens of

Flint to foment violence but to preserve law and order. . . . Go home
to your families and let the Fisher Body workers continue their peaceful struggle for the right to live!

Bob Travis was among the union men carried off to Hurley Hospital,
having received gas burns around the eyes from an exploding shell. At Hurley, after undergoing preliminary treatment, he was arrested but slipped off
by way of a rear stairway and exit. He returned to Fisher Two but left again
when two state police officers contacted him with an imperative call from
Governor Murphy, who was reported to have ordered out the troops.

The night grew steadily colder, and pickets and strike sympathizers began to fall away rapidly. The crowds on the street had dispersed and only a
knot of police remained far up the hill, waiting. A reconnaissance tour that
Roy Reuther and I made inside the plant showed an alarmingly small number of men remaining. Evidently many of the sitdowners had slipped home
for the night, seizing the first opportunity in two weeks to do so.

Reporters had told us that the city had sent to Saginaw for new supplies
of gas. What if they arrived and the police attacked again? There would be
no holding them with our small numbers, we told ourselves panic-stricken.
Roy and Vic Reuther and I talked these things over with a tired sort of des-
peration. It was 2:30 and still no word of the troops. We did not know that
the governor had recently arrived in Flint and was at the Durant Hotel at that
moment.

Suddenly, an insane thought came to us. Why not evacuate now, before a
new attack started? The plant was not worth the risk of fighting for and losing. The effect on the morale of the strike would be devastating. We even
discussed the details of the evacuation. We would announce to the press
beforehand that we were leaving voluntarily, line up the men, and let them
march out in triumph. Fortunately, the aberration was short-lived and after
a few minutes we came to our senses.

Perhaps it was the sudden vision of the picketers at the blazing sala-
mander, amazingly gay and light-hearted, that drove off these defeatist
thoughts. No more than a dozen of them were left, including two women,
one of them Genora Johnson, the wife of a Chevrolet worker who had become a leader in the Auxiliary. The small group was circling the fire jaunti-
ly, telling jokes and singing. Just then they were intoning songs of their own
making, choosing some popular ditty, then one of them would propose the
first line, another the second, the task keeping them occupied and happy. It
was not until 4 A.M. that other organizers came to relieve us.

• • •

On the morning following the Fisher Two fight, the curious began arriving early on the scene. The radio and papers had had a Roman holiday

and everyone wanted to get a look at the battleground. Before noon the workers began coming to union headquarters to sign up and soon there was a double line at the dues windows, extending out to the vestibule. This continued for several days, a consequence that General Motors had certainly not anticipated.

The National Guard did not arrive until early the following morning, but that afternoon, during a gathering outside Fisher Two, an observation plane of the Guard droned aloft. The workers looked up to it with friendliness. The sitdowners had swept the street of the debris that had been left in the wake of the fighting, but bits of glass were still palpable beneath one's shoes and the air bore a slightly acrid tang.

The pro-company crowd in Flint had spasms of fear when Governor Murphy failed to declare a state of martial law in the city as 1,200 troops marched in and 1,800 more prepared to move. No troops were sent to the plants; moreover, they were billeted at an abandoned schoolhouse in the center of town. The governor, seeing in the resounding defeat of the corporation at Fisher Two the possibility of a prompt termination of the crisis, refused any course that might wreck this chance.

General Motors officials were definitely on the defensive over the recent happenings. In response to the widespread public resentment of the attempt to starve out the sitdowners, they hastily expressed their regrets for the violence and bloodshed while contradictorily insisting that the fighting had been entirely between the police and the strikers. "Let's discuss matters equitably across the table and settle them that way," GM president William Knudsen said. "I don't want anybody to get hurt." Murphy took him at his word and arranged the conference.

The conferees went into session at 11 A.M. on Thursday, January 14, and at 3 the following morning. Murphy, grey with exhaustion, came out to announce in his rococo manner: "We have arrived at a peace."

The union had agreed to clear all occupied plants not later than the following Monday morning, when negotiations would begin, upon the reciprocal pledge of the corporation that during a period of fifteen days it would not remove "any dies, tools, machinery, material (except for export trade) or equipment from any of the plants on strike" nor "endeavor to resume operation in any such plants."

The truce terms were by no means popular with us in Flint. Our whole strike had been built around the occupation of the plants. The shift to the outside would be like disarming ourselves completely. Fifteen days constituted a terribly short security period, putting very little pressure on the company, whereas each passing day placed an increased compulsion on the union to come to terms.

Nevertheless, the union proceeded to carry out its side of the bargain, clearing the plants of Guide Lamp in Anderson and Cadillac and Fleetwood in Detroit. General Motors, on the contrary, started right off by violating the terms of the pact in encouraging the police to break the picket lines that were established at these plants and wiring the strikers to report to work on Monday, when the negotiations were scheduled to begin.

Arrangements had been made for a mammoth celebration at the Flint evacuations, which were to take place on Sunday afternoon. It had been a difficult task to convince the sitdowners into accepting the "truce"; the promise of a big, roasted chicken dinner did little to cheer them. Everyone at headquarters was likewise in a low mood and I reacted nastily when Bill Lawrence, a UP reporter, approached me breezily in the Pengelly vestibule.

"Where's Bob?" he asked.

For no reason, I lost my temper. "Can't you ever give a guy some peace?" I demanded.

"But I've got something important," he insisted.

There was something about the way he said it and looked at me that caught my notice. I took him by the side door into Travis's office.

"Bob, here's a statement Boysen is issuing tonight," he said, handing Travis a sheet. "I was nosing around their office when I saw it on the desk so I picked it up and read it. Williamson came in and said that he hadn't intended letting anyone see it until after the evacuations but since I already knew about it he said I could have a copy but to keep it quiet until tonight.[21] You might give me something on it in advance though there isn't a hell of a lot to it from what I can make out."

Travis read the short statement. Calmly he rose to his feet though his heart was thumping. "Listen, Bill, just wait here a minute, will you?" And he stepped into the adjoining room with the mimeographed sheet and got the long-distance operator on the telephone. There was some delay in finding Homer Martin but he was finally picked up at the Cass Tech auditorium in Detroit, where a "victory" celebration was being held. "Homer," Travis told him, "I just got hold of something important. It's a publicity release that Boysen is giving out tonight. Knudsen has agreed to meet with the Flint Alliance on Tuesday." He read the release to him, but Martin replied coolly: "I don't think that means anything, Bob. What's the difference if they do have their meeting—it can't have any real effect. I think you ought to go right ahead with your plans."

Travis was in no mood to argue. He replied sharply, "Like hell I will!" and hung up. Then he picked the receiver up again and asked the operator to get him John Brophy at the same number. When the latter heard Travis's news he hurried back to the auditorium.[22]

"We've got to see the governor right away," he told Martin. "This changes the whole picture."

The background to Boysen's press release was a letter he had sent to

Knudsen asking for a conference for his group with the General Motors president: "We earnestly request an appointment with you at 9 o'clock Tuesday morning, if possible, for a committee of twelve members of the Flint Alliance on which will be representatives of the vast majority of workmen of each of your Flint plants. The purpose of this meeting will be to discuss collective bargaining as it affects the vast majority of your employees."

Knudsen's reply, which was on the sheet that Bill Lawrence had brought to Travis, contained a damaging little sentence that revealed the dishonorable objective of the entire interlude: "We shall notify you as soon as possible as to a time and place for a meeting."

Thus, with one cynical stroke, would the corporation render its negotiations with the union utterly worthless before they had even begun. Its agreement to meet with the Flint Alliance would prejudice the union's fundamental demand—for sole collective bargaining—in advance, would "remove from negotiations a point on which the corporation had agreed to negotiate," as the union's official explanation expressed it.

After talking to Brophy, Travis had sped a "runner" out to Fisher One with a note for Mortimer, who was there to officiate at the evacuation proceedings. A meeting was immediately called inside and when Mortimer explained the situation and proposed that the evacuation be called off, the men cheered. "Yeah, man, that's the stuff! We stuck it out this long, let's stick till we win!"

Mortimer then announced the change of plans to the five thousand people outside who had been waiting for an hour in a steady drizzle to witness the important event. The strikers' wives were there with their children. Bud Simons kissed his wife for the photographers and clambered back into the plant.

There was an even bigger gathering at Fisher Two following this one. Vic Reuther spoke over the mike: "This is the same voice that spoke to you Monday night. I think we should christen this square for posterity. We will call it Bulls Run for it was here that we put the bulls on the run."[23]

• • •

The battle was on again. The strike had not yet completed its third week but the feeling on all hands was that we were in for a tough and stormy period. The union's top strategy board discussed plans for raising a huge war chest for the increasing needs of the strike. A request for financial aid was drawn up by Secretary-Treasurer Addes and sent throughout the country, eventually bringing tens of thousands of dollars, mainly from UAW unions.[24] The CIO as such gave much less than is usually supposed, most of its financial aid at that time still going to the organization of the steel workers.

The scene shifted momentarily to Washington, where the principals in the great struggle were called by Secretary of Labor Frances Perkins. She sent an official request to Alfred P. Sloan, president of General Motors, but he turned it down cold. Unilateral conferences went on for a short period, with Perkins talking first to one group and then to the other and getting nowhere fast. John L. Lewis felt that it was time for President Roosevelt to speak out: "We have advised the Administration that the economic royalists of General Motors . . . contributed their money and used their energy to drive the President of the United States out of the White House. The Administration asked labor to help it repel this attack. Labor gave its help. The same economic royalists now have their fangs in labor and the workers expect the Administration in every reasonable and legal way to support the auto workers in their fight with the same rapacious enemy."

But Roosevelt refused to be smoked out, and, in a one-sentence comment, he rebuked the CIO leader, "Of course, in the interests of peace there come moments when statements, conversations and headlines are not in order."

This gave the General Motors bigwigs the chance they wanted to strut off the scene while announcing their intention of reopening as many of the unstruck plants as was feasible—to "alleviate distress." Secretary Perkins responded by issuing an official request that Sloan and Lewis get together and "lay their cards on the table," which Lewis immediately acknowledged whereas the company, amazingly, refused the secretary's mandate. "The question of the evacuation of the plants unlawfully held is not, in our view, an issue to be further negotiated," Sloan wrote Perkins. "We will bargain on the proposals set forth (by the union) as soon as our plants are evacuated and not before."

The President then sought to restore the delicate balance he was maintaining. Again calling the press and again allowing himself to be quoted directly, he issued a diplomatically worded statement: "I told them I was not only disappointed in the refusal of Mr. Sloan to come down here, but I regarded it as a very unfortunate decision on his part."

• • •

The violence that broke out soon after and almost simultaneously at several plants demonstrated that the corporation had other plans than negotiating. In Detroit, the scene was the Cadillac plant where a hundred of Commissioner Heinie Pickert's riot squad went into action against the pickets (the sitdowners having left this plant as a result of the "truce") and split open several heads, including that of one woman.

The union at the Guide Lamp plant in Anderson, Indiana, experienced an even more violent attack. Significantly, it was led by members of a "Citizens' League for Employment Security," a counterpart of the Flint Alliance made up of plant foremen, backwoods Rotarians, and small-time politicos, and was openly supported by the city officials and police. When crushing the picket line, the plant manager himself assumed a heroic role. Mounting on a car top and waving an American flag, he shouted to the assorted mobsters: "It's nights like this that a city shows what's in it!"

A third blow was struck at Saginaw, organizationally a suburb of Flint. Travis's friend from Toledo, Joe Ditzel, and several CIO organizers, mainly members of the United Mine Workers, were in nearby Bay City making arrangements for a mass meeting when they were set upon in broad daylight by a large group of company men. They got back to Saginaw, supposedly under police escort, with the vigilantes following close behind.

In Saginaw, the organizers were forced into an easily identifiable Yellow Cab after being badly beaten by a mob while the police looked on benignly. With several police cars before and behind them they were rushed out of the city at sixty miles an hour, accompanied by a large group of vigilantes. Inside the Flint city limits, a gray sedan was parked, its engine running, waiting for the arrival of the motorcade. It allowed the leading police car to pass, then, as the taxi approached, the sedan swerved directly toward it, sideswiping it into a telephone pole. The organizers narrowly escaped with their lives though all were badly injured. Three required several months of hospitalization.

There was, finally, a legal phase of the corporation's attack that took the form of an amended bill of complaint and motion for injunction. It was filed in the court of Judge Paul V. Gadola, a Tory stalwart whose personal holdings had undoubtedly been carefully checked to avoid a repetition of the Black fiasco. If the unlawful seizure of the plants continued, the bill contended, the result would be "loss of the plaintiff's business and the diversion thereof to plaintiff's competitors"—and eventually bankruptcy.

• • •

To strike director Bob Travis and his aides the moment cried out for a counteroffensive to the corporation's accelerated onslaught. Travis realized that the union's undertaking would have to be spectacular. Ever since the beginning of the strike he had weighed the possibility of "taking" Chevrolet. This plant, and particularly its motor-assembly division (Chevrolet No. 4), which made engines for a million cars a year, was generally regarded as the most important single unit in the General Motors framework.

The chief obstacle to capturing Chevy 4, Travis knew, would be its great mass of company guards. The workers reported that a veritable army was in control of the plant since the reopening, all provided with new clubs and a number with guns. Together with Ed Cronk, Howard Foster, and Kermit

Johnson, three Chevy men, Travis retired to his Dresden hotel room to work out a plan, if possible, to outwit the Chevrolet plant police.

After poring over a rough, hand-drawn map[25] of the plant area and weighing the relative numbers of union members in the various factories, a tentative plan of action was worked out. It would concentrate on the three units where the union was strongest—Chevy 4, 6, and 9—and would take place at the change of shifts to assure the presence of a maximum of union forces. The three units formed an almost equilateral triangle; the distance between any two of them about three hundred yards.

The key move decided upon was a decoy action—a sitdown at Chevy 9—that would draw guards away from the other plants.[26] A big racket would be put on at Chevy 9 to increase the illusion, with pickets outside, the sound car, the women's Emergency Brigade. Shortly thereafter, things would start in the other two plants, with Chevy 6 merely mustering its strong union forces and then marching on the gargantuan Chevy 4 and helping to close it down.

Sunday evening had been set aside for a general membership meeting. Chevrolet plant manager Arnold Lenz had presented the union with a good excuse for strike action by discharging three union men during the previous week. We were delighted—the company was playing right into our hands. After an hour of talks, mainly by famous visitors, the enthusiastic gathering was declared closed to all but Chevrolet workers and the others were asked to leave. Travis took the platform amid a rapt silence. The men sensed that something important was in the works.

"Men," he began, "when the unstruck plants reopened last week we gave our pledge that we wouldn't interfere. We knew that you boys could use the money. Besides, your working wasn't going to weaken the strike anyway. But it seems that Arnold Lenz took this as a sign of weakness. He's fired several more men already and intimidated hundreds of others. Well, we've worked out some plans that we're going to discuss with the stewards. You know why we can't talk about them in the open."

The stewards and volunteer organizers, a group of a hundred or so, stayed on after the meeting broke up. They were lined up in the hall and told to pass one by one into the adjoining room, where Travis, Roy Reuther, and I by a quick exchange of eyes passed on the trustworthiness of each candidate. The thirty men thus designated were given a signed slip of paper that they were told to present at the Fisher One plant at midnight.

The purpose of this elaborate procedure was to prevent any details of the new strike plan from getting to the company. The careful timing of the action, which was to start ten minutes earlier at Chevy 9 than at the two other plants, was designed to draw off the armed guards at Chevy 4 and thus lighten the task of the union forces at this crucial plant. But everything depended on keeping the company in ignorance of these essential details.

On the way out to Fisher One, however, Reuther and I expressed some doubts to Travis about how the plan had worked out. We disagreed especially about two or three individuals whom he had approved over our veto. Travis smiled. "I wanted to get them in," he said, giving us an enigmatic look. "We're not going to tell this meeting the whole plan," he explained. "It'd be dynamite. Even if there wasn't a couple of stool pigeons among them, how would you keep thirty men from telling their friends or their wives? By tomorrow early the whole town would know about it."

He paused, studying our faces quizzically. "So here's what we'll do," he continued, coolly. "We'll tell them only that we're going to strike Plant 9 and the rest we'll keep secret. Except for the three boys that know about it already, naturally, and will have to take the lead. Your stool pigeons are going to be there. They'll run right back to Arnold Lenz with this false dope. Lenz is pretty shrewd but he'll believe it's the McCoy because of all the trouble we took to get this group chosen. That means that tomorrow at 3:20 he'll rush his armed thugs out to Chevy 9 and fall right into our trap!"

When, however, Bob stood before the stewards out at Fisher One and revealed that the project entailed the "taking" of Chevy 9, it fell like a dud. One of the men ventured a question. Couldn't General Motors get bearings which Chevy 9 produced from other places? He was quite sure that the plant at Muncie, Indiana, could supply all the bearings that GM needed.

"We've checked into all that," Travis said authoritatively. "Besides, we're not really interested in the importance of the plant. General Motors isn't going to put out cars anyway so long as Fisher One and Cleveland Fisher are kept tight. This strike is merely to show that the union hasn't demonstrated all its strength yet and that there's more to follow unless the company comes to its senses. Do you get the point?"

The men thought they did and they perked up. "One more thing," Travis said. "You boys in the other plants aren't to rush out to help Plant 9. The boys in 9 can take care of themselves. Stick to your own plant and watch for developments."

After the meeting Travis drew Ted LaDuke and Tom Klasey, Chevy 9 men, aside. "I want to tell you fellows that everything depends on the fight you can put up. We don't expect you to win out but it's absolutely necessary for you to hold the plant from 3:20 to about 4:10. Then you can walk out. You see, we're not really after Chevy 9. We couldn't tell all those fellows what our real plan was or it would be sure to get back to Lenz. What you guys are going to accomplish by your fight is to draw off all the company guards while the boys are taking *Chevy 6*. That's the plant we really want!"

Thus was the plan laid for the capturing of Chevrolet No. 4—with checks, double-checks, and triple-checks.

• • •

Around 11 the following morning, Kermit Johnson, one of the three key men in the strike plan, showed up at the union office, looking sheepish.[27] Travis fixed him with a cold stare.

"How come you aren't in the plant?"

"I overslept," Johnson smiled self-consciously.

"Can you get in at noon?"

"Sure."

"See that you do!"

But the noon hour passed and when Travis ran into Johnson again he was fit to be tied. This time the young chap had simply "forgotten" to go down in time.

"Listen," Travis told him, "you're going to get into that plant at the change of shifts if I have to throw you through a window! Even so you're not going to be able to hold back many of the day men. We can just about write them off."

At 2:30, a meeting began in the Pengelly auditorium. It had been called for the ostensible purpose of organizing a protest march on the courthouse where the injunction hearings were to start that afternoon. At 3:10, while Travis was speaking, my wife Dorothy suddenly came into the hall, looking very excited. She handed Travis a slip of paper. It was blank but Travis drew his eyes over it as though he were reading.

"Brothers and sisters," he said tensely, "I don't want you to get excited but I've just gotten word that there's trouble at Chevy 9. The guards are beating up on our fellows inside the plant. There are some pickets down there already but they can use some reinforcements. I suggest that we break up this meeting and go right down there."

The audience, more than half of them women, pushed their chairs back and dashed for the stairs. Outside, they found a long line of cars, motors running. The trip to the plant was so expeditiously accomplished, in fact, that, when they arrived, nothing had yet begun to "happen" inside the factory. The newspaper people had also been tipped off that there would be "something doing" at Chevy 9 that afternoon and a number of them were already on the spot, including movie trucks from Paramount and Pathe News.

But all this display was hardly necessary. A leak to the company from the previous midnight's meeting at Fisher One had the wished-for result. The entire armed force of the Chevrolet division had been concentrated in the personnel building right next to Plant 9, awaiting the union's "attack." The first company move came shortly before 3:30, when a large group of blue-uniformed guards filed out of the personnel building, crossed the narrow driveway, and entered Chevy 9.

It was soon evident to those outside that the strike had begun since the windows that opened to the street had shortly before been ominously shut. Suddenly, the pickets were conscious of fighting going on inside, beyond the little opaque square windowpanes. The crowd grew excited, and, when one of the windows was pushed open and a worker's bloody head appeared, gasping for air, Geraldine Klasey recognized her husband, let out a yell, and dashed across the street, screaming, "They're smothering them! Let's give them air!"

The other women followed immediately and promptly commenced smashing the windows with their sticks as blurred snatches of the inside fighting appeared, vague forms milling about eerily in a thick fog. Outside the union sympathizers were going through a hell of doubt. What was happening? After what seemed an era of waiting, it became clear that the fighting had ceased.

A strange quiet settled on the union crowd, a quiet of apprehension. The leaders, after conferring, decided that there would be no point in staying any longer and agreed that they ought to conduct their people back to Pengelly headquarters. Just then the men from inside started coming out, a number of them hurt and bleeding. They picked up several of the wounded men and took them along.

Bob Travis and I had remained at the Pengelly Building behind closed doors, each of us at a telephone. Several scouts had been assigned to different sectors of the "front" with a handful of nickels and instructions to call every five minutes. Our function was to coordinate, if possible, the actions of the several plant groups in line with the developing situation.

At a quarter of four, we still had no news about Chevy 4 except that the day shift had left the plant at 3:30 and that there was no sign of a disturbance or other happening inside. Organizer Ralph Dale was keeping us informed about this sector. The hum of motors indicated that work was proceeding normally, he said. We did not hear from him again, and the reports from Chevy 9 indicating that everything had gone off there exactly as planned left us cold.

When we could stand the suspense no longer Travis asked me to go to Chevrolet 4 and reconnoiter. It was around 4:15 and my driver and I were hastening toward the parked volunteer car that would take us there when the union caravan returning from Chevy 9 arrived. I dashed to the sound car. "How come you're back already?" I shouted to Walter Reuther. "How about Chevy 4?"

"It fell through," he replied. "The plant's working full force."

We went back to the Pengelly and climbed the stairs. The men emptied their hats of the crushed paper they had stuffed into them in expectation of meeting with police clubs. We stood around looking at one another disconsolately.

"Well, Bob, it was a noble effort anyway," CIO organizer Powers Hapgood observed with his invincible good humor.

The telephone rang. It was Ralph Dale. We could hear his excited voice rattling through the receiver: "We've got her, Bob! The plant's ours!"

"What the hell are you talking about?" Travis shouted. "Are you crazy?"

"Honest to God, Bob. I've just been talking to the boys on the inside. All the scabs have left already. The boys have begun to barricade the back doors. We're going in to help them."

We were too stunned to express our joy and were merely trying to figure it all out. What had happened? Why had we not heard about it sooner? We realized that we had underestimated the time that would be required for the plan to unfold. Also, because of Kermit Johnson's absence the strike had not been launched until the second shift was underway, and that had played hob with the original plan. And there were other miscalculations and misadventures. Yet the workers had made up for them all with a remarkable spontaneity.

• • •

Still in its broad outlines the strategem had worked out surprisingly well.[28] At 3:20, ten minutes before the end of the first shift, the night-shift men of Chevy 9 who had gathered in the cafeteria in the southwest corner of the one-story building lined up three abreast and entered the plant proper. They started circling the shop, shouting: "Strike! Strike!"

A majority of the day workers immediately shut down their machines and joined the parade. The others hastily made for the plant's exit, some without stopping for their wraps. Almost simultaneously the doors opened from the outside, and a throng of company guards came running in, all armed with big hickory sticks. Arnold Lenz himself was in the lead, closely followed by personnel director Floyd Corcoran and other top managerial and supervisory officials.

Lenz's army swarmed into the plant and followed in the wake of the union parade, howling, "Reds! Communists!" The unionists shook their fists furiously at Lenz. "You bastard!" someone cried. "We ought to tear you apart!" A flying wedge of guards split the workers' line in the center of the shop and an attack with clubs and blackjacks began. The workers were outnumbered but they had stashed away defense weapons in handy places. They spread out to break the charge up and began firing oil pump blanks and pulleys, anything that came to hand, at their attackers.

Dozens of individual fights were soon taking place in scattered parts of the shop. Several guards would isolate a striker and go to work on him. Two union men, Russell Hardy and Morley Crafts, were beaten unconscious, then tramped on while lying on the ground. Friends rushed to their aid, fought off the guards, and carried the injured men to the cafeteria. Little by little the guards retreated to the back part of the plant, where Lenz and the other officials had gathered to watch the spectacle.

At an order from Lenz, the guards produced riot guns, and fizzing shells began to explode among the workers. Ventilation having been shut off, the gas took immediate effect, and the men began coughing violently. But they held on doggedly. When the women began breaking the windows from the outside, the company group were intimidated and for a while the two sides merely stood glaring at each other. The company forces were preparing to make a final attack to drive the by-now reduced union group out of the plant. But the men spared them the trouble. At 4:10 sharp they marched out in unison, having fulfilled their task with exemplary courage and determination.

In Chevy 4, meanwhile, the day crew had gone home, and the night crew had started working. Kermit Johnson had managed to get in at the change of shifts but was able to keep only a handful of his friends from leaving the plant. With these few he hid in the balcony toilets, waiting for the men from Chevy 6.

In Chevy 6, as the 3:30 whistle blew and the machines started up, Ed Cronk went to his press, set it going, shut it off again in a minute, picked up a piece of lead pipe, took a crumpled little American flag from his pocket, and held it above his head as he ran through the shop, yelling "Shut 'er off and follow me!"

This factory, which made heavy steel parts like fenders, running boards, and splash guards, was extremely noisy. Cronk banged his pipe on things as he ran to attract attention, jumping over stationary conveyors and supply stacks that were in his way and heading for the exit. A group of foremen sought to stand him off but the powerful fellow swung his pipe and they backed away. But Cronk had traveled too fast and by the time he reached the western door he had only about thirty-five men with him.

He decided to go on with this group anyway, figuring that there was no time to go back for more. It was but a short jog to Chevy 4 and when the Chevy 6 men got there, Kermit Johnson and his small group were waiting at the door with the bad news that their part of the plan had failed to come off. "Well," Cronk said, "let's go back and get some more men then."

When they got to Chevy 6 things were really stirring. Carl Bibber's powerful gang of a hundred men from the dock—all union—were working their way through the plant and another bunch of fifty or so were marching and shouting in another section. Along with the newcomers the union men succeeded in shutting the whole works down in no time. "All right, boys," Ed Cronk shouted as once again he raised aloft his crumpled American flag, "everybody over to Chevy 4 now!"

Meanwhile, the Chevy 4 night shift had been working with agonizing tenseness. The plan as given out by the union—that Chevy 9 was the objective—had fooled few of these men. Most felt that their own plant must be involved in the action but they did not know when it would start. The entrance into Chevy 4 of the augmented group from Chevy 6 gave them their first hint. In crankshafts, Gib Rose chose that moment to step up to his buddy. "Smith, you said you was with me no matter what happened. How about it?" he asked.

"Sure!"

"Okay, as soon as I pull that button you get into the aisle and start parading and hollering."

He then reached up and pulled the switch and conveyor A-1 was dead. This was the signal for Dow Kehler, who headed conveyor A-2. In five seconds it, too, was down. When the next man saw that, he pulled the switch on conveyor A-3 and the entire division was frozen.

But the real job had only just begun. A few of the staunchest unionists got into the aisles and began marching around, crying "Strike is on! Come on and help us!" A lot of the men kept working or made a desperate effort to do so. But the ranks of the strikers grew steadily as courage added to courage. There was no physical violence. A few would merely act fierce. One enormous chap, for example, with a wrench in his fist tore down the line and yelled "Get off your job, you dirty scab!" Yet he never touched a man—all shrunk with fright before him.[29]

After a while, the several union groups that had been going through the plant joined forces, now many hundreds strong. Squads of union men were now stationed at key conveyors everywhere. Others set themselves to guard gates or mount lookout. They drove the foremen before them, shouting that they had fifteen minutes to leave the plant. The foremen yelled to the nonstrikers to mount to the balcony, no doubt hoping to organize a big enough group to take over again. But nothing came of it.

The battle was over. The enormous plant was dead. The unionists were in complete control. Everywhere they were speaking to undecided workers, many of whom reached their decision at that time and joined the sitdown. Others went home, undeterred by the strikers. About two thousand remained, and an equal number went off. But as they left by the rear exits a large number, following an impulse of solidarity, dropped their lunches into huge gondolas, half filling several of them with what proved to be a much-needed supplementary supply of food.

As soon as the strikers had driven the foremen out, they began barricading the plant's exits. By this time the high main gate on Chevrolet Avenue had been locked[30] and outside pickets and men from Fisher Two who had carried salamanders over gathered. Soon a singing, cheering picket line, including many Emergency Brigade women from Chevy 9, was marching several hundred strong before the plant. The arrival of a sound car that led the steadily increasing crowd in songs and cheers completed the happy throng.

The defense of the back doors remained the chief concern of the sitdowners, according to Howard Foster, one of the three men who had worked out the decoy strategy with Bob Travis. Foster reported that he was worried by the fact that he had only recently been changed to the night shift and hence knew few of the men. Nevertheless, he found "one man that could run a lift truck and I had him stack stock against the doors and we barricaded the whole back end of the plant and down the sides and the upstairs to prevent those fellows from coming back. We had men stationed to see that they didn't come in."[31]

When the plant was secure the men gathered at the rear windows to watch the movements of the foremen and guards who were marshaled in Chevy 8 across the narrow court. Finally, they came furtively out and dashed around the corner of the plant out of sight. They were all carrying clubs but the fight was over for them. Their leaving was the company's admission that the sitdown at Chevy 4 had succeeded.

• • •

The far-reaching consequences of the new sitdown had certain harsh and unexpected early features. Governor Murphy, who had been preparing the ground for the resumption of negotiations, thought that the renewed hostilities would again disjoint his efforts. He was furious with the union, regarding the new action as almost a personal affront.

At his command, at 9 P.M., twelve hundred National Guard troops were mounted into army trucks and moved to the Chevrolet area, taking possession of all streets and approaches. Guards, their bayonets fixed, were strung about the entire vast rectangle. Eight machine guns and 37-milimeter howitzers were mounted at strategic points overlooking the tract. The Chevy 4 sitdowners were subjected to virtual martial law.

How far would the restraint go? The first order issued by Colonel Joseph H. Lewis was to stop all those seeking access to the plant. Even the union food car was turned back and the commanding officer declared, "When the men get hungry they can go out and eat. Nobody is keeping them from going out."

This attitude of the Guard opened the question of a possible attack on the plant. I had been inside the plant for some time when I learned that a caucus was being held to decide what to do in case that happened. I barged in on the meeting and was surprised to find Walter Reuther and Powers Hapgood there, as well as Kermit Johnson and several other Chevrolet men though the caucus was apparently being run by Frank Trager, who was a stranger to me.[32] At the moment, he was developing the idea that a meeting should be called. The men should be told that in case of an attack they were not to resist but merely sprawl on the ground so that the Guard would have to carry them out.

It was obvious that Reuther was embarrassed if not displeased by Trager's exposition. Without concealing my anger, I broke into it: "What right does a bunch of outsiders have to make a decision like that? Don't you think Bob Travis and the strategy board ought to be told about it?" The argument continued for awhile and got hot at times but the question was dropped eventually. In any case, there was no attack that night.

Around 1:30 A.M., lights went out in the plant and the heat blowers likewise went dead. For a while it seemed that panic would result as the men began milling about in the dark, stumbling over each other and crashing into things. But after some minutes calm was reestablished. The men settled down for the night though it grew very cold in the plant.

At about 4 o'clock Walter Reuther and Powers Hapgood crawled under the boxcars parked along the loading dock and got past the military blockade. The National Guard had set up headquarters in the personnel building near Chevy 9. Reuther and Hapgood told the officer in control: "There are three thousand men in the plant. We've assumed the responsibility of keeping these men disciplined. But the lights and heat have been shut off and the men are making torches out of old waste. If that plant goes up in flames the company itself will be to blame."

Shortly thereafter the lights came on again and the heat somewhat later though the Guard continued to turn it off and on. The blockade on food was permanent, however. Toward dawn the picket line had dwindled to a handful, including several women of the Emergency Brigade. Soon after, a squad of troops arrived, confiscated the sound truck, and arrested the last five pickets.

All that morning efforts were made to get the governor to allow food into the plant. Shortly after noon John Brophy came from Detroit just as I arrived at the Pengelly Building from Chevy 4. I told him of the situation there. Brophy immediately got Governor Murphy on the telephone and a long and heated conversation ensued. "The good people of this country did not expect to see the governor of Michigan condemn to starvation hundreds of workers who are fighting for their elementary rights," Brophy said, his face deeply flushed with anger. "I'm sure you will be able to win the strike for General Motors that way. . . . Well, I don't see how their taking the Chevrolet plant breaks faith with you, governor. . . . I don't say that two wrongs make a right but the cases are not similar. . . . We appreciate that, governor, but it will be meaningless if at this late date you break this strike by martial law!"

Early that afternoon Colonel Lewis's attitude had undergone a complete change. Was it because of Brophy's talk with Governor Murphy? Soon after we were to learn that the reason was much more exciting than that. The corporation, overwhelmed by the new union victory, had finally consented to negotiate without preconditions.

Brophy and I joined Travis and Roy Reuther at the armory, where Colonel Lewis greeted us very graciously. "You see, gentlemen," he said, "the governor has been receiving information all night from certain sources that the new strike was entirely executed by out-of-towners who just went in and seized the plant. We understand now that that isn't exactly correct."[33]

"We're willing to go in there with you and inspect all the occupants," Brophy offered. "Any man who can't show a Chevrolet badge will be asked to leave."

"That won't be necessary," the colonel replied. "If you will do that yourselves I will take your word for it."

"And the men will get food?" Travis asked.

"I see no reason why not once that point is clarified."

We all went over the fence and into the frigid factory, where a meeting was quickly called in the cafeteria. The men were asked to show their badges and all those that wanted to leave were invited to do so. Not one took advantage of the offer. Then we sang "Solidarity," bade the men goodbye, and left.

The morning after Chevy 4, John L. Lewis took the train to Detroit. Nevertheless, when Knudsen shook hands with him at 9:30 on Wednesday, February 3, in Judge George Murphy's private offices,[34] the act by no means signified that the strike was ending or that General Motors would cease encouraging offensive acts against the union. The strikers in Flint, rather than experiencing any relaxation of their struggle, were to go through a period of extraordinary tension.

The first blow was Judge Gadola's injunction delivered the day after Chevy 4. The judge added his assurance that he would personally see to the execution of the terms of the writ on the strength of the authority over the National Guard given him—together with the sheriff and independently of the governor—by an obscure statute on the state books.

As though to demonstrate its own pacific intentions, the union declared the day of the injunction "Women's Day." Several hundred women had come to Flint from Detroit, Pontiac, Lansing, and Toledo to assist in the celebration. Those from Detroit were wearing green berets to match the red tams of the Flint women, the idea of the Emergency Brigade having spread swiftly. The women decided under the critical circumstances to march right into the heart of the city, many of them with their children.

After the parade the women hastened out to Fisher One as the injuction's deadline approached. The picket line was the biggest in Flint's history. The loop trod down the entire great length of the plant, six abreast going both ways. Continuous arrivals from out of town augmented the huge gathering, and, as traffic jammed on the highway in front of the plant while motorists slowed to watch the demonstration, the unionists had to arrange an impromptu traffic corps to keep cars moving.

The sitdowners gathered at all the windows, wearing neckcloths that could be dipped into water and rubbed protectively over their eyes in case of the use of gas in an assault on the plant. The sheriff's attack did not come off, however, and the great mustering of defenders gave joyous expression to their feelings of relief.

A few hours after the demonstration at Fisher One, reports started filtering into union headquarters that City Manager Barringer and Police Chief Wills were organizing a "civilian army" for the purpose of "shooting it out if necessary to repossess Flint for the forces of law and order." The massed picketing during the demonstration, the blocked traffic, the pickets' sticks, and the alleged bellicose acts against passersby served as the arguments for the mobilization.

The battling city manager called his "civilian army," their guns concealed beneath their hunting jackets, to a dress rehearsal. John L. Lewis accused the GM negotiators of "siccing" their dogs on the strikers while hypocritically engaging in "peace" conferences. The situation became strained and Governor Murphy had to step in, insisting that the corporation heads put a damper on their overzealous agents in Flint.

• • •

Negotiations in Detroit had meanwhile circled around the single subject of recognition, which in its abstract quality seemed terribly distant from the grim reality of the battlefront. The basic fact of union recognition had been formally accepted by the corporation when it had agreed to negotiate without any preconditon. But the extent of that recognition remained unresolved. The entire effectiveness of the bargaining procedure depended on the answer to that issue.

The UAW's strategy board early realized the necessity for a compromise in the union's demand for corporationwide recognition and offered an important concession for a quick settlement: exclusive bargaining in only the twenty struck plants where the union had demonstrated its strength. But the corporation representatives made no sign of bending to the offer. For days the negotiations stiffened along these lines. The two groups sat in separate rooms at opposite ends of Judge George Murphy's court,[34] never meeting, while the governor hastened back and forth between them, trying to keep the thin wisp of the "discussions" alive.

On February 8, the complete breakdown of negotiations seemed imminent. When the conferees left at one in the morning no arrangement had been made for their return. The governor was steeped in the depths. What an outcome after all his herculean efforts.

Murphy told the union's representatives that he would like to see them within an hour at his apartments. His manner was extremely cold as he indicated that he had a major announcement to make to them. Lewis, who had come down with the grippe during the day, went to bed, but the rest of the strategy board kept the appointment with Murphy.

They found the governor in his bathrobe and house slippers, lounging in a deep chair. His attitude had apparently changed again. He was very friendly and went into a lengthy discussion of the situation, emphasizing his own predicament. He had been eminently fair to the union but the time had come for a change and the union would have to make an important concession if it wished to avoid an attack of volcanic proportions upon itself, the Democratic party, and him.

Putting his hand on his former classmate Maurice Sugar's knee, he asked confidently: "Morrie, what do you think about it?"

"Well, I'd like to ask you a question, Frank," Sugar replied. "What exactly do you propose to do if the men don't come out?"

The governor proceeded to give a long, circuitous answer that ended in a startling revelation. He would go into the plants personally and ask the men to leave voluntarily. "And I would expect you boys to help me," he concluded.

The words were quietly spoken but contained the possible destiny of the strike, as the sudden silence of the union leaders indicated. Murphy was fully aware, as they were, of his great personal authority with the workers. But the question of the future of that authority hung in the balance and caused him to temporize. He did not, however, tell the union men that he had had a secret conference with Lewis before this meeting and had read Lewis a letter that he was sending to the auto union and that, presumably, would be made public simultaneously.

Murphy's letter was a formal demand that the union "restore possession of the occupied plants to their rightful owners," backed by the direct threat that Judge Gadola's injunction, "lawfully entered after fair and open hearing had been accorded to both parties." His writ of attachment for the bodies of the sitdowners would, in case of a refusal, be put into force by the National Guard in Flint.

Lewis had then responded to the letter with an incisive reply in which he promised to adopt the very course of action that Murphy had said would be his own during the meeting with the union men a half hour later. "I do not doubt your ability," Lewis had said, "to call out your soldiers and shoot the members of our union out of those plants. But let me say that when you issue that order I shall leave this conference and I shall enter one of those plants with my own people."[35]

Murphy must have thought hard over Lewis's words. In any case his letter was not sent and he did not read it to the union leaders that night or tell them of Lewis's sharp reaction to it. The governor kept to his bed all the following day. But the General Motors negotiators were back at recorder's court at 8:30 P.M. The pleasure of striking final poses had been short-lived for the corporation grandees.

In a couple of hours that evening the negotiators made more ground than they had in the previous eight days. The corporation finally agreed in principle to grant sole recognition for the struck plants. The question of wearing buttons inside the factory still made some trouble. Knudsen seemed to consider it a minor point but his associates disagreed. Finally, the question was settled with the strange device of Knudsen's agreeing to give the union a personal letter on the subject, from which the corporation's other negotiators could abstain.

The only remaining obstacle was the duration of the sole bargaining agreement. The union had asked for a year originally but had come down to six months. The corporation set its limit at three months. The question was still unsettled on the afternoon of February 10 when CIO counsel Lee Pressman and Mortimer telephoned Bob Travis. "We'll leave it up to you, Bob, as to how tough we can be," Mortimer said. "How long do you think the Flint people could hold out if there was a breakdown now?"

"It depends a good deal on what Murphy does," Travis replied. "Otherwise I'd say we can still keep going for a couple more weeks but the strain is getting pretty strong."

"Well, we think you ought to come down here then."

When Travis and I arrived in the evening, negotiations had shifted to the Statler Hotel. Lewis was in bed and traffic was steady in and out of his suite. All but the duration of the pact had been disposed of and conferees were hacking out the final forms of the rest. Mortimer and Pressman brought us a copy of the list of plants that were to come under the sole bargaining agreement. "Read it over carefully," they enjoined, both almost bursting with tenseness. They hung over us possessively as we read.

The two groups had finally agreed on a group of seventeen plants whereas we had expected twenty. "Where's Guide Lamp?" Travis asked suddenly. Then we noticed that only Chevy 4 had been listed, while Chevy 6 and 9 were not. The Flint guys would like that!

A pained look came over Pressman's face. "Which of those plants are sticking points?" he asked. "Let's keep it down to the absolute minimum so we won't kill our chances for the six-month clause. We haven't settled that yet!"

"That's right," Travis agreed. "Guide Lamp is the only one I'd insist on. We can take care of Chevrolet but Guide Lamp means a wedge in Anderson. That's goddam important. It means Muncie, Indianapolis, Kokomo. That's key for General Motors."

So the negotiators went back and in a half-hour returned wreathed in smiles. The six-month question had been turned over to Lewis and John Thomas Smith for the final decision. Smith, a tall, portly gentleman, came down from the twelfth floor and entered Lewis's room. We were under considerable strain for the next half hour. Finally, Smith came out again and though I scrutinized his face anxiously I could not tell how the thing had gone. But when Murphy came out of Lewis's room, beaming, he gave the thing away. He went off with the Du Pont spokesman just as Ora Gasaway, Lewis's aide, appeared. "The chief wants everybody inside," he said.

We filed in quietly and stood about Lewis's bed. The tough public figure I had expected had faded into the courteous personality that was Lewis in private. He told us of his final conversation with Smith, dramatizing the last exchanges: "So I just got up on my elbow and I looked at him and said: 'Mr. Smith, do you want your plants reopened?'—'Of course.'—'Well, then, it's six months!' And so it was." It was a delightful performance but later I thought of how inadequate the words were for so important a matter until I realized that it was not so much the words that counted but the force of character of the amazing man who had spoken them.

Aside from recognition, the settlement specified that negotiations on the other union demands would begin on February 16 and the union agreed that no strikes would interrupt these conferences. The famous single-page statement of recognition was supplemented by another curiosity of this very curious agreement, a second personal letter, this one from Knudsen to Murphy, which carried a more complete pledge of the corporation to the union: "we hereby agree with you that within a period of six months from the resumption of work we will not bargain with or enter into agreement with any other union or representative or employees of plants on strike . . . without first submitting to you the facts of the situation and gaining from you the sanction of any such contemplated procedure."

This periphrastic language constituted exclusive bargaining rights since it was unquestioned that the governor would honor the union's trust.

• • •

On arriving in Flint that afternoon, we stopped first at Fisher One for a prearranged meeting. As Mortimer read and explained the few paragraphs of the pact and its additions the faces that were glued on his were serious to the point of somberness. Then the men began firing questions. Did that mean everything else stood where it was before the strike started? How about the speed of the line? How about the bosses?

Finally, one of them defined the settlement succinctly: "What's the use of kidding ourselves? All that piece of paper means is that we got a union. The rest depends on us." When the vote was taken, not one hand was raised against accepting the pact. Then a great cheer burst from the throats of the sitdowners. It was similar at the other plants.

The evacuation began at Fisher One. The factory whistle blew a full blast, and the men began marching to the door. The crowd of thousands gathered outside joined the sitdowners for the two-mile parade to the other plants and the massive jam of strikers, sympathizers, and hundreds of cars began their singing, cheering, honking way toward town.

Night was beginning to close in on Chevrolet Avenue when the contingent appeared at the crest of the hill. The Chevy 4 leaders were standing on the high landing above the gate, a tall American flag on each side and men gathered inside the doors. As the Fisher One parade arrived, great flares suddenly lit up, confetti flew, and the enormous gates of the plant opened slowly.

The crowd was so great at Fisher Two that the thousands coming from up the hill had to stop by the bridge fifty yards away. The cheering exceeded all the bounds of hearing as the small group came out of the plant that they had defended so valiantly against the police's gas and bullets for the first great victory of the strike. A narrow path had been left open for them and then they were swallowed up in the mass.

The parade surged into Third Street bound for the center of town. It was hardly a parade, it was more like a great migration. Not a policeman was in sight anywhere though thousands of people lined the street and—for the first time in Flint—applauded and cheered a union parade. "Come on in!" the marchers shouted. Many responded and promptly had union buttons stuck onto their coat lapels.

Pengelly Hall was jammed beyond the last inch of space. The stairs and vestibules on all the floors were packed, and, when the crowd could no longer penetrate the building, newcomers massed outside until five thousand people had gathered. Sound apparatus was strung down to the second floor from the hall and was hung out of the windows facing the street, where the crowd cheered lustily everything that was said.

The great mass outside dispersed slowly but in the hall merry-making went on into the night. Around two in the morning dozens of people still stood around talking, men and women filled by the glamour of the strike and reluctant to abandon it for the humdrum of everyday existence.

Leaving, I noticed two young men near the hall door. They had been drinking, and one was trying to explain something to his friend. His words came garbled, and, as though realizing that he was not making himself understood, he shook his head violently several times. Finally, almost tearful, he exclaimed as from the very depths of his being: "Emmet, you gotta believe me! It ain't me that's talkin', it's the CIO in me!"

The Detroit Upsurge and the Chrysler Strike

While the Flint sitdown was in progress, I was so deeply absorbed in it that I lost the sense of everything else. I rarely went out to eat, stilling my hunger with sandwiches and coffee prepared in the Women's Auxiliary's alcove, refusing to be wangled into accompanying Adolph Germer, a soup gourmet, to a little place he had found on Saginaw, which served big, hot bowls of homemade quality, he assured me. As for sleeping, I got very little, but that was nothing new for me. A life-long insomniac, I did not miss lost sleep and used the night for readying material for the *Flint Auto Worker,* which was put out every three or four days.

It is hard to believe, after fifty years, that Homer Martin almost fired me during this rugged period for allegedly shirking my responsibilities. Wyndham Mortimer told me over the telephone a number of times that Martin was displeased with me, accusing me of having abandoned my editorial post. This did not disturb me because I could not believe that even so self-centered a person as he would fail to recognize that Flint was the heart of the union's destiny. Besides, the accusation was unjustified. I had put out two full editions of the *United Automobile Worker* in December, one of which, the Christmas issue, contained twelve pages laden with important tidings and had appeared just before the sitdown began.

Mortimer had come to Flint on January 17[1] and I had previously arranged to go back to Detroit with him in order to put out an edition of the International's paper, having asked B. J. Widick, editor of the *United Rubber Worker,* to do the current issue of the *Flint Auto Worker.*[2] Because Widick was on an extended leave in Flint, he was able to accept the chore and was working at it when I left. In fact, it must have come off the press soon after because when a copy arrived in Detroit, its big headline was an embarrassing anachronism: "VICTORY IS OURS—Great Gain Is Made by Truce."

Widick had predated the issue to January 15, when the agreement was reached by the two sides and had not changed it when the pact was abrogated. At any event this muddle was corrected two days later with my publication of the January 19 edition of the *United Automobile Worker.* It was almost entirely devoted to the Flint situation, featuring the General Motors "sellout" in outraged, accusative terms:

GM Breaks Word: Parley Is Off
Strikers Continue to Occupy Flint Fisher Body Plants

The big accompanying article explained the circumstances of the breakoff, countering GM's "bad faith" with the union's "good faith" because we had, according to the agreement, abandoned the other held plants at Guide Lamp in Anderson, Indiana, and those of Cadillac and Fleetwood in Detroit. The broken truce permitted me to stay on in Detroit for three more days to prepare another issue of the paper with important items that had been missed, managing at the same time to mend some broken fences. I asked Homer Martin to do a roundup exposé himself about General Motors' duplicity in the Flint Alliance affair, for example, which pleased him, or so I thought.

More gratifying was the chance this second issue gave me to describe some exciting recent organizational developments in Detroit, particularly those at the Briggs-Meldrum plant. Dick Frankensteen, the Detroit organizational director who was personally involved in this strike, was very cool with me at first, understandably perhaps. But his ruffled sensibilities must have been smoothed by the big front-page story I did about it, as well as by another piece about the settlement of the drawn-out Bohn-Aluminum sitdown in which he had likewise participated. The Bohn strike had started on December 30 and had therefore accompanied the Flint sitdowns from their beginning. This gave me a sense of retroactive guilt for which I was glad to atone.

The Briggs strike was, on the other hand, in full force when I arrived in Detroit and I got a whiff of it during my short stay. The strike had been precipitated by the mass discharge the week before of some three hundred men. It was not a sitdown, just the ordinary strike with mass picketing and violence duly furnished by Heinie Pickert's sadists. On January 18, the company announced that it intended reopening the plant the following morning. The union had been given a sample of the technique that would be used when the Cadillac and Fleetwood factories were evacuated on January 17 in accord with the GM-UAW "truce." When the union tried to set up picket lines at those plants, they were assaulted so brutally by the police that Walter Reuther had to call on the Dodge "flying squad" for assistance.[3]

Frankensteen expected big trouble at Briggs-Meldrum on the morning of January 19 and prepared for it the night before by mobilizing the Dodge workers on the afternoon shift. A leaflet was passed out telling them to come to the local's headquarters after work. Frankensteen also called the Socialist and Communist parties, the Workers Alliance, and other auto locals, alerting the latter to send their day-shift members to Briggs before they went to work. The Dodge hall was kept open all night and workers were fed sandwiches and coffee and entertained by Frankensteen's singing.[4]

At 5:30 A.M., a mass of possibly two thousand pickets got into their cars and drove in a motorcade to Meldrum, where they joined hundreds of Briggs workers and others already there, including thirty militants who had driven up from Toledo Chevrolet. A slow-moving circular line was started before the plant gate, while on the other side of the street some would-be scabs protected by a cluster of cops were gathered. A police officer yelled to Frankensteen, "You've got to leave this gate open." "If you want another Fisher Two riot then try to break this line!" he yelled back.

The police replied by laying down a tear-gas barrage. The pickets scattered and I had a curious sense that the Flint attack was actually being repeated. When the cold wind had lifted "the blue screen of tear gas," as I described it in *United Automobile Worker* on January 22, police could be seen conducting the scabs toward the gate. Frankensteen yelled, "Pickets, return to your line!" A number had already done so and were surrounding individual scabs, muscling and mooching them away from the gate. There was no violence. Even the police seemed reluctant to initiate it, discouraged undoubtedly by the great mass of pro-union workers. The scabs withdrew, hooted by the pickets.

The danger was over. Dick Frankensteen spoke over the sound car's loudspeaker, thanking the visitors for their help and bidding them to be ready for the following day. The Briggs strikers took up their posts again, led by a slight, wiry chap who had caught my notice by his serious and determined bearing, looking more like an intellectual than a worker. I asked who he was and was told his name, Emil Mazey.

However, there was no call to battle the police at Briggs a second time. The lesson of the great concentration of union force had registered a swift change of heart on the part of the Briggs management. An important point seemed to have been made: that the UAW was now powerful enough to conduct an outside strike as well as a safely cushioned inside one.

At 8:30 that morning the company got word to the union that it was prepared to talk to its representatives. Dick Frankensteen spoke to Fay Taylor, the personnel director, and negotiations with the plant committee were arranged.[5] A company statement was released advising that the whole incident had been the result of a "misunderstanding" and that all discharged strikers would be rehired when the plant reopened the next day. It is significant that the Bohn-Aluminum strike was settled at almost the same time.

Dick Frankensteen later revealed to me the curious circumstances that accounted for this simultaneity, both pacts having been arranged by John Gillespie, Harry Bennett's shadowy proxy.[6] After contacting Frankensteen at the Dodge union headquarters, the two men had driven out to the Briggs-Meldrum plant, where Gillespie went in alone to meet with the management while Frankensteen sat in his car in the parking lot. When Gillespie came out, all he said was, "Well, okay."

"Okay what?" Frankensteen asked.

"Okay, they're going to return your people. Have them all report to their jobs tomorrow. There will also be a 10 cent increase in their next pay checks."

Frankensteen was intrigued but from past experience he knew that he could take Gillespie's word. He called the Briggs strike committee together to make the announcement. Except for Emil Mazey, they were all willing to accept the offer on a silver platter. Mazey said he did not like it. What the company gave as if on its own it could also take away. But the "practical" sense prevailed. The Meldrum factory was completely organized "overnight," Frankensteen said, and "Mack Avenue" and the other Briggs plants likewise signed with the union. Then Gillespie told Frankensteen to go after Bohn-Aluminum and the union found the management there "as soft as melting butter."

In giving account of these dealings, Frankensteen tended to overplay the anecdotal side though he did not forget the battles in which he himself often played an aggressive role. But it was like carrying the ball while others ran interference for him. I did get to talk to some of the people in the strike at Bohn, especially the women, and wrote a piece in the *United Automobile Worker* on January 22 headlined "Women: Strike's Unsung Heroines." Helen Goldman and Catherine ("Babe") Gelles had organized the kitchen and chiseling committee on the Midland Steel model, they told me. They set up a group called the "Minute Women," because "at a minute's notice they can step in anywhere and serve food [for strikers]." Since the inspiration for the name seemed to be Flint's Emergency Brigade, I added a section telling how that already-famous band had been formed after the Fisher Two battle through the initiative of Genora Johnson, who, I wrote, "symbolized the spirit of fighting womanhood."[7]

• • •

When we left Flint after the strike and returned to Detroit, I was filled with expectation. In fact, the period that followed in Detroit was extraordinarily exciting, and not only for myself. A description can be found in the first issue of the *United Automobile Worker,* that of February 25, which I put out after my return. The account required eighteen pages. The leading theme was blazoned over the first page: "All the World's Talking of the Great Victory." A montage of a dozen photo snips of GM workers in action interspersed with clippings proclaimed: "Union Wins," "Strikers Cheer," "Strike Peace Hailed," and "New Life Begins."

"WORKERS POUR INTO UNION AFTER VICTORY," the inside head announced, and the story that followed might well be considered the usual exaggerated fustian yet only the style was overplayed:

> Detroit—The great G.M. strike victory has opened the floodgates of unionism to the unorganized workers of Detroit. By the thousands and tens of thousands they are pouring into the union, surpassing the wildest dreams of those who have worked and sacrificed to see the coming of this day. Strike after strike has followed upon the G.M. settlement. This upsurge of organization has not been confined to auto workers. Union headquarters have been swamped day and night with delegations from textile plants, bakeries, cigar factories, laundries, restaurants, meat packing houses and every other description of industry.

The entire staff was drawn into the wild melee. Everyone was on the telephone, meeting delegations of strikers, and trying to satisfy their insistent requests. The International had to keep people in the office twenty-four hours a day. This went on for days and weeks and in the end what had started as a gratifying confirmation turned into a nightmare. The most exacting task, besides trying to get organizers to where they were needed, was to sort out the strident demands and fit them into their proper slots. Often it was not possible to accomplish this.

One morning, a delegation of six, including two women, barged into my office, which seemed to be the only one that had no visitors at that moment. I stood up and remained standing while talking to them because I could not offer the group any seats; I held my scrapbook and pencil in my hands. I started firing the basic questions at them that we had all memorized: name of company, address, number of workers, parts produced, pay scales, grievances, and the rest. But I stopped recording after their first answer. The company's name was a give-away; it was a sausage-pickling operation. "But listen, friends, you're in the wrong place," I told them with a sympathetic smile.

"Ain't this the CIO?" one of the men demanded.

"Sure. But we're the United *Automobile* Workers. What you want is the Amalgamated Meat Packers Union."

"Is that the CIO?" he shot back suspiciously.

"No, it's the AFL. But it's a very good union," I assured him.

"Hell, we don't want no truck with the AFL," he snarled and the others muttered their assent in unison.

"But don't you understand, we don't have the *right* to take you into the UAW. The only people we can accept are auto workers."

"So you refuse to take us in?" the spokesman demanded almost inimically.

"We have no choice. If we accept you it would get us into a lot of trouble."

They looked at each other and then at me for a long, unfriendly moment. Then the spokesman softened, "Couldn't you send somebody down at least to show us how to get started? There are five hundred of us sitting down, not knowing what to do."

I could not lie to them. "I will if I can find someone," I said unhappily. "All our organizers are running around like chickens with their heads chopped off. I'll tell you what I think would be a better idea. Let me call up the Amalgamated Meat Packers."

The suggestion was vehemently rejected: "Nothing doing! We don't want no AFL union. We'd rather stay off by ourselves." I never did find out what happened to this plant. I was probably too embarrassed to check but I thought about it reproachfully for some time.

Actually, the staff of organizers did very little work in the field. Like doctors in an epidemic they did not have the time to visit individual claimants. Their efforts in the turbulent situation consisted essentially of separating out the most likely candidates for UAW affiliation and following through with them. They set up tentative locals by holding ad hoc meetings inside the plants, often with the eager cooperation of the managements, recording the outstanding grievances and getting employees back to work pending negotiations. These cases were handled by Dick Frankensteen on an assembly-line basis.

With a fistful of sheets he made the rounds of the city by geographical sections, having sent wires on ahead to a number of the companies and arbitrarily setting the approximate hour when he would be around to each. "I negotiated as many as four or five contracts a day," he recalled.[8] "Incidentally, I signed the first union-shop agreement in an automobile plant in history—at Thompson Products. And the man I signed with later had a nervous breakdown: they had to put him in an institution."

Each management expected the Dodge flying squad (now expanded to two or three units) to come roaring to their plant at any moment and to shut it down. At the L. A. Young Company, producers of cushion wiring, the plant manager asked, "You're not going to bring your flying squad here, are you?"[9] Frankensteen looked nonchalantly toward the window. "I don't know, they might turn up here." And sure enough, the squad popped up during the negotiations, having gotten the idea themselves, he assured me, of putting in an appearance as a friendly surprise to him. An hour before the end of shift, Mike Dragon would call the International from the pay telephone booth inside the plant, asking if his boys would be needed and where.

Then he would send a message to Oliver Hamel on the third floor at Dodge and by quitting time they were all ready to go.

Companies already in contact with the union anxiously sought to forestall unpleasant surprises by announcing important concessions to International headquarters. The head of F. L. Jacobs wired that he had settled all differences with the plant committee. The Motor Products bargaining committee itself telephoned to report, on the insistance of the management, that the local's secretary and vice president, who had been fired, had been reinstated. One firm, whose name I cannot recall, invited UAW negotiators to a buffet lunch at the Statler Hotel.[10]

After the meal, Frankensteen sat down with the very congenial company representatives and began reading the toll of accusations from a sheet he held in his hands. Its grim details in contrast to the comfortable setting gave an ironic twist to what he read. He ground away at the terrible conditions in the plant, the hazards to life and limb, going into scary detail about the overhead crane that ran back and forth just above the heads of the workers. He ended by demanding that all the union members who had been discharged must be returned to their jobs immediately before anything could be done.

The company men had listened respectfully but in mounting amazement to Frankensteen's outlay of accusations. None of their employees, a spokesman said at last, had to their knowledge ever said anything to the supervision about grievances. "Yes," Frankensteen inserted, "that's what all managements tell us." And as far as they knew, the company spokesman continued, there were no union members in their factory, information that made Frankensteen merely smile. And about the other conditions that had been cited, the spokesman said, they simply weren't so. As for the overhead crane, it was news to them and they ought to know their own factory. Frankensteen was invited to visit it and see for himself.

He realized then that he must have mixed up his sheets but he could not admit that, asserting bluntly that he would give the management three days to think things over and then he would get in touch with them. Back at the office, he found that the union did not have a single listed member in the plant, as the company man had claimed. Nevertheless, to save face, Frankensteen asked me to prepare a leaflet that was promptly distributed at the company's gate, calling the workers to a meeting. There was, surprisingly, a good turnout. All those who attended signed up and a decent contract was obtained with little effort.

The same could be said about any number of other firms, not only in the Detroit area but also throughout Michigan, at Lansing, Grand Rapids, Pontiac, Muskegon, to say nothing of the tidal wave that swept through Flint and the region around it. There was, hearteningly, I thought, a simultaneous upsurge of local newspapers in these centers, and they reported these developments directly. The initiators of the locals' papers often referred to the *Flint Auto Worker* as their model and wrote to ask me for advice, sending copies of their own sheets.

The Grand Rapids auto local's *Voice of Labor* furnished a special surprise in reporting the great organizational drive among the hitherto impossible-to-reach furniture workers of that city, particularly the "supposedly unorganizable Dutch and Polish workers." All were joining fast, three hundred signing up at one meeting, which was held up for half an hour by the rush of applicants who seemed overeager after having waited so long. The UAW local was forced to move for lack of space and was planning to purchase a building with three meeting halls by selling stock to members at $5 a share with a guaranteed dividend of 6 percent.[11]

The Lansing local, which had a certain base to begin with, now enjoyed an unprecedented surge, which its new paper, the *Lansing Auto Worker,* trumpeted in a huge headline: "The Greatest Union Organization Drive in History." It would have been expected that the Fisher Body plant there would be especially responsive to the Flint victory but in reality it was reflected in every other factory of this important automobile center: Reo, Olds, and Motor Wheel.

Pontiac, which likewise established its own journal, was probably the most interesting center to me because its members had gone beyond the purely inner-plant concerns to the living conditions outside. The city's notoriously poor living quarters (were Flint's any better?) had inspired a strong movement for housing improvement, passing over to strikes at rental units to hasten action. The auto union pressured local authorities to force proprietors to obtain certificates of compliance from health officers and building inspectors, otherwise no action in court would be entertained to compel rent payments. The union backed this measure with a threat to call a "holiday" at the great auto plants in case a rent striker was called to trial, promising, according to the *Pontiac Auto Worker,* that "the entire body will constitute a panel for the jury to insure that at least half of the jury will be auto workers."

This development thrilled Dorothy and me because it indicated that the victorious auto workers were already expanding their trade union action into phases of social and even political concern. It was what we had hoped that the sitdowners of Flint, with their unique experience of togetherness, would carry back into daily life in a manner that we characterized to ourselves as the "total union." This did occur in some promising ways until the process was halted by the intense internal union strife that developed inexorably after the great triumph.

Meanwhile, there was still, not unexpectedly, a tremendous backlog on the organizational side that had to be disposed of, especially in certain places. In Flint and other centers where vigorous strikes had been conducted or where the union was previously established (as in Kansas City, St. Louis, and Atlanta), this task was facilitated. But in others, it had to be started from the very beginning. In the important center of Anderson, Indiana, one almost had the sense of a community emerging from the ruins of civil war (see chapter 13). Bob Travis had successfully fought for the Guide Lamp unit at Anderson to be included among the GM plants that were granted sole collective bargaining rights in the February 11 settlement. But the Anderson union hall was at that very moment in a shambles and many of its most active members had been run out of town or were in hiding.[12]

Participants have left descriptions of these events, one of which was prepared for my wife (and is in her personal papers) by Annie Hoffman, whose husband was a worker at Guide Lamp. It supplements the account that Sophie and Victor Reuther gave me in our interview in 1938. Sophie had volunteered to help the union at Anderson when Vic was assigned there shortly after the Fisher Two battle. When he was called back to Flint to answer "inciting to riot" charges growing out of the Fisher Two battle,[13] Sophie remained in Anderson and soon became involved in company-led violence there. Vigilantes knew of her presence in town and tried to pick her up but she was hidden by courageous union men and women. She shifted from house to house every couple of hours, changing her hat and coat each time. In one home, she recalled, the woman sat facing the door with a shotgun on her knees.

When Victor returned to Indiana, he could not get through to Anderson because vigilantes blocked the roads and watched the trains for the "invasion" that was expected from Flint. He stopped at Alexandria, where the UAW had a good group, and organized a fleet of cars to accompany him to Anderson. There they reestablished the picket line at Guide Lamp in the face of the armed vigilantes who glared at them from across the road. Reuther had his sound apparatus with him and kept appealing to the picketers to avoid provocation though no one could have mistaken to whom he addressed his words. After two hours, with the plant evidently in operation, the token line was called off until the next day.

The brave group of unionists did not know how long they would be tolerated. As it happened, help would soon be forthcoming, the result of Maurice Sugar and Ed Hall's efforts with Governor Clifford Townsend.[14] They had a group of Anderson unionists with them when they met the governor in Muncie, men who had joined them on the train and warned them about the violence at Anderson. They asked them to tell Townsend about it. One burly man lifted his hand as he talked. "Governor," he said. "I lost these two fingers fighting for my country and I would do it again. But I just talked to my wife long distance and she said she's in hiding and can't go home for fear those vigilantes will kill her." Tears rolled down the big fellow's cheeks.

Maurice Sugar asked Townsend for protection by the state police to get them into Anderson but the governor replied that the state police could only be used for highway patrol, according to a law recently adopted at labor's insistence. How about the National Guard? he was asked. The Guard was also unavailable because it was occupied with a major flood in the Ohio River Valley. Finally, Sugar and Hall proposed that Townsend deputize 125 unionists to face the vigilantes. In the end, the governor promised to turn the matter over to a lawyer friend in Anderson.

It was evidence of the amazing prestige that the UAW had acquired in the industrial communities after its stunning triumph at Flint despite the countervailing efforts of the big corporations. One felt that nothing they did could halt the trend, as was attested by the news in the *United Automobile Worker* of March 20 of the organizational strides being made everywhere. In Anderson itself, the word was that at the other GM plant, Delco-Remy, meetings were being scheduled in every department by early March. Workers at the Aladdin Company in Alexandria, most of them women, started a sitdown on March 2. Those at the Rex Manufacturing Company of Connersville sat down after the mayor, William F. Dentlinger, spoke at a UAW rally. And my friend John Bartee of the Studebaker local made similar reports about Indianapolis, where Homer Martin had designated him International organizer.

• • •

However meaningful these events were to the groups involved and even to the UAW as a whole, they could not claim the attention of a truly big strike such as the general shutdown of the Chrysler factories. Still, this great conflict that seemed to be inevitable once it occurred took us all by surprise. I had heard for some days and from several individuals, including Dick Frankensteen, about the reluctance of the Chrysler workers to strike. Negotiations were proceeding, and I imagine that we all felt that they would end in an agreement, the way things usually happened with this corporation.

A three-man committee was handling the negotiations: Frankensteen, R. J. Thomas, and a man named Zimmerman from Dodge Truck. There were also twelve others, three from each local, who constituted a "strategy board" that had been voted the power to call a strike "if necessary." They did not participate in the negotiations but sat in a side room and waited for developments. After a few days they grew impatient and began to press for action though Frankensteen insisted that the rank and file in the locals were "quite passive" and not at all eager to strike. This was apparently a misstatement as far as the Dodge workers were concerned because he admitted that when the strike was finally called there was not the slightest opposition to it. It took exactly ten minutes, he said, to shut down the enormous plant with its twenty-five thousand employees.

A large number of these stayed in, most of whom, however, were soon asked to leave, the occupants being limited to 1,800 in order to minimize the feeding and billeting problem. The remainder were either assigned to picket duty on six-hour shifts or made to feel useful at other chores, especially chiseling. A flock of these teams dug up "five thousand dollars in cash and about three thousand in food, including a live cow."[15] The sitdowners seemed set for a long, comfortable vigil but were yanked out of their complacence when the company was granted an injunction ordering the occupants to leave their plants at 10 A.M. on March 17.

On the afternoon before the deadline, three of the local's leaders came to Maurice Sugar, who had handled the court procedure, and asked him what the sitdowners should do.[16] Sugar did not know any of the men and accordingly put them off without committing himself. He knew that the UAW executive board and officers were meeting in Cleveland and went into another room, where he called Homer Martin. Sugar told Martin that he could not reveal what he had to discuss over the telephone but that it was important enough to warrant Martin and Frankensteen's immediate return to Detroit. The result of their meeting that evening was that the two men made the rounds of the occupied plants during the night and told the men to sit tight despite the injunction, the way the Flint sitdowners had done.

The union's defiance brought an explosion of anger from authorities. Even Governor Murphy, who must have had a vision of the repetition of the General Motors nightmare, joined the chorus to demand the surrender of the plants. The Chrysler strikers replied in bristling words that reminded one of the Flint workers' response to threats of clearing them out of Fisher One and Fisher Two.[17]

But the Detroit police had no intention of fighting the thousands of Chrysler men inside their plants. Instead, they directed their wrath against a small cigar factory that was occupied largely by women who resisted eviction with exemplary courage. As the police served notice that they meant to continue these violent tactics, UAW people began to feel that a vigorous reply was in order to halt the brutality that patently had the Chrysler plants as its ultimate goal.

The enormous Cadillac Square demonstration of March 23 was the result of this determination. Curiously, although the crowd of a hundred thousand or more that made up this mammoth gathering consisted mostly of Chrysler workers who were not sitting in or were members of other UAW locals, the task of mobilizing these masses was in no way assumed by the International's top leadership. Running off the hundreds of thousands of announcements that were distributed at the factory gates was actually undertaken at my request by an outside group, the Civil Rights Federation, whose executive secretary, Avrahm Mezerik, delivered great bundles of them to my office, where members of the locals picked them up.[18]

During the distribution I got into a hassle with Adolph Germer, who came raging at me, his forelock blocking one eye and his forefinger waggling in my face. I realized that he reflected Homer Martin's attitude and tried hard to control my feelings. "Do you mean to say," he demanded, "that you're going to ask people to come to that demonstration even though we haven't been able to get a permit for it?" He glared at me in utter fury, then added in a voice of doom, "It's going to be a perfect setup for another Haymarket Square Massacre!"

To be frank, we were all worried about that situation but felt that the hostility of the city authorities had to be faced down. As for Adolph Germer's ominous predictions, we in Flint had become accustomed to them because he registered them about nearly every militant action that was contemplated. It had come to the point that Bob Travis refrained from telling him about most of our plans. Dick Frankensteen had other fears about the great meeting. Police could provoke a riot to cover an attack on the sitdowners in the plants. "It would be an ideal time," he declared, "for the cops to make their strike [attack] when we all have our hands full fighting at the square."

In the end the union was spared the necessity of taking any of these foreboding chances. Mayor Frank Couzens had turned down the UAW's request to use the steps of the city hall on Woodward for the demonstration. "But we gave him a face-saver," Frankensteen said, "by offering to change the site of the meeting to Cadillac Square." And the mayor then agreed to grant the permit.

A reporter from a New York paper asked him, "How come you changed your mind, Mayor?"[19]

"I told you," he replied, "there would be no questioning on that question. You are a very impertinent reporter," he added and asked the man to leave.

"I'll go," the newsman said, "but you can't take my thought away from me. You conceded because you had to!" It was a reply that cheered me when I saw it in print since it put into the record the idea that the union's intrepidity filled the hearts of its adversaries with terror. The reporter must have been a Newspaper Guild member because Frankensteen recalled that he had, on his own, intervened with the mayor to put in a speakers' platform for us at city hall.

My own contribution to the meeting was to put out a two-page special of the *United Automobile Worker.* Others had suggested a leaflet, but it seemed to me that the paper would be more impressive and would put the UAW's official seal on the event. I got Martin's consent to the flyer by suggesting that we should put a heavy-typed statement signed by him right across the page with the heading "WE HAVE JUST BEGUN TO FIGHT!"

Once the meeting was underway, no one seemed to remember all the fears and hesitancies that had almost derailed it before it started. The frightening thoughts of a riot and of the plants being invaded vanished in the face of the thunderous reality. The full stature of the UAW was overwhelmingly revealed by the unending columns of workers that kept pouring into the square, carrying their banners and greeted by the repeated roar of solidarity from the assembled crowd that kept pressing closer and closer together to make room for newcomers.

As I twisted my way through the lively mass, aided by a dozen others spread all over the square in distributing the paper, I had to pause when "The Star-Spangled Banner" began reverberating from the loudspeaker on the platform. I looked up at Dick Frankensteen and Homer Martin standing there, preternaturally aggrandized by the throng, hands on hearts, their lips moving, and their features set. I was surprised to see George Edwards at the microphone, as the strong voice hardly sounded like his. His face was taut with earnestness and it was only later that I learned how scared he was.[20] When the meeting started, Frankensteen had asked him to lead the crowd in singing the national anthem. Edwards stalled until Frankensteen became angry."Go ahead and start singing!" he muttered.

"Goddam it," Edwards blurted out desperately, "I don't remember the words!" But he had no choice. Frankensteen pushed him up to the microphone and somehow the forgotten words came back.

• • •

The magnificent demonstration accomplished one other thing that was above all else important: It set the Chrysler negotiations going. From Dick Frankensteen's account, given to me in 1938, my notes reveal an embarrassing poverty of discussion on key issues at these sessions, at least the way he remembered them. There was, however, a lot of gossip in his story about the famous personalities who were present and other similar details, however interesting they might otherwise be. Frankensteen was understandably impressed by these accessory matters but that was not the only reason for the vacuity of his report. The fact was that the contract that was obtained lacked more than it contained, as he was prepared to admit.

Frankensteen made much, for example, of the "friendship" that developed during the conferences between Walter Chrysler and John L. Lewis, who on the former's suggestion began to call each other by their first names. Such trivia impressed me as beneath consideration at the time and I did not think the better of Frankensteen for mentioning them. But somehow, on reexamining them years later and setting them up with other such intimacies that he told about, they began to assume a certain importance after all.

Governor Murphy was already on a first-name basis with the company's head, Frankensteen asserted, because he was an old friend of the family, having been the roommate of their son-in-law, Byron Foy, at the University of Michigan and their guest on a trip to Europe. It was Frankensteen's opinion that Chrysler thought that this close relationship with Murphy would be meaningful in the negotiations. When he discovered that he could not count on it, he became very cool toward the governor. "I've heard reports that it left a permanent rift between the two men," Frankensteen said. "But Governor Murphy upheld his impartiality all the way through," he added loyally.

Frankensteen revealed the transcendency that the New York financial interests had assumed in the corporation though only to poke fun at them, it seemed to me. Actually, he never spoke about the battery of "financiers and lawyers" who sat behind Chrysler at the conferences unless it was to ridicule them. "They occupied a whole floor in the Olds Hotel," he remarked, "and when they walked up to the capitol they looked like a parade of penguins." Chrysler had retired from the active direction of the Detroit plants, Frankensteen pointed out, and spent his time in New York keeping an eye on the financial end of the corporation. The facts were probably much different, as John L. Lewis seemed to think, sensing a struggle between the nominal head of the corporation and the Wall Street men and trying to give his new friend his personal support.

Frankensteen tended to corroborate this view in a certain respect. "On one occasion," he said, "we were trying to find a formula to fit their vanity and which would also be satisfactory to us. After we had been working on it for hours, Lewis suddenly turned to Chrysler and told him: 'Here you've got a million dollars worth of brains with you and they can't even write a simple paragraph!'" Lewis was also contemptuous of K. T. Keller, the man who had succeeded Chrysler as the operating head of the Chrysler plants and whom Lewis evidently considered a stooge of the fiscal team. In one joust between the two men, Keller made the mistake of being sarcastic with Lewis.

"You know, Mr. Keller," the latter growled, "you've got only one goddam thing on me and that's a few lousy dollars."

Keller tried a comeback, assuring Lewis that he was not afraid of "your bushy eyebrows."

"Mr. Keller," Lewis snapped, "I've watched you wriggle and swiggle all this time and if I were responsible for hiring stool pigeons the way the newspapers say you've been doing, I'd wriggle and swiggle too."[21]

The negotiations reached a stalemate when the corporation raised hedging arguments. As a precondition to its signing the contract, it demanded a no-strike pledge by the union. The wave of unauthorized strikes in the Flint plants that was just then receiving horrendous publicity served as Chrysler's best polemic. What was the point of the union's inscribing an agreement if it didn't live up to it? they asked. The union was damned no matter what its negotiators answered.

A more immediate point was Chrysler's insistence that the strikers abandon the plants, repeatedly threatening to halt the talks unless they did so. Most of the UAW negotiators were inclined to give in on this point, John L. Lewis in particular, Frankensteen said.[22] "He argued that we had accomplished our major purpose already and that public sentiment was beginning to turn against the union because of the continued occupation." In fact, it was no longer necessary, Frankensteen agreed, because Governor Murphy had assured the UAW that the state police would be employed to see that the plants were not operated and that machinery and equipment were not moved out of them while they were idle.

The difficulty involved in getting the sitdowners out of the Chrysler plants was to take on a great importance in the history of the UAW because of the use that Homer Martin and Dick Frankensteen made of it, spreading the word that the resistance to evacuation was a deliberate "communist plot" meant to embarrass them. The red-scare was chiefly Martin's contribution to this fable; Frankensteen's was more personal because he had convinced himself that the Mortimer-Travis-Reuther group were sabotaging "his" strike after winning "theirs" at General Motors. In my opinion, the disastrous factional fight that soon afterward began to rip the union apart was born at this time, nurtured by William Munger, an affiliate of the Lovestone Communist Party Opposition and Frankensteen's chief advisor at the Chrysler negotiations.

The rupture between the two groups seems to have developed into a fullblown plot during the twelve hours of bitter contention that Frankensteen and Martin shared getting the strikers to give up their plants. *Time* magazine for the week of April 5 ran a story on this exploit, describing how the two men started from Lansing in the evening and traveled over icy roads with a state police escort, stopping at plant after plant, haranguing, exhorting, and threatening. I imagined them emotionally exchanging their recollections after each encounter as they headed for the next, singling out some especially vicious opponent, a "red" undoubtedly.

That was not how Frankensteen recounted the experience to me a year later, however, after his break with Martin. "We had the most trouble at Chrysler-Jefferson and Dodge," he recalled, at both of which the communist influence was negligible. "At Dodge, my own plant, some of the guys called me a 'sell-out.' If the General Motors men could hold out for forty-four days, one fellow shouted, we must be a bunch of rabbits to be giving up after thirty-one!'"

Frankensteen had asked Adolph Germer and Ed Hall to go into the Dodge plant with him because he anticipated some strong personal opposition. "But the attack on Lewis and the UMW was even worse since they claimed that they had always sold out the workers. Germer got hot but he was howled down. So I took over and tried to calm them by telling them of Governor Murphy's assurance that the plants would remain closed after we left them. But the men were not rational. They were all keyed up by the rumors floating around that the court orders had been issued on the injunction writ and that the police were mobilizing to smash the picket lines after the evacuation."

When I interviewed him in 1938, Ed Hall described the situation at Plymouth when the officers arrived there early in the morning. "The guys resented being routed out of sleep in the middle of the night to be told that they had to make up their minds in fifteen minutes on a matter that would affect their whole life." The local was reputedly left-wing, including its president, Leo LaMotte, and had been reluctant to strike in the first place, considering it a mistake. Now, however, they angrily refused to give up the plant, acceding only after a long debate to Governor Murphy's personal plea to the strategy board, which LaMotte transmitted to them.

There was only one plant, De Soto, with a known communist in the leadership. He was Karl Prussian, who was also a member of the strategy board. He had been fired some months ago, with Frankensteen's collusion, he told me later in 1937, but had remained active in the local pending the adjustment of his case. The strikers had heard over the radio of the officers' decision to evacuate the plants and voted to refuse to go along unless it was okayed by a meeting of the united committees of all the locals. When Frankensteen and Martin arrived at De Soto that night on the first stop of their tour, the group rebuffed them. Frankensteen furiously accused Prussian privately that this was his doing. "On the contrary," Prussian replied, "I was in favor of evacuation but the committee here took their stand during my absence in Lansing with the strategy board."

At any event, when the De Soto strikers heard on the following day at 2 P.M. that the Dodge sitdowners had left their plant, they immediately voted to do the same. These circumstances did not alter the factional line of conduct that Martin and Frankensteen had decided upon and which they began to put into operation after the strike in a manner that soon turned out to be irreversible.

• • •

Getting the strikers out of the plants may have catalyzed the negotiations, but it hardly brought a satisfactory settlement. Frankensteen admitted as much in his introduction to a surprisingly revealing booklet that the UAW put out right after the strike, in April 1937. It is a motley of apologetic pleas, concessions, and one extravagant boast. Although it was the first contract that Chrysler had ever signed, he declared, the union had nonetheless obtained things that it took the miners forty-five years to gain. Yet all of these arguments did not palliate the union's acceptance of the no-strike pledge or the retrogressive seniority arrangement.

Frankensteen made a desperate effort in the brochure to minimize the weakness of the seniority setup. No doubt he had on his mind the sensitivity of the Dodge workers on the subject since seniority had almost provoked a big strike in the plant that previous autumn. The give-away clause on it in the new contract read: "Exceptional employees may be retained irrespective of seniority." This was an amazing reversion to the infamous "merit clause" of 1934, which for several years had furnished automobile manufacturers with the means of resisting a genuine seniority system based solely on service as well as the means to coddle anti-union favorites among their employees. Frankensteen admitted that the clause "reads very bad," then added naively that "it isn't as bad as it looks on paper." It was limited to only 10 percent of the work force, he explained, as though imposing a special disadvantaged status on two thousand workers was a minor matter.

The Dodge workers did not agree and Frankensteen later gave me an account of the dramatic manner they adopted to show their discontent. "I had never entered the Dodge local hall when they hadn't cheered me," he said. "But this time their booing was tremendous and it started below as I began mounting the steps. It became deafening when I came into the hall and I walked down toward the front feeling as if I was on my death march. It continued as I stood facing them, then suddenly a story I had read by Anatole France that I hadn't thought about in years came to my mind and I started by telling them about it." The story was about an old labor leader who had done his best to serve his people. But on one single occasion he took the unpopular side of a certain question, the correct side, and was defeated. A group who had been plotting to get him rode him out of town and taunted him on the way, "'Well, we got you, didn't we?' But the old man replied: 'No, whether I live or die it will be with a clear conscience. But you yourselves can never have that feeling again.'"

"'Therefore,'" Frankensteen concluded, "'I want to say to you tonight that whether you accept or reject the contract is your prerogative. But I believe in my position so sincerely that if the contract is rejected I will consider it a rejection of myself and my leadership and I will resign.' It brought the house down," he ended, "and they voted for acceptance almost unanimously and without discussion."

I heard Dick Frankensteen speak many times and he could be very effective. On this occasion his performance must have been one of genuine virtuosity. Yet the contract's defects remained and the Dodge workers must have thought of them often in the sequel, as he did himself when he told me the story fifteen months later, characterizing the agreement as frankly "bad."

Part Three

The UAW Defeats Factionalism and Starts Anew

GM's Counterattack at Flint and the UAW's Reply

The two-page Chrysler strike issue of the *United Automobile Worker* with its defiant heading—"WE HAVE JUST BEGUN TO FIGHT"—was the second-last one that I would do. It could not have been more than a week or ten days later that Homer Martin let it be known in his circuitous way that I was dislodged as editor, demoted to assistant under William Munger. I was scandalized though I felt better when I learned that the post had first been offered to Frank Winn, who was a professional after all and highly competent. But Winn turned the job down indignantly. However solacing this was to my self-respect, I was still faced by the debasing situation of having to work in the name of another person who, aside from his total lack of ability, had assumed a posture on the International's staff that most of us regarded as repellent.

I was hurt and angry but in no mood to fight as a number of friends advised, including Bill Davey, an officer of the Newspaper Guild. Davey, whom I knew from Cleveland, asked me to write to Morgan Hull of the national office. I did not do this until the end of May when the question was no longer moot. But the letter recalls some of the circumstances of Martin's decision. I tried to see him after my demotion to demand an accounting but he sidled out of the interview. I did learn indirectly, however, one criticism that he had raised about my work. I was accused of playing favorites with others to his detriment in the paper. The accusation led me to do a quantitative count of names mentioned and space alloted, which showed Martin leading by at least two to one in both cases.

Two Detroit papers approached me through Frank Winn for an interview, but I turned them down. However unjust I might have considered my treatment, I was too intimately bound up with the union to let myself be the cause of dissension in it. Homer Martin was the elected leader of the UAW and whatever I thought about him or his capabilities, I felt that his position ought to remain publicly inviolable. Still, I could not work for the International under the conditions that had been offered, even if the idea of giving up my relationship with the union was painful. As it turned out, however, another way appeared by which this predicament could be avoided. Dorothy and I were overjoyed by the possibility.

The Flint local needed a full-time editor of its own because of the tremendous growth of the union since the settlement, and Bob Travis asked me if I would put out the paper on a weekly basis. Since the end of the strike I had made several hurried trips to Flint to prepare issues of the *Flint Auto Worker.* Everyone assumed, I most of all perhaps, that I would resume my pre-sitdown practice of getting out these occasional numbers in addition to the International's journal. But it was soon evident that this would be unsatisfactory.

Actually, we did not feel that we were going *back* to Flint. Even after our return to Detroit, Flint's hold on us had continued. Apart from the hundreds of friends we had made there during the sitdown, there was the closeness of being at the hub of things, at the center of activity, whether in the union or as part of the community.

Detroit, in contrast, had seemed cold and unfriendly after our return there. I sensed it as a kind of resentment to the lead that Flint had taken in the organization after its brilliant victory. People at UAW headquarters smiled wanly when you talked to them about it and soon you stopped doing so. The Chrysler strike did not change things. This was *their* strike I was made to feel when I asked Dick Frankensteen to get me into one of the occupied plants, Dodge preferably, to do a story on it. He said that he had tried, but it was impossible to arrange because of the fear of a police invasion. The sitdowners were not even allowing press reporters in to write feature stories, he said. After the evacuation trouble, Frankensteen was cold, resentful, and piqued in his most sensitive spot: his egotistical self.

There would be nothing like that in Flint. I was eager to get started, to learn what had taken place in the plants since the end of the strike, and to tell that story. I attended a large stewards' meeting at Chevrolet a day or two after we arrived and heard the most vital and devoted members of the union describe how things stood. At this stage, it was apparent from reports out of Chevrolet that members of the supervision were trying to reestablish their pre-strike authority. They picked out some of their old favorites and arranged to furnish them with clubs that were stored in the superintendents' offices. One man described a foreman who would take one or two stooges off the line and walk up and down the aisle with them, cursing the union.

But the members learned to control their tempers, several of them having been fired after falling into the trap. One steward commented sensibly: "There's only one way to stop all of this, it's to organize the shop one hundred percent. How many stewards here have their departments one hundred percent? We're going to get our last man tomorrow, outside of the eight or nine company guards who we don't want anyway. The rest, all of those that were sitting on the fence, we've got them now!"

A number of the foremen recognized that the established power of the union was inevitable. "Some foremen are even voluntarily approaching stewards," another man reported, "and asking them to help set up a regular grievance procedure." A steward from the Chevy 4 crankshaft department told how the men had slowed production from 330 to 300 jobs an hour. The action had created tremendous excitement. Plant Manager Arnold Lenz was said to mutter: "You're cutting us down by more automobiles than Packard, Olds or Pontiac produce altogether!"

"The boys all say they feel five years younger," still another man said. "Lenz says, 'The boys are loafing.' The boys say, 'To hell with Lenz! A good day's work for a good day's pay.'" This quiet, deliberate method of slowing down the line was applied at all the factories, I would learn. The hourly reduction in turn-out ran from 5 to 10 percent, as was reported at the two Fisher plants, at Buick, and even among the new women unionists at AC Sparkplug.[1] Wages were not neglected, either, the major targets being classification inequalities. In the past, these had been the widespread basis for discrimination, and until the corporation agreed to a systematic adjustment on a national scale, individual pressure on a department or plantwide basis would remain the only recourse. At the UAW-GM national negotiations in March 1937, the corporation categorically opposed such an arrangement.

These negotiations were conducted on the union side by Wyndham Mortimer and Ed Hall and resulted on March 12 in what was loosely called a "supplementary contract." It was far too modest a document to deserve the name, most of it consisting of evasions by GM. Key demands like the elimination of piecework and control of the speed of production were shunted back to the individual plants, at a few of which, like Fisher One and Cleveland Fisher, substantial improvements were made. The minimum wage and the thirty-hour week were refused pointblank. Of the two points that were approved, one was merely a reiteration of the February 11 document granting sole collective bargaining. The other, seniority based on length of service, was textually granted, and the *United Automobile Worker* heralded the event with deserved effusion on March 20: "the infamous 'merit clause' under which the auto workers have suffered for over three years was wiped out forever." Discriminatory discharges, many of which went back a number of years, others associated with the recent strike, were left for individual plants to handle and "dozens" of cases had already been settled.[2]

The only new and major arrangement that emerged was termed the "grievance procedure." This called for a permanent bargaining committee of five to nine members, depending on the size of the plant. Committee members handled only the grievances of their own areas that were taken up at regular meetings of the committee with the management. The company's aim was to draw the complaints away from the work place, in particular out of control of the shop stewards, whom workers had previously depended upon for on-the-job settlements.[3]

The virtual elimination of the stewards was the one issue that worked up emotional controversy at the conference of GM locals that the UAW called to approve the March 12 supplementary agreement. Negotiators pointed out that though the stewards were not explicitly sanctioned in the agreement, neither were they eliminated. This apparently convinced most of the 250 delegates that they would just have to battle continuously for their acceptance by the supervision. But the danger of stripping the stewards of their power, Bob Travis argued, remained.[4] It would tend to destroy the militancy of the union. He tried to make up for this by demanding a large increase in the size of the permanent bargaining committee, which Walter Reuther opposed on the ground that it would make the committee unmanageable. Travis replied that the committee could be kept to a practical size but should be chosen from the stewards and hence be responsible to them. His proposal was defeated by a close vote. This had a lasting influence on the subsequent development of the UAW-GM system of negotiations.

• • •

An example of the union-management bargaining procedure under the new system (which constituted probably the first continuous sessions of their kind held at General Motors) is available in a unique set of minutes recorded at the Flint Chevrolet plant from March 8, 1937, to February 23, 1939, and which I obtained only in recent years.[5] Though kept by the union, the minutes give every evidence of being done meticulously and with commendable objectivity.

It may seem surprising that the activities described in the minutes began four days before the supplementary contract was initialed. But it is very likely that the permanent bargaining committee was precipitated into action prematurely by an unauthorized strike. Bob Travis had futilely sought a conference with Arnold Lenz, the Chevrolet plant manager, to discuss the reinstatement of a large number of workers who had been fired for union activities. This was the usual procedure after a settlement, he argued. Lenz's stubborn refusal to even talk about the matter seemed to leave no other option to the UAW leaders, who felt deeply committed to the discharged men, several of whom had been active during the sitdown.

Arnold Lenz was apparently taken by surprise by the union's decision to strike and immediately asked for a meeting. Lenz himself attended the meeting, which he seldom did in future negotiations. The union was represented by an ad hoc committee of seven because the permanent bargaining committee had not yet been elected; Bob Travis and Roy Reuther supplemented the ad hoc committee.

Of the twenty-two discrimination cases listed, fourteen were reinstated, at times with a penalty layoff of a couple of days, two weeks in the highly publicized instances of Bill Roy and Howard Tolls, who had admitted to soliciting for the union on company property. Five others were recorded as "natural layoffs," which might have meant several things, for example, a cut in staff or lack of seniority in those designated. Several men had refused to accept a transfer or a change of work and their discharges were readily adjusted. One had refused his foreman's order to climb a high ladder but it was found that he was under medical care for heart trouble. Two cases were characterized as pending while under further investigation.

Only one man was judged a final discharge by the management, Walter Reed, an old-time militant who was accused of asking to be put on the sick list during the sitdown while Chevrolet was still operating. Soon after he was "seen" (evidently on the union sound car) "broadcasting and directing union traffic," a reference no doubt to the big demonstration that took place outside of Fisher One. This negative decision, though unsatisfactory to the union, did not prevent a settlement of the conflict because of the other important concessions.

It appears to have opened the way to regular grievance proceedings. The next meeting, on March 18, witnessed the discussion of wage adjustments. New hires, the management announced, would receive 65 cents, which would be increased to 70 cents after thirty days; all others who had six months' seniority would earn 75 cents an hour. In production departments the "graduation" would be more rapid and other adjustments were being "surveyed." Most important, the union's demand for a general raise would receive a favorable reply on March 27, the company indicated.

A memorandum handed to the management three days later contained what seems to have been an afterthought. The union expected the blanket raise promised by the company for March 27 to be for 10 percent and would be based on a "set production of 300 units produced per hour." This opened the entire question of the speed of production, which had not thus far been discussed. However the great motor plant, Chevy 4, with its four thousand workers, had on its own put in a demand for an unspecified reduction and announced that "a committee of three will make a survey of speed-up in Plant 4."

The company's reply could be anticipated and, indeed, at the session of March 26, when Arnold Lenz presented the promised wage scale, he pointed out that this offer was contingent on a rate of production of 330 units.[6] The earnings of the entire corporation depended on this production level at Chevrolet, he declared, intimating that the welfare of the workers themselves was primarily bound up with this productive accomplishment.

A prolonged and animated debate followed. Roy Reuther repeated organized labor's motto of "a fair day's work for a fair day's pay" but stressed the importance of balancing profits and wages "on the ground that the bread of all men costs the same." Lenz replied that the company was willing to hire extra men in order to get the 330 units an hour, thus reducing the speed of production. But it was not possible to do this everywhere because of the frequent lack of space for additional machinery or men, so he offered to bring the company's required rate down to 320 units.

Despite this apparently satisfactory settlement, the relations between the management and the union by no means leveled out. In fact, within a week, on April 5, the strike at Chevrolet was resumed—this time on the basic issue of wages—resulting in a resounding victory that, according to the *Flint Auto Worker* of April 15, added "tens of thousands of dollars every week" to workers' pay checks.

After ten days of heated negotiations conducted by ten representatives chosen from every production plant in the company, hourly raises of at least 10 cents and as high as 27 cents were registered in practically every department and on every operation. A minimum of 95 cents was established in the motor division at Chevy 4. Workers, who had waited for years to receive the top rate for their category, were given prompt increases to bring them up to that level. And all of this would come while the speed of the line was being firmly controlled. The supervision was instructed to iron out all speed-up conditions called to their attention, the April 15 article concluded.

Considering these important concessions, one might have expected that lesser grievances could be adjusted out of hand. But such was not the case. Hardly more than a month later, according to the conference minutes of May 22, the company-union relationship had assumed a strong sense of conflict. A blowup occurred at the June 4 session, where the company group was led by H. E. Coen, the assistant plant manager. The subject was cleanup time. Committeeman Fred Grant of Plant 8 complained that the men were not permitted to stop work to clean up around their machines before the whistle. They were docked six minutes for doing so, which would seem to be of no great moment. However, it caused minor revolts in two of the plants, where the men quit work at the whistle without turning off the machines. Coen called this "a very childish act" because shutting off the machines was part of a man's job. Ed Cronk of Plant 6 replied that if the company refused to pay the men for cleaning up before the whistle he did not see how they could be expected to shut the machines off on their own time. The argument grew personal and Cronk is reported in the union's own minutes to have "made some very crude and vulgar statements." Whereupon Coen decided that the conference "had gone out of control [and] the management's representatives retired from the conference."

There was a kind of voluntary cynicism about the company's replies thereafter that seemed to be intended to infuriate the union's bargainers. When, for example, on July 1, a committeeman complained that a foreman in his department did the work of a regular employee as well as supervisory duties, the management side replied that this practice (long condemned by the union) was permissible if the foreman wished "to render temporary assistance to the men."[7]

Proof of the ineffectualness of the bargaining procedure thereafter shows up distinctly in a study of the replies to grievances reported in the minutes. By my count, of ninety complaints brought to conference, only twenty-nine were accommodated, almost without exception those of minor, if not trivial, importance. For example, nine grievances were considered in the period from July 15 through 22. Only two were accepted. One was the request for a few extra fans during a heat wave; the other involved a safety warning that railroad cars were being switched on company ground without the aid of a brakeman. Refused, on the other hand, were such bids as the reconsideration of two demotions and a modest wage bonus in the grueling heat-treat department.

A near-breakdown in relations is revealed in the minutes of the August 26 session, when H. E. Coen reverted to the unsettled grievance of "lost time" on what was called the "hoodline" in Ed Cronk's plant, which had recently erupted once more. Coen reminded the union delegates of the way these men "had tried to force the management into allowing a wash-up period before the whistle blew by deliberately quitting early," whereas employees were paid to work from whistle to whistle and were expected to do so. "But now," he observed sadly, "after a real attempt at collective bargaining, the men in this particular plant without resorting to the proper bargaining channels, quit work early. Actions such as these cause one to feel that all the effort expended toward making a success of collective bargaining has been to no avail."

There is the impression of a foreboding pause at that point, as Coen prepared to outline the conclusion of this disturbing matter. The workers on the hoodline, he continued, were then told that the time lost due to their quitting before the whistle would be deducted from their pay checks. And they had started a slow-down in retaliation. "Production," he said, "dropped the first night from 100 to 94 percent and on the second night to 77 percent, which is a severe loss. Press switches were greased (to delay handling) and gauges were tampered with, causing an increase in scrap. Such actions can only be described by the word 'sabotage,'" Coen observed somberly.

It seems curious that in the absence of Ed Cronk, unaccounted for in the minutes, to find Coen making a sarcastic reference to him, a remark which was not caught up by the other committeemen. Recently, he remarked, while Cronk was in Detroit attending a UAW class for new leaders, "no disturbances were reported in this department, which had operated at 100 percent, whereas upon his return such instances had started to recur." In the light of the detailed circumstances, Coen concluded, the company had decided "that the night shift would be advised at 3:30 P.M. today (which was actually within a few minutes) that unless production was restored to 100 percent, with the understanding that the men were to work at their machines from whistle to whistle, the night shift on the job would be dismissed and the balance of this model (which had but a few weeks to go) would be run out by the day shift, which had maintained production throughout the difficulty with the night shift."

The union committee was faced by a painful dilemma. Some of them were openly opposed to the slow-down tactics at Plant 6. In fact, Junior Sanders, a second representative at the present bargaining session, had earlier revealed that a number of the workers at the plant, including himself, supposedly, "would like to work until the whistle blows." One wonders what any of the more militant committeemen present thought about this damaging admission made in the presence of the management representatives. Surely it encouraged Coen to issue his naked threat to the night crew of Chevy 6, who would no doubt prefer to swallow their wrath rather than take a layoff of two weeks or more.

In the language of the minutes, the union committee declared that they "did not condone actions of this kind and requested permission to investigate this grievance." Permission was granted and the committeemen left the meeting, hurried to Plant 6, and, following their "investigation," production was restored—to 101 percent efficiency!

• • •

Despite H. E. Coen's self-serving, benign appraisal of the bargaining procedure at Chevrolet, it is obvious from the recounted antagonisms that the attitude of the Chevrolet management toward the union was only superficially congenial. Moreover, we must remember that the few top officials engaged in the negotiations were only a small part of the managerial apparatus. We learn absolutely nothing about the rest—the foremen, the superintendents—those who could make the workers' lives a constantly recurring misery. It was their attitude that explained the conduct of such men as Ed Cronk, who appears in the minutes as exaggeratedly antagonistic and impossible to get along with. There is, however, another medium available to us that suggests a different explanation for this bellicosity. It is found in the copious reports of worker correspondents to the *Flint Auto Worker*.[8] Here, in any case, one could learn from their own words how the workers felt about things.

The UAW-GM antagonism that prevailed after the strike was sustained by an almost unanimously negative press. Important national newspapers again became interested in Flint, but the interest was no longer sympathetic as had been the case during the sitdown, with its unique and picturesque features. Out-of-town reporters with whom we had become congenial returned to Flint to write "before-and-after" stories. But their chief interest, we learned, was in interviewing GM officials, who told them about the chaos that unionists were precipitating inside the plants by constant wildcat strikes that disrupted production despite the corporation's serious efforts to make a success of collective bargaining.[9]

One felt that some of the reporters were merely interested in erasing the memory of their earlier enthusiasm. They paid little heed to our replies to the arguments of the corporation officials or to our explanation of the corporation's failure to reeducate their supervision to the requirements of the new situation inside the plants.

I happened to be the butt of one of these reporters, Paul Gallico, whom for personal reasons stemming from my youth, when I read some of his pieces in leading slick magazines, I favored during the strike by arranging for him to have the first chance to write an inside account of the sitdown at Fisher One, where he was allowed to stay overnight. He rewarded me for my sentimentality by putting me into a novelette in which a double of Bob Travis was the hero. The strike leader became the cat's-paw of a dubious character, an aggressive, talkative, curly-haired type—in short, me. When this objectionable individual appears on one occasion, a reporter asks a colleague, "Who is that?" The reply is a grunt and a shrug of shoulders: "There's one of them in every strike!" But the burden of the story centers on the strike leader's disillusionment, which is brought about by a lovely newspaperwoman who disproves for him his exaggerated beliefs in the allure of unionism, thus casting doubt on the merits of the strike itself and the reality of its accomplishments.

The role of workers' correspondents in the *Flint Auto Worker* was already established before the strike. They were necessary because of the way the paper had to be put out during my weekend visits to Flint, when I would work over the prepared notes and contributions of volunteers from the plants. This activity had lapsed during the sitdown because strike news had engrossed attention. Problems from inside the plants were reduced since most were either on strike or closed because of it. All this was abruptly changed when work started up again under new conditions and challenges, a completely new world, in fact.

After my permanent installation in Flint, the development of the worker correspondents took on major importance, evolving rapidly into a widespread medium of communication by volunteer contributors from all the plants and many of the larger departments. Their efforts were linked to some extent by the weekly meetings that I set up at the Pengelly Building for each shift on the day of the deadline. During these lively sessions we read and discussed the contributions. At the request of a number of the correspondents I started a weekly class in journalism for each of the shifts, as an item in the issue of June 2 reminds me.

During the first two or three months after the sitdown the references to mean or uncooperative foremen were the most popular items and the commentaries were apparently quite effective. There is much evidence that these sarcasms brought results. The nastiest of bosses disliked being pilloried in print. Whereas in the past they might have enjoyed the reputation for being tough, they began to realize that things had changed and even the company no longer expected them to ride herd on workers.

One of our best reporters, a man from Chevy 2 who signed himself "Publicity Pat," told of one foreman who was reported to him of having made insulting remarks about the aggressiveness of the workers in another department, boasting about what he would do if he was boss there. Pat put it to the man himself who tried to pass it off as a joke. "He begged and cajoled us not to publish the item. Needless to say, it was published." Pat commented: "Now the *Auto Worker* is an all-powerful little paper and through it we can express our views regarding shop conditions and bosses bull-dozing union men, also the policy of our young and powerful organization. Remember, it's read by all of Flint, including the big shots of General Motors."

Pat's last remark was corroborated by a number of correspondents from the other plants. A Fisher Two man wrote in the May 25 issue: "Certain foremen were noticed reading our union paper in the cafeteria recently. Pretty good paper, isn't it boys?" A Buick No. 11 correspondent observed, "Foremen are asking for their copy of the *Auto Worker*." He suggested taking a vote about putting them on the mailing list. A reporter from AC Sparkplug noted, "We understand that the last paper caused quite a bit of discussion among the supervision." Just before the strike, he explained, the company union requested time-and-a-half pay for Sunday work and was "turned down flat." Two weeks ago, he added, a complaint on the same subject had appeared in the *Flint Auto Worker*. "Shortly after that we were told that time and a half would be paid for Sunday work."

Standard Cotton, the small shop that produced cushions for GM and shared the sitdown with us, credited the paper for having corrected one of its most dangerous working hazards. It was our "constant barrage of publicity," Chairman Carl Thrasher reported, that won a modern ventilation system for the workers, a number of whom had previously developed bronchial trouble because of its lack. Due to the agitation of the *Flint Auto Work-*

er, a deputy state inspector had visited the shop and ordered the management to make the installation within a month, Thrasher wrote on April 29. "Our thanks to the staff of the *Flint Auto Worker* for their aid in this matter."

The correspondents' reports of changes in conditions during the six-month period after the strike would reward a study by historians. Periodically, spokesmen for the different units prepared round-ups of improvements. The issue of April 29 summarized the gains at Fisher One, the most spectacular of which no doubt was the slashing of the speed of the line, from 450 units a day before the strike down to 372.[10] "Wherever a job was considered very tough, extra men were added," the shop committee explained to me. Piecework was wiped out in most departments and innumerable safety and sanitary features were installed. Wages, of course, had not been neglected, having been raised on a plantwide scale between 10 and 15 cents an hour. "Most important is the sense of security," one member observed. "You feel that you have something to say about conditions," another added, "while before you took what they gave you and kept your mouth shut."

Fisher One enjoyed the advantage of having begun to build up its strength several months before and especially during the great sitdown. Changes came more slowly at Buick and AC Sparkplug, which had missed that primary source of learning.[11] It was perhaps significant that a majority of the unauthorized strikes listed in the *Flint Auto Worker* occurred at these two units, indicating that such confrontation was essential to instill respect for the union among the supervision. On April 15, a month after the supplementary agreement was signed by General Motors, several short stoppages were still "needed" at Buick to force the management to observe its provisions. A sitdown at factory No. 12 "was instrumental in getting us our first meeting with the management," a correspondent wrote, while another strike was required at department 07 to win such obvious things as repairs in a dangerously ripped-up floor, a light-signal to call for the carry-away truck, and replacements for antiquated equipment.

The situation at AC Sparkplug, where women workers predominated, was in many ways even more backward. "Why did the girls sit down in plant 2?" one of them asked rhetorically in our issue of April 15. "They knew that this weapon was to be used only as a last resort. They didn't sit down because they wanted to lose five hours pay. They sat down because the conditions on the line . . . were so unbearable, so wretched, that they just couldn't stand it any longer! The company would not supply the kind of tape that the girls wanted. Doesn't that seem like a small thing to cause girls to sit down and lose money?" She seemed to pause as though raising her brows to her interlocutors and then resumed:

But did you ever work on a production line that ran so fast . . . that the tension of your body and your nerves wouldn't relax even over a weekend? Did you ever work that fast and on top of that have the constant irritation of . . . having stock stick to your fingers because the company wouldn't give you the kind of tape that would make your work easier? Tape that grew into a nightmare. Did you ever have to cut porcelain during your lunch hour because a machine had broken down? . . . Did you ever have to run your machine through lunch hour? . . . Did you ever have to work without a rest period [toilet] till 2:30? Did you ever have to drop 88 shells a minute and inspect them at the same time? No, You Never Did! But the AC girls did, and that's why they sat down. And these are the results:

1. A 20-minute rest period divided into two. 2. No more work before or after the whistle or during lunch. 3. Re-timing of the line. 4. Extra relief girl from 8:30 to 10:30 and 1:00 to 3:00. 5. White smooth tape instead of the sticky black. 6. A better distribution of gloves. 7. No more pushing trays down the line.

• • •

Reports from inside the plants were only one phase of the paper. From the start, I planned to devote major attention to city news, which would not only be interesting to our readers but could also give a different slant to things than did the ineffable *Flint Journal*. A handicap was my total ignorance of local politics, but I began to devote some time to it and was helped by my contact with Philip C. Klein, whom I had met at one of the weekly meetings of the city commission.[12]

We had come to Flint just when some interesting things were taking place in that body, which had switched to a pro-union stance since the UAW victory. Klein told me that a majority of the nine commissioners had recently been led to adopt that viewpoint by two of them, Joe Shears and Oliver Tappin, and had then agreed that their first task was to depose John Barringer and Jim Wills as city manager and police chief.[13] Bob Travis and Roy Reuther were deeply involved in this stratagem and I met the two designated successors, William Findlater and Police Captain Twohey, in Travis's office, on separate occasions. In nominating Findlater to take Barringer's post, Shears recalled that he had been purchasing agent at Buick for a number of years before being let out in 1932. "GM gave him a rotten deal after his long service," he said.

Travis thought a good deal about getting the union involved in the political life of the city and spoke to Philip Klein about an idea of setting up a political machine organized by wards around the shop stewards. A concrete development presented itself that spring in the form of a campaign for the replacement of three members of the Flint school board. A list of three candidates was hurriedly thrown together for a "labor slate," though

Jay Greene, vice-chairman of the Fisher One strike committee, was the only actual worker on the slate. The other two men, however, had strong pro-union reputations. Dr. C. C. Probert had gone into Chevy 4 during the sitdown and silenced the false reports that were being circulated about an epidemic of pneumonia among the men. Loren Herrlich, a pharmacist, was a well-known liberal who pledged to fight for "academic freedom for teachers and pupils" and for opening school auditoriums for civic meetings, an important objective at the time.

This slate was presented without organizational preparation due to the lack of time. I was unable to give the candidates the kind of play in the paper that I would otherwise have done. The campaign excited Dorothy and me since it fitted the plan that we had already begun to think about during the strike, of helping to establish what we called a "total union." Thus, at a general stewards meeting at Chevrolet I seized the opportunity of urging participation in the election: "The time has come when we must be 'union' in the Pengelly Building, 'union' in the shop, 'union' when we go shopping and 'union' at the ballot box."[14] I got a good hand but we lost the election. Our labor candidates got merely 50 percent of the score of the lowest winner. We did not despair, however. We would do much better the next time. But there was no next time, for all at once we had our hands full fighting an all-out attack launched by the city's resurgent anti-union forces.

After the strike, the organizational tide had swept through Flint into every craft and trade, most of them without any connection to the automobile industry. Bars, restaurants, hotels, and department stores were all bitten by the sitdown bug, in which the UAW organizers or more often just freelancing members got involved. A sit-in at the J. C. Penney retail store, a type of the old five-and-dime, attracted large crowds that watched the women clerks through the store's wide display windows, skating, dancing, and cooking meals. This did not spare them, however, from eventual rough treatment by the police, who were now taking orders from the associated businessmen of Flint, recently organized into what was euphemistically termed a "Law and Order League," a name covering a pernicious anti-union bias.[15]

A number of attacks on small strikes, ending in a violent assault on the pickets at the Durant Hotel, where a UAW volunteer was killed, marked an anti-union rebirth that seemed aimed directly at the UAW. This was corroborated by the unprovoked fatal shooting of a Buick worker, John Pastva, near the Pengelly Building after a meeting there. The policeman who fired the shot claimed that Pastva, a gentle man and popular unionist, was acting "suspiciously" while walking toward his car.[16] Various other events fitted into the pattern of a generalized offensive. The Flint school board discharged five pro-labor teachers.[17] William Findlater's accession was controverted by a change of vote of one of the commissioners, ostensibly a union man, Frank Ringlein, which also made it possible to bring Jim Wills back as police chief.[18] Soon after, a flurry of court orders against other strikes finally provided the signal for a direct blow at the auto union.

The criminal charges of "inciting to riot" rising out of the Fisher Two Battle of Bulls Run against Bob Travis, Victor and Roy Reuther, and me, which we had assumed from private General Motors assurances would be allowed to lapse, were suddenly brought back to life and put on the active judiciary calendar of the circuit court. It is strange that in my report of the "hearing" I frivolously disregarded the danger that was involved, poking fun at the "ridiculousness" of the proceedings, which I characterized as a "pathetic drama." We were represented by Maurice Sugar. County prosecutor Joseph Joseph presented almost two dozen witnesses, most of them police officers who often disagreed among themselves on the simplest points. Even the judge derided the preparation of the case. "All the property that was destroyed according to your own witnesses," he told Joseph, "was one broken window and you haven't proven that the union was responsible for that either."

We all assumed that the charges would be dropped and as week followed week and we heard nothing more about the matter we concluded that this had quietly occurred. We were shocked to learn at the end of May that although charges had been dropped against three of us, Victor Reuther had been indicted for the full count, the penalty for which was five years' imprisonment. We woke up with a start. Victor came to Flint from Anderson, Indiana, to help organize his defense, especially to line up the witnesses since the trial date had been set for only ten days later, June 7. I ran a lead story on the case, telling of the defense meetings being scheduled by the various UAW units and picking up the words of a member at a Fisher Two rally as a heading that became our slogan: "As long as Vic Reuther is under fire, the General Motors strike has not been won!"

The article raised the image of the countless innocent victims in labor's long litany of struggle: "Though it is hard to believe that an innocent man can be railroaded to prison for a long sentence, the labor records are full of similar cases in which the charges were no more serious or the proof more substantial than in the present instance. . . . Workers must remember that the scales of justice are usually weighted against them or their leaders. The only assurance that Vic Reuther will not be railroaded to a long prison sentence is a roar of protest from them."

The UAW's counterdrive climaxed in a great demonstration at Kearsley Park on June 5, two days before Vic Reuther's trial was to open. On the previous day, ten-minute sitdowns at all the auto plants were scheduled for the two shifts. "Longer shut-downs will not be tolerated by the committeemen," it was scrupulously specified to avoid blame for encouraging "wildcats" by these demonstrations. During the protest stoppages, each factory was to conduct a rally at a prearranged spot inside the plant, and right after work a larger meeting was to be held in the vicinity of each plant to whip up attendance at the citywide mass gathering on June 5.

Even the *Flint Journal* called the Sunday meeting the largest demonstration in Flint's history. Michael J. Burke, president of the local AFL council, many of whose units had suffered from police attacks and other repressive measures, had called on his people to join the auto workers' rally. Homer Martin was the featured speaker, but the three Reuther brothers, assuming the podium one after the other, took the laurels from him. After the gathering the entire throng of forty thousand, directed by two thousand UAW shop stewards, formed a line of march for a torchlight parade through the heart of the city, all units marching under their own banners. Spectators often eight and ten deep crowded the sidewalks.

It was all done in the grand style that the union had evolved during the great sitdown. Except that it happened before the demonstration, the retreat of the anti-union surge insofar as Vic Reuther was concerned brought us a thrill of gratification when it was announced that the charges against him had been summarily dropped.[19] The abrupt decision was indubitably intended to discourage participation in the demonstration. This it failed to accomplish and the thrust of the great rally was proudly transformed from a defensive manifestation into a reassertion of the union's soaring power.

The first National Council meeting, United Automobile Workers Federal Labor Unions, Detroit, July 9–14, 1934. George Lehman is in the line at left, fourth from the front, behind him is Ed Hall. The first person on the right is Homer Martin, behind him is Fred Pieper. (The Archives of Labor and Urban Affairs, Wayne State University)

UNITED AUTOMOBILE WORKER

Special Convention Number   MAY, 1936.   Detroit, Mich.

UNION WINS SELF-RULE

Dillon Out; New Officers Elected

FIRST DEMOCRATICALLY ELECTED OFFICERS of United Automobile Workers. Left to Right: Wyndham Mortimer, First Vice Pres.; Ed Hall, Second Vice Pres.; Homer Martin, President; Walter N. Wells, Third Vice Pres.; George Addes, Secretary-Treasurer.

AFL HEAD ENDS TRIAL PERIOD

"I am here to perform my duty as President of the the American Federation of Labor, to carry out the decision of this convention of the A. F. of L. and the Executive Council, to end now the administration of your affairs by men appointed by the A. F. of L., to terminate the probationary period and to place the destinies of this great organization in your hands."

These words, of President William Green, which 40,000 auto unionists have awaited—yes, impatiently—for over two years, were finally heard on the first day of the South Bend Convention, April 26. A great ovation of the assembled delegates greeted this statement, which formally established the complete autonomy of the auto union. Immediately upon the utterance of these words, President Dillon, Green's appointee of last August, was automatically relieved of his office, and by the suggestion of the President of the A. F of L., the Convention proceeded to elect a temporary chairman. Vice President Homer Martin was unanimously picked for this honor.

Without delay, the delegates then got down to the business of the Convention the first of its kind ever held by the auto workers under completely democratic rule.

COUGHLIN MAKES UNITY APPEAL

In a spectacular manner Father Coughlin walked into a party of delegates at the United Automobile Workers' Convention Thursday night in South Bend.

The radio priest had not planned to attend the convention. He was en route from Chicago to Detroit, stopping here for dinner.

Invited to Speak

Richard Frankensteen, head of the Detroit Automobile Industrial Workers organization, and friend of Father Coughlin, who attended the convention, persuaded the radio priest to speak.

He approved industrial unionism along the lines that the organization here is being directed. He said men are not paid on a basis of what they produce but on a basis of existence.

The greatest interest is being manifested in this burning issue by the workers at Hudson's. The place and exact time of the meeting are to be announced later

Martin President; Mortimer, Hall, Wells, Addes Also Chosen

MAKE PLANS FOR MAMMOTH DRIVE

One of the key points in the program adopted at the South Bend Convention for building the International Union was the decision to inaugurate a great organization drive in the industry, particularly in its heart, the State of Michigan.

Details were left in the hands of Executive Board, though the following plans were specified:

1. Prominent speakers, like John L. Lewis, Charles P. Howard, and other outstanding proponents of industrial unionism, be brought into the auto centers.

2. Organization Committees be set up by the General Officers wherever they are needed.

3. Credentials issued to voluntary organizers upon recommendation of the District Councils.

Widest Publicity

4. Widest possible publicity, through press, radio, sound cars, etc.

5. Enlistment of all liberal and civic-minded groups for assistance.

OFFICERS' SALARIES DRASTICALLY REDUCED

The salaries of all five General Officers were set at $3,000 per annum. This represents a big cut compared with the sums paid last year, the President having formerly received $6,500 and the Vice-President and Secretary-Treasurer, $4,500 each.

The present salaries thus total up to $15,000 or a saving of $500 over those in the past; whereas two extra General Officers will be available for our International despite this reduction.

With the termination of the "probationary period," the question of the election of officers came immediately upon the agenda of the Convention at South Bend. After the constitution of the International had been changed increasing the number of officers to five, this important matter was taken up.

Those elected to office need no introduction to the auto workers of this country. They have all been in the forefront of the battle for the International from the time the original federal locals were set up, and later took up the cudgels for complete democracy.

Homer Martin, former vice-president, was elected president by acclamation. Wyndham Mortimer, president of the powerful White Motor local and the Cleveland Auto Council, was designated first Vice-President. Ed Hall, of Milwaukee, outgoing Secretary-Treasurer, was chosen second Vice-Presidency; while the third Vice-Presidency went to Walter N. Wells, of Detroit, who has been very active in the movement of that city. George Addes, of the famous Toledo local, will fill exceedingly well the most important of all—Secretary Hall's shoes hereafter, keeping the books and finances of the International in order.

It is hard to imagine a better set of honest, upright and aggressive leaders to direct the affairs of the International Union during the coming year.

6. Raising of a "war chest" of $250,000, of which at least $75,000 must come from the affiliated locals of the International Union.

7. Request aid of all local, central and state bodies of organized labor.

8. When necessary, councils of correlated plants shall be established by the General Executive Board for the purpose of discussing negotiations and compiling data on hours, wages and working conditions.

Research Dept. to Aid

A Setting up of Research Department in cooperation with the Educational Committee to help compile such data. Locals shall do this on individual scale as well.

This is the plan. By adopting it, the convention showed that the International Union means business. The next few weeks and months ought to witness the unheard of undreamt of stores of energy, under the guidance of the General Officers and Executive Board, which will mean that our union has finally gone to bat with the tremendous problem of organizing the tens of thousands of unorganized auto workers. But only the completest cooperation and self-sacrificing efforts will bring this aim to a successful termination.

HUDSON LOCAL VOTES ON MERGER QUESTION

Detroit—A special meeting of the Hudson Local of the Associated Automobile Workers of America (A.A.W.A.), headed by Arthur Greer, is being called for May 22, for the purpose of exploring and discussing the question of amalgamating with the International Union.

INDEPENDENTS IN UNITY BANQUET

Working at lightning speed, the General Officers of our International, elected at South Bend, arranged a banquet on Wednesday evening, May 6, only four days after the closing of the Convention in honor of the three independent unions which have expressed themselves through their representatives as favoring amalgamation.

Present were Richard Frankensteen, head of the A. I. W. A. with a number of members of the Executive Board of his union. Arthur Greer and two others from the Hudson local of the A. A. W. A. and three representatives of the M. E. S. A.

Speakers Call for Unity

Speaker after speaker rose to his feet, telling with deep feeling how he had been waiting for this day with great longing and expectation. After listening to these men from all the most important auto unions in the industry, it was almost impossible to understand why such a meeting of friendship and solidarity could not have taken place long before this.

President Martin, in a most stirring address which closed the banquet, said that the time and the reason for disunity were past, and he invited the representatives of the independents to come into the fold so that working together, the common obligation of all to the auto workers and their families could finally be met.

Day of Unifing Closer

This banquet brought the great day of ultimate unity closer than ever, though it was pointed out that a number of matters, some of them technicalities, had to be settled beforehand.

Pengelly Building, Flint UAW headquarters, where Wyndham Mortimer opened organization campaign in early June 1936. (Flint Public Library)

Picketing strikers dance in the street during the Kelsey-Hayes Wheel Company strike, December 23, 1936. (The Archives of Labor and Urban Affairs, Wayne State University)

Fisher Two strikers defend their plant against violent attack by the police in the "Battle of Bulls Run," January 11, 1937. (The Archives of Labor and Urban Affairs, Wayne State University)

Members of the Women's Emergency Brigade marching outside of Chevrolet Plant No. 9 in Flint on February 1, 1937. At the far left are Dorothy Kraus and Walter Reuther. (The Archives of Labor and Urban Affairs, Wayne State University)

The formal signing of the contract agreement between the United Auto Workers Union and General Motors Corporation. At the desk, left to right: Wyndham Mortimer for the UAW, Michigan Governor Frank Murphy, William Knudsen for General Motors, and John Dewey for the National Labor Relations Board. (The Archives of Labor and Urban Affairs, Wayne State University)

Bud Simons, strike leader at Fisher Body Plant One, reads the news of the strike settlement to the strikers. (The Archives of Labor and Urban Affairs, Wayne State University)

The Cadillac Square demonstration against the court injunction ordering strikers out of Chrysler plants, March 23, 1937. (The Archives of Labor and Urban Affairs, Wayne State University)

Strike leaders arraigned for "inciting to riot" during the "Battle of Bulls Run."
Left to right: Victor Reuther, Bob Travis, Roy Reuther, Maurice Sugar, Henry
Kraus, and Judge Edward D. Mallory. (The Archives of Labor and Urban Affairs, Wayne State University)

Richard Frankensteen being beaten by Ford Motor Company Service Department personnel during the "Battle of the Overpass" on the Miller Road overpass, May 26, 1937. Walter Reuther was also badly beaten here. (The Archives of Labor and Urban Affairs, Wayne State University)

International Union
United Automobile Workers of America
AFFILIATED WITH THE AMERICAN FEDERATION OF LABOR

GENERAL OFFICERS

HOMER MARTIN . . . . President
WYNDHAM MORTIMER . . . . . . First Vice-President
ED. HALL . . . . Second Vice-President
WALTER N. WELLS . . . . Third Vice-President
GEO. F. ADDES . . . . Secretary-Treasurer

GENERAL OFFICES
801-5 HOFMANN BLDG.
DETROIT, MICH.
Cadillac 5146-7-8-9

March 27, 1937

Mr. Jay Lovestone
c/o P. Michael
131 W. 33rd Street
New York, N. Y.

Dear Jay:

I was delighted to get your last letter, as I am always delighted to receive your letters.

I read with a great deal of interest your articles. It seems
to me that they strike the key-note in the whole situation.

I realize we have many things to straighten out in our International Union before it is a well organized and solidified
union. However, let me reassure you about Brother Brown, as
I am sure that he will be kept on the payroll one way or
another. At the present time, I can defend his remaining on
the payroll because of the necessity for organization and his
success in that. However, I have already recommended his being
placed on the payroll of the CIO and will keep him on the
International payroll until the CIO accepts him. I am sure that
he can be kept on one or the other of these payrolls; at least I
am determined that we shall not lose him. As you may well
realize, this was a maneuver by certain parties to keep our boys
out of the International Union and out of strategic positions,
where they could mould the organization along proper lines.

I appreciate more than I can tell you your expression of pleasure
at the successful outcome of our Cadillac Square meeting. This
was almost spoiled, however, by the action of the Conference for
the Protection of Civil Rights, headed by Mezerik. May I say
that only the quickest possible and most determined action on
our part saved the meeting and made it a tremendous success.
Bill perhaps will explain other matters to you.

Wishing you every success in your work, I am,

Fraternally yours,

Homer Martin

Homer Martin
General President

HM:VF
IUUAWA

The UAW Splits into Two Opposing Camps

16

Eighty UAW activists were unavoidably absent from the Kearsley Park concourse because they were delegates to an important two-day conference of representatives from all UAW General Motors plants. Present at Detroit were 517 envoys from twenty-seven centers. Their task was to outline the new contract that would be presented to the corporation on August 11, the expiral date of the original six-month agreement that John L. Lewis had torn from the clutching fingers of GM's DuPont lawyers on February 11, 1937.

"Flint's great delegation of eighty was cheered resoundingly as it stood up in answer to the roll call," the *Flint Auto Worker* of June 10 reported in proud comment on that event. The delegates elected a permanent "Committee of Seventeen" to stay on in Detroit and coordinate the demands that had been put forward and then negotiate on them with the corporation. Flint's group had been granted four posts on this negotiating committee: Louis Baraty, Buick; Patricia Wiseman and Bert Harris, Fisher One; and Bob Travis, who was named for the Chevrolet delegation, which could not agree on its member. He later retired when that unit designated David Dow for the position.

The carefully chosen negotiating committee never did get to carry out its assigned task, however, as a new situation developed within the International that hampered it as well as various other developments. Flint seemed to be at its center, which cut short the sense of euphoria that prevailed after the great Kearsley Park demonstration, when we had assumed that the attack on the union had been halted. It had merely changed its character, which was harder or even impossible to combat because it was led by the president of the UAW.

Homer Martin's antagonism had already surfaced a month or so earlier. The warning signal had come soon after the Chrysler strike, when several members of the International's staff were fired. The first victims, Victor Reuther and I, were notified on the same day. Other discharges followed soon after, and their choice suddenly made us aware that sides were being lined up, characterizing what would soon develop into a pervading factionalism.

It was not until a year later that we were to discover, from a batch of letters that were mysteriously brought to the office of Maurice Sugar, the labor attorney, that a non-union person was the controlling influence that propelled Martin into launching this affliction that was to plague the UAW for two terrible years.[1]

The background of Jay Lovestone prepared him extraordinarily for the role of master factionalist that he was to play within the auto union. Formerly the national secretary of the Communist party, he had been expelled in 1928 after a sharp internecine conflict and had founded his own group, the Communist Party Opposition (CPO). The various activities of this "party" and the way Lovestone succeeded in winning Martin to its banner are beyond the scope of the present work. But it is important to know the almost fictional ascendancy that he won over Martin and the manner in which he imposed his baneful influence on the UAW through Martin.

There is one letter of the several hundred in the Lovestone file, which I carefully annotated when Maurice Sugar acquired it, that is revelatory of the way he functioned. Dated June 17, 1937, the letter was addressed to Lovestone from George Miles, his coordinator of operations in the UAW.[2] Miles wrote of the Flint local's recent endorsement of five general officers for re-election at the forthcoming convention. This was "extremely disquieting," Miles observed, describing the plan he had worked out for nullifying it and which Glenn Shadduck, a Chevrolet worker and member of the CPO, whom Martin had recently put on his personal payroll, would carry out by organizing a "backfire . . . of adopting resolutions, statements, etc." against Bob Travis's "unity of all constructive elements" program.

A month later, in a letter dated July 29, George Miles refers dourly to the frightening successes of the "Unity Group" in the elections of delegates from the Flint units to the convention. Especially shocking to him were the results at Chevrolet, where the Lovestone group had its only base and where the entire pro-Martin slate (including Shadduck and other CPOs) was defeated almost two to one. Miles angrily comments that Martin shared in the blame for this rout because he had allowed Bob Travis's entire "machine" in Flint to remain intact "although it should have been smashed immediately."

This bad news did not discourage Lovestone's hopes for the Milwaukee Convention, however. He was counting on one powerful factor for winning a sweeping victory there: the enormous prestige that Martin had acquired during the General Motors strike. A great part of his fame stemmed from the barnstorming trip that John L. Lewis had suggested to him, meaning actually to get him away from the negotiations.[3] Martin had, as a result, won acclaim and headlines in all the auto centers that he had visited and had become the symbol of the great sitdown, not only to the general public but also to the UAW membership.

Thereafter, he felt that he could do anything he set his mind to. He had early won Dick Frankensteen over and now introduced him to Lovestone, with whose followers Frankensteen was already working at Ford. A big majority of the UAW executive board, animated chiefly by Fred Pieper, backed Martin in support of the clean-sweep program that he expected to put across at the Milwaukee Convention that summer against the Mortimer-Reuther-Travis group. But his chief hope lay in the tenfold increase in the UAW membership, a majority of whom were in new locals that would come to the assembly thinking of Martin as the unchallenged standard-bearer of the great union.

The first blow aimed at the Flint leadership was classic: a charge of financial mismanagement during the strike. It would have been a miracle if some accounts had not become tangled up in all the commotion. But what the anonymous accuser had failed to take into account was Bob Travis's experience as president of the dynamic Toledo Chevrolet local. "I signed every check," Travis explained, "every [bill] that was over one dollar. . . . I wouldn't sign it unless it was for something and was [made out to] the people that got it." His secretary, Olga Richards, audited every bill that got a check. Smaller expenditures came out of the petty cash, each outlay no matter how small being noted.[4]

As soon as Travis heard from Detroit that his books were to be examined, he insisted that this be done by two certified accountants who must be designated by George Addes. They spent several days looking over the wads of papers that had been amassed and announced that the strike records were several hundred dollars in the black. But the experience had made up Bob's mind about a primary necessity. The Flint local would have to hold elections without delay for officers and a board into whose hands he could pass all administrative responsibilities. Membership of Local 156 was rising by several thousand a week; soon thirty thousand members would be paying a dollar dues every month.

Nominations for officers were set by the local but before they took place, the Lovestonite group at Chevrolet led by Ted LaDuke, Tom Klasey, and Glenn Shadduck began a campaign opposing them with the covert support of Homer Martin, as Bob Travis intimated in a report to the International's executive board.[5] "I received a communication from Brother Martin," he wrote, "[advising] the postponing of the elections," who came up to Flint in person to see that this would be done. "I told Brother Martin that . . . the local union had postponed the nominations for one week." Martin then sent Anthony Capellini, a CIO organizer, to prevent the nominations at the following meeting. But "the membership . . . were in no mood to keep coming to meetings every Sunday," Travis said. Capellini and his few supporters were brushed aside and the nominations were held, reported the *Flint Auto Worker* on April 15.

The great number of nominees from all the divisions of Local 156 demonstrated the popularity of the ballot. There were no fewer than seven candidates for president and five each for recording secretary and second vice president. Primary elections to cut down the number of candidates were held the following week but Martin again intervened, demanding that the final voting be postponed. The reason he gave was that the executive board was preparing a plan for the organizational structure of large amalgamated locals, which would include Local 156.

It was a danger signal, we all felt, clearly revealing Martin's intention to split the local into its five components, as his most vocal supporters in Flint had been demanding. These included, besides the Chevrolet Lovestonite group, members of the old pro-Dillon crowd, mainly from Fisher One, followers of Bert Harris, and other suspected former Black Legionnaires.

Yet Travis realized that he could not defy the executive board openly and in a forthright statement that was published in the April 23 issue of the *Flint Auto Worker,* he declared his acceptance of a "temporary postponement" of the final elections under the two conditions that he had announced at the previous meeting of the local: "I said then and I repeat now that I would not be a party to any plan that would split the local apart or that would take away from our members their inalienable right to vote for and elect their officers."

Travis outlined the reasons for the necessity of prompt elections. "Innumerable difficulties were rising . . . the responsibility for everything fell upon myself and the other organizers. Often we had to make arbitrary decisions. . . . But there was something else that entered in, about which I have never before spoken. That was the obstruction and even sabotage of a few of the old officers.[6] If it had not been for the assistance of our General Secretary-Treasurer, George Addes, the local would have had to close its offices long before this."

Homer Martin's design in breaking up Local 156 was undeniably politically motivated. Fractured into several smaller units, the huge Flint local could more easily be controlled. This was already happening at Fisher One, where Bert Harris's group, encouraged by Martin and Fred Pieper, were challenging the leadership of Bud Simons, Walter Moore, and other members of the plant committee who had come out of the sitdown strike.[7]

In the other units, however, Martin's plan to split the local was looked upon askance. Within a few days of the meeting at which Travis warned against this danger, most of them took action not only against disuniting

Local 156 but also in expressing their loyalty to Travis and Roy Reuther, who were considered to be the intended victims of these maneuverings. In a resolution adopted unanimously on April 20 by the AC Sparkplug unit, this accusation was raised in so many words: "Whereas we believe that there is a conspiracy to take either or both Robert Travis and Roy Reuther out of Flint." In addition to AC, the big Buick plants No. 6 and No. 12, as well as Chevrolet No. 2, quickly expressed strong support for local elections and backing for Travis and Reuther. Other similar actions followed.

It was almost three months after the "temporary postponement" of the local elections, however, before the international executive board announced its decision about them. This occurred at a mass meeting of five thousand held at IMA Auditorium on July 10, the ruling being that the status of Local 156 would be held in abeyance until the Milwaukee Convention decided the issue of the organizational structure of large amalgamated locals.

Meanwhile, the board established a kind of tutorial control of the local under the permanent supervision of a five-man committee. It consisted of three pro-Martin board members (Fred Pieper, Russell Merrill, and Delmond Garst), plus Glenn Shadduck, the Lovestonite Chevrolet member and Martin's most fervid supporter, and Bob Travis. The decision of the board, as announced at the IMA Auditorium, was approved without opposition by the big assembly, reported the *Flint Auto Worker* on July 14.

This temporary retreat was, of course, carefully prepared with the rank and file by the leaders of the union, as Bob Travis indicated in a talk. "We recognize the authority of the executive board," he asserted, "and we will support their decisions . . . even though we may disagree with [them]." The *Flint Auto Worker* of July 14 further reported that the board's postponement had caused a "great amount of disappointment," which had been embodied in "a large number of wires . . . asking for a reconsideration. However," it concluded solicitously, "these by no means signify a tendency to split the ranks of the union."

There had obviously been a significant change in the attitude of the Travis-Reuther group. Its note of defiance was gone. Although several attempts had been made to force the issue of the elections, these were abruptly abandoned. We were, frankly, profoundly disturbed by the developing factionalism in the union, which we were now aware was being fostered by external intrigue. Our constant appeals for unity, as reflected, for example, in the *Flint Auto Worker* of June 30, grew more and more frantic. "The spirit of factionalism which had for weeks been undermining the local's unity," I wrote fervidly in describing a local meeting, "was wiped away amid thunderous cheers and a unanimous pledge to devote the entire energies of the local to fighting our enemies"—that is, General Motors.

And yet, despite our expressed concern, we did not avoid doing things that would inevitably encourage disunity. Thus, at the mass meeting at the IMA Auditorium, where the local had formally registered its compliance with the executive board's decisions, Roy Reuther and Ralph Dale made the startling announcement that they were resigning from the International's staff. Reuther explained that they had been notified by Martin of their pending transfer and the audience cheered when he revealed that the two men had decided to remain in Flint "until their tasks are completed." A motion was proposed immediately that the two organizers be placed on Local 156's payroll as business representatives. It was adopted by acclamation.

The *Flint Auto Worker* carried Reuther's letter of resignation. In it he declared that he did not question the authority of Martin or the board but that he did "question the wisdom of this move" just when the local was "in the midst of solidifying the gains of the UAW . . . and training the thousands of new recruits as disciplined, loyal members of our union." We all felt that Reuther's decision was fully justified and that Martin's action, besides being potentially harmful, was dictated by factionalism. That the Chevrolet unit, to which Reuther was attached, approved of his decision was soon after verified in the elections for Milwaukee delegates, when his name topped the list of twenty-five candidates.

● ● ●

No one was more susceptible than I to irate responses to challenges by the other side. However, most responses remained shut up within me despite the many temptations that my position on the paper presented to enable me to get them off my chest. Nevertheless, I gave way in the end and was roundly pummeled for it. I had become aware sooner than most others, I believe, of the subtle role that the Lovestonite William Munger, the International's research director and more recently editor of the *United Automobile Worker,* played in fomenting a partisan split in the union. It was through the paper especially that he began to assume the ideological leadership of the Martin-Frankensteen group.

Unauthorized (wildcat) strikes proved handy instruments toward this end. For two or three months after the sitdown they were quite prevalent in Flint and could thus be readily blamed on the organizers that were functioning there. This censure was the more effective since the wildcats were at first virtually impossible to control, given the volatile circumstances existing among Flint's forty thousand inexperienced workers. They came at a particularly bad time, moreover, when the union was trying to establish stable relations with the corporation. No one reading the *Flint Auto Worker* of that period could doubt the earnest efforts of the UAW leaders to solve this problem.[8]

But the opposite conclusion would be drawn from consultation of Bill Munger's *United Automobile Worker*. In the issue of June 19, for example, it reported that the executive board had called for disciplinary action in unauthorized strikes, with the Flint local clearly in view. In the July 3 issue, Homer Martin was quoted as blaming his shakeup of the Flint local on "wildcat strikes." On July 17, his letter to William Knudsen, president of General Motors, was cited, pledging the union's unrelenting struggle against the UAW members and leaders who fomented them.

This conciliatory tone toward the corporation proved to no avail because GM's financial record for the June quarter had just been published and showed that it had suffered a 25 percent decline in profits for that period over 1936, from $88 to $66 million. In his reply to Martin's letter, Alfred P. Sloan pertinently blamed the loss on the UAW's irresponsibility. Martin answered testily that the union had shown "better control over its members than General Motors [had] over its board of supervisors." But at this point Bill Munger took the matter into his own hands, in effect contradicting the forthright words of the UAW president and assessing full blame to the auto union for the situation: "We frankly recognize . . . the destructive role which has been played by certain elements within the ranks and in the officialdom of the union."

This groveling self-inculpation roused my disgust and anger to the point that I decided to reply to Munger's insinuations in the only editorial that I ever signed since I wanted to place the full responsibility for it upon myself. Moreover, in order to avoid a partisan interpretation, I made no reference to Munger's article, addressing myself instead to Sloan's letter and titling my reply "Cut in Profit Benefits Community." Thus, in taking the bull by the horns, I admitted that wages had in fact been increased—and company earnings correspondingly decreased—by the aggressive policy of the union. That was our goal, I asserted, and the result was that business was booming in Flint and in other automotive centers.

"The average wage increase in this city's plants," I wrote, "was at least 15 cents an hour." For forty-two thousand workers, this added up to $250,000 more in their pockets each week, available for spending. Everyone in town benefited by this gain, even the local businessmen. "Can the businessmen see that? Or will they join law-and-order leagues and try to destroy the . . . prime mover of this improved situation, which is the union?"

The pleasure that this outburst brought me was short-lived, even though I had expected some kind of disciplinary reprimand from the executive board's five-man committee in Flint. It came in the form of the paper's being placed directly under their control. Thereafter, I was required to turn over to them the final makeup sheets before sending them to the press. In the very next issue (August 14, no. 34), Fred Pieper informed me that I would have to change the masthead to *Flint Edition, United Automobile Worker* and eliminate the heading of the lead editorial, "Unity Imperative to Win GM Pact," as well as two of its paragraphs, beginning: "They say that we are merely playing politics before the convention," and then going on to expand in the rest of the piece on "the need for unity."[9]

The editorial was signed "R. C. Travis" but it was I who actually wrote it. The required change in its heading was easy, a substitute of "Solidarity" for "Unity" as also in the alteration of a subhead. In the text, I enjoyed using the crossword puzzle technique of finding synonyms for wherever *unity* had been used: "stick together," or "close cooperation," or "harmony." And I most enjoyed the final message about the coming convention, which could not possibly have been more "unity"-like but which passed my board of examiners without a murmur: "If we come out of it split into two separate camps no one but the workers will suffer. There must not be any two sides about it! We have no serious fight among ourselves. We must therefore get together at all costs, consolidate our ranks and leadership, to obtain those things in the shop that we are striving for!"

Pieper's sensitivity about the word *unity* was, of course, understandable. It had become loaded with convention significance since the launching of two opposed caucuses, one of which was known as the Unity Group. Still, I continued to argue with him disingenuously about the appropriateness of the word, which was just as meaningful to the auto workers as "solidarity." Wasn't it contradictory to expunge it from the vocabulary?

Sensing that I had caught his interest, I continued to develop my dialectic by giving it a personal note. Pieper himself had frequently used the word "unity" I told him, and, getting hold of a recent issue of the *Flint Auto Worker,* I showed him its triple-banked heading in boldface caps: "UNITY PERFECTED—LOCAL FACES G.M. WITH SOLID RANKS." Then I read the lead to him: "'The spirit of factionalism which had for weeks been undermining the local's unity was wiped out amid thunderous cheers. . . .' And this is what you said in this very same article," I continued, having noticed his smile, "'Workers in General Motors are faced with a problem today which will call on all the resources of our great International, and which demands that unity and militance of action for which Flint's name is famous.'"

I searched his eyes expectantly. But it was all unavailing for Fred Pieper was too much of a politician to allow egotistic gratification to interfere with strategy. Perhaps I tried to press the point too hard when I brought out another issue of the paper in which I quoted him as putting the brakes on the local's Progressive Group, the other pre-convention caucus that had been launched weeks before the Unity Group.[10] What I should have realized was that this was probably before Pieper had been affiliated with the PG himself. But he was surely lined up now, for it was getting close to convention time and he had to make sure of his own reelection to the executive board. There was strong opposition to him in his district at Atlanta, we had heard, and he would need the support that Martin and Frankensteen could give him. Surely it would not come from left-wingers like Mortimer or Hall.

• • •

The UAW's first caucus, the Progressive Group, was set up in June by Dick Frankensteen under the strong urging of Bill Munger and of Jay Lovestone himself. The first meetings were informal affairs and attended mainly by Frankensteen's followers and several Lovestonites or fellow-travelers.[11] Walter Reuther got wind of one of the meetings that was held in the basement of the Hofmann Building on Woodward Avenue, where the UAW offices were located.[12] He went there casually but was stopped at the door. His only interest, he told the doorkeeper, was to plead with those present about the danger of these divisive groups. But the rebuff convinced him that the only way to get that idea across was to set up a caucus in opposition.

A number of others had the same idea and early in July the first meeting of the Unity Group was held. Its chief purpose was to endorse a slate for the convention that was more or less dictated by its name, or so we thought in Flint when we called for the reelection of the five International officers. Bob Travis had anticipated this step by proposing that slate at a local meeting (which had raised George Miles's ire), accompanying it with an accolade to the officers' "magnificent job that [will] go down as one of the most brilliant in all labor history." It was "unanimously adopted," I reported in the *Flint Auto Worker* of June 16 and probably did not think that any of this was "factional." Roy Reuther spoke for Travis's motion, I added.

One would expect that the five officers would be endorsed by the Unity caucus two weeks later. In the interim, however, the matter was fully discussed and a more reasonable distribution was adopted, as Walter Reuther reported for the group's steering committee.[13] It consisted of what he termed an "all-inclusive slate," which was made up of the original officers minus Walter Wells and plus Dick Frankensteen and R. J. Thomas. Neither Reuther nor Bob Travis were on the slate nor were they ever suggested for it though many people at the caucus must have thought that either one or both had as much claim to such a distinction as did the new candidates.[14] But in the eyes of Unity's leaders the slate was meant to be a broad accommodation among the union's leading groups, not a reward for merit. The "left" simply had too many individuals who had made outstanding contributions in the sixteen months since the South Bend Convention.

In his report to the caucus, Walter Reuther told of contacts that were attempted with the Progressive Group, once at a caucus that it held at South Bend. The Unity Group chose a committee of nine to go there and present its "program of unity" to the big gathering. They were not allowed into the meeting, however, and one of the interlocutors at the door took the line that "a good fight will strengthen the union." Another Unity delegation that tried to speak to a second Progressive caucus was again stopped at the door and given twenty minutes to prepare its "concrete proposals," which would be read to the meeting before the vote on whether to admit the delegation was taken. Reuther rapidly jotted down some remarks about how important it was that the two groups work out a program for "abolishing all factional fights," ending with Unity's "unified slate" of six candidates. The proposals were tabled without discussion though one significant thing did emerge from Unity's intervention. When the Progressive Group chose its slate, Russell Merrill defeated R. J. Thomas for one of the five candidates. Thomas threatened to quit the caucus and join Unity. To keep peace in the family Merrill retired in his favor.[15]

In their talks to the Unity caucus of July 24, Mortimer and Hall told of the virulent campaign that Martin's expanded corps of more than 150 "organizers" were putting on all over the country.[16] Their reports gave a disheartening foretaste of what could be expected at Milwaukee. Mortimer described how the daily press was being fed red-baiting fantasies about him that stemmed directly from the International office. On one occasion, when he contacted the *Detroit News,* they equivocated in printing a retraction or even a personal reply. Mortimer was also blamed for all the unauthorized strikes though he had practically no contact with the rank and file. Homer Martin had seen to that.

All the talk about unauthorized strikes was a hoax, Ed Hall charged; there had been no unauthorized strikes to speak of in months. General Motors was just yapping about them to prop up its demand for the right to discipline the workers, with the blessings of the union. Hall revealed that the seventeen-man GM committee that was supposed to be working on the new contract was no longer functioning. Most of its members had been put on the International payroll to politic for the Progressive ticket. The rest had gone home in disgust.

Contestation had taken hold of the executive board as well, whose meetings Reuther described to me as resembling brawls on a football field. He was often the target, probably because he was the typical quarterback, small and cheeky. He described one time when the board was discussing the large number of delegates that Flint was sending to the convention (the majority of whom were Unity) and Homer Martin raised the question of economy. Reuther snapped, "You've got your nerve talking about economy when you've been putting dozens of men on the payroll for political purposes." Martin rushed at him "like a mad bull," Reuther said. "I ducked and picked him up and threw him over my shoulder. He was kicking his feet and pounding on my back. They had to pull him off." Poor Lloyd Jones, a Unity man, was not as adept as Reuther in self-defense. On the same occasion he passed a remark that Dick Frankensteen considered a slur. Although about one and a half times the size of Jones, Frankensteen walked over to him and told him to stand up. Jones did so and Frankensteen hit him square on the mouth, splitting his lip.

In the board meeting in Milwaukee before the convention, things were in turmoil. Convention committees were being chosen, a task that the UAW constitution assigned to the general officers. But Martin arbitrarily turned it over to the board, on which he had a large majority. Hall and Mortimer walked out of the meeting, checked out of the hotel, and went to the airport.[17] Mortimer flew back to Detroit while Hall took a plane to Indianapolis, where he had been asked by the GM local to attend a meeting with the management.

George Addes caught him on the telephone when he arrived in Indianapolis. "Listen," he said, "these birds are really ready to throw you out. We think you'd better come back. Mort and Walter are flying back from Detroit." Reuther had walked out of the board meeting for a different reason. The Ford organizing committee had arranged to hold a second distribution of UAW literature at River Rouge after the first one had been crushed by a gang of thugs and servicemen in the "Battle of the Overpass" on May 27. Reuther asked to be excused from the board session so that he could participate in the new distribution, which was understandable considering the part he had played in the first one. But the board turned down his request, threatening him with expulsion if he went to Detroit. "I told them to go to hell," he recalled bitterly.

The executive board's position was truly reprehensible in the case of Walter Reuther because he had been so terribly mauled at the first distribution.[18] It was a wonder that neither he nor Dick Frankensteen, on whom the Ford bruisers had concentrated their savage assault, was permanently crippled. Many of the distributors, including a number of Detroit's Emergency Brigade, which had been modeled on Flint's group, were badly hurt, worst of all Tony Marinovich, the husband of Irene Young, a leader of the Ternstedt local, his spine being fractured when he was thrown from the steps of the overpass.[19]

We in Flint, who had been overwhelmed by the first reports of the attack, were greatly relieved to see the photos in the papers the following morning. One picture in particular cheered us and I ran a copy of it in the *Flint Auto Worker* on June 2. It showed Reuther and Frankensteen sitting side by side, faces bruised, while Dick was stanching Walter's bleeding ear with his handkerchief. I recall Roy Reuther and myself scrutinizing the photo with pleasure. It was as though we were willing to forget their pain if they were willing to forget their animosity. I said as much in the caption: "And this cool, clear thought remains: We must be a solid phalanx of determination and power. We have had our petty little differences but these shrink to insignificance before the threat of Capital's mailed fist."

But Dick Frankensteen continued building his caucus nevertheless with total disregard of the character of those he mustered. In Flint, the Progressive Group absorbed the worst elements of the Dillon days, a number of whom would have their white or black hoods stored in the garret. Some of them stuck with Homer Martin to the bitter end of a nearly shattered union. It was at Fisher One that they were strongest, having been well organized in their terroristic group long before the strike. They had only gone into retreat when the Black Legion was exposed. Now, encouraged by Martin and under the whip of Bert Harris, they took advantage also of the resentment to the sectarian tendencies of the left-wing group that had led the sitdown at Fisher One as well as the guilt feelings of those who had not participated in it. Their success can be gauged by the fact that Harris's slate made almost a clean sweep in the vote for convention delegates.[20]

It was the only plant where this happened. Except for Fisher Two, which was able to keep clear of factional division at that time, all the other units endorsed Unity candidates by big majorities. Even at Chevrolet, where Martin's Lovestonite adherents like Ted LaDuke, Tom Klasey, and Glenn Shadduck were most prominent, their Unity opponents took twenty-four of the twenty-five places by an average margin of 3.5 to 2.[21] The only exception was Jack Little, a scrappy chap who would assume a bellicose role in the ferocious hostility that later developed in the UAW at Flint.

The Buick division's Unity sweep was even more impressive than the one at Chevrolet and the same was true of the results at AC Sparkplug.[22] The *Flint Auto Worker* of July 29 described how when the booths at Chevrolet closed at 2 on Saturday morning, five hundred candidates, watchers, and tellers ripped their left-over slates into shreds and threw them into the air while the whole crowd sang "Solidarity." The article commented ardently: "All concerned agreed that this was the end of slates and caucusing at the Chevrolet Division."

This dream likewise would remain unrealized. Solidarity would be far from the sentiments of the majority of the delegates at Milwaukee. Despite the scrupulous and conscientious efforts of most leaders of the Unity caucus, the convention would be unavoidably riven because that was the set plan of the organized majority, the Progressive Group. But one soothsayer had a halcyon vision of that assembly since to him the factional conflict in the UAW was the path to power, as he revealed in a letter to "Dear Homer." The letter reveals the incredible authority that its writer, Jay Lovestone, enjoyed with the president of the UAW. "Here is a memorandum giving the gist of some of the things we discussed the other day," he started and then went on for five typed pages, organizing the convention and the union that would emerge from it under his protégé's triumphant leadership. The missive was dated August 3 but would not become known to us and to the rest of the UAW for more than a year.

Lovestone had the answers for everything. Regarding the difficulties with General Motors, he said: "Concretely, I have in mind John L. and you speaking on a national hookup on labor's answer to the responsibility challenge as given in the renewed agreement [what 'renewed agreement'?] with the G.M.C." Then he took up the various departments of the International and assigned the personnel that would direct them, starting with a man named "Polier as general counsel." The publicity department was "weak" (poor Frank Winn), but "I have in mind one of the people to whom you ought to give consideration."

And so it went on, one by one, with all his other choices: the Women's Auxiliary which was already solidly disposed of in the hands of an old Lovestonite, Eve Stone; as were research and the International journal in those of the insidious William Munger. Lovestone had even thought of an anthem for the union, a "special song and music" that would be composed by "one of America's outstanding music composers," explaining as though to a neophyte: "There is great value to be attached to an Auto Worker song, with life, with power in it and with specially written music instead of borrowed or stolen notes. When you say the word, I will have the composer get on the job."

Homer did so, and the promised chant was sounded at the convention. But as far as I could notice, it did not make much of an impression there though Munger filled two whole pages of his convention edition with it. The delegates were far more concerned with the fierce struggle going on for control of the International, which at any event was to a considerable extent a consequence of Jay Lovestone's fertile brain.

The Milwaukee Convention

When the convention opened at Milwaukee on Monday morning, August 23, the Unity delegates (many of them, anyway) were ridden by a deep sense of anxiety. Several of us had tried to make up tables of the comparative strengths of the two sides. Two of the tables are now in my personal files, one that I compiled and the other compiled by an unidentified person whose estimates were too optimistic to be taken seriously even then. The point was that only a fraction of the 256 locals (almost two thousand votes) that were eventually accredited were known to any of us in the Unity Group.

The other side had the means of being better informed, with a more strongly organized caucus and with Homer Martin's 150 special "organizers" hired for that purpose from all over the country. Dick Frankensteen had made statements to the press claiming a 55 percent advantage in Detroit, which might have been correct. His air at the convention was enormously self-assured. His huge athlete's frame was resplendent in a light summer suit, his moist, ruddy face exuberant. Dozens of Progressive Group people buzzed all over the Schroeder Hotel's reception hall, pinning their colored insignia onto delegates' lapels, which they accepted without objection. All these people were unknown to us and we felt that this was no longer "our UAW" but a mass of strangers.

It was a reprieve to get into the auditorium and find the several large Unity delegations, wearing their overseas caps, gathered at their assigned places: Flint, the West Side Local, Seaman Body, Allis-Chalmers.[1] It was already past the scheduled opening hour but George Kiebler, president of the host local, did not call the assembly to order until 11 A.M. After the invocation, he read an inane wire from President Roosevelt, which nonetheless received a prolonged ovation in which all delegates joined. Then came the reading of the names of the four major committees: rules, credentials, constitution, and resolutions. The tenseness took hold again.

We in Unity listened carefully, knowing that the four lists were the nuclei of inevitable conflict. I jotted down the names and was not surprised to find that there were fifteen on each list, divided unmistakably into Progressive (PG) and Unity adherents, ten and five each. That was the way Homer Martin had willed it by ruling that the executive board members (whom he controlled ten to two) would share nominations with the general officers. The Unity leaders had discussed whether they ought to challenge this illegal procedure on the convention floor, remembering the disastrous use Frank Dillon had been able to make of this advantage at the Detroit Convention two years earlier. But they decided against it since to do so would start the convention off in a spirit of conflict. But the conflict came on anyhow.

Meanwhile, our ears and eyes were alert for any hint of encouragement by speakers from CIO affiliates. Leo Krzycki of the Amalgamated Clothing Workers on that first morning gave our avid hearts a thrill by calling on the delegates "to go out of this convention hall solidly united," bringing cheers from the Unity crowd.[2] That afternoon, Ora Gasaway of the United Mine Workers, whom Martin identified as John L. Lewis's "representative," elicited an even more excited response with what appeared to be a clearly pertinent allusion to our outlook: "When you leave this convention, leave here with that emblem still upon your breast that some of you now have in the form of 'Unity' for the future."[3]

Our optimism was corroborated when we read in the *Detroit News* on the following day, August 24, Dick Frankensteen's worried reply to a question of Archie Robinson's about the report that Lewis was coming to the convention to bring about a compromise. "John L. Lewis," he asserted, "is interested in the policy of an organization but [will] not attempt to dictate or interfere with an election in the automobile union."[4] Nevertheless, Frankensteen arranged for the convention to cancel its scheduled evening session in order to conduct a pep rally of his caucus, telling his people to corral as many delegates from the outlying districts as they could; there would be plenty of food and drinks. At the rally, Frankensteen called on Larraine Loewe, a representative from the International Ladies Garment Workers (ILGWU), whom Martin had invited at Jay Lovestone's suggestion. She was a rousing speaker and spent most of her time redbaiting. She narrated how communists had tried to destroy the ILGWU until David Dubinsky booted them out.[5]

After the opening ceremony (an inheritance from the AFL) of escorting Homer Martin to the platform, the Unity people joined in the noisy demonstration that lasted a whole hour. The delegates blew whistles, shot off capguns, and shouted themselves hoarse.[6]

We were fully convinced that factionalism was expiring when, following this exhilarating experience, Ora Gasaway delivered a prepared address that bore the imprimatur of his chief, hammering away on the need for unity in terms that could hardly be misread. "I realize that you could adjourn this convention and caucus from now until Saturday morning [and] you wouldn't be a damn bit closer than you are now. . . . [It] is my judgment that you had better go into executive session . . . and thresh it out and then when you open the doors that you will go out in one body."[7]

It was a wise message, but it had not converted everyone in the house, far from it. Almost immediately after Gasaway's talk, Stuart Strachan, chair of the credentials committee, reported that there were several challenges to the seating of delegates. They had caused a sharp confrontation among the committee's members, who were solidly lined up into majority (PG) and minority (Unity) clusters. By pleasant surprise the majority dropped its challenges against Roy Reuther and Lloyd Jones just before giving its report, no doubt because of the weakness of its position. But it maintained its objections to Stanley Nowak, whose case went back to committee after the discussion on it took up most of the convention's time that morning.[8]

The final two cases of the committee, more than provoking differences of opinion between the two sides, involved issues of real importance. One concerned the seating of Morris Field of the Dodge local, a friend of Dick Frankensteen's and a reputed follower of Jay Lovestone, to whom Frankensteen had pledged to get Field elected to the executive board. In fact, Field's name had been listed by the *Detroit News* as one of the four Detroit men backed by the PG caucus.[9]

Minority spokesman George Edwards explained to the convention that his group did not object to Field as a delegate, but rather to the method by which he was designated.[10] Field was never actually elected a delegate, Edwards said. He had run for the post as representing the Dodge Machine Shop, where he had formerly worked before Martin appointed him as an International organizer. Out of 111 votes cast in that department, Morris Field received only eleven. But Frankensteen promptly arranged for the naming of five alternate delegates from the local and designated Field as the "first alternate." Soon after, one of Dodge's forty-four regularly elected delegates retired and Field was substituted for him. It was this type of manipulative procedure that the minority committee asked the convention to clarify while waiving its opposition to the seating of Morris Field.

Frankensteen sharply reprimanded Edwards for making a "report of propaganda" and not of facts though he did not gainsay the basic truth of what Edwards had presented.[11] It was probably correct that Edwards had a motive in making public these rather sordid facts about a candidate for the board on the PG ticket. As such, moreover, the Field case eventually became involved in the credentials committee minority's challenge against another majority ruling. This was its refusal to seat eight additional delegates from Fisher One of Flint, which developed into the convention's most agitated controversy that continued to trouble it until its final hour.

• • •

Even more than the credentials committee's operations, the Unity people found the actions of the constitutional committee cause for concern. Unity had prepared a set of contradictory recommendations that they considered essential to prevent the International's trend toward centralized control.[12] This aim was admitted by Homer Martin in his interviews with the press, where he argued for the necessity of a strong union on the UMW model. Mortimer, Hall, Travis, and other Unity leaders, though accepting the need for discipline in a vastly spread-out organization such as the UAW, maintained that local autonomy and democratic expression must be preserved to the fullest possible extent within that framework.

Unity feared that there would be insufficient time to explain the fundamental issues at stake. Two days of the convention's allotted six had passed and the constitutional committee had not yet appeared. It was meeting regularly, as we heard from its Unity members, who reported that bitter conflicts were taking place on various subjects. The danger was that the amended constitution would be incomplete at convention's end and would have to be left in the hands of the executive board, which we all feared would not be much better than the outgoing one. The minority members of the committee decided to prepare a couple of mimeographed sheets titled "For a Democratic Constitution" and to distribute them among the delegates.[13] Sensitive about being accused of a factional act, the group explained in its memo: "You are entitled to the facts . . . which you could not get in any other way under the rules" and listed majority and minority proposals "where fundamental differences exist."

We began to suspect a conscious design to waste time during the convention's unfolding sessions, especially through speeches by eminent individuals whose long-winded effusions could not be controlled. An idea of the time consumed by nine speakers in the first three days can be obtained by a count of the pages that their addresses occupy in the *Proceedings:* thirty-five of 105, exactly a third. Most delegates, who had never attended a convention, probably considered this arrangement normal. So, too, did they meekly accept the constant intercalations of the chairman, not only in the introduction of speakers but also in comment on every subject, often lengthy, which became frankly partisan when the convention began to take on a fractious tone.

The partisan spirit of the PG revealed itself defiantly on the convention floor as though it were something to be proud of.[14] A motion by a Pontiac delegate that all members be asked to "refrain from wearing any factional insignia" was ruled out of order by Martin.[15] A resolution presented by Forrest Woods of Studebaker for the unified resolutions committee, calling for the abolition of caucuses, was smothered by disingenuous arguments: by Martin asking "what constitutes a caucus"; by Frankensteen's outraged assertion that the resolution was "as undemocratic as anything could be"; by H. O. Hurley of Bendix charging that it was in defiance of the Bill of Rights guarantee of freedom of assembly; and by a paean of praise for caucuses as such by John Ringwald of Chevy Gear and Axle: "There has never been a convention held that had good constructive thought come out of it but that there were caucuses held before the convention."[16] One wondered, hearing all these dicta, what had happened to the paternalistic plea of Ora Gasaway-Polonius that seemingly had evoked such universal accord.

Unity decided to force the issue of the convention's getting down to business.[17] Kenny Cole of the Toledo Chevrolet local, a soft-spoken, intelligent person who never antagonized anyone, was given the job. Shortly before the adjournment of the afternoon session of the third day, he moved "That this convention request that the constitution committee bring in as near a full report as possible tomorrow morning, and that the convention stay in session until the constitutional changes or amendments are properly taken care of."

Martin ruled the motion out of order. The constitution committee, he declared, expected to have a full report the next morning anyway. But his features suddenly took on a tight-lipped, angry alteration as he added, "I would like to say there has been . . . a lot of deliberate interference with the work of the constitution committee. I don't want to have to say more about that, but I can tell this convention a rather sordid story if these parties do not desist from their activities."[18]

There was something especially unpleasant about this threat because it apparently meant that Unity would have to fight on personal rather than substantive grounds.[19] The "exposure" came that same evening, moreover. Dick Reisinger had made a motion for a night session on the same basis as Kenney Cole's rejected motion: to expedite the convention's work. The night session was approved but served little purpose since, after a couple of resolutions were disposed of, another loquacious speaker was trotted out to consume a full hour of the convention's dwindling time.[20]

Isidore Polier, the speaker, was no ordinary attorney, as Homer Martin's glowing disclosure of his many merits revealed. I was ignorant at the time of the plot between Martin and Jay Lovestone to use Polier's appearance to launch him as a substitute for Maurice Sugar as the UAW's general counsel. His speech was very competent and informative on the important subject of labor and social legislation but it was wasted on the impatient Unity delegates, who were eager to get down to work.

Nevertheless, had they searched for it, they could not have found a more inopportune voice to express their chafing than John Anderson's. The irascible Scotsman made the additional faux pas of including the chairman in his diatribe: "I have to raise objections to so many longwinded speeches from the platform, such as the last speaker made, as well as the chairman speaking extemporaneously. I thought we came here to transact business and we have set a long-distance record for sitdown strikes. . . . I think it is highly fitting and proper that the chairman bear in mind the tremendous expense of this convention and that those seats here · are not for company. . . . I would like the chairman to inform this convention if 70 percent of our time is going to be taken up listening to speeches from outsiders."[21]

Anderson's blast brought "tremendous cheering," as the *Detroit News* reported on August 26, followed by boos on the part of PG mainstays who hastened to succor Martin. He did not need the help, letting loose the tirade that he had promised earlier. It brought the convention's brawling mood to its highest pitch. "Brother Anderson," he said, "I am going to answer you in your own kind. Go down to your committee and get Nat Ganley and some of the rest of the obstructionists, who have absolutely been hindering the work of these committees. Go down and ask them why these committees are not ready to report. Go down and ask five men on the constitution committee why a minority has held up the work of this convention."[22]

He made it sound like some nefarious communist plot though he was actually referring to the occasional counterproposals that the minority group on the committee had to make because convention rules did not allow contesting reports to be brought out on the floor. The Unity leaders had decided that this situation must be clarified to the delegates and Walter Reuther felt that the time had come to do it.[23] Explaining how Martin had contrived to give his group a two-to-one control of all committees, he declared, "I think the chair [is] very unfair . . . to say that any person or any small minority is obstructing the report of that committee. . . . They have a majority on every committee, the committee on credentials, the committee on constitution, etcetera. . . . If the constitution committee is ready to report—and they have a majority—and we *don't* have a majority—then what in the hell is stopping the report at this time?"

The matter was left in abeyance as the night session adjourned. But the following morning, Thursday, August 26, when the session began with David Dow, chair of the constitution committee on the podium and ready to report, Unity members felt a distinct satisfaction. Nonetheless, they indicated that they were prepared to continue the struggle for a voice for minority committees on the convention floor. David Dow had hardly gotten started reading the constitution when Nat Ganley took a point of order on procedure to explain "that the only way to get both sides of the story and the disputed points is to hear the full report of the majority of the committee and the minority and then take it up seriatim."[24]

But Martin was ready for it, replying sharply that number 12 of the convention's rules allowed merely for "concurrence or non-concurrence from the floor" on a committee's report. Those opposed could speak against it, and if voted down the report went back to the committee. Lou Baraty of the minority was equally prepared for this response and moved that the rule be suspended to allow for the reading of the minority report. But, like a player on a tennis court, Martin was primed for this move also. "The rules which you have adopted provided the method by which they can be amended," he asserted. "The motion is to amend the rules by suspending."

The motion was defeated on a voice vote because Unity members realized that they could not possibly muster the two-thirds tally on a roll-call needed for an amendment. Martin then nailed down this procedure as the one he would follow thereafter, insisting that "any change in the report of the committee constitutes a substitute or amendment."

Bob Kanter of the West Side Local and Unity spokesman on the rules committee then interposed: "This question was discussed in the rules committee and I was given to understand . . . that minority reports would be permitted on this floor. Now if it is the interpretation of the chairman that minority reports will not be given, then I . . . request this convention to refer this rule back to the rules committee for an interpretation."[25]

Martin summarily ruled Kanter's "motion" out of order and in a display of firmness called the convention back to business by asking for a vote on Article II of the constitution. Actually, the article had already been adopted unanimously. Nevertheless, when the aye-and-nay vote was taken again, there was clearly a doubt regarding the result. Martin quickly asked if "the division of the house" was desired. Something in his manner as he looked around at the PG floor leaders indicated that there might have been some plan cooking among them. One of them, George Rose, of Racine, observed, "I say that on all questions on which we are [too evenly] divided we should have a roll-call vote."[26]

Martin replied eagerly: "Are there a sufficient number requesting a roll-call vote?" And, checking the forest of raised hands, he replied to his own question: "There are more than 250 delegates evidently desiring a roll-call vote on this question before the house."

It became perfectly evident then that he was in a big hurry to get the roll-call vote underway and the only possible reason could have been that the PG group had decided to register its superiority on a favorable question.

Unity members sought to stop him on his headlong course because they were by no means eager to have a showdown vote as yet. Bob Travis tried to point out that the question was not on the article in the constitution itself but Martin persisted in the procedure he had laid down: "For your clarification you are voting upon the motion of the chairman to adopt Article II of your present constitution under the heading, 'Objects.' The only motion before this house is the motion of the chairman to adopt. That has been moved and seconded."

It was not until Emil Mazey, a minority member of the constitution committee, intervened that Martin was compelled to abandon the senseless course he had assumed. "The minority committee has no opposition to Article II," Mazey shouted. "The motion on the floor was whether the minority committee was to be heard. There is absolutely no opposition to this article."

Martin's features took on a chagrined and innocent look. "If there is no objection, why the delay?" he asked, scoldingly. And realizing that the PG's plot to get a roll-call vote was scotched, he called out: "Are you ready for the question?" And the unopposed Article II was once more adopted unanimously.[27]

But it was only a momentary hold-up to his purpose. Who could have known that another opportunity would come on a silver platter from the "opposition"? Bob Kanter had not forgotten that the important point he had raised was still unanswered. "I rise to a point of order," he said. "My point of order is that I requested a ruling from the chair on whether or not any rule or all the rules may be suspended by the convention."

"Yes, by a two-thirds vote of the body, as covered by the rules," Martin replied.

"I appeal from your decision," Kanter shot back, holding his gaunt stance erect. It was clear that the appeal was a Unity decision but it reopened the chance of PG's getting its roll-call vote and under especially favorable conditions it seemed to me.

"You are not appealing from my decision," Martin answered calmly, "you are appealing from the rules you have established." And he immediately turned the chair over to Ora Gasaway to denote that he as a party to the debate was ready to defend his interpretation.

Kanter spoke first and made what I felt was a clear exposure of the issue. Rule 24, he admitted, held that the rules could only be amended by a two-thirds' majority roll-call vote of the convention. However, he added, "a motion to suspend the rules is not a motion to amend the rules." In fact, he pointed out punctiliously, there was nothing in the convention's rules altogether that dealt with their suspension. But that matter was taken care of by rule 20, which stated, *"Roberts' Rules of Order* shall be the guide on all matters governing this convention not herein provided."

"I therefore will read from *Roberts' Rules of Order,*" Kanter said, and he opened the little book concealed in his tapering hands to the page divided off by a slip of paper and began reading slowly, emphasizing every syllable: "'The motion to suspend the rule may be made at any time when no question is pending; or while a question is pending, provided it is for a purpose connected with that question.'" And he drew the pertinent conclusion, that "a motion to suspend Rule 12 is in order at the present time."[28]

Acting chairman Gasaway's summary of Kanter's presentation seemed to leave little doubt that he agreed with it. But Martin disregarded it along with Kanter's argument, repeating the same words he had used over and over—"that a suspension of the rules constitutes a change of the rules"—to which he sought to give an overwhelming sanction, "These rules . . . have been adopted by every international union in the United States or in the world. These rules have been adopted from time immemorial."

He seemed on the point of taking a vote when Forrest Woods made a motion for a roll call. There it was, the move I had apprehended, supplied by the vaunted parliamentarian of the Studebaker local. Gasaway asked if there were 250 delegates who approved and judged that the number that stood up exceeded twice that many. As arrangements were being made, delegates began raising worried questions, "What exactly was being voted on?" Walter Reuther, referring to the "general confusion," asked if he could have "one minute . . . to clarify this issue" but was disregarded.

Taking the vote lasted more than two hours, then the tabulation began. The official hour of adjournment was well past, but the delegates were reluctant to break up for lunch until the count had been announced. But by 1:30, hunger triumphed over "mathematics," as Gasaway observed, and it was agreed "by unanimous vote" to declare the session in recess for forty-five minutes. The afternoon session had no sooner reassembled when George Addes read the vote: "1,032 votes to sustain the chair, 729 opposed."[29]

•   •   •

It was a staggering blow for Unity. The Martin-Frankensteen caucus had proved its domination over the convention by a margin of 58 to 42 percent. We had, of course, assumed that we were in the minority but not to that extent, a gap of three hundred delegates. Unity people had fought ardently in the committees and on the floor, hoping to win a few delegates here and there by their reasoning, by their sincerity. But it was now limpid clear that the difference could not be bridged at this convention. Thereafter, we realized, the issue was foregone. Everything we had feared could happen. The Unity officers would be driven from their posts and in the rout a number of board members would probably swing over to the other side. Martin and Frankensteen would acquire a stranglehold on the union, more potent and certainly more dangerous than Frank Dillon had ever possessed.

Still, the Unity minority was by no means prepared to give up the fight. It is not difficult to account for this persistence. The struggle to win autonomy had been long and arduous; the excitement of democratic experience, however brief, was not lightly surrendered. Because the future was fated to be contested sharply, it was imperative to prepare for it, and no place was better than at the convention and no task more apposite than strengthening the democratic rights in the constitution. Although all of this was not spelled out at the time, much of it was felt instinctively.

One of the measures by which the PG caucus sought to consolidate its power was through the method of representation at conventions.[30] Because Unity had its concentration in the bigger locals and the PG controlled a great flock of smaller ones, the latter proposed a basis of representation that cut down the vote of the great units by approximately four-fifths, under the catch-all argument of "democratic rights" for the small locals. It was an obvious attempt to convert a self-serving tactic into a policy, which struck a majority of the delegates as unsavory. After brilliant contributions from Bob Travis, Walter Reuther, Lloyd Jones, and especially Tracy Doll of the Hudson local, purportedly an independent but actually close to the PG, Homer Martin closed the debate through his usual practice of violating the chairman's role of impartiality. His reward was a booming defeat of the majority's proposal.

This amazing setback, coming so soon after its smashing roll-call victory, jolted the PG's forces, who were flabbergasted to discover that the Unity minority was not quite ready to curl up in a corner. On the contrary, it was clear that it had won new supporters who were probably alerted by the warning in the memorandum that Unity had distributed. The constitution committee continued reporting a series of sections on which there were no disagreements until the fundamental question of the number of vice presidents was reached. Unity had proposed that the number be raised from three to five and once more the atmosphere became charged.

Homer Martin had the misfortune to suggest at this particular moment that, to save time, all controversial sections be shunted aside for later consideration while those "not in controversy" should be taken up first.[31] Ordinarily, this probably would have been accepted without further ado, but when Martin asked the committee's chair, David Dow, to proceed along those lines, a thunder of vociferation from the suspicious delegates rocked the hall. Chairman Dow did not help things by assuming an aggressive tone: "If you think for one moment you are going to make a loud clamor [with] a loud yea and nay . . . you are wrong. From now on it is going to be a roll-call vote and nothing else." He might have added that the convention would have to go on until Labor Day.

Martin hardly had the time to comment on David Dow's genial warning when a delegate ran up to him and whispered something of seemingly breathless importance into his ear. It was the news that John L. Lewis, who had arrived at the hotel half an hour earlier, was ready to come to the hall, escorted by a reception committee of International officers and board members. As the party came through the doors, the assembly rose in unison as though by command, waving their banners and cheering lustily.[32] The cheering went on for twenty minutes, during which the convention was gloriously and thoughtlessly united, majority and minority, Progressives and Unity. We were all cheering for the union, for its fabulous achievements, for which, if credit were due to any single man, it was this man.

Yet when, after a glowing eulogy by Martin, from which, surprisingly, the typical pulpit exaggerations were absent, Lewis began to speak in his deep bass voice, the delegates swiftly fell into a profound silence as they set themselves to listen to the great man's message.[33] Strangely, as had happened two years before in Cleveland, I did not hear Lewis's speech for the first minutes. Or perhaps what I did hear was obscured by the very intensity of my effort to call forth from his words an ardently desired meaning, some unlikely reference that would give us a glimmering hope.

But suddenly I was aware of the fascination of Lewis's words that compelled attention. He was talking to the auto workers with an incomparable intimacy. Surely no renowned labor man coming from the outside had ever spoken to union men and women in that fashion. Lewis's humanity, his sensitivity, shone forth in his words. It was he who had a debt of gratitude toward them, he said, for helping him realize a life-long dream that had seemed doomed to non-accomplishment but for them. These two thousand men and women, and the hundreds of thousands beyond them, had conducted perilous combats, had demonstrated unlimited fortitude, and had won incredible victories that this powerful man above all others could esteem. And he loved and honored them for it.

It was this meaning that one felt in John L. Lewis's presence on that day and that I treasured as I listened to him, not with my ears but with my whole heart. Then, all at once, his words seemed to acquire a different resonance, somehow more pragmatic, down to earth. He was conversing with his listeners about their union and its problems. He was well-informed about them but it was amazing that he would be interested in such trivial matters. They should not hold conventions every year, he advised. They should not expect to settle all their problems at one swoop. They should avoid quarrels and he told them why:

Every newspaper in America is watching this convention. Every politician . . . in this country is watching this convention. Why? Well, because they are measuring the success and the future of the CIO by what this convention does. I don't think you delegates should take too seriously the political rivalry. . . . But I don't think you should permit yourselves to be brought into a position . . . of being engaged in . . . political rivalry to the point where the public may believe that that rivalry may affect the integrity of your union.[34]

And suddenly, the extraordinary words that many had hoped for, others feared, were there:

I know all of your officers personally. They all look like pretty good officers to me. . . . I have sat in conference with all of them, I have sat in wage negotiations with all of them, I have stood on public platforms with all of them. . . . What do you want out of officers? What does anybody want an officer to do except to administer the affairs of the union honestly and go out and increase the strength of the union? They have done that thing once, twice, thrice, ten-fold and more. . . . I think the formation of this great union . . . has been one of the most outstanding accomplishments that labor anywhere in the world has ever done before. . . . And I think that the officers . . . who led you through that enterprise . . . are deserving of your commendation.[35]

Then, lest some fastidious listeners might interpret his praise selectively, Lewis explicated his espousal in a modern legend of surpassing charm.

You know, there used to be a great tight-rope walker years ago before the time we were born whose name was Blondin and he carried a man on his back on a steel cable across Niagara Falls—a remarkable feat. Well, suppose I had been that man on Blondin's back and after Blondin had carried me across while I held my breath and shut my eyes and held on to him for dear life, suppose I had said to Blondin by the time he had carried me over to the Canadian side: "Blondin, I am dissatisfied with you; I am dissatisfied with you, Blondin, because back there a hundred-fifty yards when you were right over the center of the Horseshoe Falls, you leaned too far to the left," or, "Blondin, you leaned too far to the right."

The entranced crowd broke into a roar of laughter and whistled with delight. Lewis looked at them from beneath his famous, heavy brows, and when the crowd was once more silent, quietly, insistently, he drew his conclusion, which they already knew. "As far as I am concerned, I am for the officers of the United Automobile Workers because I think that they have crowned themselves and your union with glory in the degree of their achievement. I simply say this in passing as an honest tribute . . . and not with any desire to affect your own individual judgment." But no one in the audience believed his last remark. Lewis had told them what they ought to do about their officers and most of them were now convinced that he was right.

• • •

Heartening signs of their comprehension came fast, starting at the afternoon session right after Lewis's appearance. Both sides were eager to show their willingness to compromise on previously controversial points.[36] Ernest Nation of Toledo Chevrolet (Unity) was on his feet before Homer Martin had the chance to rap his gavel. He moved that the convention follow Martin's contested suggestion about taking up noncontroversial sections of the constitution first and leaving other issues for later.[37] Then Stuart Strachan reported that the credentials committee had voted unanimously on Stanley Nowak's claim to a seat. This left but a single unsettled case on the committee's roster.

Soon after, the constitution committee came back to announce that the majority had agreed to an important compromise on the question of representation at conventions by conceding Unity's view that all locals without exception would receive "one vote for every hundred members."[38] A few minutes later, the same committee reported that the hotly disputed issue of the vote by 50 percent of members being required on a referendum for special conventions had been cut to 25 percent. And, finally, the arrangement of biennial instead of annual conventions was conceded by Unity, as John L. Lewis had specifically advised.

Important above all, moreover, was the alteration in Martin's attitude, as illustrated in the discussion of the section on presidential powers. Chairman Dow had moved the adoption of Article X, section 1, paragraph 2, which called for the filling of vacancies in the International office by the president.[39] The motion was seconded when Martin asked that the section be referred back to the committee. "There have been a great many things said about . . . my desire to have powers of this sort," he explained as he began to read a recent editorial from the influential *New York Herald-Tribune* titled "The Issue at Milwaukee": "'We may be over-simplifying the issue between the two factions fighting for supremacy at the convention of the United Automobile Workers of America, but from this distance it appears to concern the choice between an international union administered as a centralized autocracy, on the model of the United Mine Workers, and one whose local units retain some degree of autonomy.'" Then Martin commented indignantly on the editorial, studding his talk with eulogies of John L. Lewis and the UMW. "All I want," he said, "and all I ask for is an international executive board with power."

It was at this point that the convention was made aware of some offstage events that had actually begun right after adjournment following Lewis's appearance.[40] Dick Frankensteen suddenly entered the hall and on a point of personal privilege made a few highly mysterious remarks, ending with a special request. "I would like to say," he remarked, "that I have just left John L. Lewis and he [asked] Brother Ora Gasaway . . . to explain something to this convention, and I move . . . that Brother Gasaway convey the message from John L. Lewis . . . that Brother Lewis asked to be conveyed." His rather garbled words were in keeping with the emotion that was plainly written on his face.

Ora Gasaway undertook to carry out his assignment but no one was any the wiser for it after hearing him. He referred to Lewis's praise of the International officers, then implied that there had been some pained comments by certain members of the executive board who had apparently been left out of his commendatory remarks and made a sweeping explanation: "President Lewis makes it emphatically clear that he in his reference refers to the lowest member in your union, the local union, the international executive board and the officers of the . . . International Union."

These words were so much gibberish to the delegates, who had expected to hear what the fate of the officers would be. I happened to know from Mortimer what the tentative terms were but it was not until months later, in 1938, that Frankensteen gave me a detailed account of what had actually taken place outside of the convention. While he had listened to Lewis's speech, he said, he felt that he had fallen into a trap. After adjournment, he had passed Lewis in the lunchroom but had merely nodded to him. But their tables were close and Frankensteen decided on the spur of the moment to tell him how he felt: "If you planned to crucify me, Mr. Lewis, you've certainly done a wonderful job. I can beat Mortimer and Hall and the whole outfit but I can't beat John L. Lewis and the CIO too!"

Lewis rose from his seat and called Frankensteen out into the hall. "Dick, what did I say that made you feel that way?" he asked. Frankensteen told him that he was not an officer, only a board member. But he was a candidate for office so Lewis's speech was, by inference, an attack on his candidacy.

"Dick, if I've hurt you," Lewis said, "there's always an executive position open for you in the CIO."

"I'm interested in staying with the auto workers" was the reply. Lewis then called Gasaway out and, in Frankensteen's presence, instructed him to correct the impression that Lewis had given in his speech and to say that he had meant to say that all the officers, including the executive board, had done an excellent job.

The more rabid members of the PG caucus were not satisfied with Frankensteen's personal accommodation and almost convinced him that they ought to go right ahead with their plan to clean the Unity crowd out. They were still confident of winning, they insisted. That evening, the CIO bigwigs, including Gasaway, Dubinsky, John Brophy, and others, held a roundtable with a few selected men of the two groups. Bill Munger accompanied Frankensteen and Martin on the one side, with Mortimer and Hall on the other. The CIO officials made a strong bid for an inclusive slate while Martin and Frankensteen remained noncommittal.

After the roundtable, they talked the matter over at length. Frankensteen claimed that he was not convinced but Martin wavered, saying that the inclusive slate was the best way out. "We'll have a majority of the officers and the board so we'll be in control." He tied the knot by promising to make Frankensteen his assistant president (as Jay Lovestone had suggested) at the first session of the executive board right after the convention.[41] The office would give Frankensteen priority over all the others, so he agreed. "But it was a hell of a job selling it to the men," he admitted. "They threw back at us all the arguments we had given them."

It was not until the morning of the sixth day, August 28—supposed to be the last day of the convention though it was not—that the settlement of the major controversy was attained. As arranged by the CIO representatives, David Dubinsky opened the question to the delegates. "I believe that a base of agreement was found that should be satisfactory to the entire convention," he affirmed, adding that he could not specify any details because group leaders had not yet had the opportunity to consult with their delegations.[42] He did add, however, as if letting it slip out, that they had accepted the idea for "unanimous decisions on each and every matter that comes before the convention," which sounded like an old-time labor leader's mode of settling an internecine quarrel.

Ora Gasaway, who followed, lifted the veil somewhat more by revealing that it was the CIO's suggestion that the delegates choose "sufficient officers . . . to carry on between now and the next convention. . . . Therefore, we believe you should have five vice-presidents instead of three and twenty members of the international executive board."[43] After Gasaway had finished at 10:10 A.M., Homer Martin announced that the convention would recess for an hour, during which the two caucuses could consider the CIO's proposal.

Curiously, both caucuses were open to the press; on August 28, the *Detroit News* reported on speakers at each of them. It described the PG caucusers as being wrought up. "We won't compromise!" they kept shouting. The *News* quoted Mortimer as saying: "Nothing would make me more happy than to see the convention adopt the compromise." Unity's decision was reached in thirty-five minutes, the paper reported.

But two more hours passed without any decision by the Progressive caucus. At 1 P.M., Mortimer announced, evidently by official advice, that the recess had been extended until 2. The disgusted and ravenous Unity delegates went out to eat.

The convention did not reconvene until 2:25, the Progressives having taken four and a quarter hours to make up their minds. Homer Martin turned the gavel over to Ora Gasaway because the election of officers was to follow right after the decisions of the two caucuses had been announced. Martin, of course, was a candidate, albeit unopposed. In taking the chair, Gasaway assumed a posture that made one feel that there had been a final hitch at the PG caucus though it did seem a good sign that the big fifty-by-twenty-foot placard with the names of the PG slate on it had been hauled down from the front of the hall. "Well," Gasaway asserted pointedly, "we are going to find out now whether men will do what they say they will do or not." And he called on Dick Frankensteen.

Frankensteen set his jaw and tilted his heavy chin. "On behalf of the Progressive caucus I wish to make clear that we are ready and willing to accept the proposal of Brother Gasaway on behalf of John L. Lewis." Then he added defiantly, "I want to assure the delegates who have been in the other caucus that I am not a horse thief." He received a cold stare from several Unity people whom he looked at and then said, "I should likewise say that we do not feel that Brother Hall or Brother Mortimer are horse thieves."

Mortimer followed with assurances that "the Unity caucus stands ready now, as it always has, for harmony and cooperation in the International Union."[44] The election of officers followed, and all were acclaimed by unanimous votes except Ed Hall, against whom several delegates asked that their negative ballots be recorded.[45]

When the election of the officers was completed, Forrest Woods, certainly by previous arrangement with Ora Gasaway, moved that the unanimous election of executive board members should follow. Gasaway, disregarding the loud outburst of objections, insisted that this was the "judgment of President Lewis." The shouts of "no, no, no" grew in vehemence and Gasaway made the curious request that delegates should at least "have a little vote," without explaining how this could be done. Only when John Milkent of Kenosha-Nash pointed out to him that the procedure was unconstitutional because board members were not elected by the convention directly but by separate districts did Gasaway reluctantly abandon his proposal.

As the delegates were being sent off to their various district caucuses to elect their board members, Henry Clark of the Flint Buick division quietly tossed a monkey wrench into the convention proceedings.[46] Things halted for one short moment when he asked that the body reconsider the allotment of Michigan's seven board members by adding one more representative to that number. He would be a black man, Clark declared, and would be chosen in a special election after the convention by the vote of all black auto workers in the state. President Martin, smiling hypocritically, ruled the proposal out of order. But it would come up again and again in varying forms at future UAW conventions.

The afternoon session was recessed to allow the districts to meet and elect their board members. At the opening of the night session at 8:45, Acting Chairman Gasaway announced that the Michigan delegation would need two more hours to "tabulate" its votes, so the sessions were adjourned until Sunday morning.

During the next two sessions, the convention devoured a mass of unfinished business; the resolution that perhaps drew the most notice was the organization of Ford.[47] Other measures did not win the full attention of the delegates, however, who waited anxiously for the credentials committee's report on the seating of the eight additional Fisher One delegates. The question had been left dormant for several days, and Unity people feared that it would not be disposed of when the convention adjourned.

The question was unique since the Fisher votes were necessary for the election of a Flint candidate to the board.[48] The extent of Martin's control of the incoming executive board also depended upon it. After the district caucuses of the previous evening, the results showed that the Progressive Group would have a board majority of sixteen to eight. It was considerably better than the former ratio of ten to two but still far from a reassuring basis of work. Walter Reuther and the other elected Unity board members were already thinking about whom they might swing over to their side. Tracy Doll seemed the best bet. Charles Millard, the board member from Canada, was another possibility.

But there was one other choice, rightfully Unity's, that had gone over to the other group due to the banning of the eight "delegates" from Fisher One. This was Morris Field, who had won his post because of that ruling. Michigan's seven elected board members had obtained the following scores: Charles Madden, 558; Tracy Doll, 553; Loren Houser, 553; Lester Washburn, 544; Walter Reuther, 537; Leo LaMotte, 525; and Morris Field, 524.9. The eight Fisher delegates had tried to get into the Michigan caucus but were stopped by Bert Harris's group. Those eight votes would have elected the candidate the Flint Unity majority had put up, they contended. They demanded that the Field election be annulled and the choice be given to the legitimate contestant.

Once the Michigan caucus vote was known, the issue between the two sides became as taut as it had ever been. Unity must get the matter on the convention floor by pounding away at it. The Progressives must head it off; all of their leading floor people were assigned tasks in that crucial operation. But it was Martin himself who proceeded to take the lead with a remarkable display of stalling. He poured out an unabating stream of observations; he had a grab-bag full of interruptions.

As the Sunday afternoon session had gone past the half-way point and the Fisher One question had not yet been brought to the floor, Unity leaders became desperate. Bob Travis, as head of the Flint delegation, asked if the credentials committee was ready to report on the question.[49] Martin replied innocently, "I don't know. I will ask the credentials committee. Is the credentials committee ready to report?" But there was no reply from Stuart Strachan, the committee's chair, who obviously was not in the hall. George Edwards replied sarcastically for him, "Yes, the credentials committee has been ready to report for three days." It became evident that Stuart Strachan and the rest of his majority were in hiding.

Martin looked around expectantly for any other lurking committee chair, then cried out with undisguised joy, "The publications committee is ready to report, and we will hear from that committee!" Fitting into his design, the committee's report dealt with the "Publication of Local Papers" and was aimed at their suppression.[50] Some of the leading Unity locals were concerned with the issue and thus might have their attention drawn away from the Fisher One affair. This included the West Side Local and Flint, as well as a couple of others, Plymouth, for example, whose weekly journal had already fallen under the threat of being banned by the International office.

In fact, the committee's report was non-concurred in by minority member Pat Early, one of our star correspondents on the *Flint Auto Worker,* which could hardly have been otherwise when one reads the first "whereas" of the committee's resolution: "Whereas, the publication of local papers is deemed inadvisable at this time because of the fact that the International, the local, and every member of the UAWA are liable in any damage suit they might incur for slander." The resolution suggested that the International journal should, by expanding, absorb all the communicative requirements of the union and thus eschew these dire eventualities. It was just so much eye-dust meant to conceal the true issues involved, the right of the locals to self-expression and the free development of independent thought.[51]

Entering into the debate, Martin gave an emotional, blood-curdling interpretation of the danger of damage suits: "We can be sued to the extent that it would bankrupt this International Union, bankrupt every person here, and take your home and everything you have by the courts of this country."[52] The cries of "no!" mingled with ridiculing laughter caused him to lose his pose of patience. When the delegates also derided his suggestion that the question be turned over to the incoming executive board, he became pallid with wrath and shouted menacingly: "It does not make . . . one bit of difference whether you vote it up or down. The general executive board now has the power to do it, as adopted in this constitution." The slip of raw arrogance received its due then and there. The question was called for and the roar of "no's!" left no opening for a call for a standing vote.

The sharp setback should have given Martin reason for pause. Still, the question involved was of minor importance and he could have been content to have gained another hour of delay. The afternoon session was speeding to its end and the opposition were not a whit closer to their major goal of reversing the Fisher One decision. When Bill Cody and John McGill once more took up the call for the credentials committee's report, Martin responded deviously, "I understand they will be ready in just a few minutes. While [they] are getting ready . . . I will ask that the resolutions committee make a very brief report."[53]

When it had finished, Martin put on a worried air and called out, "Is the credentials committee ready to report? Brother Stuart Strachan?" He looked around as though he had just seen Strachan somewhere. The pantomime was catching and a number of the delegates started to do the same. Finally, as though resignedly, Martin designated David Dow, who was at hand and who, without further delay, began to give the constitution's "final report."[54] It was a nice long one and Nat Ganley brought up a number of important things that, were it were not for his well-organized notes and phenomenal memory, might have been left out. In the end, Martin, who had all but cursed Ganley on the floor for his "delaying" tactics, was thanking him profusely while David Dow addressed him as "Nat."

It was 5:35 when Walter Reuther moved that the credentials committee be found by getting the sergeants-at-arms after them, slipping in at the end of his motion the significant addition "that the names of the executive board members elected to Michigan shall not be declared elected until the credentials committee has first reported and that report acted upon by this convention." The addition was meant to prevent Morris Field from being snuck in and obligated before Fisher Body's eight Unity delegates had been accredited and cast their votes for Field's opponent. Homer Martin declared the motion out of order.

Amid "considerable confusion," Reuther remained standing and cried out, "Mr. Chairman, I rise to a point of order," probably intending to appeal the chair's ruling. But John A. Carnahan of Port Huron, Local 127, in response to an unmistakable signal, made a motion to adjourn.

Five minutes earlier, Martin had turned down such a motion with the remark "I don't think these delegates want to adjourn." But now, for his own reasons, he accepted Carnahan's motion, and when several delegates noisily demanded the floor, he refused to recognize them, alleging that "the question of adjournment is not debatable." He called for a voice vote and quickly declared the motion adopted. The convention was adjourned at 5:40 P.M., and the question of the eight hapless Fisher One delegates was carried over to the final session.

• • •

Homer Martin opened the Sunday night session at 8:15 with the announcement that the credentials committee was ready to report. The delegates set themselves to listen to this long-deferred account only to learn that Martin himself intended to give them a lengthy rundown on it before it was delivered. Soon the delegates were expressing their displeasure, their interruptions continuing until one shouted in a trumpeting voice: "Give us that report!"[55]

Finally, Martin stepped aside, but when Stuart Strachan made his presentation it was incongruously out of keeping with all the commotion and distemper that had preceded it. The report turned out to be as bland as faucet water. There was no argument, no explanation even, merely the flat declaration that after hearing a "large number of witnesses, including Brothers Travis and Pieper," the committee had decided that "there has been no evidence . . . presented . . . which would in any way make us feel that the [former] general executive board's ruling be any way changed." A motion to that effect was made and seconded.

The minority committee was taken aback. Joe Ditzel asked if the minority report was now in order. "Brother Edwards has the minority report," he explained.

"Go right ahead, Joe," Martin replied, "You have the floor." And he meant exactly that because for the next ten minutes he absolutely refused to recognize Edwards despite angry shouts from the delegates: "We want Edwards! We want Edwards!" Martin finally called on Bert Harris instead. As a delegate from Fisher One, Harris had the merit at least of presenting substantive arguments from the majority side.[56] He made one important point, that all of Flint's other units had elected alternates, whereas Fisher One had refused to do so. This was the basis of its contention that the eight additional votes granted Fisher One after the audit of the local's books should be prorated among the fifteen already elected Progressive delegates.

After Harris had finished, Martin resumed his stalling but seemed to be startled by the sharp reprimand from Alan Strachan, the brother of the committee chair, who always reminded people to call him by his first name so that he would not be mistaken for his despised sibling.[57] "Mr. Chairman," he said, "I demand that the minority part of that committee be heard."

Martin tried to pass it off with innocent surprise. "May I say I recognized Brother Joe Ditzel, speaking for the opposition?" But the shouts thundered, "We want Edwards! We want Edwards!" And Martin finally granted him the floor.

Edwards's report was attention-riveting. Martin tried to break its hold on the delegates by intermitting a personal remark: "Brother Edwards, may I interrupt you to say . . . that an amalgamated union . . . cannot speak for a plant relative to the election of delegates." But he received a staggering rebuke: "Mr. Chairman, that is the point of issue here and I propose to state it. I didn't think I should be called upon to debate with the chair but rather with the members of the majority committee."

Point by point Edwards recounted the sequence of the controversy, how, on July 10, the Flint local voted to send a full slate of ninety-one delegates, carrying one vote each. Since an audit of the per capita payments by the five divisions would require several weeks, preliminary estimates were made to permit immediate elections while allowing for adjustments in the number of delegates assigned after the results of the audit were known, Edwards explained. Thus, "if any group was entitled to fewer delegates . . . they would be cut from those receiving the lowest vote. If any group was entitled to more delegates these would come from those next highest in order."

Edwards went on, aware that he held the delegates' undivided attention. "This is exactly what has been done in the Fisher case. The eight Fisher delegates who are here demanding seats are men [and one woman, Pat Wiseman] who were elected . . . as the next highest on the list of candidates." Then he corroborated these details by quoting from an article in the *Flint Auto Worker,* published several days before the Fisher elections and listing the forty-one nominees from that unit.

The executive board's supervisory committee at Flint were aware of this arrangement, Edwards further pointed out, since they were at the local meeting when it was adopted and had approved it then. He quoted from verbatim notes of Fred Pieper, chair of the committee, to that effect.[58]

After Edwards had finished, Martin would not permit a vote as he maundered on from one subject to another. What he said made no sense and was not meant to make sense. Let them shout. Let them howl. Then, when they were distraught with their anger and their disgust, all at once he stopped and called out to them: "Are you ready for the vote? All those in favor say 'Aye.' Those opposed, 'No!' The 'Ayes' have it."[59]

Very few delegates realized what had happened. Mortimer had taken the floor but apparently was not aware either of what had taken place. He made an ardent plea for a "fair hearing" for both sides. He did not realize that it was too late. Homer Martin had ended the need for all discussion.

Delegates were beginning to apprehend what had occurred. There were cries of "roll call, roll call." But Martin had no intention of allowing a roll-call vote or any other kind of vote. And he proceeded to explain to the assembly why a vote was no longer necessary, that he had the incontrovertible proof that this was so. "I made a decision as chairman," he repeated, "and may I say to you also that there is a machine, an electrically equipped machine in this building that registers the vote 'Aye' and 'Nay.'" He looked around as though expecting to be congratulated, then with triumphant pride he repeated his announcement while pointing to an apparatus on a table: "Let me tell you—this machine registered the vote, and the operator here can tell you that that machine scientifically decides the question. The answer of this machine was 16 to 12 in favor of the decision."

After Martin's astounding revelation, there was a pause as the delegates took in the situation. Auto workers have an innate respect for any mechanical device and their first thought concerns how it works. But Joe Ditzel was full of indignation. "Are you going to register a vote according to a machine which will tell which side can yell the loudest?" he demanded.[60] Another Unity man from the Allis-Chalmers local followed: "If there is democracy, are we going to leave it go to a machine?" He insisted on a roll-call vote as the human alternative, whereas Maurice Steinhardt, a mechanic at Flint Chevrolet, cast doubt on the capacity of a machine to distinguish between aye and nay.

Martin stood his ground, trying to announce the next order of business, but his voice was drowned out "by loud and continuous shouts of protest" (this and subsequent quotations are taken from the convention's *Proceedings*). "I know you don't want me to speak," he called out. "Where will the convention be next year?"

"There were cries of 'No! No!' and the noise increased."

"Where will the convention be next year?" he repeated.

But by now the convention was in total disorder. "A number of delegates were standing on tables and tables and floor were pounded with sticks and there was a general condition of disorder." I felt that the convention would break up in a riot and I was not the only one. Delegates were yelling at each other. Some blows were exchanged.

"I think all of you realize," Martin started saying but "was interrupted by cries of 'We want Reuther! We want Reuther!'" Yet Martin visibly had no intention of recognizing Reuther, who was standing in the aisle, pumping his hand. "There are literally hundreds of men and women that have never spoken," Martin said. "I am going to recognize them."[61]

A delegate from Toledo yelled, "Why in the hell don't you call on the president of Local 12 . . . Brother Kramer?"

The drumbeat sounded: "We want Reuther! We want Reuther!"

Bert Harris, evidently on a sign from the chair, rose to make a motion but "was unable to proceed because of the noise." Yet Martin knew what it was, "There is a motion before the house," he proclaimed. "The motion is. . . ." But "the noise assumed such proportions the president was unable to make himself heard."

Still unrecognized, Walter Reuther had begun speaking, and his words are recorded in the *Proceedings:* "I want to appeal from the decision of the chair on the last vote . . . accepting the report of the credentials committee."[62]

Martin appeared to be in doubt about what to do with the appeal when

George Addes rose from his seat on the podium and took the matter into his hands. His dark features were set in grim severity. "The papers have . . . headlines that fists are flying in the U.A.W. of A. convention, and here we are again this evening in a state of disorder. Regardless of what the decision of the chair is—I am not saying the decision is fair or unfair—but the decision has been made, the convention has made a decision, and in order to have the harmony and unity which we all desire . . . let the decision stand as it is."

There were cries of "no, no," but Addes disregarded them and repeated his solemn admonition: "Let the decision stand as it is. Certainly a rising vote or a roll call is not going to clear up the situation and I want to appeal to each and every one of you . . . for the sake of the preservation of this organization, that you abide by the decision of this convention."[63]

Addes's simple and deeply earnest appeal caught on at last with the agitated delegates. Walter Reuther himself was convinced that the moment for retreat had come and added his endorsement to accepting Martin's decision while insisting that this be done "under protest": "I can see now we are not going to work it out here," he conceded. "Let us settle down and all get back to our respective districts and fight to make this organization stronger." Then he ended with a direct appeal to the other side: "I say on behalf of my group, let us forget the Unity caucus and let us forget the Progressive caucus and think only of the automobile workers and the CIO, and let us go out of here unified and solid." The convention's last acts seemed to sustain this desperate plea.

The next convention city was chosen from half a dozen nominations, the vote appropriately favoring the city of George Addes, the peacemaker: Toledo. Even Homer Martin put aside his own home town, Kansas City, and plumped for the Ohio auto center, a solid Unity town, where, he declared with much truth, "the International Union was practically born."

The convention could hardly have ended on a more hopeful note, however tenuous. A delegate moved that all unfinished business be turned over to the executive board and the motion was adopted without discussion, a thing that would have been utterly unthinkable half an hour earlier.[64]

Homer Martin then asked for a motion to adjourn. But Nat Ganley, the "chicken-flicker from New York," according to Dick Frankensteen's anti-Semitic description, who was the sharp-eyed custodian of the constitution committee, reminded the chair that the newly elected executive board (including Morris Field) had not yet been installed. Apologetically, Martin turned the chore over to the CIO's remaining representatives, Ora Gasaway and Leo Krzycki, the latter administering the obligation, and the former adjourning the convention "sine die."

A Short-lived Mirage of Peace

18

Despite its agitated ending, the Milwaukee Convention left a heartening impression on the Unity Group. Our International officers had been reelected. Our position on the executive board had been strengthened. And, most important, the union had not been smashed as many of our members had considered likely. This positive outcome, we freely acknowledged, was due to the intervention of John L. Lewis, who had, moreover, given every indication of remaining a direct and steadying influence in the union.

Unity's satisfaction can be gleaned from the postconvention issues of its two leading local newspapers, those of Flint and Detroit's West Side Local. Both acclaimed the "harmony" that had been established at Milwaukee. Walter Reuther's *Conveyor* struck me as going a bit too far in commenting, on August 31, 1937, that "union democracy was effectively preserved," although I realized that its seemingly exaggerated confidence was probably justified by the comparative security that this local enjoyed.

We in Flint, on the contrary, did not even possess local autonomy. There was nothing to indicate that the new executive board would remove the controlling five-man committee from our backs. Nor would the strong PG groups at Fisher One and Chevrolet cease their disruptive activities under the committee's cloak. It was with the former group chiefly in mind that I added a warning note in an inner page of our paper, a note that will strike contemporary readers as strangely contradictory of the "harmony" proclamation of my leading article on the front page.

It was deceptively titled "Clarification of the Fisher One Convention Controversy." But the text was partisan, starting with the charge that the decision to ban the eight additional Fisher One delegates had deprived Flint of its rightful representative on the International's executive board. This would seem reason enough to explain my making the facts of the dispute known to our members. The only problem was whether doing this could be accomplished without arousing antagonism.

That was virtually impossible to achieve and the fact was that I did not even make the effort. I argued, on the contrary, that the reason for running the article was the appearance in the previous number of the International journal of the "complete quotation of President Martin's arguments" during the convention debate. Hence, I wrote, it was "no more than democratic" to let our people read George Edwards's minority report, upon which Martin had made the ruling that had threatened to break up the convention until "leaders of the Unity group called on their followers to accept [his] decision."

I realized that William Munger would not allow this article to pass but had no idea that he would cancel the entire "Flint Edition," which appeared as a four-page, wrap-around of the *United Automobile Worker.* For some reason for which I cannot account, the paper was actually printed (with my article included) though it was "withheld from circulation," as Munger revealed in the following issue, September 18, of the International journal.[1] His decision must have been taken belatedly since there would have been no reason to go to the expense of running the paper off the press were it not intended for distribution.

Even before this issue of the Flint Edition had been "suppressed," I sensed that its final occlusion was inevitable, at least as far as I was concerned.[2] Munger's article quoted me as stating in the Detroit papers of the previous day that I "intended to publish the paper elsewhere anyway." According to the *Detroit News,* I had said, "We haven't the support of the Flint local yet in making this move but we feel confident we can get it. . . . We merely want a paper that will be free from the dictates of the International office."

These self-assured assertions were belied by a staggering succession of announcements issued by UAW headquarters during the following days. On September 19, Homer Martin was quoted as saying in the *Detroit News* that he planned to "reorganize" the Flint local. On September 21, the same paper reported that Bob Travis and I had been summoned to appear before the executive board in Detroit. We drove down together and, as I recorded in my notes, Bob intended to demand that a court stenographer be present at his hearing and that he be allowed to read a prepared statement. I do not recall if these requests were granted. At any event, we can gather from the *News* that he appeared before the board on September 23 and that on the following day Martin announced that he would be transferred out of Flint.

Bob made a flippant remark about going on a hunting trip to Manitoba but must have changed his mind since he was present at the Flint local's meeting that Dick Frankensteen in his capacity as "assistant-president" called two days later. Here, Frankensteen announced Bob's transfer officially and Bob replied, "I accept the authority of the union." Then he added, "I hope that I will be assigned to organizational work at Ford."[3] The big crowd at the IMA Auditorium applauded but Frankensteen, who was the director of the Ford organization drive, did not take Bob up on the offer. He also had the poor judgment to choose this moment to report that the local was several thousand dollars in the red.

This ragged tale was quickly challenged by several angry members who demanded the floor. But Frankensteen abruptly adjourned the meeting with the announcement that another session would be held the following Saturday to take up the question of splitting the local into its separate plant divisions.

The Flint meeting was, in fact, the signal for a general shakeup in the International. Early the next week, Homer Martin reported that half of the UAW's two hundred organizers and staff members would be let go. Economy was his given reason. However the first ten victims he named were Unity people, including several of its outstanding members: Vic Reuther, Bob Kanter, Stanley Nowak, Mel Bishop, and Frank Winn. A separate item in the *News* reported that I had left Flint. "He is no longer on the payroll," it added, without mentioning that it was the Flint local's payroll and not the International's that was meant. The source of the information was also not given and I never did learn on whose authority I was separated from my last job with the UAW.

Martin had announced the sweeping purge from his suite in the downtown Eddystone Hotel, where all through the day he was said to have dictated letters and statements. He did not sleep at the hotel, merely using it for "privacy," as he explained. Word soon started arriving that protests had begun pouring in at International headquarters in the old Hofmann Building, and the following morning, September 30, when he entered the hotel at 9, a delegation was waiting for him, demanding a meeting.[4] He shook hands all around and said that he would see them in a little while; he would let them know when. After "two or three hours" the group sent a small committee up to remind him. The spokesman knocked several times at the door and then rapped loudly. Finally Martin opened it a few inches and stuck a gun out through the aperture.

The press gave only Martin's version of the incident, which he altered several times, first denying then admitting that he had pulled the gun. He thought that they were thugs, he said in the *Detroit News* of October 1. "I knew if they broke down the doors they might have stepped in with gats. I don't own a gun. I never carry one. There was a 32-calibre automatic pistol in the room. I picked it up and went to the door. I didn't know whether the gun was loaded. In fact I wouldn't have known how to use it in any case."[5]

This self-serving language that carried things right back to the pre-Milwaukee days was not apt to efface such shrieking newspaper headlines as the one that appeared in the *Detroit News* on October 9: "UAW 'Rebels' Picket Martin—President of Union Pulls Gun." Especially outraged was the union delegation that was the butt of the attack, which was compounded by a virulent statement, headed "Martin Condemns Hoodlum Tactics," in the *United Automobile Worker*. The incensed group, who identified themselves as members of Reuther's West Side Local 174, demanded that the paper print their reply. When this was rejected they prepared a seven-page account of the incident and mailed it to all locals, with the "sincere request" that it be read before their membership.[6]

A covering note by Richard H. Eager, chair of the Ternstedt unit of Local 174, pointed out that Martin was aware that there was no danger of physical harm to him because the delegation had asked the telephone operator downstairs to announce them. There was absolutely no effort made to break down the hotel room door, he added.[7]

The memorandum explained that the delegation intended to discuss the deteriorating conditions at Ternstedt with Martin, as well as to protest the dismissal of "some of our oldest, most experienced and most capable organizers." One, Stanley Nowak, was in charge of Ternstedt and had helped build the union there to the strength of ten thousand members. Recently, the management had begun a reckless campaign of speedup, wage cuts, and discrimination. After two months of fruitless efforts by the bargaining committee, the union decided, on Nowak's suggestion, to take a premonitory strike vote. Martin fired him soon after. The committee charged that this was done as a concession to the Ternstedt management, which had been demanding Nowak's removal for months because of his aggressive leadership. The accusation seemed to fit into the conciliatory pattern of the UAW's attitude toward General Motors, which was featured in a heading of the International journal of September 18, 1937: "Union, Corporation Agree on Outlaw Strike Formula—Executive Board Gives Assurance of Responsibility."

The article shocked many members of General Motors locals when they realized that the union leadership had finally knuckled under to the corporation's demand that it "be allowed to discharge, or otherwise discipline, union members . . . guilty of instigating unauthorized strikes. The UAW also obligated itself to take effective disciplinary action against those responsible." It was amazing to learn, moreover, that during the two months of attempted negotiations between the union and the corporation, the latter had adamantly refused to discuss the union's prepared body of demands until such a commitment had been made. According to the assurance of the front-page banner—"CLEAR WAY FOR GM REVISION"—this discussion would now get underway without further delay.

A month later, on October 18, at a gathering of the chairmen of the bargaining committees from sixty GM plants, it soon became evident that progress in these negotiations had been practically nil. This was admitted in the statement from Homer Martin to the committee chairmen that Bill Dowell, national head of the negotiating committee, later read to newspaper reporters: "if General Motors is unwilling to make concessions, the locals [should] be ready to take action." The negotiating committee, later called the "Committee of 17" had been elected on June 6, in Detroit, at the big conference of representatives from all General Motors plants.

"However," Dowell added in a statement to the newsmen, "the UAW does not wish to convey the impression that there will be a strike in General Motors." He may have had in mind the sharp rebuke that the UAW leadership had received for "irresponsibility" during the first CIO convention that had begun a few days earlier in Atlantic City. A resolution presented by Sidney Hillman, president of the Amalgamated Clothing Workers, was aimed directly at the auto union: "We want to bring to industry a sense of confidence that contractual relations with labor will not disturb industry." In an interview with the *Detroit News* on October 12, 1937, Hillman was more explicit: "The UAW has ceased to be an asset of the CIO. It has become a distinct liability and will continue so as long as its irresponsible acts continue."

• • •

It was an open secret a month later, when a great conference of 282 delegates from all the General Motors UAW locals assembled in Detroit, that an acceptable contract had not been extracted from the corporation.[8] In fact, newspapers were already predicting the day before the sessions opened that delegates would turn down GM's offer. On November 11, the *Detroit News* reported "on good authority" that the company's negotiators had warned that they had granted all the concessions that they possibly could.

There were conflicting ideas about what the conference would decide to do under the circumstances. Some thought that the delegates would vote to strike; others felt that this was doubtful with the holidays coming on. A semiofficial viewpoint, apparently inspired by William Munger, held that the economic situation made a stoppage impossible. Automobile production was falling, some plants were already on a four-day week, and companies were in a very favorable position with regard to the union.

Delegates arriving on the morning of November 14 heard that GM and UAW negotiators had met the night before for a last bid at improving the company's offer. The talks had gone on, it was said, without a break, from 2 to 10:25. The seriousness of the effort was highlighted by the report that Homer Martin had sat through the entire session, after which he had made an amazing statement to the press to the effect that the talks had attained "a point late Friday night when a tentative agreement on the main points of the contract had been reached."

Unity's delegates, however, were prepared for a battle. The West Side Local's GM units—Ternstedt and Fleetwood—had brought along a memorandum of "instructions" that actually were directed at themselves but they distributed copies to all the delegates. It was headed "These Points Must Be in the New GM Contract." The document's opposition to granting GM disciplinary powers over UAW members was categorical.

Bill Dowell opened the sessions by reading his report of the UAW-GM negotiations, verbatim copies of which had been distributed among the delegates.[9] But it was only when Dowell read GM's replies slowly and emphatically that their appalling emptiness was brought home to them.

General Motors had answered no to everything—to sole bargaining rights, to recognition of the stewards' system, to corporationwide seniority in case of decentralization, to the seven-hour day and thirty-five-hour week, to uniform classification of operations and standardized pay rates, and to revision of timing operations. After counting off ten of the points Dowell realized that he had left one out. The company's answer to the request for vacations with pay, he hesitated, was "No!"

The conference adjourned after the reading and Dowell reopened it in the afternoon with a frank admission that he had already heard many complaints about the agreement during lunch time. He reminded the delegates that the committee had taken no position on it. "We told General Motors as late as last night before we got up and walked out of the conference that certain provisions that they were trying to write into the agreement just would not be accepted by the delegates." In fact, he added, President Martin had written them a letter last night to that effect, a revelation in disaccord with the glowing statement that Martin had given to the press.

The delegates were not placated by these soft words. A delegate from Pontiac named Johnstone started off by taking strong exception to General Motors' negative response on the question of decentralization, "which afflicts us sorely at this time." He ripped into Dowell's blank remark that "we have not been able to arrive at anything which would tend to solve that problem." That, Johnstone charged, was due to a lack of "militance." Ever since General Motors got that statement from the UAW on unauthorized strikes, he affirmed, "it is sitting back with a smile of smug complacency. . . . I want to say that it amazes me . . . that any committee would have the incomparable effrontery to bring us back less than we [have] at the present time." He ended by moving "That we reject the report of the committee and recall them." There was no vote taken on the motion, perhaps because the conferees were not ready to take so ultimate a decision.

Another delegate then demanded to know who had given the executive board the right to allow General Motors to "determine the guilt" of any worker, to act as "judge, jury and prosecutor?" His local, Number 329, he complained bitterly, already had one member who was suspended for thirty days and "who is walking the streets and his family hungry because of the arbitrary decision handed down by the international executive board." His emotion almost beyond control, Delegate Parrish asked, "Do you think that is just?" Furious cries came back, "No! No!"

Bill Dowell tried to continue with his report, a thankless job. He kept reminding the delegates that the "agreement" was not final and advising them to think it over carefully that evening and come back the following morning with ideas about how to "turn the heat on General Motors."

Earl Anderson, a delegate from the Southgate plant in Los Angeles, interposed artfully, "I would like to ask [the chairman] what he means by 'turning the heat on' and in what way we will do that?"

Dowell swiftly began backtracking. "I don't want to be an alarmist," he hesitated. "I am not well enough up in the business world to know what the economic conditions are. There are certain factors that point to a reduced schedule in the automobile industry." He halted abruptly as though realizing that he had gone beyond his depth, then promised hastily that the next day people from the CIO who were familiar with such matters would be present to answer all their questions. This namby-pamby reply roused the ire in Delegate Chiesa, a member of the big PG Local 235 of Detroit, which was supposed to be staunchly lined up with Martin. "This sounds to me," he erupted, slapping the sheets in his hand, "like something sent to a little baby to play with. . . . This is a crime to the working-class of General Motors. I make a motion we send this back to General Motors!"

This angry outburst coming from one who could hardly be considered a harebrained leftist must have hoisted a danger signal to floor leader John Ringwald of the pro-Martin forces, who made a sudden motion for adjournment. No one opposed it. Even the Unity people realized that there was no point in pressing the issue since it was plain that the delegates were overwhelmingly convinced about rejecting the pact.

• • •

Unity's intuition was proved correct on the following morning, when the conference chair, Stuart Strachan, a PG leader, opened the session by proposing that it be adjourned until that afternoon. The Committee of 17, he explained, had been meeting almost all night and were in the process of putting the finishing touches to their recommendations.[10] "I think an agreement has been reached by all parties," he said reassuringly, and Bob Travis of Unity made the motion to recess.

When the conference reconvened at 1:30, delegates did a double-take when the credentials committee, a majority of which was PG, proposed that seven challenged delegates from Flint, all Unity, should be seated. Seven top people, including Roy Reuther, Gib Rose, Kermit Johnson, and Pat Early, were included.

Carried forward by the placatory mood of the delegates, Martin assumed his famous fiery oratorical style. He was by no means opposed to strikes, he assured them. On the contrary, "Any time we can improve the condition of the workers by striking, then for heaven's sake strike and stay on strike until we get what we are after. . . . I want to make that clear, that as president of this International Union, you are not going to have a lot of trouble getting authorization for strikes."

A delegate [name not given]: Will you back it up?
President Martin: You can have it in writing.
A delegate: Yeah, after it is won.
President Martin: You know that kind of stuff doesn't get anybody anywhere.

But Martin was not going to let himself be baited. The simmering discontent of the delegates roused by the nullity of what had been gained from General Motors could be ignited too easily. With renewed aplomb, he informed the assembly that the Committee of 17 had a program that it would communicate to them. It had been adopted by unanimous vote. But first he wanted to read a letter that he was going to send to William Knudsen. The corporation's proposed agreement, he had written, did not "insure a just and workable relationship" with the union. "Our membership is definitely of the opinion that your proposals fail even reasonably to achieve such a result and even in many respects weaken the existing provisions of our present agreement." For these reasons, "the delegates were unanimously of the opinion that your proposals are unsatisfactory and voted [to reject them]."

The Committee of 17, through its chair Bill Dowell, then presented its program: rejection of the corporation's proposals; reaffirmation of the union's determination to obtain an agreement consistent with its original demands; and "that immediate steps be taken through the International Union under the National Labor Relations Act, to establish the union as the exclusive bargaining agent for the employees of the General Motors corporation." Martin, in reply to a question, declared that the statement granting GM the right to discipline those responsible for unauthorized strikes would also be withdrawn.

A motion was adopted to reject the agreement. President Martin asked the delegates to repeat the vote by rising to their feet, cheerily calling on the visitors in the balcony to join in, as though in celebration of some proud event. "The motion is adopted by unanimous vote," he gloated. A delegate

sought to carry the explosive impulse along with a motion that the conference adjourn and that "all go home." "No, no!" voices cried out, as many
considered that much still remained to be done. With only a few hours of
the second and last day left, nothing at all had been accomplished except for
the acknowledgment of a failure.

The delegates were boiling with angry thoughts to which they wanted to
give vent about conditions in their plants. The speedup that they described
made one think of the situation existing before the GM sitdown.[11] Delegate
Silver K. Parrish of Local 329 said that they would have to get a raise of half
a dollar an hour to make up for the extra work that General Motors was
squeezing out of them. "The point I'm trying to get through is this: Are we
going to notify the company that the wage-slashing through speedup is going to [have to] stop until these negotiations are finished?"

"The line is running so very fast," Delegate Glovak of Local 235 verified, "that you see the men puffing like steam engines and they look to the
committee to do something . . . but the management says they can do nothing about it. . . . They [the management] are fighting Carter Glovak, and
why? Because he told the men: 'Do what you can, and what you can't do,
let the line go to the dogs!' I told them that."

Delegate Johnstone of the angry Pontiac delegation, whose sharp displeasure with the new agreement had released the delegates' furious criticism of it, called for a forthright disavowal of the Committee of 17. The
union ought to go back, he advised, to the men "who negotiated the original
contract that is superior to the one which has been read to us. Let us use
some of the brains that enabled us to gain the position that we had under the
former contract. These men will lead us out of the wilderness. . . . Let us
elect a strike committee." The implied praise of Wyndham Mortimer and Ed
Hall did not please President Martin at all: "I think all of us here know that
we are not dealing with kids' play, that we have a job in which this matter
of calling names and of raising personalities . . . must be forgotten."[12]

The peace offering seemed sincere and Walter Reuther, speaking for the
Unity side, decided to take Martin at his word.[13] Admittedly, firing the Committee of 17 was not the answer. The negotiators were not to blame for the
weakness of the new agreement. The fawning attitude of the UAW's leadership was at fault. "We ought to reaffirm those things we want in the agreement," Reuther argued, "and then send the committee back with specific
instructions and set a limited time in which we will negotiate." He proposed
a broad campaign of publicity against layoffs, violation of seniority, lead-
poisoning, and the speedup system. "Let us put the corporation on the spot
and bring the whole thing out in the open by issuing weekly bulletins in
General Motors locals. . . . We must let General Motors know that we are
building up a fighting spirit."

The session ended with a report on perhaps the only noncontroversial subject that could be handled peacefully before any UAW meeting at that time: the organization of Ford.[14] Dick Frankensteen, director of the Ford drive, delivered a lengthy report about the meeting that had just been held by seventy-five delegates from every Ford plant in the country. He ended with an exuberant promise: "I am going to devote all that I have in me to this drive. I want your support, all of it, Unity and Progressive, all of us together, and I think with that support that the task that all of us recognize must be done will be done."[15]

The most heartening thing about this talk was no doubt those final words, the call for unity, for the end of factionalism, coming from the man who had done more than any other person to foment and sustain it. In fact, it was the one assurance that factionalism might indeed be eradicated.

•   •   •

The final session on Sunday evening gave ample play to the new spirit of coexistence. It opened with the reading of a wire to the conference from the unemployed committee of the Cleveland Fisher Body Local 45, reporting the permanent layoff of a thousand workers: "Situation desperate. We demand that conference take immediate action. Work must be shared by all employees by seniority. . . . Protect your future. Please grant the floor to our spokesman, Brother Brooks."[16]

The request was promptly granted and Brother Brooks proceeded to outline the decentralization policy of General Motors. As the minutes summarize, "he pointed out that thousands of workers in the Fisher plant have been laid off. . . . This work has been sent out to various plants throughout the country, particularly the plant located in the city of Grand Rapids."

It is surprising that this key problem of decentralization should have waited until the last hours of the conference to appear and then by a reminder from outside. Yet it had occupied the minds of many delegates, as the response to the Cleveland wire would quickly demonstrate. Bill Dowell cited the Pontiac Fisher plant, which, he said, had cut back to twenty-eight hours because of the layoff of 1,350 men whose jobs had gone to a newly built plant at Linden, New Jersey. Harry Sanders of Toledo Chevrolet followed with a famous case to which I have alluded in chapter 9.

Vice-President Wyndham Mortimer, who over the years had studied "technological improvements" and other causes of work displacement, next took the floor to report on his findings. The problem of decentralization, he reminded the delegates, had been raised with General Motors at the March negotiations, but the company was not at all responsive. He listed five courses of action that could be considered: (1) "That workers who have done the work . . . shall go with the work wherever it goes"; (2) that sharing the work "was all right to a certain point, but you cannot carry it too far";

(3) force the government to keep these people on their jobs by "[taxing] the companies that are making these huge profits to pay the bill"; (4) "raise the hourly rates and reduce the hours"; and (5) "organize the unorganized plants throughout the country."[17] These suggestions opened a broad discussion. Claude Henson, speaking for the Pontiac local, added three other suggestions: establish corporationwide seniority, a national uniform GM wage scale, and full cooperation by GM locals doing similar work regarding their production schedules.[18]

After Mortimer's program with the Pontiac local's amendments was adopted, the discussion continued on how pressure must be put on General Motors to force its adoption. A proposal that all UAW locals be called upon to hold special meetings on the following Sunday afternoon was considered too static by John W. Anderson, president of the Fleetwood unit of the West Side Local. In its place, he offered an idea of "establishing the authority of the union." This would be accomplished by proclaiming a "national labor day for General Motors" that would take the form of a short stoppage, the day and hour being kept secret until the last minute, when it would be announced by a strategy committee comprised of Martin, Mortimer, and Dowell.[19] The plan met with instantaneous approval. As Walter Reuther observed:

> I believe the effectiveness of this program lies in the fact that you have power under control, disciplined power. If the plants in Flint, Pontiac, Saginaw . . . went down with a bang and the workers had a meeting . . . let me tell you when that old switch went up again at the second hour, that union would be a stronger union than it was when the switch was pulled. . . . Just picture those boys in Flint, in Chevrolet 4 and Fisher 1. They will sit down right where they sat down last winter and they will feel the same power as they felt then, and General Motors will know about it.[20]

This vote released a freshet of enthusiasm. Homer Martin painted a picture of the General Motors "big boys" holding a conference of their own at that very moment. "I can well imagine that they are scared because this delegation has shown a sense of solidarity that they . . . had hoped would not develop."[21] Then he paused and added with solemn emphasis, "Today is the beginning of the end of factionalism in the UAW." Whereupon the delegation began spontaneously to sing "Solidarity Forever," the minutes report. Walter Reuther, declaring Martin's words "the best thing I have heard since I have belonged to this union," seized the moment to propose a meeting of the two factions to consolidate the newfound concord, to work out all differences and "get down to earth and get a good GM agreement and organize Ford."[22]

The union was wise to General Motors, Martin pitched in. "We know that they have already determined a long time ago not to give us any improvement in the agreement. We discovered that this week but we have got the stuff, we think, that will make this world sit up and take notice when we tell them about it. . . . They are going to recognize this union and treat us decently or we are going to be worse than a case of itchy hives. . . . If I have to authorize a strike tomorrow or the following week, General Motors has got it coming and they are going to get it!"[23]

Strikes were threatening at Pontiac and Saginaw, a request to stop using scab steel being produced at the Republic Steel Company. Henry Clark of Buick's foundry seized the euphoric moment to offer the resolution he had long been hugging close on discriminatory practices against black workers at his plant and other GM units: "All foundry workers shall be considered as [full-fledged] employees of the corporation, regardless of race or color, and shall be given an equal opportunity to be transferred from plant to plant and promoted according to their seniority and ability to do other work."[24]

Walter Reuther moved for a review of the program of action that the conference had adopted in support of its negotiators by instructing the general officers and the executive board to assemble a new conference, not later than sixty days hence, "at which time we shall receive reports of the progress made on the negotiations." In approving the motion, delegates were aware that it silently implied possible strike action that could be taken at the height of production on the new model if the results were unsatisfactory at that time.[25]

Bob Travis, in coordination with Reuther's motion, offered as the final decision of the assembly a motion regarding a wide publicity program that would be initiated in support of the negotiators.[26] He presented it in the form of a panel of accusations "indicting" General Motors on seven counts: speedups, discriminations, provocative actions by officials, chiseling on wages, disregard of safety and health, decentralization, and violation of seniority. "I move further," he said, "that each and every day press statements be given out . . . in conjunction with the weekly bulletin," an idea that Walter Reuther had suggested. Travis's motion was adopted unanimously.

The session was finally ready to adjourn at 10:15 P.M. and President Martin bade the delegates to prepare for the parade that he had earlier suggested, regardless of the lateness of the hour and the inclement weather. "All of us who have our coats can form in the ranks here and we will march out and around the square and we can sing 'Solidarity Forever!' as we go."[27]

Recession and Unemployment: The Locals Revolt

Whatever lessons the delegates carried home from these exhilarating happenings, the Pontiac group was the first to put them into execution. Martin's constant baiting of their representatives during the sessions was forgotten in his final sanction of militant action, which they regarded as aimed directly at themselves: "'If I have to authorize a strike in every plant next week, if I have to authorize a strike tomorrow or the following week, GM has got it coming and they are going to get it!' [applause]."[1]

A strike started at the Pontiac Fisher Body plant the next night and was reported in the *Detroit News* on November 16. Dorr Mitchell, a union spokesman, declared to the paper that the strike was "spontaneous" and due to the company's refusal to stagger employment and restore the jobs of five hundred men laid off the previous week. He also cited the speedup and other grievances.

The strike was a sitdown and the union seems to have met with some opposition since occupants welded the gate and forced those who wanted to leave to return to the plant though a few managed to climb over the fence. The sitdowners decided to evacuate the factory on the morning after, however, when Mitchell announced that the management had agreed to a conference "this afternoon." The 2,500 occupants marched out in a group at 8:30.

The sitdown started again at 3:30 that afternoon, when workers were told that the company had taken disciplinary action against four leaders of Monday's strike: George Method, the plant chairman, and three members of the shop committee. Further discharges would follow, the management warned, basing this additional penalty on the GM-UAW "agreement" for punishing fomenters of unauthorized strikes, albeit that putative agreement had been angrily disavowed by the just-ended conference. The local's leaders responded by planning to spread the strike to a second plant, Pontiac Motors.

But the corporation found allies at the union's highest levels. Fred Pieper hurried to Pontiac and insisted in the name of the International executive board that the strikers must return to work. William Munger, editor of the UAW journal, announced bluntly that the stoppage was unauthorized. Homer Martin, he said, was in southern Illinois visiting his mother, who was ill, but Munger had arranged for him to issue a statement by telephone, in which Martin gave the corporation renewed assurance of his opposition to unauthorized strikes and, by inference, approved its disciplinary actions at Pontiac.

Returning to Detroit the next day, Martin called the executive board into extraordinary session to consider the crisis while issuing an angry statement against the strikers: "No small group of workers who think they can do as they please can close a plant and stay within the pale of the union," the November 21 *Detroit News* reported him as declaring. The board moved to Pontiac on the suggestion of some members that it would be "impressive . . . to show the earnestness . . . with which they regarded the situation."[2] That evening, President Martin resumed his admonitions to the Pontiac workers at a meeting of "two thousand." After displaying his forensic talents for half an hour, he felt that he had won over his auditors and asked those to stand who agreed that the sitdowners must abandon the plant. Only half the audience got up.

Visibly shaken, Martin changed his line. It was impossible for the union to give formal authorization to the strike, he pleaded, since General Motors would use that as an excuse to refuse to negotiate a new contract. But if the strikers ended their sitdown promptly, the union would be in a strong position to bargain with the corporation. The meeting ended in a deadlock.

After touching base at the executive board session, Homer Martin retired to his hotel room, leaving the hot potato in the hands of the board members, who had decided to remain in session until the plant was evacuated. At some time after 1 A.M., according to the board's minutes, the Fisher Body bargaining committee and officers of the local union appeared and George Method and Arthur Law, the local's president, gave a report of "the entire situation." "After much general discussion it was finally mutually agreed that the Fisher Body committee would depart to the plant for the sole purpose of evacuating [it] and that they would report to the board within an hour."

They never reappeared. Meanwhile, a battle raged among the board members about what action should be taken. Walter Reuther, whom I interviewed in 1938, reported that Unity board members felt that the union must first authorize the strike to strengthen the strikers' negotiating position. But the Unity members were swamped by the big pro-Martin majority that wanted to order the men back to work under threat of expulsion from the union. As the night wore on, Reuther felt that the strikers grew distraught by the rumors that were passing, some to the effect that the strike would be authorized, others that it would not. In the end, "their morale was broken" and it was uncertain what course they would take.

Martin and his intimates provided the newspaper with a different story. L. B. Netzorg, an International representative on Martin's personal staff, reported that he had come to his hotel room to wake him well on into the morning and told him that the moment was propitious for him to talk to the strikers. Martin got dressed and, without notifying the executive board, which had left a standby group in session, entered the plant. He had been warned, he told the press on November 22, that the strikers were in a nasty mood and he might get hurt. But Martin bravely courted the danger, Netzorg related. An hour later he emerged, smiling, from the plant, five hundred men in his wake.[3] The vote to leave had been unanimous, he said.

The plant remained closed as the management and the bargaining committee engaged in sustained negotiations. General Motors was adamant on the union's major demands for the reemployment of 1,350 laid-off workers and the abandonment of its plan to shift a considerable part of the work to Linden, New Jersey.[4] After two days of discussion, a mutual agreement was reached to turn the dispute over to an arbiter. A local meeting of a thousand members received the news in silence, the *Detroit News* reported on November 23, despite the combined efforts of Martin, Frankensteen, and Reuther to stir their enthusiasm. The negative result of the arbitration award some time later confirmed this skepticism.[5] Thereafter, discontent in the local was such that Homer Martin found it necessary to name Charles Madden, Pontiac's executive board member, as its administrator with full powers.

• • •

Though the two union caucuses on the executive board had split sharply on the procedure to follow in the Pontiac strike, this did not produce a rift between them serious enough to reestablish the violent factionalism existing before the conference of November 13-14. So the Unity people felt, at any event, as they prepared for the "peace meeting" between the two caucuses that Walter Reuther had proposed to the conference and which, in the euphoria of its final hours, was accepted.

Documents exist that the Unity side prepared for the meeting, including ideas for the program to be proposed as well as a running report by some anonymous person of the meeting itself.[6] The last archive particularly reveals that individuals on both sides argued the desirability of putting an end to factionalism and the possibility of accomplishing that goal. Dick Frankensteen's approach is particularly significant.

It was evident, however, from the start that many members from the PG side were unenthusiastic about the whole effort. The Lovestonites and those close to them were undisguisedly antagonistic to it, as the pilfered correspondence of Jay Lovestone with his lieutenants in the UAW would one day reveal. Peace between the two auto union factions was the last thing that Lovestone wanted since it was incompatible with his personal ambitions about the UAW. Homer Martin's placatory final words at the November 13–14 assembly had filled him with dismay. He referred derisively to it as the "Halleluyah Conference" and observed about the "peace meeting," "I don't think anything but black shadows will come out of [it]."[7] Lovestone insisted that the meeting should take place "without commitments" and with a group of "non-softies" on the PG side. Naturally, there was a majority of his people on the list of names he proposed.

Their influence at the gathering was quickly registered by a motion to limit the discussion. Walter Reuther had led off by introducing the Unity program, copies of which were distributed.[8] Fred Pieper skimmed the program with his sharp eyes and rejected it instantaneously on the grounds that the entire list concerned matters of union policy, over which the International's executive board had sole jurisdiction. The Lovestonites lent their support to this viewpoint but the Unity program received help from an unexpected source. It came from Dick Frankensteen, who suddenly began reading an agenda that he said he had prepared and which, as the unnamed keeper of the Unity minutes recorded, was "practically identical" with their own. It was readily adopted as the "basis of discussion." In fact, despite Fred Pieper's warning, the talk that followed covered every conceivable subject that was before the union.

Some of the opinions expressed were sharp and even antagonistic in a personal way.[9] Yet the meeting ended with the adoption of Unity's proposals that the two sides choose five men each for future contact and that another such meeting be slated soon.

Unity had every reason to be content with the outcome. The anonymous author of the Unity memorandum was sanguine in his summary of the session. His conclusion was that, outside of Pieper and the Lovestonites, some of the PG were definitely ready for peace: Martin, Frankensteen, Dowell, Thomas, and Dobrzynski, who was connected with the Ford organization committee.

The reaction of the Lovestone-Pieper group was, of course, the antithesis of this view. The Lovestone correspondence unfurls a flurry of activity to halt the "peace" momentum. Jay Lovestone had already foreseen its dangers after the GM Conference and had hit upon a stratagem to scotch its progress by fomenting a rift within the Unity Group.[10] In a letter written on December 3, Lovestone reveals to Francis Henson that he had been meeting with Norman Thomas, the nation's outstanding socialist and its candidate for president, and had told him of the closeness that had been building up between the socialists and communists in the UAW. Thomas was, he said, deeply disturbed and asked Lovestone to prepare a memo that he could use at the next meeting of the National Executive Committee of the Socialist party.

Lovestone outlined in his letter to Henson the proposals he would make to Norman Thomas: the socialists were to break with the Unity caucus; they were to announce this rupture in the press; and they were to fire Carl Haessler, the editor of the *Conveyor,* the weekly publication of the West Side Local. In return, the socialists in the UAW could expect to receive "all considerations."

This exchange of views is the first known manifestation of an attempt involving the national leadership of the Socialist party to disrupt the united front between socialists and communists (and their sympathizers) within the UAW. Efforts of the Lovestonites to encourage such a rupture intensified demonstrably during the following period. Among the ploys they used were political issues, the most successful being the attitude toward war, where the similarity of outlook of the CPO and the Socialist party in contrast to that of the Communist party was exploited dexterously.

Nevertheless, intra-union partisanship still remained the strongest basis for establishing alliances, which Jay Lovestone certainly realized. A couple of weeks after he reported his contact with Norman Thomas to Henson, Lovestone wrote to him again, describing Thomas as "worried sick" by the maneuvers of Dick Frankensteen.[11] Henson had probably given Lovestone this idea by telling him that the frequency with which Frankensteen received "CP delegations" was becoming a standing joke in UAW headquarters. The delegations included not only John Anderson and Nat Ganley, who were UAW local leaders after all but also top CP political figures like Will Weinstone, state organizer of the party, and Bill Gebert.[12]

The fact was that Dick Frankensteen was experiencing great anxiety about how the Dodge local elections were panning out. In truth, the PG candidates' chances looked so bad that he began sounding out Unity leaders about composing a united slate. It was the pressure of individuals close to the CPO (Morris Field, for example) that allegedly routed this accommodation and Frankensteen ended by fielding a ticket comprised only of PG members.

• • •

After the short interlude of peace-seeking, the UAW's factionalism seemed to be reestablishing itself. There were some indications of changes in the lineup but the blight remained and, indeed, continued to grow. One wonders how this could have been the case in view of the steady deterioration of economic conditions, which gave members far more serious things to worry about.

At its quarterly session of January 12–13, 1938, the International executive board took official cognizance of the recession by adopting a pessimistic resolution to the effect that although increased productivity had raised industrial output 22 percent and profits 17 percent above pre-depression levels, eight and a half million workers remained unemployed and actual suffering existed among auto workers.[13] The UAW reflected this situation organizationally and financially.[14]

The union "is facing a grave economic crisis," George Addes revealed to the executive board in a "secret" report, asking them to instruct the general officers "to make whatever reductions in employees and expenses as are necessary . . . and if budget exceeds income the budget be *graduated downward* [emphasis added] within the limits of our income—if necessary without notice." Under no circumstances, he added, should the International sell $100,000 of its U.S. government bonds, which Martin had done in the recent past, without the sanction of the executive board. This warning was indubitably aimed at Martin's extravagance, which even some of his supporters deemed necessary to control.

There were indications that a number of the board members were inclined to forget factional lineups due to their concern over the economic situation. It was surprising to read in the board minutes, for example, that approval for the controversial Ludlow Amendment was adopted without opposition. The amendment called for a constitutional change that would require a national referendum before the United States could engage in any overseas war.[15] Much space had been devoted to this proposal in the *United Automobile Worker,* mainly in pursuit of factional advantage by the Lovestonite editor Bill Munger.[16] Yet nothing of the sort was reported at the board session after Morris Field presented his resolution.

The sense of congeniality continued throughout the entire session and was commended in a final motion by Charles Madden, the PG board member from Pontiac, asking "that President Martin be given authority to make a statement in regards to the harmony existing in the International board." This diplomatic turn of phrase was meant to disguise a direct order to Martin, for whom the UAW's peace surge had evidently ended and who had given signs of being suspicious about the loyalty of some of "his" members on the board.

We can understand this attitude better if we read "Inside the CIO," a series of syndicated articles by the journalist Benjamin Stolberg that had begun to appear in the national press during the executive board's session. Martin had undoubtedly known about them before they were published since they were written with the help of Jay Lovestone, whose correspondence refers to the articles. Starting on January 10, 1938, the first half of the twelve pieces dealt with the UAW. The articles were so brazenly slanted, so meshed with pure invention, that only the most prejudiced person could have taken them seriously. Martin, however, vainglorious as he was, could hardly resist the appeal of being depicted as an intrepid modern knight battling for true American trade unionism against communist disrupters.

Homer Martin's unwavering purpose was a "strong, powerful, progressive and contractually-responsible" union, Stolberg wrote, and he inferred that Martin had the prestige to attain that goal at Milwaukee and would surely have done so had he not been so "desperately anxious" to establish peace in the union. The journalist described Martin as working closely with John L. Lewis, whom he credited with having helped draw up the new contract with General Motors. But Martin was "brow-beaten" into abandoning this agreement at the November Conference, "which was packed by the Unity opposition."

The Lewis-Martin intimate collaboration was unquestionably Jay Lovestone's brainstorm, meant to get his protégé off the hot spot with Lewis after Martin made a disastrous speech in Rockford, Illinois, which the *Chicago Tribune* quoted at length on December 3, 1937. Martin had thought that the talk, delivered to the UAW District Council, was private, but a reporter was in a side room and took it all down in shorthand. It was a slashing cut at the CIO, which, he claimed derisively, received per-capita tax only from the UMW, the UAW, the Rubber Workers, the ILGWU, and the ACW (Amalgamated Clothing Workers). These big internationals were supporting paper unions controlled by the Communist party. David Dubinsky of the ILGWU was not going to pay any more per capita to the CIO, Martin said, and neither was he.

John L. Lewis was outraged, and Jay Lovestone was distraught by these quoted utterances.[17] Lovestone urged Martin to write an apology to Lewis, which Martin did. Yet the apology did not spare him a withering going-over from Lewis at the meeting of CIO presidents that took place at that time. Reading from a clipping about the Rockford speech, Lewis commented, "If Homer Martin wants to take this matter before the rank and file workers at the next UAW convention, I will accept the challenge."[18]

Nevertheless, Lewis was too responsible a person to allow the rift to widen, and he invited the UAW's executive board to come to Washington for its January session. Martin readily agreed but changed his mind in angry reaction to an article headed "Lewis Calls UAW Parley" in the *Detroit News*. Martin wanted to show the world who was running the UAW.[19]

Apparently Martin had recovered his verve after the Stolberg articles appeared. A few days after the series ended, he was asked to do an interview with the *New York Herald-Tribune,* which he eagerly accepted.[20] We learn about its contents from the open letter that the Unity officers and board members wrote him immediately after the interview was printed, asserting that it ended any remaining hope for peace. It was nothing but a red-baiting slur directed against them, they stated, and it resumed all the repudiated accusations of their responsibility for unauthorized strikes and the lack of union discipline.

They cited the explosive, off-the-cuff pronouncements that Martin was in the habit of making, drawing attention in particular to "your January statement favoring wage cuts under certain circumstances." While later purporting to deny these remarks in the *United Automobile Worker* of January 22, Martin ended by repeating them even more incisively: "However, we all recognize that there are certain companies which are thrown into a bad competitive situation, which, if the workers refuse to give consideration to the facts in the case, might bankrupt the company."

It was amazing how many companies considered themselves eligible to the escape clause in Homer Martin's declaration. Some were prepared to expose their books to the UAW negotiators to prove that they were close to economic collapse. This was not only true of companies that were negotiating on new contracts but also of others whose pacts still had time to run but asked that they be reopened so that deserved alterations could be applied.

• • •

In fact, the auto industry was indeed in a bad way and getting worse by the week, judging from the headlines and statistics in the *United Automobile Worker.* "UAW to Lead Mighty Protest against Layoffs and Hunger," it announced on January 29, and a week later, "200,000 Demonstrate." The site was Cadillac Square, which less than a year earlier had witnessed a similar gathering. But the shouting was no longer for "Recognition" and "Improved Conditions," but for "Adequate Relief!"

The UAW's most active department was now the welfare committee headed by Dick Leonard, a Chrysler man. His appointment as welfare director was bannered in the UAW paper of December 18, 1937, which defined his job as "Mobiliz[ing] for Relief." The magnitude of the task could be envisioned by the partial statistics of layoffs in Detroit as of January 8, 1938, thirty-six thousand in nine auto plants. And these figures leapt upward, unabated, until the plants resembled the autumn change-of-model doldrums instead of the high-production throb of early winter.[21]

Soon, the new welfare committee was given a semi-independent status in the International, from which it quickly evolved into the WPA Auxiliary Union, which was chartered as a subsidiary of the UAW, covering unemployed members who obtained government jobs. The purpose was to stave off an expected attempt by the left-wing Workers Alliance, which the CIO favored, or even a revived communist-led Unemployed Council to take over the field of the jobless. The danger was that many UAW members would fall into their fold, as Jay Lovestone early began to warn Homer Martin and Dick Frankensteen.[22]

Unemployment was the great concern, not only in Detroit but also in all other auto centers.[23] Cleveland set up unemployment bureaus. Women's Auxiliary members at Pontiac became official investigators of the relief needs of families. The Pontiac local organized a flying squad to fight evictions, as did the Detroit Motor Products union and others. The West Side Local conducted victorious rent strikes. Saginaw set up a canteen and fed a thousand people a day with the aid of contributions from merchants. The Flint local fought garnishments that were being deducted from its members' pay checks, as well as the unfair sharing of the available work at Chevrolet.[24] The major action in Flint, where forty thousand were on relief, was a mammoth parade followed by a meeting of 7,500 at the IMA Auditorium.

The companies did not seem too concerned about these activities on behalf of the unemployed. On the contrary, they saw the economic crisis as an opportunity to strengthen their own positions in the plants against those workers lucky enough to still have jobs. It was a miscalculation based on a mode of thinking that was a year out of date, as the workers in a number of plants at Detroit would demonstrate in the early spring of 1938. The West Side Local's numerous parts plants figured prominently in this educational process.

The tie-in with Homer Martin's offer to make wage adjustments had appeared early in that local's negotiations for new contracts. At one of the companies, Gar Wood, Martin had personally intervened to make a reduced-wage arrangement that other managements brought up thereafter, including the managements at Timken, Federal Screw, American Brass, and many more. "A lot of them who had not thought of asking for wage adjustments did so now," Walter Reuther told me.[25]

The critical point was reached with the tough Federal Screw management, which demanded "consideration" even though the company had tripled its profits in 1937. The union countered with an offer to take a 5 cent an hour cut in the form of a loan that the company would repay. It was refused. The local then said it would allow a cut of 10 cents, which would be repaid out of profits. This, too, was turned down. The union then threatened to strike, but the company bluntly announced that a 10 cent cut would go into effect whether or not immediately. It was apparent that it was spoiling for a fight. Reuther was convinced that the company had an understanding with Mayor Richard Reading to keep the factory running with the help of Commissioner Heinrich Pickert's practiced scab-herding police.[26]

Because I was ill and laid up at the time, I did not get down to the strike but it was described to me in great detail by leading participants, including Walter Reuther, and especially by Stanley Nowak, the organizer in charge of the plant, and George Edwards, who was assigned to the strike by the West Side Local. All three accounts coincided in giving the struggle a unique character that led me to dub it "a neighborhood in revolt."[27] These people lived in the vicinity of the plant and often worked there. They were largely of Polish extraction and Nowak developed a close affinity with them.

The strike at Federal Screw began on a Monday morning, March 28, and the majority of the factory's three hundred employees joined the picket line. There were only twenty-five scabs, who were ushered into the plant by a police force at least as numerous as the strikers. The union's plan was not to interfere with the passage of the non-strikers but to go after them when they were leaving at the end of the shift and try and discourage them from returning the next morning. There was some violence that first afternoon: a few strikers were clubbed and some of the scabs were roughed up. The following day the police corps was doubled, and the pickets were outnumbered too badly to become aggressive, except for a few hotheads who got clouted for their intrepidity.

The big turmoil started on the third afternoon. There were five hundred police, the union estimated, and only half as many pickets though their numbers would be augmented by workers from Kelsey-Hayes, George Edwards recalled. But the union depended mainly on the auxiliary aid coming from the neighborhood. The "strategy," Stanley Nowak explained, was to let the few scabs leave quietly from the plant's three exits and hurry toward their parked cars on Livernois, escorted by the police. The main concentration of pickets gathered in the half-dozen cross streets, waiting until the scabs passed. Then they began throwing the missiles that they had stashed away.

The police battalion, including several mounted officers, came after them. But the pickets vanished into alleys and back yards while youngsters hidden behind garages and armed with BB blow pipes began aiming their tiny pellets at the horses' legs. Some of the neighbor women helped fleeing union men get away. The mounted policeman who chased Stanley Nowak ran his horse up onto a porch during the pursuit, but the woman who lived in the house opened the door and pulled Nowak in. He told of another woman who had a handsome garden trimmed with white-faced bricks, which she dug out one by one and handed to a picket, who heaved them from behind a fence.

All of the scabs and eighteen policemen were reported to have been hospitalized on that day. But a good many pickets were also badly hurt. The *United Automobile Worker* on April 2 described the assault on one union man who, it said, was not expected to live: "Percy Keyes, a Negro worker, was on the lawn of a house on Otis street, a block from the plant, with some other people. The police suddenly rushed in; the others ran but Keyes quietly put up his hands. Instead of arresting him, they clubbed him down, beating him viciously about the head and body. Then they picked him up by the arms and legs . . . and savagely kicked him. Then they dropped him to the ground unconscious, but after a time his body began to twitch and they began to club him all over again."[28]

Taken to Harper Hospital, Keyes "was found to have a broken back and probably skull fracture, a fractured knee-cap and innumberable serious bruises and internal injuries." Homer Martin and Walter Reuther appeared before the Detroit Common Council to protest the savage violence of the police. Using the occasion to correct the impression of his ill-fated wage-cut pronouncements, Martin demanded: "Is this a part of the general plan of the manufacturers to break the union's resistance to wage slashing . . . to start the ball rolling to further prostitute [sic] the wage levels of the factory workers?"

After the battle, however, Federal Screw put up the white flag, agreeing to a truce while parleys went on and promising not to attempt to operate the plant. A week of serried negotiations followed, and the *Conveyor* of April 12 was able to announce that an agreement had been reached. Together with sole collective bargaining, a complete steward system, plantwide seniority, no layoffs until the work week had been scaled back to thirty-two hours, and other concessions, the major demand, which had released the bitter struggle was given top prominence in the banner headline "Federal Screw Pact Restores Old Pay Rates."

This headline typified the current status of the UAW, when a militant left-wing local had to content itself with a defensive settlement with a small company. It clarifies the union's continuing failure to win a satisfactory contract with General Motors. After that corporation had unilaterally cancelled the old agreement on January 11, the UAW signed a "new" one with it on March 12 but the agreement was basically unchanged but for a few minor adjustments in the grievance procedure, reported the *United Automobile Worker* on March 12, 1938.

The Unity group gave a harsh evaluation of the contract, which was no doubt widely shared, in its weekly letter of March 24.[29] The General Motors workers, it stated, "have been forced several steps backward by a new supplementary agreement signed by President Martin without consultation with the workers involved. It is . . . a bitter surprise to thousands of our membership to find that an agreement has been reached, signed and put into effect without their having any knowledge or say as to its contents." It was, in effect, a mode of procedure that was contrary to the most elementary democratic traditions of the UAW.[30]

• • •

Convinced that their efforts to rid the union of factionalism were vain, Unity leaders decided to hold an extraordinary national caucus on March 12 to discuss what could be done about the critical situation in the UAW. All the union's important problems and shortcomings were taken up at length but the subject that seemed to dominate the session was the local elections that were being held. Results of a number of them were already available. They "reflected the deep resentment against the policy of the administration," the Unity letter commented after the caucus.

There is available a considerable collection of these election results which, on the whole, reveal a sharp shift from PG to Unity leadership in the locals.[31] This was remarkable considering that the elections were held in March 1938, barely seven months after the Milwaukee Convention, where the Martin-Frankensteen forces had ridden herd over Unity. The results indicated a significant change in the lineup of forces in the UAW that would eventually bring about a radical shake up in the union's top leadership. I titled the summary I prepared for Unity "A Pastor Losing His Flock."

Most revealing of the new trend were the PG's reversals in former strongholds. In Detroit, one of the biggest surprises was at Chevrolet Gear and Axle, where the thuggish John Ringwald was defeated. Other striking setbacks were dished out to two pro-Martin vice presidents. One, Walter Wells, was swept out of office at Detroit Gear; the other, a more important PG figure, R. J. Thomas, was beaten badly by Bill Marshall, the Unity incumbent, at Chrysler Local 7. Most startling of all was the PG defeat at Dodge, with thirty thousand employees Detroit's most important automobile manufacturing establishment after Ford, which shifted sides in electing a majority of Unity officers.[32]

On the national scale, the elections followed the same pattern with one outstanding exception—Flint. Unity remained in control at Bendix (Carl Shipley), Toledo Local 12 (Dick Gosser), Cleveland Fisher (Charles Beckman), and the Cleveland Auto Council (Dick Reisinger). In Saginaw, the group won in three locals out of four, as well as in Bay City, where Charles Madden and Bill Dowell were described as being "thrown out of the hall" for trying to sell the new GM agreement to the members.

Meanwhile, former PG bastions fell one after the other. Ed Hall's friend Bill Cody beat Frank Kiebler at Seaman Body in Milwaukee and board member Russell Merrill lost the seat at Studebaker that he had held since the union was founded. Frank Tucci, the Lovestonite board member from the East Coast, could not even get a second to his nomination at Tarrytown. Only on the West Coast did board member Irvan Carey hold his GM local in Los Angeles for PG until word of the new agreement arrived. At a special meeting, a Unity contact wrote to Mortimer, Local 216 adopted a resolution "in a rage," demanding a new convention "to get rid of Homer Martin and his gang."

The four locals won by the PG outside of Detroit (except for Pontiac, which Charles Madden held firmly for Martin) could have been in the Unity column but for untimely internecine quarrels that broke out in that group. At Kenosha, there was a disturbing additional factor, the refusal of the Socialist party to back John Russo, the Unity candidate for the presidency of the state UAW council, while running George Nordstrom on an independent third ticket. This allowed John Milkent, the PG contestant, to win easily. The Socialist party of Wisconsin was engaged in a conflict with some leading CIO officials (for example, Emil Costello, the state president), whom it identified as "communists."

A similar mutinous spirit had surfaced in Detroit with Emil Mazey, head of the important Briggs local. He had even nominated Martin for state president of Labor's Non-Partisan League (LNPL) and had backed one of Martin's most reactionary henchmen, a man by the name of Connibear, for another office. The motivation of Mazey's support for Martin was largely their concordance of views on the war question, in which Mazey, though not a socialist, had aligned with certain national leaders of the Socialist party who joined the Lovestonites in launching a peace movement. It was a plot that CPO representatives in the UAW used assiduously to split the SP and CP "sympathizers" in the Unity group.[33]

• • •

The difficulties that appeared in the Flint local elections were the most disturbing of all these Unity-splitting manifestations. Here it seems undeniable that Roy Reuther was to blame since he had decided to run for president of the big amalgamated local and refused to retire when widespread opposition to his candidacy began to be expressed. "It will be a vindication of Bob and Roy and all the work they did," his friends countered. The strongest objections came from the Buick members, who maintained that Reuther was too controversial a figure and proposed instead a leading rank-and-filer such as John McGill of Buick or Gib Rose of Chevrolet, both loyal Unity men who were very popular and capable.

The matter could not be settled by the local crowd, and as the date of the primaries approached, a small delegation of top Unity men—Mortimer, Hall, and Travis—came to Flint to try to effect a compromise accommodation. The discussion, some of which I managed to record, went on for hours. In particular, John McGill's arguments struck me as very much to the point though they were not very helpful in bringing about an understanding.

"What I am going to say," I jotted down as he began to speak, "I am going to say as an honest trade unionist even if I have to walk out of that door all by myself after I've said it." Then he turned directly to Roy Reuther: "A lot of people are just sick and tired of fighting about you. At every meeting of the Joint Council, some point or other comes up about you that ends in a wrangle that uses up all the time when we should be discussing more important business. I believe," he continued while turning to the others present, "that Roy Reuther as a real union man should drop into the background rather than continue to disturb things. I for one would refuse to be a member of any slate where his name stands at the top."

McGill's talk resulted in turmoil. Ed Hall and Mortimer tried to calm things down while seeking to remain impartial. But in the end they indicated that they favored Roy's candidacy. Bob Travis was of the same opinion but was more outspoken. "Things have come to a pretty pass," he said angrily, "when people who claim they are Unity come asking for our support yet they won't give anything in return."[34] The moment was tense. I was surprised at Travis's lack of tact. John McGill rose and put on his coat and a number of others did the same. The next day Buick held a caucus of their own and picked a third slate headed by McGill.

The results of the primaries, though disappointing, were not hopeless. None of the three presidential candidates got the required majority. Nevertheless, the split seemed to favor Unity in the runoffs, the votes being distributed as follows: Jack Little (PG), 2,322; Roy Reuther (Unity), 2,063; and John McGill, 1,068.[35] Because McGill would be automatically out of the finals, there was ample room for optimism. The McGill-Geiger group promised to throw its strength to the Unity candidates, but the results produced a shattering surprise.

The total of ballots soared from 5,500 to more than twice that number and their distribution was completely modified. Jack Little defeated Roy Reuther by the stunning count of 7,540 to 4,080, almost two to one. What could have happened? One thing seemed evident: the Buick group had not kept its word to back Reuther. Yet this would fall far short of accounting for the deficit in the ballots that he received.[36]

The split in Unity was the basic reason though it must have worked differently on different kinds of people. Nonpoliticals would have tended to believe the charge that Unity was dominated by a coalition of communists and socialists, thus verifying the effectiveness of Homer Martin's rantings. Most significant perhaps was the loss of confidence by nonattached voters in candidates engaged in an innergroup quarrel. Something must be wrong, they would think, if they could not agree among themselves. Whatever the case, the Flint elections were a deeply disquieting experience that should have been a warning to us, especially in view of subsequent events that closely involved the Unity cause.

A Split in Martin's Ranks

20

The first thing that did occur was extraordinarily favorable to Unity's fortunes: nothing less than Dick Frankensteen's break with Homer Martin and the Progressive Group and his switch to Unity. His decision was not received with satisfaction by all of our people, however, though most came around to it eventually. There were some important exceptions, nonetheless, whose recalcitrance put a new stamp on the UAW's subsequent history.

Though the chief inspiration for Frankensteen's move was the adverse results of the March local elections, that was not the only factor involved. A growing rift with Martin had become evident for some time due to Martin's outrageous handling of the union's affairs and his increasing attachment to the henchmen of Jay Lovestone on the International's staff.

Frankensteen continued to air his idea of "outlawing factionalism," talking about it to anyone who would lend an ear. He even gave DeWitt Gilpin, a writer for the *Daily Worker,* an exclusive interview on the subject, which was accompanied by a photograph.[1] According to Frankensteen, Gilpin had told him that the pope had recently advised French Catholics to accept the communists' "outstretched hand" and though he was not a Catholic, it struck him as a plausible excuse for accepting the anomalous publicity for his program and himself.

Everyone in the UAW seemed to be looking for unconventional allies. Even Homer Martin stretched a hand out to several Unity leaders before the January 1938 board session. The idea had come to him from George Addes, who had decided to talk to him about what he considered a dangerous plan that Fred Pieper planned to bring before the board. With the goal of gaining extended powers for his "finance committee," Pieper proposed to cut into the duties of the president, the secretary-treasurer, and the other officers and to set his committee up as a superpower over the UAW by controlling its finances.

Pieper's excuse was the catastrophic pitch in the union's exchequer over the past six months, when it had slumped from more than $400,000 to $100,000. Everyone acknowledged the grim necessity of cutting the budget but Martin felt personally threatened by Pieper's auditing, which showed that Martin's expenses ran to $80 a day in addition to salary. His pack of menials and his bodyguard also cost the union several more thousands a month. The new International headquarters at the Griswold Building and its elegant furnishings, particularly in Martin's huge office, which had required an outlay of $18,000, were, on the other hand, safe from Pieper's threatening shears. His social outlook upheld that kind of expenditure as proper and even indispensable; the UAW president's office must be as elaborate, he argued, as that of any corporation head.

Nonetheless, Martin appeared to sense dangers in the plans of the bustling Pieper, toward whom he always acted with such deference that it began to be whispered that Pieper "had something on him." Martin's reply to Addes was to ask him to arrange a secret meeting between themselves and the other Unity officers. It happened that only Addes and Ed Hall could come and the two men were stunned by Martin's geniality. He began by saying that he had agreed to a request of Mortimer's about giving a donation to Tom Mooney and was authorizing an immediate cash gift of $5,000.

It was a shrewd way to begin the talk, but it was not necessary to win Addes and Hall's support to the list of resolutions that Martin had prepared to set before the board, which he read: (1) Get rid of the Pieper committee; (2) send Pieper back south; (3) lay off organizers on the basis of seniority plus accomplishment; (4) remove Dick Frankensteen as assistant president; and (5) remove him as head of the Ford drive.

Hall and Addes were particularly taken with the first three points but they were not too displeased with the last two either. From their partisan view, they were still inclined to welcome any opposition to Frankensteen. They were aware that he seemed to be changing but they mistrusted the sincerity of the ambitious man.

Even Mortimer was behindhand in appreciating the significance of Frankensteen's break with Martin. He told me, his eyes squinted with mischief, of a conversation that he had had with Martin's Lovestonite administrative assistant Francis Henson, who had "felt him out" by telling him that Martin was afraid of the bloc that Dick Frankensteen was forming with the Communist party. Mortimer asked: "Why would the Communist Party do that? Frankensteen is far worse than Martin. After all, Homer is just a nut but Dick is a fascist!"[2] Mortimer said that Henson was delighted. He seemed totally unaware of the effect that such talk might have on re-mending Frankensteen's rift with Martin.

Yet there was no real danger that such an event would take place since the politically oriented Frankensteen realized that the union was headed for catastrophe under Martin's leadership. The local elections of March had convinced him that a radical change was in order. This can be gathered from the letter that he sent to all the general officers and executive board members on April 21.[3] It was an updated, fully developed version of his original conception of "outlawing factionalism" and it was so well written as to win the accolade of "astute" from George Miles, Lovestone's sharpwitted ambassador to Homer Martin's court. Frankensteen's letter covered the entire range of economic, political, and organizational objectives of the union.

All caucuses must be "abandoned immediately" under pain of disciplinary action, he began. Then the letter went on to the program itself: active support of the policies of the CIO; organization of the unorganized, in particular in the competitive shops, at Ford, in aviation, and of the unemployed; maintenance of wages, hours, and working conditions, especially a determined opposition to wage cuts;[4] opposition to wildcat strikes; support to the Wage and Hour Bill and Roosevelt's Appropriation Bill for the Unemployed; full backing for the reelection of Governor Murphy and building Labor's Non-Partisan League; autonomy of the local unions; and democratic procedure.

The official reply to Frankensteen's memorandum came in the form of a slashing attack in the *United Automobile Worker* of April 30. Without mentioning his name, the news story described it as a "desperate attempt of the chronic factionalists . . . to wage war in the name of peace." They were called "Machiavellian politicians" and "wolves who bleat like sheep." Martin himself was quoted as charging that his enemies were applying a "'trojan horse' tactic in seeking to enter the rear door as a faction to end factionalism." His statement contained a veiled threat that we all missed at the time: "when opposition . . . degenerates into opposition for its own sake, no union can tolerate [its] continuance and must take such measures as are necessary to preserve the organization and maintain its integrity."

Meanwhile, Martin's Lovestonite advisors drafted a counterprogram for him to present to the international executive board for its approval. Except that it lacked Frankensteen's prescript for outlawing caucuses, it was not essentially different from the latter's memorandum. It was, however, more neatly packaged into "twenty points" and as such would serve Homer Martin as a banner that would mask the draconic acts he would undertake against his opponents in the following weeks.[5]

• • •

It all started deceptively enough on June 5 with Martin calling the executive board into special session "to consider and ratify a contract [for a group insurance plan] which has been negotiated in accordance with the instructions of the executive board." It was explained in his letter that this task could be completed expeditiously and that the board members would be able to return to their districts by June 9 since the insurance plan was the only subject to be considered. There was something about the insurance plan, a concoction of the devious Fred Pieper, that troubled a number of the board members.[6] Why the big rush? they asked themselves suspiciously. When they were assembled on June 8, a motion was presented that the agenda of the meeting be expanded so that corollary subjects, including the status of Pieper's finance committee, could be discussed.

Martin was sharply opposed to the extension. But when the vote was taken, the motion to add to the agenda was surprisingly adopted. It was Martin's first defeat by the board since he had taken office in April 1936 and he was shaken. He abandoned the session, accompanied by a majority of his associates and never returned to it. The *Detroit News* of June 10 gave the vote as eleven to eight, with five members absent. It named Walter Reuther, who was home after a tonsillectomy, as one of the latter.

Walter Reuther released a statement from his sick bed on the same day that cast doubt on how his own vote might have gone. "I am entirely unacquainted with the details of a reported controversy in the UAW," he stated. "If the rumored 'putsch' [Martin's word] had any foundation it will be fought bitterly by every honest UAW member." He seemed thus to be taking Martin's part in the dispute, referring approvingly likewise in his statement to the board's recent endorsement of Martin's twenty-point plan "to eliminate factionalism and lay a basis for a healthy union program."[7]

Nevertheless, the board went on with its augmented business program. A committee was set up to prepare the additional agenda that night and the following morning several resolutions were presented that the remaining members adopted.[8] The chief of these dealt with the insurance plan itself. Because of the importance of the subject for the UAW membership, it stated, the matter should be given careful and thorough study. It was recommended that the plan should be referred to the CIO, whose ideas would be pooled with the UAW's into a resolution that would be submitted to the next International convention.

Martin accused "the opposition" of "staging a coup." In a press statement on June 10, 1938, he repeated almost the exact words of the board's resolution, however, maintaining that "the proposed group insurance plan . . . is a matter of fundamental importance to the entire CIO," and hence that "we think it better to go over the matter in close collaboration with the CIO leaders in Washington." Therefore, he announced, as though it was his original intention, that the executive board meeting that he "adjourned yesterday" would reconvene on June 11 at the United Mine Workers headquarters in Washington.

The board's new majority, with Dick Frankensteen as their spokesman, had refused to recognize Martin's adjournment, insisting that no one had the right to take that action except themselves once they were in session, but they were nonetheless all at the new meeting place on the specified day.[9] No one could quite understand why Martin had chosen this particular venue for his controversy with the board. It was as though he were designating Lewis as the arbitrator.

It was soon apparent, however, that Martin had no intention of making peace with his opponents. Taking the offensive immediately in Lewis's presence, he delivered a long and bitter assault on the five general officers (excluding only R. J. Thomas), charging them with having mounted a revolt against him in disregard of his twenty-point program of harmony that the board had endorsed unanimously. Therefore, he had decided to suspend the five officers and to put them on trial before the executive board (over which he would have regained majority control by the suspensions).

John L. Lewis was described as arguing strenuously against this decision and declaring "that in his opinion no evidence had been submitted that showed a violation of the 20-point program or any good union principle and that the only differences were minor administrative ones which could easily be adjusted."[10] But his counsel was not heeded and two days later Homer Martin publicly announced the suspension of the five men.

They reacted swiftly, their first concern being to protect the union's treasury. Secretary-Treasurer George Addes, by decision of "the five," contacted the banks where the International had accounts, reminding them that all checks had to carry his signature as well as Martin's. On that same day, June 14, the five officers were summarily expelled from International headquarters, being allowed to take only their personal belongings with them. They were hardly in a position to challenge these orders since Martin had installed what the *Detroit News* of June 15 called "strong-armed squads" or "goons" at the Griswold Building.

It was from his home that Addes had to carry out, on June 16, the next step that "the five" had decided upon. They would ask the locals to halt their payment of per-capita tax to headquarters and to mail their checks to Addes's home. Some days later he explained to local financial officers that this step had been taken with the understanding of the union's bonding company and that the checks were being held in safe keeping. By July 15, he was able to report that the checks received up to that date totaled $12,000. Many other locals decided to withhold their per capita altogether.

On June 18, the five officers expanded their counteraction by calling on the locals to adopt two resolutions, one protesting their suspensions and requesting their reinstatement, the other demanding a special convention if the corrective acts were not taken by July 1.[11] And on June 21, the officers sent a general letter of elucidation of the crisis to the locals, which started with the ringing words: "Our union is in danger! Our great union, which we have fought for and built, which has brought industrial freedom, security and other great improvements into our working lives, has been placed in jeopardy by the recent action of President Martin and those associated with him on the international executive board."

The letter then went on to detail the circumstances that led to this crisis. "Can President Martin actually think," it asked, "[that] it is unconstitutional for a majority of the board to vote against him? . . . But once [his] majority was endangered, he was apparently ready to go to any extremes to retain his autocratic control. Already he has suspended five members of the 24-man board. He has threatened six others with suspension. . . . The duty of all of us is clear and inescapable. We must fight for the reestablishment of democracy in our union."

The response to this appeal, which was supplemented by the officers' direct contacts through letters, telephone calls, or personal visits, was fast and abundant. Aside from the two major resolutions, which largely predominated, other proposals were offered, most frequently a call for the intervention of John L. Lewis, who was asked, for example, to take charge of the trials of the accused men. The per-capita strike was at times supplemented by a measure regarding a local's own bank deposits in order to protect them from possible seizure by Martin, by having them placed in the custody of several elected members. A few locals refused to reach a decision until they had heard spokesmen from the two sides. The Studebaker group asked that every local be allowed to have a witness at the trial to report back to his people since the executive board could not be trusted to "render an impartial verdict."

An estimate was made at the time of the comparative strength of the pro and con reactions to the officers' campaign. It was taken by someone at a large meeting of the executive boards of the Detroit locals that was held on July 22, a few days before the trials began.[12] Most of the bigger Detroit locals are listed as having voted for the officers. This included the West Side Local, Hudson, Plymouth, Chrysler, Murray Body, the two tool-and-die unions, and others. Those voting against included only three important groups: Chevy Gear and Axle, Packard, and, surprisingly, Dodge, Frankensteen's local. In the last case, however, several big departments had taken favorable positions and a meeting of three thousand that was held shortly thereafter overwhelmingly endorsed the officers after a debate between Frankensteen and Frank Reid, the PG president. I calculated the comparative strength of the two sides at the July 22 meeting of the Detroit executive boards. The ratio backing our side was overwhelming: 145,000 to 30,000.

Unfortunately, these rough figures failed to distinguish a third persuasion that was by no means negligible. It was led by Walter Reuther and his associates, who differed quite widely among themselves, however, regarding the course of action to be taken in behalf of the officers.[13] Reuther projected a more cautious policy—that of paying the per-capita tax to Martin "under strong protest," as his local had done and of taking no steps regarding a special convention until all other efforts to reestablish peace had been exhausted. In any case, he insisted on permitting the trial to proceed, which was ambiguous since it seemed to assume that the officers could have been "guilty." Emil Mazey, on the other hand, was opposed to extending any help at all to the embattled officers. "A plague on both your houses" was the burden of his thinking, which was expressed even more extravagantly by some other Reutherites as "Throw the two sides out!"[14]

• • •

The trials of the officers were unexpectedly divided into two parts, George Addes's starting three weeks ahead of the others. The reason for this was apparent since his authority over the union's finances had to be nullified. On July 7, at 3 P.M., he was presented with the charges and told that he would have to take the stand the following morning at 11.[15]

When he appeared before the "court," he asked immediately for an extension to prepare his case. It was refused. He then asked for a court stenographer "so that an accurate record of the trial could be taken." This was likewise refused, as was his request for a copy of the trial's proceedings. Martin's executive board had already posted the rules that would govern the trial, one of which denied the right of an individual board member to interrogate a witness directly, requiring instead that his question must be submitted in writing to the general counsel of the International (a Martin appointee), who, "if agreeable," would pose it for him.

After allowing this farce to go on for half an hour or so, Addes announced that Martin and his board "majority" could not be considered an impartial jury since they had prejudged his guilt by approving his suspension. "I consequently ask that the CIO be allowed to name an impartial trial committee." When this request was turned down, Addes withdrew from the hearing.

Six of the board members followed him soon after. The thirteen remaining members promptly declared him guilty and stripped him of his office. Then, in an unbelievably vindictive act that was in violation of the UAW constitution, they deprived him of his membership in the union, which he had held since the summer of 1933.[16]

In retrospect, I find these proceedings hard to credit. One would expect that there would have been some sharp challenges by Maurice Sugar, the well-known labor attorney who represented the officers in this entire affair.

I myself was closely associated with them during this period though I was not admitted to any of the trials. I believe that the other officers were not permitted to assist at Addes's hearing either. The explanation of this amazing situation was that Martin's executive board did not trouble itself about legalistic irregularities. It was evident that Addes was not allowed to have legal counsel or he would surely have mentioned his friend Sugar's presence at the trial in the account that he gave of it in his radio talk over WJR on July 21.[17]

Maurice Sugar was very much present, however, at the trial of the other officers that began three weeks later, as well as in the preparatory work that had to be done for it. His hand is obvious, for example, in the alterations of the seventeen rules for the conduct of the Addes case that were originally prepared by Martin's general counsel, Larry Davidow, who had changed them now to correct several gross deficiencies that Addes had pointed out during his trial. Thus the rules were amended to allow the officers to have their own counsel, who would be permitted moreover to cross-examine opposing witnesses, and to provide for a court reporter.

The accusations against the officers were summarized in a letter that Homer Martin sent them on June 29, 1938, listing nine charges, the first of which contained a compendious statement of his complaints: "That you have, with others, conspired by carrying on divers acts, over a period of time, for the purpose of personal and factional gain, to disrupt . . . the International Union, to interfere with its proper functions and to bring about a state of chaos within the membership." In support, Martin listed a few overt acts that were supposed to illustrate the charges.[18]

The officers replied that these fantastic accusations were "so vague, so general and indefinite as to make impossible the preparation . . . of a proper and adequate defense." Hence they demanded a "particularized statement": When, where, how, and by whom was each dastardly act engaged in? When, where, how, and by whom were the alleged dangerous public statements made? What exactly constituted the "disruptive activities" with which they were charged? In what way did they "divert sums of money from the International Union?"

This voluminous requisition must have given Martin and his board members pause since the board replied by instructing the UAW's prosecutor, Larry Davidow, to furnish the officers with the "supplemental bill of particulars." They tried to put an aggressive front on their concession with a demand of their own for a "verified answer" by the officers to the charges. The answer was to include "all affidavits and exhibits in support of their pleadings." The officers snapped back on the next day that the requirement was illegal: "It requires the defendants to disclose their evidence before having been confronted with the evidence of the prosecution. It recognizes affidavits as evidence. It is obviously intended to permit of a prosecution without the prosecutor being obliged to produce witnesses against the defendants. It permits ex parte action."

The defense then offered a single accusation against the accusers, turning back their attack against themselves and rebutting the charge of "conspiracy" that had been imputed to the five officers by declaring that "such conspiracy as existed was a conspiracy between President Homer Martin and an irresponsible, disruptive political adventurer and intermeddler of New York; that in this conspiracy were a number of persons in prominent positions in our union, all of these positions having been [procured] through the direct appointment or influence of Homer Martin; that with rare exceptions such appointees . . . are not auto workers. And that it was . . . this conspiracy which the union has been . . . encountering [and] which we have been attempting to eliminate from our union."

The reference was, of course, to Jay Lovestone and his corps of followers in the UAW, whom union activists had been aware of for some time. What was new was that voluminous documentary proof of the collusion between Homer Martin and this group had become available only days before the trials began. The last sentence of the previous quotation gives the impression that this evidence had been in the hands of the officers for a considerable length of time during which they had been "attempting to eliminate" the conspiracy from the union. This was a deliberate misstatement made for forensic effect.

• • •

Maurice Sugar would eventually reveal how the "Lovestone correspondence" was put into his hands, brought to his office and turned over to his receptionist by an unknown person who left immediately.[19] He told about this in a letter that he wrote years later to Wyndham Mortimer. "I don't know the exact date," Sugar said, "but it must have been in August, 1938, shortly after the 'trial' of the five, as you will note from the enclosed." He added at the end of his letter, "I think, Mort, you will find practically all the answers you want . . . right where I found them, that is, in the bulletin issued by you, Frankensteen, Hall and Addes in August 1938. I am enclosing this bulletin."[20]

The bulletin was prepared by me, as Mortimer narrates in his book. Actually, Sugar was in part responsible for my assignment. He telephoned me one morning at the apartment that we were subletting from Avrahm and Marie Mezerick and asked if he could come over. He was carrying a well-filled briefcase when he arrived and his first words, spoken at the door with his typical mysterious smile, were: "What would you say if I told you that I have here in this briefcase some letters that will spell the end of Homer Martin in the UAW?"

I shrugged noncommittally since I was accustomed to Sugar's dramatic manner. "I probably would say, 'You must be dreaming.'"

He took his pipe out of his mouth. "Well, it's a fact, as you yourself will be convinced when you've looked them over."

Before showing the letters to me, he gave me a short summary of their contents. "What I want you to do is stand by while these letters are being photostated. We'll have two copies made and you'll be able to work with one of them to write a brochure. I'll make good use of the other. But first I'm going to put the originals away in a safe place."

He had already arranged for the printer and there was a two-man "guard" standing outside while the photostats were being worked on. I started reading them as they came off the flat-press and was swiftly seized by an emotion of mixed incredulity and apprehension. I kept looking outside to make sure of the guards. I told the printer that I wanted him to conceal the originals as soon as he was done with each batch.

It was a huge relief when, several hours later, Sugar returned to drive me home with a great bulging envelope clutched under my jacket. With his own copy he prepared, as I would learn soon after, the brief that would serve as the major defense of the five officers. As for my own use of the letters, after reading and re-reading them I was convinced that the proper medium for telling the UAW members their overwhelming story would be a newspaper rather than a brochure. The officers agreed and decided to send bundles to every local in the country.

I sketched out an eight-page tabloid as though I were at my old job of putting out the *United Automobile Worker.* All that would be missing was the masthead, instead of which I would set a triple-banked banner: "AN APPEAL TO THE MEMBERS OF THE UAW!" It was my intention to go beyond the revelations of the Lovestone letters and give members some facts about their union that their supposed International journal had been hiding from them. One article would tell of the fake crisis that Martin had created at the June executive board meeting and that had served as his excuse to suspend the officers. Another would expose the reeking details of Fred Pieper's plot with the convicted crook Frank Cohen to put over a fraudulent insurance plan on UAW members. In still another I would tell of the surge of support that was accumulating on behalf of the officers, support that by that date counted locals with a membership of two hundred thousand.

The Martin-Lovestone conspiracy would not be neglected to be sure though the tabloid could not match the enormous detail that Maurice Sugar used in his defense brief. The singular importance of the tabloid was that it was the only medium that would carry the story to the members. I presented the principals in the plot by posting their portraits in the center of page one with a heading that asked "WHO IS PRESIDENT OF THE U.A.W.A?" to which the subheads replied, "He Pulls the Strings" (over Lovestone's photograph), and "He Makes the Moves" (over Martin's).

An accompanying piece scouted Martin's denial of the authenticity of the letters by quoting the telegram that Maurice Sugar had received from Lovestone's New York lawyers demanding the return of "certain documents . . . which were stolen from his apartment . . . which have been incorporated by you in affidavits before the executive board of the United Automobile Workers Union and which have been released by you, according to press statements to newspapers. . . . [Signed] Davidson and Mann, 122 East 42nd Street, New York City."

Among the sample letters that Sugar released to the press, the tabloid reproduced in full what was unquestionably the prize of them all. It was from Homer Martin to Jay Lovestone and bore the delectable salutation, "Dear Jay," which was to become a password among UAW wags. It was initialed at the lower left "HM:VF" ("Homer Martin by Vivian Fox," his private secretary) and on the right below it bore his signature, which locals were asked to compare with those appearing on letters that they might have received from Martin.

The letter was dated March 27, 1937, revealing that the Martin-Lovestone intimacy had been in full bloom eighteen months earlier. It was concerned with a snag that had arisen in their shared domination of the auto union. Involved was a man named Irving Brown, a member of the national executive committee of Lovestone's party, whom Martin had appointed to the important post of the UAW regional director in Baltimore. The international executive board, however, had decided to remove him, the reason given being that he was not an auto worker. Accordingly, Martin wrote "Dear Jay" reassuringly that Irving Brown would be kept on nevertheless. "I am determined that we shall not lose him. As you may well realize, this was a maneuver by certain parties to keep *our boys* [emphasis added] out of the International Union and out of strategic positions where they could mould the organization along proper lines."

The letter was matched by another that illustrated the amazing reach of influence that the Lovestone clique exerted within the top UAW administration. Homer Martin had been asked to join other trade union leaders in signing a petition to President Roosevelt to call upon him to lift the embargo on arms to anti-Franco Loyalists in Spain. It was an estimable initiative, but George Miles, Lovestone's ambassador to the UAW, feared that it might cause "numerous protests" to pour in. "Now do you think Homer should sign?" he asked his chief and repeated the question in bigger letters at the bottom of the letter: "Wire reply—Yes or No."

The trial of the officers did not begin until July 25 and there was just enough time for me to get two columns about it into the paper.[21] I was particularly pleased to tell about the big delegation of local presidents from Detroit, Toledo, Cleveland, and other centers; they had appeared, demanding the right to sit in on the sessions. They had been enraged by the report of the farcical manner in which George Addes's case had been conducted and wanted to prevent a repetition. They waited all day but Martin refused to see them and finally ordered them out of the building, reviling them as "communists and disrupters." When they refused to leave, Fred Pieper called in some of Martin's guards from the hall and fisticuffs followed. The irate men issued a statement that I ran in the tabloid: "Since the Martin majority on the board is afraid to conduct the trials of the suspended vice-presidents in the open before the elected representatives of the UAW local unions, it is plain that a frameup is being schemed by Martin and his ring. The verdict is cut and dried. We denounce this travesty of justice and democracy and call on all UAW members to continue the struggle for fair dealing and the rights of the individual members against the power-mad Martin dictatorship."

The atmosphere of the trial was tense. Once, when Sugar declared that Martin had called Pieper a stool pigeon in Pieper's own presence, board members of the two sides rose as though ready for battle, yelling and brandishing their fists. Such reports from the inside of the trial are rare. Martin published a record of the proceedings, but so much was expurgated from it that the account is almost worthless concerning what actually took place.[22] Its 115 pages consisted overwhelmingly of affidavits, exhibits, newspaper articles, executive board resolutions, letters, and only two live items pertaining to the trial itself: Davidow's opening statement and the testimony of the single witness that Davidow called, F. J. Michel, the board member from Wisconsin.

There is not one word in it from the officers' side, not even the opening statement by Maurice Sugar. When he tried to break in to make that statement, his mere "interruption" was obliterated from the printed booklet. Those few words were recorded originally in a press statement that I possess, however.[23] Also expunged was another angry "interruption" to Davidow's charge that Vice-President Walter Wells and George Addes had on one occasion tried to force the members of the Norge local at Muskegon "to adopt an agreement which proposed to accept a ten percent cut in wages." Quoting from my notes:

Mr. Addes [interrupting]: You're a God damned liar.[24]
Mr. Davidow: We propose to show. . . .
Mr. Morris Field: Just a moment there, Brother Chairman. I wish the
reporter to be sure to write down the statement of Brother Addes, call-
ing our counsel a God damned liar, put it down just like that.
Mr. Addes: I want it recorded like that.

Despite the official record's silence, Maurice Sugar did manage to get
some licks in when cross-examining Davidow's one and only witness.
Board Member Michel had, for example, testified that the plot of the officers to take over the union was masterminded by the communists. Sugar
asked him what a communist was. A disrupter and a stool pigeon, Michel
replied.

"Is Dick Frankensteen either of those?"
"No."
"So he isn't a communist?"
"No."

"So we'll need a third category for these officers," Sugar commented,
since Michel had testified that other officers were either "known communists" or "reputed communists."

He also cross-examined Michel at some length about the Unity letters
that we had put out in March of that year. Davidow in his bill of particulars
had described them as "poison pen letters," which he invited Michel to identify as an "effort to establish a dual organization" and their request for small
donations from Unity adherents to defray the expense of the letters as "col-
lecting regular dues."[25] Michel obligingly complied with these suggestions.
But when Sugar read the letters to him sentence by sentence, he could not
point to much that was wrong with them and Sugar even got him to admit
the truth of some things that were said.

After several days of stalling, Martin suddenly suspended the trial and
announced that when it would reopen in a week no further witnesses would
be called. "The trial thereafter would be conducted merely on the basis of
affidavits," he declared. The purpose was evident, Sugar observed caustically. "You cannot cross-examine an affidavit." The defense was required
to answer the so-called "proofs" that the prosecution had prepared in printed form before the trial reopened. It was given until Wednesday, August 2,
to do so. But the printed manual did not arrive from the International's office until Thursday, August 3.

Nevertheless, the defense's answer was handed in on August 2 at the
specified time, 4 P.M. Sugar had not needed the manual to prepare it since
the officers had agreed that they would disregard the lies and insults that it

would contain and confine their reply to an exposé of the Martin-Lovestone "conspiracy" that Sugar would assemble from the captured correspondence. There is a copy of this brief among my private papers. It consists of fifty-four typed sheets and four photographs that Sugar had selected, with his comments, and is presented over the officers' signatures. A few of these pages together with the four photos were prepared as a press release and a larger selection of the "evidence" had, of course, been presented in the eight-page tabloid that I had put out.

I reported in that paper how the trial ended: "Martin's kangaroo court went through its paces. Vice-Presidents Ed Hall, Dick Frankensteen and Wyndham Mortimer were removed from their posts and expelled from the union." And I added how, in a tricky gesture meant to underscore the magnitude of the others' guilt, Walter Wells was let off with a three-month suspension. But Wells reacted with anger to this dubious distinction: "I shall never give up the fight for an honest, democratic and decent union."

• • •

Wells's declaration of loyalty was appreciated but the other officers realized that nothing but a joint struggle could win their reinstatement.[26] Locals' activities that had been initiated after the officers' suspensions had to be intensified. Their appeals to John L. Lewis and the other CIO leaders must be pursued. The central location for planning became Ed Hall's apartment, which was well located, in the center of town, and had a big living space unencumbered by an excess of furniture. Ed's wife established an atmosphere of effortless hospitality by simply disregarding what was going on, not serving drinks or anything else, and allowing visitors to shift for themselves. When Hall got hungry and his wife was out he made no bones about boiling a half-pound of potatoes for himself, mashing them with a wad of butter, and eating them without letting it interfere with business.

I became a constant habitué at the apartment for the rest of the summer. I arrived after eating my own lunch at our apartment, which was within walking distance. Without thinking about it, I assumed the job of coordinator of assignments, mainly because of my innate orderliness, which had benefited from my experience during the Flint sitdown. I had developed the practice there of jotting down all important things that needed doing on individual slips of paper, which I then tore up when the tasks were carried out.

The major task of the officers was to speak to the locals. Two of them would often attend the important meetings. Though it was summer and fewer regular meetings were scheduled, many special get-togethers were called during the crisis. In addition, the officers had their own contacts and a number of the arrangements were made through them. After a month or so of hectic activity, however, their dedication flagged. Only Frankensteen and

Mortimer kept up their drive. Frankensteen loved speaking to groups, big or small. For Mortimer, it was part of the job that had to be done. More important to him though, I believe, were the countless letters that he typed to people all over the country. Still, when he had to make a speech it was always concise and to the point, however undramatic.

Frankensteen, on the contrary, was a dynamic speaker. He was a would-be actor who made up that way for the career he had missed by getting involved in the labor movement. Ed Hall was also an effective platform performer, which was not the case with George Addes, who despite his intense sincerity seldom inflamed his auditors. He preferred doing radio talks, perhaps since he could give them "in private." The locals donated funds for these talks by the officers.[27] I wrote most of the broadcasts and accompanied the officers to the studio, which I considered to be an important adjunct of the job.

I have often been asked how Dorothy and I lived during this period. The officers could not pay me since they were not paid themselves. Besides, I do not think that it ever occurred to them that I expected to be paid. There is a letter in my files from Hall to Mortimer, who had reminded Hall of some expenses I had incurred on his account. Ed referred drolly to "our sensitive friend" and promised to take care of the matter. No doubt the fact that I had worked for the UAW had given these men the habit of depending upon me to do things for them.

I had learned early in life the truth of Polonius's apothegm. But Shakespeare's foolish old man had not gone on to explain about the subconscious link between asking favors and loss of memory. Maurice Sugar had intimated to me several times that the officers had agreed to deduct a small percentage from their accumulated back pay when they were reinstated to be divided between us on a two-to-one basis. They must have changed their minds when their big checks came or perhaps they had simply forgotten about their promise.[28]

In fact, it would have made no difference to us under the circumstances.[29] Dorothy and I had agreed that we would see this terrible crisis through to the end, come what may. Our union, on which we had labored as though it were a personal creation, was at stake. We had no other choice. Fortunately Dorothy had a WPA job and it was enough to keep us going while I continued doing what we both considered an indispensable task.

There were times when this self-imposed duty took on a curious character. At one low point during that sweltering summer, a couple of the officers grew despondent and began sloughing off their responsibilities. Only Mortimer and Frankensteen remained faithful to their assignments. It may have been partly out of appreciation for this that Dorothy and I became more intimate with Frankensteen and his wife, Mickey. We went to movies together and once took a trip to Frankenmuth, where Frankensteen treated us to the famous chicken dinner—"all you can eat for a dollar." We were astonished to see him gobble two whole birds, which he did without the least self-consciousness and disregarding every rule of etiquette, encouraged by the adoring looks of his wife. Their taste in movies, however, was more difficult to share. Once we attended a gooey musical with Jeannette McDonald and Nelson Eddy and were dismayed when, after the first screening, Frankensteen begged us to stay on for a repeat performance.

The other officers had, meanwhile, taken to fishing. They went out late at night and slept most of the following day. Disgusted, I decided to go with them and try to bring them to their senses. We had two boats with outboard motors. In addition to Hall and Addes, several others were along, including Leo LaMotte, president of the Plymouth local. We were on Lake St. Clair, which is a big piece of water, and all I remember is our constant efforts to keep out of the path of the huge freighters or their wash. There was no fishing that night.

After a while most of the men curled up on the boat bottoms and went to sleep. I stayed awake, of course, lest one of the steamers came our way. Toward dawn we decided to go back in but the motor on our boat would not start and Addes and Hall took turns rowing. There was an all-night diner in a house off the bank and we went there for breakfast. We were all ravenous but no one was quite as hungry as Hall, who ordered "a dozen scrambled eggs and a load of rashers." When the Greek waiter brought in the food in two trips, Hall's plate was missing. "How about my order?" he growled.

The man raised his thick black brows and stared at him. "I thought you was fooling!" he said after a long pause.

Hall stomped out and waited for us in the car. Somehow there were no more fishing trips after that. So, in a way, I seemed to have accomplished my purpose after all.

•   •   •

A great number of people came by Ed Hall's apartment during those days—board members, local leaders, and rank-and-filers. But Walter Reuther and his group were noticeable by their absence. A great coolness in their relations with the old Unity crowd had set in. Actually, the rift had started quite some time back during the officers' suspensions or even earlier. It was Dick Frankensteen's break with Homer Martin and the circumstances that surrounded that action that started the coolness though the Lovestonites had some success also in making inroads among the "socialists," particularly on the peace issue. There was an open fight, for example, at a meeting of the Joint Council of the West Side Local on the question of sending delegates to the Washington Anti-War Congress which was fostered by Martin (guided by Lovestone) and the national Socialist party. The Reuther group at Local 174 won out but they had to join with pro-Martinites like Stuart Strachan and John W. ("Little John") Anderson, president of the Fleetwood unit, to do so.

Dick Frankensteen was too gregarious to remain a loner. He had assimilated so thoroughly with Unity that it seemed that he had always been with us. To the Reutherites this was sheer opportunism based on Martin's decline and inevitable replacement. But Reuther's friends were far from thinking that Frankensteen would be an improvement. In fact, when they looked over the field they saw none of the old officers as an inspiring candidate. They never mentioned aloud the idea that Walter Reuther would be exactly that but the thought was in their minds.

I have recorded several indications along these lines in my notes, one of which surfaced at what I incorrectly termed a "socialist caucus." People attended from Flint, Saginaw, Pontiac, and Detroit, about sixty-five in all, I was told. Flint was particularly well represented and I was surprised by some of delegates who were there, for example Jay Green of Fisher One, Irene Mitchell, and especially Terrell Thompson, who would soon be elected the first president of the Chevrolet local after the split-up of Local 156. Thompson and I had recently become quite friendly, at his initiative. It was he, in fact, who wrote me about this caucus. It is in one of a series of letters in his careful hand that I still have. I cannot account today for his having contacted me originally unless it was because my name and address had been mentioned in one of the Unity letters as a mail-drop.

Among the Detroit people cited as being at the caucus were Walter Reuther, George Edwards, Bill Marshall, Emil Mazey, Ed Hertz, and, surprisingly, Leo LaMotte, who was close to our group but somehow got invited to this meeting. Terrell Thompson described the purpose of the gathering as a discussion of what to do about the officers' expulsions. The idea of peace at all costs came up strongly. Thompson himself asked, "What if peace fails?" But George Edwards, who was in the chair, shrugged it off. "What I mean," Thompson came back, "is what if Martin follows up, as he's threatened to do, by suspending the six Unity executive board members?"

Edwards suddenly came to life. "Then we'll fight like hell!" What he meant, it was clear, was that they should fight for Reuther if for nobody else.

Bill Marshall, president of Chrysler Local 7, gave this preference a sweeping extension: "I say, let's clean them all out and put a new bunch in with Reuther or Tracy Doll as president." And, more amazing still, he proposed a motion, which was adopted, that they start gathering signatures of support and that a committee of five be set up to prepare and circulate the petitions.[30]

Another example of this campaigning was provided by Roy Reuther, who gave it an unpleasant slant. Someone had invited him to Cleveland to talk to the CIO Council about the suspensions. Many people there were shocked that he came to Mortimer's hometown and made the callous remarks that he did, such as: "There must be peace in the organization even if some individuals have to lose their jobs." And he did not shirk at naming Mortimer and Frankensteen as being chiefly responsible for the union's emergency though my notes do not indicate that he touted his brother as the one who could pull it out of the flames.

Walter Reuther's availability for high office came into the open at the Michigan State CIO convention, where the split in Unity became painfully evident. I missed this meeting since I was in New Jersey on a job for Bob Travis but I received detailed reports from Dorothy and Ed Hall.[31] Their accounts made the campaigns for state offices sound like a comedy of errors made up of plots and counterplots, broken promises, and other alleged skulduggery.

Hall described how the whole thing got started at a small meeting at Walter Reuther's home on the evening before the weekend convention opened. Present there were Hall, Reuther, Mazey, Marshall, LaMotte, and Lloyd Jones, the last apparently being the one who proposed Reuther for the state presidency. Hall said that he agreed to go along until the next morning, when he overheard Ben Fischer, a national officer of the Socialist party, say that the post would be a "stepping-stone" for Walter to the UAW presidency.[32] That made Hall boil. If that was the case, he told himself, then he'd see to it that Reuther got neither post and decided to back Adolph Germer for the state's chief executive.

He made a couple of telephone calls and then broke the bad news to Reuther that Germer was a candidate for the presidency. Reuther said that he would not run against Germer if he was sure that he wanted the job. "Okay," Hall agreed, "let's get up a committee and ask him." The two of them, plus Marshall, Jones, and John Anderson went to see Germer, who told them "confidentially" that he had received instructions "from Washington" that in order to avoid factionalism in the State CIO he was to "allow" his name to be put up as a candidate. Reuther must have done a double-take since that was the Communist party's line. But he raised no objection and stepped out of the race.

However, the trouble erupted with the choice of the secretary treasurer. "I didn't want Walter there either," Hall explained, "so I decided to nominate Vic Reuther for the job." This split Unity right down the middle since many of its delegates were committed to Dick Leonard for that office and for the same reason of avoiding any factional individual in that post! Dick Frankensteen's people were also strongly for Leonard, who was a Chrysler man. But a number of Unity members who were not in the Reuther camp nevertheless felt an obligation to support Victor. This included Curt Murdoch of Packard and even John Anderson, who said that he had given his word and would not double-cross his friends.[33]

The upshot was an overwhelming victory for Leonard, 340 to 180 though Unity had counted its strength at the convention as a ratio of 350 to 250. Emil Mazey's big Briggs delegation walked out in great dudgeon. This imperiled the vote for the five vice-presidencies, of which Unity figured it would take three. But its candidates, Marshall, Jones, and Ed Geiger of Buick Flint, were all defeated by pro-Martin men. The convention ended in bitterness. It was a harsh augury. Everyone accused everyone else of selling out. In the end, personal favoritism was strengthened whereas the coherence of Unity suffered.

Things came to a head at a Unity caucus in Toledo on August 15.[34] There, Walter Reuther offered a resolution in opposition to a special convention, proposing instead that the UAW quarrel be taken to the CIO convention in November. His resolution received a small vote but the meeting decided to call a broader conference five days later so the issue could be resolved by a more representative group.

The attendance at the gathering on August 20, likewise held in Toledo, was almost as big as a convention. There were 702 "delegates" present representing seventy locals that had an estimated membership of 244,500.[35] The discussion was limited to two resolutions. The first, aimed at Homer Martin, called upon John L. Lewis to designate an administrator over the UAW. The resolution was opposed by a certain number of delegates, largely associated with the Reuther group, who sought to amend it by restricting the administrator's powers and term of service.[36] A committee that had been to see Lewis during the five-day interim reported that they had the impression that he was ready to step into the UAW but were convinced that he would never do so if strings were attached to his course of action. Accordingly, the original resolution was adopted without opposition.

The second resolution called for a special convention in seventy-five days and the election of a "convention committee" immediately from the floor to make the necessary arrangements. The Reuther group was fundamentally opposed to this proposal as they had been when it was first aired at the time of the officers' suspensions. This time Victor Reuther carried the ball, announcing that he had a substitute resolution to present. George Addes, the conference chair, was apparently acquainted with Victor's substitute and told the body that he considered it out of order since it negated the purpose of the original resolution. Nevertheless, in order to uphold democratic procedure, he had decided to allow Vic to read the resolution.

Then a strange thing happened. Some delegate or other appealed the decision of the chair and when the vote was taken the appeal was overwhelmingly upheld. There could be no mistaking that, beyond Victor, his brother Walter was the target of this action. My notes about the incident record the "sad look" on Vic's face when the delegates roared out their refusal to hear his substitute resolution read. The delegates were, in any event, correct in gauging John L. Lewis's mind on the first resolution. Shortly thereafter he sent Philip Murray and Sidney Hillman to Detroit to assume the problem of the reinstatement of the expelled officers.

The CIO Steps In, the UAW Starts Anew   21

Without doubt, the strong showing of the local union representatives at Toledo in support of a CIO mediation, which a delegation of Unity leaders had promptly carried to Lewis in Washington, encouraged him to take this step. A week before Murray and Hillman left for Detroit, he prepared the way for them by perfecting a plan that he mailed to all UAW locals. "I . . . urge you and the membership you represent," he wrote, "to study this proposal carefully and to take action urging your International executive board to accept [it]," the August 28, 1938, *Detroit News* quoted him as saying.

The proposal brought sharp rebukes from Homer Martin and his supporters, who, in the same issue of the *News* charged that "Lewis has cast aside the role of umpire and has stepped into the situation as a partisan." After Martin gave a shocking talk to the Wisconsin UAW District Council, that body adopted a resolution "vigorously protesting the unwarranted . . . interference of Lewis" and invited its locals to do the same, noted the *Detroit News* on August 29. The council also asked the International to stop paying per-capita tax to the CIO. Martin took to the air to keep fanning the flames.[1]

But his effort was hardly enough to change the minds of the major part of the aroused UAW membership, which continued to support CIO intervention. I reported new additions to our fold in letters to my wife, who was at Mackinaw Island for several weeks because of her hay fever. Strong pro-Martin locals like Chevy Gear and Axle and Chrysler Hyde Park had switched sides, I told Dorothy on September 3. "Even Mazey has okayed the CIO plan."

At the beginning of September, Philip Murray and Sidney Hillman arrived in Detroit and began holding caucuses with the two sides of the embattled union. "Our boys see them tomorrow morning," I wrote to Dorothy on September 4, adding that the two men had appeared before the executive board that afternoon, where they "did a slick job." Nevertheless, I confessed that except for Walter Reuther, we—that is, the Unity majority—"are dead certain that peace with Martin is impossible."

The talks went on for several days more and nothing happened to make us change our minds. "The officers are going ahead with plans for the convention," I announced on September 7, which seemed to be in keeping with what the CIO representatives themselves desired since Mortimer had seen John Brophy in Toledo over Labor Day and been told by him to "Go ahead and send out your convention calls." They were in fact ready to go but had been held back to give the UAW executive board every chance to make up their minds about the CIO plan. "I still hold little hope," I wrote on September 10.

On the day before, however, without our having heard about it, there had been a break in Martin's ranks. Several of his board members began to waver under the persistent impact of the CIO leaders' arguments. Four members declared themselves ready to sign Lewis's plan. Surprisingly, two of the converts were men that would be least expected to change: R. J. Thomas, Martin's assistant president, and Delmond Garst, one of his oldest friends. They were joined by Charles Millard of Canada and Charles Madden of Pontiac. But the revolt was short-lived and Martin was able to tell Murray and Hillman on September 12, in the presence of the supposed rebels, that his board majority was unanimous in its opposition to the plan. In fact, he said, an executive board meeting would be held on the following afternoon to make the decision formal. The press was so advised.

But on the following morning the board meeting was called off. Soon after, Martin's scheduled radio talk in which he was supposed to announce the negative decision was canceled because of "illness." I saw him that afternoon and he did look sick. Delmond Garst was standing a little behind him and raised his hand slightly and wagged his fingers to me in acknowledgment of his shift. The Unity leaders decided to disregard these signs and continue to present an aggressive stance. On September 13, I wrote to Dorothy about a new national conference that was scheduled to be held shortly in Toledo, which would unite all pro-CIO forces.

Martin's loss of his majority was discussed freely in the press, which spoke of the "defections of five erstwhile supporters . . . on the union's executive board [as having] left Martin unable to regain control of the body." They would not let him break off the negotiations with Murray and Hillman, it was further reported in the *Detroit News* on September 14. On September 15, the *News* described Martin as "seeking desperately to regain his board majority." A mass of his followers had been summoned from various cities to put pressure on the board but to no avail. It took a final test of strength and only three of eighteen "available" members opposed the CIO's plan, according to the *News* of September 16. Finally, Martin himself announced in the *Detroit Free Press* on September 17 that the vote to endorse the plan was unanimous.

A deft shift of line was devised by his Lovestonite staff to give the impression that Martin had gained everything for which he had fought. The *United Automobile Worker* hailed the settlement: "UAW Autonomy Safe—Bond Strengthened Between CIO, UAW." The story was ludicrously self-laudatory. "President Homer Martin," it said, "made and won a valiant battle to keep the autonomy of the UAW intact while . . . preserving and strengthening the union's bonds with the CIO, of which it is the very heart." Murray and Hillman lent their imprimatur to the cover-up by signing a joint statement with Martin and the board.

Did they seriously think that they had won their struggle with the slippery man? A lengthy report that they issued several months later to the UAW membership would imply that they did. It described the agreement that had been reached setting up a four-man committee—Murray, Hillman, Martin, and Thomas—that would undertake the solution of the union's differences. They would only tackle problems that were referred to it. Their role was strictly advisory. No recommendation could become effective without the approval of the executive board.

The "coordinating committee" went to work immediately. Twenty-eight conflicts were referred to it (90 percent of them by Martin himself). Investigators were sent into the field to meet with hundreds of officers and members of twenty-six locals, many of them of outstanding importance: Plymouth, Packard, Allis-Chalmers, the West Side Local. On November 19, the committee handed in its recommendations, which dealt with every type of issue. These proposals were endorsed unanimously by the executive board and by Homer Martin, who addressed glowing praise and "appreciation" to Murray and Hillman.

But it was all a false front since the overwhelming success of the CIO's plan meant that he had lost the executive board irretrievably and that his only recourse was to seize the union into his own hands. This conclusion was already surfacing at the time of the CIO's first national convention that took place on November 14 and 15 in Pittsburgh. I was at this important gathering, mainly at the insistence of Mortimer, who was already in Pittsburgh when he wrote me that "You'll never forgive yourself if you miss it." He enclosed a small check, hardly ample for the journey but enough to snap me out of my doldrums.

My being there, especially the letters I sent to Dorothy, have helped cue me in on the last gyrations of Homer Martin. The executive board were all present and met intermittently during the convention. In one letter I describe a hilarious near-fight between Martin and Ellsworth Kramer after Martin called him "'a goddam son-of-a-bitch of a liar' . . . Kramer went for him and Murray grabbed Martin by the tail as two or three others held onto Ellzie while he yelled unmentionable things. Ellzie is going around now saying he's biding his time. Homer tried twice to shake hands with him but he refused," I wrote to Dorothy on November 15.

The board were solidly lined up against Martin and one of their most important decisions was to break up his machine. Several of the top Lovestonites on the staff were among those fired when all national departments were put in the hands of the vice presidents: Women's Auxiliaries (Eva Stone); Research and Publication (Bill Munger); and Ford Organization (Ziggy Dobrczinski). Only Morris Field held on to his post as educational director. I wrote that he was "voting 100% with our people." But Tucker Smith, Martin's collaborator in the Socialist party–Lovestonite anti-war movement, was sacked, as were various others, including Elmer Davis, my erstwhile friend from Cleveland who had been Martin's chief bodyguard for several years.

While Homer Martin attracted quite a lot of curious attention at the convention, John L. Lewis gave him short shrift despite Martin's sycophantic attempts to play up to him.[2] "Words cannot express . . . our everlasting appreciation . . . not only to the CIO but to you personally," Martin declaimed. He spent most of his time camped in the visitors' section, however, surrounded by his goons.

I was in Mortimer's hotel room when Mike Quill of the New York Transport Workers Union came in and gave us a revealing account of a session that he, Harry Bridges, and several others had had with Lewis. Lewis told them that Homer Martin had asked David Dubinsky for a loan of $75,000 and had almost convinced him until Lewis heard about it. He telephoned Dubinsky and warned him that he would expose his dealings with Jay Lovestone if he gave Martin the money. He was able to back the threat, he told his visitors, because of information that he had obtained from reading Lovestone's correspondence in the memorandum that the UAW officers had recently sent him. "If David had given Homer the money," Lewis commented, "he would have had two unions in his 'independent movement' today though Homer doesn't have any army left any more."

No one at the Pittsburgh Convention seemed to have any idea about who Martin's successor would be though it was taken for granted that he was on the way out. But Dick Frankensteen did not allow the matter to remain in the dark and was quite successful in pushing his own candidacy. Luck was with him. Someone suggested on one occasion that the assembly ought to sing "Hold the Fort!" but nobody offered to take the lead, probably because they did not know the words. But Frankensteen knew them (a great surprise to me) and happily stood forward and sang two whole verses in his fine tenor.

His performance was a sensation. This must have inspired Heywood Broun, the newspaper columnist and head of the Newspaper Guild, when he was giving a humorous talk on how to get publicity. He pointed out that it was necessary to have a short name to start with, like "Lewis," that fitted neatly into a headline. "Frankensteen wouldn't stand a chance," he said, as the crowd, disagreeing, applauded loudly.

Lewis's major address was the high point of the convention for me. "By medium of an attack on the Nazi government for its atrocities against the Jews," I paraphrased it for Dorothy, "he launched a great plan for the defense of democracy throughout the world and pledged the aid of the twenty million CIO members and their dependents whenever the fascists attempted to spread to the western hemisphere."

The chief topic of conversation in Pittsburgh was the recent elections; everyone was disturbed by the poor results. At our dinner table, one night, Mortimer and I were called on to account for Frank Murphy's defeat.[3] Mortimer blamed the Socialist party and I added the role of Homer Martin and the Lovestonites, quoting from the letters, which I knew almost by heart. Harry Bridges, Joe Curran, and others gave the reasons for the defeats in their bailiwicks until it became apparent that we were all missing something that we probably did not want to admit, a national turn to the right.[4] "Everybody's been blaming local circumstances for these defeats," I said. "I think they're all individual rationalizations for events that had a national cause."

I did not get the chance to finish my thought because John Strachey, the English writer, had just taken a seat at our table and did it for me. He told of hearing the same discussions everywhere while touring the country and had concluded that they revealed a distinct weakening of the New Deal spirit. Faces were suddenly sobered by his words but no one offered a contrary opinion.

There was one disturbing impression that I carried away from the convention. Mike Quill had referred to it when telling Mortimer of the delegation that had seen Lewis. They had wanted to talk to him about the rumors that John Brophy would be removed as the CIO's organizational director, which would be considered a blow at the progressives. But Lewis had given them no satisfaction and it would eventually become known that Brophy was to be replaced by Harvey Fremming.[5] The little I knew about Fremming was not reassuring and his appointment struck me as possibly auguring an important change of course in the CIO.

• • •

Despite the devious role that Homer Martin had played at the convention, Philip Murray and Sidney Hillman reported that the auto union "was again on the path of progress."[6] They were accordingly stunned when they read a press statement that Martin released a few weeks later, on December 31, 1938: "A so-called Coordinating Committee has been set up which takes away the autonomy of our union by delegating the constitutional autonomy to this so-called Coordinating Committee of four" (two of whom were R. J. Thomas and Homer Martin himself).

It was a declaration of war against the CIO, as Martin confirmed on January 20, 1939, by announcing the suspension of fifteen general officers and executive board members, whom he charged with a "conspiracy" of turning over "the membership, moneys, books, property and assets of the International Union and its locals to the CIO." On February 6, he and the five remaining board members filed a bill of complaint in the circuit court of Wayne County, Michigan, listing a long body of indictments against the fifteen suspended men, the most serious one of which concerned the Ford Motor Company.[7]

Homer Martin, the complaint explained, had recently been engaged in highly promising negotiations with that company, talks that "on or about January 1, 1939," had ended in a "tentative understanding and agreement" calling for the reinstatement of six hundred or more discharged Ford workers and the establishment of local and national collective bargaining committees. These brilliant results, however, were wrecked by the obstructive efforts of the fifteen suspended officers in league with the CIO, whereupon the Ford Motor Company had "refused to go further in the matter."[8]

These exaggerations, if not downright falsehoods, hastened Murray and Hillman's publication of their report, dated February 9, 1939, on the accomplishments of the coordinating committee.[9] The report is of particular interest because it contains details unmentioned by Martin about the Ford negotiations, which the CIO leaders decided they had to divulge because of Martin's accusations.

"A few weeks ago," they wrote, "[Martin] announced that he was about to complete an agreement with the Ford Motor Company. The members of the UAW executive board . . . knew of these meetings but knew nothing of what was transpiring at them . . . [and] felt the time had come for him to share his secrets with the duly-elected spokesmen of the automobile workers." This, they said, he refused at first to do but later agreed to meet with the board. He then "demanded the right to continue his talks with Bennett and Ford." The board saw this as a trap but the CIO leaders urged them to grant the request. "We wanted to see," they explained, "whether Martin really had achieved something or was merely trying to sell a pig in a poke." The board accordingly consented to Martin's request but when he found that he "could not produce" the expected results, he turned on them and claimed that they had "wrecked" the agreement. Then he followed through with his mass suspensions.

These actions had, of course, destroyed the whole purpose of the coordinating committee, that of establishing peace in the UAW, Murray and Hillman asserted. "We have reluctantly been forced to the conclusion that Martin does not care for the continued existence of an automobile union unless he can exercise his dictator-mania in running the organization. His chaotic, irresponsible dealings . . . are the natural expressions of a man whose ruthless ambition drives him to wreck what he cannot rule." They called upon UAW members to support the special convention, which the executive board had scheduled for March 27, 1939, in Cleveland, as the only way out of this situation.

The board felt that it had to legitimize its position by taking official action against Martin. He was promptly impeached and his trial was set for March 11. It was held with Martin in absentia, of course, but testimony was taken from a great number of witnesses, a majority of them officers and board members but also quite a few local leaders whose groups had shocking experiences with him. Some of those who volunteered to testify had traveled along with Martin until it was politically perilous to do so any longer.

Among these, R. J. Thomas probably had most to reveal because he was the last of the six officers to abandon Martin. The CIO leaders had suggested that he serve as acting president until the convention. This was accepted though some board members did not like the argument that they offered: that his recent association with Martin gave Thomas a nonfactional posture that would appeal to those UAW members who had stuck with him until recently. Nonetheless Thomas's testimony was often invaluable. He described, for example, how he had accompanied Martin when they met with Father Coughlin during the previous suspensions. Martin's "prosecuting attorney," Larry Davidow, had also gone along.

The radio priest suggested that they ought to see Harry Bennett, Ford's personnel director and head of the notorious Service Department, intimating that he could make the contact for them. Coughlin castigated the other UAW officers, who were all communists or fellow-travelers, he said, and he displayed a special animus for Dick Frankensteen, whom he described as a Jew. Coughlin told Martin that the UAW would be much better off were it not connected with the CIO and that if he quit the CIO he would get support from sources he did not suspect existed as well as a contract with Ford. It was agreed that Martin should write a letter to Harry Bennett, which he did, Thomas said.

There was a second meeting with Coughlin two weeks later, Thomas continued, from which Larry Davidow was excluded.[10] But the editor of *Social Justice,* Coughlin's propaganda sheet, was there and the priest promised Martin that there would be an important article about him in the next issue (and there was). Coughlin reported that he was arranging a meeting for Martin with a large group of priests at the Shrine of the Little Flower and he wanted Thomas or Martin to name all the communists that they knew to be in the CIO and UAW. Martin asked if the meeting would be off the record and Coughlin promised that every priest would take an oath on it. But the revelations were turned over to the Dies Committee, Thomas testified, though he had avoided attending the meeting.

The Ford deal was the key feature of Martin's trial because the board feared that many members might take seriously his claim of having been close to signing a contract with Ford when his enemies cut the strings. Hence the testimony of several members of the Ford locals was highly valued. Two of them—Paul Ste. Marie and Percy Llewellyn, officers of the River Rouge Local 600—were able to furnish information of the negotiations between Martin and Harry Bennett.

John Gillespie, Bennett's agent, was present at the conference that took place in Detroit on November 9, 1938, where preliminary details of the "tentative agreement" that Martin had vaunted were revealed to committees from three Ford locals, those at River Rouge, Kansas City, and St. Louis. It was difficult, however, to get any straightforward information about this agreement from either Martin or Gillespie, all those who had been at the meeting reported, which indicated that what they had to offer was insubstantial at best.

"We asked Gillespie just what kind of an agreement would Ford offer," Paul Ste. Marie testified.[11] "He parried the question half a dozen times" and finally replied that the UAW must have "implicit faith and confidence" in Ford and that the agreement would have to be privately arranged "without any witnesses, without any writing." Despite this misty vagueness, Martin praised the "understanding" enthusiastically. He told those who attended the conference that it should be reassuring to them that Ford agreed to deal with the UAW only as long as he, Martin, was its president, deftly ignoring the fact that this gave him a permanent grasp on his shaky job. "Homer," Gillespie would ask him, "how long is it going to be before you tell the executive board to go to hell and kiss your ass!"

Martin was clearly delighted by these references to his importance. He boasted to the representatives from the three locals, without realizing the serious implication of his words, that Harry Bennett had offered him a closed shop contract if he would take the UAW out of the CIO and either go into the AFL or independent. Bennett offered to put thirty thousand Rouge workers into a meeting for Martin to organize; he also would place his entire Service Department at Martin's disposal at any time or place required. Ste. Marie was asked what the representatives from the Ford locals thought about the company's offer. "They thought it was lousy," he replied. "I believe the Kansas City and St. Louis committees were tempted to throw Gillespie out of the window." He explained that there would be no representation plan except as it was operated by Martin and Bennett: no committeemen, no stewards, in short, no grievance procedure.

Paul Ste. Marie was told that he could have any job in his department (the tool-and-die shop) that he wanted if he went along with the agreement. When he received his card calling him back to work on January 19, 1939, he decided to test the seriousness of the whole arrangement by wearing his UAW button when he entered the department. "I wore it in plain sight right above my work apron so that everybody could see it. But I conducted myself in such a way that nobody could accuse me of doing anything else but company work. I didn't say a word to anybody but I noticed that the men were tickled pink to see somebody in there wearing a union button." He worked two full days but on Tuesday, January 23, at 8:30 or 8:45, he was suddenly surrounded by twelve servicemen, who "very unceremoniously rushed me out of the plant."

After Llewellyn and Ste. Marie held the stand for many hours, it hardly seemed necessary to call on other witnesses. The revelations of all the crimes and follies of Homer Martin were almost superfluous but a number of the witnesses wanted to clear their conscience.

Martin was found guilty by unanimous vote. Dick Frankensteen made a motion to reaffirm Thomas as acting president until the convention. He may have been asked to do so by the CIO leaders and complied in a spirit of good sportsmanship.

• • •

As a matter of fact, candidates were already in the field against Thomas. These individuals had been opposed to Homer Martin from early on; they were men from the Unity camp, whose unison was quite badly splintered by this time, however. Dick Frankensteen considered himself the most logical choice. I had heard him say as much at the CIO convention. He ruled out as competitors Mortimer (too old), Ed Hall (too controversial), or even George Addes (who was "satisfied" to continue as secretary-treasurer). Frankensteen did fear Walter Reuther, but I would have disagreed with him because I knew that Reuther had lost a large part of his potential support by his failure to give the endangered officers the help they deserved. More and more, this resulted in Reuther's being pushed toward the conservative side. He ended by supporting Thomas for the presidency.

This trend was illustrated incisively in a conflict that grew out of one of the decisions of Murray and Hillman's coordinating committee. According to its printed report, "It recommended in the Allis-Chalmers local, Milwaukee, the right of the International Union to *restrict* and *eliminate* those who would use the local for Communist Party purposes." This was to be accomplished by putting an administrator over the local who would be designated by F. J. Michel, the ultra-conservative board member from Wisconsin. The appointee promptly carried out the assignment by removing all officers, outlawing local meetings, and turning over important subsidiary posts to company unionists. He also halted payment of per capita to the state CIO council, an act Michel condoned by arguing that a number of other locals were doing the same because the council was communistic.

This situation had been tolerated by this very militant local and by its displaced president Harold Christoffel until just before the Cleveland Convention, when the administrator decided to appoint the local's delegates. The dispute that resulted came before the international executive board, where Ed Hall offered a motion to withdraw the case from the coordinating committee and settle it in the board. Thomas declared the motion out of order and Hall appealed his decision. Reuther supported Thomas, saying that he had discussed the case with the CIO leaders and did not want to give them "a kick in the teeth." Mortimer countered by saying that he, too, had talked with Hillman, whom he quoted as suggesting, "Do anything you want with Allis-Chalmers. I don't want to hear any more about it. I am sick of it."

During this exchange, Thomas was called out to answer a long-distance telephone call. He returned, looking crestfallen, and reported that it was from Phil Murray, who insisted that he settle the Allis-Chalmers case "peaceably if possible." Ed Hall demanded sarcastically whether Thomas had the impression that Murray felt he had been given "a kick in the puss." Thomas stalled: "Not if it's settled peaceably." The upshot was a substitute motion: If everything else failed, then a balanced committee (Michel, Field, and Ellsworth Kramer) should go to Milwaukee and conduct free elections for the delegates. The motion was adopted by a close count, with Reuther voting against.

The Allis-Chalmers affair was significant because it previewed the atmosphere that would prevail at the Cleveland Convention as well as of the conduct of some of the leading people who would be there. Whatever else could be said about Dick Frankensteen, his defense of Harold Christoffel had displayed a surprisingly firm attitude on red-baiting. He was taken sharply to task for this by Fred Pieper, who said that the Allis-Chalmers leader had "a pipeline to Moscow." Angrily referring to the often-repeated slur that Pieper was a GM stool pigeon, Frankensteen declared, "I'd rather have a pipeline to Moscow than to General Motors." Pieper swallowed and took it. All that happened, according to my notes, was that "the remark was wiped clean from the record."

The fact was, however, that Frankensteen had been making up to the Communist party for some time, no doubt in the hope of winning its support for his candidacy. Like a number of other people, I knew that he had seen Bill Gebert, a national leader of the Communist party, after distancing himself from Homer Martin early in 1938. But Frankensteen was in for a rude awakening regarding these expectations, as was I for that matter, because the awakening occurred in our apartment.

The Frankensteens and my wife and I had planned to go out together one afternoon and he telephoned to make arrangements to pick us up in their car. He asked me if it would be all right if he met Bill Gebert for a few minutes in our apartment before we left. "He just called," he explained, "wanting to make an appointment for this afternoon but I told him we were going out. So I thought it would be most convenient to see him at your place for a short time. I'll leave Mickey in the car. I hope you don't mind."

As a matter of fact, I did but I didn't say so. Gebert arrived shortly before Frankensteen and I was more annoyed than ever to discover that he was accompanied by Roy Hudson, a tall, long-legged seaman whom I knew by name as a top communist official. I was relieved when Frankensteen arrived only a few minutes later and showed no sign of removing his heavy blue overcoat.

I recall these details because of the curious way he stood looking down at Hudson, who had resumed his seat in the center of the front room. Frankensteen was surprised though not displeased, I felt, probably thinking that Hudson's presence was a good omen to his purpose. But his satisfaction was promptly erased by a flush of discontent as he listened to Hudson's hurried words, which he delivered without introduction. Moreover, their meaning was crude and undisguised. The UAW was faced by a critically important situation at the coming convention, Hudson said. The future of the union was at stake. All self-seeking considerations must be put aside. The CIO had saved the union from certain disaster. All responsible leaders should realize that and act accordingly. Frankensteen listened with unconcealed displeasure, finally breaking into the aggressive tirade, his plump cheeks deeply suffused with color. "Am I to understand, Mr. Hudson, that you're trying to tell me that we must all support Thomas for president?"

"Precisely."

"Well, Mr. Hudson, all I can say is that I think you are one hundred percent wrong!" And he turned abruptly to Dorothy and me, who were standing, coats on, close to the door in an obvious urge to avoid involvement and, on my part at least, to reveal my vexation. "We ought to be going," Dick said to us. "Mickey will be wondering what happened to me."

"Just pull the door shut when you leave," I told Gebert.

• • •

Homer Martin left the UAW proscenium with dramatic fanfare. He held his own convention in Detroit on March 4, 1939, at which he was the one and only star. Ten pictures in his personal *United Automobile Worker,* which was stripped of its CIO emblem and halted publication soon after, show him broom in hand "house-cleaning" the UAW, greeting an adoring female member of the Kansas City local "who knew him when," shaking hands with four black delegates, being given "two trips around the hall" on the backs of loyal supporters and receiving "secessionists" from Reuther's local.

By its own printed figures, the convention had "official delegates" claiming only 64,700 members in a union with more than three hundred thousand adherents, based on 647 delegates registered for 243 locals. Many delegates were of dubious representativity, moreover, compared to those from the same locals who would be in Cleveland three weeks later. The group picture of Martin's new executive board of seventeen further exposed the fragility of his strength. Only three of the original members were left, all "representing" numerically small regions.[12] Flint was the only important center in which Martin still had some standing and he tried to seal its support by granting it two executive board members: Jack Little of the Chevrolet local and Jerry Aldred of Fisher One. But even this backing was already being challenged in Flint.[13]

• • •

The wakening came three weeks later, on March 27, with the opening of the Cleveland Convention of the UAW-CIO at the Hollendon Hotel. My lengthy diary of that event records the "marvelous spirit" that prevailed there.[14] This may have been an overstatement, but it was true of the beginning, anyway, when a band gayly played a succession of state anthems.

An enthusiasm of different type was roused when Dick Coleman in the name of the California delegation presented the convention with a facsimile copy of the original pardon of labor's most famous prisoner, Tom Mooney. The delegates cheered lustily, then gave three hip-hip-hoorays for California Governor Culbert Olson. A reference to what was to become the convention's most hotly debated issue slipped in when the band played "On, Wisconsin!" and a number of delegates from that state pointed to Ed Hall, who rose to his feet and received loud cheers.

When, soon after, Acting President R. J. Thomas pounded his gavel to open the session officially, he got only mild applause. But his introductory words were acclaimed: "This organization is going to live on!" He then listed its accomplishments since the Milwaukee Convention (the list was exaggerated): more dues collected; more and better contracts; wages maintained despite the depression. And he affirmed the UAW's loyalty to the CIO rather than to Henry Ford, a reference to the repudiated Homer Martin that all present understood.

On the second day, the part that the CIO would play at the convention was made explicit when it was announced that, at the request of Philip Murray and Sidney Hillman, a closed session would be held. The CIO leaders presented some unpleasant truths to the delegates. They were present, they said, to prevent any splits in the organization and if necessary to dictate what must be done toward that end. Soon after the closed session ended, a delegate of the Dodge local (Dick Frankensteen's) registered a protest on the convention floor to a statement that had been attributed to it by the *Cleveland News*. All the delegates had applauded the CIO leaders, it stated, except those of Local 3, who "sat quietly as Murray and Hillman delivered their thrusts against the communists." The local affirmed its loyalty to the CIO amid loud applause, the *Proceedings* reported on March 29.

This inverse publicity was hardly required by the CIO officials, who had, without opposition, won the sway over the delegates that they themselves had.demanded. The closed session gave them a unanimous vote of confidence and asked for their continued advice. I recorded having heard a number of friends (in particular those from the Cleveland Fisher Body local) saying that they would do anything that the CIO men suggested. It was a rash promise and most of those who made it would later break it. Others, on the other hand, would take prompt advantage of the situation to open their attacks on the five officers, as though to designate them as the targets at whom the CIO leaders were aiming.

Their first thrust came during the officers' reports. Certain members of the rules committee, which handled the reports, belonged to the "clean-sweep" group and were in a position to make difficulties for the officers. Fault was found, for example, with Frankensteen's account of his work with the Ford organization committee and he had to rewrite his report. Similarly, Walter Wells was told to rewrite his report on aircraft organization. Most of the reports were thus delayed a day or two while members of the committee kept asking when the officers would be ready to report. In the end, some of the delegates must have had the impression that the officers were remiss in their responsibilities or engaged in a cover-up.

Such was not the case with George Addes, however, who received tremendous applause when he first appeared at the podium and continued to get a big hand every other time he returned, if only to read a wire or make an announcement. It was plain that the delegates wanted to impress the CIO leaders with their support for Addes's candidacy, especially after one of the local newspapers carried the story that Addes had been pushed aside by them in the choice for the president.

Accordingly, they whistled and stamped their feet every time Addes appeared. Victor Reuther made a psychological blunder when he protested against these "unnecessary demonstrations" so the enthusiastic displays for

Addes merely increased in fervor. In Addes's report, he explained the difficulties that there had been in controlling the International's finances under Homer Martin, when an enormous deficit of $370,000 had accumulated. He ended by warning, "We must wipe out the last vestige of that destructive factionalism which our ex-president and his eastern advisor [Lovestone] introduced into our union." That gave his supporters the occasion to cheer again, "unnecessarily."

The other officers in their reports continued the general line that Addes had adopted. Dick Frankensteen gave details of how the Ford campaign had been sabotaged by Martin's Lovestonite minions. Ed Hall's talk was more personal; he took the bit in his teeth to answer jibes about how the officers had voted on the executive board in favor of receiving the back pay they had lost during their suspensions. What was wrong about that? he asked. Didn't every auto worker fight for the wages that were due him? His report was approved unanimously, as was Mortimer's. But after the vote was recorded, a member of Chrysler 7 (Thomas's local) named Dynes went to the microphone to register his opposition.[15] Ellsworth Kramer of Toledo 12 angrily moved to strike this remark from the record, which was done.

These Pecksniffian snipes of the Reuther group did them more harm than good, many felt. Walter Reuther seemed to realize this, I observed, when I sat near him and Bob Kanter during the discussion on resolutions. When the resolution came up on an amendment to the Neutrality Act along the lines suggested by the CIO, calling for a boycott of the aggressor nations and cooperation with the democracies, Walter Reuther whispered to Kanter, "Are you going to talk on this?" Kanter replied: "No." Next was the resolution on Labor's Non-Partisan League that praised Roosevelt's social legislation and called him a great humanitarian. Reuther's concern shifted to Emil Mazey, who remained in his seat, however, checking his papers. Only on the resolution approving the coming conference at Lima regarding "the furtherance of the Good Neighbor Policy" in the Americas did Mazey react, but it was merely to register his negative vote. As I watched him, I could not help but admire his consistency; he expressed his viewpoint even though he knew it might have a negative effect on his popularity.

Meanwhile, the duel between the two groups came down to earth as the race for officers began. Delegates started passing around incongruous slates that mixed the most unlikely teammates. One of these prompted George Addes to intervene. Asking for the floor on special privilege and holding a sheet in his hand, he asserted: "I have never been or will not be a member of any group or caucus." It was a "brilliant coup," I recorded, and it caused "great cheering," as I am sure almost anything Addes said would have done. A day later, what I incorrectly called the "SP caucus" (it was much broader than that) was set up in one of the hotel parlors, and everyone was invited to pick up a little broom. The idea of the "clean sweep" was aimed at the officers but many adherents of our side got brooms and snake-danced around the hotel, yelling "Addes is our leader, he will be approved!"

These hijinks went on into the early hours but did not appear to have any physical effect on the delegates. The following morning, the great task of remaking Martin's repressive constitution got underway. The delegates studied each new section with a searching eye. If it was good, they cheered; if it was dubious or inadequate, they sent it back. The aim was to secure democratic rights on every level of the organization, with special emphasis on the locals. A two-thirds vote of the executive board was required to revoke local charters.[16] A limit of thirty days was set on the imposition of a local administrator, then elections must be held. Far from being banned, local papers were encouraged. The power of the International president was limited to "administrative authority" and that only between sessions of the executive board, whom he was ordered to consult on any major issue.[17] As one delegate commented, "You might as well elect a wooden Indian."

When Article 8, section 1 of the constitution came up, the assembly began to buzz. The article was regarded as the convention's most controversial issue since it involved the fate of the vice presidents and everyone knew that there would be a battle. The crowd was stunned when, before anyone had the chance to say a word for or against the committee's proposal, the officers took the lead and effaced themselves. All endorsed the CIO's recommendation to eliminate their posts. Ed Hall typically made a joke of it: "The convention is evidently the clearing house for vice presidents." Mortimer explained how the CIO leaders had to consider various suggestions for handling the matter. One held that the five officers be retained; another that they be reduced to three; still another that they be cut to one. "So," he ended with an ironic smile, "we felt that if all of us were removed, we would all go home satisfied. But if we went on record as opposing the CIO it would be one of the greatest calamities in American labor history." I did not take Mortimer's exaggerated words seriously.

The delegates were charmed by such self-abnegation. The officers themselves seemed to be pleased with it, forgetting for the moment perhaps that it was tantamount to an admission of complicity in Martin's disruption and an acceptance of the verdict of the clean-sweep group. What then would happen to the presidency? They seemed not to realize that they had weakened their voices by eliminating themselves from office, which would soon compel them to put up a disagreeable fight against the CIO's inflexible choice for the top post.

But the amiability of their present act sufficed for the occasion. Delegates queued up at the microphone to purvey their praise, while Reuther gave it a special meaning that was recorded in the *Proceedings* of April 2: "No one can try to interpret this as a victory for any group. It is a victory for the whole union." A motion was proposed and adopted by a rising vote: "We commend the International officers for their loyalty and faithful devotion to the UAW and the CIO during their suspension from office."[18] It was, in effect, an answer to the clean-sweep group.

• • •

It was soon apparent that the question of the presidency was far from settled despite the constant pressure exerted by the CIO leaders. Their emphasis had been on the officers since it was from them that an opponent to Thomas would in all probability come.[19] Soon enough the contest broke out on the convention floor. Displays of partisanship were let loose at any slight excuse. A delegate motioned that the delegates give Thomas a rising vote of thanks for conducting the sessions "very democratically" but many did not rise. I noticed that those from Bendix, Buick, California, and others demonstratively held their seats. Then a group started parading and shouting, "Thomas is our leader, we shall not be moved!" The second time around they were drowned out by "Addes is our leader!" The clean-sweepers yelled, "We want Thomas!" but this was blurred by a roar of "We want Addes!" and by pounding on the tables.

The convention had plenty of work to do and was moving along with the all-important constitution. But a strong sense of dissatisfaction prevailed among the delegates due to the continued delay in the election of officers. Four days, five days, six days passed, and the time had not yet been set. It was an open secret that the delay came from the CIO leaders, who apparently were not yet confident of a Thomas victory. Even those in the pro-Thomas camp, particularly the rank-and-filers who were not on the inside of the intensive back-door confabs, began to show their impatience. A week had already passed despite the night sessions that had been held almost every day. The tired, disgusted delegates voted down an extension of that night's session beyond the usual 10 o'clock limit that had been set.

Sidney Hillman, who, it was said, was working with the constitution committee, sent a request through Dick Frankensteen that this action should be rescinded and that the convention should keep going that night until the committee had brought in its report on a very important subject, the reapportionment of the board members. Chester Mullins, though a delegate from Walter Reuther's local, led the fight to turn Hillman down: "Let's tell them all to go to hell!" he shouted. Thomas rebuked Mullins, saying that he sounded like Homer Martin. He could have eaten his words when Mullins retorted: "I'm as loyal to the CIO as you are any day!" Hillman's supported motion to extend the night session was defeated overwhelmingly, I recorded, "with almost all SP [meaning pro-Reuther] locals voting against."

Even Bob Travis, who remained a convention favorite throughout, was hooted down when he tried to speak for the extension of the night session. It was a pity since he wanted to tell the delegates about an agreement that had been reached by all groups, with Hillman's blessings, about a plan to bring the eliminated vice presidents into the executive board. This would be accomplished in the following manner. Frankensteen was assured of winning a post in Michigan but Mortimer and Hall could get in only by reapportioning the board districts. Wisconsin would get two members instead of one, the extra post going to Hall. Mortimer's arrangement was more complicated, requiring the joining of East Ohio (Cleveland) to the Eastern District.[20]

But the plan fell through, one reason probably being Reuther's reluctance to give his opponents so strong a hold on the new board. Hillman himself must have foreseen this danger and had gone along with the reapportionment plan merely to tie the officers' consent to Thomas's candidacy. The maneuver splintered when Hillman's double-dealing was exposed at a meeting that Mortimer, Hall, and Travis had with him that same evening. I was outside Hillman's room at the time and could hear Hall shouting in anger. Then he came bursting through the door, which he clacked after him, a sound I can still hear.

I was told, of course, about what had taken place inside. Hall had become furious with Mortimer and Travis when they admitted to Hillman that, come what may, they would never engage in an open fight against the CIO. Hall had remained intransigent and demanded of Hillman what the CIO leaders would do if the convention refused to go along with Thomas. Hillman replied calmly: "We would call a press conference and announce that the Communist Party had taken over the UAW."

That was when Hall rose up in fury. "You'd really do that, would you? What would be the fuckin' difference between you and Homer Martin then?"

After the convention session had ended, a large number of delegates assembled in the hotel lobby. Tempers were explosive. The constitution committee had appeared after all yet had nothing to offer but ordinary sections for discussion. When they ended their report, the delegates broke up the session, shouting: "Enough is enough!" Ed Hall joined them in the lobby and peppered them up still further, sizzling the CIO leaders. The word went around: "We're going to meet in Room 284." In a little while, the crowd was so dense there that they moved to the Cypress Room, then out of there to the ballroom nearby.

A few of us tried to calm things down. "No attacks on the CIO," we urged. Ed Hall had meanwhile cooled down somewhat and left soon after. Carl Shipley of Bendix was helpful in his way by using the occasion to make a campaign speech because he had decided to run against Thomas for president. He probably hurt his chances by spending a lot of time developing the theme that the trouble was all due to the fight between two political parties though he had the good sense to not identify them.

Finally, a motion was adopted to call Hillman down to answer their questions. Most of those present thought that he would not have the guts to come. The word was passed around that if he did show up he should be greeted with utter silence and certainly not applauded. The sensible and likable Joe Ditzel of Toledo Chevrolet was designated as spokesman and right after that Hillman did appear, looking as bright and friendly as could be. Ditzel quietly told him what was on the fellows' minds. Chiefly, they wanted to know whether the delegates had the right to choose their own officers or did they have to accept men who were picked for them?

Hillman's approach was to deny categorically that the CIO was giving any orders. He spoke of the necessity of bringing the various groups together and handled the question of the communists deftly by declaring that it was bad for political parties to interfere in a union's affairs but that he was opposed to inserting anything like that into the constitution or to red-baiting. He pointed out that the CIO leaders had intervened on only two issues, explaining their position on the elimination of the vice presidents and why they had favored adding one board member to Wisconsin. Was that so terrible? He went on suavely, interminably, until the men's eyes began to glimmer. They had hardly slept for days. Hillman ended by talking their anger to sleep.

He also spoke about general subjects: the need for unity in the labor movement, the attacks on the CIO, the miners' strike. He won his audience so completely that he was able to answer a direct question on Addes's candidacy. Addes had made one serious mistake, said Hillman, he had become linked with a certain political group, "for reasons beyond our control" (an expression that I never could figure out). Accordingly, Addes's election to the presidency would do the UAW great harm by playing into the hands of its enemies. I was overwhelmed to note the effect that these remarks had on the men. Some of Addes's most ardent partisans seemed to have been taken in by Hillman's performance. It was past 2 in the morning when the caucus broke up.

It was a good deal later and I was still up, not even thinking of sleep, sitting in a deep chair in the lobby and feeling utterly disconsolate. I thought of spending an hour or so on an article about the convention for the *New Masses* that Maurice Sugar had wished on me but I had no desire to do.[21] Suddenly, Sugar was standing before me, smiling broadly with his pipe clutched between his teeth. What did he find to be so happy about? "You look blue," he commented, taking a seat beside me. "Let me cheer you up.

I've been with George Addes for the last couple of hours and I think we've got the thing licked."

The idea was a speech that Addes would give at the first appropriate time. Sugar and he had worked it out; the speech would be "short and snappy," hitting all the high points. Then, as soon as Addes finished and got his usual big hand, someone would be primed to make a motion to suspend all business and hold elections immediately. The delegates were sick and tired of stalling; they wanted to get it over with and go home. I was not very encouraging but Sugar obviously did not need that kind of a boost.

No part of their plan came out as intended. George Addes did speak early in the session but on a resolution on strikes and, curiously, he got no applause when he came to the podium. What was more, he never did give the rousing speech that Sugar had told me about, probably having changed his mind about the whole idea. The motion about the elections was not presented until that afternoon, but it was the Reuther group that did it, evidently counting on the advantage gained by Hillman's performance at the previous night's caucus to put Thomas across. Yet the motion was defeated overwhelmingly, which is difficult for me to understand unless perhaps because delegates no longer felt urgent about the vote since they had accepted Thomas's designation as unavoidable.

When Hillman arrived later that evening, it was to say goodbye because, as he explained, he had been invited to attend the "peace" meeting between officials of the AFL and the CIO. The delegates rose, cheering, all past resentment apparently forgotten. His short talk was full of the usual commonplaces, declaring that the UAW would now be more "unified," more "solidified" to face employers, I recorded in my diary. He admonished the delegates that the CIO would continue to employ every measure to keep politics out of the organization, while he still denied that it had interfered in any way in the elections.

• • •

It was not until the following afternoon that the voting took place. Addes was given a big hand when nominated for president. He came to the podium and, with involuted phraseology, explained his foreknown decision: "I want to at this time express my sincere appreciation to all of the delegates who desire to have me run for the office, but I think for the best interests of this union, for the best interests of the labor movement as a whole and particularly the CIO, I have taken my position in not accepting the nomination for president." There was "loud, prolonged applause," I recorded in my diary, in acknowledgment of the courageous action of an honorable man.

Carl Shipley, the protest candidate, got more applause when nominated than did Thomas, as did even the third candidate, Frank Tuttle, an amiable man famous for his letters to the editor of the *Detroit News*. John Anderson, in calling out the vote of his group, Tool and Die Local 155, rubbed in the bitter truth that everybody knew: "Twenty-three votes *for the CIO*—and Thomas."[22] The final count was Thomas, 1,233; Shipley, 403; Tuttle, 59.5.

The nomination of Addes for secretary-treasurer aroused a spate of nostalgic excitement. He was elected by acclamation. Then the convention quickly subsided into indifference. An insouciance took hold of the delegates, which could have given the impression to the unknowing that they were in accord with the election's results. Only about three-fourths of them had remained to the end, however. Some had to leave because their round-trip tickets required it and Indiana's delegates left early "to take care of" Homer Martin, who had scheduled some activities in their state. Some of the bigger locals donated hundreds of dollars to smaller groups that had run out of funds but had pledged to stay until the last section of the constitution had been disposed of. When this happened, the constitution "was adopted as a whole" amid great cheering, as though to mark some historic event.

My own task was still unfinished. I had been working fitfully on the *New Masses* article and had wired A. B. Magil, its editor: "Convention adjourns this afternoon. Can you hold space for article arriving Monday?" My chief problem was to sum up the events without giving them the negative slant that my own feelings dictated. The communist editors would, no doubt, want nothing but praise for the convention, but I decided nevertheless to adopt the line that the clean-sweep group had flagrantly endangered the unity of the union, which had been saved largely by important concessions of its most responsible leaders: Mortimer, Addes, Frankensteen, Hall, and Travis.

These men had made the greatest sacrifices. They had given up the presidency, the vice-presidencies, and, in the end, the board memberships-at-large as well. The other side had claimed to be stalwart CIO champions but had made no contribution at all to a peaceful solution, whereas Eddie Levenson, their "publicity man" and the future editor of the UAW journal, had handed out unofficial press releases that always linked Addes with the Communist party and Thomas with the CIO. But the CIO could not have accomplished its decree, which by whatever name one gave it was nothing but a purge, without the consent of the Mortimer-Addes group. It was utterly false what the newspapers were saying, that this unity was bought at a price exacted by the Communist party: control of the executive board.

The board members were elected as always by the democratic vote of the delegates in their respective districts. No one, not even the CIO, could be said to have been capable of predetermining the results of these elections. The voting for the seven board members in Detroit and Michigan, on which I kept a fairly close count, was a good example of this basic truth. The Communist party was supposed to have told "its people" to vote for Walter Reuther as being representative of the union's "constructive forces." This may have been true even though the results hardly bear out such a directive. Still, the communists claimed after the voting that Reuther by himself would not have been reelected were it not for their support.[23] Reuther, it is true, shared top honors with Frankensteen in the final count, but an important part of his vote, besides that of his followers, undoubtedly came from the conservative elements rather than from the Unity people of whatever political outlook.

In Detroit, only five of the ten Unity locals gave Reuther any votes at all.[24] John Anderson, on the other hand, a self-acknowledged communist, received support from nine of the ten. Five of these locals were considered to be communist-influenced, but only two of them cast any ballots for Reuther: L. A. Young and Tool and Die Local 157. Among the three other Unity locals that backed Reuther, only Murray Body, led by his friend Lloyd Jones, gave him as high a vote as it did the other Unity candidates. The other two gave him only partial support: one-half of the delegates from Chevy Gear and Axle and one-third of those from Dodge.

The Flint locals did somewhat better for Reuther though I do not have the voting records of all their units. Fisher One, a more conservative local since the decline of the left following the big sitdown, gave him thirty-four votes against a top count of thirty-nine to a Flint candidate by the name of McAlpin. Three of the four delegates of the AC Sparkplug local, which was socialist-influenced, voted for Reuther; two voted for Frankensteen; and all four voted for McAlpin. In Local 156, a remnant of the former amalgamated local, Frankensteen and LaMotte topped the list while Reuther got only about half of Frankensteen's vote. But his poorest showing was at Buick, where only one of the nine or ten delegates supported him, the others voting for the full Unity (and communist-preferred) list of Frankensteen, La-Motte, Anderson, and Curt Murdoch of Packard. Reuther's weakness here was, no doubt, due to the bitter memory of Roy Reuther's candidacy for president of the amalgamated local two years earlier, which had resulted in a disastrous split.

Finally, it is important to note that the eleven pro-Reuther locals in Detroit gave an overwhelming majority to their own choice of candidates, with Reuther's vote leading the slate in most cases.[25] Unity men got scattered votes in only five of these locals, in two of which, both small units, they equaled the count of the pro-Reuther slate. But in the three remaining unions they were swamped: by three to one in Local 306, by two to one in the big West Side Local, and by eight to one in Emil Mazey's Local 212 (Briggs). The roundup of the above results illustrates one solid fact: the split of Unity and the Reuther group.[26]

• • •

Soon after the executive board elections had been tabulated, the convention broke up, and delegates hurried to leave, after having spent several days more in Cleveland than they had planned. As usual, I was a straggler. There were people to whom I had a last important word to say or from whom I needed to get some information. The thought of starting work on the book that I had considered writing for the past five years suddenly gave many of them new status as possible sources.

When they finally freed themselves from me, I still had to copy a letter that I scribbled to A. B. Magil containing last-minute additions to the article I had sent off the day before. I had just finished it and was sealing the envelope at the reception desk when John Anderson appeared, looking very impatient if not disgusted. "Quit stalling," he barked. "You've got to leave with the rest of us."

I realized that something was up and asked him what it was.

"Fred Pieper is out with a little gang of well-wishers. They want to mess you up."

"Why me?" I asked, hardly believing him. "What did I do to him?"

He gave me an ironic look and took hold of my arm. "You must have done *something.*"

It was dark outside and chilly but there was no sign of Pieper or any other inimical body. Instead, a loudly talking group of friends stood a bit down the street near a couple of cars. And the little non-event seemed to have missed me.

In retrospect, I tried to make sense of it. It struck me that I had not benefited personally from the convention to be blamed for any one else's woes. Fred Pieper and others of his stripe had, to be sure, been big losers. Though he never deserved it through positive accomplishment, he had held an important post in the union for a number of years and his loss of status must have been a very serious blow. He was the kind of person, perhaps, who could have thought of making someone "pay" physically for his loss. But he was a notorious coward, having swallowed the insult of being called a stool pigeon a dozen times without ever assailing his accuser. It would be different with me, he must have thought.

Curiously, it was mainly other losers that he most hated, whereas he in certain respects was on the winning side since the progressives had been pushed aside.[27] Mortimer, Hall, and Travis had lost far more than he. The two former vice presidents had, it was true, been promised important posts by the CIO leaders though they had not yet been told where or what these would be. One could expect that they would be at outlying points, where Mortimer and Hall could not finagle their return to power or exercise their great influence to the detriment of the winners. And that was the way things worked out. The labor movement, unfortunately, is no different from any other social entity: its memory is short.

As for myself, I had in recent months begun to feel half-forgotten and now the break would be complete. Except for my wounded ego, I did not much mind that. I was disgusted with what had taken place at the convention and was even highly displeased with the officers for accepting their fate without putting up a battle. I was enraged with the Communist party for the defeatist influence that it had sedulously sought to exert after hypocritically declaring that it was staying aloof from the choice of officers at the convention.[28]

There should have been a fight on the floor, I felt, against the shameful conduct of Murray and Hillman. It was entirely in keeping with the worst traditions of old craft unionism and recalled the experiences we had with Francis Dillon and Bill Green in Detroit four years earlier. The AFL officials had prepared for it by expelling a number of militant unionists, thus assuring the rise of Homer Martin. The CIO leaders had been slicker but the results were the same. They had destroyed the careers of some of the finest people in the auto union and opened the way to Homer Martin's close associate, a man of unknown character or quality. It struck me that the path ahead was fraught with peril.

And thus my last efforts, however slight, to be useful to the union that I loved had gone for naught. Strangely, I was not too sad about that, perhaps because I was relieved to be quit of it. I would never link my life to a union again, certainly not to the UAW.[29] Meanwhile, my task was to write its story as I had shared it. Could I do this without revealing the bitterness that I felt? I thought that I could since no matter what had happened, my deep belief in the union was still alive and would be forever, perhaps. The living spirit of the UAW had not been damaged by what had happened in Cleveland. I could verify this by the many heartening pictures that I carried off in my notes, which I had continued recording all through the wracking event.

This was my habit, for I had been preparing for this book for five years, gathering a huge jumble of scribblings and memorabilia I sent ahead to Beaver Island at the northern tip of Lake Michigan, which Dorothy and I had discovered on one of her yearly escapes from hay fever. The postmistress there, Mrs. Pischner, with whom she had become friendly, had rented a cabin for us for $25 a month at the southern end of the island near the lighthouse. The cabin lacked running water, electricity, gas, and other conveniences, but it gave us five glorious months, June through October, for me to write my book.

First came six chapters of the background history, which I would eventually abandon but which have served as a nucleus for the present work. I had by this time taught myself to type and, after getting started on what I soon realized would be the central feature of the book, it seemed that I could go on forever as I poured out the "chronicle of the dynamic auto workers," later titled *The Many and the Few,* the story of the great Flint sitdown strike.

It was this event above all, I felt, that auto workers must remember. There would never be another like it. They had matured during the forty-four days of struggle as few workers had ever done, which prepared them for the enormous trials through which they would come successfully.

Now, after fifty-odd years, the UAW still celebrates its greatest victory. The positive accomplishment of the Cleveland Convention, I recognized, was that it had made it possible to preserve this memorable tradition by re-establishing the integral strength of the organization that had created it.

Notes

Chapter 1:
Looking for a Strike

1. Mortimer devotes some attention to the TUUL union in *Organize! My Life as a Union Man* (Boston: Beacon Press, 1971).

2. The local's minutes, which are in the White Motors Papers in the Archives of Labor and Urban Affairs at Wayne State University, show a big jump in quality when the change was made.

3. It was Harvey Brown, an officer of the Machinists Union.

4. Mortimer, *Organize!* 58.

5. Mortimer, *Organize!* 60–61.

6. In *The Automobile under the Blue Eagle* (Ann Arbor: University of Michigan Press, 1963), Sidney Fine adopts in toto the White Motor Company's version of this contention. He tells of its great losses since 1930, adding sympathetically: "Despite this fact, the company in August 1933 . . . had boosted wage rates 10 percent." But the union was unappreciative: "Early in December 1933 . . . Federal Labor Union 18463, which seems to have been infiltrated by communists or at least by communist sympathizers, voted to strike unless the company raised wages, improved working conditions, and recognized the union" (212–13). As I have shown, there was no such malicious invasion of White Motors. There was, on the contrary, a voluntary unification of two groups, admittedly with differing ideologies, which remained permanently merged thereafter.

Chapter 2:
The Growth of the White Motor Local

1. The White Motor local's minutes are now in the Archives of Labor and Urban Affairs, Wayne State University.

2. Document now in Kraus Collection, Archives of Labor and Urban Affairs, Wayne State University.

3. The report is in the Archives of Labor and Urban Affairs, Wayne State University under the heading of the White Motor local.

4. The UAW locals were unanimously bitter about the Auto Labor Board's (ALB's) record in handling the great number of union discrimination cases. Sidney Fine disagrees with this judgment, however: "If the ALB did not produce the 'hell of a big change' in employer-employee relations that [Leo] Wolman thought it had, it did nevertheless leave its mark on the automobile industry. It secured the return to employment of several hundred workers who but for its intervention might have remained without work" (*Blue Eagle*, 414). This quantitative estimate of discrimination misses certain fundamental factors. The restoration of their jobs to a few hundred of the several thousand workers long after they were discharged failed to correct other great losses incurred by the local unions involved, a number of which were destroyed during the great impulse of early 1934. This could have been prevented only if a strike had been called at that time. The ALB was set up to prevent such action and its influence was deleterious both on that occasion and subsequently. Seeking a partial vindication for this, as Fine attempts to do, does not furnish a valid historical appraisal of the ALB's harmful role or explain the universal disapprobation of the ALB that labor organizations, including the national AFL itself, felt.

Chapter 3:
Cleveland Starts a Movement for an International

1. The fight took place on June 19. Louis was first knocked down by Schmeling in the fourth round; he was knocked out in the twelfth.

2. In the roll call of the AFL convention in San Francisco, in October 1934, are recorded the following delegates from automobile unions: John Bartee, Federal Labor Union (FLU) 18310, South Bend (five votes); Edward Stubbe, FLU 18463 (sixteen votes); Frank Johnson, FLU 18512, Flint (sixteen votes); Rudolph Anderson, representing three locals at Racine, Wisconsin, FLU 18785, FLU 18525, and FLU 19241 (a total of nine votes); and Melvern P. Russell, Racine FLU 19188 (three votes).

3. Stubbe's intervention is reported in American Federation of Labor, *Proceedings of the Convention,* San Francisco, October 1934, 595ff, including the words "applause in enthusiastic manner" on page 598. The resolution he presented is listed on pages 581–82.

4. See the oral history of Bud Simons, September 6, 1960, Archives of Labor and Urban Affairs, Wayne State University.

5. I later learned that Weileder was referring to the Socialist Labor party, against which he seemed to have a grudge. I had never heard it mentioned before although I did later.

6. Sidney Fine refers to a letter on this subject that Green wrote to Dillon on December 25, 1934, giving as the source the Green Letterbooks (*Blue Eagle,* 405 and n75).

7. Lehman was out of town on National Council business.

8. The Works Progress Administration (WPA) was a federal project of "made work" designed to combat unemployment.

Chapter 4:
The AFL's Bogus Plan for a National Auto Strike

1. Actually, I was the author of the document and I called the first section a Preamble to account for its curious wording.

2. By the "International committee" was meant the unofficial group promoting the International Union.

3. In *Blue Eagle* (323–25), Sidney Fine lists the Cleveland local with five other AFL units, chiefly in Fisher Body plants, that disregarded the boycotts.

4. An important part of this correspondence is in the Kraus Collection, Archives of Labor and Urban Affairs, Wayne State University.

Chapter 5:
Cleveland's Unions Take the AFL at Its Word

1. The White Motor local leaders even gave President Black the opportunity to talk to its members at a great meeting that the company arranged at the Public Music Hall in Cleveland.

2. *Cleveland Plain Dealer,* May 22, 1935. The paper also ran the statement that I had prepared for Mortimer and Reisinger, which was the only strike release I was allowed to issue. It was an indirect reply to the company's insistence on its tireless efforts to reach a peaceful agreement. After saying that the company was supposed to come up with a counterproposal but did not do so, the union spokesmen reported that "Negotiations with the White Motor company reached the strike stage after many weeks' conferences with management in which every effort was made by the strike committee to arrive at a settlement."

3. The committee's hands were tied by a motion that Lehman had put across by a vote of 134 to 121 shortly before the strike, that no one was to make statements to the press unless they were previously approved by a local meeting. It was a ludicrous gesture aimed at Mortimer, who, in a careless answer to a reporter during the negotiations, had remarked that a strike was "possible." The *Cleveland News* had reported Mortimer's reply as a definite decision to strike. I set out to get the paper to correct this, which it at first refused to do. But a leader of the Newspaper Guild, Elmer Fehlhaber, arranged for the *News* to publish a letter by Mortimer, which was run verbatim with the heading "What Mr. Mortimer Really Said."

4. It was a round-up of the strike published on June 29, 1935.

5. Sidney Fine (*Blue Eagle,* 523) corroborates this universal viewpoint of peaceful strike and accomplishment despite the fact that he characterizes its

leader elsewhere as an "undeviating follower of the communist line" (303). He notes in particular that "the union, after examining the company's books, did not insist on a general wage increase," a very uncommunistic way of acting, it would seem.

Chapter 6:
The Toledo Chevrolet Strike

1. *Strike Truth,* April 26, 1935 (James Roland and Joseph Ditzel coeditors), Oversize Folders Box, Kraus Collection, Archives of Labor and Urban Affairs, Wayne State University.

2. This was done by Max Kampelman in *The Communist Party vs. the CIO* (New York: Praeger, 1957), 64, published twenty-two years after the Toledo strike. Nevertheless, Sidney Fine (*Blue Eagle,* 391) picks up Kampelman's lead uncritically.

3. Most of these details of the developing Chevrolet strike stemmed from interviews that I later obtained from Roland and Travis.

4. The transmissions were headed for final assembly plants in Kansas City, St. Louis, Norwood, Ohio, and Flint.

5. As quoted in *Strike Truth,* April 26, 1935.

6. In Kraus Collection.

7. *The New Militant,* May 14, 1935.

8. Fine, *Blue Eagle,* 401–2.

Chapter 7:
The AFL Imposes an Unacceptable International
on the UAW

1. See Fine, *Blue Eagle,* 405 n75. All of this was unknown to us at the time.

2. See Box 8, Kraus Collection, Archives of Labor and Urban Affairs, Wayne State University, for a letter dated July 31 to Killinger, preferring charges against him in the name of the "General Organizer of the American Federation of Labor" (that is, Dillon).

3. ACLU report by Lyle W. Cooper, Marquette University, and Max E. Geline, attorney.

4. "Statement of the Progressive Delegates to the Convention," Box 5, Kraus Collection.

5. Roland and I sat together during the early days of the sessions and he regaled me with stories about the Chevy strike. He left the convention soon after, however, which was fortunate for our group because my familiarity with him had not gone down well with members of the big Toledo local.

6. International Union of United Auto Workers, *Proceedings of the Convention,* Detroit, 1935, 15ff.

7. *Proceedings,* 29.

8. *Proceedings,* 18–19.

9. *Proceedings,* 34.

10. *Proceedings,* 35–39.

11. *Proceedings,* 40–44.

12. Forrest Woods later told me in a personal interview that he had strongly opposed Martin's candidacy. "All the National Council members had pledged not to run against Dillon. . . . After the convention many of us were even more bitter with him for having stayed in the race. Otherwise we would have elected the other officers as well as the executive board. This way we got nothing."

13. *Proceedings,* 61–64.

14. *Proceedings,* 64–66.

15. *Proceedings,* 70.

16. *Proceedings,* 71.

17. *Proceedings,* 72.

18. *Proceedings,* 73–74.

19. *Proceedings,* 77ff.

20. *Proceedings,* 107, and personal notes.

21. My viewpoint at the time on the so-called independent unions did not much differ from the convention resolution fostered by the Dillon forces, which attacked them all virulently, the "Coughlin Union" in particular. This retrogressive attitude was completely altered by the time the South Bend Convention was held eight months later, largely because of the influence of the newborn CIO.

Chapter 8:
The Industrial Unions Support the UAW's Protest

1. Mortimer, *Organize!* 88–89.

2. See Kraus Collection, Archives of Labor and Urban Affairs, Wayne State University.

3. The Mechanics Educational Society of America was an "independent" union largely made up of skilled workers, particularly tool-and-die mechanics.

4. Even the *Daily Worker* seemed stunned by the change in Lewis. Just before the convention, it had warned its readers against the attempts of such leaders as Lewis and Sidney Hillman to take control of the industrial unionism movement. Their real purpose, it avowed, was "to behead it." But after seeing the new Lewis in action, Bill Dunne, the communist paper's leading writer, grew dithyrambic about him, asserting that he constituted a Götterdämmerung for the AFL craft leaders, that is, a "twilight of the gods."

5. American Federation of Labor, *Proceedings of the Fifty-fifth Convention,* Atlantic City, November 1935, 523ff.

6. *Proceedings,* 537.

7. *Proceedings,* 726–27.

8. Mortimer, *Organize!* 92–93.

9. *Proceedings,* 735.

10. *Proceedings,* 732–33.
11. *Proceedings,* 734–35.
12. *Proceedings,* 729.
13. *Proceedings,* 732.
14. *Proceedings,* 745.
15. *Proceedings,* 732–33.

Chapter 9:
Lewis Chooses Cleveland to Launch the CIO

1. Mortimer says that I accompanied him to Washington to see Lewis (*Organize!* 98). This was not the case. We had talked about my going, but only in addition to the auto workers' delegation. I could not swing the expense, however.

2. Dubinsky and Lewis were the only representatives of industrial unions on the AFL Executive Council.

3. American Federation of Labor, *Proceedings of the Fifty-fifth Convention,* Atlantic City, November 1935, 574.

4. *Proceedings,* 742. Frank Martel was a leader of the International Typographical Union, which put him in a rather delicate position with respect to the Detroit Federation of Labor, the majority of whose affiliates were craft unions. On the other hand, his own union, a leading member of the CIO, as well as his personal opinions, would have registered a strong pull in the other direction.

5. *Proceedings,* 727.

6. The conflict over the granting of the Toledo Local 12's charter is recounted in detail by Homer Martin in the South Bend Convention's *Proceedings* (119–21). Several of his arguments are corroborated, apparently unwittingly, by Dillon himself, in his report to the convention, notably through the correspondence it reproduces between the Detroit UAW office and the Toledo local.

7. I described this experience of the Toledo Chevrolet workers in an article titled "General Motors Strikes Back," published in the *Nation* of December 25, 1935, under the pseudonym H. S. Grant.

8. The leader of the Norwood clique was Bill Black, its erstwhile president and once a leading progressive. Black's sudden, mysterious turn became understandable several months later when the La Follette Committee exposed him as a probable Pinkerton spy.

9. One of these was Paul Porter, the editor and publisher of *Kenosha Labor,* with whom we had maintained friendly relations for some time. His printer put in a bid for the job of publishing the journal; others were made by publishers of labor papers in Flint and Detroit. A letter dated April 27, 1936, addressed to Porter by the *Milwaukee Leader,* giving "quotations for publishing of the proposed Auto Worker's official publication," indicates that the matter was already well underway. Original in Box 6, Kraus Collection, Archives of Labor and Urban Affairs, Wayne State University.

10. In Box 5, Kraus Collection.

11. Dillon's reference is to the edition of March 1936.

Chapter 10: The South Bend Convention

1. For Green's speech and other matters taken up by him, see International Union of Automobile Workers, *Proceedings of the Convention,* South Bend, 1936, 10–24.

2. *Proceedings,* 7. For Dillon's entire speech, see 6–8; for other interventions, see 23–24.

3. *Proceedings,* 122.

4. *Proceedings,* 217.

5. See the published list of resolutions. The late number—Resolution Number 177—hints at a belated arrangement of this issue.

6. The nomination of Martin as temporary chair was made by previous arrangement by Dick Reisinger of the White Motor local. *Proceedings,* 24.

7. See Francis Dillon's "Report to the Convention," *Proceedings,* 5–22.

8. Roderick McDonald, Dillon's spokesman, admitted this reason for splitting the Toledo local (*Proceedings,* 122).

9. *Proceedings,* 34. Travis's minority report was befuddled by a substitute motion, an amendment, and an amendment to the amendment, before it could prevail.

10. *Proceedings,* 74–75. The original letter is in Box 5, Kraus Collection, Archives of Labor and Urban Affairs, Wayne State University.

11. The Dillon supporter was F. J. Michel, who, as board member from Wisconsin, would play a leading role during the following years in Martin's anti-progressive majority.

12. *Proceedings,* 45–46.

13. *Proceedings,* 38–39.

14. *Proceedings,* 48–49.

15. *Proceedings,* 52. The link between the three vice presidents and reduced officers' salaries established a tradition that helped maintain the rank-and-file character of the UAW.

16. *Proceedings,* 71.

17. *Proceedings,* 72. The results of the voting for first vice president were: Mortimer, 138.599; Merrill, 90.696; and Shipley, 3.6.

18. Davis's motives were beyond calculation at this juncture because they were so mixed up with devious schemes.

19. The resolution, Number 183, was submitted by Local 139, Cleveland, in the name of Frank C. Scheepers (*Proceedings,* 124).

20. *Proceedings,* 127–28.

21. *Proceedings,* 128–29.

22. *Proceedings,* 129.

23. *Proceedings,* 129.

24. *Proceedings,* 125–26.

25. *Proceedings,* 132.

26. *Proceedings,* 133.

27. *Proceedings,* 133–34.

28. *Proceedings,* 129–30.

29. *Proceedings,* 132.

30. *Proceedings,* 134.

31. *Proceedings,* 232.

32. *Proceedings,* 147–48.

33. The expression came from Walter Reuther. He added, "but in actuality we can get all the people who work in our respective plants . . . in our organization and they will stay there" (*Proceedings,* 171).

34. I was delighted by the prominence that Reuther was winning. We had come to know each other in Cleveland during the previous autumn, when he was making a speaking tour in northeast Ohio under the auspices of the Socialist party and the Friends of the Soviet Union, a nonpolitical organization that was quite prominent at the time. He spoke about the two years that he and his brother, Victor, had spent touring in Europe and East Asia, but chiefly about the year and a half they worked at an automobile factory in Gorki. One of his talks was given at the White Motor local.

35. I later learned that Leo Krzycki of the ACW and a prominent Milwaukee socialist intervened with Roy Speth of that city, who was chair of the credentials committee, on behalf of Reuther. See oral history of Roy Speth, Archives of Labor and Urban Affairs, Wayne State University.

36. *Proceedings,* 247. Homer Martin was markedly friendly to Walter Reuther from the chair. The chief reason for this was Martin's wish to be thought of as sympathetic to the Socialist party, a desire he evidenced by other acts. For example, he invited Norman Thomas as a speaker and seized the occasion to praise him warmly. He also put Tucker P. Smith on the program to speak on workers' education. Smith, a leading socialist, was head of the well-known Brookwood Labor College. He terminated his hour-long talk with an offer of almost $5,000 in scholarships for UAW members.

37. The full names of these organizations were the Automotive Industrial Workers of America, the Mechanics Educational Society of America, and the Associated Automobile Workers of America.

38. *Proceedings,* 96–97.

39. *Proceedings,* 137–38.

40. Martin had been in touch with Coughlin while still a preacher in Kansas City and had joined the National Union for Social Justice, as appears in a letter he wrote to the radio priest, addressing him as "Dear Father" and telling him how Martin used Coughlin's talks in his own sermons. (In Homer Martin Papers, Archives of Labor and Urban Affairs, Wayne State University.)

41. Archie Robinson, in the May 1 *Detroit News,* quotes Coughlin as telling him that he was on the train from Detroit to Chicago and had stopped off at South Bend for lunch at the Hoffman Hotel. Robinson continues with the un-

likely story, probably given to him by Frankensteen, that the priest was seen by some UAW delegates, who ran and told Martin. Martin then got Frankensteen and they rushed over to the hotel to invite Coughlin to speak at the "banquet" (smoker). Robinson was there, too, and quotes Coughlin liberally in the article.

42. Frankensteen's lengthy speech to the convention is given in full in the *Proceedings,* 138–44.

43. *Proceedings,* 145.

44. *Proceedings,* 243.

45. *Proceedings,* 238.

46. The Tucci letter is in Box 5 of the Kraus Collection.

47. The eastern district included New York, Pennsylvania, New Jersey, and Connecticut. The southern and western districts, each likewise covered by a single board member, were even more immense, including Georgia, Tennessee, Louisiana, and West Virginia for the southern; and Arkansas, Iowa, Missouri, and California for the western. The states included by the UAW's geographers were evidently those that had at least one auto local at that time.

48. Two Flint delegates whom the La Follette investigators identified were Dick Adlen and Delmar Minzey, the latter from AC Sparkplug. Adlen, a substitute delegate from Chevrolet, was chosen by subterfuge to replace Ted LaDuke by Arthur "Frenchy" Dubuc, president of the local, who was also later exposed as a spy. Adlen's legitimacy was challenged by Lester Washburn of the credentials committee. The case was discussed lengthily before the delegates (*Proceedings,* 66–69), with Adlen and Minzey as the chief witnesses.

49. *Proceedings,* 164–65.

50. *Proceedings,* 214.

51. *Proceedings,* 214–15.

52. *Proceedings,* 162. Its inspiration was the Gorman resolution proposed at the October AFL convention in Atlantic City.

53. Dick Reisinger, chair of the resolutions committee, enthusiastically carried out this exhortation in the following months by helping to organize a Farmer-Labor party in Cuyahoga County. Similar engagements were undertaken by members of other UAW locals, for example, by John Bartee of the Studebaker local.

54. *Proceedings,* 201.

55. These resolutions appear in the *Proceedings:* La Follette, 226; Olympic Games, 225; Scottsboro Boys, 202; Tom Mooney, 200; and National Youth Administration, 224.

56. *Proceedings,* 177, Resolution Number 72; quotation from Dillon, *Report to the Convention,* 45.

57. *Proceedings,* 225. The original resolution was presented by the White Motor local, which had a large proportion of elderly workers who were extraordinarily sensitive on the speedup question and had fought to eliminate piecework.

58. The committee changed the sum assigned to UAW locals from $25,000 in the original White Motor resolution to the unrealistic amount of

$75,000. Delegate Bill McKie, a discharged Ford worker who was to devote the rest of his life to organizing the River Rouge plant, presented a resolution (*Proceedings,* 219) calling for a Ford unionizing fund. Most delegates would have thought it a far cry at that stage of the organization.

59. The numbers of dues-payers are arithmetic approximations that I made based upon the 35 cent monthly per-capita tax for each member, which the International collected.

60. The five Flint locals averaged $53.35 per-capita payments each month for the previous six months, according to the secretary-treasurer's records. That would be the payment for approximately 170 members.

61. *Proceedings,* 253.

62. The interventions of the five delegates are recorded in the *Proceedings,* 253–54.

63. The intervention of John Bartee is recorded in the *Proceedings,* 254–55.

64. *Proceedings,* 259.

65. *Proceedings,* 261.

66. *Proceedings,* 265.

Chapter 11:
The Organization Drive Gets Underway

1. It was not until August that I finally received my appointment after high praise from Martin by wire and letter for the July issue (July 16, 18, 1936, Kraus Collection, Archives of Labor and Urban Affairs, Wayne State University). I never received any other contract but Dorothy and I decided that we should go to Detroit to live, at least temporarily. The rush of events during the next few months decided the matter permanently for us.

2. For example, in a statement in the *Detroit News* of August 4, Homer Martin said that the membership was increasing at an "unprecedented pace" and that old and new members were "coming back by the thousands." He claimed that the UAW's membership had doubled to eighty thousand in four months, with forty new local charters issued. This would average a thousand members per local although the entire International did not have more than three or four locals with as many as a thousand members.

3. The heading was not based on much concrete evidence though the *Detroit News* of September 5, 1936, announced that the Detroit and Wayne County Federation did protest the suspensions, whereas Mortimer reported to me that the Flint Federation had voted to maintain the UAW delegates in full standing.

4. Executive board members were paid no salary; hence, granting them an organizer's post was considered remuneration for the responsibility they assumed. However, it was almost always at half-pay, which had to be supplemented by some local group or groups since an organizer was not supposed to work in the plant.

5. Smith accused Hall of helping Dillon break the picket line during the Motor Products strike that occurred during the months before the South Bend Convention.

6. MESA units in Cleveland and Toledo soon after opened negotiations with the UAW. At the former, they were conducted by Dick Reisinger, whose task was facilitated by the fact that a leader of the MESA, Bert Cochran, had taken the initiative for the merger through correspondence with Mortimer.

7. Not long after, in a radio talk, Frankensteen announced that the amalgamation had been completed and that twenty-six AIWA locals, three MESA locals, and one AAWA local had joined the UAW.

8. Frankensteen's accusation was drawn from the La Follette Committee's proceedings (273), which stated that "the Board's decision found that the [Fruehauf] company had violated the Act by . . . employment of the detective agency for espionage purposes. The Board found that the workers had been discharged because of their union activity and that the company's policy was to disrupt the local union of the UAW and so to defeat collective bargaining." For Frankensteen's radio talk, see "Radio Speeches," July 17, 1936, 10:15 P.M, Box 6, Kraus Collection.

9. A full-time organizer earned $40 a week and was expected to keep expenses at a minimum—and George Addes saw to it that he did so. Frankensteen was paid $48 as chief organizer for Detroit. Part-timers got $20–25; a few who continued at their jobs earned only $10. By mid-autumn there were thirteen full-time organizers on the payroll, nine of them in Michigan, and nine part-time men, five in Michigan. The CIO eventually paid the salaries of three additional UAW organizers though a few more of their own men were sent in by the big internationals, especially during the great strikes.

10. See the articles signed by George Addes in the *United Automobile Worker,* August, September, October 1936, which give full details.

11. The letter, now in the Kraus Collection, was from Lindley Crossthwait and Bill Black and circulated before the latter was exposed as a company agent. I never learned how Mack had obtained the letter.

12. Henry Kraus, *The Many and the Few: A Chronicle of the Dynamic Auto Workers* (Los Angeles: Plantin Press, 1947; repr. Urbana: University of Illinois Press, 1985), 30.

13. There was an exchange of letters between Martin and Addes, dated October 10–19 and November 9, 1936, which I annotated, showing this effort by Pieper, which proved unsuccessful at the time though several months later he did get to Flint and established an administratorship over the local with Martin's blessings. The letters are among my private papers.

14. Working closely with Pieper were Russell Merrill and F. J. Michel, the board member of Wisconsin.

15. The exposure of the Black Legion, which lasted two months, spread from Detroit to Pontiac, Muskegon, and other cities and was heard by several one-man grand juries.

16. Poole's wife denied this testimony emotionally (*Detroit News,* May 23, 1936).

17. This remark was made by Harvey Davis, who, according to Dayton Dean, was the key figure in the Silas Coleman murder. He was a "colonel" in the Black Legion.

18. It was not until a year later that I was vindicated in this little argument when the UAW paper reported that a radio talk by John L. Lewis had been censored because of an attack Lewis made on Davey, whom he characterized as "the infamous governor Davey." The story appeared in the August 1937 issue of the paper, when I was no longer connected with it.

19. Mortimer prepared a paper for the International officers that is now in the Kraus Collection. Dated September 27, 1936, it tells of his difficulties with alleged Black Legion members in Flint. He also turned over to the officers a confession by Harold Hubbard, a worker at Fisher One, of membership in the Legion. The confession is also in the Kraus Collection.

20. *Flint Journal,* August–September 1936. Hubbard's disclosures were the result of a one-man grand jury hearing conducted by Circuit Court Judge Edward D. Black, who attained infamy during the Flint sitdown (Kraus, *The Many and the Few,* 113). Black summoned seventy witnesses but kept most of their testimonies secret.

21. The memorandum is now in the Kraus Collection though it was not in my possession when I wrote *The Many and the Few* from 1939 to 1941.

22. The GM official referred to was Harry W. Anderson, vice president in charge of personnel. See Kraus, *The Many and the Few,* 37, for Anderson's letter that had been published by the La Follette Committee.

23. The Nellie Compton incident is described in Kraus, *The Many and the Few,* 37.

24. Tice Woody gave an amazing reason for having joined the Black Legion (*Detroit News,* June 4, 1936): to get support for his Republican candidacy for the state legislature. He claimed that he quit the Legion when he was double-crossed in favor of another man.

25. *Detroit News,* June 13, 1936. The Cass Tech meeting, it was reported, had been organized by the Conference for the Protection of Civil Rights, a broadly based organization that recently had been founded to combat the Duncan-Baldwin bill, which aimed at curbing freedom of speech and assembly under the sanction of punishment for criminal syndicalism. The conference played a helpful role to the UAW during the great sitdown.

26. Christopher Johnson, in *Maurice Sugar: Law, Labor, and the Left in Detroit, 1912–1950* (Detroit: Wayne State University Press, 1988), claims (183) that Sugar furnished this information to Martin, which he had derived by interviews with Motor Products strikers. I did not know about these interviews at the time though I was aware of Sugar's interest in the Black Legion. I had obtained from him a copy of chapter 7 ("The Black Legion in the Unions") of his unpublished "Memorandum on the Black Legion," now in Box 7 of the Kraus Collection.

27. The source of this material is Sugar, "Memorandum on the Black Legion," chapter 7.

28. See Kraus, *The Many and the Few,* chapter 3.

29. This is revealed particularly in the correspondence of Benjamin Allen. See the letters from Benjamin Allen to John J. Abt, counsel of the Subcommittee, of December 5 and 16, 1936, Kraus Collection.

30. Most of the following account of the Owosso Convention was drawn from an unpublished manuscript that I prepared immediately following that assembly.

31. This campaign is described in Johnson, *Maurice Sugar,* 188–90. It should be mentioned, however, that Dick Frankensteen and his two "teammates," Edward Ayres, president of the Graham-Paige local, and Vincent Klein, treasurer of the Chrysler-Kercheval local, chose to run for state representatives on the Democratic ticket.

Chapter 12:
The First Victories

1. An eyewitness, J. Bouissounouse, described the Paris sitdowns excellently in the July 1936 issue of *Survey Graphic.*

2. *Survey Graphic,* July 1936.

3. The functions of the banner committee escape me, perhaps they were to prepare slogan-bearing placards.

4. In those early days, the affidavit was greatly used by auto unions that found it difficult to establish the credibility of their statements. I can vouch for the fact that the union people took these affirmations very seriously and that they could in general be trusted.

5. These and other actions are described in the November 1936 issue of the *United Automobile Worker* and stem from reports made at an organizers' meeting of November 23 that I annotated. Louis Adamic, with whom I spoke at length when he visited Detroit around this time, reflects these effervescent days in an excellent piece in *The Nation,* December 12, 1936.

6. In the letter, dated November 3, that I wrote to "all officers and members of General Motors locals," I asked for "items of speedup, stretchout, elimination of operations, displacement of men, lengthening of hours, cutting of pay, withholding of bonuses, etc." (Box 7, Kraus Collection, Archives of Labor and Urban Affairs, Wayne State University).

. 7. The letter from Bob Travis to Henry Kraus, dated October 30, 1936, dealing with the first issues of the *Flint Auto Worker,* is in the Kraus Collection.

8. See Kraus, *The Many and the Few,* 47–55; also chapter 13 of this volume.

9. The Bendix local, after lengthy negotiations, had wrung a contract from the company several months earlier on the threat of a strike. The contract included recognition, seniority adjustments, a small blanket raise, and other concessions. It was one of the rare concrete achievements that I could record that summer in the paper.

10. *United Automobile Worker,* December 1936, 12. More extensive parts of the "Diary of a Sit-Down Striker" were published fifty years later in 1986; see Dave Elsila, ed., *We Make Our Own History: A Portrait of the UAW* (Detroit: UAW Education and Publications Departments).

11. The complete agreement as quoted in the December 10 edition of the UAW paper contained only the following items: "The management agreed to

recognize the Automobile Workers as the bargaining agent for its membership; not to grant concessions to any other group not granted to Local 9; to establish a board of review with equal representation from the union and management to pass on grievances; to give a day's notice of layoffs; and a minimum of two hours' employment for any employee called to work."

12. UAW press release by Frank Winn, November 25, 1936, Kraus Collection. Winn reported that "practically all daily papers featur[ed] the incident," meaning the strike.

13. The UAW's executive board analyzed the situation of union organization in GM plants and found a number of key units extremely weak. See Kraus, *The Many and the Few,* 74.

14. A copy of this letter is in the Kraus Collection.

15. Using various disguises, the following locals promised to strike: Toledo Chevrolet, Janesville, St. Louis, Kansas City, and Norwood. The November issue of the *Flint Auto Worker* ran their replies. Regarding the Kansas City strike, see Kraus, *The Many and the Few,* 74–75.

16. Kraus, *The Many and the Few,* 71.

17. The vote was as follows: For the Pieper motion: Pieper, Michel, Garst, Merrill, Willis Marrer of Norwood, and Kennedy. Against were Jones, Soltis, Reuther, Washburn, Tucci, and Frankensteen. The incident is described in Kraus, *The Many and the Few,* 73.

18. Exhibit 1835 is on page 5461 of La Follette Committee Report, "Hearings before a Subcommittee of the Committee on Education and Labor," in *Violations of Free Speech and Rights of Labor,* Vol. 15-A, 75th Cong., 2d sess., pursuant to S.R. 266, 74th Cong., Part 15-A, November 18, 1937.

19. The Kraus Collection (Box 7) contains a sheet with the scores of all who participated in the membership drive contest conducted by the Midland unit and Local 155, listing recruits from June to October 1936. John Anderson leads with fifty-six but Jim Howe is a close second with forty-four. No other contestant comes near these totals.

20. Workers not involved in the sitdown became active in other strike activities, notably visits to other locals' meetings. This was an exciting experience for the participants, who usually received ovations when the "Midland Steel sitdowners" were announced.

21. Our armed guards were cited in an article by Harold P. Marley, in the *Christian Century,* January 6, 1937.

22. These and other similar questions became burning issues during the great sitdown strike at Flint. The UAW's preoccupation with them at Midland served as an instructive manual for many union activists in other places.

23. From the personal interview I had with Reuther late in 1937, which was also the source of much other material in this section.

24. The "fainting spell" was always told as a real event thereafter. George Edwards defended this bit of falsified reporting when I interviewed him two years later: "The fainting story was invented but it's become historical so it can no longer be changed." Edwards evidently did not know about the supposed victim having had a real swoon, as Victor Reuther reports in *The Brothers Reuther* (Boston: Houghton Mifflin, 1976), 135. George Edwards, Victor Reuther,

and Merlin Bishop, the International's part-time educational director, had all obtained jobs at Kelsey-Hayes shortly before the strike and so were able to play important parts in it. Bishop mimeographed a sixteen-page account of the strike "immediately following the settlement." A copy is in Box 1 of the Merlin Collection, Archives of Labor and Urban Affairs, Wayne State University.

25. Walter Reuther gave me the following account about a year later. It was probably changed somewhat in the retelling but this was the way I recorded it from him. During the sitdown proper, I was often at Kelsey-Hayes and scribbled my own notes for use in the *United Automobile Worker.* Regarding the kitchen and the activities of the women, Dorothy Kraus has been my chief source. Her personal papers contain much material from the Kelsey-Hayes, Midland Steel, Bohn Aluminum, and other Detroit strikes of the period. She has also turned over to me most of the documents from the Kelsey strike that are in Box 7 of the Kraus Collection, for example, the report of donations gathered by the chiseling committee.

26. In *Detroit in Perspective* 4 (1980): 74–90, Frank Boles assigns Danzik's role to a man he identifies as Charles Demong, whom he designates as the Kelsey-Hayes personnel manager. Victor Reuther speaks of Danzik, although he spells the name as "Danzig."

27. The issue of women sitdowners was settled in each strike by its own circumstances. Kelsey-Hayes (and Bendix) allowed for separate quarters for the women, which was not the case at Midland. But the decision in the latter to ban women subsequently raised some controversy and the *United Automobile Worker* was concerned about explaining it, arguing that women had work to do at home and children to care for, as though they did not have the same problems when they went to their regular jobs. More to the point, the UAW's leaders were sensitive about the "morality" issue, at which the newspapers kept hammering away.

28. This narrated incident was recorded by Dorothy Kraus in her notes. She had become closely attached to Sophie Guzik, admiring her strength of character and working-class militancy.

29. Dorothy and I had early decided that it was not proper for more than one member of a family to receive the union's money.

30. Victor Reuther identifies the letter as having been written by Merlin Bishop (*The Brothers Reuther,* 138). The original is in Box 7 of the Kraus Collection. It is curious that neither Victor Reuther nor Merlin Bishop mentions Dorothy's participation in the Kelsey-Hayes strike. Frank Boles cites several pertinent documents in the Kraus Collection that came from her, stemming from her activities in the Kelsey strike.

31. *Detroit News,* December 16, 1936, as well as December 17 and 21 for other quotations that follow.

32. George Edwards used this method of defense as a model when helping to erect the inner barricades for the Chevrolet Four sitdown at Flint on February 1, 1937, as described in Kraus, *The Many and the Few* (218). See also his article in the *United Automobile Worker,* January 22, 1937, which anteceded the Chevy 4 strike.

33. The original menu is in Box 7 of the Kraus Collection.

34. The sitdowners' defense inside the factory was organized by Merlin Bishop, he claims, in his sixteen-page memorandum. The paper, notes the author, was "dictated immediately following settlement," which could account for the extravagant remarks and descriptions it contains. For example, Bishop says that when the strikebreakers came in, he contacted the picket captain, "who within an hour" reinforced the local's picket line with about four thousand union sympathizers from locals that were meeting that night, which would have been a fantastic feat. See Box 1, Bishop Collection, Archives of Labor and Urban Affairs, Wayne State University.

35. Several of these incidents were likewise described to me by George Edwards, also a direct witness and participant. For example, he reported that it took about three hours for the outside sympathizers to assume their full strength, certainly a more reasonable estimate than Bishop's figure.

36. Details of these negotiations were recounted to me by Walter Reuther and Dick Frankensteen at the time of their occurrence and more in detail a year or so later when I interviewed them both, separately.

37. George Kennedy had practically invited Bennett to take such action by telling the press that he would not oppose it (see the *Detroit News,* December 23). I was reminded of this fact by Frank Boles in his article in *Detroit in Perspective.*

38. As a matter of fact, plantwide adjustments of 3 to 8 cents an hour were obtained in the upper brackets within a few weeks after the strike.

39. One of the people from whom I heard it directed against Reuther himself was Sophie Good, Vic Reuther's wife though I do not recall whether her husband shared this view. Somehow I did not mind it so much coming from her since I attributed it to her left-wing, Polish, working-class background.

Chapter 13:
The Great General Motors Sitdown

1. This chapter is a highly abbreviated version of *The Many and the Few.* There are a number of changes in wording as well as observations on the accounts of other participants. The primary difference lies in the elimination of detail. Nevertheless, because of the historical importance of the Flint strike and the role it played in the development of the union, a full report of its main features is included.

2. The body's official name was the Sub-Committee of the U.S. Senate Committee on Education and Labor: Violations of Free Speech and the Rights of Labor. It was chaired by Senator Robert M. La Follette, Jr., of Wisconsin, whence its name.

3. The first letter is dated July 10, 1936, and they run to November 10, 1936. They are in the Kraus Collection, Archives of Labor and Urban Affairs, Wayne State University.

4. Adolph Germer claims credit for having persuaded Mortimer "to leave Flint in hopes that the move would restore stability." Germer may have urged

Mortimer to take this step but it was not by any means the reason he made up his mind to do so. The reluctant decision was his own, as he indicates in his letter in the Kraus Collection, dated October 22, 1936, and sent from the East to Bob Travis, who had urged Mortimer to return to Flint because things there were beginning to "pop." Mortimer wrote in part: "I know that Flint is the most important point in the whole organization campaign, and I feel I can do more good there, yet it is also true that other places need attention as well." It was Mortimer's rationalization for having left Flint in order "to keep peace in the family." See Kraus, *The Many and the Few,* 30.

5. Also included were Harry Van Nocker, Jay Green, Clayton Carpenter, and Vic Van Etten and, among the women, Marie Schlacter and Pat Wiseman.

6. It was to become a separate local paper eventually. It was issued only occasionally at first but appeared several times a week during the sitdown.

7. Actually, wages at this time at Fisher One and in the auto industry in general were relatively superior to those elsewhere. Weekly earnings in the auto industry were $36.16, the highest in the country. The hourly wage of 79.3 cents was 40 percent higher than the national average for twenty-five manufacturing industries, according to government statistics.

8. The following famous incident has been reprinted in anthologies, most recently in the U.S. Information Agency's *American Perspectives* (Washington, D.C.: Government Printing Office, 1990), 113–17. The "bow" was a supporting angle-iron welded across the top of the roof structure of the auto body.

9. This was the department in which the main welding and soldering work of the assembly process took place.

10. My friend, Jerome Strauss, who worked in the tool-and-die department at Cleveland Fisher, told me that after the strike started General Motors had begun to make duplicate dies for Cleveland and Flint body stampings at Fisher 23, Detroit. Then, fearing a strike there, GM shifted this work to the "safer" plant at Pontiac. It took three months to make these dies, Strauss said, which indicated how far ahead GM was planning.

11. Almost twenty-five years later, Bud Simons declared that the moving of the dies incident was all a hoax that Bob Travis had invented with Bert Harris, leader of the press-room group. See Simons's oral history of September 6, 1960, Archives of Labor and Urban Affairs, Wayne State University. Travis, Simons said, was worried that the current flat-glass strike at Toledo would shortly force Fisher One to close, thus wrecking the sitdown plan. It is highly questionable whether Travis would entrust such a role to Bert Harris, a former Black Legion suspect and a dubious character at best. Also amazing was the idea that Travis would do this without telling any of the rest of us about it.

12. Roy Reuther had been sent up to Flint about a month earlier to assist Travis in his rapidly expanding task. He was acquainted with Flint, having taught union classes there in the early period of the NRA from 1934–35 under the Federal Economic Recovery Agency.

13. Van Nocker's journal is in the Kraus Collection.

14. The kitchen committee eventually engaged several dozen members, most of them women, in the various details of its work. Dorothy Kraus's several orga-

nizational tasks occupied most of her time but she functioned as Bob Travis's overall supervisor of the kitchen. Other women, strikers' wives (for example, Hazel Simons, Donna Devitt, and Bessie Taylor), were involved with its practical features. Those like Lottie Krank, who worked at Fisher One and were not permitted to sit in, contented themselves with doing other outside work. But this was not the case with Pat Wiseman, who deeply resented being excluded from the sitdown and maintained a one-woman picket line throughout the strike.

15. Fisher Body 2, a small assembly plant on the other side of town, had struck independently some hours earlier than Fisher One.

16. In his oral history of November 22, 1960, in the Archives of Labor and Urban Affairs at Wayne State University, Adolph Germer lays claim to having been responsible for a number of initiatives that no one knew about during the sitdown. He takes credit for the idea that Judge Black might have been a GM stockholder. Whereupon, Germer says, Lee Pressman declared that he was going back to New York (which never happened) to look into the matter. Pressman then sent a wire (evidently from New York) that the judge owned "218,000" [*sic*] of such stock. After the union exposed this fact, Germer concludes, the company decided that "they could not resist the organization any longer and they began to recognize it and they have had relations with them ever since." Hence the strike should have ended then and there! Despite its wholly contradictory character, Sidney Fine accepts Germer's claim, giving a strange reason: "Pressman has generally been given credit for having suggested that Black might be a GM stockholder," he observes, "but I have preferred to rely on Germer's contemporary account," meaning his diary (*Sit-down: The General Motors Strike of 1936–37* [Ann Arbor: University of Michigan Press, 1969], 381 n45).

17. A Pinkerton agent by the name of Peterson, who was in charge of spies at the Flint Fisher Body plants, testified at the February 1937 hearings before the La Follette Committee that he had a spy sitting down at Fisher Two who "came out after a while," adding significantly that "when he came out he told about how many men were in there." See La Follette Committee, "Report," vol. 5; see also under "Clark," another Pinkerton official, 1761.

18. The Fisher Two bodies were sent across the street by way of an overhead conveyor to Chevy 2, a final assembly plant where cars were prepared for the regional market.

19. In *The Many and the Few* (128–29), I name Bruce Manley and Hans Larsen as leading the group that took over the gate. Sidney Fine quotes the La Follette Papers, Box 124, "Flint Affairs," as naming Roscoe Rich for this task (see *Sit-down,* 344 n8). I have no means of verifying this matter and am, accordingly, dropping any reference by name to the responsible person or persons though Roscoe Rich, in an oral history of July 6, 1978, does identify himself with "guarding the stairs."

20. The La Follette Committee's reports are replete with evidence that General Motors paid for gas shells and guns furnished to the Flint police. Dated as late as November 28, 1936, bills for many thousands of dollars worth of purchases are listed linking the names of James V. Mills, Flint police chief, Arnold Lenz, Chevrolet plant manager, and others.

21. This was Floyd Williamson, a highly paid publicity man who worked for the Lawrence Will Advertising Agency of New York, which had been hired to handle the Flint Alliance's public relations.

22. John Brophy, the CIO organization director, had assumed the task of keeping close tabs on Martin. In the memoirs he wrote years later, Brophy was confused about the details of this incident; he writes that it was he who got the "leak" from Bill Lawrence though he himself was in Detroit at the time. Fine (*Sit-down,* 396 n68) confirms the version in *The Many and the Few,* referring to a letter that Lawrence wrote him on May 1, 1967.

23. The quotation is from the *Flint Journal,* January 18, 1937, a photocopy of which is in my private files. The conflict at Fisher Two was thereafter referred to as the "Battle of Bulls Run" by unionists and can be found in this form in innumerable citations by UAW people. However, in *Sit-down* (4), Fine changes the name of this event to the "Battle of the Running Bulls," saying merely "as the union was later to name it." He does not, however, reveal when this identification took place or upon whose authority.

24. Donations to the UAW's Strike Fund from January 1 to February 9, 1937, totaled $40,201.88. The four biggest donations were from Toledo Local 12 ($10,000); Studebaker Local 5 ($6,000); Flint Local 156 ($1,354.84); and Hudson Local 154 ($750).

25. This was probably the map that Roy Reuther said he drew; see Fine, *Sit-down,* 398 n6.

26. I did not know at the time I wrote *The Many and the Few* that Bob Travis credited Kermit Johnson with the idea for the decoy, which, according to Fine, Travis reported in an interview on December 10, 1964 (*Sit-down,* 267, 398 n6).

27. My account of Kermit Johnson's role in the taking of Chevy 4 has been criticized both on grounds of personal antagonism and on a factual basis. I admit that it was impermissible for me to write that his failure to go to work either that morning or at noon was "a case of funk" (*The Many and the Few,* 200). But the fact remains that he did miss going to work on time and consequently failed to carry out his part of the take-over plan. The record that Johnson himself left of his actions on that day is incontestable verification on this score. It first appeared in the Chevrolet Local 659's *Searchlight* commemorative issue of February 11, 1959, more than twenty years later.

He opens his account by describing how he "walked through the plant gate *that afternoon* [emphasis added], February 1, 1937." He goes on, "Now at exactly 3:10 P.M., I was upstairs in the toilet. . . . I had nothing to do but wait and hope that everything was moving according to schedule." Johnson had "nothing to do" because he had already missed out on his own role in that schedule. At 3:25, he continues, he went down to the main floor to watch for the arrival of Ed Cronk from Plant 6. "I couldn't understand why Ed and his men weren't here: they were long overdue." Yet he should have known that they could not possibly have been there at 3:25 because they did not start work on the night shift until 3:30 and only then could they get busy closing down their plant.

Actually, it was a good deal past 3:25 when Johnson went downstairs and the Chevy 4 night shift was going full force. It was at least 3:45 when Cronk arrived, accompanied by twenty men. Johnson asked him rather ungraciously "where in the hell the three hundred men were that he had guaranteed to bring with him." They thus decided "to go back to Plant 6 for reinforcements" and, disregarding the stiff fight that the men had been putting on there led by Carl Bibber, "Polack" Joe Stoyall, and others, Johnson concludes, "Luckily, we encountered little opposition . . . and in a short time we were back in Plant 4 with hundreds of determined men."

28. Fine's outline of the plan differs in several important respects from the one in *The Many and the Few.* He reports, for example, that Bob Travis decided to make a significant last-minute change in the plan by telling Ed Cronk not to take his men from Chevy 6 to Chevy 4, but to Chevy 9 (*Sit-down,* 268). Fine does not say, however, where he got this astonishing information, which is contradicted by all other accounts. Its source, however, is hinted at when Fine reports that this alleged alteration by Travis was countermanded by Merlin Bishop, who was in a sound car on the hill overlooking Chevy 6 when Cronk came out of that plant (*Sit-down,* 270). Who gave Bishop the authority to overrule a supposed order of the chief organizer of the strike in Flint? The whole story, which undoubtedly originated in Bishop's pregnant imagination, is recorded in his oral history as taken by Jack W. Skeels on March 29, 1963, as Fine has noted in *Sit-down* (419). Oral history in the Archives of Labor and Urban Affairs, Wayne State University.

This authentication by Fine of Bishop's information is the more surprising when one reads his oral history and notes the extravagant way he describes the working out of the Chevy plan, especially the part that he ostensibly played in it (interview with Jack W. Skeels, 22): "So when [Cronk] came out with his small following, I advised him from the bluff with the mike . . . to go into Plant 4 and close it down. In the meantime, Roy [Reuther] with his sound car had created so much commotion that all the police force, the ambulances, the police cars and the guards went out of the main plant [Chevy 4] which we wanted and over to Plant 9, just as our strategy had anticipated. Meantime I pulled around in front of Plant 4 and instructed them as to how to take over," Bishop went on. "We had sent out calls to as far away as Toledo and Detroit. . . . People left their plants, jumped in their automobiles, did not even take time to notify their wives and came to Flint. By six or seven o'clock they were coming in cars and going over the fence, helping to barricade Plant 4."

29. In *The Many and the Few* (215), I identify this huge person as Kenny Malone. That is an error, as Malone indicated in an interview with Stephen Peets in preparation of Peets's BBC film *Yesterday's Witness* in 1975. Malone says that when he went to work at Chevy 4 that afternoon, "I met some guys and they told me that the trouble was going to be in 9 [so] I didn't go into 4, I went . . . to 9." It was only after the men were driven out of Chevy 9 that he went back to Chevy 4 "and by that time Plant 4 had already been taken." In an interview on July 29, 1986, with Neil Leighton and me, Kenny Malone explained that the role I describe in the book was his brother Pat's, not his. "Well, you know," he excused me, "we looked a lot alike and a lot of times we were mistaken" (43).

30. The stairs at this plant going up to the entrance from the street sidewalk no longer exist.

31. In *The Many and the Few* (218), I wrote that George Edwards of the Detroit West Side Local was in charge of this work because I saw him occupied with it when I went into the plant after it was captured. It appears, however, that the insiders had already done much of this work, as Howard Foster reported in his interview with Stephen Peets of the BBC. Kenny Malone told Neil Leighton and me that when he got back to Chevy 4, he got hold of a pickup truck with a battery-operated hoist and helped stack stock against the back doors "until it run out on me."

32. Frank Trager was national labor and organization secretary of the Socialist party, I later learned.

33. This story was probably fabricated by the same National Guard officer who had given the press the fantastic tale that the strikers were holding five hundred "loyal" workers as hostages.

34. Judge George Murphy was the brother of the governor.

35. As quoted by Lewis himself at the UAW's convention in St. Louis in July 1940.

Chapter 14:
The Detroit Upsurge and the Chrysler Strike

1. His reason for coming is fully described in Kraus, *The Many and the Few,* 161–64, as well as in chapter 13 of this volume. He came to officiate at the evacuation of the Fisher One and Two plants, which was suddenly called off.

2. B. J. Widick had come for a short stay like so many others but was caught in the whirl of events and could not pull himself away until his name was included among those charged with inciting to riot during the Battle of Bulls Run and he was legally advised to leave the state.

3. There are various sources for this incident, including my interviews with Walter Reuther and Mike Dragon, as well as accounts in the local press. The Dodge "flying squad" was a group that had been set up some months earlier for the purpose of supplying quick support for UAW strikes when needed.

4. The main source of information about the Briggs-Meldrum strike is from my interview with Dick Frankensteen, to which I have added details from my own observations.

5. In my story in this issue of the paper I use a different name for the personnel director, Dean Robinson. I cannot account for this discrepancy.

6. The revelations about John Gillespie's role in the Briggs and Bohn strikes came from my interview with Dick Frankensteen.

7. *United Automobile Worker,* February 25, 1937. The article went on: "During the famous battle of Fisher Two, she was right there among the men, defying the bullets and gas of the cops and fighting back with all that was in her. . . . Mrs. Johnson remained with the strikers all through that eventful night,

helping to cheer them by leading them in singing. Two songs that appear elsewhere in this paper were composed at this time, largely through her inspiration."
It is pertinent to quote this passage because in recent times Genora Johnson
(Dollinger) has claimed that the papers I edited contained no mention of wom-
en, particularly of herself.

8. Frankensteen's claim of signing as many as five contracts a day was
hardly exaggerated. In an article in the *United Automobile Worker* of March
20 George Addes reports applications for sixteen new contracts during that
week.

9. L. A. Young's assembly line of 150 workers sat down on February 18,
while the rest of the plant continued to work. The strikers presented no demands, evidently waiting for the union's representatives to come and talk things
over with the company. See the *Detroit Free Press,* February 19, 1937.

10. Dick Frankensteen's account of this experience with the anonymous
company, as given in his 1959 oral history in the Archives of Labor and Urban
Affairs at Wayne State University, varies considerably from the one he gave me
in our interview in 1938. I am not claiming precedence. However, it has been
my experience that delayed interviews frequently have the tendency to exaggeration or of complacent boastfulness.

11. This desire to own their own headquarters was to be heard among UAW
locals frequently during this period, possibly reflecting the loss of private
homes, a common experience with workers during the depression.

12. For a short description of the Anderson Guide Lamp violence, see
Kraus, *The Many and the Few,* 184.

13. The charges were dropped against Roy Reuther, Bob Travis, and me, but
they were maintained against Victor Reuther in what for a while looked like a
concerted plan to make him a scapegoat due to his absence in Indiana.

14. The facts of my interview with Maurice Sugar shortly after this incident
took place were later corroborated by certain details that Ed Hall revealed when
I interviewed him in 1938.

15. The description of the organization of the Dodge sitdown came from my
interview with Dick Frankensteen. The donor of the cow, he said, was Mary
Zuk, the organizer in 1935 of the famous women's meat strike in Detroit. She
was a member of the Hamtramck common council.

16. This account was given to me by Maurice Sugar when I interviewed him
in 1938.

17. Kraus, *The Many and the Few,* 233.

18. Such details may give the impression of organizational looseness in the
International, which was to some extent true during this period. Moreover, the
recent experience of the Flint sitdown had given us the habit of independent
action, which had evidently infected some of the Detroit locals, particularly the
progressive ones.

19. It is a pity that the newspaper source of this incident has been lost, especially since the reporter turned out to be pro-union.

20. The source for this is my interview with George Edwards in 1938.

21. Lewis's remark about the Chrysler stool pigeons was probably a refer-

ence to the public hearings that the La Follette Committee had been conducting in Washington, which received wide publicity. A pertinent personal detail was the exposure of a Dodge worker and militant member of the union, John Andrews, as a Corporations Auxiliary spy; he was also the former close friend of Dick Frankensteen's, who participated in the revelations.

22. Frankensteen's view is corroborated by *Newsweek* (April 3, 1937), which suggests that Lewis was eager to get back East to negotiate the UMW contract.

Chapter 15:
GM's Counterattack at Flint and the UAW's Reply

1. For example, the *Flint Auto Worker* on April 3, 1937, reported a drop in speed at the Fisher One North unit from fifty-five to fifty-two jobs an hour.

2. Reinstatements at Chevrolet and AC Sparkplug ran to more than two dozen in a ten-day period. Eighteen were rehired at Chevy, including men who were discharged upon returning from Anderson, Indiana, where they had gone on a solidarity mission and been jailed there (*Flint Auto Worker*, March 3, 1937).

3. Many retired workers, in oral histories recorded as many as thirty years later, praised the superiority of the steward system in the handling of grievances and in animating the union in the shop.

4. See the oral history of Bob Travis taken by Neil O. Leighton, University of Michigan-Flint, December 13–15, 1978.

5. A photocopy of these minutes that the union kept was recently made available to me by Shirley Foster, the widow of Howard Foster, a member of the Chevrolet local for many years and one of the three men who, together with Bob Travis, worked out the strategy of the "Capture of Chevy Four."

6. The company's wage scale ran from 90 cents to $1.05 an hour, evidently for production work.

7. This was an old grievance that class-conscious workers often raised against foremen, who sought to obliterate the gap between the workers and themselves, whereas union men wanted to keep foremen where they felt they belonged, on the company's side.

8. An almost complete set of the *Flint Auto Worker* for the period during which I edited it and beyond is available at the Flint public library.

9. Emily Clark Brown, who conducted an excellent study of the UAW members' relations with management after the Flint sitdown, interviewed representatives of both sides and drew the following conclusion: "Although the factors involved were highly complex, in most cases the attitude of the management seemed to be the one most crucial factor in determining the character of the development." The quotation is taken from an article that probably appeared in the *Detroit News* during June 1937.

10. The drop in production from 450 units had begun before the big strike as a result of the union's first successes in the plant.

11. Louis Baraty, Buick chairman, presented an excellent roundup of the

gains in that unit in the June 10 edition of the *Flint Auto Worker.* He made a thorough study of wage raises that brought annual earnings up by $384 to $576 for production workers; big gains were won also by common laborers and employees in assembly, parts, heat-treat, foundry, and tool and die, as well as by women workers. I had prepared a similar summary for Fisher One in an earlier issue (April 29), gathered from a dozen interviews.

12. One letter from Klein to me is in the Kraus Collection, Archives of Labor and Urban Affairs, Wayne State University. Among my personal files is a handwritten summary headed "Philip Klein's notes on Flint politics." It contains several items, including one identifying the professional status of the commissioners; another shows the preponderance of bankers and businessmen on the city's leading committees.

13. *Flint Auto Worker,* March 3, 1937.

14. The typed minutes of the stewards' meeting are in my personal papers.

15. An article in a July issue of the *United Automobile Worker* reveals the openly anti-union program of the Law and Order League of Flint. It quotes a spokesman, Raymond French: "In case of a strike we will protect the right to work if the police ask us to. . . . If we are asked to protect the peace we will naturally be armed and deputized." Another leader, Rudolph Eckert, had once been a member of the Friends of New Germany, a fascistic organization.

16. Ed Geiger, an officer of the Buick local, praised Pastva as a loyal union man who had served steadily on the picket patrol at Fisher One though he worked at Buick (*Flint Auto Worker,* June 16). Another union member, Edwin B. Green, wrote to the paper (June 30) and identified the trigger-happy Officer Grimes as having been, with Green, a member of the Ku Klux Klan, and "who became a part of the riff-raff that formed the Black Legion . . . after the decent Americans had shaken the Klan."

17. The Flint UAW local conducted an energetic but unfortunately unsuccessful campaign on behalf of the reinstatement of the teachers.

18. On the contrary, the recall campaign conducted against Frank Ringlein a couple of months later was aided by the resurgent strength of the UAW and by the mobilization of the stewards at Buick in the Ward 6 district. This recall was successful; it was only the second time in Michigan's history that this had taken place, according to the *Flint Auto Worker* of July 22, 1937.

19. The excuse that Special Prosecutor Clifford A. Bishop gave for dropping Victor Reuther's charges was a legalistic accommodation: The riot act at Fisher Two had not been read to the strikers by the proper authorities (*Flint Auto Worker,* June 2).

Chapter 16:
The UAW Splits into Two Opposing Camps

1. In a letter dated January 22, 1966, from Maurice Sugar to Wyndham Mortimer, which is in my personal files, Sugar wrote: "The Lovestone corre-

spondence came into the possession of the Union in the following manner: One day my receptionist came into my office with a package. She said that a man had handed it to her, saying that it was for Mr. Sugar. He left immediately. She did not know who he was. Neither did I. When I examined the contents of the package I grasped their importance. They were authentic—I had no doubt about that. I immediately got in touch with Addes. And that's how it happened. I don't know the exact date, but it must have been in August, 1938, shortly after the 'trial' of the five suspended general officers, as you will note from the enclosed."

2. The endorsement of the five officers by Local 156 is reported in the *Flint Auto Worker* of June 16, 1937.

3. Mortimer described this incident to me soon after it took place. See Kraus, *The Many and the Few,* 265–66.

4. See the oral history of Bob Travis taken by Neil Leighton, University of Michigan-Flint, December 13–15, 1978, 77–78.

5. "Herewith is report submitted by R. C. Travis to the executive board for their consideration and decision on the question of the recent elections in Flint, Michigan." In author's personal files.

6. The old officers of Local 156 dated from Mortimer's period in Flint, when he had arranged for the separate units to be joined into one local. They had continued to hold these posts though Bob Travis had shunted them aside during the big strike. Originally, thirteen members were on the Flint local's executive board of 1936. According to a La Follette Committee report of November 16, 1937, three of these men were Corporations Auxiliary agents and "at least two other members were Pinkerton spies" (70).

7. New elections at the Fisher One unit were not held until late in May 1937, when the following officers, most of them close to Harris, were designated: Henry Wilson, chair; Harold Hubbard, vice-chair; Arliss Freeman, sergeant-at-arms; and Bert Harris, Ed Carpenter, and a man named McSwain, committeemen. Reported in *Flint Auto Worker,* May 25, 1937.

8. A few of the many pertinent examples are the following: April 3, 1937, page 2: after a strike at Buick, it was agreed "that the men in factory no. 11 would take up all grievances in the proper manner in the future." April 29, page 3: "Travis Calls for Firm Union Discipline." June 2, page 4: a letter from Bob Griffith, probably from Fisher Two, "calls for Curb on Sitdowns." June 16, page 1: an article on strike settlement at Chevrolet Grey Foundry, Saginaw, reports that "the men unanimously agreed not to strike again no matter what controversy arises, but to follow out the agreement."

9. The canceled page is in Box 10 of the Kraus Collection, Archives of Labor and Urban Affairs, Wayne State University.

10. A Unity member at a meeting had asked Pieper whether it was "legal" for the other group to pass out leaflets marked "Progressive Group of Local 156." Pieper replied, "There is no Progressive Group within Local 156, only Local 156 itself." There were "tremendous cheers," the paper reported. The questioner continued, "Does that mean that anyone who passes out literature

other than that dealing with union business is subject to suspension or expulsion?" Pieper responded, "Yes."

11. When I interviewed him, Frankensteen mentioned the following men as among those present at these early caucus meetings with him: Morris Field, Morris Silverman, Ziggy Dobrzynski, and Bill Taylor.

12. This account is from my interview with Walter Reuther.

13. Reuther's report is one of several documents from this caucus that are in my personal files.

14. Ralph Dale, the able and alert friend of Ed Hall who had been assigned to Buick as organizer during the sitdown and had remained there, encouraged that unit to propose Travis and Walter Reuther as general officers of the International but on Travis's demurrer the matter was dropped.

15. Strong pressure had to be exerted on Merrill to drop out of the race, as is reflected in an affidavit signed by three top leaders of his South Bend coterie: John H. Bartee, the UAW's organizational director for Indiana, and Leslie R. Tower and Charles H. Wilson, UAW organizers assigned to that state. The three men testified that on July 6, 1937, Merrill "did say to us during a discussion of the coming convention and the fact that he and Richard Frankenstein [*sic*] were contemplating their candidacies as Vice Presidents of the International Union of the [UAWA], when asked what he would do in the case they lost, that 'we will start a cessation [secession] movement from the I.U.A.W. of A.'" A copy of the original affidavit is in my personal files.

16. Verbatim copies of the talks by Mortimer and Hall are in my personal files.

17. From my interview with Ed Hall. Mortimer's participation in this irresponsible act can only be explained by the overwrought situation of the time.

18. The "Battle of the Overpass" and its sequel, the suit filed by UAW victims against the Ford Company, are developed in detail in Johnson, *Maurice Sugar,* 223–26.

19. Reuther, who had organized a group of "five hundred" from his own West Side Local for the second distribution, did not participate in the handout after all but went back to Milwaukee to the board meeting in answer to George Addes's urgent telephone call. The distribution went off peaceably, with a large number of watchers, some of them official observers, including the spunky Mrs. Gifford Pinchot.

20. Our eyes boggled when we saw Paul Treadway's name among the victors at Fisher One though we were not surprised to see Bert Harris's. Pat Wiseman was not elected but Marie Schlacter was. Not a single one of the left-wing group who led the sitdown was included. Several of them challenged the results, however, and the case became a hot issue at the Milwaukee Convention.

21. The full results of the election of convention delegates at Chevrolet appear in the *Flint Auto Worker,* July 29, 1937; those at Fisher Two are recorded in the issue of August 5, 1937.

22. The Buick results appear in the *Flint Auto Worker,* July 22, 1937; those at AC Sparkplug are recorded in the issue of July 29, 1937.

Chapter 17:
The Milwaukee Convention

1. My visual memory of the convention, aside from its great mass of almost two thousand delegates, was a blaze of color. It was the first assembly at which overseas caps, for forgotten reasons, had been universally adopted, each local suiting its own fancy in color and lettering. The Emergency Brigades of the Flint and Detroit auxiliaries added to the chromatic pattern with their red and green berets and armbands, while the Packard women sported gleaming white shirts and blue sashes.

2. International Union of United Automobile Workers, *Proceedings of the Convention,* Milwaukee, 1937, 9.

3. *Proceedings,* 18.

4. The information is from an interview with Nicholas (Mike) Dragon, Frankensteen's friend, who was highly informative about the activities of the PG caucus at the convention. Spreading falsehoods about leading Unity people was a major feature of their efforts. Travis was an important target, his alleged mishandling of funds being a chief accusation. We had prepared in anticipation a fourteen-page booklet, which Flint's Unity delegates chipped in to pay for. Titled "Flint, a True Report," it listed the local's outstanding accomplishments since the strike. Copy in the Kraus Collection, Archives of Labor and Urban Affairs, Wayne State University.

5. *Proceedings,* 19.

6. *Proceedings,* 34.

7. *Proceedings,* 39.

8. *Proceedings,* 42–45.

9. *Detroit News,* August 23, 1937. The newspaper listed the four choices of the PG caucus for the executive board from Detroit as Morris Field, Loren Houser, Ed Ayres, and John Ringwald. Only the first two were elected.

10. *Proceedings,* 41–42.

11. *Proceedings,* 43.

12. The *Detroit News,* August 18, 1937, provides statements on the subject by Homer Martin and Ed Hall.

13. I possess a copy of the memorandum prepared by Unity in my personal files.

14. *Proceedings,* 63.

15. *Proceedings,* 83.

16. *Proceedings,* 84–85.

17. *Proceedings,* 90.

18. *Proceedings,* 90.

19. *Proceedings,* 91–92.

20. *Proceedings,* 96–102.

21. *Proceedings,* 106.

22. *Proceedings,* 106. David Dow, chair of the committee, backed Martin in his accusation of sabotage of its work by minority members. Despite the fact

that two CIO leaders, Ora Gasaway and Frederick Umhey (executive secretary of the Ladies Garment Workers) had helped draw up a "tentative constitution to guide us . . . this opposition has argued [against] it all the way down the line," he charged (*Proceedings,* 110).

23. *Proceedings,* 106–7.

24. *Proceedings,* 111.

25. *Proceedings,* 112.

26. *Proceedings,* 113.

27. *Proceedings,* 114–15.

28. *Proceedings,* 115.

29. *Proceedings,* 121.

30. *Proceedings,* 137ff. The majority's voting system would grant one vote for the first two hundred members, a second vote for the next three hundred, and one vote for every five hundred thereafter. Bob Travis gave examples of the unfair distribution of voting strength that would result from this system. Thus the Dodge local (PG), with twenty thousand members, would get forty-one votes instead of two hundred, whereas forty-two small locals with a total of a thousand members would get forty-two votes.

31. *Proceedings,* 154–55.

32. *Proceedings,* 156.

33. Martin introduced Lewis as "the most outstanding labor leader of all time . . . [who] represents for us a new hope, a new life, a new being in this country." Thus committed, he could hardly contradict whatever Lewis might propose regarding the UAW's internecine quarrel. *Proceedings,* 156–66.

34. *Proceedings,* 162.

35. *Proceedings,* 164–65.

36. *Proceedings,* 166.

37. *Proceedings,* 168.

38. *Proceedings,* 169–70.

39. *Proceedings,* 172–74.

40. *Proceedings,* 178–79.

41. References to Jay Lovestone's thoughts have their source in his letters.

42. *Proceedings,* 202.

43. *Proceedings,* 203–6.

44. I recall one discordant topic, however, that was discussed in a huddle at the Unity caucus: Walter Reuther's opposition to Lloyd Jones's reelection as executive board member. He said that Jones was not "board caliber." He managed to win out in the end and Jones's name was absent from the list of those elected. This rejection pained me since I had a sincere and affectionate regard for Jones and felt that he was unjustly downgraded by intellectuals because of his unsophisticated manner.

45. *Proceedings,* 210–11.

46. *Proceedings,* 214.

47. In the vote on the resolution calling for an aggressive drive at Ford, Walter Reuther presented a dramatic interlude in the form of a "secret" member from Rouge, after warning news photographers not to take shots of him. "I

recommend, Mr. Chairman," he ended, "a standing vote on this resolution." Martin eagerly entered the act: "Are you ready for the vote? Let's stand up!" He played a different role in suppressing resolution 147 calling for the adoption of "Solidarity Forever" as the "official theme song" of the UAW. His negative ruling on the voice vote caused loud objections but he explained that "we want a song of our own," having in mind the "anthem" that his mentor Jay Lovestone had arranged for his friend, the "eminent composer," to create.

48. The executive board member that the Flint delegates proposed was Louis Baraty, president of the Buick unit. Flint had voted sixty-three to twenty-one for Baraty, who was Unity's candidate.

49. *Proceedings,* 257–60.

50. *Proceedings,* 261ff.

51. *Proceedings,* 263.

52. *Proceedings,* 265.

53. *Proceedings,* 266.

54. *Proceedings,* 267–73.

55. *Proceedings,* 275–77.

56. Harris claimed that when his unit received word that the eight delegates were being added to its group, eight hundred signatures were gathered within an hour to a statement denying their legitimacy.

57. *Proceedings,* 277–80.

58. *Proceedings,* 280.

59. *Proceedings,* 282–83.

60. *Proceedings,* 283–84.

61. *Proceedings,* 284.

62. *Proceedings,* 285.

63. *Proceedings,* 286.

64. *Proceedings,* 289.

Chapter 18:
A Short-lived Mirage of Peace

1. A copy of the Flint Edition, dated September 11, 1937, is in my personal papers.

2. Six weeks later, the International's executive board made the ban on local papers general. All but one knuckled under despite some initial resistance. Mark Belian, editor of the *Kelsey-Hayes Picket,* called it a "usurpation" of the right of free speech and said he would continue publishing until his membership stopped him, reported the *Detroit News* of November 11, 1937. The *West Side Conveyor* put up the stiffest fight, the local Joint Council announcing in the *Detroit News* on November 14 that until Martin "explains in what way the local would benefit by suspending publication, we will continue . . . the *West Side Conveyor.*" It did, in fact, keep going for a number of months.

3. On November 5, 1937, Travis was sent to Muncie, Indiana. Six months later he was dropped from the UAW payroll and went to work for the CIO.

4. Martin and the delegation have described the following incident in contradictory versions.

5. On October 8, Martin sent a long, personal letter, a copy of which is in my files, to all UAW locals, describing the gun incident: "As president of your international union, my life has been threatened many times. . . . My first thought was that I was set upon by a gang of thugs; therefore, when the door was about to be broken down, I opened it myself, and stood ready with a gun to protect my life."

6. A copy of the request, dated October 19, 1937, is in my files.

7. Martin had opened the door and stuck his gun into the ribs of Daniel Gallagher, chair of the Timken plant.

8. I did not attend this conference though I interviewed several of its leading participants soon after. In mid-October, Dorothy and I, May and Walter Reuther, and Frank Winn had driven to New York, with a weekend stopover at Reuther's parents in Wheeling, West Virginia. While the rest of us remained in New York, Reuther went off for a day or two to attend the CIO Convention in Atlantic City. Later, when the others returned to Detroit, I stayed on in New York for a few more days, thus missing the GM-UAW conference.

9. The detailed reports that follow are from the *Proceedings of the UAW-GM National Conference, November 14–15, 1937,* Box 12, Kraus Collection, Archives of Labor and Urban Affairs, Wayne State University.

10. The Committee of 17 had been elected at the June 5–6 UAW Conference of GM locals and functioned in the "negotiations" that followed.

11. *Proceedings,* 53.

12. *Proceedings,* 54.

13. *Proceedings,* 56.

14. *Proceedings,* 70. Frankensteen in his report was silent about the serious mistakes that had been made in the Ford drive and gave no indication that this situation would be changed.

15. *Proceedings,* 71.

16. Once opened, a number of delegates took up the question of layoffs. Fisher 37, Detroit, employed only half as many men as the year earlier due to "progressive operating methods" and speedup. Janesville Chevrolet reported that its management was trying to do the same work with reduced manpower, but pieceworkers were having "a hard time to make out." Janesville Fisher Body had 117 fewer men than a year before. The union asked to replace piecework with a straight hourly rate, which was refused. Saginaw reported conditions "much the same as before we had an agreement"; the management was "just as overbearing as ever." Indianapolis said management's attitude was "that the union is on the way out." Speedup was being applied wherever possible. Work was at reduced schedule, seven hours a day, but the reporter ended strongly: "Our local is determined to preserve the union and we stand ready to do anything to accomplish that end."

17. *Proceedings,* 72–73.

18. *Proceedings,* 75.

19. *Proceedings,* 77.

20. *Proceedings,* 78.

21. *Proceedings,* 79.

22. This proposal of Walter Reuther's was omitted from the *Proceedings.* However it, and other significant details of this discussion that also were cut, are recorded in my personal notes.

23. These remarks are diametrically opposed to those Martin made to the press on the evening before the conference opened.

24. *Proceedings,* 85.

25. *Proceedings,* 86.

26. *Proceedings,* 88–89.

27. *Proceedings,* 90. Martin's reference was to the square called Grand Circus Park.

Chapter 19:
Recession and Unemployment

1. These words were left out of the *Proceedings,* as were various others but I recorded them in my notes from other sources.

2. The quotation is from the "Special Session of the UAWA International General Executive Board," November 21, 1937, which is in my personal papers.

3. The highly responsible Frank Winn deflated this eulogistic account in a letter to the labor editor of the *New York Times,* Louis Stark, who had drawn uncritically from it in his written report of the evacuation. "I don't want to go into detail on the Netzorg evacuation incident," Winn wrote, "except to say that the men, disgusted by the attitude of the [executive] board, had already voted to leave the plant, and most of them had left, when Netzorg got there. The only ones there were about 75 who had been left behind to clean up the plant. Netzorg hurriedly called Martin and these 75 were the ones who 'meekly' followed Martin from the plant." Winn's letter, dated December 5, 1937, is in Box 12 of the Kraus Collection, Archives of Labor and Urban Affairs, Wayne State University.

4. Quoted by a local representative, Odin Johnson, in the *Detroit News,* November 20, 1937.

5. Nevertheless the *United Automobile Worker* hailed the Pontiac retreat as a great accomplishment, on November 27, adding that "Early resumption of bargaining on a national scale was indicated" while acclaiming Martin for his "strong stand."

6. These papers were in a batch turned over to me many years ago by John Anderson, president of Local 155.

7. Jay Lovestone to Francis Henson, December 3, 1937. I have a copy of these "Lovestone Letters," furnished me by Maurice Sugar, which I used to prepare an eight-page newspaper that will be discussed later. The same material is evidently available in the Archives of Labor and Urban Affairs at Wayne

State University, according to Johnson; see *Maurice Sugar,* 318 n7, a reference to the thirty-one-page brief in the Maurice Sugar Collection, Boxes 27–28, that Sugar used in defending the suspended officers.

8. A mimeographed copy of the Unity program, or at least one version of it, is among my papers.

9. As an example of the freeness of the discussion, when Bill Munger accosted Walter Reuther with illegally continuing to publish the *West Side Conveyor* at a time when all other locals were putting out their papers as covers of the folded-in International journal, Reuther replied that his local had asked the International to send someone out to tell them what such an arrangement would cost. This had not been done thus far. He invited Munger to their next meeting to take care of this unfinished business.

10. Jay Lovestone to Francis Henson, December 3, 1937.

11. Jay Lovestone to Francis Henson, January 5, 1938.

12. Francis Henson to Jay Lovestone, January 3, 1938.

13. "Minutes of Second Quarterly Meeting of the International Executive Board, IUUAWA, January 12–23, 1938," 25. The International's secretary-treasurer's report is on page 42.

14. "Minutes of the International Executive Board," 32–33. Addes's figures describing the UAW's "grave economic crisis" were suppressed but we are fortunate in having a compendium of the union's financial situation in a letter that Mortimer wrote to John L. Lewis on October 22, 1937. The general fund, he revealed, had declined from June to October from $428,000 to $100,000. Income for July was $107,000, outgo was $144,000; for August, $102,000 and $174,000. The condition would continue to deteriorate.

15. Wyndham Mortimer later claimed that he and several others had voted against the Ludlow Amendment resolution; the UAW's journal printed a note on his declaration.

16. Munger's aim was to promote a rift between "socialists" and "communists" in the Unity group by exploiting the anti-war question. He made what was considered a big scoop by getting Mortimer to debate him on the question in the columns of the *United Automobile Worker* on March 12, 1938.

17. Francis Henson to Jay Lovestone, January 3, 1938. Henson also enclosed a letter that Homer Martin had written to John L. Lewis on December 23, apologizing for the Rockford, Illinois, incident.

18. Quoted in Henson to Lovestone, January 3, 1938.

19. See Henson to Lovestone, January 3, 1938.

20. Martin's interview in the *Herald-Tribune* appeared on February 3, 1938. The officers and other board members of the Unity Group wrote their letter a few days later. The copy in my files bears no date.

21. By April 9, according to the UAW Research Department, twenty-three of Detroit's automobile manufacturing and parts plants were down to sixty-nine thousand workers from a normal count of 250,000. The count for the biggest plants was devastating: Ford Rouge, eighty-seven thousand down to ten thousand workers; Dodge, 24,500 down to seven thousand; three Chrysler plants, 22,900 down to 7,500; Plymouth, eleven thousand down to seven thousand;

Packard, fifteen thousand down to 6,500; Hudson, 14,500 down to five thousand; Chevrolet Gear and Axle, 11,900 down to 4,550; and Ternstedt, closed. Cleveland was also badly hit, with the Fisher Body plant there reporting half of its men laid off due to technical "improvements." One of the "most drastic" of these was the new "merry-go-round conveyor system for the turret-top roofs." See Harold C. Read in *United Automobile Worker,* January 15, 1938.

22. In a December 20, 1937, letter to Dick Frankensteen, Jay Lovestone discusses the matter at length, outlining a program of action for the UAW against the recession and advising that Frankensteen and Martin, along with Bill Munger, go to Washington to see Roosevelt on the subject. See also Jay Lovestone to Francis Henson, December 3, 1937.

23. The activities listed in the following paragraph were gathered from articles in the *United Automobile Worker,* the Flint Edition, and the *West Side Conveyor,* January through April 1938.

24. Minutes of the Chevrolet bargaining committee with plant management, Flint, March 24, 1938, in my personal papers, a gift of Shirley Foster.

25. As reported by Walter Reuther in his personal interview with me; Federal Screw and American Brass ended in violent strikes.

26. In a press statement of March 30, 1938, Walter Reuther declared, "It is obvious that Federal Screw is not acting on its own initiative. General Motors has told it to reduce prices 15 percent if any more orders are to be placed. This is a test case for the entire wage structure in the auto industry. If the employers succeed here they will chop wages everywhere else." In Box 12, Kraus Collection.

27. The description probably stems from Reuther, who, in a protest hearing before the Detroit Common Council, is quoted as saying, "It was the infuriated neighbors, more than anyone else, who had fought the police. . . . Women and children, maddened by the vicious police provocation [who] were mercilessly beaten down when they tried to defend their most elementary rights." *United Automobile Worker,* April 2, 1938.

28. The report about Percy Keyes (or Key), which was attributed to Homer Martin, was taken from a press statement of Walter Reuther's.

29. Mimeographed letter signed "UNITY," dated March 24, 1938. Five such letters that were mailed to group members in March and April 1938 can be found in Box 13 of the Kraus Collection.

30. Wyndham Mortimer and Ed Hall, as chief negotiators of the original April 1938 agreement, wrote Homer Martin on March 10, 1938, that the new "agreement" was "open to most serious criticism." Letter in Box 13, Kraus Collection.

31. In addition to my personal notes, Box 13 in the Kraus Collection contains several informative items regarding these elections.

32. Frankensteen had depended on receiving a clean sweep in his own local to make up for all the other upsets. His failure to do so was a heavy blow and undoubtedly a determining factor in his change of camps soon after. Five of seven PG officers at Dodge were defeated by a 2.5 to 1 vote. Of the five important Detroit locals that retained their PG officers, three were close or only dubi-

ous victories. Curt Murdoch, the Unity candidate at Packard, lost by only 250 votes out of 5,500. At Budd Wheel, the PG men declared themselves neutral, while those at Chrysler Highland Park were considered friendly to Unity. On the contrary, all Unity triumphs in Detroit were conclusive: West Side Local, four to one; Briggs, three to one; Plymouth, two to one; and L. A. Young, two to one. Figures are lacking for the two Tool and Die Locals 155 and 157, but their victories were no doubt decisive, as was that of Murray Body. Even the former PG Hudson local, which had long assumed a neutral stance, elected a slate sympathetic to Unity.

33. The leading socialist in this collaboration was Tucker P. Smith, a member of the SP national committee and former director of the defunct Brookwood Labor College, which Roy and Victor Reuther and other socialists had attended before their UAW careers. Homer Martin appointed Smith as the executive secretary of the UAW's Keep America Out of War Committee, which was in charge of recruiting auto local delegations to the Anti-War Congress held in Washington on May 28–30, 1938. Smith remained on the UAW payroll for many months, his tenure extending beyond the rupture of most other UAW socialists with the Martin-Lovestone alliance. The congress's call proclaimed that "Our people oppose fascism at home but a war against fascism abroad will bring fascist dictatorship at home."

34. The Detroit Unity people had been asked for financial help, which was essential in the Flint campaign because Martin amply supplied the PG forces.

35. These results included only three of the Flint divisions: Chevrolet, Buick, and AC Sparkplug. I have no figures for Fisher Two and Fisher One already had a separate charter.

36. Some years later, another curious element came to my notice in the form of a letter that is mentioned in my notes. In the letter, Carl Thrasher of the Standard Cotton local, and a supporter of John McGill's, said that he had written to an eastern Catholic newspaper to claim that it was a member of the faith that routed Roy Reuther in the Flint election.

Chapter 20:
A Split in Martin's Ranks

1. There were actually two articles in the *Daily Worker,* one appeared on January 5 and another on January 10, 1938.

2. Mortimer's opinion was evidently based on Frankensteen's earlier association with Father Coughlin, who had recently admitted his sympathy for Hitler.

3. In a letter to Bob Travis, dated June 3, 1938, Mortimer wrote: "As a result of these elections, Frankensteen saw that Martin was through and so he began looking around for a new alignment, with the result that we had a meeting in my house at which time Frankensteen's letter was drawn up and the decision was made to send it to all board members."

4. Frankensteen's reference to the fight on wage cuts was a swipe at Martin,

who had gotten into hot water by offering them to companies that were hard-hit by the recession.

5. Martin and his Lovestonite advisors were not the only ones who had the idea of matching Frankensteen's effective anti-factionalism program. Walter Reuther, a few weeks later, issued what he called "a program to end factionalism by removing the causes of factionalism," which he explained as follows: "You can't get rid of factionalism until you've organized Ford, the competitive shops, etc." He got the joint council of his local to endorse the program, then sent it with an introductory letter to all locals in the country.

6. Fred Pieper was aware that the contract must be signed quickly since the company handling it had been accused of fraudulence in the past and its contact man with the UAW, Frank Cohen, was a convicted crook on several counts. The *New York World Telegram* had run an exposé of this background in October 1937 and these things would inevitably become known to the executive board, Pieper feared.

7. Reuther's reference to a "putsch" could have been quoted from a statement by Martin's publicity writer. A copy of Reuther's press release is among my personal papers. A letter from George Miles to Jay Lovestone, dated June 10, 1938, seems to indicate a coordination of the two releases. Miles writes: "Homer telephoned this morning . . . asking for Reuther's phone number and then spoke to him asking for a statement."

8. In my own notes about these additions to the agenda, I recorded that Mortimer went to Walter Reuther's house the night before the board meeting to show him the resolutions that had been prepared and obtain his approval. This would seem to invalidate the claim that friends of Reuther's later made that Frankensteen and the Communist party tried to pull a coup d'état during Reuther's absence from the board session.

9. Details are contained in three press statements by Dick Frankensteen appearing in the *Detroit News* of June 8, 1938.

10. This description of Lewis's reaction was given in a letter addressed to UAW members by the suspended officers and dated June 21. The letter began with the words "Our union is in danger" and then proceeded to give the background of the incident. A copy of the letter is in my personal files.

11. The convention would be called, it was later explained, in accordance with the UAW constitution, which required a referendum of the membership.

12. I made a list of locals outside Detroit that in one way or another showed sympathy for the officers' cause: Buffalo, Toledo 12 and 14, Atlanta 34, Studebaker 5, Bendix 9, White Motors 32 and Cleveland Auto Council, Oakland 76, Los Angeles District Council, Allis-Chalmers 248, Seaman Body 75, Flint (Buick and Chevy 4 and 5, nights), Windsor, Canada 502 and Canada District Council, and Bay City 362 (after turning down Reuther's call for "peace" based on Homer Martin's twenty-point program).

13. The suspended officers eventually abandoned the per-capita tax strike when the drive for the special convention became very strong and they realized that the voting strength of nonpaying locals would be weakened seriously at the convention. But the Reutherites continued to contest the special convention it-

self until it became inescapable when Homer Martin openly defied the CIO and the CIO leaders openly backed it.

14. The *Socialist Call* chose this moment to attack Mortimer, whom it linked with the Communist party as being responsible for the UAW's troubles. Vic Reuther was so angered that he demanded a retraction. A confidential Socialist party report issued at this time, which is in my files, warned against the danger of dual unions, one headed by Martin and Pieper, the other by the CP and Frankensteen. "Hardly a happy choice," the report observed.

15. The circumstances of Addes's trial are described in a July 15 letter sent by the five officers with the unqualified approval of the six minority board members to all UAW locals. The circumstances were also reported in the radio talk that Addes gave over WJR in Detroit on July 21, a copy of which is in my private papers.

16. Article 17 of the UAW constitution specifically reserved the right of expulsion from the union to the locals. It would, of course, have been impossible to obtain such an action against Addes from his own Toledo Local 12.

17. The talk was the first of a series that the officers gave during this crisis, several of which I helped write, Addes's talk in particular. I still have a copy of it with several minor changes in my hand as well as whole sections that evidently were crossed out when the talk was found during a practice reading to be longer than the fifteen minutes allowed.

18. The charges and supporting "evidence" consisting of affidavits, newspaper clippings, and other printed material, as well as the testimony of the single witness, F. J. Michel, were published in a manual carrying the date of August 3, 1938. Not a word is contained in the manual that was offered by the other side.

19. Sugar's letter, dated January 22, 1966, is among my private papers. He was wrong, however, in saying that he had obtained the Lovestone correspondence after the trial of the officers; he used it during the trial to telling effect.

20. Mortimer, *Organize!* 161.

21. Although I could not sit in on the trial, I, along with a number of other UAW people, spent most of each day at the hotel where it was held. The hotel gave us a room where board members would give us up-to-date reports and where I gathered copies of documents that were distributed to the press.

22. "Charges against Richard Frankensteen, Ed Hall, Wyndham Mortimer, Walter N. Wells, George F. Addes, and Affidavits and Exhibits in Support Thereof." It is dated August 3, 1938.

23. Strangely, the press statement was put out by the Publicity Bureau of the UAW on July 27, with an explanatory note: "Following is the opening statement by Larry S. Davidow, prosecuting attorney, before the UAW trial, now in progress at the International Union offices in Detroit."

24. Addes's angry words are also in the July 27 press statement.

25. It was Jay Lovestone's idea that the Martin forces should refer to the Unity Group as the "Dual Union Group." He and his followers use this reference several times in correspondence.

26. It was not Martin's only attempt to disrupt the unity of the officers.

Shortly before the trial, he made a secret visit to Governor Frank Murphy, who was on Mackinac Island for a rest. Martin asked the governor to tell Frankensteen that if he denounced the Communist party he would be reinstated. I later learned from Frankensteen that Murphy passed the word to him, but he turned the offer down, explaining that he was in this fight with the other officers and that they were pledged to stick together to the end. Murphy told Frankensteen: "I knew you would say that, Dick, and I said as much to Murphy. I told him that I regarded you as one of my best friends." Then he advised Frankensteen to go on the air and tell the whole story to the public. Murphy offered to raise the money for him and outlined the entire speech for him, Frankensteen said. Murphy even told him to condemn red-baiting. It seems worthwhile mentioning in this regard that Carl Haessler, who while editing the West Side Local's *Conveyor* continued to write for the *Federated Press,* a national circular, and ran a piece in the latter maintaining that only the "Communist party" had joined with Dick Frankensteen in the new alliance.

27. The bill for Addes's first talk, $125, was paid for by his Toledo Local 12. In my notes there are a number of other such entries that do not usually specify a particular speaker's name. The Tool and Die Local 157 was one of them. Among the most generous donors were the Allis-Chalmers Local 248 and the Plymouth Local 51. The former voted $125 for the first broadcast over WJR and then up to $250 a week thereafter. At Plymouth, the local approved its executive board's radio payments while asking that it use discretion, indicating that the board had probably started out on a rather ambitious program.

28. Not all of them forgot. Among my papers is a receipt for $268 drawn up by Maurice Sugar to Mortimer on December 19, 1938, which is marked "Fees and expenses for expulsion of officers." There is no equivalent in my name from Mortimer but he knew that I would never accept any money from him.

29. Several letters that I wrote to Dorothy when she was up North indicate that this question roused some bitterness in me. In one, dated September 13, are included the following observations: "I wish to gosh they'd settle the row. I'm fed up on it all ways. . . . It makes me feel cold to see how little the greatest personal sacrifice registers with even the best of them. . . . Of course, if the split comes I'll be needed again and I suppose I'll drown my Weltschmerz again in work. . . . I've got to see it finished, that much I know. And everything else must wait on that."

30. The committee consisted of Emil Mazey, Bill Marshall, Walter Reuther, Ed Hertz, and Leo LaMotte. Marshall had certainly thrown in the name of Tracy Doll as a cover because no one would have thought of him as a serious candidate for the presidency.

31. Travis was working for the United Mine Workers' District 50, a sort of catchall affair that organized workers unclaimed by any other union. A plant he had been working on had scheduled a labor board election and he had asked me to come and put out a paper for it. Hall's information came during the lengthy interview I had with him several months later; Dorothy's in the form of letters while I was in the East.

32. Ben Fischer was one of the socialists who tried to develop relations

with Lovestonites in the UAW. There is in my personal files a confidential report dated June 7, 1938, from Fischer to the Socialist party's national office. Fischer writes: "The anti-war congress in Washington has had a very good effect on our work. Martin is now working as closely with us as with any single group. . . . The chances that we would be isolated because of our opposition to Murphy is less now than ever before. . . . This will give us a freer hand in the unions and will hinder the development of hysteria for Murphy and against the socialists."

33. John Anderson claimed that it was he who nominated Victor Reuther despite the decision of a caucus, reportedly called by communist delegates, which endorsed Germer and Leonard for the two major offices.

34. A report on the caucus is in a carbon of a letter in my private files, dated August 15, 1938, from Mortimer to "Dear Frank" (probably Frank Slaby of the Oakland, California, GM Local 76).

35. A typed report of the conference, on the same paper and done on the same machine, was no doubt prepared by Mortimer. I can recognize his typing from little idiosyncrasies like the use of a semicolon instead of a colon in the salutation. The conference report is in Box 14 of the Kraus Collection, Archives of Labor and Urban Affairs, Wayne State University.

36. The committee that went to Washington to see Lewis consisted of Paul Miley; Earl Tallman, president of the Hudson local; Dick Frankensteen; Walter Reuther; and Mortimer, who reported to the August 20 conference that the committee was unanimously agreed "that President Lewis was ready to step into the situation."

Chapter 21:
The CIO Steps In, the UAW Starts Anew

1. This is reported in the *Detroit Times,* August 29, 1938, and in a talk Martin gave on the radio on August 30, which was reported in the September 3 edition of the *United Automobile Worker.*

2. Nevertheless, in Lewis's report to the convention, he mentioned warmly the fact that the CIO had helped settle the UAW's factional controversy. When this section was read, the delegates applauded it loudly.

3. Mortimer told of Emil Mazey's open opposition to Murphy, choosing the election period to plump for a labor party. Victor Reuther was even more direct. In charge of the Ternstedt unit, he was said to hide away the bundle of pro-Murphy tabloids assigned to it that Labor's Non-Partisan League had printed. When accosted by Irene Young, secretary of the Ternstedt unit, he replied: "I'm not doing anything to help the Democratic Party!"

4. A lot depended on what facts you chose to use. In Detroit, for example, Stanley Nowak had won a brilliant victory for the state senate, despite (perhaps because of) Homer Martin's open opposition. Another important victory of a pro-labor candidate was that of Rudolph Tenerowicz, mayor of Hamtramck, for the U.S. Congress. And in Flint, fourteen of seventeen candidates endorsed by labor had come out ahead in the primaries.

5. Fremming was head of the Oil Workers. According to my information, his candidacy was being pushed by conservatives, and he was conducting a red-baiting campaign against Brophy.

6. Murray and Hillman are quoted from the four-page summary of their report of February 9, 1939, on the record of the coordinating committee up to that date.

7. The five remaining board members were Irvan Carey, Frank Tucci, Loren Houser, Lester Washburn, and Charles Madden. There were three others that Martin did not suspend but who, for reasons of their own, soon joined the fifteen others by voluntary self-exclusion: F. J. Michel, Russell Merrill, and Walter Wells.

8. Quoted from the "bill of complaint" that Martin had printed; it is dated February 6, 1939. The portion devoted to Ford is found in sections 56–60.

9. On the same date, Martin wrote an introductory letter to the bill of complaint, which indicates manipulation of this date because the Murray-Hillman statement contains other material drawn from the bill of complaint.

10. Although he had converted to Christianity, Davidow's parents were Jewish.

11. These details are derived from a long, almost verbatim report in my tiny handwriting on eleven sides of large sheets. The report, headed "Testimony before the executive board, rooms 616 and 644, Hotel Hollenden, March 11, 1939," is in my personal files.

12. The original members were Frank Tucci, eastern United States; Irvan Carey, California; and Lester Washburn, western Michigan.

13. I possess a photocopy of the Flint-Chevrolet local's executive board minutes from the early period given to me by Shirley Foster. A special meeting of the board was held on February 25, 1939, just before the Martin convention, indicating that this local was sending delegates there. The names of the twenty-four local board members were listed in these minutes but nine names were subsequently crossed out when the individuals in question evidently decided to return to the UAW-CIO. Some Cleveland delegates also attended Martin's convention, especially people from Fisher Body. Bob Bates was rewarded with a leading post in the WPA and Elmer Davis, Martin's bodyguard, became a board member.

14. My major source of information about the Cleveland Convention, even more important than the *Proceedings,* which are located in the Archives of Labor and Urban Affairs at Wayne State University, has been my handwritten diary of some forty pages, which is among my private papers.

15. Bill Marshall, one of the most hostile members of the Reuther group, was president of the Chrysler 7 local.

16. The powers of the executive board were greatly strengthened to read as follows: "The international executive board shall have executive, legislative, and judicial powers over all affairs," whereas the previous constitution conceded these powers to the president, who consequently encroached on every other branch.

17. Many of the other constitutional changes and key resolutions adopted were directed against Homer Martin's unscrupulous concessions to the employ-

ers. An example was Resolution Number 62, which ordered the incoming executive board to issue a public statement to the effect that, whenever the automobile companies violated contracts, the UAW would "authorize the necessary action required to protect the interests of the workers concerned." This was linked with Martin's notorious campaign against wildcat strikes and his granting of power to General Motors and others to discipline union members.

18. According to my diary, the motion was offered by a delegate by the name of Ralston from the Studebaker local.

19. In *Organize!* (162–63), Mortimer describes how Murray and Hillman sought to influence him by telling him that Earl Browder, the head of the Communist party, was for Thomas. Browder and several other CP officials tried to do the same, but when Roy Hudson told Mortimer that Thomas was John L. Lewis's choice, Mortimer as good as called him a liar.

20. Other proposals were to make the officers board members at large or to guarantee them important posts as national directors. Yet no real effort was made to carry out these "offers," certainly not by the CIO leaders who would have been able to obtain their adoption.

21. The *New Masses* was a communist-oriented magazine prominent in the thirties. The article appeared in the issue of April 1939, probably under an assumed name.

22. Carl Shipley's votes are interesting to study in the *Proceedings* since, among other things, they reveal locals that disregarded the dictates of CIO leaders, including a number of Unity units. Shipley got most of his votes from Indiana (Studebaker and Bendix, mainly) and Wisconsin. The Nash local of Kenosha gave him all its votes except one, whereas Seaman Body (Ed Hall's local) voted for him unanimously. The left-wing Allis-Chalmers Local 248 split its vote between Shipley and Thomas. Important groups from other states also gave ballots to Shipley. Toledo 12, Addes's local, gave all but one delegate's votes to him. Local 76 of Oakland, California, gave him all its votes. In Detroit, Packard 190 divided its votes, and Chevy Gear and Axle 235 gave all but one to Shipley. Surprisingly, Mortimer's Cleveland locals did not fully support the CIO's candidate; even one of White Motors' delegates, Ed Stubbe, cast his ballot for Shipley. The smaller Local 217 gave all its eight votes to him. But the biggest break in Cleveland was at Fisher Body, which sent half of its delegates to Martin's convention: Bob Bates, Louis Spisak, Jack Barskites, Ralph Rocco, and James Nolan. The five who came to the Cleveland Convention—Charles Beckman (the local's president), John De Vito, Jerry Strauss, Morris Gottlieb, and Bert Foster—went loyally down the CIO line.

23. The votes received by the four elected board members from Detroit were: Frankensteen, 657; Reuther, 652; Leonard, 574; and LaMotte, 557. John Anderson was next in line with 462 votes, tied with a man named Ryan. The votes that other well-known Detroit men received were: Pat Quinn (Dodge), 441; Tracy Doll (Hudson), 387; and Curt Murdoch (Packard), 327. The elected up-state board members were: Art Case (Buick Flint); Reuben Peters (Bay City); and William McAuly (Pontiac).

24. The ten Unity locals were: Murray Body, Plymouth, Packard, Dodge,

Chevy Gear and Axle, L. A. Young; Tool and Die 155 and 157, and Locals 205 and 208.

25. The eleven pro-Reuther locals in Detroit were: Chrysler 7, Fleetwood 15, Local 140, Hudson 154, West Side 174, Briggs 212, and Locals 203, 227, 262, 306, and 490.

26. It was said at the time that a distinct majority of the board members were Unity men. But changes came so fast in the following year or so—changes, too, in the viewpoint of leading figures like Thomas, Addes, Frankensteen, and others—that it would be impossible for me to verify these claims, particularly as I lost close contact with the UAW soon after the convention.

27. I think that Fred Pieper not long after the convention obtained a job with the CIO in the South.

28. An editorial to that effect appeared in an issue of the *Daily Worker* published during the convention.

29. I had been offered jobs with two locals as editor of their journals, both of which I turned down.

Index